SUPERVISION
SETTING PEOPLE UP FOR SUCCESS

Carlene Cassidy
Anne Arundel Community College

Robert Kreitner
Arizona State University

SOUTH-WESTERN
CENGAGE Learning™

Australia · Brazil · Japan · Korea · Mexico · Singapore · Spain · United Kingdom · United States

SOUTH-WESTERN
CENGAGE Learning™

Supervision: Setting People Up for Success
Carlene Cassidy
Robert Kreitner

To Laura—this would not have been possible without your love, support, and thoughtful reviewing.—C.C.

With love to my precious little family—Margaret and our two cats, Yahoo and Sweetie Pie.—R.K.

Senior Acquisitions Editor: Michele Rhoades

Development Editor: Suzanna Smith Bainbridge

Editorial Assistant: Ruth Belanger

Marketing Manager: Clinton Kernin

Marketing Communications Manager: Nathan Anderson

Project Manager, Editorial Production: Susan Miscio

Print Buyer: Doug Wilke

Permissions Editor: Katie Huha

Text Researcher: Mary Dalton-Hoffman

Production Service: Matrix Productions

Text Designer: Adriane Bosworth

Photo Manager: Jennifer Meyer Dare

Photo Researcher: Sarah Evertson

Cover Image: © iStockphoto.com/simonkr

Compositor: PrePress PMG

Library of Congress Control Number: 2008925594

For product information and technology assistance, contact us at **Cengage Learning Academic Resource Center, 1-800-354-9706**

For permission to use material from this text or product, submit all requests online at **www.cengage.com/permissions.** Further permissions questions can be e-mailed to **permissionrequest@cengage.com**

ISBN 13: 978-0-618-86213-9

ISBN 10: 0-618-86213-7

South-Western Cengage Learning
5191 Natorp Blvd.
Mason, OH 45040
USA

Cengage Learning products are represented in Canada by Nelson Education, Ltd.

For your course and learning solutions, visit **www.cengage.com.**

Purchase any of our products at your local college store or at our preferred online store **www.ichapters.com.**

Printed in the United States of America
1 2 3 4 5 6 7 12 11 10 09 08

Brief Contents

Contents

CHAPTER 5

Setting Your New Hire Up for Success: Orientation   118

CHAPTER 6

Appraising and Rewarding Performance   148

CHAPTER 7

Training: Begin with the End in Mind   176

CHAPTER 8

Motivation and Coaching—It's Okay to Have Some Fun!   206

CHAPTER 9

Building a Positive, Creative, and Productive Work Environment   234

CHAPTER 10

Communication: Around the World in 60 Seconds   266

CHAPTER 13

Legal and Ethical Challenges for Today's Supervisors   350

Straight Talk from the Field: Jan Donald   351

CHAPTER 14

Harnessing the Power of Information Technology and the Internet   376

Straight Talk from the Field: Lisé Johnson   377

Preface

This book is anchored to the belief that everyone has the potential and capacity to succeed. Productivity researchers tell us that opportunities to succeed need to be more abundant in today's workplaces. Supervisors, by virtue of their pivotal location in organizations, are in an excellent position to address that challenge. By recognizing the unique talents and potential of their team members and providing them with motivating work and instructive leadership, supervisors can promote both individual and organizational success. As the title of this book indicates, we believe that one of the essential roles for supervisors is to **set people up for success**.

The white-water rafters on the cover symbolize contemporary work teams. Conditions can change quickly and supervisors need to anticipate what's ahead so that they can adapt to the situation or rapidly change course if necessary. They also need to prepare their team members by providing the necessary resources (organizational equivalents of a paddle, a life jacket, and training). The rafters will achieve their ultimate goal of successfully navigating the river and getting through dangerous water by working together and following the feedback and guidance of their leader. Inspiring supervisors foster positive work environments where everyone knows their job and "keeps paddling."

Supervisors contribute to team and organizational success by leveraging individual strengths and placing people in positions that take advantage of their unique skills, talents, and interests. Supervisors set their employees up for success by hiring wisely and providing necessary training, coaching, feedback, and professional development. In addition, they collaborate with their teams to clarify a common vision and build commitment to shared goals. Effective supervisors are comfortable with diversity and with empowering their team members to innovate, solve problems, and demonstrate initiative.

We wrote this book for current and future supervisors in large and small profit and nonprofit organizations alike. We also wrote it for entrepreneurs set on building their own thriving businesses, and for all others who will eventually interact with supervisors. In other words, we wrote this book for **you**. The next generation of supervisors will need to function at a high level while navigating a rapidly changing and, in some cases, quite volatile work environment. Our goal is to set supervision students up for success by providing useful information and practical tools in a concise and readable package.

Through our combined experience as business owners, executives, educators, and consultants, we have had the opportunity to provide supervisory training for many hundreds of employees in a wide variety of organizations including American Express,

Honeywell, Motorola, Double Tree Hotels, State Farm Insurance, the Hopi Nation, Caterpillar, U.S. Steel, Johns Hopkins Health System, and Lifetime HealthCare. In addition, we have learned an incredible amount from our students during our combined thirty-plus years of teaching at community colleges and universities. We have incorporated these experiences into a practical, hands-on style textbook. *Supervision: Setting People Up for Success* combines informative reading with real-world examples, knowledge-to-action features, case studies, and interactive activities. Just as the white-water rafters enjoy the thrill and exhilaration during their ride downriver, we hope you enjoy your journey to becoming a successful supervisor!

Business School Accreditation Standards Are Integrated and Supported

As we developed this book, we strived to meet the accreditation standards for the top two accrediting organizations for business schools: AACSB International (The Association to Advance Collegiate Schools of Business) and ACBSP (The Association of Collegiate Business Schools and Programs). Both of these organizations advocate a focus on excellence in business education. We have incorporated features and content to facilitate teaching excellence and outcome-focused learning. Recommended topics for "general knowledge and skill areas" that are covered in this textbook include: leadership, communication, ethical reasoning, analytical skills, information technology, diversity and multicultural understanding, teamwork skills, and reflective thinking.

Essential Topics for Current and Future Supervisors

Students studying supervision will quickly realize that the supervisory role involves a broad range of responsibilities. In this textbook, we address a wide array of topics that are relevant for supervisory students. We present these through concise conceptual and theoretical explanations so students understand the foundation information. We also give students the opportunity to explore these concepts through real-world examples and experiential learning activities to encourage practical application of their new knowledge and emerging skills.

These essential topics include:

- Organizational and management structures and the importance of supervisors
- Understanding the supervisory role—trainer, planner, scheduler, motivator, coach, controller, leader, recruiter
- Team building:
  - Common ground and vision
  - Goal setting, SMART goals, and keys to success
  - Leveraging individual strengths
  - Empowering your team
  - Motivation and rewarding achievement
  - Working with virtual teams
- Leadership styles, situational leadership, and the supervisor as servant leader
- Delegation and empowerment

- Fostering a culture of accountability
- Outcome measures and assessment methods
- The planning process—involving your employees, connecting to the mission, and contingency planning
- Time management, the A-B-C priority method, and the 80/20 principle
- Retention—strategies, alternative work schedules, and impact
- Job analysis, defining core abilities and updating job descriptions
- Recruitment, realistic job previews, pre-employment testing, interviews, reasonable accommodations, legal issues, and the PROCEED model for employee selection
- New employee orientation, the buddy system, clarifying expectations, training plans, and the 5:15 report
- Performance appraisals—making them relevant, timely, and legally defensible
- The "no surprises" approach to supervision
- Employee compensation and rewards—linking rewards to performance and discovering what matters most
- Beginning with the end in mind, training methods, variables that impact individual learning, modeling, experiential learning, skill development versus factual learning, and measuring results
- Generational differences and how they impact contemporary supervisors
- Employee motivation, myths, and motivators
- Coaching—guiding employees when learning a new task, skill, or information, and connecting the "how" with the "why"
- Feedback techniques—timing, content, and delivery
- Developing peak performers, the importance of a positive self-image, and a winning attitude
- Cultivating creativity, encouraging new ideas, developing creative thinking skills, and "design-thinking" models
- Fostering a positive, productive work environment
- Healthy habits and their impact on stress and absenteeism
- How conflict and failure can be good at work
- Cultural diversity and the impact on workplace communication
- A communication continuum with five strategies, plus communication techniques
- Challenges supervisors face, and solutions:
  - Getting underachievers back on track with action plans
  - Handling performance problems with progressive discipline
  - Discovering the source of negative conflict and turning a negative into a positive
  - Workplace violence and the HARM model of assessment
  - Employee theft—creating checks and balances

- Substance abuse and drugs in the workplace—recognizing the signs and understanding how to legally manage the situation
- Bad attitudes, poor hygiene, and other undesirable characteristics—handling without comprising anyone's personal integrity or self-image
- Practicing the philosophy of "trust but validate"

- Staffing—estimating, forecasting, and planning
- Scheduling strategies and the evaluation of today's scheduling alternatives
- Staying out of jail—employment and labor laws every supervisor needs to know
- Ethical decision making and strategies for encouraging ethical conduct
- Harnessing the power of technology and the Internet to become more efficient and effective supervisors:
  - Protecting systems and data
  - The pros and cons of productivity tools and computer surveillance
  - Recruiting and communicating on the Internet
  - Intranets as an organizational tool

Key Features of This Book

The practical "how to" writing style throughout this book is one of the distinguishing characteristics that sets it apart from other textbooks.

Supervision: Setting People Up for Success is built around the fundamental training principles presented in Chapter 7. The training process begins with an explanation, followed by a demonstration, then discussion and experiential learning activity. The trainer and, in the case of this book, the professors, provide feedback, facilitate further discussion if necessary, and encourage repetition (practice, practice, practice). As a result, we have incorporated the following key features to provide a comprehensive learning experience:

- Chapter **learning objectives** provide the reader with an explanation of what they will be learning—this learning tool reinforces the training philosophy of "beginning with the end in mind" and is outcome-focused.
- Chapter-opening vignettes—**Straight Talk from the Field**—feature fifteen supervisors from various companies and industries around the United States. These "guest speakers" provide real-world examples that resonate with students and bring the material to life through their candid personal experiences.
- **Key terms** are bold within the text to assist students in mastering new vocabulary and concepts. These terms are repeated in the margin on the page in which they appear, for greater emphasis. They are also listed at the end of the chapter with text page notations.
- The **Knowledge to Action** activities are a unique learning tool incorporated throughout the book. Each chapter contains several Knowledge to Action scenarios and questions designed to allow students to reflect on what they have just learned and to apply their new knowledge. Through these engaging individual or group activities, students discover why the information is relevant and how it can be used in the workplace. These are outstanding focal points for class discussion.

- Major **Points of Emphasis** are repeated in margin notations in a larger, bold font to draw the student's attention to key concepts and lessons. While this is a rather unique feature for textbooks, it has been used by journalists for years.

- **They Said It Best** inserts provide students with inspiring and informative quotes from highly respected contemporary and historical figures—many of whom students are likely to recognize.

- **Questions for Reflection** encourage students to assess their understanding of the material and to practice how this new knowledge can be applied.

- Every chapter includes a **You Decide** case study that provides students with real-world scenarios related to subjects presented in that chapter. These case studies challenge students to apply what they have learned, think critically, problem solve, and practice their supervisory skills and knowledge. The questions at the end of each case study can be assigned as homework to individuals or handled as a group project for discussion.

- The **Hands-On Activities** at the end of each chapter include a wide range of experiences such as Internet research and personal interviews. These activities are designed to encourage students to include in their learning experience *new* knowledge from *new* sources beyond this book, their classmates, and the instructor. These projects will help students to further develop their research, analysis, and communication skills—all of which will benefit them as supervisors.

- The **Supervisor's Toolkit** is another unique component to this book that has practical application for the class and beyond. Each of the supervisor's toolkit activities can be assigned separately. In addition, they can be combined throughout the course of the academic term to culminate in a Supervisor's Toolkit Portfolio. Students are encouraged to retain their supervisor's toolkit resources beyond their academic experience and continue to use them in the workplace.

- **Self-assessment tools and surveys** are included throughout the book, particularly in Chapter 15. These tools help students increase their self-awareness and develop "emotional intelligence." In addition, these tools are designed for future use by the students when they become supervisors. They can use these tools to better understand their employees, which can help facilitate their supervision and coaching.

Complete Teaching and Learning Package

For students, *Supervision: Setting People Up for Success* includes excellent tools for learning. In addition to the outstanding pedagogical features within the text, this program also provides students with:

- A comprehensive **companion site** that can be accessed at www.cengage.com/management/cassidy. This is a free companion site that includes features such as *Straight Talk* supervisor bios, glossary terms, chapter outlines, and more.

- Value-added content available through WebTutor provides students with access to interactive quizzes, flashcards, video clip support, PowerPoint slides of lecture outlines, and more.

For instructors, this book is delivered with an outstanding package of teaching materials including:

- **Instructor's companion website** at www.cengage.com/management/cassidy: This password-protected site provides valuable resources for designing and teaching your course. Website content includes PowerPoint slides, electronic files from the *Instructor's Resource Manual*, text-specific video segments and DVD guide, additional assessment tools and forms for student engagement, and more.

- **Instructor's Resource Manual**, prepared by Professor Elaine Madden, contains chapter objectives, lecture outlines, case interpretation/solutions for You Decide case studies, potential responses to the Questions for Reflection, and much more. Teaching tools and special class exercises are provided to help faculty expand on the text material. Types of learning tools include case studies, role-plays, and key issue expansions.

- The **Test Bank** includes more than 1500 true/false, multiple-choice, short answer, and essay questions. Page references are indicated for every question, as are designations of either *factual* or *application* so that instructors can provide a balanced set of questions for student exams. Each question is also tagged based on AACSB guidelines.

- **ExamView.** Available on the Instructor's Resource CD-ROM, ExamView contains all of the questions in the printed Test Bank. This program is an easy-to-use test creation software compatible with Microsoft Windows. Instructors can add or edit questions, instructions, and answers, and can select questions (randomly or numerically) by previewing them on the screen. Instructors can also create and administer quizzes online, whether over the Internet, a local area network (LAN), or a wide area network (WAN).

- **Premium PowerPoint slide presentations.** PowerPoint slides have been specially developed for this book to enhance the teaching and learning experience. The Premium PowerPoint slides embed multimedia content including graphics, tables, weblinks, and video clips.

- **Instructor's CD-ROM.** Key instructor ancillaries, including the *Instructor's Resource Manual*, Test Bank, ExamView, and PowerPoint slides, are provided on CD-ROM, giving instructors the ultimate tools for customizing lectures and presentations.

- **WebTutor for Blackboard/WebCT.** Jumpstart your course with customizable, rich, text-specific content within this Course Management System. Access a wealth of interactive resources in addition to those on the companion website to supplement the classroom experience and further prepare students for professional success. This resource is ideal as an integrated solution for your distance-learning or web-enhanced course.

- **DVD.** Each chapter contains a video segment to support the specific chapter topics. The *Instructor's Resource Manual* provides specific information about each video segment. A DVD guide also provides lecture support and can be found on the instructor's companion site.

Your Feedback Is Needed and Appreciated

We have written this book for you! We are all part of a team to help set supervision students up for success. Through our years of teaching, training, and supervising, we have received valuable feedback from students, professors, co-workers, and employees. This feedback has been essential to our drive for excellence and continuous improvement. Please e-mail your comments, compliments, criticisms, questions, and suggestions for improvement to carlenecassidy@verizon.net.

Acknowledgments

We both want to take this opportunity to recognize the individuals from Houghton Mifflin Company, Cengage Learning, and Matrix Productions who have contributed enormously to this project. A hearty thank you to the following key contributors: Lisé Johnson (who was responsible for putting this author team together and setting us up for success), Michele Rhoades, Suzanna Bainbridge, Danny Bolan, Susan Miscio, Sara Planck, Sarah Evertson, Merrill Peterson, Tom Lewis, Mary Dalton-Hoffman, Nathan Anderson, Ruth Belanger, Clinton Kernin, Doug Wilke, Katie Huha, Adriane Bosworth, and Jennifer Meyer Dare.

We also want to gratefully acknowledge the following academic reviewers. Your insightful comments, questions, and suggestions for edits, additions, and deletions helped shape this book. We hope you recognize your specific contributions when reviewing the finished book!

David Batts, *East Carolina University*
Wm. Hugh Blanton, *East Tennessee State University*
Dennis Brode, *Sinclair Community College*
Gary Bumgarner, *Mountain Empire Community College*
Helen Davis, *Jefferson Community and Technical College*
Neil Hinton, *Hocking College*
Gail Knell, *Cape Cod Community College*
J. Howard Kucher, *University of Baltimore*
Robert D. Lewallen, *Iowa Western Community College*
Elaine Madden, *Anne Arundel Community College*
Noel Matthews, *Front Range Community College*
Gerald McFry, *Coosa Valley Technical College*

Patricia Mielke, *Western Technical College*
Ranjna Patel, *Bethune Cookman University*
Ed Robinson, *Robert Morris University*
Lewis Schlossinger, *Community College of Aurora*
Joyce L. Suber, *Washtenaw Community College*
Frank G. Titlow, *St. Petersburg College*
Brandi Ulrich, *Anne Arundel Community College*
Kevin A. Van Dewark, *Humphreys College*
Thomas Waite, *DeVry University*
Deb Walsh, *Western Technical College*
Joyce Walsh-Portillo, *Broward Community College*
Teri L. Weston, *Harford Community College*
Michael R. White, *University of Northern Iowa*

A very special thank you goes out to our chapter-opening vignette contributors. They are busy people who generously took time to share their experiences and wisdom with the readers of this book. They know what it is like to take the heat day in and day out on the managerial firing line, so they are as "real-world" as you can get. Thank you for stepping up and building practical bridges to the supervision classroom.

To the next generation of supervisors—we wish you all the best on your journey to becoming successful supervisors.

Personal Notes from the Authors

FROM CARLENE CASSIDY:

To my current and former students, employees, co-workers, and supervisors—words cannot describe how much I have learned from all of you. Thank you for helping me to grow and develop throughout my career. To my family and friends—thank you for your encouragement, patience, and understanding. To Brookie, Christopher, Robert, Katie, Connor, and Erin—thank you for being wonderful sources of inspiration through your curiosity, enthusiasm, and incredible ability to help me see the world with a fresh perspective. Finally, to my partner on this project—Bob, your wisdom, guidance, and mentoring combined with your incredible expertise are a true gift. A gift I am very grateful to have received.

FROM BOB KREITNER:

Textbook writing is hard work that requires teamwork and leadership. This project has allowed me to work with a dynamic team of professionals—from co-author, to editors, to production specialists—that is made up of *great* leaders. At key points, each stepped forward to take charge and give the project positive traction. I greatly admire and appreciate Carlene's desire to learn, willingness to work hard, and ability to maintain her "never quit" attitude. No matter how much white water we encountered, she just "kept paddling." Each of these remarkable team members has taught me that the future looks very bright. I am extremely grateful for the honor of being on this team.

SUPERVISION
SETTING PEOPLE UP FOR SUCCESS

CHAPTER 1

Supervisors Are Vital to Organizational Success

Learning Objectives

1. Describe a typical organizational pyramid and identify where supervisors are positioned in most organizations.

2. List the five functions of management and discuss the functions supervisors are most likely to be responsible for.

3. Identify and briefly explain various aspects of the supervisor's role.

4. List essential skills and knowledge needed for a supervisor to be successful.

5. Identify trends impacting businesses and briefly explain the effect on supervisors.

6. Discuss organizational basics, including four characteristics common to all organizations and organizational charts.

7. Describe how a small company or entrepreneurial venture's organizational structure and supervisory responsibilities may be different from those of a larger organization.

Straight Talk from the Field

Saminda Wijegunawardena, P.M.P., is a project manager at Pixar Animation Studios in Emeryville, California, where he is responsible for the production engineering team.

QUESTION . . .

What are the most essential skills for supervisors or managers to be successful?

RESPONSE . . .

My view of the most important skills for a supervisor or manager has evolved significantly through my career. Fundamentally, it reflects the transition from my sense of being a supervisor whose focus was managing work to a manager whose goal is leading a team. In the latter, quality work emerges as a byproduct of a high-functioning team, but in the former, while you may initially produce good work, you are not cultivating the interpersonal relationships of a healthy team.

As you can imagine, varied instances of interpersonal conflict, both passive and active, emerge in the workplace and can corrode an otherwise healthy and skilled team. Detecting the root causes of these systemic issues may be difficult because of individual attitudes towards power or entitlement within the workplace that can cloud perception.

I feel emotional intelligence (including emotional awareness) can be the most invaluable skill a supervisor/manager can possess in resolving these problems. The abilities to effectively organize, cast/delegate, monitor, and coordinate work are of course important core skills. But the ability to function with emotional intelligence in all these aspects is the distinguishing factor from simply getting things done to building a fertile team that continues to perform well in changing, challenging environments.

Work is done by people and people do not stop having feelings because they are at work.

For me, emotional intelligence is simply knowing who you are. If you do your best in this pursuit, you are able to interact genuinely and rationally with your team by removing your own personal projections from those interactions. You are then able to listen more openly and objectively to your team members, encouraging them to do the same. You can then reflect and take proactive steps to strengthen those relationships and employ skills in motivating and coaching your team members in this aim.

As my career has progressed, I have been fortunate to supervise more and more skilled, talented people. The only thing that has remained consistent is the types of relationship issues that arise. Developing an emotional intelligence quotient (increasing emotional awareness) has become for me an integral step in developing into a strong manager and leader.

Chapter Outline

S upervisors are essential to any organization that depends on people to achieve success. To grasp the role of supervisors in today's workplace, you will need a working definition of *management*, an awareness of typical supervisory responsibilities, a common managerial vocabulary, and a basic framework for understanding business organizations.

> *Supervisors are essential to any organization that depends on people to achieve success.*

With that in mind, this chapter will provide you with examples of organizational structures including large corporate structures, small businesses, and entrepreneurial ventures. You will also learn about organizational charts and the characteristics common to all organizations.

In every organization, at least one person needs to take on the role of supervisor. We will discuss the various responsibilities a supervisor has within an organization, how supervisors fit into the management pyramid, and essential skills for successful supervisors.

This chapter will also touch on some of the trends impacting contemporary organizations and managers, including technology, the global economy, and diversity in the workforce. Several chapters of this textbook will expand on these topics.

Supervisors and the Organizational Pyramid

management
the process of working with and through others to achieve organizational objectives in a changing environment.

Before we provide a general overview of a supervisor's responsibilities, we will first discuss where a supervisor fits into the management structure of the typical organization. **Management** is the process of working with and through others to achieve organizational objectives in a changing environment. Supervisors are an

> *Supervisors are an integral part of the management team and process.*

integral part of the management team and process. The legal definition of **supervisor** is:

> any individual having authority, in the interest of the employer, to hire, transfer, suspend, lay off, recall, promote, discharge, assign, reward, or discipline other employees, or responsibly to direct them, or to adjust their grievances, or effectively to recommend such action, if in connection with the foregoing the exercise of such authority is not of a merely routine or clerical nature, but requires the use of independent judgment.[1]

In the workplace, it is common to hear the words *manager* and *supervisor* used interchangeably.

Organizations are frequently characterized as a pyramid (see Figure 1.1 for an illustration of this concept). In the upper portion of this pyramid, there are three levels of management: (1) top, (2) middle, and (3) lower. Each of these levels is explained further in the following sections. Managers at all levels are highly interdependent and they must all communicate with one another effectively in order to focus on and achieve key organizational goals and objectives. In addition, it is important to note that we are using the organizational pyramid as an instructional tool to illustrate common management responsibilities. Keep in mind that every business and nonprofit organization is different. Therefore, you can expect to discover many variations on this pyramid theme, depending on the organization's purpose, structure, and prevailing leadership style. Generally speaking, the trend today is away from top-down, command-and-control management and toward bottom-up participation and empowerment.

Top Management

Top managers are also referred to as *executives* and the organization's *senior leadership team*. As Figure 1.1 indicates, there are fewer people in top-management positions. Job titles frequently mentioned in this category include:

- Chief executive officer (CEO)
- President
- Chief operating officer (COO); chief financial officer (CFO)
- Senior vice president; vice president

supervisor
an individual who typically has the authority to hire, direct, promote, discharge, assign, reward, or discipline other employees.

FIGURE 1.1 The organizational pyramid

- General manager
- Division head

Responsibilities include:

- Strategic planning (one- to ten-year plans)
- Major financial and operational decisions
- Organization-wide personnel and human resource decisions
- Major public relations and marketing messages
- Overseeing major emergencies and crisis management events

Middle Management

Top management takes the lead in casting the organization's vision and strategic mission. Middle managers, in turn, are responsible for translating strategies into operational plans and deciding who will do what and when. Most organizations will have more middle managers than top managers and more lower managers than middle managers.

Job titles for middle managers include:

- Functional manager
- Product-line manager
- Department head
- Store manager

Responsibilities include:

- Intermediate planning (six months to two years)
- Logistical and operational decisions
- Budget decisions
- Facilities planning
- Staffing and human resource decisions
- Handling isolated crisis management events

Lower Management

Supervisors are usually positioned in this level of management. Although this is the lowest level of management, many would argue that supervisors are vital to daily operations and organizational success.

Job titles for lower managers include:

- Unit manager
- Branch manager
- Department supervisor
- First-line supervisor
- Shift manager or supervisor
- Team leader
- Project manager

Responsibilities include:

- Operational planning (one week to one year)
- Meeting production goals/quotas
- Customer service
- Coordinating staffing and work schedules
- Personnel and job-assignment decisions
- Organizing training, orientation, and team-building activities
- Unit-level facilities/resource planning and purchasing
- Day-to-day and local crisis management
- Enforcing job safety regulations and accident reporting

In most organizations, the majority of the employees are positioned at the bottom of the organizational pyramid as nonmanagerial workers. Where U.S. labor laws apply, these nonmanagerial employees are often referred to as *nonexempt* employees. This means they are covered by labor laws that, among other things, require overtime pay for working extra hours. Accordingly, managers and supervisors are typically called *exempt* employees who do not receive overtime pay for working extra hours. Lower-level managers or first-line supervisors have regular contact with employees and, in many situations, customers. Therefore, they have responsibility for day-to-day operations, which are essential to organizational success. In addition, supervisors interact regularly with middle managers by providing them with status reports and performance updates, while also receiving guidance and direction regarding organizational goals and operational plans. In organizations where participative management is practiced, supervisors may also interact with top management.

KNOWLEDGE TO ACTION

1. Why do you think supervisors are important to organizations and their management structure?

   _____

2. Imagine that you work for a large retail store such as Best Buy or Home Depot and the company decides to eliminate all lower-level management positions. What do you think would be the impact on the employees and the customers?

   _____

Managerial Functions and Supervisory Roles

managerial functions
general administrative duties that need to be carried out in virtually all productive organizations.

For nearly a century, the most popular approach to describing what managers do has been the functional view. It has been popular because it divides the management process into distinct activities and duties that can be taught and learned. **Managerial functions** are general administrative duties that need to be carried out in virtually all productive organizations.

Fayol's Universal Management Functions

Henri Fayol, a French industrialist turned writer, became the father of the functional approach in 1916 when he identified the five managerial functions depicted in Figure 1.2:

1. Planning
2. Organizing
3. Commanding
4. Coordinating
5. Controlling[2]

Fayol claimed that these five functions were the common denominators of all managerial jobs, whatever the purpose of the organization. For example, head nurses in hospitals, military commanders, the CEO of Exxon, department store managers, and high school principals all perform the same basic management functions, according to Fayol's view. Critics of Fayol's functional perspective say that it unrealistically portrays the management process as an overly rational and orderly process (e.g., managers plan on Monday, organize on Tuesday, etc.). For example, what do you suppose Fayol would make of the following situation at Cranium, a game and toy company? Co-founder Richard Tait, a former Microsoft executive, explains:

> People get to choose their own title. When Whit Alexander and I first created Cranium, we wanted to make sure everything about our company was fun, so we decided to give ourselves creative job titles—I am the Grand Poo Bah, and he's the Chief Noodler. Now all new employees we hire are empowered to develop their own special title. Our CFO is Professor Profit, and our head of the toy business is the Viceroy of Toy . . .
>
> You have to create an environment for people to be creative and innovative. My office has a glass wall, and I'm right near the front door, so I'm the official greeter. The walls are brightly colored, and we have music playing everywhere. Even the way the offices are arranged is incredibly collaborative—there's no sense of departments[3]. . . .

Make no mistake, Tait and his fellow managers at Cranium perform Fayol's five management functions. They just do it in a fast-paced, creative, and rather disorderly fashion. In this regard, the typical manager's day is probably a lot like yours—overloaded, hectic, and busy.

FIGURE 1.2 Five functions of management

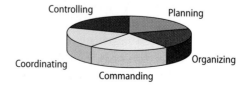

Supervisors Play Many Roles

Supervisors who are committed to setting their employees up for success wear many hats.[4] The supervisor's role encompasses Fayol's five functions along with a wide variety of duties and responsibilities. The following is a brief explanation of the more common supervisory roles and responsibilities. Each of these areas will be discussed in more depth in subsequent chapters.

TRAINER

As a **trainer**, supervisors teach employees and coworkers new information and skills. One of the keys to any new employee's success is being prepared to do his or her job. This requires proper orientation and training. Effective supervisors realize that training is an ongoing process. Although it is emphasized for new employees, all employees benefit from periodic training and professional development opportunities.

PLANNER

A **planner** evaluates goals, objectives, and future needs to prepare plans that provide the necessary resources and action items to achieve success. In most organizations, upper management is primarily responsible for broad strategic planning, and middle managers and first-line supervisors handle the implementation or execution of those plans. A key to success is to have plans for achieving department-level goals and objectives. This includes planning for training, staffing, purchasing, advertising, evaluation, and more. Important components of planning include goal setting, defining critical success factors, and developing tactics for getting your employees involved.

SCHEDULER

As a **scheduler**, a supervisor prepares the schedule to ensure that proper staffing and resources are available to meet production or customer needs. In organizations both large and small, supervisors need to productively arrange human, material, and informational resources. In addition, supervisors are responsible for scheduling facilities, inventory, and equipment to maximize efficiency and provide exceptional quality and/or service.

MOTIVATOR

Supervisors also serve as **motivators** who inspire their employees to perform at their best and achieve a common goal. One of the hardest things to define, but one of the most important roles for a supervisor, is that of motivator. To inspire their teams to work together, managers and supervisors need to recognize that each person is unique and that everyone is not motivated by the same incentives and rewards. For example, Starbucks has many part-time employees who need to feel like full-fledged members of the coffee shop giant. Chairman and CEO Howard Schultz explained to *Business 2.0* how his company tries to exceed his part-timer's expectations so they will be motivated to do the same for customers:

> We provided comprehensive health care as well as equity in the form of stock options to all employees. For the first time in America's history, not only did part-time workers

trainer
a person who teaches employees and coworkers new information and skills.

planner
a person who evaluates goals, objectives, and future needs to prepare plans that provide the necessary resources and action items to achieve success.

scheduler
a person who prepares the schedule to ensure that proper staffing and resources are available to meet customer needs.

motivator
a person who inspires people to perform at their best and achieve a common goal.

This supervisor values her employees' opinions. By being involved in planning sessions, they are more likely to achieve desired team results. Meaningful participation can be a powerful motivator in today's complex and fast-paced workplaces.

© Keith Brofsky/Getty Images/UpperCut Images

Supervisors should spend time coaching all of their employees.

coach
a person who guides employees with instruction, feedback, and encouragement.

controller
a person who measures quality and performance.

leader
one who sets the tone for the organization, creates the vision, and inspires others to achieve.

recruiter
one who assists in identifying potential job candidates, screening applications, interviewing, and hiring new employees.

have a stake in the financial outcome of the company, but they had the kind of health-care programs that gave them the sense of security and a psychological contract with the company that the company was not going to leave people behind.[5]

COACH

A **coach** is a person who guides employees with instruction, feedback, and encouragement. Effective supervisors coach their employees. Coaching goes beyond motivation, as described above, by guiding employees, helping them to focus on their "high pay-off" activities, providing positive feedback, allowing them to learn from their mistakes, and celebrating successes. In addition, it is important for supervisors to spend time coaching all of their employees—the top performers as well as the underachievers.

CONTROLLER

As a **controller**, a supervisor measures quality and performance. Control does not have to be negative or unpleasant. In fact, positive and proactive supervisors realize that their job is to focus on controlling quality and keeping things headed toward organizational goals and objectives. Success needs to be measured, so deviations can be corrected. Effective supervisors involve their employees in developing tools to assess quality and performance. By involving employees, supervisors share the responsibility for control with their team. Ultimately, the supervisor is responsible for the performance of her or his unit. However, the process of involving team members makes assessing quality and performance a much more open and positive experience.

LEADER

A **leader** sets the tone for the organization, creates vision, and inspires others to achieve. Supervisors set the tone for their employees. This includes everything from attitude to behavior. We have all heard the advice, "lead by example." This is essential for supervisors because their employees will look to them to establish moral and ethical values; create a positive, pleasant work environment; communicate in a professional manner; and use technology appropriately—all the while staying focused on organizational goals, production standards, and customers' needs.

RECRUITER

Recruiters assist in identifying potential job candidates, screening applications, interviewing, and hiring new employees. Supervisors are involved in many aspects of recruitment. In a small business, the supervisor may handle all elements of recruiting—including advertising, screening applications, interviewing, and hiring. In larger organizations, supervisors generally partner with specialists in the human resources department to accomplish all of these tasks.

Essential Skills for Successful Supervisors

Supervisors need to be passionate about their jobs, with a strong desire to do the work, help other people succeed, and accept additional responsibility. Individuals who apply for supervisory positions simply because they want to earn more money are usually not successful. In addition, as we learned from Saminda Wijegunawardena at the beginning of this chapter, supervisors should be confident in their ability to interact and communicate effectively with other people. One of the skills Mr. Wijegunawardena considered to be instrumental to his success is emotional intelligence. The following section provides an overview of essential skills for supervisors, including emotional intelligence. We will explore each of these skills in more detail in future chapters.

Communication Skills

Depending upon the circumstances, supervisors may communicate with their employees, customers, suppliers, managers, representatives from government agencies, banks, labor unions, the media, consumer advocacy groups, and the general public. Every day, supervisors encounter an opportunity to exchange information with others. To be effective, supervisors need to understand their audience, be clear about the message they wish to convey, and actively seek feedback. The following communication capabilities are essential:

- Listening
- Interpreting nonverbal communication

"Look! Another message to decipher from management."

© Ted Goff

- Articulating their point, both orally and in writing
- Projecting a positive demeanor

Communication skills for supervisors are so important that Chapter 10 is devoted solely to this topic.

Entrepreneurial Thinking and Creativity Skills

Organizations are moving at a rapid pace and change is the norm rather than the exception. This type of environment requires supervisors to be quick on their feet. Entrepreneurial thinkers tend to stand out as supervisors. They adapt quickly, are creative problem solvers, and develop new ideas to increase productivity, enhance quality, increase profits, and/or expand market share. They are opportunistic, meaning that they know when the time is right to make a change or try something new.

Decision-Making Skills

Supervisors make decisions every day. Some are routine and others more complex, with significant short-term and longer-term consequences. Regardless of the type of decision, supervisors need the ability to gather information, validate facts, identify consequences, analyze data, and stay focused on the goal. Of course, those decisions need to be ethical ones that are in the best interest of the organization and society.

Technical Skills

This involves the whole package of technical job skills, including computer skills. For example, if you have plans to become an executive chef, you need to possess all of the culinary and kitchen management skills to handle this responsibility, train your employees, and solve problems as they arise.

Team-Building and Leadership Skills

Doris Christopher, founder of The Pampered Chef, attributes much of her success to the team of people who work for her company.[6] Recruiting, training, and motivating a group of individuals to work together to achieve a common goal requires a well-developed team. In addition, a team needs a leader like Doris Christopher who can inspire, motivate, and adapt quickly.

Political Skills

When you see or hear the word *political*, do you immediately think of elected officials in public office? In the workplace, political skills focus on positive attributes including the ability to build long-term relationships of trust with others. Just as good politicians understand the needs of their constituents, politically savvy supervisors understand the needs of their employees, boss, organization, and internal and external customers.

With this knowledge, supervisors are better prepared to make good decisions, to be responsible, and to be accountable. Effective supervisors are diplomatic and they know how to get things done through support, cooperation, and effort from others. Managers and supervisors who are politically naïve can get shortchanged. Consider this situation, for example:

> I've been working at my current job as a marketing manager for about a year now, and one thing is bugging me. Every time I propose a strategy or a solution in a meeting, someone else at the table repeats it, in somewhat altered form—and ends up getting the credit for having thought of it. This is no trivial problem, since in my department, year-end bonuses are based on how many of each person's ideas have been put into (profitable) practice.[7]

THEY SAID IT BEST

Honesty is the cornerstone of all success, without which confidence and ability to perform shall cease to exist.
—MARY KAY ASH, Founder of Mary Kay Cosmetics

Source: Chip Bell, *Managers as Mentors* (San Francisco, CA: Berrett-Koehler Publishers, Inc., 1998), 146.

Delegation Skills

Delegation is the process of sharing authority and responsibility with others. Supervisors need others to get things done. This requires delegating tasks and authority to the right employees. It also requires preparing employees to succeed with delegated tasks.

Computer/Technology Skills

Computer information systems are commonplace in today's small and large organizations. Some industries, such as financial services and banking, would be hard-pressed to function without computers. Others, such as the local deli, could still function, although less efficiently. Regardless, supervisors can increase their own personal efficiency and effectiveness along with the performance of their teams if they understand computer technology and information systems and how these tools can be used to benefit both individuals and the organization.

Emotional Intelligence and Self-awareness

Daniel Goleman's 1995 book, *Emotional Intelligence*, popularized a concept psychologists had talked about for years.[8] Whereas one's standard intelligence quotient (IQ) deals with thinking and reasoning, one's emotional intelligence quotient (EQ) deals more broadly with building social relationships and controlling one's emotions.[9] **Emotional intelligence** has been defined as:

> . . . good old street smarts—knowing when to share sensitive information with colleagues, laugh at the boss's jokes or speak up in a meeting. In more scientific terms, . . . [emotional intelligence] can be defined as an array of noncognitive skills, capabilities and competencies that influence a person's ability to cope with environmental demands and pressures.[10]

delegation
the process of sharing authority and responsibility with someone else.

emotional intelligence
noncognitive skills, capabilities, and competencies that influence a person's ability to cope with environmental demands and pressures.

Increasing your self-awareness is an important aspect of developing emotional intelligence. With emotional intelligence, supervisors are able to position themselves and their employees in situations that reduce negative emotional responses and increase the likelihood of positive interactions.

Administrative Skills

Supervisors spend a lot of time organizing, scheduling, planning, preparing and managing budgets, conducting performance appraisals, monitoring quality and key indicators, and processing paperwork or online forms. All of these activities require an understanding of basic business functions and the related legal issues as well as the ability to effectively execute in each of these areas.

Time Management Skills

Yes, supervisors wear many hats. This requires excellent organization and time management skills, including the ability to prioritize, say "no," and manage an ever-changing schedule. According to research, it can take up to 25 minutes to regain focus from even the slightest interruption. This time is valuable to the individual and the organization alike, so coping with interruptions is another skill that supervisors need to master. The following are commonly used tips for preventing and handling interruptions.

- Check e-mail a few times a day, rather than responding to every new message.
- To avoid visitors, stand up to talk with them, get rid of comfortable chairs (except your own), and try closing the door.
- Control your time. Respond to the person who says, "I just need a couple of minutes of your time" with a polite "not now," and schedule time for him/her to come back.
- Use the phone or e-mail. If you can avoid a meeting or a visit, pick up the phone or send an e-mail and encourage others to do the same.[11]

Trends Impacting Supervisors

There are several trends impacting organizations and supervisors. Many of these involve how work is getting done. As technology continues to advance and the population ages, supervisors are likely to experience firsthand the impact of one or more of the trends discussed below. Three prominent trends impacting businesses include (1) an increasingly diverse workforce, (2) globalization, and (3) technology.

Diverse Workforce

diversity
a wide range of individual characteristics.

Many think of **diversity** strictly in terms of race, gender, and ethnicity. However, our definition is much broader, with a wide range of variables. These variables include attitudes, perspectives, opinions, gender, age, ethnic background, language skills,

FIGURE 1.3 What generation are you?

Generation	Birth Years
Baby Boomers	1946–1964
Generation X	1965–1980
Generation Y (Millennials, Nexters)	1981–2000

Source: Based on discussions in Linda G. Keidrowski, "Whose Generation Is It, Anyway?" *Small Business Times* (February 2, 2008), http://www .biztimes.com/news/2008/2/8/whose-generation-is-it-anyway, (accessed on April 12, 2008); and Anne Houlihan, "The New Melting Pot: How to Effectively Lead Different Generations in the Workplace," *Supervision* 68 (September 2007): 10–11.

education, work experience, socio-economic status, religion, sexual orientation, disabilities, and alternative family structures (for example, single parents or caregivers for children and parents).

Here are a couple of examples of workforce diversity:

1. Age diversity: Some baby boomers are staying on the job longer than they anticipated, while others are reentering the job market and ultimately working side by side with the Generation X and Y populations. (See Figure 1.3 for a breakdown of these generations by birth year.) These groups have more differences than just their age or physical appearance. Their work ethic may be different, their perceptions of quality may vary, and the way they learn and work often are not the same. Supervisors need to bridge the gap and recruit, train, inspire, motivate, and retain all of their employees, regardless of their ages.

2. Work experience: In today's workplace, former military personnel are highly prized potential employees. Some of the reasons include their strong work ethic, leadership skills, their ability to handle stress, and their ability to adapt quickly.[12]

KNOWLEDGE TO ACTION

Age diversity creates opportunities and challenges for supervisors. To explore this concept further, answer the following questions after visiting Duke University's Personal Assistance Service (PAS) website at http://www.hr.duke.edu/pas/.

- Select the *Supervisor Resources* link on the left-hand column
- Select *The Multigenerational Workplace* link on the lower right
- Review all five parts:

1. What are some of the characteristics described in *Part 2. Description of the four distinct work groups* that apply to your generation?

2. How should work expectations differ for each generation (see *Part 3. Work performance expectations for these different groups*)? What suggestions does the PAS website have for supervisors regarding work performance expectations?

Advances in computer technology, combined with high energy costs, have led to a significant increase in telecommuting. Telecommuting gives employees the opportunity to work from home by connecting with the office via computer and phone. By avoiding rush hour traffic, this telecommuter enjoys flexibility, and time and cost savings. This arrangement can also reduce employers' overhead expenses for office space. Experts suggest that, when possible, telecommuting employees dedicate a separate area of their home for working.

© Marili Forastieri/Getty Images/Digital Vision

outsourcing
is when a company or government agency contracts with an unrelated firm to complete work that was previously done internally.

off-shoring
the practice of having activities completed in a foreign country.

As you can see, the increased diversity of our workforce creates opportunities and challenges for supervisors. Successful organizations have learned how to integrate diversity into their corporate culture by leveraging individual strengths and talents to develop a more innovative, creative, and effective workforce.

Globalization

The concept of globalization has created challenges and opportunities for supervisors. Globalization is:

> . . . the creation of international strategies by organizations for overseas expansion and operation on a worldwide level. The process of globalization has been precipitated by a number of factors, including rapid technology developments that make global communications possible, political developments such as the fall of communism, and transportation developments that make traveling faster and more frequent. These produce greater development opportunities for companies with the opening up of additional markets, allow greater customer harmonization as a result of the increase in shared cultural values, and provide a superior competitive position with lower operating costs in other countries and access to new raw materials, resources, and investment opportunities.[13]

One of the outcomes of globalization is a change in how and where work gets done. Outsourcing and off-shoring practices have increased as companies have contracted different aspects of their operations to outside firms in an effort to increase profitability. This includes contracting with specialty companies across town and with businesses located in another part of the United States—or even in another country. Manufacturing jobs have been one of the first to be directly impacted by this movement. As a result, many U.S. workers have seen their jobs eliminated as their companies moved operations overseas or subcontracted to foreign manufacturers. This trend has expanded to include a variety of industries ranging from computer call centers to tax preparation services.

OUTSOURCING

Outsourcing refers to an operational shift when a company or government agency contracts with an unrelated firm to complete work that was previously done internally. "One result of outsourcing is that the location of work shifts, and associated jobs migrate, outside the company." However, this "redistribution of jobs among employers, but does not necessarily reduce the number of jobs in the United States."[14]

OFF-SHORING

Off-shoring, according to the National Academy of Public Administration report, refers to the shifting abroad of business activities or processes and can be a subset of outsourcing if the supplier is located in a foreign country.[15]

Companies choose outsourcing for various reasons. Potential benefits include cost savings, increased productivity, and expanding to a 24/7 operation.[16] However, along with these potential benefits, outsourcing and off-shoring also create new challenges for supervisors, such as quality, communication, and privacy issues.[17]

Technology

Consumer expectations have changed in tandem with technological advances. We live in a society that expects instant gratification and immediate access to information. As with other emerging trends in business, this presents opportunities and challenges. Innovations such as online just-in-time training provide supervisors with some much-needed relief. Technology has also led to improved communication with employees, has streamlined processes, and has developed ways for businesses to more accurately measure success.[18]

In addition, technology has provided a mechanism for companies to help improve their employees' lives. Telecommuting and the "virtual office" are two ways companies are providing schedule and location flexibility by taking advantage of technology.[19] Of course, these opportunities create new challenges for supervisors, including monitoring quality and productivity, while keeping the virtual team connected and focused on organizational goals. Providing motivational and technical support for remote workers is another major challenge.[20]

A closer look at technology and productivity also leads to the question about how much time employees are spending on their computers searching the Internet, instant messaging friends, or watching videos on YouTube. Employees are also likely to identify some downsides to technology, such as the "Big Brother" syndrome, wherein bosses engage in classic micromanagement (e.g., constantly looking over employees' shoulders) with the help of their computers.[21] For example, supervisors in the delivery service industry can now use their computers and global positioning software to monitor the exact location of their employees throughout the day. The "Snooping Boss" problem has also become an issue for many supervisors, as employees believe they are being spied on by employers, who have electronic access to their e-mail, keystrokes, Internet searches, and voice mail.[22]

The Supervisor's Organizational World

Supervisors need to know about organizations because organizations are formed to accomplish what individuals cannot do by themselves. An **organization** is defined as a cooperative social system involving the coordinated efforts of two or more people pursuing a shared purpose.[23] In other words, when a group of people formally agree to combine their efforts for a common purpose or a shared goal, an organization is formed. There are, of course, exceptions to this definition. For example, if two individuals agree to push a car out of a ditch, the task is simply a one-time effort based on an immediate need to resolve a problem. No real "organization" has been created.

However, if the same two people decide to pool their resources to start a towing service, an organization *would* be created. The "coordinated efforts" portion of our definition, which implies a degree of formal planning and division of labor, is present in the second instance but not in the first.

Common Characteristics of an Organization

organization
a group of people combining efforts for a common purpose.

All organizations—large or small, profit or nonprofit, government agency, privately held, or publicly traded—have common characteristics. According to Edgar Schein, a prominent organizational psychologist, all organizations share four characteristics: (1) coordination of effort, (2) common goal or purpose, (3) division of labor, and (4) hierarchy of authority.[24]

COORDINATION OF EFFORT

Coordination of effort involves two or more people coordinating mental or physical efforts to accomplish a task. You probably have heard the phrase, "two heads are better than one." Individuals who join together and coordinate their mental and/or physical efforts can accomplish great and exciting tasks. Building the great pyramids of Egypt, conquering polio, sending manned flights to the moon—all of these achievements far exceeded the talents and abilities of any single individual.

The coordination of effort allows the group to take advantage of individual strengths and expertise, making the team far more efficient and effective.

On a smaller scale, think about the level of planning and coordination required to throw a big party or an elaborate wedding. These tasks also require a coordination of effort that actually multiplies individual contributions. In other words, if one person attempted to do everything, it would take much longer and the results would likely be of lesser quality than if a group of individuals collaborated. Coordination of effort allows the group to take advantage of individual strengths and expertise, making the team far more efficient and effective.

COMMON GOAL OR PURPOSE

A **common goal** (sometimes called a *purpose*) is something of mutual interest that members of an organization strive for. Coordination of effort cannot take place unless those who have joined together agree to work toward a common goal. A common goal or purpose gives the organization focus and its members a rallying point. For example, let us consider Starbucks again. In 2006, *Fortune* magazine reported CEO Howard Schultz's ambitious growth plan: "the head of the world's largest coffee-shop chain said he plans to more than triple the number of stores, to 40,000, with half in the U.S. and half overseas."[25] Imagine the huge implications for hiring and training.

DIVISION OF LABOR

Division of labor is the process of dividing tasks into specialized jobs.

By systematically dividing complex tasks into specialized jobs, an organization can use its human resources efficiently. Division of labor permits each member of the organization to become more proficient by repeatedly doing the same specialized task. However, overspecialized jobs can cause boredom, alienation, and disinterest as employees master their tasks and come to believe that they are not being challenged or given enough variety. This can also leave an organization understaffed if an expert quits or is out on sick leave.

The advantages of dividing labor have been known for a long time. One of its early proponents was the pioneering economist Adam Smith. While touring an eighteenth century pin-manufacturing plant, Smith observed that a group of specialized laborers could produce 48,000 pins a day. This was an astounding figure, considering that each laborer could produce only 20 pins a day when working alone.[26]

Now, imagine for a moment you are the supervisor at the local Starbucks. You can assign one employee to take care of an entire order from entering it into the cash

coordination of effort
the process of two or more people coordinating mental or physical efforts to accomplish a task.

common goal
something of mutual interest that members of an organization strive for.

division of labor
the process of dividing tasks into specialized jobs.

When employees work together to achieve a common goal, they frequently enjoy better outcomes than if they worked independently. This is called *synergy* (or the 1 + 1 = 3 effect). Whether they are brainstorming about new ideas or solving a problem, real teamwork gives individuals with diverse skills, experience, and knowledge the opportunity to make unique contributions for the benefit of all.
© Comstock/Jupiter Images

register to preparing the drink—or you can use a division of labor to specialize with one person taking the order, a second working the cash register, and a third preparing the drinks. Each of these tasks requires special training. After a lot of practice, the person typically feels like she/he has mastered that job. At this point, the organization is considered to be operating in a highly efficient manner. Keep in mind, however, that this is also the point where many employees get bored doing the same thing all day and ask to do something else. This leads to the opportunity for cross-training.

HIERARCHY OF AUTHORITY

Hierarchy of authority is the formal organizational structure that defines positions of authority and decision making. According to traditional organizational theory, if anything is being accomplished through formal collective effort, someone should be given the authority to see that the intended goals are carried out effectively and efficiently. Organizational theorists have defined authority as the right to direct the actions of others. Without a clear hierarchy of authority, it is difficult, if not impossible, to coordinate effort. Accountability is also enhanced by having people serve in what is often called the **chain of command,** which defines who reports to whom. For instance, in a typical ski shop, the store manager has authority over the parts supervisor, the repair supervisor, and the sales supervisor, who in turn has authority over the sales associates. Without such a chain of command, the store manager would have the impossible task of directly overseeing the work of every employee in the store.

hierarchy of authority
the formal organizational structure that defines positions of authority and decision making.

chain of command
the order of authority that defines who reports to whom.

Properly structured, hierarchy can release energy and creativity, rationalize productivity, and actually improve morale.

The idea of hierarchy has many critics, particularly among those who advocate flatter organizations with fewer levels of management.[27] Organizational theorist Elliot Jacques has answered those critics as follows:

> . . . there is a widespread view that managerial hierarchy kills initiative, crushes creativity, and has therefore seen its day. Yet 35 years of research have convinced me that managerial hierarchy is the most efficient, the hardiest, and in fact the most natural structure ever devised for large organizations. Properly structured, hierarchy can release energy and creativity, rationalize productivity, and actually improve morale.[28]

What is significant about this quote is the last sentence. In this textbook, you will learn how to set your people up for success by providing the right balance of structure and independence while leading them toward a common goal.

From the "big picture" perspective, successful organizations balance coordination of effort, common goal or purpose, division of labor, and hierarchy of authority to achieve their goals. How this is structured depends on the organization's size, its employees, the operation, and type of industry. A large *Fortune* 500 company such as Procter & Gamble, headquartered in Cincinnati, Ohio, has multiple divisions that include multiple layers of management. In contrast, a small business, such as the award-winning Bicycle Sport Shop in Austin, Texas, has fewer levels of hierarchy and only one or two divisions of labor. However, all of the elements of an organization are present within both organizations, which allows each to achieve success in a highly efficient and effective manner.

Organizational Charts

An **organizational chart** is a diagram of an organization's official positions and formal lines of authority. In effect, an organizational chart is a visual display of an organization's structural skeleton. With their usual boxes and connecting lines, organizational charts (sometimes called *organizational tables*) are a useful management tool because they are a blueprint for deploying human resources.[29] Organizational charts are common in both profit and nonprofit organizations.

Every organization has two dimensions, one representing **vertical hierarchy** and one representing **horizontal specialization**. Vertical hierarchy establishes the chain of command, or who reports to whom. The organizational chart from a grocery store shown in Figure 1.4 provides an excellent visual tool to describe hierarchy. The chart lets everyone in the company know who reports to whom, which is important for supervisors and their employees.

organizational chart
a visual display of an organization's official positions and formal lines of authority.

vertical hierarchy
another term for "chain of command."

horizontal specialization
various divisions of labor across an organization.

entrepreneurial venture
a new or emerging start-up business.

The Entrepreneurial Venture

Up to now, we have focused our discussion on models that are quite likely to exist in large organizations. However, entrepreneurs and small businesses make up a significant portion of our economy. Therefore, just like a large *Fortune* 500 corporation, an **entrepreneurial venture** needs to establish a formal organizational structure to achieve long-term success. In addition, someone in the company

FIGURE 1.4 Grocery store organizational chart

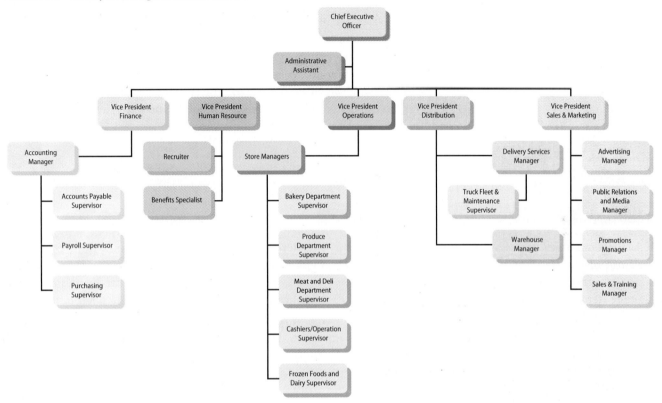

needs to accept the supervisory role. Typically, the business owner assumes these responsibilities.

What may be different with a new venture is fewer resources and greater responsibility. For example, when Doris Christopher started *The Pampered Chef* in the basement of her home in the Chicago suburb of River Forest, she had to do it all. Ms. Christopher said of those early days, "In my one-woman show, I did everything from answering the phone to emptying wastepaper baskets."[30] Twenty-five years later, The Pampered Chef has approximately 1,000 employees and over 70,000 independent "Kitchen Consultants" to accomplish the same tasks—just on a much larger scale in a much more complex organization.[31]

As you can see, during the start-up phase, companies often rely on the founders to handle multiple roles. In small companies, communication is typically more frequent and informal because there are fewer people to reach and feedback is often immediate. In addition, smaller organizations can usually adapt and change more quickly because decisions can be made on the spot rather than requiring a committee or board approval. Therefore, smaller organizations are often more flexible than large organizations.

Many large companies are striving to benefit from the economies of scale that come with their size, while maintaining the small company style and corporate culture, which is typically more creative and nimble.

What's Ahead

Present and future supervisors need to master the supervisory skills mentioned in this chapter, while also learning to balance the needs of the company with the needs of their employees. Emerging trends create opportunities and new challenges for achieving personal and organizational goals. The remainder of this book will provide you with new information and many tools, techniques, and strategies to improve your supervisory skills and help you set your employees up for success. The future is yours. Go for it!

SUMMARY

1. Management structures are frequently described in the form of a pyramid where there are three levels of management: (1) executives are at the top, (2) middle management is next, and (3) lower-level managers at the bottom. Supervisors are usually positioned in the lower level. Although they are at the bottom of the organizational structure, many would argue that supervisors are most important to the day-to-day operation of a business. Each level of management is unique, with independent responsibilities; however, all managers must communicate with one another effectively to remain focused on appropriate organizational goals and objectives.

2. Managerial functions are general administrative duties that need to be carried out in virtually all productive organizations. The five functions of management are: (1) planning, (2) organizing, (3) coordinating, (4) commanding, and (5) controlling. Supervisors perform all of these functions to a certain extent, spending most of their time coordinating and organizing day-to-day operations.

3. Supervisors are often described as "wearing many hats." This is because the supervisor's role typically includes (1) trainer—teaches employees and coworkers new information and skills; (2) planner—evaluates goals, objectives, and future needs to prepare plans; (3) scheduler—prepares the schedule to ensure that proper staffing and resources are available to meet customer needs; (4) motivator—inspires people to perform at their best and achieve a common goal; (5) coach—guides employees with instruction, feedback, and encouragement; (6) controller—measures quality and performance; (7)

leader—sets the tone for the organization, creates the vision, and inspires others to achieve; and (8) recruiter—assists in identifying potential job candidates, screening applications, interviewing, and hiring new employees.

4. Supervisors need to possess a variety of skills to achieve success. The most common skills include: (1) communication, (2) entrepreneurial thinking and creativity, (3) decision making, (4) technical, (5) team building, (6) leadership, (7) political, (8) delegation, (9) computer, (10) administrative, and (11) time management skills, all performed with emotional intelligence.

5. Successful organizations are embracing many emerging trends, such as increased workforce diversity, which extends beyond gender and ethnic background to include age, language skills, education, work experience, socio-economic status, religion, sexual orientation, disabilities, and alternative family structures. In addition, technology, globalization, outsourcing, and off-shoring are having an impact on today's supervisors. One important factor to note is that each of these variables creates opportunities and presents new challenges.

6. All organizations share four characteristics: (1) coordination of effort, (2) common goal or purpose, (3) division of labor, and (4) hierarchy of authority. Organizational charts provide a visual diagram of an organization's official positions and formal lines of authority; they also establish the chain of command, or who reports to whom.

7. What may be different with a new entrepreneurial venture or small business—compared to a large organization—is

that there are fewer resources and greater responsibility for the owner(s). During the start-up phase, companies often rely on the founders to handle multiple roles, including supervisory responsibilities. Smaller organizations can usually adapt and change more quickly because decisions can be made on the spot rather than requiring a committee or board approval, which is often the case in a large organization. Therefore, smaller organizations are often more flexible than large organizations.

TERMS TO UNDERSTAND

chain of command, p. 19
coach, p. 10
common goal, p. 18
controller, p. 10
coordination of effort, p. 18
delegation, p. 13
diversity, p. 14
division of labor, p. 18
emotional intelligence, p. 13

entrepreneurial venture, p. 20
hierarchy of authority, p. 19
horizontal specialization, p. 20
leader, p. 10
management, p. 4
managerial functions, p. 7
motivator, p. 9
off-shoring, p. 16
organization, p. 17

organizational chart, p. 20
outsourcing, p. 16
planner, p. 9
recruiter, p. 10
scheduler, p. 9
supervisor, p. 5
trainer, p. 9
vertical hierarchy, p. 20

QUESTIONS FOR REFLECTION

1. Which of the various supervisory roles is most appealing to you?
   a. Explain why.
   b. What skills do you currently have that provide you with the capability to do this part of the job successfully?
   c. What skills do you need to develop or improve to be successful in this area?
2. What are six of the essential skills supervisors need to have in order to set their employees up for success?
   a. Pick three of these.
   b. Provide an example of how these skills are used by supervisors to be effective in their jobs.
3. How do you think technology advances are impacting supervisors?
   a. Provide two examples of how technology may be making a supervisor's job easier/more efficient.

   b. Provide two examples of how technology may be creating new challenges for supervisors.
4. One of the common characteristics of organizations is the coordination of effort.
   a. What does the phrase, "two heads are better than one" mean to you?
   b. Provide a personal example of a situation where the coordination of effort led to positive results.
5. Division of labor and work specialization may lead to positive outcomes, but it also may have negative consequences.
   a. What are potential benefits to an organization that uses work specialization?
   b. What are some potential downsides to work specialization?

ORGANIZATIONAL CHARTS

1. Find organizational charts for four different types of organizations.
   a. A large (more than 500 employees) regional or national for-profit company.
   b. A small (under 100 employees) local for-profit company.
   c. A nonprofit organization.
   d. A government agency.
2. What do the organizational charts have in common?
3. What is different about the organizational charts you found?

4. Is the chain of command obvious and clear for each organization?
5. How are these organizational charts helpful to supervisors working for these companies?

THE IMPACT OF GLOBALIZATION

Form teams of three or four to respond to the following questions.

1. How has globalization impacted your local community?
2. Who in your group is wearing an article of clothing that was not made in the United States?
3. How does the shift in manufacturing overseas impact each of you as consumers? And as future supervisors?

Interview an Expert

Select a supervisor or manager (any business is fine). Be sure to include the contact name, phone number, company name, and address. Also include why you chose this particular individual. After the interview, conclude your assignment with a summary of how you can apply what you learned to your own personal growth and development as a supervisor. In other words, answer the question, "What can you learn from this person that will make you a better supervisor in the future?"

SAMPLE QUESTIONS

1. Describe the nature of this business.
2. Why did you choose to get involved in this type of endeavor?
3. What background is required to do your job?
4. Describe a typical day for you.
5. What are the challenges you face in this type of business?
6. Are there any trends or changes you foresee in this business?
7. Are there any employee challenges you would like to discuss?

8. Is teamwork used on a daily basis here and, if so, how?
9. How do you manage stress?
10. Can you describe your leadership style or the style of your boss/company?
11. How important is the financial aspect of business to your position?
12. Can you provide me with an approximate salary for your position?
13. What is the benefit package for managers?
14. Do you have unions here and, if so, how do they affect the way you do business?
15. Is there anything you would like to add that we did not discuss?

You may use these questions or any others you think may be appropriate to the business you are reviewing. Schedule the appointment ahead of time and try to limit your interview to 30 minutes. Be sure to thank the manager and send a follow-up (written) thank-you note within three business days.

CASE STUDY 1.1
Hiring a New Day Care Supervisor

Katie has decided to expand her day care business. She currently has one location that is licensed to care for 12 children between the ages of 6 months and 5 years old. Her center is open from 8:00 A.M. to 5:30 P.M. Monday–Friday. Her current customers are asking for Saturday hours and extended hours so that she would open at 7:00 A.M. and close at 9:00 P.M. In addition, she has a waiting list of seven children. Finally, the local military base is about to add 5,000 new jobs, so Katie believes that there will be even greater demand for her services.

Katie's expansion plans include tripling the size of her current space. She also plans to extend the hours of the center to 7:00 A.M. to 9:00 P.M. Monday–Friday and 8:00 A.M. to 4:00 P.M. on Saturday. In addition, she is going to open another location across town that will be closer to the military base. This new location will accommodate up to 36 children.

Katie will continue to run the main location. She is getting ready to hire a supervisor for the new location. She has identified two candidates as finalists for the position. Both candidates meet all of the local legal requirements

for working at a day care center. Shawn has a bachelor's degree in early childhood development as well as extensive experience working in a day care center, but he has never been a supervisor. The other candidate, Elizabeth, has a degree in elementary education with a teaching certificate that includes pre-K, which qualifies her to work in a day care center. She has been a supervisor for five years at a local Chuck E. Cheese pizza restaurant that caters to children, but she has never worked in a day care center.

Questions

1. What will be some of the new supervisor's responsibilities?
2. What are the most important skills for this person to have before he/she is hired?
3. Describe the type of person Katie should hire.
4. Whom would you hire—Shawn or Elizabeth? Why?
5. In what areas will Katie need to provide training for this new person?

SUPERVISOR'S TOOLKIT

The supervisor's toolkit section of this book appears at the end of each chapter. It is designed to provide current and future supervisors with exercises, information, and tools that can be used throughout their career. These activities will involve self-assessment exercises as well as information-gathering experiences. All of these may be used to explore personal strengths, knowledge, and attributes. In addition, many of the exercises will be useful to supervisors working with their employees now and in the future.

Continue your exploration of The Multigenerational Workplace at Duke University's Personal Assistance Service website at http://www.hr.duke.edu/pas (remember to select the links specified on page 15).

1. What are seven points to consider in managing the multigenerational workforce (see *Part 4*)?
2. What do members of each of the various generation groups have in common?
3. Why is it important to be aware of the commonalities as well as the differences?
4. What do you think is most relevant in *Part 5. Distinct ways each group responds to the workplace*?
5. Are these stereotypes about various generations an absolute guide for supervisors to follow? Why or why not?
6. How will you use this information to be a more effective supervisor?

CHAPTER 2

Leadership and Teamwork Essentials

Learning Objectives

1. Define leadership, list the qualities of an inspiring leader, and describe what it means to develop your people.

2. Identify and discuss basic leadership theories and models and describe the servant leadership philosophy.

3. Describe the characteristics of groups and list the six stages of group development.

4. Discuss the characteristics of teams, identify strategies for leading effective teams, and discuss methods for supervising a virtual team.

5. Explain the empowerment process and describe some of the benefits.

6. Explain delegation and describe the benefits, barriers, and steps to effective delegation.

Straight Talk from the Field

Barbara Schwenger-Huffman is Senior Human Resources Services Manager for San Francisco-based Williams-Sonoma, Inc. She is responsible for leading the human resources, training, and development functions for Williams-Sonoma customer care centers (call centers) in Camp Hill, Pennsylvania; Oklahoma City, Oklahoma; and Las Vegas, Nevada.

QUESTION: *What does it take to be an effective leader of in-person and virtual teams?*

RESPONSE:

*T*hus far in my career, and even earlier in school, I have fallen into leadership roles quite naturally. I was fortunate to have early leadership learning experiences to gather skills and to begin building my leadership repertoire. Coupled with a strong sense of responsibility and passion for each job, I thought I had the basics of leadership figured out. Of course, I would need to make adjustments to my style, depending upon the organization and the people I was working with, but found that my general skills adapted easily enough from place to place. However, once I started leading remote teams, I found that what got me there would not keep me there. My skills and practices from the traditional work setting needed to evolve. Virtual leadership situations place even greater demands on planning and staged executions, on defining objectives and expectations, on communicating in general, and upon your ability to flex supervisory style for the unique abilities of each team member.

In the past, one of my favorite aspects of leading teams was getting deeply involved and offering hands-on solutions to challenges. I prided myself in understanding the teams' needs and being able to jump in and complete the task at hand when necessary. This allowed for some success in terms of quick accomplishments and in creating change. While I enjoyed being connected with and able to motivate a team that may have been struggling, this mode of operation required that I use caution so as not to inadvertently become a micromanager. Another drawback to my highly hands-on style was that while I was doing the job for my team, I did not always leave myself enough time for planning and performing my own tasks.

For the last few years, I have had the good fortune of leading virtual teams. The members of my team are also leaders of intact teams in their location. Striving for successful and productive teams while leading from a distance, via the phone, e-mail, and occasional visits has required a change in my leadership behaviors and style. In doing so, I believe I am becoming a more conscientious leader. No longer can I rely on micromanager habits, leading by "popping in" or managing the environment by keeping abreast of water-cooler chatter. Instead, more thoughtful communication and planning skills are required.

Here are my five tips for leading in-person and virtual teams:

1. Plan to be flexible with your leadership style. This is a good practice regardless of your team location, and an essential skill for virtual supervision. Because my main goal is to have those I lead be productive and successful in their respective locations, I am more deliberate in identifying where each individual is in their development and what support the location requires of them. For some, daily coaching and planning calls filled with guidance and support are necessary. Others may require only weekly meetings to report their progress and respond better to being challenged with additional tasks.

2. Long-distance leadership means that it is often literally impossible to be that hero-leader who jumps in and saves the day. Instead, ask questions about and explore what a team needs to move forward and then challenge the team to take the appropriate action. Often I find that teams much prefer operating this way. What team doesn't want to own the success of solving its own problem?

3. In the past, I enjoyed reading a situation in the moment and relying upon my ability to react correctly no matter what came my way. This means I may have missed opportunities in terms of planning, predicting, and establishing desired results. With a virtual team, it is imperative to give definition to everything from next steps in a project to satisfactory performance criteria.

4. Plan and choose words and actions that make your intentions clear to team members. Without mutual eye contact to "read" how your message is being received, the ability to shift and clarify in the moment may be lost. As I learn more about and then consider each team member's preferences and needs, I find the potential barriers of long-distance communication dropping away.

5. Leadership requires strong listening skills. You will want to listen for meaning, not just for words. Particularly with virtual leadership. During conference calls, take time to fully listen and understand each participant prior to responding. This may require asking clarifying questions or possibly asking team members to repeat themselves. The quality of your telephone technology should be considered in communicating with your team. You may have to wait until others have finished speaking and revisit a topic from earlier in the conversation before getting clarification. Interestingly enough, this forced waiting and revisiting often creates new and better solutions, and does not allow a leader to inadvertently shut down productive peer discussion.

Although my goals are still the same—productive teams that contribute to the bottom line while working in a healthy environment—being a virtual team leader makes me ask myself: Why am I here? How can I be helpful to my team? Once I began approaching leadership in the "helpful mode" and literally started asking "how can I help?" (vs. telling), I found that team results and relationships improved.

Chapter Outline

This chapter will introduce you to common leadership traits and qualities, many of which Barbara Schwenger-Huffman just mentioned. As we embark on our journey to learn about leadership, it is important to note that leadership is not an exact science and that leadership traits, qualities, and styles are simply examples identified by leadership scholars. Keep in mind that many great leaders do not possess all of the attributes mentioned. As you reflect on your own personal leadership qualities, remember that each leader is unique. You may not have some of the characteristics described in this chapter, but that does not mean you do not have the potential to be a great leader. Remember that developing your own personal leadership style and honing your leadership skills will take time and focused effort. Finding ways to practice leadership skills both on and off the job can help present and future supervisors develop their abilities. For example, serving in campus, community, or religious organizations will give you an opportunity to experiment with different leadership styles in a variety of situations. Like riding a bike, leading effectively is learned only by doing.

Beyond personal leadership, supervisors are frequently expected to lead teams. Teamwork is essential to achieving organizational goals in an effective and efficient manner. At the heart of good teamwork is the team's leader, who often is the supervisor. Therefore, it is important to understand leadership traits and skills as we begin to study how to become effective supervisors who can lead others, including diverse and virtual teams.

In this chapter, you will learn about various leadership styles, theories, and models, and what it means to be a servant leader. In addition, you will be introduced to leadership skills—including delegation and empowerment. You will also learn about strategies to build a cohesive team. High-performance teams need highly effective leaders. Take the next step toward learning how to become that high-performance leader.

 Leadership

Leadership is the process of inspiring, influencing, directing, and guiding others to participate in a common effort.[1] To encourage participation, leaders supplement any authority and power they possess with their personal attributes, visions, and social skills.

There are many leadership theories, traits, and expert opinions about what is (and is not) most effective. There is no perfect definition or theory. The purpose of this section is to have you think about your own theories and preferences as you begin to develop a personal leadership style that is going to work for you in various situations you may encounter. Keep in mind that developing as a leader takes time, commitment, and the ability to learn from your mistakes. Just as there is no perfect leader, there is no magic potion you can take to become a successful leader. You may wonder, "When will I know if I have become a good leader?" There are two rather simple answers to this question: (1) when people follow and (2) when you are developing more leaders.

Developing as a leader takes time, commitment, and the ability to learn from your mistakes.

As an inspiring example, consider what happened when Van Jones, a Yale Law School graduate and activist in Oakland, California, made these remarks in San Francisco at a recent gathering of community leaders called Advancing a New Energy Economy in California:

> "What is considered green is usually for the eco-elite. . . . But if we are actually going to meet the challenge of global warming, we are going to have to weatherize millions of homes and install millions of solar panels. That's millions of new jobs. We need to connect the people who most need the work with the work that most needs to be

leadership
is the process of inspiring, influencing, directing, and guiding others to participate in a common effort.

done." It's one of his favorite themes: the need to expand the green movement beyond "lifestyle environmentalists," with their hybrid cars and other eco-status symbols. The audience cheered. "Van Jones, he's a rock star," says Tim Rainey, director of economic development at the California Labor Federation.[2]

Qualities of an Inspiring Leader

Figure 2.1 provides two lists of the qualities and characteristics of inspirational leaders. The first list is from the *leader's* perspective. This list was developed from a series of interviews of high-performing leaders. The second list, the *follower's* perspective, was compiled from a survey of followers.[3]

One of the common elements you will notice in these lists is agreement on the importance of "people skills." Clearly, both leaders and followers value effective communication skills. This includes the ability to articulate their vision using storytelling and other techniques to bring the idea to life, the ability to listen effectively and not do all the talking, and an effort to minimize the use of jargon. **Jargon** is informal terminology unique to a business or industry that is often not understood by new employees, customers, and people outside the organization.

FIGURE 2.1 Qualities of inspiring leaders

Source: Council for Excellence in Management Leadership, Inspired Leadership Research Project (Research conducted by the Chartered Management Institute), *Inspired Leadership: Insights into People Who Inspire Exceptional Performance* (United Kingdom: DTI, UK Government, 2006), 5.

jargon
informal terminology unique to a business or industry, often not understood by new employees, customers, and people outside the organization.

Qualities of Inspiring Leaders

From the Leader's Perspective

- Strong communication–storytelling and listening
- Passion for learning and intense curiosity
- Focus on developing people
- Able to have fun and remain very energized
- Strong self-belief, coupled with humanity and humility
- Committed to giving something back and to making a significant difference
- Clarity of vision and ability to share it with their people
- Dogged, often "relentless" determination
- Very strong focus on priorities
- Not afraid to show some vulnerability
- Regular use of reflective periods
- Almost universal dislike for jargon
- Passion for and pride in what they do

From the Follower's Perspective

- Genuine shared vision
- Real confidence and trust in their teams
- Respect for employees and customers
- Commitment to developing people
- Clear standards of ethics and integrity
- Willingness to take risks

Notice that the lists include personal attributes. Respectful, ethical, passionate, determined, energetic, confident, and humble are among the characteristics of inspirational leaders.

Another item that appears on both lists is the idea of developing people. This is absolutely essential for supervisors. One of the primary roles of supervisors is to get work accomplished through other people. In order to set people up for individual success in their jobs, a supervisor should be committed to helping each person develop and grow.

What Does It Mean to Develop People?

Making a verbal commitment to developing people is not enough. Supervisors need to take action. The first step involves learning about your employees and their skills, knowledge, education, goals, and dreams. The next step is to meet with your employees individually to create a development plan that is consistent with their personal goals and that will also help the organization to achieve its goals. By investing in your employees, you are investing in your company. Remind yourself that, if you take the time to learn about your employees but don't take the time to act on the information, more harm will come than good.[4]

The plan you create may include action items such as the employee enrolling in training classes, taking some college courses, job shadowing, sitting in on meetings, working on special projects, cross-training, and/or accepting more responsibility.

One of the keys to success in any organization is *trust*. When supervisors are trying to develop their people, it is important that they provide the necessary training and resources. As trust grows among team members, supervisors no longer need to work side-by-side with their employees. However, they should routinely meet with their employees, as this supervisor is doing, to solicit their feedback and provide guidance and coaching when necessary.

© Jetta Productions/Getty Images/Iconica

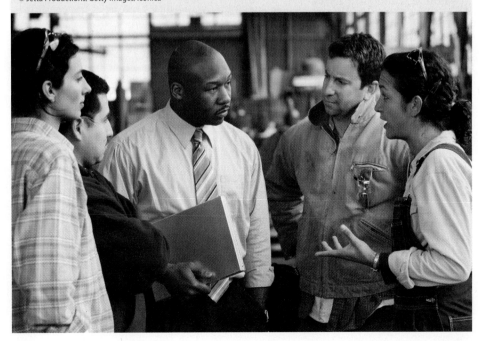

Supervisors will frequently assess employee skills and prepare an action plan or professional development plan as part of the annual performance evaluation process.

It is necessary for supervisors to find a way to develop their people to the point where they can have confidence and trust in their ability to do their jobs without constant supervision.

Supervisors will frequently assess employee skills and prepare an action plan or professional development plan as part of the employee's annual performance evaluation.

As a supervisor, it is important for you to be patient as you work to develop your people into more effective employees and potentially future supervisors and leaders. Learning new skills and taking on new assignments are processes that take time and commitment. When you schedule training, choose days and hours that are less busy to provide ample time for questions and review. As you learned in Chapter 1, coaching and training are essential roles of a supervisor.

It is necessary for supervisors to find a way to develop their people to the point where they can have confidence and trust in their ability to do their jobs without constant supervision. Later in this chapter, we will discuss techniques for empowering your team and delegating effectively.

Leadership Theories and Models

Scholars have spent decades studying various leadership theories and examining the traits, behaviors, and approaches that are used to effectively lead people. We will explore some basic leadership theories that have been developed over the years.

Behavioral Styles Theory

This perspective of leadership is probably the most widely recognized. Rather than focusing on individual traits of successful leaders, behavioral leadership theorists examine patterns of leadership behavior, called **behavioral leadership styles**. The three classic styles of leadership behavior are (1) authoritarian, (2) democratic, and (3) laissez-faire (or *hands-off*). Each has strengths and limitations.

AUTHORITARIAN

Authoritarian leaders retain all authority and responsibility. They assign people to clearly defined tasks, and there is primarily a downward flow of communication. This leadership style tends to stress prompt, orderly, and predictable performance. However, it can also stifle individual initiative and breed resentment.

DEMOCRATIC

Democratic leaders delegate a great deal of authority while retaining ultimate responsibility. Work is divided and assigned on the basis of participatory decision making. An active, two-way flow of upward and downward communication is common. Democratic leaders typically enhance personal commitment through participation. However, this approach can be very time-consuming.

LAISSEZ-FAIRE

Laissez-faire leaders grant responsibility and authority to a group of individuals. Group members are told to work problems and challenges out themselves and to do

behavioral leadership styles
patterns of leadership behavior.

authoritarian leader
one who retains all authority and responsibility, assigning people to clearly defined tasks; there is primarily a downward flow of communication.

democratic leader
one who delegates authority while retaining ultimate responsibility, arranging to have work divided and assigned on the basis of participatory decision making; active two-way communication is common.

laissez-faire leader
one who grants responsibility and authority to a group of individuals, who are told to work problems out themselves; communication is primarily horizontal among peers.

the best they can. Communication is primarily horizontal among peers. This approach permits self-starters to do what they think is necessary and appropriate without interference or direction from their leader. However, in the absence of direction and guidance from their leader, groups may become unfocused and drift aimlessly.

For a number of years, theorists and managers hailed democratic leadership as the key to productive and happy employees. Eventually, however, their enthusiasm was dampened when critics noted how the original study relied on children as subjects and virtually ignored productivity. Although there is a general agreement that these basic styles exist, debate has been vigorous over their relative value and appropriateness. Practical experience has shown, for example, that the democratic style does not always stimulate better performance. Some employees prefer to be told what to do rather than to participate in decision making.[5] This can be the result of cultural differences, as was the case when the world's largest television maker was created by the merger of China's TCL Corp. and France's Thomson.

> In China, says one TCL official, "if the leader says something is right, even if he is wrong, employees will agree with him. But in foreign companies, they will not agree with him. We have two different cultures.[6]

Table 2.1 provides an overview of each of these leadership styles along with their strengths, weaknesses, and examples of situations where each approach may be used in the workplace.

Situational Theories and Models

Convinced that no one best style of leadership exists, some management experts have identified situational or contingency thinking as a more effective approach. The common element in all theories of **situational leadership** is this: successful leadership occurs when the leader's style matches the situation. Situational leadership advocates stress the need for flexibility to adapt one's leadership style to the situation. They reject the notion of a universally applicable style. Research is underway to determine precisely when and where various styles of leadership are appropriate. Three different approaches to situational leadership are introduced and discussed here: (1) Ken Blanchard and Paul Hersey's model, (2) Fred E. Fiedler's contingency theory, and (3) the path-goal theory.

Situational leadership practitioners stress the need for flexibility to adapt the appropriate leadership style to the situation.

situational leadership
the concept that successful leadership occurs when the leader's style matches the situation.

Blanchard and Hersey's situational leadership model
a leadership model based on four different leadership styles or characteristics: directing, coaching, supporting, and delegating.

BLANCHARD AND HERSEY MODEL

Ken Blanchard and Paul Hersey have been called the pioneers of situational leadership.[7] The framework for **Blanchard and Hersey's situational leadership model** is based on four different leadership styles or characteristics: (1) directing, (2) coaching, (3) supporting, and (4) delegating.[8] As we progress through this book, we will define these terms and you will discover how important these skills are to supervisors in today's workplaces.

Blanchard and Hersey place a great deal of emphasis on the concept that "no single all-purpose leadership style is universally successful."[9] They provide this overview of situational leadership:

TABLE 2.1
Behavioral Leadership Styles

	Authoritarian	Democratic	Laissez-faire
Characteristics: Authority	Leader retains all authority and responsibility	Leader delegates a great deal of authority while retaining ultimate responsibility	Leader grants responsibility and authority to group
Work assignments	Leader assigns people to clearly defined tasks	Work is divided and assigned on the basis of participatory decision making	Group members are told to work things out themselves and do the best they can
Communication	Primarily a downward flow of communication	Active, two-way flow of upward and downward communication	Primarily horizontal communication between peers
Primary Strengths	Stresses prompt, orderly, and predictable performance	Enhances personal commitment through participation	Permits self-starters to do things as they see fit without leader interference
Primary weaknesses	Approach tends to stifle individual initiative	Democratic process is time-consuming	Group may drift aimlessly in the absence of direction of leader
Examples	Urgent/emergency situation such as a team of firefighters responding to a call. The leader takes control and assigns other firefighters specific tasks and responsibilities.	Planned change such as a restaurant that wants to extend its hours to provide lunch service as well as dinner service. Employees are involved in menu planning and promotional ideas.	Routine staffing such as a team of homecare nurses responsible for round-the-clock, on-call scheduling, to respond to after-hour phone calls. The nurses negotiate among themselves to accommodate personal preferences and vacation days.

KNOWLEDGE TO ACTION

You must always be sure to choose a behavioral leadership style that is appropriate for the situation. For example, imagine that you are the supervisor of a grocery store. The power goes out and there are no generators. There are close to a hundred customers in the store and the cash registers are not working.

1. Which behavioral leadership style would be best for this situation? Explain your answer.

2. After the crisis is resolved, the regional manager asks that you create an emergency plan for your store that specifically addresses how to respond during a power outage. Which behavioral leadership style will you use in preparing this plan? Explain why.

Successful leaders can adapt their behavior to meet followers' needs and the particular situation. Effectiveness depends on the leader, the followers, and situational elements. Leaders must be able to diagnose their own behavior in light of their environments.[10]

The variables or environmental factors Blanchard and Hersey are referring to include the nature of the organization and the employees' skills and level of readiness. The point is that effective leaders need to be able to assess their organization, the situation, their employees' abilities, and their employees' *willingness* to follow. In addition, these leaders need to adapt their personal leadership style and approach to fit the circumstances, or they need to modify one or more of the situational elements.[11]

Supervisors have a leadership role within an organization. To be successful using the Blanchard and Hersey model, supervisors need to shift styles to handle the situation and accommodate the needs of their employees. For example, imagine you are the supervisor of a bank branch. When you hire a new employee and she is scheduled to open the bank for the first time, your leadership style needs to be directive. As you build trust in the employee and her confidence and level of readiness increase, you can shift to coaching, supporting, or delegating leadership styles. This process is like changing clothes to suit the weather. Why wear shorts and flip-flops in a blizzard?

FIEDLER'S CONTINGENCY THEORY

Although Fiedler's contingency theory is closely aligned with Blanchard and Hersey's situational leadership model, there are unique aspects and distinct differences that are worth exploring. Among the leadership theories discussed so far, Fiedler's is the most thoroughly tested. It is the product of more than 30 years of research by Fred E. Fiedler and his associates. **Fiedler's contingency theory** gets its name from the following assumptions:

> The performance of a leader depends on two interrelated factors: (1) the degree to which the situation gives the leader control and influence—that is, the likelihood that [the leader] can successfully accomplish the job; and (2) the leader's basic motivation—that is, whether [the leader's] self-esteem depends primarily on accomplishing the task or on having close supportive relations with others.[12]

Regarding the second factor, the leader's basic motivation, Fiedler believes leaders are either task-motivated or relationship-motivated. These two motivational profiles are roughly equivalent to managers and supervisors being primarily concerned about *production* or about *people*.

A consistent pattern has emerged from many studies of effective leaders carried out by Fiedler and others.[13] As illustrated in Figure 2.2, task-motivated leaders seem to be effective in extreme situations when they have either very little control or a great deal of control over situational variables. In moderately favorable situations, however, relationship-motivated leaders tend to be more effective. Consequently, Fiedler and one of his colleagues summed up their findings by noting that "everything points to the conclusion that there is no such thing as an ideal leader."[14] Instead, there are leaders, and there are situations. The challenge, according to Fiedler, is to analyze a leader's basic motivation and then match that leader with a suitable situation to form a productive combination. He believes it is more efficient to move leaders to

Fiedler's contingency theory a leadership model based on the notion that a leader's performance depends on the likelihood that the leader can successfully accomplish the job and the leader's basic motivation.

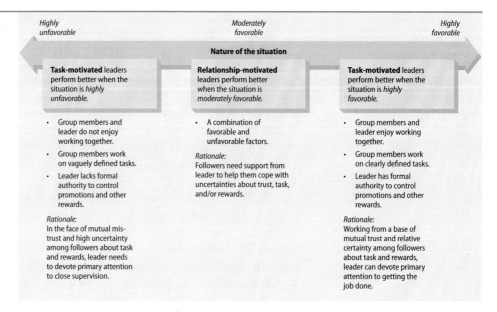

FIGURE 2.2 Fiedler's contingency theory of leadership

a suitable situation than to tamper with their personalities by trying to get task-motivated leaders to become relationship-motivated, or vice versa. Referring again to our clothing metaphor, this is like taking your shorts and flip-flops and moving to Florida to avoid a winter in Minnesota.

PATH-GOAL THEORY

Another situational leadership theory is the **path-goal theory**. This theory gets its name from the assumption that effective leaders can enhance employee motivation by (1) clarifying the individual's perception of work goals, (2) linking meaningful rewards with goal attainment, and (3) explaining how goals and desired rewards can be achieved. In short, leaders need to motivate their followers by providing clear goals and meaningful incentives for reaching them. Path-goal theorists believe that *motivation* is essential to effective leadership. To take it a step further, motivation is essential for successful supervision. You will be introduced to motivational theories and practical applications in subsequent chapters.

> *Path-goal theorists believe that motivation is essential to effective leadership.*

According to path-goal theorists, leaders can enhance motivation by increasing the number of opportunities for their employees to earn personal rewards for goal attainment. This level of achievement will also increase personal satisfaction on the job as well. To set their employees up for success, leaders should provide a clear path to goal attainment, make necessary resources available, and eliminate potential barriers. [15]

Situational variables include personal characteristics of employees, environmental pressures, and demands on employees. These will vary from situation to situation and, in some cases, from day to day. Thus, path-goal proponents believe supervisors need to rely on four different leadership styles, choosing the one that is best suited to the situation. These four leadership styles are (1) directive, (2) supportive, (3) participative, and (4) achievement-oriented.

path-goal theory
a leadership model that suggests that leaders motivate their followers by providing clear goals and meaningful incentives for reaching them.

1. Under the **directive leadership style**, managers tell people what is expected of them and provide specific guidance, schedules, rules, regulations, and standards.[16] This leadership style is often used when employees are new, lack experience, and need direction. It is also common in situations that require quick decisions and have a sense of urgency, such as a team of firefighters responding to an emergency call.

2. Under the **supportive leadership style**, managers treat employees as equals in a friendly manner while striving to improve their well-being. This style may be appropriate, for example, in a professional office setting such as an accounting firm where knowledgeable employees perform the majority of the work. They typically do not need much direction or guidance. However, they want to be treated with respect and they want to know they are valued.

3. Under the **participative leadership style**, managers consult with employees to seek their suggestions and then seriously consider those suggestions when making decisions. This style of leadership is often used in organizations where the employees understand the organization and can contribute creative ideas that will help the company grow and succeed.

Supervisors should adapt their leadership style to the situation. In urgent situations, such as firefighters responding to an emergency, the supervisor needs to use a directive leadership style to quickly take control of the situation. After the emergency is over, it is useful to switch to a more participative leadership style during the debriefing session.
© Dwayne Newton/PhotoEdit

4. Under the **achievement-oriented leadership style**, managers set challenging goals, emphasize excellence, and seek continuous improvement while maintaining a high degree of confidence that employees will meet difficult challenges in a responsible manner.[17] Any organization that is goal oriented is likely to use this leadership style at some point in time.

COMPARING FIEDLER'S CONTINGENCY THEORY WITH PATH-GOAL THEORY

The assumption that managers and supervisors can and do shift situationally from style to style clearly sets path-goal theory apart from Fiedler's model. Recall that Fiedler claims that managers cannot and do not change their basic leadership styles.

Although research on the path-goal model has produced mixed results,[18] the experience of Leonard D. Schaeffer, former CEO of Wellpoint Health Networks, based in Thousand Oaks, California, validates the path-goal contention that leaders do in fact change leadership styles:

directive leadership style
a leadership style in which managers tell people what is expected of them and provide specific guidance, schedules, rules, regulations, and standards.

supportive leadership style
a leadership style in which managers treat employees as equals in a friendly manner while striving to improve their well-being.

participative leadership style
a leadership style in which managers consult with employees to seek their suggestions and then seriously consider those suggestions when making decisions.

achievement-oriented leadership style
a leadership style in which managers set challenging goals, emphasize excellence, and seek continuous improvement.

As the company has changed, I've gone through my own transformation as chief executive. The top-down, autocratic style I had to adopt to turn around the business gave way to a more hands-off style that focused on motivating others to act rather than managing them directly. And more recently, I've been going through yet another shift—away from the participative mode and toward what I call a reformer style of leadership in which the chief executive's role is to represent the company's interest on a broader stage.[19]

Another valuable contribution of path-goal theory is its identification of the achievement-oriented leadership style. As managers and supervisors deal with an increasing number of highly educated and self-motivated employees, particularly in advanced technology industries, they will need to become skilled facilitators rather than just order-givers or hand-holders.

KNOWLEDGE TO ACTION

1. Select a situation from your work or an extracurricular group you are involved with. Choose a situation that will ultimately lead to change, such as a new sales campaign, a fundraiser, or a recruitment drive. Describe the situation.

   _____

2. Which situational leadership style do you think would be most effective in the scenario you described above? Explain why.

   _____

3. What variables did you consider when selecting a leadership style?

   _____

Toward Servant Leadership

Let us conclude our discussion of leadership by exploring the intriguing concept of the servant leader and tackling the issue of a single best leadership style.

Servant Leadership

In addition to a working knowledge of the various leadership theories we have just discussed, aspiring leaders should consider what it means to be a servant leader.[20] This is where Robert Greenleaf's philosophy of the *servant leader* enters the picture as an instructive and inspiring springboard. The **servant leader** is an ethical person who puts others—not herself or himself—in the foreground. Greenleaf spent forty years working for AT&T before retiring in 1964. In 1970 he wrote his first essay titled, "The Servant as Leader," which was eventually published as a small paperback book.[21] As a devout Quaker, Greenleaf wove humility and a genuine concern for the whole person into the philosophy of leadership he developed during his career at AT&T.[22] Important characteristics of the servant leader include the following:

- *They are servants first.* Servant leaders are motivated by a natural desire to serve, not to lead. They must make a conscious choice to *aspire* to lead. People who are leaders are responding to an innate drive to acquire power or material possessions.

servant leader
an ethical person who puts others—not herself or himself—in the foreground.

- *They articulate goals.* A servant leader gives certainty and purpose to others by clearly articulating a goal or, in today's leadership parlance, a vision.

- *They inspire trust.* Followers are confident of the leader's values, competence, and judgment. He has a sustaining spirit (entheos) that supports the tenacious pursuit of a goal.

- *They know how to listen.* The true, natural servant leader responds to any problem by listening first. You can discipline yourself to learn to listen first, and thus become a natural servant. Here, Greenleaf draws on the prayer of St. Francis: "Lord, grant that I may not seek so much to be understood as to understand."

- *They are masters of positive feedback.* The servant leader always offers unqualified acceptance of the person, although she doesn't necessarily accept the person's effort or performance.

- *They rely on foresight.* No leader ever has all the information necessary to make major decisions. But servant leaders have an intuitive sense that they use to bridge information gaps. Their ability to detach from day-to-day events allows their conscious and unconscious to work together to "better foresee the unforeseeable."

- *They emphasize personal development.* A servant leader views every problem as originating inside, rather than outside, himself. To remedy any "flaw in the world," the process of change starts in the servant, not "out there." Notes Greenleaf, "This is a difficult concept for that busybody, modern man."[23]

One person who embodies the servant leader philosophy is John Wooden, who coached the UCLA men's basketball team to an astounding ten national championships: "The great thing about Coach Wooden is that he is what he is," former player Bill Walton says. "This is a man with no pretensions. He is a humble, giving person who wants nothing more in return but to see other people succeed."[24]

In addition to legendary leaders like Coach Wooden, there are also servant leaders walking the halls of many companies and organizations today. One of the skills these leaders have in common is the ability to foster a work environment that embraces the elements of servant leadership. These include focusing on developing their people and service to others, sharing their power and delegating decision-making authority, and creating a sense of community.[25]

Who is a servant leader? Greenleaf said in the *Servant as Leader* that the servant leader is one who is a servant first. He wrote:

> It begins with the natural feeling that one wants to serve, to serve first. Then conscious choice brings one to aspire to lead. The best test is: do those served grow as persons; do they, while being served, become healthier, wiser, freer, more autonomous, more likely themselves to become servants? And, what is the effect on the least privileged in society; will they benefit, or at least, not be further deprived? [26]

Obviously, Greenleaf was looking beyond profit and productivity to a higher ideal. However, more than thirty years after writing his essay, his philosophy is still relevant in today's business world. Supervisors who act as servants set their people up for success. They provide their people with the necessary resources, tools, and training to get the job done. They support the development of their employees intellectually, physically, and emotionally. They recognize that their workers

Supervisors who act as servants set their people up for success.

are people, not just objects to complete a task. This concern for individuals and their well-being, combined with a clear vision, good systems, and excellent communication skills, is a strong indicator that the servant leader will ultimately achieve positive, high-quality team outcomes.

What Is the Ideal Leadership Style?

You have just learned about several leadership behaviors, theories, models, and styles. With the wide variety of options, it can be somewhat overwhelming to try and figure out which style is best. Put your mind at ease because there is no such thing as the ideal leadership style. In fact, the best answer to this question is, *"It depends."* Choosing the appropriate leadership style depends on many variables, including your own personal style, the level of readiness of your followers, the organization, and the situation itself. Lieutenant General William J. Lennox Jr., former Superintendent of the U.S. Military Academy at West Point summed this concept up nicely when he said:

> *A good leader has a number of styles that he or she uses depending on the situation.*

A good leader has a number of styles that he or she uses depending on the situation. If you're in a "must perform" environment, where time is short and the objective and process are complex, you have to be more assertive and you have to point people in the right direction and assign jobs and be very centralized. If you are in a less stressful environment, ideally you ought to be able to back off, allow subordinates to use their creativity and initiative: in this case, the job usually gets done a whole lot better.[27]

Groups

What is a group? From a sociological perspective, a **group** can be defined as two or more freely interacting individuals who share a common identity and purpose.[28] We will expand this definition to specifically address formal groups in the workplace. Following common practice among managers and supervisors, we use the terms *group* and *team* interchangeably as we explore the characteristics of mature groups and the six stages of development for new groups or teams.

Formal Groups

A **formal group** is a group created for the purpose of doing productive work. It may be called a *team*, a *committee*, or simply a *work group*. One person is normally granted formal leadership responsibility to ensure that group members carry out their assigned duties. Frequently, supervisors are recognized as the group leader for their division, location, shift, or production line.

group
two or more people who share a common identity and purpose.

formal group
a collection of people created to do something productive.

Characteristics of a Mature Group

Like children who mature into talented adults, groups undergo a maturation process before becoming effective. We have all experienced the uneasiness associated with the first meeting of a new group, be it a class, club, or committee. Initially, there is uncertainty about objectives, roles, and leadership combined with a lack of mutual understanding, trust, and commitment among the new group members. The prospect of cooperative action seems unlikely in view of the defensive behavior and potential differences of opinion about who should do what. Typically, someone steps forward or is assigned to the leadership role, and the group begins to make progress toward eventual maturity. A working knowledge of the characteristics of a mature group can help supervisors envision a goal for the group development process.

If and when a group takes on the following characteristics, it can be called a *mature group*:

1. Members are aware of their own and each other's assets and liabilities.
2. These individual differences are accepted without being labeled as good or bad.
3. The group has developed authority and interpersonal relationships that are recognized and accepted by members.
4. Group decisions are made through rational discussion. Minority opinions and dissension are recognized and encouraged. Attempts are not made to force decisions.
5. Conflict is over substantive group issues such as group goals and the effectiveness and efficiency of various means for achieving those goals. Conflict over emotional issues regarding group structure, processes, or interpersonal relationships is minimal.
6. Members are aware of the group's processes and their own roles in them.[29]

Supervisors serving as group leaders will typically rely on one or more of the leadership styles, discussed earlier, to guide a group from its early, immature beginning into a mature group.

Six Stages of Group Development

Experts have identified six distinct stages in the group development process: (1) orientation, (2) conflict and challenge, (3) cohesion, (4) delusion, (5) disillusion, and (6) acceptance.[30] See Figure 2.3 for an overview of the stages as they relate to the level of maturity of the group. Each stage confronts the group's leader and contributing members with a unique combination of problems and opportunities.

STAGE 1: ORIENTATION

Attempts are made to "break the ice." Uncertainty about goals, power, and interpersonal relationships is high. Members generally want and accept any leadership at this point.

STAGE 2: CONFLICT AND CHALLENGE

As the emergent leader's philosophy, objectives, and policies become apparent, individuals or subgroups advocating alternative courses of action struggle for control. Many groups never continue past stage 2 because they get bogged down due to emotionalism and infighting.

FIGURE 2.3 Group development from formation to maturity
Source: Adapted from Linda N. Jewell and H. Joseph Reitz, *Group Effectiveness in Organizations* (Glenview, IL: Scott, Foresman, 1981), 20. Used with permission of the authors.

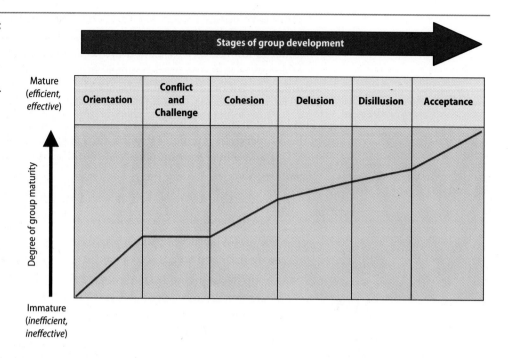

STAGE 3: COHESION

A "we" feeling becomes apparent as everyone becomes truly involved. Any lingering differences over authority, structure, and procedures are resolved quickly. This stage is usually relatively short.

STAGE 4: DELUSION

A feeling of "having been through the worst of it" prevails after a rather rapid transition through stage 3. Issues and problems that threaten to break this spell of relief are dismissed or treated lightly. Members seem committed to fostering harmony at all costs. Participation and camaraderie run high as members believe that all the difficult emotional problems have been solved.

STAGE 5: DISILLUSION

Subgroups tend to form as the delusion of unlimited goodwill wears off, and there is a growing disenchantment with the way things are turning out. Those with unrealized expectations challenge the group to perform better and are prepared to reveal their personal strengths and weaknesses if necessary. Others hold back. Tardiness and absenteeism are symptomatic of diminishing cohesiveness and commitment.

STAGE 6: ACCEPTANCE

Members' expectations are more realistic than ever before. Since the authority structure is generally accepted, subgroups can pursue different matters without threatening group cohesiveness. Consequently, stage 6 groups tend to be highly effective and efficient.

Supervisors can help their team members progress through this process by discussing the six stages with them. This awareness can reduce time-wasting problems and inefficiencies. However, just as it is impossible for a child to skip being a teenager on the way to adulthood, teams will find there are no shortcuts to group maturity. Some emotional stresses and strains are inevitable along the way.[31]

Teams and Teamwork

Contemporary organizations form synergistic teams of individuals with specialized skills. Ideally, the whole will be greater then the sum of the parts. When this assembly-line worker is done on this engine, the engine will move down the line to the next technician. Thanks to the combined efforts of many specialists, a high-quality motorcycle will soon roll off the assembly line.
© Keith Myers/MCT/Landov

synergy
the idea that the whole is greater than the sum of its parts.

cross-functional team
a task group staffed with a mix of specialists who are focused on a common objective.

The concept of synergy best captures the meaning of "team." **Synergy** is the idea that the whole is greater than the sum of its parts. There are many examples of synergistic relationships. Reese's Peanut Butter Cups are popular because they are a tasty combination of peanut butter and chocolate. For an industrial example, consider the Harley-Davidson Motorcycle manufacturing plant in York, Pennsylvania. The various factors involved in producing a motorcycle include design specifications for each of the different motorcycle's parts, people, assembly, painting, and testing. None of these factors alone can give you an exciting ride down the road. It requires synergy—all the factors brought together properly—to give you that ride. Key to the factory's synergy are synergistic teams that coordinate their efforts and communicate with other members of the organization to efficiently produce high-quality motorcycles.

Synergistic teams of specialists from different areas are the organizational structure of choice today. For instance, IBM's CEO, Samuel J. Palmisano, staked the future of his giant corporation on teams, starting at the top:

> For generations . . . [the] 12-person body presiding over IBM's strategy and initiatives represented the inner sanctum for every aspiring Big Blue executive . . . [In 2003], the CEO hit the send button on an e-mail to 300 senior managers announcing that this venerable committee was finito, kaput. Palmisano instead would work directly with three teams he had put in place the year before—they comprised people from all over the company who could bring the best ideas to the table. The old committee, with its monthly meetings, just slowed things down.[32]

Thus, teams and teamwork are vital group dynamics in the modern workplace.[33] In this section, we explore teams and teamwork by discussing cross-functional teams, strategies for developing effective teams, and specific suggestions for supervising a virtual team.

Cross-Functional Teams

A **cross-functional team** is a task group staffed with a mix of specialists who are focused on a common objective. The ultimate goal is to perform as a synergistic team where the group members collaborate to achieve a better result. This structural device deserves special attention here because cross-functional teams are becoming commonplace in today's workplace.[34] A cross-functional team is typically based on assigned rather than voluntary membership. It is quite different from the functional department approach, which can have problems integrating and coordinating between units. Boeing, for example, relies on cross-functional teams to integrate its various departments to achieve important strategic goals. The giant aircraft manufacturer thus accelerated its product development process for the Boeing 777 jetliner. Also,

Boeing engineer Grace Robertson turned to cross-functional teams for faster delivery of a big order of customized jetliners to United Parcel Service (UPS):

> When UPS ordered 30 aircraft, Boeing guaranteed that it could design and build a new, all-cargo version of the 767 jet in a mere 33 months—far faster than the usual cycle time of 42 months. The price it quoted meant slashing development costs dramatically.
>
> Robertson's strategy has been to gather all 400 employees working on the new freighter into one location and organize them into "cross-functional" teams. By combining people from the design, planning, manufacturing, and tooling sectors, the teams speed up development and cut costs by enhancing communication and avoiding rework.[35]

This teamwork approach helped Robertson's group stay on schedule and within budget, both vitally important achievements in Boeing's battle with Europe's Airbus to be the world's leading aircraft maker.

Cross-functional teams have exciting potential. But they present management with the immense challenge of getting technical specialists to cooperate and work effectively together.

Developing Effective Teams

Diversity is an important characteristic for organizations and teams. However, it may create some challenges as your team members' differences can lead to misunderstandings and/or miscommunication. Therefore, it is important for supervisors to consider each of the following areas when developing their team: (1) build trust, (2) establish ground rules, (3) develop common ground and establish clear communication channels, (4) value diversity, and (5) leverage individual strengths.

BUILD TRUST

Trust is a key ingredient for any successful team. **Trust** is a belief in the integrity, character, or ability of others, and it is essential if people are to achieve anything together in the long run.[36] Sadly, trust is not one of the hallmarks of the current U.S. business scene. In fact, 90% of adults surveyed indicated that corporations cannot be trusted to look out for the interests of their employees.[37] To a greater extent than they may initially suspect, supervisors heavily influence the level of trust in their work groups and teams.

Trust is a fragile thing. As most of us know from personal experience, trust grows at a painfully slow pace, yet can be destroyed in an instant with a thoughtless remark. Mistrust can erode the effectiveness of work teams and organizations. To develop long-term relationships of trust, supervisors need to embrace the six ways to build trust featured in Figure 2.4.

KNOWLEDGE TO ACTION

As a supervisor, you must build trust with your employees and coworkers. Consider and discuss five specific action items that you can do in the next week to help build trusting relationships with your team.

FIGURE 2.4 Six ways to build trust
Source: Adapted from Fernando Bartolomé, "Nobody Trusts the Boss Completely— Now What?" *Harvard Business Review* 67 (March-April 1989): 137–139.

Six Ways to Build Trust

1. **Communication**. Keep your people informed by providing accurate and timely feedback and by explaining policies and decisions. Be open and honest about your own problems and mistakes. Do not hoard information or use it as a political device or reward.

2. **Support**. Be an approachable person who is available to help, encourage, and coach your people. Show an active interest in their lives and be willing to come to their defense.

3. **Respect**. Delegating important duties is the sincerest form of respect, followed closely by being a good listener.

4. **Fairness**. Evaluate your people fairly and objectively and be liberal in giving credit and praise.

5. **Predictability**. Be dependable and consistent in your behavior and keep all your promises.

6. **Competence**. Be a good role model by exercising good business judgment and being technically and professionally competent.

FIGURE 2.5 Team ground rules

Team Ground Rules

Every team has unique personalities, goals, resources, and timelines. This list is intended as a starting point. Each team should take time to draft ground rules that are relevant and meaningful for the situation. Feel free to add to this list, delete, and/or modify.

1. Keep an open mind.

2. Give constructive feedback directly and openly.

3. Stay focused on clear objectives, directions, and project plans.

4. Acknowledge problems and deal with them.

ESTABLISH GROUND RULES FOR YOUR TEAM

When dealing with a diverse group of people, supervisors need to put a great deal of emphasis on communication. The first step is to establish ground rules for the team. (See Figure 2.5 for practical tips.) Keep in mind that every team has unique personalities, goals, resources, and timelines. Team leaders should kick-off the first meeting with a discussion of ground rules that are relevant and meaningful for the situation.

DEVELOP COMMON GROUND AND CLEAR COMMUNICATION CHANNELS

Team members need to have a clear purpose, goal(s), understanding of available resources, and background information such as budgets, and deadlines. They also need to understand expectations. In addition, team members need to know how to communicate with one another and with the team leader. Supervisors want to foster an open line of communication where the channels for feedback and suggestions are easy and clear for team members. Frequent updates and verification that everyone has the same understanding are important. Cultural differences, gender, age, educational level, and work experience are just a few of the variables that lead to misunderstandings and unnecessary conflict among team members. As the team leader, take the extra

trust
a belief in the integrity, character, or ability of others.

time to be sure everyone is on the same page. Clarifying expectations up front can reduce wasting time later.

VALUE DIVERSITY

In addition to cultural differences, you may have different levels of experience and education on your team. This requires you to communicate everything in a format that can be easily understood by everyone. The people on your team who are more advanced may get bored if there is too much time spent providing basic information. Consider conducting a separate meeting or briefing for individuals who need more time or a more lengthy explanation. Age differences can bring about great ideas, but they can also be the sources of frustration and stereotyping.

A difficult task for team leaders is to get all of the team members to value diversity rather than create biases, stereotypes, or negative energy. Begin by sharing how and why each person's unique qualities and characteristics are valued. Launching team meetings with a brief activity allows team members to get to know one another in a fun and educational way. As the team leader, it will be your job to make sure everyone knows that their ideas, opinions, and suggestions are valued.

A great example of this is from a story told by a sales associate working at a local bookstore where all the other employees were at least fifteen years older. His supervisor created an environment where everyone was valued and treated with respect. At a team meeting, the group was brainstorming about different ideas for expanding the store's video, gaming, and DVD offerings. The young man said he felt very safe and comfortable making a suggestion in front of his older, more experienced coworkers. When he shared his idea for a section featuring anime, many of his colleagues did not know what he was talking about; however, his supervisor encouraged them to listen and learn. The young man explained the animated-entertainment movement that has captured the attention of many young people. He continued with a recommendation to advertise in the local high school and college newspapers to announce the store's new offerings. The supervisor supported his recommendation. Had his supervisor not created an environment that embraced diversity, this young man may not have felt safe making this suggestion and ultimately the store would have lost out on what turned out to be a profitable idea.

LEVERAGE INDIVIDUAL STRENGTHS

Supervisors do more than just lead teams in developing lines of communication and guiding decision making. In fact, the majority of the time, supervisors are leading their teams to execute and achieve results. Therefore, the supervisor needs to know each team member's skills, knowledge, talents, interests, goals, dreams, values, and motivations. In addition, they need to know if each employee is properly trained, ready to take on the task, and understands the value and

One of the keys to supervision is to know your employees' abilities.

importance of the job. One of the keys to supervision is to know your employees' abilities and where they excel. This will allow you to assign individuals to tasks and roles that take advantage of their strengths. This is a crucial component of setting your people up for success. In addition, supervisors who assign tasks based on skills and ability benefit the organization by leveraging individual strengths to create an efficient and effective team.

Virtual Teams

A **virtual team** is a physically dispersed task group that interacts primarily by electronic means.[38] Telephones and voice mail, e-mail, videoconferencing, Web-based project software, and other forms of electronic interchange allow members of virtual teams from anywhere on the planet to pursue a common goal.[39] It is commonplace for virtual teams to have members from different organizations, different time zones, and different cultures.[40] The steps to forming a virtual team—providing members with the tools to do their jobs, building trust, and motivating the team—follow many of the steps mentioned previously. However, as Ms. Schwenger-Huffman mentioned at the beginning of this chapter, supervisors who lead virtual teams face some unique circumstances. This section provides the following practical suggestions for managing virtual teams: (1) forming the team, (2) preparing the team, (3) building teamwork and trust, and (4) motivating and leading the team.[41]

FORMING THE TEAM

The initial step for every team is the selection of team members. Once the group is formed, it is essential to clarify the purpose for the team. Consider the following suggestions when forming a team:

- Develop a team mission statement along with teamwork expectations and norms.
- Agree on project goals and deadlines.
- Recruit team members with complementary skills and diverse backgrounds who have the ability and willingness to contribute.
- Get a high-level sponsor to champion the team and/or project.
- On the company intranet or project Web page, post a biographical sketch, contact information, and "local time" matrix to familiarize members with one another and their geographic dispersion.

PREPARING THE TEAM

The next stage in team development involves identifying and providing the necessary resources and information to prepare the group. In addition, you need to be sure all team members are comfortable using the agreed-upon tools to achieve the goals of the group.

- Make sure everyone has a broadband connection and is comfortable with virtual teamwork technologies (e.g., e-mail, instant messaging, conference calls, online meeting and collaboration programs such as WebEx, and videoconferencing).
- Establish hardware and software standards for compatibility.

virtual team
a physically dispersed task group that interacts primarily by electronic means.

- Make sure everyone is comfortable with synchronous (interacting at the same time) and asynchronous (interacting at different times) teamwork.
- Get individuals to buy-in on team goals, deadlines, and individual tasks.

BUILDING TEAMWORK AND TRUST

One of the keys to successful groups is team chemistry. When individuals respect and trust one another, they will work better as a team. The team leader's role is to facilitate the team-building process in an effort to develop a cohesive group. Facilitation of team development includes:

- Make sure everyone is involved (during meetings and overall).
- Arrange periodic face-to-face meetings, team-building exercises, and leisure activities.
- Encourage collaboration between and among team members on subtasks.
- Establish an early-warning system for conflicts (e.g., gripe sessions).

MOTIVATING AND LEADING THE TEAM

Every member of your team is unique—their strengths, interests, values, and motivators will be different. The challenge for team leaders is to use individual strengths to achieve a group goal while providing rewards that are appealing to everyone. To keep your team focused and inspired, consider the following:

- Post a scoreboard to mark team progress toward goals.
- Celebrate team accomplishments both virtually and face-to-face.
- Begin each virtual meeting with praise and recognition for outstanding individual contributions.
- Keep team members' line supervisors informed of their accomplishments and progress.

Empowering Your Team

As you have read before, supervisors are responsible for getting work done through other people. When you achieve a high level of trust and confidence in your team members, you should be able to empower them to achieve goals and objectives without constant supervision. People generally resent having their supervisor looking over their shoulder and telling them every move to make.

What Is Empowerment?

empowerment
making employees full partners in the decision-making process and giving them the necessary tools and rewards.

Empowerment occurs when employees are adequately trained, provided with all relevant information and the best possible tools, fully involved in key decisions, and fairly rewarded for results.[42] Those who endorse this key building block of progressive management view power as an unlimited resource. As Frances Hesselbein, a widely respected former head of the Girl Scouts of the USA, puts it, "The more power you give away, the more you have."[43] The challenge for today's supervisors is to understand how and why to empower their employees.

THEY
SAID IT
BEST

When you fully empower people, your paradigm of yourself changes. You become a servant. You no longer control others; they control themselves. You become a source of help to them.

—STEPHEN R. COVEY

Source: Stephen R. Covey, *Principle-Centered Leadership* (New York, NY: Fireside, Simon & Schuster, 1991), 256–257.

Why Empower Your Team Members?

Empowering your team achieves a variety of positive results. It enables your employees to serve customers more efficiently and it provides the supervisor with more time to focus on other aspects of their job.[44]

Many see an empowered corporate culture as a place where all employees, regardless of their position or title, accept responsibility for their own and the organization's performance.[45] The essence of empowerment is to train your employees so they understand the organization's values, policies, procedures, and their role in achieving the desired outcomes. One of the goals is to allow employees to make decisions without checking in with their supervisor. An excellent example of this can be experienced with retail giant L.L. Bean. If a customer has a product that has failed (for example, a broken zipper), every employee at L.L. Bean has been empowered to handle the situation. Every employee has been trained in L.L. Bean's mission, values, policies, and procedures and they have been empowered to take action to support each of these. The employee who is presented with the failed zipper knows that she can either offer to have it repaired or allow the customer to choose a replacement. The employee does not need to check with a supervisor. It is at her discretion to do what is necessary to make sure the customer leaves satisfied and remains loyal to L.L. Bean.

Getting Started: Taking the First Steps Toward Empowering Your Team

Empowering your team takes time, training, desire, commitment, vision, and trust. Lieutenant Colonel Martin Tillman, instructor of program management and leadership with the Defense Acquisition University at Fort Belvoir, Virginia, has identified seven key considerations related to empowering a team:

- Not everyone wants to be empowered
- There must be a common vision/strategic direction
- Convey the strategic direction in a manner that inspires and helps people to see their role in its accomplishment
- Gain your subordinates' trust
- Build on shared values
- Strive for complete business process/vision alignment
- Don't forget to use the right tools[46]

You have already learned about developing a common vision that appeals to everyone. Part of this process is letting people on your team know how their skills and knowledge contribute to the success of the team. Gaining subordinates' trust (and learning to trust your subordinates) takes time. To gain and keep trust, you always want to be honest with your employees. If they catch you in a lie, they are unlikely to ever trust you again. In addition, follow through on promises. If you tell an employee you will do something by a certain day, plan to deliver a day or two earlier than promised. That way, you can still deliver on time even if something unexpected happens (e.g., you get sick or your computer crashes). One of the best ways to build and reinforce trust relationships is to have frequent, open, and honest communication.

Another point Colonel Tillman makes is to use the right tools. This includes everything from communication tools to problem-solving tools to motivational tools. As we have discussed, it is essential that you get to know your employees as unique individuals so you can be effective in selecting the right tools.

KNOWLEDGE TO ACTION

1. Why do you think L.L. Bean has empowered its employees to make independent decisions that ultimately have financial consequences?

2. What steps do you think L.L. Bean took in the process of empowering its employees and also setting them up for success?

Effective Delegation

Delegation is the process of assigning duties and responsibilities to another individual and giving him/her the necessary decision-making authority to be successful in the completion of assigned tasks.[47] Although the individual completing the work is accountable to the supervisor, the supervisor has ultimate accountability for the quality of the work and overall performance of the team.

What Is the Difference Between Empowerment and Delegation?

Many use the terms *empowerment* and *delegation* interchangeably. There is certainly overlap and the steps to implementation are fairly similar. However, empowerment is more broadly focused on a philosophy, a culture, and an overall thread running through an organization. Delegation involves sharing direct authority and responsibility for specific work with your employee(s). It is one step toward empowering your employees.

Why Delegate?

As you learned in Chapter 1, supervisors wear many hats and have a wide variety of responsibilities. Most successful supervisors choose to delegate authority and responsibility to their employees. Delegation can provide two major benefits: (1) it allows you to train and develop your employees and (2) it increases the efficiency and effectiveness of the entire team.[48] It can be a challenge for supervisors to motivate and inspire their employees when they practice delegation. Employees sometimes perceive delegation as simply having more work "dumped" on them. However, if done properly, delegation is an effective way to make more time available for supervisors to plan, train, coach, and motivate. In addition, employees who desire more challenge generally become more committed and satisfied when they are given the opportunity to take on more responsibility or tackle significant problems.

Conversely, a lack of delegation can stifle initiative. Consider the situation of a California builder:

> [The founder and chairman] personally negotiates every land deal. Visiting every construction site repeatedly, he is critical even of details of cabinet construction. "The building business is an entrepreneurial business," he says. "Yes, you can send out people. But you better follow them. You have to manage your managers."
>
> Says one former . . . executive: "The turnover there's tremendous. He hires bright and talented people, but then he makes them eunuchs. He never lets them make any decisions."[49]

Supervisors who are perfectionists have a tendency to micromanage and avoid delegation. As a result, they have problems in the long run when they become overwhelmed by minute details.

Delegation Is Not Relinquishing Responsibility

The delegation process is not a quick fix for a supervisor's time management dilemmas. Former President Harry Truman is said to have had a little sign on his desk that read, "The Buck Stops Here!"[50] Supervisors who delegate should keep this in mind because, although authority may be passed along to people at the lower levels, *ultimate* responsibility cannot be passed along. Thus, delegation is the sharing of authority, not the abdication of responsibility. Even seasoned business executives can forget this. For example, Chrysler's former CEO Lee Iacocca fell victim to this particular lapse:

delegation
giving others additional responsibilities, authority, and the necessary tools.

When the company started to make money, it spent its cash on stock buybacks and acquisitions. For his part, Iacocca was distracted by nonautomotive concerns.

[Iacocca] concedes that while he kept his finger on finance and marketing, he should have paid closer attention to new model planning. "If I made one mistake," he says now, "it was delegating all the product development and not going to one single meeting."[51]

Iacocca corrected this mistake before he retired by getting involved in the design process, which led to a positive outcome as customers responded favorably to Chrysler's bold new designs.

Getting Started with Delegating

There are several reasons why supervisors generally do not delegate as much as they should:

- Belief in the fallacy, "If you want it done right, do it yourself"
- Lack of confidence and trust in lower-level employees
- Low self-confidence
- Fear of being called lazy
- Lack of planning
- Vague job definition
- Fear of competition from those below
- Reluctance to take the risks entailed in depending on others
- Lack of controls that provide early warning of problems with delegated duties
- Poor example set by bosses who do not delegate[52]

Managers can go a long way toward delegating effectively by recognizing and correcting these tendencies both in themselves and in their fellow managers and supervisors.[53] Since successful delegation is habit forming, the first step is usually the hardest. Properly trained and motivated people who know how to take initiative in challenging situations often reward a delegator's trust with a job well done.[54]

As you embark on this journey to learn effective delegation skills, remember that delegation takes time, planning, patience, and frequent communication. Therefore, it is important to be thoughtful and purposeful in your approach to delegation. Consider following these steps:

1. **Assess Employees' Readiness:** Assess the level of readiness of your employee(s) before you decide to delegate.

2. **Choose What to Delegate:** Identify a specific task, job, or responsibility that can be delegated. Choose something that is relatively straightforward, fairly simple to teach, and can be easily measured or monitored. Imagine for a moment that you are the supervisor of a call center that responds to customer service phone calls. Your shift ends at 10:00 P.M. Each evening you have a closing procedure that includes transferring the telephones to a remote operator, printing a call summary report for the shift, setting the alarm system, and locking up. Rather than delegating all of your responsibilities at once, you may choose to delegate them one at a time. This will allow you to first train someone on a simple task such as transferring the phones. Let this individual

try it for a few nights, then make sure proper procedures are being followed simply by placing a test call.

3. **Prepare Training Materials:** Once the task is identified, prepare a detailed document that explains the process or job in detail. Include any guidelines, forms, contracts, limitations, or parameters. For example, you may choose to delegate product purchasing to one of your employees. However, you need to create a limitation that any purchase over, say, $500 requires your signature. After a trial period, you may choose to increase the dollar amount based on performance, trust, and confidence.

4. **Identify Performance Measures:** Determine how you will measure success. Remember, delegating does not mean you are no longer accountable for the end result. Therefore, you need to identify a method to verify that the work is being completed and continues to meet the same quality standards. Determine when and how you will monitor progress.

5. **Train Employees:** Meet with employees when there is plenty of time to train them, let them practice while you are there to assist, and provide them with ample opportunity to ask questions.

6. **Let Employees, Customers, and Vendors Know:** Communicate with everyone who is connected with the task to let them know you have delegated authority to someone new. Explain how training will take place and how they should communicate any concerns or questions. The entire team needs to be on board and supportive of the newly delegated person.

7. **Give It Meaning:** When communicating with team members, take a few extra minutes to explain why you are choosing to delegate to someone and how this continues to support the vision, mission, and goals of the organization.

8. **Set Your Person Up for Success:** Set the proper tone—realize that your employees will probably make mistakes. Let them know it is okay to ask questions. You also want them to report any problems to you right away. It is far better to be made aware of potential problems than to hear about it weeks later from an irate customer or concerned boss. This requires that you make it "safe" for them to report issues to you. The first time you yell at them or discipline them will likely be the last time they are forthcoming with bad news. Find the proper balance and be patient.

9. **Follow Up:** Check in with your employees, review their work and reports, and go over the performance measures discussed in step 4.

10. **Celebrate Success and Give Credit:** Give credit where credit is due. Servant leaders and successful supervisors get satisfaction from seeing their subordinates succeed. Employees always appreciate being recognized and thanked. Take time to acknowledge your employees' contributions and achievements.

Delegation requires that delegators follow up.

Once supervisors have developed the habit of delegating, they need to remember this wise advice from Peter Drucker: "Delegation . . . requires that delegators follow up. They rarely do—they think they have delegated, and that's it. But, they are still accountable for performance. And, so they have to follow up, and have to make sure that the task gets done—and done right."[55]

SUMMARY

1. Leadership is the process of inspiring, influencing, directing, and guiding others to participate in a common effort. Some of the qualities of inspired leaders are (1) ethical, (2) committed to making a difference and developing their people, (3) excellent communicators, (4) focused on their vision and priorities, (5) confidence and trust in their team, (6) determined, (7) passionate and proud of what they do, and (8) able to promote a shared vision.

2. There are many leadership theories and expert opinions about which leadership style is most effective. There is no perfect definition or theory and there is no ideal leadership style. Choosing the appropriate leadership style depends on many variables, including your own personal style, the level of readiness of your followers, the organization, and the situation itself. There are three well-known behavioral leadership styles: (1) authoritarian, (2) democratic, and (3) laissez-faire. In addition, there are three different approaches to situational leadership: (1) Ken Blanchard and Paul Hersey's model, (2) Fred Fiedler's contingency theory, and (3) the path-goal theory.

The servant leader is an ethical person who puts others first—not herself or himself—in the foreground. The essence of Greenleaf's servant leadership philosophy is that a leader's role is to serve his/her followers. One of the characteristics servant leaders have in common is the ability to foster a work environment that embraces the elements of servant leadership. These include (1) focusing on developing their people, (2) service to others, (3) sharing their power, (4) delegating decision-making authority, and (5) creating a sense of community.

3. A group can be defined as two or more freely interacting individuals who share a common identity and purpose. A formal group or team is created for the purpose of doing productive work. One person is normally granted formal leadership responsibility to ensure that the members carry out their assigned duties. Frequently, supervisors are recognized as the group leader for their division, shift, or production line. Experts have identified six distinct stages in the group development process: (1) orientation, (2) conflict and challenge, (3) cohesion, (4) delusion, (5) disillusion, and (6) acceptance.

4. Synergy is the idea that the combination of many parts creates a better end result. Therefore, synergistic teams bring together diverse individuals to achieve a positive outcome. An example of a synergistic team is a cross-functional team that is a mix of specialists who are focused on a common objective. Team development involves (1) building trust, (2) establishing ground rules, (3) developing common ground and establishing clear communication channels, (4) valuing diversity, and (5) leveraging individual strengths. A virtual team is a physically dispersed task group that interacts primarily by electronic means such as telephones and voice mail, e-mail, videoconferencing, Web-based project software, and other forms of electronic interchanges. There are some unique circumstances facing supervisors responsible for managing virtual teams, including (1) forming the team, (2) preparing the team, (3) building teamwork and trust, and (4) motivating and leading the team.

5. Empowerment occurs when employees are adequately trained, provided with all relevant information and the best possible tools, fully involved in key decisions, and fairly rewarded for results. Some of the benefits of empowerment include enabling employees to serve customers more efficiently and providing supervisors with more time to focus on other aspects of their job. This process takes time, training, desire, commitment, vision, and trust.

6. Delegation is the process of assigning duties and responsibilities to other individuals and giving them the necessary decision-making authority to be successful in the completion of their tasks. However, it also requires supervisors to follow-up. Delegation can provide two major benefits: (1) it allows supervisors to train and develop employees and (2) it increases the efficiency and effectiveness of the entire team. Delegation takes time, planning, patience, and frequent communication. Ten steps to follow when delegating tasks include (1) assess employee readiness, (2) choose what to delegate, (3) prepare training materials, (4) identify performance measures, (5) train employees, (6) communicate changes, (7) make it meaningful, (8) foster success, (9) follow up, and (10) celebrate success and give credit.

TERMS TO UNDERSTAND

achievement-oriented leadership style, p. 37
authoritarian leader, p. 32
behavioral leadership styles, p. 32
Blanchard and Hersey's situational leadership model, p. 33
cross-functional team, p. 43
delegation, p. 50
democratic leader, p. 32

directive leadership style, p. 37
empowerment, p. 48
Fiedler's contingency theory, p. 35
formal group, p. 40
group, p. 40
jargon, p. 30
laissez-faire leader, p. 32
leadership, p. 29
participative leadership style, p. 37

path-goal theory, p. 36
servant leader, p. 38
situational leadership, p. 33
supportive leadership style, p. 37
synergy, p. 43
trust, p. 44
virtual team, p. 47

QUESTIONS FOR REFLECTION

1. There are many different leadership theories and no ideal leadership style. Explain what "it depends" means to you in the context of choosing the best leadership style.

2. What are some of the differences between the three behavioral styles of leadership (authoritarian, democratic, and laissez-faire)?

3. What are three steps you can take today to practice servant-leadership skills? Explain.

4. Describe a synergistic team that you have observed or been a part of.
   a. Why was it synergistic?
   b. What were some the benefits?
   c. What were some of the challenges?

5. Why are team ground rules important? What are some of the most important ground rules to consider?

HANDS-ON ACTIVITIES

VALUING DIVERSITY

Read the following diversity statement from Google Corporation's website and answer the questions that follow.

Google Celebrates Diversity

As the billions of pages in our index show, Google is a great believer in inclusiveness.

Google aspires to be an organization that reflects the globally diverse audience that our search engine and tools serve. We believe that in addition to hiring the best talent, the diversity of perspectives, ideas, and cultures leads to the creation of better products and services. This diversity of our employees and partners serves as the foundation for us to better serve our diverse customers and stakeholders all over the world.

Diversity plays a large role in the way we're developing our engineering organization around the world. We're building a large worldwide office presence to establish ample global representation among our engineers, and we're applying that same focus to establish a balanced representation of employees at Google. In the end, these efforts help us more accurately and relevantly represent our users, and our continued success depends on the best minds working from different perspectives and insights.

—Alan Eustace, Google SVP, Engineering & Research

Google considers diversity a business imperative. We foster diversity through awarding scholarships, outreach in K-12 initiatives, partnerships, and striving to perfect a work environment that is inclusive, supportive, and collaborative.

Source: Google Corporation's website, © 2008 Google. Viewed April 19, 2008. http://www.google.com/support/jobs/bin/answer.py?answer=55998.

1. What impact do you think this statement has on Google's current employees?

2. How do you think this statement affects Google's ability to recruit new employees?

3. The last paragraph states, "Google considers diversity a business imperative." Explain why you think diversity should be a business imperative for Google or any other company.

LEADERSHIP

1. Identify a public leader who you think demonstrates one of the behavioral leadership styles.

   a. Whom did you identify?

   b. Which of the behavioral leadership styles does he/she demonstrate? Explain your answer.

2. Identify a public leader who you think demonstrates one of the situational leadership models.

   a. Whom did you identify?

   b. Which of the situational leadership models does he/she demonstrate? Explain your answer.

3. Identify a public leader who you think demonstrates servant leadership and explain your answer.

4. Which of the leaders you identified in questions 1-3 would you want to follow? Explain your answer.

Interview an Expert

Select a leader to interview. This may be a supervisor, manager, project leader, or team leader at your work or someone you know from another business or nonprofit organization. After the interview, document what you gathered from the person during the conversation and conclude with a summary of how you can apply what you learned to your own personal growth and development as a leader and supervisor. In other words, answer the question, "What can you learn from this experience and what new information will make you a better supervisor in the future?"

SAMPLE QUESTIONS

1. What was your path to a leadership position?

2. How would you describe your leadership style? (You may want to share information you have learned in this chapter.)

3. How has your personal leadership style helped or hindered your ability to lead?

4. How has your leadership style changed over the years? Why?

5. What are your suggestions for effectively leading a team that is physically located together?

6. If applicable, what are your suggestions for effectively leading a virtual team?

You may improvise and add or edit questions to fit the situation or the circumstances of your interview. Schedule your interview ahead of time and try to limit it to about 15 minutes. Remember to send a thank-you note to the person you interview.

YOU DECIDE

CASE STUDY 2.1
Delegation

Connor is the housekeeping supervisor at a five-star hotel. His company is committed to a corporate culture of empowerment. The company is completing construction on a conference center adjacent to the hotel. Connor has been asked to take responsibility for all of the recruiting,

hiring, and training of new housekeeping staff for the conference center while also maintaining his current job as housekeeping supervisor.

Fifteen people work for Connor. Christopher has been with the hotel for twelve years. He is a reliable,

---

high-performing member of the housekeeping department. In fact, he has been selected as employee of the year two out of the last three years. Although he has never been responsible for supervision or training, he has taken a supervision class at the local community college and he has expressed an interest in taking on more responsibility. Connor realizes that he cannot do everything himself. So he plans to delegate some responsibilities and authority. He believes Christopher is ready to lead the hotel housekeeping team.

Questions

1. How would you recommend Connor begin the process of delegating?

2. What are some of the potential barriers?

3. What can Connor do to set Christopher up for success?

4. What responsibility, if any, will Connor have for the hotel housekeeping department once he has delegated responsibility and authority for day-to-day operations to Christopher?

SUPERVISOR'S TOOLKIT

Complete this survey of your own skills inventory, interests, goals, and motivators. With this knowledge, you can be more focused on your own career planning and academic goals. In addition, you should have all of your employees complete this inventory. This will allow you to learn more about your employees. The results can be used as a tool to work with each person to prepare a professional development plan.

1. What are your goals and expectations for work?

2. What skills do you have and how would you rate your level of proficiency for each (beginner, intermediate, advanced)?

3. What do you like doing the most? Why?

4. In what areas would you like to improve?

5. Would you like more or less responsibility? Explain.

6. What motivates you?

7. What do you want to get out of this job (e.g., social interaction, new skills, money)?

8. Identify three work-related performance rewards that are meaningful to you.

You can list specific skills or knowledge that are unique to your workplace and you can add or edit questions to meet your needs.

CHAPTER 3

Planning, Goal Setting, and Achieving Results

Learning Objectives

1. Explain what a well-written organizational mission statement should accomplish.

2. Describe the planning process, list three different types of plans, and explain why it is important to link planning with the organization's mission.

3. Explain the importance of goals, list four different types, explain how to write SMART goals, and create your own personal goals.

4. Describe two tools for prioritizing.

5. Explain the planning and control cycle and discuss the importance of assessing performance and measuring outcomes.

6. Explain how supervisors can increase accountability to achieve positive results.

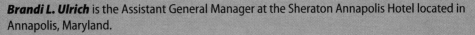

Straight Talk from the Field

Brandi L. Ulrich is the Assistant General Manager at the Sheraton Annapolis Hotel located in Annapolis, Maryland.

QUESTION . . . *How are planning and goal setting used in your organization?*

RESPONSE . . .

In the hospitality industry, there are goals for virtually every area of our operation. We have annual revenue goals and guest satisfaction goals. We have monthly occupancy and RevPar (revenue per available room) goals. We have daily goals of meeting all our guests' needs and flawlessly executing all the plans for the day. With so many goals to meet, we spend a lot of time planning and then revisiting and revising our plans.

Due to the diverse nature of our goals, we use all three types of plans: strategic, intermediate, and operational. Strategic plans are developed around our annual goals and are revisited on an annual basis. The strategic plan is tied to our annual revenue goals and our budget.

We use intermediate and operational plans on a daily basis to help us achieve our daily goals and other easily measurable successes. To illustrate our use of planning, try to imagine a high-occupancy day at a hotel. For example, let's say we have 200 rooms in our hotel and, on Friday night, 180 of them are occupied with 100 scheduled to check out on Saturday. The posted check-out time at our hotel is 11 A.M. That same Saturday, there are 80 rooms checking in that are a part of a large wedding party. While no promises have been made, the wedding ceremony begins at 1 P.M. and the bride has been told that we would do everything possible to get her guests into their rooms prior to 1 P.M. Since we need 80 rooms and only 20 will be ready first thing Saturday morning, we need to create a plan to get 60 rooms cleaned and ready by 1 P.M. on Saturday.

In this situation, our primary goal is to keep the bride and her guests happy. One way to do this would be to have all the rooms cleaned by 1 P.M. We can put a plan together to do this, which would include having all housekeepers on hand Saturday morning and having additional staff from other departments standing by to help. However, there is still a large uncontrollable variable in our plan: When will the 100 departing guests check out on Saturday morning? If they all check out early in the morning, our plan to have the rooms ready will be feasible. However, if all the guests decide to sleep in, have a leisurely breakfast, and check out around 11 A.M., our plan has a lower chance of success.

Luckily, our goal is to keep the bride and her guests happy and not necessarily to have everyone in their rooms by 1 P.M. In instances like this, a back-up plan or contingency plan is always created to serve as an alternative method of reaching our goal. In this situation, we might offer the wedding guests somewhere to store their luggage if their room was not ready before the wedding began. We may also designate a room or another area of the hotel where wedding guests could change or freshen up prior to the ceremony. Since the goal is to keep these guests happy, we try to anticipate all of their needs and have solutions ready to meet them.

In the hospitality industry, every day is different than the one before. It is one of the things that can make a career in hospitality so exciting and dynamic. Teamwork is crucial, and each day presents new challenges and opportunities for improvement. If we do not plan effectively, it would be very difficult to deliver a great experience to any of our guests, which is the ultimate goal of any hotel, especially ours.

59

Chapter Outline

Planning is an essential component of the supervisor's role. In this chapter, you will be introduced to various types of planning and strategies for achieving desired results. We begin our discussion with an overview of the organizational mission—the cornerstone of the planning process. We then provide an overview of planning, followed by a discussion of the goal-setting process. Later in the chapter, you will learn about assessing performance, the importance of measuring outcomes, and being accountable for results.

Organizational Mission

To some, defining an organization's mission might seem unnecessary. But the opposite is true. An organizational mission has been compared to a map because it provides direction and defines the primary purpose of the organization. Without a clear mission, some organizations simply drift along. Others lose sight of their original mission. Sometimes, an organization, such as Bluedot Software, Inc., finds its original mission is no longer appropriate. So Bluedot's CEO Craig Barberich guided a mission change that turned a consulting firm into a software vendor utilizing e-commerce tools.[1] Periodically redefining an organization's mission is both common and necessary in an era of rapid change.

A clear, formally written, and well-publicized statement of an organization's mission is the cornerstone of any planning system.

A good **mission statement** generates a positive image for all the organization's stakeholders and provides a focal point for the entire planning process. A clear, formally written, and well-publicized statement of an organization's mission is the cornerstone of any planning system that will effectively guide the organization through uncertain times.

The following satirical definition by Scott Adams, the *Dilbert* cartoonist, tells us how *not* to write an organizational mission statement: "A Mission Statement is

mission statement
defines the primary purpose of an organization, generates a positive image, and provides a focal point for planning.

FIGURE 3.1 Sample mission statement

The Mission of Southwest Airlines

The mission of Southwest Airlines is dedication to the highest quality of Customer Service delivered with a sense of warmth, friendliness, individual pride, and Company Spirit.

To Our Employees
We are committed to provide our Employees a stable work environment with equal opportunity for learning and personal growth. Creativity and innovation are encouraged for improving the effectiveness of Southwest Airlines. Above all, Employees will be provided the same concern, respect, and caring attitude within the organization that they are expected to share externally with every Southwest Customer.

January 1988

Source: Southwest Airlines website, http://www.southwest.com/about_swa/mission.html (accessed April 19, 2008). Courtesy Southwest Airlines.

---

defined as a long, awkward sentence that demonstrates management's inability to think clearly."[2] This sad state of affairs, too often true, can be avoided by a well-written mission statement.

A well-written mission statement should accomplish the following:

1. *Defines* your organization for its key stakeholders.
2. Creates an *inspiring vision* of what the organization can be and can do.
3. Outlines *how* the vision is to be accomplished.
4. Establishes key *priorities*.
5. States a *common goal* and fosters a sense of togetherness.
6. Creates a *philosophical anchor* for all organizational activities.
7. Generates *enthusiasm* and a "can do" attitude.
8. *Empowers* present and future organization members to believe that *every* individual is the key to success.[3]

A succinct example comes from Alan Brunacini, the long-time chief of the Phoenix, Arizona, Fire Department. He boiled his department's mission down to five words: "Prevent harm, survive, be nice."[4] (See Figure 3.1 for another good example.)

KNOWLEDGE TO ACTION

Read the Southwest Airlines mission statement to answer the following questions.

1. Does the mission statement define the primary purpose of the organization? Explain why or why not.

_____

2. What is the philosophical anchor for all organizational activities?

_____

The Essentials of Planning

As you learned in Chapter 1, planning is one of the five functions of management that supervisors are frequently responsible for, or at least involved in. Planning is an ever-present feature of modern life, although there is no universal approach to it. Virtually everyone is a planner, at least in the informal sense. We plan leisure activities after school or work; we plan what to cook for dinner; we make career plans. Personal or informal plans give purpose and direction to our lives. In a similar fashion, more formalized plans enable supervisors to organize their resources to achieve organizational purposes. A **plan** is a specific, documented intention consisting of an objective and an action statement. The objective portion is the end result or desired outcome, and the action statement represents the means to that end. In other words, objectives give supervisors targets to shoot at, whereas action statements provide the arrows for hitting the targets. Properly developed plans tell *what, when*, and *how* something is to be done.

Supervisors may encounter a wide variety of formal planning systems on the job. Regardless of the various tools that are available, sound planning involves certain essential characteristics. Among these common denominators are three types of planning, the organizational mission, goals and objectives, priorities, and the planning/control cycle.

Types of Planning

Typically, planning begins at the top of the organization pyramid and filters down. The rationale for beginning at the top is the need for coordination. It is top management's job to state the organization's mission, establish priorities, and draw up major policies. However, as we will learn later in the chapter, effective leaders recognize the value of involving all levels in the development process. After the mission statement, priorities, and major policies are established, successive rounds of strategic, intermediate, and operational planning can occur. Figure 3.2 represents an idealized picture of the three types of planning, as carried out by different levels of management. Keep in mind that even in small organizations where there may not be multiple layers of management, all three levels of planning still need to occur.

Gary Kelly (left) is the CEO of Southwest Airlines. When explaining how his company distinguishes itself from the competition, he said, "One of Southwest's rituals is finding and developing People who are 'built to serve.' That allows us to provide a personal, warm level of service that is unmatched in the airline industry." It is evident from this photo that the employees of Southwest airlines appreciate Kelly's people-centered approach as they give him an enthusiastic greeting. (Quote: *Spirit Magazine*, August 2008, http://www.southwest.com/about_swa/?ref=abtsw_gn)
© Matthew Staver/Bloomberg News/Landov

STRATEGIC PLANNING

Strategic planning is the process of determining how to pursue the organization's long-term goals with the resources expected to be available. A well-conceived strategic plan communicates much more than general intentions about profit and growth. It specifies *how* the organization will achieve a competitive advantage, with profit and growth as necessary byproducts.

FIGURE 3.2 Types of planning

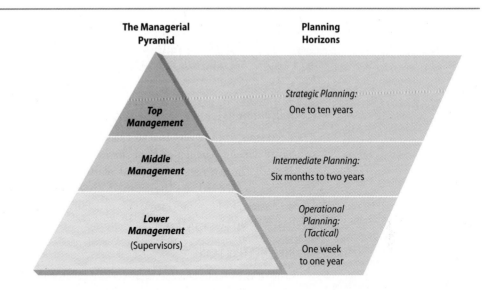

Nonprofit organizations need strategic plans every bit as much as for-profit organizations. However, the objective may be slightly different. Rather than focusing on earnings, nonprofit groups may focus on how to achieve their goals and also sustain/increase financial and human resources while continuing to serve.

Strategic plans usually cover a time period of one to ten years. Because of this extended period of time, strategic plans tend to be more general in nature. As we discussed in Chapter 1, top-level management is usually responsible for strategic planning. This is the first stage of planning. Goals and objectives developed during the strategic planning process are further refined and put into action during the other levels of planning discussed next.

INTERMEDIATE PLANNING

Intermediate planning is the process of determining the contributions subunits can make with allocated resources.[5] It is referred to in some organizations as *tactical planning*.

Intermediate plans usually cover a time period of six months to two years. Because the duration of time is much shorter than the strategic plans, intermediate plans are more detailed. Frequently, mid-level management is responsible for this phase of planning. However, depending on the size of the organization, supervisors and other lower-level managers may be involved.

OPERATIONAL PLANNING

Operational planning is the process of determining how specific tasks can best be accomplished on time with available resources.

Operational plans usually cover a time period of one week to one year. They include everything from preparing production and staffing schedules to budget planning. Supervisors are frequently responsible for preparing these detailed plans. Thus, several aspects of operational planning will be explored further in subsequent chapters.

plan
an objective plus an action statement.

strategic planning
determining how to pursue long-term goals with available resources.

intermediate planning
determining subunits' contributions using allocated resources.

operational planning
determining how to accomplish specific tasks with available resources.

The Planning Process

Successful organizations view planning as an ongoing process rather than a one-time event.

The planning process involves many people at many levels. Successful organizations view planning as an ongoing process rather than a one-time event.

WHO DOES WHAT?

Each level of planning is vital to an organization's success and cannot effectively stand alone without the support of the other two levels. As Figure 3.2 illustrates, the time periods for the various types of planning overlap, since their boundaries are elastic rather than rigid. As mentioned previously, supervisors are often responsible for operational planning. However, it is fairly common for middle managers to assist in drawing up these plans.

IMPLEMENTING PLANS

One of the challenges facing most organizations that engage in the planning process is successfully implementing their plans. It is not uncommon for businesses to prepare a strategic plan and then put it on a shelf, never to be looked at again.[6] One of the keys to making the best use of a strategic plan is to commit to the next two levels of planning. This should provide the details for implementation, including goals and objectives, priorities, outcome measures, and follow-up plans. We live in a rapidly changing world that requires organizations to consistently assess their strategic, intermediate, and operational plans to make sure the plans are still relevant.

We live in a rapidly changing world that requires organizations to consistently assess their strategic, intermediate, and operational plans to be sure the plans are still relevant.

CONTINGENCY PLANS

As we learned from Brandi Ulrich in the chapter opener, having a contingency plan is an important part of effective operational planning. Contingency plans are often referred to as *Plan B*. In other words, a **contingency plan** is a back-up plan that is prepared just in case a situation does not turn out as expected. Preparing a contingency plan begins by anticipating what could go wrong (e.g., a busy student doesn't hear the alarm and misses a big exam). Asking your team for input during this process can reveal scenarios and/or variables that you may not have considered. The next step is to identify potential solutions to each item identified. Ms. Ulrich's contingency plan for her wedding party scenario provides a good example of this process and how to plan for uncontrollable variables.

WHY CONNECT THE MISSION TO PLANNING?

Organizations with employees who understand the mission and goals experience a much greater return on investment of time and resources in preparing a strategic plan.[7] If you think of the mission as the purpose and direction for the organization, then it naturally makes sense to begin the strategic planning process by asking the question, "How do we continue to achieve our mission?" The ultimate goal in planning is to craft strategies for fulfilling the mission.

INVOLVING YOUR EMPLOYEES

Increasingly, organizations are involving employees from all levels in the strategic planning process. Direct participation in strategic planning gives employees

contingency plan
a back-up plan prepared for a defined scenario or set of circumstances.

a sense personal ownership and a feeling of responsibility for results. Human nature is such that people want to have a sense of belonging and purpose that is greater than just themselves.[8] This desire to contribute to something bigger helps explain why employees generally respond well to being involved in the strategic planning process. Also, as you learned in Chapter 2, employees are looking to follow leaders who are genuine and trustworthy. When mutual respect and trust between employees and upper management exists, strategic planning is a powerful process for uniting everyone in the organization and moving forward together to achieve the mission.

In addition, supervisors and employees are better prepared to link their weekly and monthly operational plans with the strategic and intermediate plans if they are involved in the development of these longer-range plans. In short, they "get it."

VIRTUAL TEAM MEMBERS

Do not forget about your virtual team members. As just discussed, trust is a necessary ingredient for successful strategic planning, yet it is often one of the most difficult areas to develop with virtual team members. According to business author and expert Ken Blanchard, virtual teams should have a shared vision, purpose, and values. To build a foundation of trust, team members need to respect one another, value individual strengths, contribute to the success of the team, and hold each other accountable for outcomes.[9] This requires a systematic approach and frequent, formal communication.

It is essential that you determine when and how you can get your virtual team members involved. They will not have the benefit of hearing casual conversations in the hallway or over lunch, so you must provide a communication mechanism for them to ask questions, verify information, and stay connected to the process. One way to achieve a high level of consistent communication for everyone in the organization is to create a private Web page for the planning process where team members can post documents, provide input, read meeting minutes, and stay abreast of due dates and overall progress.

THE BENEFITS OF EMPLOYEE PARTICIPATION

Successful execution of any plan—be it strategic, intermediate, or operational—requires the understanding and commitment of those directly involved. One of the best ways to get their buy-in is to allow them to participate in the planning process. One of the byproducts of their participation is a more thorough understanding of how their tasks support the execution of the strategic plan. In addition, by getting employee input, the overall plan is stronger thanks to suggestions and ideas from those who are usually closest to customers and/or products. Ideas that percolate up from the bottom frequently yield the best results. Finally, by including employees from all levels of the organization, the planning process becomes part of the culture. This makes it less threatening and more inclusive. Employee morale is better and outcomes tend to be positive.

Supervisors, such as the one seen here, who ask for their employees' input and suggestions are very likely to deliver better results. Why? Team members who are fully involved in planning and design activities typically feel more committed to the department, the project, and the organization. This ultimately leads to goal achievement and employee retention.

© AsiaPix/Photolibrary

Goals and Objectives

goal
a commitment to achieve a measurable result within a specified period.

Just as a distant port is the target or goal for a ship's crew, objectives are targets that organizational members steer toward. Although some theorists distinguish between goals and objectives, managers and supervisors typically use the terms interchangeably. A **goal** or an objective is defined as a specific commitment to achieve a measurable result within a given time frame. Many experts view goals and objectives as the single most important feature of the planning process. They help managers, supervisors, and entrepreneurs build a bridge between their dreams, aspirations, visions, and an achievable *reality*.

The Importance of Written Goals

Carefully prepared goals benefit employees, supervisors, and upper management by serving as targets.

From the standpoint of planning, carefully prepared written goals benefit employees, supervisors, and upper management by serving as targets and measuring sticks, thus fostering commitment and enhancing motivation.[10]

TARGETS

Without goals, managers at all levels would find it difficult to make coordinated decisions. People quite naturally tend to pursue their own ends in the absence of formal organizational goals and objectives. Fred Smith, the founder and CEO of overnight delivery giant FedEx, learned about the power of goals and feedback to get people moving in the right direction when he served as a U.S. Marine company commander during the Vietnam War.

> My leadership philosophy is a synthesis of the principles taught by the Marines and every organization for the past 200 years.
>
> When people walk in the door, they want to know: What do you expect out of me? What's in this deal for me? What do I have to do to get ahead? . . . They want to know how they're doing. They want some feedback. And they want to know that what they are doing is important.[11]

Meaningful feedback is impossible without a goal target.

MEASURING STICKS

An easily overlooked, after-the-fact feature of goals is that they are useful for measuring how well an organizational subunit or individual has performed. When appraising employee performance, supervisors need an established standard against which they can measure performance. Well-defined, measurable goals enable supervisors to weigh performance objectively on the basis of accomplishment, rather than subjectively on the basis of personality or prejudice.

COMMITMENT

The process of getting an employee to agree to pursue a given goal gives that individual a personal stake in the success of the enterprise. Thus, goals can be helpful in encouraging personal commitment to collective ends. Without individual commitment, even well-intentioned and carefully conceived strategies are doomed to failure.

These sailors would never dream of navigating difficult waters without charting a course. They know their final destination and they chart a path to arrive there safely. Supervisors in organizations of all types and sizes face a similar challenge. They need to work with their employees to define measurable goals and identify the best pathways to success.
© Danita Delimont/Alamy

MOTIVATION

Well-written goals represent a challenge—something to reach for. As such, they provide a motivational aspect. People usually feel good about themselves and what they do when they successfully achieve a challenging objective. Moreover, goals give supervisors a rational basis for rewarding performance. Employees who believe they will be equitably rewarded for achieving a given goal will be motivated to perform well.

Types of Goals

Most people divide goal setting into two basic categories: work-related and personal. We will focus this discussion on four different types of work-related goals: regular work, problem-solving, innovative, and development.[12] Keep in mind that most organizations will develop team goals in each of these categories as well as encourage employees to develop individual goals in support of the team's goals. You will have the opportunity to practice writing goals in the Supervisor's Toolkit activity at the end of this chapter.

REGULAR WORK GOALS

Regular work goals are most frequently associated with intermediate and operational plans. Managers and supervisors will work with their team members to develop goals that focus on the primary business unit's activities. Objectives often involve quality and efficiency. Other categories may include increased productivity and expanding market share.

PROBLEM-SOLVING GOALS

Problem-solving goals may be perceived as reactionary, the implication being that you have a problem that needs to be solved. However, the problem may be an anticipated one. For example, a supervisor may know she is planning on taking three months for maternity leave beginning in early October. She is anticipating a problem—when she goes on maternity leave, who will take her place as supervisor? To address this situation, the supervisor develops a problem-solving goal: train and mentor three current employees to be prepared in six months to perform her duties during her absence.

INNOVATIVE GOALS

In a rapidly changing economic environment, companies large and small are constantly striving to stay ahead of their competition. One way to do this is by introducing new products or services. Another way is to improve what already exists. This may be achieved by lowering costs, making processes more efficient, using resources more effectively, or discovering new products or services. Every business unit should develop at least one important, innovative goal.

DEVELOPMENT GOALS

As emphasized in Chapters 1 and 2, one of the primary roles of supervisors is to develop their employees. The first step in this process is to work with your team to identify changes that may require increased training, such as a planned upgrade to technology tools. This is likely to lead to a team goal. Here is an example: By the end of April, every team member will be proficient in the use of the new computer program and will be able to work independently on the new system. The next step is for each employee to write individual development goals. Everyone has room for improvement—it may be gaining new product knowledge or developing better communication skills.

KNOWLEDGE TO ACTION

Brainstorm with your classmates to develop a list of development goals that are appropriate and relevant for this class.

1. _____

2. _____

Writing Goals

Anthony P. Raia, an authority on goals and objectives, recommends that "as far as possible, objectives are expressed in quantitative, measurable, concrete terms, in the form of a written statement of desired results to be achieved within a given time period."[13] In other words, goals represent a firm commitment to accomplish something specific. A well-written goal should state what is to be accomplished and when it is to be accomplished. In the following examples, note that the desired results are expressed *quantitatively*, in units of output, dollars, or percentage of change:

- To increase hybrid car production by 240,000 units during the next production year.
- To reduce bad-debt loss by $50,000 during the next six months.
- To achieve an 18% increase in Brand X sales by December 31 of the current year.

SMART GOALS

Another common approach to goal setting is developing SMART goals (Specific, Measurable, Achievable, Realistic, and Time bound).[14] See Figure 3.3 for an explanation of SMART goals.

Although the SMART goals approach is widely accepted, its structure may be too restrictive for the development of innovative goals. Innovation implies trying something new and unknown, which by nature creates ambiguity and uncertainty.[15]

KNOWLEDGE TO ACTION

Rewrite the following bad examples of goals to be SMART goals.

1. Prepare my résumé.

   _____

2. Improve sales.

   _____

3. Get better grades.

   _____

FIGURE 3.3 SMART goals

SMART Goals

- **Specific**—Clearly state the desired outcome.
  - A good example: arrive to work ten minutes prior to the start of my shift every work day.
  - A bad example: be early to work.
- **Measurable**—Goals should be quantifiable using common measures such as dollars, unit count, or percentage.
  - A good example: Increase sales by 10% for the month of January.
  - A bad example: increase sales.
- **Achievable**—Be sure that the person has the necessary authority, resources, and control to achieve the goal.
  - A good example: complete and submit the scholarship application form before the April 21 deadline.
  - A bad example: receive a scholarship for $20,000 (this is a bad example because you do not control the scholarship selection committee).
- **Realistic**—Unrealistic goals can have a negative impact on a person's self-confidence and motivation. Setting smaller, realistic, incremental goals is a more effective strategy.
  - A good example for a person new to running: be able to run one mile without stopping to walk within thirty days.
  - A bad example for a person new to running: run a marathon in three months.
- **Time bound**—In addition to being measurable, goals need to have end dates. This provides parameters and makes it clear when to measure.
  - A good example: apply for open supervisor's position by Friday.
  - A bad example: become a supervisor.

ACHIEVING YOUR GOALS

Many people are excellent at writing goals but fail to prepare a written plan for achieving their goals. To achieve success, consider following the seven steps listed below. In addition, when setting goals with teams or individually, try using the goal-setting approach in the Supervisor's Toolkit at the end of this chapter to facilitate the goal-planning process.

- **Write down your SMART goal or objective**. As we just discussed, your goal has to meet each of the SMART elements. Ask yourself the following:

  1. Is it specific?
  2. Is it measurable?
  3. Is it achievable yet challenging?
  4. Is it realistic?
  5. Is it time bound?

- **Visualize the end result**. You often hear athletes such as professional basketball players describe how they use visualization to prepare themselves. For example, they picture the shot in their mind before they step up to take a free throw. The same technique can help you achieve your goals as well, by picturing what you want the end result to be. For example, one of your long-range goals may be to graduate from college. A visual image representing achievement of this goal might be you walking across the stage to receive your diploma dressed in your cap and gown, with your family and friends cheering wildly. Also, write down a couple of affirmations. These are sentences or phrases that reinforce your visual image (e.g., "I am smart. I work very hard. I love tough challenges.").

- **Give it meaning**. Identify why achieving this goal is useful and important. How does it support the mission and strategic plan of the organization? What are the benefits of achieving this goal to you and/or the company?

- **Prepare a detailed action plan**. Identify incremental steps toward achieving the goal. List specific tasks along with target dates for completion, as well as the resources you will need.

- **Prepare a plan to address potential obstacles or threats**. Identify everything that could create a barrier to completing each task. Develop a list of contingency plans for each, so you can stay on track with no excuses for failure.

- **Define measures**. Identify how and when you will measure progress to be sure you achieve your SMART goals.

- **Assess results**. If there are deviations, put corrective action plans in place. If you are achieving desired results, celebrate incremental success.

> **THEY SAID IT BEST**
>
> *You can have unbelievable intelligence, you can have connections, you can have opportunities fall out of the sky. But in the end, hard work is the true, enduring characteristic of successful people.*
> —MARSHA EVANS, Executive Director of Girl Scouts of America
> *Source: Lorraine A. Darconte, ed., Lessons for Success (New York: MJF Books, 2001), 46.*

Maximizing Success

Several factors influence personal achievement, including everything from effective time management to a positive attitude. Learning from mistakes and following Brian Tracy's *7 Cs of success* listed in Figure 3.4 can also help you achieve your goals.

THE POWER OF A POSITIVE ATTITUDE

Set an example for your employees with a positive attitude, and let them know how much you believe in them and their ability to achieve their goals.

Regardless of what type of work you do, having a positive attitude will make it more likely that you will achieve your goals. As the saying goes, "If you think you can, you will; if you think you can't, you won't." Believe in yourself, your dreams, and your goals. Set an example for your employees

FIGURE 3.4 Seven secrets to success

7 Secrets to Success

Management consultant Brian Tracy has identified seven core principles (the 7 Cs of success) to help you achieve maximum personal success:

1. **Clarity**—know who you are and what you want.
2. **Competence**—be good at what you do.
3. **Constraints**—know what is getting in the way and immediately alleviate it.
4. **Creativity**—use innovative thinking to solve problems.
5. **Concentration**—focus on completing the most important items on your list each day.
6. **Courage**—have the courage to begin, to get outside your comfort zone, to endure, and persist in pursuit of your goals.
7. **Continuous Action**—try new things, learn from mistakes, and try again.

Source: Brian Tracy, "7 Secrets to Success," Entrepreneur, February 2007, 96–101.

with a positive attitude, and let them know how much you believe in them and their ability to achieve their goals.

MISTAKES HAPPEN—WHAT NEXT?

Remember that mistakes will happen and employees will not always act or respond the way you might in a similar situation. Failures and mistakes are the learning opportunities for a better tomorrow. This applies to individuals as well as to companies. By planning and being proactive, you can minimize mistakes and reduce their impact. However, it is impossible to control every element of every day. One of the things that defines who you are as a supervisor is how you handle mistakes. It doesn't matter what the mistake is; what matters is what you do with it and what you learn from it.

KNOWLEDGE TO ACTION

Imagine that you are the supervisor at a car wash. One of your employees is vacuuming the inside of a customer's car when he spills a soda resting in the cup holder.

1. What immediate action can you take to minimize the impact of the employee's mistake?

   _____

2. What can you do after the customer leaves to reinforce an environment where you encourage employees to learn from mistakes?

   _____

3. What proactive steps can you take with your entire team to reduce the likelihood that this type of mistake will reoccur?

   _____

TIME MANAGEMENT

One of the greatest challenges people face in achieving their goals is time management. Time management specialist Amy Jones has seven strategies to help you stay the course:

- **Get off to a great start**. This includes written goals, an action plan, good work habits, and overcoming procrastination.

- **Stay on track**. Prioritize your list, do the most important items first, and start your day early.

- **Pace yourself**. Incorporate proper balance and plan your schedule to do your most important work during your most productive/creative time of day.

- **Get assistance from others**. Delegate when possible and seek out expertise and support from others.

- **Make those all-important pit stops**. Review and evaluate progress with your team, make necessary adjustments, regroup, and restart.

- **Keep your eye on the finish line.** Remain focused on what you are trying to accomplish, be results oriented, and maintain priorities.

- **Celebrate in the victory lane!** Take time to acknowledge a job well done and share the credit with those who helped.[16]

The thrill of victory! Ernst F. Van Dyk joyfully celebrates a hard-won success. As the winner of the men's wheelchair division of the 2008 Boston Marathon, Van Dyk beautifully illustrates basic success strategies presented in this chapter–have the courage to begin, get out of your comfort zone, persist in pursuit of your goals, and take time to celebrate a job well done.
© Jim Rogash/Getty Images

Prioritizing

Defined as the ranking of goals, objectives, or activities in order of importance, **prioritizing** plays a special role in planning. By listing long-range organizational objectives in order of their priority, top management prepares to make decisions regarding the allocation of resources. Limited time, talent, and financial and material resources need to be channeled proportionately into more important endeavors and away from other areas. The establishment of priorities is a key factor in managerial and organizational effectiveness. Strategic priorities give both insiders and outsiders answers to the questions, "What is most important to us?" and "How should we act and react during a crisis?" In addition to long-range strategies, priorities also need to be established for day-to-day operations and activities. Students who increase their commitment to classes in which they are doing poorly know about the power of prioritizing.

The A-B-C Priority System

prioritizing
ranking goals, objectives, or activities in order of importance.

Despite time-management seminars, day planners, and personal digital assistants (PDAs), establishing priorities remains a subjective process that is affected by organizational politics and value conflicts.[17] Although there is no universally acceptable formula for carrying out this important function, the following A-B-C priority system is helpful.[18]

A: ***Must do*** objectives that are *critical* to successful performance. They may be the result of special demands from higher levels of management or other external sources.

B: ***Should do*** objectives that are *necessary* for improved performance. They are generally vital, but their achievement can be postponed if necessary.

C: ***Nice to do*** objectives that are *desirable* for improved performance, but not critical to survival or improved performance. They can be eliminated or postponed to achieve objectives of higher priority.

The 80/20 Principle

Another proven priority-setting tool is the **80/20 principle**, also known as *Pareto analysis*. "The 80/20 principle asserts that a minority of causes, inputs, or effort usually leads to a majority of results, outputs, or rewards."[19] Care needs to be taken not to interpret the 80/20 principle too literally—it is approximate. To understand this concept better, consider that most organizations generate about 80% of their revenue from just 20% of their customers. Yet they often focus too little of their time and resources on this fruitful 20%.

To further illustrate this point, consider for a moment the supervisor responsible for training ten new telemarketers. Imagine the amount of time and effort invested in training these new employees. Each person receives roughly the same amount of initial training, followed by one-on-one training for those who need more help. Two of the new employees emerge as top performers. In fact, they are responsible for 80% of the group's total sales, although they received the least amount of one-on-one training. Therefore, it is important for supervisors to understand and be aware of the 80/20 principle when evaluating and rewarding performance.

Avoiding the Busyness Trap

Supervisors should not confuse being busy with being effective and efficient. Results are what really count.

80/20 principle
the concept that a minority of causes, inputs, or efforts tends to produce a majority of results, outputs, or rewards.

The A-B-C priority system and the 80/20 principle are two simple yet effective tools for establishing priorities that can help managers and supervisors avoid the so-called busyness trap.[20] In these fast-paced times, supervisors should not confuse being busy with being effective and efficient. Results are what really count. Activities and speed, without results, are a costly waste of time. By slowing down a bit, having clear priorities, and taking a strategic view of daily problems, busy supervisors can be successful *and* "get a life."

Finally, supervisors striving to establish priorities amid many competing demands would do well to heed management expert Peter Drucker's advice—that the most important skill for setting priorities and managing time is simply learning to say "no."[21]

*"I've got a lot on my plate right now. For starters, I need to sharpen
my pencil, refill my coffee and get a new comb."*

The Planning and Control Cycle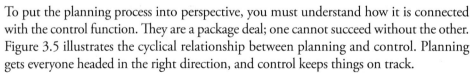

To put the planning process into perspective, you must understand how it is connected
with the control function. They are a package deal; one cannot succeed without the other.
Figure 3.5 illustrates the cyclical relationship between planning and control. Planning
gets everyone headed in the right direction, and control keeps things on track.

The planning/control cycle begins with the development of the strategic plan.
Next, intermediate and operational plans are created. As these plans are carried out,
the control function begins. When the preliminary or final results deviate from the
original plan, corrective actions are necessary. When planned activities are still in
progress, the corrective action plan can get the organization back on track before it is
too late. Deviations between final results and plans, on the other hand, are instructive
feedback for the improvement of future plans. As you can see in Figure 3.5, the
planning and control cycle is ongoing. The steps in the cycle are:

1. **P**lan—formulate strategic, intermediate, and operational plans.

2. **E**xecute—implement the plans.

3. **A**ssess—measure milestones and compare results with plans.

4. **C**orrect—take corrective action if deviations exist; improve future plans.

Getting Started

Our focus in this section is going to be on operational planning. This is the level
of planning where most supervisors are heavily involved. These plans answer the
questions: Who? How? When?

FIGURE 3.5 Basic planning and control cycle

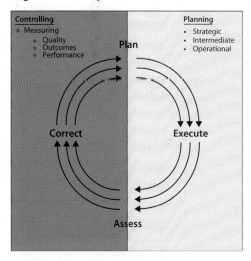

As you learned previously, all planning should begin by reviewing the mission of the organization. The next step is to clearly understand the strategic and intermediate plans developed by upper management. These plans provide a context for the goals and objectives the team will be striving to achieve in the operational plans.

There are many approaches to planning. The following are some basic steps to help you get started.

INVOLVE YOUR EMPLOYEES

Provide your employees with as much detail as possible. Let them know how important their contributions are to the planning process. Getting them involved from the beginning will increase the likelihood of successful execution of the plan. Use brainstorming techniques, surveys, and other tools to get your employees' input, ideas, and suggestions.

REVIEW MISSION AND PURPOSE

Everyone on the team must understand both the organizational mission as well as the business unit's mission and purpose. In addition, as their supervisor, you can

> *Everyone on the team should be able to answer the question, "Why does the work I do make a difference?"*

help them to realize how your team contributes to the overall success of the organization. Everyone on the team should be able to answer the question, "Why does the work I do make a difference?" Some call this having a "line of sight." For example, there is an old story about two men digging a trench. When asked what they were doing, the first replied, "I'm digging a trench." The other man leaned on his shovel for a moment and said, "I'm helping to build the foundation for a hospital."

UNDERSTAND THE STRATEGIC AND INTERMEDIATE PLANS

Everyone on the team must understand these plans and know what is expected of their business unit. One way to emphasize the value and importance of the team is to invite the company president or other senior executive to your team's kick-off meeting. Ask this person to provide an overview of the strategic plan and to reiterate the contributions your team makes to the overall success of the business.

DEVELOP SMART GOALS AND OBJECTIVES

Goals and objectives take time to develop. Remember to give your team members ample time to brainstorm, research, and analyze alternatives. This step can take anywhere from a few days to several weeks.

IDENTIFY NECESSARY RESOURCES

Again, working with your team, determine necessary resources to achieve your agreed-upon goals and objectives. Resources include facilities, equipment, materials, labor, and any other items necessary to get the job done.[22]

PREPARE A TASK LIST AND TIMELINE

List each step in the process to achieve the agreed-upon goal. Estimate how many labor hours it will take, over what period of time. It is also important to identify any related or dependent tasks. Scheduling and resource management will be reviewed in more depth in subsequent chapters.

ESTABLISH PLANS TO MEASURE PROGRESS

The next stage in planning is defining how you will measure progress and final completion. This includes establishing due dates, deadlines, and milestones. This step also requires the individuals and the team to predetermine how and when they will compare their progress to the original plan. If this is left to chance and not scheduled ahead of time, it will often be forgotten or put on the bottom of the priority list. When you finally get around to measuring progress, it may be too late.

DEVELOP AN ACTION PLAN

This stage is critical to the success of the plan. Each person on the team should know his/her roles and responsibilities. This is where the team decides who is going to be handling each task, when the task will start, and when the task needs to be finished. Team members should also know by now what, if any, additional resources they will need to successfully complete their assignment. Remember, a major aspect of setting your people up for success is making sure they have the right tools to get the job done.

CELEBRATE SUCCESS

One of the steps many new supervisors forget is to stop and celebrate success. Don't wait until the entire plan is achieved. Celebrate incremental achievement. This may be as simple as buying pizza for the team when the first milestone is achieved. The act of recognizing progress and performance will reenergize the team and keep members motivated. One excellent strategy is to ask team members for their ideas and suggestions for rewards (both incremental and upon final completion). Be sure to establish some parameters (budget, time, etc.) otherwise, they may suggest a trip for the entire team to Hawaii when your budget can only afford a Hawaiian-themed party in the cafeteria! In the big picture of planning, celebration needs to be done—but not overdone.

Assessing and Measuring Performance Outcomes

Imagine studying hard all semester and never getting a grade. Progress needs to be measured. On the job, this requires supervisors to determine how the organization will assess and measure performance. The variables that should be defined should answer the questions: What? When? How? This means that you and your team will decide *what* to measure (remember, measures need to be specific and quantifiable); *when* to measure (for example, daily, weekly, and/or monthly); and *how* to measure progress. This may include measuring quality using sampling techniques, comparing actual progress with target due dates, or other methods. Deciding how you will measure depends on what you are measuring.

To bring this all together, let's look at the case of two restaurant owners and one of their managers:

> Brooke and Robert own four restaurants in the Dallas area. In their strategic plan, they have an objective to double the number of restaurants they own over the next five years. Another objective is to increase revenue in their existing locations by 15% per year.
>
> Grahame is the manager of one of the restaurants, a Japanese steakhouse and sushi bar that only serves dinner. Included in his intermediate plan is a goal to open the restaurant for lunch six days a week. He linked this to the strategic plan based on the assumption that expanding operating hours should contribute to increased revenue.
>
> Grahame's next step is to develop an operational plan to achieve the goal of opening for lunch. He pulled together his team for a kick-off meeting. He invited Brooke and Robert to attend the meeting for the first thirty minutes. Their role was to review the company mission and go over the strategic plan. Brooke and Robert also used this opportunity to thank all employees for their efforts, to compliment Grahame's leadership, and to reinforce how valuable each person is to the overall success of the restaurant.
>
> Grahame used the second half of the meeting to begin the process of developing goals and objectives. Over the next three weeks, the team brainstormed, researched, and analyzed the opportunity to open for lunch. Here is the SMART objective they wrote: "By July 1, we will be open for lunch from 11:00 A.M. to 2:00 P.M. from Monday— Saturday, serving at least fifteen entrees on our lunch menu."
>
> Their next step was to outline all of the tasks involved in achieving this goal, along with the necessary resources. In addition, team members agreed to track their performance in reaching this goal by meeting weekly to review the original plan and compare their actual progress to the activities and milestones outlined previously. Finally, they discussed each person's role, responsibilities, and due dates.

As you can see, this approach follows a logical, sequential order of events. However, this type of comprehensive planning requires excellent communication and frequent updates. If members of your team are not on site or in the same location, it is essential that you use information technology and other methods to keep your virtual team members engaged and involved in the planning process.

FIGURE 3.6 Seven steps to cultivate an accountability-based culture

Seven Steps to Cultivate an Accountability-Based Culture

Step 1: Establish the organization's top three objectives. They should be clear, concise, measurable, and attainable.

Step 2: Assign each team member individual goals and tasks.

Step 3: Ask each team member what he or she needs to win.

Step 4: Agree on what the leader (you) will do to help. Meet individually and agree on how you will help. Why? Because you're responsible to people, not for them.

Step 5: Follow up. Meet with team members individually on a preplanned scheduled basis to discuss results. Positive results generate a dialogue about what led to the desired outcome, deviations lead to corrective planning—what will be done to get back on track, when, and what help is needed.

Step 6: Share lessons learned. Meet with the entire team on a regular basis to discuss lessons learned.

Step 7: Reward results. When objectives are achieved, reward performance.

Source: Bob Prosen, "How Leaders Increase Accountability and Results," *Supervision* 68 (March 2007): 13–15.

Increasing Accountability for Results

> *What gets measured gets done.*

As best-selling author and management expert Tom Peters said, "What Gets Measured Gets Done."[23] All of the topics we have discussed in this chapter lead to one thing: *results*. In other words, getting things done. Every organization—profit or nonprofit, large or small—ultimately needs to achieve results if it is going to remain competitive. Keys to success include maximizing individual performance and creating highly effective and efficient teams. In addition, if your teams can function at a high level with very little day-to-day direction, you will be free to focus on other aspects of your role as supervisor. This type of high-performance team usually has a sense of ownership where individuals hold themselves and their team members accountable.

To foster a culture of accountability, there should be a high level of trust and mutual respect. This provides a solid foundation for open and honest communication. Seven steps to cultivate an accountability-based culture are presented in Figure 3.6.

Involving team members in the planning process will reinforce their commitment to your organization's goals. Team members also should have an opportunity to suggest how their performance will be measured. Fairness dictates that everyone knows exactly when and how their performance will be measured. Ideally, in high-performance teams, members assess their own performance and report their progress back to the team. Of course, this assumes that the goals are specific and measurable, both quantitatively and qualitatively. Most people do not want to disappoint their teammates. Teamwork and personal accountability are powerful motivators.

SUMMARY

1. A good mission statement generates a positive image for all of the organization's stakeholders and provides a focal point for the entire planning process. The mission statement (1) *defines* the organization, (2) *creates* an *inspiring vision* of what the organization can be, (3) outlines *how* the vision is to be accomplished, (4) establishes key *priorities*, (5) states a *common goal* and fosters a sense of togetherness, (6) creates a *philosophical*

anchor for all organizational activities, (7) generates *enthusiasm,* and (8) *empowers* present and future organization members to believe that *every* individual is the key to success.

2. Planning is the formulation of future courses of action. Properly developed plans tell *what, when,* and *how* something is to be done. Essential aspects of planning include (1) linking the organizational mission, (2) incorporating all types of planning, (3) incorporating goals and objectives, (4) setting priorities, and (5) following the planning and control cycle. Three levels of planning are (1) strategic planning—determining how to pursue long-term goals with available resources; (2) intermediate planning—determining subunits' contributions using allocated resources; and (3) operational planning—determining how to accomplish specific tasks with available resources. The planning process includes each level of planning. One level cannot effectively stand alone without the support of the other two levels. Typically, supervisors are responsible for the third level—operational planning. Involving employees in the planning process will help them feel a sense of belonging and purpose that is greater than just their individual goals. This desire to contribute to something bigger is one of the reasons why planning is a powerful process for uniting everyone in the organization and moving forward to achieve the mission.

3. Goals are considered by many experts as the single most important feature of the planning process. They help managers, supervisors, and entrepreneurs build a bridge between their dreams, aspirations, visions, and an achievable *reality.* In addition, they serve as targets and measuring sticks, which foster commitment and enhance motivation. There are four different types of goals and objectives: (1) regular work, (2) problem-solving, (3) innovative, and (4) developmental. Well-written goals and objectives are SMART goals (Specific, Measurable, Achievable, Realistic, and Time bound). They represent a firm commitment to accomplish something specific, including what is to be accomplished and when it is to be accomplished.

4. Prioritizing is the process of ranking goals, objectives, or activities in order of importance. Establishing priorities remains a subjective process, and there are no universally acceptable formulas for carrying out this important function. However, there are two methods that supervisors have found helpful: the A-B-C priority system, which categorizes objectives on the basis of criticality (*must do, should do,* and *nice to do);* and the 80/20 principle, which asserts that a minority of causes, inputs, or effort usually leads to a majority of results, outputs, or rewards.

5. The planning and control cycle is ongoing. It begins with preparing strategic, intermediate, and operational plans. Planning gets the organization headed in the right direction, and control keeps the team focused on the goals and objectives of the plan. As plans are carried out, the control function begins. This may include corrective action and instructive feedback for the improvement of future plans. The four steps in the planning and control cycle are: (1) plan—formulate strategic, intermediate, and operational plans; (2) execute—implement the plans; (3) assess—measure milestones and compare results with plans; and (4) control—take corrective action if deviation exists; improve future plans.

6. Increasing accountability and achieving positive results can be accomplished by creating highly effective and efficient teams that function at a high level with very little day-to-day direction. This type of high-performance team usually has a sense of ownership whereby individuals hold themselves and their team members accountable. Begin by (1) involving everyone in the planning process; (2) creating awareness about the organization's mission, purpose, and strategic plan; (3) asking for individuals to share their ideas and suggestions; (4) incorporating feedback into the planning process and giving proper credit; (5) assigning people to tasks that will make the best use of their skills, knowledge, areas of expertise and interest; (6) minimizing internal competition; and (7) celebrating success.

TERMS TO UNDERSTAND

80/20 Principle, p. 73
contingency plan, p. 64
goal, p. 65

intermediate planning, p. 63
mission statement, p. 60
operational planning, p. 63

plan, p. 62
prioritizing, p. 72
strategic planning, p. 62

QUESTIONS FOR REFLECTION

1. Describe the three different types of planning.
   a. Which level is most likely to involve supervisors?
   b. What do you think would happen to an organization that only did one or two of these?
2. Explain your understanding of the planning process. Provide examples of specific steps a supervisor can take to involve employees.

3. Describe the A-B-C method for prioritizing and provide an example for each level.
4. Why is time management relevant to the discussion regarding goal setting? What are seven steps you can take to improve time management?
5. What are three steps you can take to encourage employees to be accountable for their goals and performance?

HANDS-ON ACTIVITIES

MISSION STATEMENTS

1. Find organizational mission statements for three different types of companies.
   a. A hospitality-related business (hotel, restaurant, or conference center)
   b. A nonprofit service-oriented organization (health care, education, or environmental)
   c. A manufacturing company (parts and/or production)
2. What do these mission statements have in common and what is different?
3. Pick the mission statement you think is best and use it to answer the following:
   a. Does the mission statement define the organization?
   b. Does it create an inspiring vision of what the organization can be and can do?
   c. Does it outline how the vision is to be accomplished?

d. Does it establish key priorities?
e. Does it state a common goal and foster a sense of togetherness?
f. Does it create a philosophical anchor for all organizational activities?
g. Does it generate enthusiasm?
h. Does it empower present and future organization members to believe that every individual is the key to success?

PERSONAL MISSION STATEMENT

Write your own personal mission statement. If you are not sure how to get started, try using the Mission Statement builder on the Franklin Covey website. Visit www.franklincovey.com, then select the link for *library and resources* where you will see the link for the *Mission Statement Builder*. This is also an excellent activity to do with your employees.

Interview an Expert

Select a supervisor or manager to interview. After the interview, document what you gathered from the person during the conversation and conclude with a summary of how you can apply what you learned to further develop your planning and goal-setting skills.

Sample questions

1. What type of planning are you involved with (strategic, intermediate, and/or operational)?

2. How do you involve your employees in the planning process?
3. How have planning and goal setting contributed to success in your organization?
4. How does your organization use individual and team goals? Are there any special rewards or recognition for goal attainment?

5. What are your suggestions for effectively setting personal and team goals?

You may improvise and add or edit questions to fit the situation or the circumstances of your interview.

Schedule your interview ahead of time and try to limit it to about 15 minutes. Remember to send a thank-you note to the person you interview.

YOU DECIDE

CASE STUDY 3.1
Goal Setting

Doug is the general manager of a regional painting and home improvement contractor business. He has been working hard to create a goal-oriented environment. He is meeting with his painting-crew team leaders. One of the problems they are experiencing is a high number of complaints that require crews to return to the customer's home or office for additional work or cleaning. Currently, crews are returning to 37% of job sites to respond to complaints. Doug's team leaders have identified a goal: "Improve Customer Service and Reduce Customer Complaints." Doug takes the time to explain SMART goals and has the team leaders go back to reword their goal so it meets the SMART criteria. They come back with the following: "Our goal is to reduce customer complaints to 15%."

Their next step is to identify specific tasks that will help them achieve this goal. They make a lengthy list that includes everything from better upfront communication with customers to increased training for their painters. One of the items that they are implementing is a customer satisfaction checklist that will be used 100% of the time with all customers. Each painting crew will go over the checklist

in detail with customers to be sure that they are satisfied before the crew leaves the worksite. The expectation is that this will get potential problems resolved so the customer will not need to call after the fact to complain.

The team leaders agree to monitor the use of the checklist on a weekly basis with their crews. Doug will monitor the number of complaints on a monthly basis to see if they begin to decline.

After the first month, Doug reviews the number of customer complaints and discovers that the percentage of complaints has actually increased.

Questions

1. Does the revised goal meet the SMART criteria? If yes, explain why. If not, revise it so it does meet the criteria.

2. How would you recommend Doug handle this situation? Explain in detail the steps he should take.

3. What can Doug do now to help his crew leaders be successful?

SUPERVISOR'S TOOLKIT

Review the goal-setting section of the chapter prior to developing three personal SMART goals. These can be related to your work, school, or life.

Develop a list of action items to achieve your goals and remember to schedule time to achieve each of the items. In addition, schedule time for follow-up to be sure you are on track to achieve your goals.

This technique should be added to your supervisor's toolkit. This tool can be used with individual employees to help them develop personal goals. It can also be

an effective approach when you work with teams to develop team goals.

Remember to ask yourself the following:

1. Is it specific?
2. Is it measurable?
3. Is it achievable yet challenging?
4. Is it realistic?
5. Is it time bound?

CHAPTER 4

Recruitment, Selection, and Retention

Learning Objectives

1. Explain why recruitment and retention are important to supervisors and describe the tangible and intangible costs of employee turnover.

2. Describe what should be done prior to placing a job advertisement, including determining core abilities and writing a job description.

3. Discuss legal issues supervisors should be aware of during the recruiting and hiring process.

4. Identify various methods for creating a successful recruiting effort, including strategies for attracting a diverse group of candidates.

5. Identify and briefly explain the seven steps in the PROCEED model of employee selection.

6. Describe strategies and techniques for deciding whom to hire, including developing selection criteria, creating a decision matrix, and preparing for in-person and virtual interviews.

7. Explain alternative scheduling options such as job sharing, flex-time, and telecommuting and discuss the impact on employee retention.

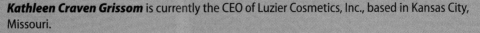

Straight Talk from the Field

Kathleen Craven Grissom is currently the CEO of Luzier Cosmetics, Inc., based in Kansas City, Missouri.

QUESTION . . .

What are the secrets to your success in recruiting and retaining loyal employees?

RESPONSE . . .

Luzier Cosmetics has three Guiding Principles that have guided all decision making for over 85 years. Created by our founder, Thomas L. Luzier, they are (1) Keep Faith, (2) Service Above Everything, and (3) Quality Survives. These principles have been faithfully adhered to since 1923. We've had many different people, with many different philosophies, walk through our doors throughout the years, but the common thread has always been the commitment to uphold these principles. These principles apply to anyone associated with Luzier Cosmetics: our staff, our consultants, our customers, and our vendors. When it comes to employee retention and loyalty, our numbers tell the story. Currently, 20% of our employees have been with us for at least 44 years, 40% have been with us for 35 years, 60% have been with us for over 20 years, 70% for over 15 years, and 80% for over 10 years. The same holds true for our consultants and customers. Our Guiding Principles foster incredible loyalty.

Keep Faith!

It is not enough to hope to be a success; you must expect to be a success. Luzier has been in operation through many wars, the Great Depression, changing fads, and changing views on skin care. When you are expecting success, each of these challenges becomes an opportunity for growth. Never settle for less! Being a good supervisor doesn't mean having all of the answers. It means relying on and valuing the participation and initiative of every single person. It also means that you can make or break the mood of the day. A positive attitude coupled with the expectation of success keeps everyone moving forward. Let the people working with you know you have faith in them and that you expect them to be successful. Their diverse backgrounds and experiences are where some of the best ideas come from. Believe in them. Always expect good things from people. Life has an amazing way of meeting your expectations—good or bad. So, why not make

them good? As the old saying goes: from a small acorn grows the mighty oak.

Service Above Everything!

We are passionately committed to helping others. We are in the "self esteem" business. We help people feel better about themselves every day. We are here to serve the people who work with us. When you are passionate about helping others, it is really easy to enjoy what you are doing. When you really believe that you are making a difference in people's lives, your enthusiasm becomes contagious. This commitment to service doesn't just apply to our customers and consultants; it applies to how we treat our employees and vendors as well. It's how we do business. We are sincerely interested in all of our employees. The more interest we show in helping our employees, the more interest they show in helping us. We make sure that they have everything they need to do their jobs effectively. We expect them to be a success. We are continuously looking for ways to create more satisfied employees. We want them to enjoy what they are doing because this comes through when they are helping our customers. We know that if they are treated well, then they will treat our customers well. It's the Golden Rule, and it works.

Quality Survives!

In our business, product quality is a must. Quality means more than just using the highest quality ingredients and ensuring product quality. Quality means having integrity in everything you do. Throughout the ages, there has never been a better business policy than absolute truthfulness. Honesty, integrity, and sincerity—always! All people want to be treated with dignity and respect. In all things, we do what we say we are going to do. We may not always agree with one another, but in all things we are *open and honest. We listen to each other and we constantly talk to one another. We make sure everyone knows what is expected of them and we remind each other constantly. We welcome the passionate exchange of ideas on company issues.*

With these Guiding Principles, you can't help but to set people up for success. You fundamentally expect it from them.

You're ready to give them whatever they need to become a success and, with a steadfast focus on integrity, you can't help but have loyal and dedicated employees. When you are passionate about helping others, they will want to help you.

Chapter Outline

Recruitment and retention efforts are often the supervisor's responsibility. Although some organizations may have a team of human resource professionals to coordinate the recruitment, hiring, and retention efforts, these activities cannot happen without some level of supervisory involvement. In fact, supervisors are frequently the first point of contact for potential job applicants. Therefore, it is essential that you have a basic understanding of the hiring process. Employee retention is another area where supervisors play a significant role. In fact, more than one in ten employees who voluntarily left their job did so because of their relationship with their supervisor.[1] As a result, we will spend time introducing you to a few strategies that can have a positive impact on retention. This chapter will provide best practices for the stages of hiring and retention.

Why Are Recruitment and Retention So Important?

Employee turnover is when employees leave a company either because they are asked to or they choose to leave voluntarily. The high cost of employee turnover is one reason why recruitment and retention is important. **Recruitment** is the process companies use to find and hire qualified workers. **Retention** refers to the efforts by a company to keep employees—the opposite of turnover. Experts estimate the average cost of turnover to be equivalent to one year's salary.[2] Although situations vary, there are some common costs associated with having to replace employees.

> The high cost of employee turnover is one reason why recruitment and retention is important.

Tangible Costs of Recruitment

The easiest recruitment costs to identify and quantify are the **tangible costs** of hiring an employee. Estimates of the average cost per new hire range from $4,000 to more than $7,000 per new employee.[3] These estimates include tangible costs such as advertising, screening, interviewing, testing, orientation and training, new employee setup, and travel.[4]

ADVERTISING

Regardless of the medium selected, there are several costs inherent to advertising. Among them are the time and potential consulting costs associated with writing the advertisement and the actual cost to place the ad. Costs for print ads will vary depending on variables such as the size of the ad, the location, the duration, the day of the week, and the type of publication and its circulation. Online advertising includes other options and variables that determine overall pricing.

SCREENING POTENTIAL CANDIDATES

Someone needs to screen every résumé and application to determine if the candidates meet the minimum criteria and should be considered for the position. This cost is either incurred internally by a human resource specialist or supervisor. Alternatively, the company may choose to outsource this activity to a company specializing in candidate searches.

INTERVIEWING

Depending on the position and the organization, candidate interviews may be handled by just one person or by a selection committee. Another approach is to use a two-tiered system whereby the initial interview is conducted by one person—typically someone in human resources—and the final interview is conducted by the supervisor or manager. Regardless of the organization's approach, there will be costs absorbed by the company in the form of lost productivity for the individuals involved in the interviewing. In addition, their lack of availability may adversely affect their team's performance.

TESTING

Pre-employment tests vary depending on the position and the organization. Tests being used by employers today include everything from personality and psychological

employee turnover
employees leaving a company either because they are asked to or they choose to leave voluntarily.

recruitment
efforts by a company to find and hire qualified workers.

retention
efforts by a company to keep employees, the opposite of employee turnover.

tangible costs
expenses that are easily defined and measurable.

tests to skills and aptitude tests. In addition, some states allow employers to conduct drug tests, background checks, and other measures to learn as much as possible about an applicant before making an offer.[5] Most of these tests have an administrative cost as well as an investment of time and effort by the organization.

TRAINING AND ORIENTATION

The cost of training new hires varies depending on the type of work and the level of experience or readiness new employees bring with them. Some jobs require extensive education and training before an applicant will even be considered, such as an airline pilot. Other jobs may require little or no experience, such as an entry-level retail job. However, all of these positions require, at a minimum, some company training because all employees need to learn the specific tools and techniques used by their new employer. Beyond the basics, training costs will vary considerably depending on the position and the employee.

Although orientation is often grouped together with new hire training, its scope is geared more toward corporate culture. It also focuses on company policies, procedures, and common personnel-related items, such as benefits and paid time off. It is important to distinguish orientation from training because orientation includes additional tangible costs separate from job-specific training activities. Tangible costs for orientation include expenses for the persons conducting the orientation or training as well as wages for the new hires during orientation and training.

NEW EMPLOYEE SETUP

At a minimum, all new employees need to be added to the payroll system. In addition, they may require computer access, building access with keys or codes, and special equipment such as scanners, vehicles, or uniforms. The time and money it takes to get all of the necessary items in place for a new hire can be substantial. In some cases, new employees are required to incur some of the costs, such as purchasing their own uniforms.

TRAVEL EXPENSES

In highly competitive markets where the organization is seeking the best-qualified candidate in either a national or international search, it is fairly common for companies to pay for applicants to travel for an interview. Additionally, the company may agree to pay for their new employee's relocation expenses. Travel expenses also may be incurred if the company sends an employee to a conference or job fair to recruit and/or interview prospects.

Intangible Costs of Employee Replacement

Intangible costs are more difficult to identify and measure than the more obvious tangible costs. These "hidden" costs include the cost of reduced performance by the person leaving, cost to pay an experienced person to take on additional work when a position is vacant, a decline in productivity as a result of increased stress of team

Word of mouth and personal referrals are often excellent ways to recruit new employees. However, many job seekers continue to use local newspaper employment ads.
© David Young-Wolff/PhotoEdit

intangible costs
expenses that are not easily defined or measured.

members during the vacancy period, lower productivity for the new employee, cost of reworking errors by the new person, and increased supervision to coach the new hire.[6]

Other intangible effects of turnover include the impact on employee morale. If your company is a revolving door of employees, it is difficult to build a strong, cohesive unit. In addition, while positions sit vacant the other workers must fill in the gaps, which can often lead to frustration and burnout.

> *Other intangible effects of turnover include the impact on employee morale.*

REDUCED PERFORMANCE OF EMPLOYEE LEAVING

When an employee makes a decision to leave, she typically gives the employer at least two weeks' notice to provide time for the employer to hire a replacement. However, from the time she decides to leave, which may be a long time before she actually resigns, the employee enters into what is often called the "short-timers" mentality. Such employees often lose interest, motivation, and ultimately productivity and performance.

COSTS OF COVERING DURING THE VACANCY

As the saying goes, "The show must go on!" In most organizations, when an employee leaves, the work still needs to get done. In some work environments, such as a restaurant, other staff members are usually asked to work extra hours, which can lead to overtime costs and employee burnout. In other work environments, employees are simply asked to do more work in fewer hours, which can lead to people skipping lunch or—even worse—cutting corners and impacting quality.

LOST PRODUCTIVITY FROM STRESS

When an employee leaves, stress can be a concern for the remaining team members. Depending on the reason for the employee's departure, this can be a major issue. For example, if a highly respected and well-liked employee leaves because of an irresolvable conflict with his supervisor, the rest of the team may expect the work environment to grow more and more unpleasant, which can lead to increased stress and a decline in productivity.

LESS PRODUCTIVITY FOR THE NEW HIRE

Most new hires will go through a transition period when they are learning specific job skills and organizational procedures relevant to their new position. Typically, employees will take a few weeks or even months to progress through this stage before they reach maximum productivity. This "ramping up" period will depend on the complexity of the work and the amount of experience the new employee has prior to being hired. Supervisors will often say things like, "I just hired a new person who has great experience, so I'm really hoping that she can hit the ground running." Certainly, seasoned veterans in the field will ramp up far more quickly than novices, but it is unrealistic to think that they will reach their optimal performance immediately.

THE COST OF REWORK

Inevitably, most new employees will make some mistakes. The time and effort it takes a more experienced employee to correct a newcomer's errors and complete the work is

When an employee has decided to quit, productivity usually declines. While the above situation may be a bit extreme, the point is clear—once an employee knows they are leaving, a "short-timers" attitude will likely prevail.
© John-Francis Bourke/Getty Images/Riser

an anticipated cost of bringing in a new employee. Excellent training and good checks and balances can help minimize errors, but it is difficult to eliminate them entirely.

INCREASED SUPERVISION

During a new hire's initial training period, a supervisor typically spends more time with this person coaching, mentoring, answering questions, and helping him handle difficult, complex, or new situations. As the employee becomes more proficient in his job, such supervisory coaching time diminishes.

The Impact of Retention

Combine the cost of turnover with the fact that today's workers are changing jobs more than ever before, and you have a significant financial issue. A 2008 survey, conducted by Harris Interactive® on behalf of Spherion Corporation, indicated that 38% of currently employed workers "are likely to look for a new job in the next year, an increase of six percentage points since December 2007."[7] Another Spherion® Workplace Snapshot survey conducted by Harris Interactive® reported that 21% of U.S. workers made a voluntary job change in 2006.[8] See Figure 4.1 for the top reasons why U.S. workers voluntarily changed jobs. Organizations with recruitment strategies that include plans for retention typically have lower rates of employee turnover. Aiming for 100% retention may be an unrealistic goal, but every organization should have a specific goal or target for employee retention.

FIGURE 4.1 Top reasons why U.S. workers changed jobs

Top Reasons Why U.S. Workers Voluntarily Changed Jobs in the Past Year

1. Growth & Earnings Potential	30%
2. Time & Flexibility	23%
3. Financial Compensation	22%
4. Culture & Work Environment	22%
5. Benefits	12%
6. Supervisor Relationship	**10%**
7. Training & Development	9%
8. Management Climate	9%

Source: Spherion® press release, *Workers on the Move: Nearly One-Quarter in the U.S. Voluntarily Changed Jobs Last Year, According to Latest Spherion Survey* (Ft. Lauderdale, FL, January 11, 2007), viewed April 26, 2008 at http://www.spherion.com/press/releases/2007/snapshot-voluntary-job-change.jsp. Reprinted by permission.

The impacts of effective employee retention programs include improved performance, higher job satisfaction, improved teamwork, and increased productivity.

Keep in mind that retention is not just about keeping employees, but keeping them productive. The impacts of effective employee retention programs include improved performance, higher job satisfaction, improved teamwork, and increased productivity.[9]

KNOWLEDGE TO ACTION

Figure 4.1 provides the results of a survey indicating why U.S. workers voluntarily changed jobs. Examine the figure, then answer the following questions:

1. What are some reasons why workers choose to change jobs that are *not* listed in the survey chart?

_____

2. Using the survey results in Figure 4.1 and your list above, which of these items do you think a supervisor can influence in his or her effort to retain productive employees?

_____

Prior to Recruitment: Defining Core Abilities and Writing Job Descriptions

There are three main reasons why a company chooses to recruit. The first and most common is to replace a worker who has left the company. Another reason is because the organization is growing or expanding hours of operation. In this situation, the company is adding staff to existing job categories. Fortunately, the job descriptions already exist and supervisors have prior experience recruiting for these positions. This experience provides a good starting point. The third reason for recruitment is the creation of *new* positions as a result of organizational growth and expansion. This situation is far different from the first two recruitment scenarios because it requires a careful examination of job duties, core abilities, and the preparation of a job description. We will explore these processes in more detail later in this section.

Before a company places an advertisement to hire someone for a new position, it needs to conduct a **job analysis** to identify task and skill requirements for a specific job. This process frequently includes the identification of core abilities as well. A job analysis should be done for all new positions. It is important to periodically review job analysis data for existing positions to be sure they are current. Figure 4.2 provides a list of questions to ask when conducting the job analysis.

Periodically review the job analysis data for existing positions.

The next step is to prepare a comprehensive **job description** that documents expectations, tasks, and responsibilities—as well as education and skill requirements—for a specific job. This process involves a variety of activities, such as defining the job duties; identifying the necessary skills, knowledge, personal attributes (attitude, personality, style, etc.), education, and experience required; deciding on the compensation level; and determining the work schedule. Job descriptions for existing positions need to be updated as necessary.

Determining Core Abilities

Taking the time to identify the **core abilities** for a position will provide a considerable return on your investment. One of the keys to effective hiring is setting clear expectations. When you understand what it takes to do a job, you will be able to articulate this to potential candidates so they know from the beginning what is expected. In addition, having a comprehensive list of core abilities is useful in developing the job description and interview questions.

Having a comprehensive list of core abilities is useful in developing the job description and interview questions.

FIGURE 4.2 Questions to ask during the job analysis

job analysis
identifying task and skill requirements for specific jobs by studying superior performers in related jobs.

job description
a document that outlines expectations and skill requirements for a specific job.

core abilities
a list of technical and behavioral skills and personal attributes required for a job.

Questions to Ask During the Job Analysis

- What are the future directions/objectives of the local area?
- What are the responsibilities of the position?
- Is the position academic or professional/general (does the role require knowledge of the teaching and learning environment)?
- What is the length of appointment and/or service fraction?
- What are the specific tasks and how will they be done?
- Why do they need to be done?
- What impact will there be on other positions in the area?
- Where will the work be done? (physical location)
- Who are the clients and what are their needs?
- How is the work is currently organized?
- Who will the position report to?
- Will any positions report to this position?
- What are the minimum knowledge and skills required to do the position?
- What equipment or working aids are required?

Source: "Job Analysis," UniSA Human Resources Unit viewed on April 26, 2008 at http://www.unisa.edu.au/hrm/employment/remuneration/job_analysis.asp.

Begin this process by consciously looking at the position from two perspectives: the employee's frame of reference and your customers' view of the organization. Customers include both internal and external customers. Whenever possible, include people who represent these different areas. Begin by drafting a list of the core abilities you think are necessary for the position, then ask for feedback from various people who will work with the person you will hire. Invite suggestions for additions, edits, and perhaps deletions. In addition, ask for assistance in defining methods for measuring each item.

Identify the physical and mental tasks required and outline how the job will get done. This may include listing specific equipment used and standards or methods.[10] You are preparing a competency-based document that should include a list of specific and measurable skills.[11] These core abilities can be broken down into three categories: (1) technical skills, (2) behavioral skills, and (3) personal attributes.

TECHNICAL SKILLS

List all of the specific technical skills required for the job. For example, let's say you are preparing a core abilities document for a bank teller. The technical skills may include the following:

1. Knowledge of bank products and services, such as investment products (e.g., savings/checking accounts), lending services (e.g., mortgages), safe deposit boxes, and vault operations.
2. Basic math skills, such as the ability to add, subtract, calculate percentages, and understand compounding and amortization.
3. Computer skills, such as basic keyboarding, word processing, and spreadsheets.

BEHAVIORAL SKILLS

List all of the desired behaviors for a person in this position. Continuing with the bank teller example, behavioral skills may include the following:

1. Demonstrating professionalism, such as dressing and appearing comfortable in appropriate business attire.
2. Conducting oneself in a confident professional manner, such as making eye contact, listening without interrupting, always remaining calm, and treating people with respect.
3. Responding in a timely and appropriate fashion by being punctual and meeting deadlines.
4. Working with customers and coworkers quickly, efficiently, and accurately.
5. Learning quickly and having the desire to acquire new knowledge and skills.
6. Demonstrating effective problem-solving and dispute resolution skills.
7. Thinking critically and analytically.

PERSONAL ATTRIBUTES

List the qualities and characteristics that are necessary for the person in the position to be successful. Again, using the bank teller as an example, personal attributes may include the following:

1. Being friendly and helpful.
2. Demonstrating integrity and honesty and understanding the need to maintain customer confidentiality.
3. Being respectful and valuing diversity (e.g., treating everyone the same regardless of education, age, gender, disability, sexual orientation, religion, ethnic background, and other personal characteristics).

The bank teller example is not comprehensive. It is simply intended to provide you with a few ideas for items that may be included in a core abilities document. As you can see, many of these items can be observed and/or evaluated during the interview process. Other items, such as honesty, may require additional research, such as checking references.

Writing a Job Description

As defined previously, a job description provides specific information about the responsibilities and duties for the position. It also includes essential skills and desired qualifications, along with information about the organization and its culture.[12] The process of writing a job description is similar to preparing a core abilities document. It can be helpful to involve others, such as employees and customers. One of the benefits of having a written job description in place is that it allows both the supervisor and the employee to clearly understand what the individual will be doing on a regular basis. In addition, it is an excellent resource during the recruitment process because

This bank teller is demonstrating many of the skills and attributes that are on her list of core abilities. She is serving her customer in a pleasant fashion during the course of the entire transaction. That's service her employer and customers can bank on!
© Kayte M. Deioma/PhotoEdit

it allows candidates to learn about the position and know ahead of time what will be expected of them. Clear expectations from the beginning can boost job satisfaction and, ultimately, employee retention. In this section, we will discuss components that should be included in every job description, regardless of the type of position.

JOB TITLE

A good job title is concise and descriptive. It should reflect the organization's culture and values and give others a clear idea of what the employee does. For example, in a retail clothing store, the person responsible for working the floor and answering customers' questions is commonly referred to as a *salesperson, customer associate,* or *fashion consultant.* The title should fit the circumstances. Calling someone with little or no experience in the business a fashion consultant could be misleading. However, that title could be perfect for someone at a high-end store who has years of fashion-related experience.

POSITION DESCRIPTION

This section provides a brief narrative description of the position, the employee's goals and responsibilities, and major job functions.[13] It previews the Job Specifications section of the job description.

REPORTING AND ORGANIZATIONAL STRUCTURE

The question answered by this section is: Where does the person filling this position fit in the organizational hierarchy? For a supervisory slot, those positions reporting directly to the individual should be listed.

ORGANIZATIONAL VALUES AND CULTURE

In this section, unique characteristics of the organization and expected behavior, attitudes, and values are specified.[14] This may include value-oriented items such as honesty, integrity, respect, creativity, and diversity and product/service-oriented items such as quality, customer loyalty, and safety. A brief overview of the corporate culture and management's philosophy will give anyone reading the job description (e.g., employees, prospective applicants, management, and customers) a sense of the character traits required for this position.[15]

DESIRED QUALIFICATIONS

Here, specific qualifications for the job are listed, including number of years of experience, education, specialized skills, certifications, licenses, knowledge, and personal attributes. There will be more qualifications for highly specialized positions; by contrast, entry-level positions typically have fewer qualifications.

REQUIREMENTS

What are the physical and mental requirements for the job? This important information helps interviewers ask precisely the right questions. Physical requirements might include the ability to lift a certain amount of weight or stand for an extended period of time. Mental requirements may include items such as working in a high-stress environment, handling customer complaints on a regular basis, working alone, or working in a fast-paced environment.

JOB SPECIFICATIONS AND REALISTIC JOB PREVIEWS

This section lists essential tasks, duties, and responsibilities for the position. Listing them in order of priority may be appropriate. The core abilities document is a good reminder of what to include. If you expect people to continuously learn or contribute to team projects, include this in the job specifications. Be specific and list the types of jobs/tasks the employee will need to complete. The idea is to minimize confusion by eliminating ambiguity.[16] Providing what experts call a **realistic job preview** contributes to employee job satisfaction and decreases turnover. The goal of a realistic job preview is to provide prospective employees with a better understanding of the job they are applying for by including details about day-to-day activities. It should include the positive and appealing aspects of the job, as well as the negatives, such as frequent travel, repetitive tasks, and cleaning responsibilities.[17] See Table 4.1 for alternative ways to deliver realistic job previews.

TABLE 4.1
Realistic Job Preview Methods

Delivery Method	Description	Pros	Cons
Direct observation	Individual shadows a person on the job and has the opportunity to observe and ask questions.	Inexpensive; remains current.	Can be difficult to schedule. Potentially awkward or invasive to customers and employees.
Meetings with current workers and/or customers	Meeting with various constituents to learn about the company and the job.	Portable, does not have to be on the job site; access to information from knowledgeable source(s); remains current.	Can be difficult to staff. Requires employees to be away from their jobs.
Videos	Shows people on the job working.	Consistent, high-impact view of the job.	Expensive. May not remain current for long if work/tasks change.
Brochures	Printed publication with positive and negative aspects of job.	Information presented in text and photos, fairly easy to update; highly portable and easy to distribute.	Passive learning—lacks hands-on experience or demonstration. Requires expertise to create.
Web-based	Positive and negative aspects of job presented online. May include text, photos, and video clips.	Portable; relatively inexpensive; easy to update frequently.	Requires expertise to create and maintain. Not all applicants have Web access.
Internship or volunteer program	Hands-on experience working at the company.	Provides employer with opportunity to assess the individual and the person to evaluate the company.	Time consuming to coordinate and train.
Hybrid	Combines one or more of the methods previously mentioned.	More thorough and accessible.	Requires frequent review and updating of all forms to remain current and consistent.

Source: Adapted from Susan O'Nell, Sherri Larson, Amy Hewitt, and John Sauer, "RJP Overview," Minneapolis: University of Minnesota, Institute on Community Integration (April 30, 2001): 1-9, http://rtc.umn.edu/docs/rjp.pdf (accessed April 26, 2008).

Finalizing the Job Description and Keeping It Current

Once you have completed the first draft of a job description, ask other team members and customers to review it and provide feedback. Make appropriate changes. It also needs to be kept current. A perfect time to reevaluate a job description for updating is during each person's annual performance review.

What if You Do Not Have a Job Description?

Many small businesses and nonprofit organizations have never taken the time to write job descriptions. If you work for one of these companies and you do not have a job description, write your own. Follow the steps outlined above, beginning with core abilities, and prepare a job description that reflects the work that you do. Clearly indicate that it is a draft and review it with your boss.

Legal Issues: Diversity and Testing

Every person in the organization should be aware of several legal issues related to the recruitment process. People have argued that only those directly involved in the process should be properly trained. However, every employee could potentially create a legal liability situation. For example, you may not legally ask applicants certain personal questions related to a disability. If a candidate arrives for an interview a little early and is waiting out in the reception area, your receptionist could legally expose the company while simply making conversation. The receptionist may notice that the applicant parked in a handicap parking spot out front and ask about the person's disability. If the person is not hired, she could potentially raise this as an issue. Therefore, it is better to err on the side of too much training and include everyone in your recruitment training.

Every person in the organization should be aware of legal issues related to the recruitment process.

As key members of the management team, supervisors should never engage in illegal discrimination. It is important to note that, in the U.S., there are specific federal laws in place to protect all workers as well as certain groups of individuals that have historically been the victims of discriminatory treatment at work. These include the Equal Employment Opportunity Law, the Americans with Disabilities Act of 1990, and the Age Discrimination in Employment Act of 1967. In addition, the Fair Labor Standards Act (FLSA) establishes minimum wage, overtime pay, recordkeeping, and child labor standards. The following discussion about these laws and the recruitment process is intended to provide an overview of these topics. Chapter 13 covers additional information, resources, and legal issues that are relevant for supervisors.

realistic job preview
gives job seekers a realistic idea about positive and negative aspects of a job.

equal employment opportunity laws
federal laws prohibiting employment discrimination based on personal characteristics.

Equal Employment Opportunity

Although earlier legislation still applies selectively, the landmark **Equal Employment Opportunity (EEO) laws** prohibit employment discrimination based on characteristics such as race, color, religion, sex (gender), national origin, or disability in the United States.

Many EEO laws are based on Title VII of the Civil Rights Act of 1964. Subsequent amendments, presidential executive orders, and related laws have strengthened this broad umbrella of employment protection.[18]

In addition, many states and municipalities also have enacted protections against discrimination and harassment based on sexual orientation, status as a parent, marital status, and political affiliation. For information, contact the Equal Employment Opportunity Commission (EEOC) District Office nearest you, or visit the EEOC website at http://www.eeoc.gov.[19]

What all this means is that supervisors cannot refuse to hire, promote, train, or transfer employees simply on the basis of the characteristics just mentioned. Nor can they lay off or discharge employees on these grounds. Selection and all other personnel decisions must be made solely on the basis of objective criteria, such as seniority or the ability to perform. Lawsuits by individuals and fines by agencies such as the EEOC are powerful incentives to comply with EEO laws. There have been guilty verdicts and settlements through the years. For example, in 2005 the clothing retailer Abercrombie & Fitch was required to pay $40 million dollars to Latino, African-American, Asian, and female applicants and employees after being charged with discrimination. As a result of the settlement, Abercrombie & Fitch was also required to establish policies and programs promoting workforce diversity.[20]

KNOWLEDGE TO ACTION

1. Why is it important for supervisors to be aware of Equal Employment Opportunity laws?

_____

2. Suppose that James is the supervisor at a motorcycle manufacturing plant. He is interviewing candidates for an assembly position on the manufacturing line. One of the applicants is a woman named Sue. During the interview, James tells Sue that the company has never hired a woman in his department because the job requires too much heavy lifting. Based on her prior experience working in a tractor manufacturing plant, it appears that Sue has the necessary qualifications for the job. However, James chooses not to hire her because she is a woman.

   a. Based on the information given, do you think Sue has been discriminated against? Explain why or why not.

   _____

   b. If Sue decides to file a discrimination lawsuit, do you think James' company could be liable in this case, even though James himself made the decision? Explain why or why not.

   _____

Affirmative Action

affirmative action program (AAP)
a program for actively seeking, employing, and developing the talents of groups traditionally discriminated against in employment.

A more rigorous refinement of EEO legislation is affirmative action. An **affirmative action program (AAP)** is a plan for actively seeking out, employing, and developing the talents of those groups traditionally discriminated against in employment, typically women and minorities.[21] Conventional AAPs seek to eliminate employment discrimination with the following four methods:

- Active recruitment of women and minorities.
- Elimination of prejudicial questions on employment application forms.
- Establishment of specific goals and timetables for minority hiring.
- Statistical validation of employment testing procedures.

Like any public policy that has legal ramifications, the EEO/AAP area is fraught with complexity. Varying political and legal interpretations and inconsistent court decisions have sometimes frustrated and confused managers and supervisors.[22] Legislated social change, however necessary or laudable, is not without pain. Much remains to be accomplished to eliminate the legacy of unfair discrimination in hiring and workplace decisions.

Diversity Goes Beyond Race and Gender

One authority on the subject, R. Roosevelt Thomas, Jr., views diversity as more than just race, gender, and ethnicity. In his opinion, diversity encompasses additional personal attributes such as education, age, background and upbringing, and personality differences. However, many employment laws focus on protecting women and minorities. They do not consider the additional elements Thomas mentions. As a result, many white males are left to wonder where they fit into the government's definition of diversity.[23]

Diversity advocates want to replace all forms of bigotry, prejudice, and intolerance with tolerance and, ideally, *appreciation* of interpersonal differences.[24] They also want to broaden the focus to include recruitment and retention of a diverse collection of people. The case for increasing diversity has moved from legal compliance to the realization that a diverse workforce is good for business.[25] Joe Watson, the founder and CEO of Virginia-based StrategicHire.com, an executive search firm, is a proponent of greater diversity. During a recent interview, he said, "If you want to satisfy clients and customers from diverse backgrounds . . . you need a diverse mix of employees who are more likely to understand them. Diversity can also stimulate creativity: People from various cultural and ethnic backgrounds offer different perspectives that can spur innovation."[26]

Periodically, as with the case of Abercrombie & Fitch, we are reminded of just how much remains to be done.

Accommodating the Needs of People with Disabilities

From the perspective of someone in a wheelchair, the world can be a very unfriendly place. Curbs, stairways, and inward-swinging doors in small public toilet stalls all symbolically say, "You're not welcome here; you don't fit in." Human disabilities vary widely, but historically, people with disabilities have had one thing in common—unemployment. Consider that today, more than 54 million Americans—nearly 20% of the U.S. population—are disabled. One in five disabled adults has not graduated from high school, and more than 70% of disabled people between ages 18 and 55 are unemployed.[27]

To put this information into perspective, we will simply compare unemployment data. An astounding 70% of people with disabilities are unemployed, compared with an overall unemployment rate that has remained around 5% for the last twenty years.[28] Clearly, there is a large gap in employment opportunities. Keep in mind that reducing the unemployment rate for people with disabilities is not just about jobs and money. It is about self-sufficiency, hopes, and dreams.[29] With the reauthorization of the Rehabilitation Act of 1973 and the enactment of the **Americans with Disabilities Act of 1990 (ADA)**, people with disabilities hoped to get a chance to take their rightful place in the workforce.[30] The ADA "makes it unlawful for an employer to discriminate against a qualified applicant or employee with a disability. The ADA applies to private employers with 15 or more employees and to state and local government employers." Section 501 of the Rehabilitation Act establishes the same protection for federal employment.[31]

As the data indicate, people with disabilities still have a lot of catching up to do to reach parity in employment. However, upon reading a recent report by Stan Newman, founder of the American Alliance for People with Disabilities, employers may soon be changing their recruiting tactics. According to Newman, people with disabilities may in fact be more productive and reliable than their coworkers.[32] The organization, Art for A Cause, based in Birmingham, Michigan, recognizes this—since 2000, it has been employing individuals with mental and physical disabilities such as cerebral palsy, muscular dystrophy, and autism. Art for A Cause was projected to reach $2.5 million in sales in 2008. Company founder Lisa Knoppe Reed explains why her company has decided to hire people with disabilities: "We don't employ them because we feel sorry for them but because everyone deserves a chance to work, and they do a great job."[33] Once this type of information reaches more supervisors and recruiters, we are quite likely to see more active recruiting of people with disabilities.

The ADA, enforced by the EEOC, requires employers to make **reasonable accommodations** to the needs of present and future employees with physical and mental disabilities. Reasonable accommodations cannot create "undue hardship" for employers, such as significant financial costs or difficulty of implementation.[34] In addition, employers are not required to modify the job responsibilities or essential skills required to perform the job. The expectation is that employers make a concerted effort to provide accommodations that will allow employees with disabilities to be successful. See Figure 4.3 for examples of reasonable accommodations that may be implemented during the hiring process.

Consider the following example to illustrate the concept of reasonable accommodation:

> John is blind and applies for a job as a customer service representative. John could perform this job with assistive technology, such as a program that reads information on the screen. If the company wishes to have John demonstrate his ability to use the computer, it must provide appropriate assistive technology as a reasonable accommodation.[35]

New technology is making reasonable accommodation easier for employers.[36] Large-print computer screens for the visually impaired, Braille keyboards and talking computers for the blind, and telephones with visual readouts for the deaf are among today's helpful technologies. Here are some general policy guidelines for employers:

Americans with Disabilities Act of 1990 (ADA)
a federal law prohibiting employers from discriminating against qualified applicants or employees with disabilities.

reasonable accommodations
accommodations for employees with disabilities that do not create "undue hardship" for employers.

- Audit all facilities, policies, work rules, hiring procedures, and labor union contracts to eliminate barriers and bias.

- Train all supervisors and managers in ADA compliance and all employees in how to be sensitive to coworkers, employment candidates, and customers with disabilities.

- Do not hire anyone who cannot safely perform the basic duties of a particular job with reasonable accommodation.

FIGURE 4.3 Reasonable accommodations

Source: U.S. Equal Opportunity Commission, "Job Applicants and the Americans with Disabilities Act," EEOC website, http://www.eeoc.gov/facts/jobapplicant.html, last updated March 21, 2005 (accessed April 26, 2008).

Reasonable Accommodations

Reasonable accommodation can take many forms. Ones that may be needed during the hiring process include (but are not limited to):

- Providing written materials in accessible formats, such as large print, Braille, or audiotape

- Providing readers or sign language interpreters

- Ensuring that recruitment, interviews, tests, and other components of the application process are held in accessible locations

- Providing or modifying equipment or devices

- Adjusting or modifying application policies and procedures.

Microsoft Corporation employee Kelly Ford works in one of the company's labs in Redmond, Washington. Here we see Ford, who has been blind since birth, testing a program that provides audible feedback about what is being displayed on a Web page and also displays Web page information on a "Braille display" that can be read by touch. As part of his job, Ford also manages a team of people who are working to improve Web page browsing for all users, not just those with disabilities.

© AP Images/Ted S. Warren

Team up with your classmates to discuss accommodations for the scenarios below. You may want to review the U.S. Equal Employment Opportunity Commission online resource, "Job Applicants and the Americans with Disabilities Act," at http://www.eeoc.gov/facts/jobapplicant.html for more information about reasonable accommodations.

1. Jamy is the supervisor of a customer service call center. Her employees use telephones and computers to conduct their work. She is currently recruiting, and one of the qualified applicants is considered legally blind. What accommodations do you think Jamy should consider for this person?

   _____

2. Erin is the supervisor of a college advising department. She is currently recruiting for a new advisor. During walk-in advising, the advisors use a computer that is positioned on an elevated counter at eye level for an average-height person standing. One of the qualified applicants is confined to a wheelchair, making it impossible for him to access this computer. What accommodations do you think Erin should consider in this situation?

   _____

With lots of low-tech ingenuity, a touch of high tech, and support from coworkers, millions of people with disabilities can make meaningful contributions in the workplace.

Employment Selection Tests

EEO guidelines in the United States have broadened the definition of an **employment selection test** to include any procedure used as a basis for an employment decision. This means that, in addition to traditional pencil-and-paper tests, numerous other procedures qualify as tests, such as unscored application forms; informal and formal interviews; performance tests; and physical, educational, or experience requirements.[37] This definition of an employment test takes on added significance when you realize that in the United States the federal government requires all employment tests to be statistically valid and reliable predictors of job success.[38] Historically, women and minorities have been victimized by invalid, unreliable, and prejudicial employment selection procedures. Similar complaints have been voiced about the use of personality tests, polygraphs, drug tests, and AIDS and DNA screening during the hiring process.[39]

Hiring Young Workers

More and more high school students are entering the workforce every day. Many of these young workers are under the age of 18, which means that there are limitations on the types of jobs they can perform, their working conditions, and the hours they work. The federal legislation governing child labor is the **Fair Labor Standards Act (FLSA)**, which is a federal law that establishes minimum wage, overtime pay, recordkeeping, and child labor standards.[40] In addition, state and local jurisdictions may have more restrictive rules and laws. The U.S. Department of Labor enforces the FLSA, and each state has a department of labor to enforce its own laws.[41] Prior to

employment selection test
any procedure used in the employment decision process.

Fair Labor Standards Act (FLSA)
a federal law that establishes minimum wage, overtime pay, recordkeeping, and child labor standards.

Prior to hiring workers under the age of 18, supervisors should verify that they are eligible based on both federal and local laws.

hiring workers under the age of 18, supervisors should verify that they are eligible based on both federal and local laws.

Workers 40 Years of Age or Older

For supervisors, this topic is important from a recruitment perspective as well as day-to-day management. Many supervisors have job applicants and employees who are 40 years of age or older. Therefore, it is important to be aware of the **Age Discrimination in Employment Act of 1967 (ADEA)**, which prohibits employment discrimination against persons 40 years of age or older. The EEOC enforces this law.

Recruitment Strategies

In his best-seller *Good to Great: Why Some Companies Make the Leap and Other's Don't*, Jim Collins uses the metaphor of a bus when referring to an organization and its employees.[42] He believes that a busload of great people can go just about anywhere it wants. But a bus filled with confused and unruly passengers is destined for the ditch. It is also important to have the right people on the right bus at the right time moving in the right direction. In other words, supervisors need to match employees' talents with tasks and responsibilities and organizational goals in an efficient and effective manner. Recruiting employees with the necessary talent or potential to be productive is essential. A recent survey of CEOs reinforces the importance of getting the right people on the bus and keeping them there.

Match employees' talents with tasks and responsibilities.

When asked what they likely will look back on five years from now as the key to their success, the number one response was, "Getting and retaining talent."[43] In this section, you will be introduced to various strategies to consider in pursuing this important goal.

Recruiting for Diversity

The ultimate goal of recruiting is to generate a pool of qualified applicants for new and existing jobs. One of the challenges is creating an applicant pool that is demographically representative of the population at large if diversity is to be achieved. A casual review of recruiting ads reveals abundant evidence of corporate diversity initiatives. Monica Reed, at Prudential in Newark, New Jersey, explains the rationale:

> Our corporate culture is diverse, because that brings a variety of new ideas and perspectives into the company. We also want to sell to a diverse audience, and someone who sees a recruitment ad that focuses on diversity may also become a customer.[44]

Age Discrimination in Employment Act of 1967 (ADEA)
a federal law prohibiting employment discrimination against persons 40 years of age or older.

Recent research about the top five most frequently used search methods has revealed a major surprise about recruiting for diversity   Personal referrals turned out to be the best way to land a job. In a recent survey of 703 people, 61% said they had found their most recent job via "networking/word of mouth."[45] The message to supervisors is clear. Your employees will talk to their friends and family about their job. They are quite likely to encourage them to apply for an opening if they feel good about the company, their supervisor, and the nature of their job.

Recruiting in a Competitive Market—Selling the Job

Many people think of recruitment as finding potential employment candidates. However, recruitment is also about the job of selling your company and your position to prospective applicants. Most supervisors, managers, and human resources professionals do not list "salesperson" on their own job description. However, the reality in today's competitive recruiting environment is that supervisors need to be able to sell the position to the best candidate. In fact, 51% of hiring managers said they feel they must *sell* jobs to candidates. This is according to a 2006 global study of more than 3,700 job seekers, 1,250 hiring managers, and 620 staffing directors in five global regions.[46] See Figure 4.4 for examples of how companies are bringing their marketing and recruiting efforts together. The overriding point is to answer the question, "What makes your organization unique?" It may be the challenging work, unique opportunities, flexible scheduling, or better pay. Identify something that makes your job opening better than the others.[47]

THEY SAID IT BEST

I'd rather do something interesting, solve an interesting problem, than do something boring and get rich.

—LOUIS MONIER, Internet Entrepreneur

Source: Lorraine A. DarConte, *Lessons for Success* (New York: MJF Books, 2001), 164.

Online Recruiting

Using online recruiting websites such as Monster, CareerBuilder, Craigslist, or social networking sites like LinkedIn provides access to thousands of people at a relatively low cost (or in some cases no cost). However, the downside can be an overwhelming

FIGURE 4.4 How to bring marketing and recruiting together
Source: Adapted from Ryan McCarthy's "'Help Wanted' Meets 'Buy It Now': Why More Companies are Integrating Marketing and Recruiting," *Inc. Magazine*, 29.11 (November 2007): p. 51–52.

How to Bring Marketing and Recruiting Together

1. **Sponsor community-oriented events.** Charity walks and bike rides, for example. You can distribute recruiting materials while identifying your business with good deeds.
2. **Look for ways to promote recruiting events** as you promote a product launch or winning an award.
3. **Involve some of your junior employees in the interview process.** New employees typically have a high level of enthusiasm and a fresh perspective.
4. **Treat every job candidate like a potential customer.** Every hiring manager should spend a few minutes during an interview making a concise but direct sales pitch.
5. **Think of every "help wanted" listing as a marketing opportunity.**

response, leading to a time-consuming and often frustrating process of identifying qualified applicants. Companies such as Protuo and ZoomInfo are using surveys and data-gathering techniques to streamline the search process.[48] Regardless of the tool, the key to online advertising is creating a specific posting and being prepared to take time to narrow down the candidate pool.

In addition, companies are using their corporate websites to attract candidates. In some cases, they are expanding out into popular websites for students to recruit applicants. For example, Ernst & Young recently purchased a page on Facebook for a sponsored group page dedicated to recruiting. The use of websites such as Facebook allows employers to reach talented candidates worldwide.

Organizations can bolster their staffs by using social networks to find just the right skills wherever they are needed. For example, Ning, a Silicon Valley startup with 10 nationalities represented among its 27 employees, follows blog postings and other cybertrails to find the most qualified candidates. The company provides software tools for consumers to build their own social networking sites, and it was through its own software that Ning located Fabricio Zuardi, living in remote São Carlos, Brazil. He had used Ning's tools to build a social networking site for people interested in music. Ning engineers liked what he was doing and engaged him in an online conversation. One day, Zuardi had the very pleasant surprise of finding a job offer from co-founder Marc Andreessen in his e-mail inbox. "For anyone in the world, the American dream is more accessible now," says Zuardi.[49]

Of course, many online venues provide space for critics to post negative information about your organization.[50]

Also, a word of caution for all students and job seekers: employers have access to the Internet too! Posting photos, videos, or blogs that may seem entertaining or fun at the time could come back to haunt you later if they are viewed and perceived as unprofessional or worse by a future employer.

 **KNOWLEDGE TO ACTION**

…the Pew Internet and American Life Project said 47% of U.S. adult Internet users have looked for information about themselves through Google or another search engine. That is more than twice the 22% of users who did in 2002. About 60% of Internet users said they aren't worried about the extent of information about themselves online, despite increasing concern over how that data can be used. Americans under 50 and those with more education and income were more likely to self-Google—in some cases because their jobs demand a certain online persona.

1. How carefully do you control and monitor what a potential employer, customer, or coworker could learn about you by doing a Web search? (For example, do you have any embarrassing content on Facebook or MySpace?)

2. Is it ethical for a potential employer to check you out on the Web before making a hiring decision? Explain.

Source: "More Americans Search Selves on Web," *USA Today,* December 17, 2007, 1B.

The Promise and Controversy of Video Résumés

Another emerging trend is the use of video résumés. This practice started with job seekers posting their video résumés on YouTube in 2006, but it is a growing market with companies like WorkBlast, MyPersonalBroadcast, and HireVue offering video résumé services to employers and prospective candidates. In addition, well-established online recruiting sites such as CareerBuilder.com offer free video résumé services.[51] Video résumés can be a great resource, particularly if you are recruiting for a specialized position that requires travel for interviewing. Video résumés can provide a lot of information about the candidate's communication skills, creativity, energy level, and style. In addition, they can be structured so the candidate is answering a series of questions simulating a live interview.

Employers need to heed the recent legal opinion about video résumés from Garry Mathiason, a senior partner at leading employment firm Littler Mendelson in San Francisco, California. Mathiason says, "Employers should never require video résumés from candidates. That's tantamount to asking questions about race or age."[52]

Job Fairs

Local high schools, colleges, and universities frequently host job fairs. For a relatively small fee, you can set up a table to attract prospective candidates. Another successful approach is special job fairs with themes or target audiences, such as a job fair at a union hall in an effort to attract union members to fill certain positions. In addition, special job fairs for military veterans are frequently held around the country.

Postings

Many employers successfully attract applicants with signs posted in the front window of their store, at the cash register, or on bulletin boards. In addition, contractors and others with company vans or trucks have posted Help Wanted signs on their vehicles. This is one of the least expensive recruitment methods available, and you just never know when your next employee may walk through the door. This can be a particularly effective method for retailers, because people who like to shop at a particular store might also like to work there. Billboards are another medium companies have used to post recruiting advertisements. In an aggressive recruitment effort, online insurance provider Esurance posted a recruitment advertisement on a billboard placed right next to a competitor's call center.[53] This is a rather unique situation, yet very creative and potentially very effective.

Referrals

Word-of-mouth advertising is both effective and inexpensive. In fact, it can be up to 75% less expensive than traditional advertising or placement agencies.[54] In addition, employee referrals lead to greater retention because they have already passed the first test—peer approval. Rewards for employees who make a referral come in various forms, including cash, gift certificates, company apparel, and other fun prizes. Many organizations disburse the reward in increments, giving the referring employee half upon the new hire's start and the other half after three or six months of employment. One potential downside of referrals is less diversity, because employees tend to refer people from within their own social circles.[55]

Beyond your own employees, consider seeking recommendations from your suppliers and customers. Both of these groups have a vested interest in seeing your business succeed. They are also inclined to refer prospective candidates they believe will make a good fit and do a good job.

Special Events and Outreach

In highly competitive markets, companies have gone to great lengths to attract the top talent. This includes everything from the low-cost approach of treating a prospective candidate to lunch to more expensive and extravagant events such as Ernst & Young's Utah rafting trip for soon-to-be accounting graduates or the wine tasting and baseball games sponsored by Blackboard to recruit technology candidates in the Washington, DC, area.[56]

Outreach includes recruiting through professional organizations. For example, if you are seeking an accountant, you may want to contact your state's association of certified public accountants to learn how you can reach their members, who are quite likely to be qualified for the position.

Retirees and mothers are two groups of workers who are returning to work. Employers are reaching out to these potential employees because they are perceived as mature, experienced workers. One of the challenges for supervisors is finding the right balance, because many of these returning workers may want to work part-time or require a flexible schedule.[57]

KNOWLEDGE TO ACTION   Brainstorm with your classmates to prepare a list with no fewer than six different types of jobs and your suggestions for recruiting for each position.

Employee Selection: The PROCEED Model

Del J. Still, a respected author and trainer, summarizes the employee selection process with the acronym PROCEED, in which each letter represents one of the seven steps involved (see Figure 4.5). This model encourages supervisors to take a systems perspective, from preparing to hire to the final hiring decision.

FIGURE 4.5 Still's PROCEED model

Source: Adapted from Del J. Still, *High Impact Hiring: How to Interview and Select on line Outstanding Employees,* 2nd ed., rev. (Dana Point, CA: Management Development Systems, 2001): 43–44

Employee Selection Process: Still's PROCEED Model

Step 1: Prepare

Identify existing superior performers.

Identify the competencies or skills needed to do the job.

Create a job description for the position; if one already exists, review and update as necessary.

Draft interview questions and/or scenarios.

Step 2: Review

Review questions for legality and fairness.

Step 3: Organize

Select your interview team.

Determine your method for interviewing.

Assign roles to your team and divide questions.

Step 4: Conduct

Gather data from the job candidate.

Step 5: Evaluate

Determine the best matches between the candidates and the job.

Step 6: Exchange

Share data in a discussion meeting.

Step 7: Decide

Make the final decision.

Check references prior to making an offer.

The Selection Process

Human Resources experts commonly compare the selection process to a hurdle race. The whole selection process can become quite complex and drawn out at companies such as Google, where rapid growth means steady hiring:

> A team of nearly 50 recruiters divided by specialty combs through résumés, which applicants must submit online, then dumps them into a program that routes those selected for interviews to the proper hiring committee and throws the rest in the electronic trash. Interviewing for a job is a grueling process that can take months. Every opening has a hiring committee of seven to nine Googlers who must meet you. Engineers may be asked to write software or debug a program on the spot. Marketers are often required to take a writing test. No matter how long you have been out of school, Google requires that you submit your transcripts to be considered. The rigorous process is important partly for the obvious reason that in high tech, as on Wall Street, being the smartest and the cleverest at what you do is a critical business advantage.[58]

Equal employment opportunity legislation in the United States and elsewhere attempts to ensure a fair and unprejudiced race for all job applicants.[59] The first two hurdles are résumé screening and reference checking; both are very important because false information is found in up to 40% of job applications.[60] Frequently, supervisors make a decision about whom they

It is essential that you always check references prior to making an offer.

want to hire and want to move as quickly as possible; however, it is essential that references always be checked prior to making an offer.

One of the challenges with contacting prior employers for a reference on an applicant is that the company representative may not be forthcoming with information about the individual for fear of a lawsuit. However, many states are now enacting legislation to protect employers in an effort to allow organizations to provide truthful job references.[61] If you are asked to check references for a job applicant, be sure to review your company's policy as well as state laws pertaining to job references.

Background checks for criminal records and citizenship status verification are more essential than ever in an age of workplace violence and the strict enforcement of immigration laws, which can result in heavy fines. For many government jobs and positions with contractors doing business with the government, security clearances are also required. Other hurdles may include psychological tests, physical examinations, interviews, work-sampling tests, and drug tests.

Criteria and Decision Matrix

With the job description and core abilities clearly defined, your next steps are to develop selection criteria and create a decision-making matrix. Keep in mind that these are tools to assist in the hiring selection process; they should be used in conjunction with some of the other recruiting methods discussed in this chapter, including interviews, demonstrations, presentations, pre-employment tests, work product reviews, and reference checks.

PREPARING SELECTION CRITERIA

When preparing selection criteria for the first time, it is helpful to have the job description and core abilities documents readily available. The process begins with writing a list of the major skills, experience, and knowledge required for the position.

Once you have the list, sort it in order of priority, listing the most essential skills first, followed by the skills for which you are willing to provide training. For an example of a selection criteria priority listing, see Table 4.2, a template for an insurance company recruiting a software engineer. At the top of this list are computer programming skills and experience working with the software programming languages the company uses. Knowledge of the insurance industry is at the bottom of the list. The supervisor has determined that programming skills are essential to the job, and industry knowledge is secondary. This is a good approach, as few applicants will meet every qualification you have established.

USING THE DECISION MATRIX

The selection criteria list can be expanded to create a very useful decision matrix. To use the list as part of a decision matrix, give each item a weighted value. The more important the skill is to the position, the higher the weighted value should be. It is common for the total weighted values to add up to an even number such as 100, 150, 200, or 500. The goal is to put scoring emphasis on the skills, knowledge, and experience that you deem essential for the position.

TABLE 4.2
Sample Selection Criteria and Decision Matrix Template (Insurance Company/Software Engineer)

Selection Criteria	Weighted Value	Candidate #1		Candidate #2		Candidate #3	
		Raw Score	Weighted Score	Raw Score	Weighted Score	Raw Score	Weighted Score
3–5 yrs programming experience							
Expertise using .NET							
Experience writing vbscripts							
Expertise using C#							
Expertise using Java							
Experience with Microsoft Suite of products							
Proficiency creating Crystal Reports							
Demonstrated ability to document coding process							
Knowledge of the program development cycle							
Ability to gather user requirements							
Demonstrated experience preparing end-user training documents							
Experience training end-users							
Knowledge of Insurance Industry							
Weighted Total							

This tool is intended to assist in the selection process; it is to be used in conjunction with other recruiting methods including interviews, reference checking, demonstrations, presentations, and review of work product.

Instructions for using this template:

1. List the skills, experience, and knowledge you require for the position.
2. Write the list in priority order with the most important on top and progressively working down to the least important. This may be difficult, as you may feel that everything is important.
3. Assign each criterion a weighted value.
4. As you are reviewing applications, use the scoring matrix to help you narrow down your applicant pool to the top candidates.

Assigning weighted values and raw scores are both rather subjective. Therefore, it is important that the selection committee agree on the weighted values prior to reviewing any applications. In addition, the committee should decide on a formula for assigning raw scores. Most raw scores are assigned on a scale of 1 to 5. To illustrate how this is done, use the selection criteria for the software engineer in Table 4.2.

TABLE 4.3
Completed Selection Criteria and Decision Matrix Template (Insurance Company/Software Engineer)

Selection Criteria	Weighted Value	Candidate #1		Candidate #2		Candidate #3	
		Raw Score	Weighted Score	Raw Score	Weighted Score	Raw Score	Weighted Score
Min. 3 years programming experience	25	3	75	5	125	2	50
Expertise using .NET	20	5	100	5	100	5	100
Experience writing vbscripts	20	0	0	5	100	5	100
Expertise using C#	20	5	100	2	40	0	0
Expertise using Java	20	5	100	5	100	0	0
Experience with Microsoft Suite of products	20	5	100	5	100	5	100
Proficiency creating Crystal Reports	15	0	0	5	75	0	0
Demonstrated ability to document coding process	15	5	75	5	75	0	0
Knowledge of the program development cycle	12	0	0	5	60	0	0
Ability to gather user requirements	10	0	0	5	50	5	50
Demonstrated experience preparing end-user training documents	8	0	0	0	0	5	40
Experience training end-users	8	0	0	0	0	5	40
Knowledge of Insurance Industry	7	0	0	0	0	5	35
Weighted Total	200		550		825		515

The supervisor has determined that the applicant should have at least three years of programming experience. The selection team decides on the following scoring formula:

Number of Years of Experience	Score
0–2	0
3	1
4	2
5	3
6	4
7+	5

When using the decision matrix, every person who is involved in the selection process must understand and agree to the criteria and the scoring formula. See Table 4.3 for an example of a completed selection criteria and decision matrix for recruiting a software engineer for an insurance company.

In the example given in Table 4.3, it is evident that Candidate #2 has more of the essential skills for the position. Candidate #3 is strong in the end-user training and documentation as well as industry knowledge. However, the supervisor believes that it will be easier to train the new hire in these areas rather than teaching the person new software programming skills.

Pre-employment Testing

As mentioned earlier, employers require job candidates to take several different types of tests. Often times, they use pre-employment tests because they are required to by law or union rules. In other instances, employers use pre-employment testing because they have found that the results help predict the future success of the candidate.

Pre-employment tests may be job specific and technical in nature. For example, a fiber optics company requires candidates to take a vision test to rule out color blindness because recognizing colors is an essential skill for the job.

Other tests assess behavior, thought processes, and analytical skills. In fact, there are more than 2,500 cognitive and personality tests available to employers.[62] After doing some research, a trucking company based in Dayton, Ohio, learned that truck drivers with multiple delivery sites in a day are more successful if they are social and interact well with people. In contrast, truck drivers who have long distances to travel with limited social interaction are typically more introverted and quiet. As a result, this company now uses pre-employment assessment tests for social skills. The outcome was outstanding: driver turnover has fallen to 22%, compared with the industry average of 116%.[63]

Employers may also require other pre-employment assessments, such as drug tests, criminal background checks, or rigorous psychological testing. Typically, an employer conducts these tests to help identify the candidate who will achieve long-term success in the organization.[64] However, with over 2,500 tests to choose from, there is a strong possibility that the employer may not select the test most appropriate for its particular situation and needs. Combining relevant industry research with assessments will often yield more reliable and desirable results.

Before deciding to use any pre-employment test or assessment, be sure it is legal. Different states and local jurisdictions have different rules and laws regarding pre-employment screening. Also, be sure to select evaluation tools that match your corporate culture and are appropriate for the position. This type of screening can be perceived by candidates as invasive and personally offensive, which may lead to well-qualified candidates withdrawing their applications.

> *Before deciding to use any pre-employment test or assessment, be sure it is legal.*

Interviewing

Interviewing involves assessing job candidates by asking them questions about their work experience and potential. This topic warrants special attention here because it is the most common tool for selecting employees. Managers and supervisors at all levels are often asked to interview candidates for job openings and promotions. Preparing for and then interviewing potential candidates takes time, organization, and planning. This process begins by writing down questions for telephone, in-person, or virtual interviews. Although you will have the opportunity to adapt your questions to the candidate and the situation, you want to be sure you cover the same basic questions with each applicant so you have a consistent baseline for comparison.[65]

DEVELOPING INTERVIEW QUESTIONS

Interviewing is like a test. As most teachers will tell you, they create the questions expecting specific answers or seeking certain types of information. Developing good

interviewing
assessing job candidates by asking questions about their work experience and potential.

interview questions requires a comprehensive understanding of the core abilities, job description, and responsibilities. Therefore, it is best to not delegate this job to someone outside of the department. However, a human resource specialist can be very helpful in working with you to craft questions that will assess a candidate effectively.

In writing questions, minimize the number that can be answered with a simple yes or no. Instead, try to develop open-ended questions to get the candidate talking. In addition, seek to learn more about the candidate's past performance and behavior, because this can be an excellent indicator of future conduct.[66] Create your questions to assess those skills and abilities you previously determined were essential to the job. For example, in our previous example with the bank teller, we determined that problem-solving skills were necessary. To evaluate a candidate's problem-solving capabilities, ask her a hypothetical question such as: "Today, a customer came into the bank demanding access to his safe deposit box, but he didn't have the key. How would you handle this situation?" Another approach would be to ask the candidate to describe a problem she was confronted with at work and share how she handled it.

Proceed to develop several behavior-oriented questions that focus on essential skills and abilities for the job. Remember the legal limitations and only ask questions that are relevant to the job, leaving out any personal questions such as marital status, religion, politics, or children.

PHONE INTERVIEWS

Many recruitment initiatives involve telephone interviews. This technique is often used if there are several desirable candidates and/or if costly travel may be required. Phone interviews are typically limited to three or four questions. In addition to paying attention to the quality and content of candidates' answers, you also want to listen for passion, energy, and enthusiasm.[67]

IN-PERSON INTERVIEWS

Several clues to a person's behavior and professionalism are revealed before you even meet him. For example, how did he treat the person on the phone who scheduled the interview? How did he treat the person who greeted him when he arrived for the interview? Also, notice how the person is dressed—is it appropriate for the position? Does he seem comfortable?[68] Next, notice how he responded to you. Did he reach out to shake your hand? Did he have a firm (not too firm) handshake? Was his demeanor and communication professional and confident? Did he make eye contact with you when introducing himself?

Observing a candidate's **nonverbal communication**, such as facial expressions, posture, eye contact, and other body language, during the interview can also reveal a lot about her feelings, confidence, and personality. Also, notice if the candidate leans forward or becomes more enthusiastic when sharing a story or information about an experience she seems passionate about. If a candidate shows no energy or enthusiasm during the interview, take that as a warning sign.

Let candidates know at the beginning of the interview that you will be taking notes to help you recall specific information later. In addition, share with them that you have prepared some questions ahead of time that you will be asking all of the applicants so you have a consistent process for evaluating candidates. Conclude the

nonverbal communication
facial expressions, posture, eye contact, and other body language.

interview by asking if the candidate has any questions and also by clarifying the person's expectations for the position. Your goal is to hire someone who is not only going to fill a vacancy but also contribute to the organization's success as a high-performer.

Other approaches to hiring include peer interviews and team selection. These strategies can be excellent for long-term retention and for getting everyone on the team committed to the success of the new hire. Coworkers who have a voice in the hiring process are far less likely to complain about newcomers and far more likely to help them acclimate to their new position.[69]

VIRTUAL INTERVIEWS

With the emergence of video résumés, it is not surprising that there are now companies offering video interviewing systems. Typically, the candidates are asked a rather generic set of questions. They record their answers using a Webcam in their home or at an employment agency offering this service. One of the advantages for the employer is the freedom and flexibility to watch the virtual interviews at a convenient time and place. An advantage for the job candidate is the opportunity to view the recording and make improvements before submitting a final version.[70]

Retention Through Alternative Work Scheduling

Learning about retention begins with understanding why people leave their jobs. One of the major reasons workers leave, according to research, is to find a job that provides more time and flexibility. Career growth and increasing earnings potential is another one of the top reasons cited in the survey.[71] (Refer back to Figure 4.1 for a list of the top reasons why U.S. workers voluntarily change jobs.) Combine this high percentage of workers in transition with the cost of employee turnover, and retention becomes a significant financial issue for any organization. As you can see, several of these items are within a supervisor's sphere of influence, such as time and flexibility, culture and work environment, supervisor relationship, and training and development. We will examine each of these in more detail in subsequent chapters. In this section, we focus on location and time flexibility.

One retention item that you may want to consider during the recruitment process is alternative scheduling. Busy people want flexibility in their work lives. There are four common types of nontraditional scheduling: telecommuting, job sharing, flextime, and a compressed work week schedule.

Telecommuting

telecommuting
connecting to one's office via computer technology while working at home.

Decades ago, futurist Alvin Toffler used the term *electronic cottage* to refer to the practice of working at home on a personal computer connected to an employer's place of business. More recently, this practice has been labeled **telecommuting** because work—rather than the employee—travels between a central office and the employee's home, reaching the computer via cable modem, phone lines, or satellite. The advent of overnight delivery services, low-cost fax machines, e-mail, high-speed Internet access, and wireless connectivity, combined with telephone/cell phone communication, has broadened the scope of telecommuting. According to a recent study, an estimated 12.2 million employees telecommute full-time and approximately 45.1 million Americans conduct a portion of their work at home.[72] While some organizations have a team of workers who are full-time telecommuters, other companies reserve this flexibility for employees who have been with the organization for a year or two.[73]

Job Sharing

Job sharing is when one job gets done by two people. The reasons for creating this type of arrangement vary almost as much as the scheduling structures. Companies in a down market may downsize by consolidating two jobs into one. In an effort to keep talented people, they set up a job sharing arrangement. More often, however, job sharing arrangements are set up to accommodate employees who request a reduction in their hours on the job. To keep their valued workers, companies are growing increasingly receptive to this arrangement.[74] Job sharing schedules may have one worker covering Monday to Wednesday and the other working Wednesday to Friday (each working a half day on Wednesday, for coordination purposes). If one worker wants to take a week off for vacation, the other employee makes arrangements to cover the full week. In other companies, job sharing is broken down in larger increments such as full weeks or even months of rotating on and off the job.

Flex-time and Compressed Work Week

Flexible scheduling, or **flex-time**, is when an employer permits an employee to work a modified schedule while still achieving the hours necessary to equate to a full work week. For example, some companies offer a compressed work week whereby an employee works four 10-hour days or works five 9-hour days and then takes a day off every other week. Flex-time also includes modified hours, allowing an employee to arrive early or late and leave early or late. These arrangements are often made to accommodate child care needs, commuting issues, or class schedules for those taking college courses.

Making Alternative Scheduling Work

There are many benefits to allowing employees to work at home, job share, or modify their schedules. However, all of these situations require careful planning. Establishing clear expectations on everything from communication, accountability, and performance to who is responsible for maintaining computer equipment for the telecommuter. Many employees who take advantage of alternative schedules also accept the reality that they must remain accessible even if they are not in the office. When companies begin to offer scheduling flexibility, it is a good idea to start with a pilot program with one or two employees for a short time, such as three to six months. In addition, it is important to communicate what is happening with everyone in the

job sharing
a situation in which one job gets done by two people.

flex-time
when an employer permits an employee to work a modified schedule.

TABLE 4.4
Telecommuting and Alternative Work Scheduling: Benefits and Potential Problems

Benefits	Potential Problems
1. Significantly boosts individual productivity.	1. Can cause fear of stagnating at home.
2. Saves commuting time and travel expenses (lessens traffic congestion and parking lot demands).	2. Can foster sense of isolation, due to lack of social contact with coworkers.
3. Taps broader labor pool (such as mothers with young children, workers with disabilities, retired people, and prison inmates).	3. Can result in competition or interference with family duties, thus causing family conflict.
4. Eliminates office distractions and politics.	4. Can disrupt traditional supervisor-employee relationship.
5. Reduces employer's cost of office space.	5. Can cause fear of being "out of sight, out of mind" at promotion time.

organization.[75] As you can see in Table 4.4, there are many positive outcomes from alternative work scheduling approaches such as telecommuting. But there are also many potential problems that need to be addressed.

As you learned earlier in this chapter, one of the top reasons why employees leave a job is time and flexibility. Therefore, it seems logical that the more willing you are to provide workers with an alternative work schedule, the more likely you are to recruit and retain top talent.

SUMMARY

1. The high cost of turnover is one of the major reasons why recruitment and retention are important to supervisors and employers. Tangible costs include (1) advertising, (2) screening, (3) interviewing, (4) testing, (5) training, (6) orientation, (7) new employee setup, and (8) travel expenses. Intangible costs include (1) less productivity for the new employee, (2) cost of rework for increased errors by the new person, (3) increased supervision to coach the new hire, (4) cost to pay experienced person to take on additional work during vacancy period, (5) lost productivity from stress of team members during vacancy period, (6) the cost of reduced performance by the person leaving, and (7) the impact on employee morale.

2. Before placing an advertisement to hire a new employee for a new position, it is necessary to conduct a job analysis to determine core abilities by identifying task and skill requirements for specific jobs. In addition, it is important to prepare a comprehensive job description—a document that outlines role expectations and skill requirements for a specific job. This process involves a variety of activities, including defining the job duties;

identifying the necessary skills, knowledge, personal attributes (attitude, personality, style, energy level, etc.), education, and experience required; deciding on the compensation level; and determining the work schedule.

3. Legal issues that impact the recruitment process include (1) Equal Employment Opportunity (EEO) laws, which prohibit employment discrimination on the basis of race, color, sex, religion, age, national origin, disabilities, and, in some states, sexual orientation; and (2) affirmative action programs (AAPs), which attempt to seek out, employ, and develop the talents of groups traditionally discriminated against in employment, typically women and minorities. AAPs amount to a concerted effort to make up for *past* discrimination. EEO laws, in contrast, are aimed at preventing *future* discrimination. Typical AAPs attack employment discrimination with the following four methods: (1) active recruitment of women and minorities, (2) elimination of prejudicial questions on employment application forms, (3) establishment of specific goals and timetables for minority hiring, and (4) statistical validation of employment testing procedures.

Additional laws that impact the recruitment process include (1) the Americans with Disabilities Act of 1990 (ADA), which requires employers to make reasonable accommodations to meet the needs of present and future employees with physical and mental disabilities, and (2) the Fair Labor Standards Act (FLSA), which establishes minimum wage, overtime pay, recordkeeping, and child labor standards. In addition, employment selection tests—defined as any procedure used in the employment decision process—also have legal ramifications for employers.

4. The ultimate goal of recruiting is to generate a pool of qualified applicants for new and existing jobs. One of the challenges today is creating an applicant pool that is demographically representative of the population at large if diversity is to be achieved. Recruitment strategies include (1) proactive methods, (2) students, (3) advertising with traditional media outlets such as newspapers, magazines, radio, and television, (4) online recruitment, (5) video résumés, (6) billboards and postings, (7) personal referrals, (8) special events, and (9) recruitment agencies.

5. Still's PROCEED model for employee selection provides a methodical step-by-step approach to the employee selection process. The seven steps are (1) prepare, (2) review, (3) organize, (4) conduct, (5) evaluate, (6) exchange, and (7) decide.

6. Prepare selection criteria using the job description and core abilities documents to create a list of the major skills, experience, and knowledge required for the position. Prioritize the list with the most essential skills at the top. Next, prepare the decision matrix by giving each item a weighted value. The more important the skill is to the position, the higher the weighted value should be. Determine what (if any) pre-employment tests will be used. Write interview questions and prepare for telephone, in-person, or virtual interviews.

7. The cost of employee turnover and retention is a significant financial issue for any organization. Several retention items are within a supervisor's sphere of influence, including time and flexibility, culture and work environment, supervisor relationship, training and development, and management climate. Time and flexibility can be addressed with alternative scheduling arrangements such as telecommuting, job sharing, and flex-time.

TERMS TO UNDERSTAND

affirmative action program (AAP), p. 96
Age Discrimination in Employment Act of 1967 (ADEA), p. 101
Americans with Disabilities Act of 1990 (ADA), p. 98
core abilities, p. 90
employee turnover, p. 85
employment selection test, p. 100

Equal Employment Opportunity (EEO) laws, p. 95
Fair Labor Standards Act (FLSA), p. 100
flex-time, p. 113
intangible costs, p. 86
interviewing, p. 110
job analysis, p. 90
job description, p. 90

job sharing, p. 113
nonverbal communication, p. 111
realistic job preview, p. 94
reasonable accommodations, p. 98
recruitment, p. 85
retention, p. 85
tangible costs, p. 85
telecommuting, p. 112

QUESTIONS FOR REFLECTION

1. What are some of the tangible and intangible costs of turnover?

2. Describe the Equal Employment Opportunity laws and how they impact supervisors during the recruiting process.

3. Explain why recruiting for diversity is important and identify a few effective strategies for attracting a more diverse pool of candidates.

4. Explain how the use of online recruiting tools and video résumés might benefit the employer.

5. What is considered to be one of the most effective recruiting methods? Explain your answer.

6. Describe telecommuting and identify steps an employer should take to ensure long-term success for the telecommuting arrangement.

HANDS-ON ACTIVITIES

JOB DESCRIPTION

Evaluate a sample job description. You may use one from your work or you may use one from an employment website such as www.careerbuilder.com or www.monster.com. Choose a job that you are familiar with and critique the job description.

1. What important components are included in the job description?

2. What components are missing?

3. Draft content to complete this job description.

INTERVIEWING QUESTIONS

1. Write a list of questions you would want to ask if you were hiring for the position described in the previous section.

2. Write a list of questions you cannot ask an applicant.

Interview an Expert

The purpose of this exercise is to learn from an expert the best practices he/she has developed for recruiting talented people and what not to do. Identify a person to interview who has extensive experience hiring employees. Your goal is to learn from this person's experience. You may use the questions listed below and/or develop your own. After your interview, prepare a brief summary of the conversation and list their recruitment best practices.

Questions

1. What is one question you ask of every applicant, regardless of the position?

2. How do you assess the candidate's professionalism, reliability, honesty, and integrity?

3. Do you use any pre-employment tests? If yes, please describe what tests and why you selected them. If no, why not?

4. What are some examples of questions you have asked to learn more about a candidate's behavior patterns?

5. Who in your company is involved in the interviewing process?

6. Do you ask all of the candidates for the same position the same questions? Please explain.

7. What other screening or evaluation do you do?

8. Which recruiting strategies/advertising tools are most effective for attracting a diverse candidate pool?

9. What questions are off limits, which you will never ask?

You may improvise and add or edit questions to fit the situation or the circumstances of your interview. Schedule your interview ahead of time and try to limit it to about 15 minutes. Remember to send a thank-you note to the person you interview.

YOU DECIDE

CASE STUDY 4.1
Alternative Scheduling

Laura is the regional vice president for a large insurance agency serving Texas, Mississippi, Louisiana, Florida, Georgia, and South Carolina. Her company has fifteen offices located in metropolitan areas in all six states. Due to the rise in claims, the company is experiencing financial constraints. Laura has been asked to reduce costs.

She is considering laying people off; however, the company actually needs more staff to keep up with the volume of phone calls and accounts requiring processing. With the exception of her salespeople and claims adjuster, the rest of her employees spend their work days sitting in offices on the telephone with clients and prospective clients while also processing claims and accounts on the computer. She feels strongly that she needs to keep the talented people she has, but she also knows she needs to reduce costs by closing some of the offices or at least reducing the amount of space the company leases, thus reducing overhead costs.

Questions

1. What are some alternative scheduling options Laura could use to keep her employees while also reducing costs?

2. Pick the option you would recommend to Laura. What are the potential benefits and the potential problems with this option?

3. How should Laura proceed?

SUPERVISOR'S TOOLKIT

Create the following for a job of your choice—this may be the job you currently hold or your dream job.

1. Job Analysis and Core Abilities
   Conduct a job analysis and list the core abilities for the job, including technical and behavioral skills along with desired personal attributes.

2. Job Description
   Include the following elements:
   a. Job title
   b. Position description

   c. Reporting and organizational structure
   d. Organizational values and culture
   e. Desired qualifications
   f. Job requirements—identify any physical or mental requirements for the job.
   g. Job specifications—list the essential tasks, duties, and responsibilities for the position.

3. Selection Criteria and Decision Matrix
   a. Prioritize your list, putting the most essential items at the top of the list.
   b. Assign weighted values to each item.

CHAPTER 5

Setting Your New Hire Up for Success: Orientation

Learning Objectives

1. Explain the importance of planning new employee orientation.

2. Describe steps you can take prior to your new employee's first day to begin the process of setting your new hire up for success; identify items to include on a pre-arrival checklist.

3. Explain the importance of discussing expectations held by the new employee and describe strategies for clarifying these expectations during the orientation period.

4. Describe who and what should be included in the new hire's orientation plan, including both the general company overview and the job-specific orientation.

5. Discuss basic elements of a good orientation training plan. Identify topics to include in the new hire's plan and discuss the value of a buddy system to help the new employee acclimate to the job and the corporate culture.

6. Identify methods for measuring and reporting progress.

7. Describe the benefits of discussing performance expectations and reviewing the performance appraisal process during orientation.

8. Explain how orientation training plans can be modified to accommodate the virtual employee.

Straight Talk from the Field

Heather Herrod is the Slot Marketing Manager at the Monte Carlo Resort & Casino, in Las Vegas, Nevada.

QUESTION:

How do you help employees acclimate to the corporate culture at the Monte Carlo Resort & Casino and what steps do you take to set them up for success?

SUPERVISOR RESPONSE:

When I describe my job to people outside of the gaming industry, their ears often perk up as they think of all the movies and TV shows out there that glorify Vegas and the casino industry. Some people ask, "How can I break into the gaming industry?" Perception often strays from reality when it comes to the gaming/hospitality industry. It is not necessarily hard to find a job in this industry, but the perception of the kinds of jobs available and the ideal job can be unrealistic. It is important to realize when you are looking for a job, in any industry, that you may not necessarily find your dream job right off the bat. Making a sacrifice or taking a position that could lead to a career is more important than taking a job for the wrong reasons.

As a Slot Marketing Manager, I have hired several employees and learned valuable lessons in the process. I recently read Jim Collins' book Good to Great and liked his metaphor of the organization as a "bus." He says the key to organizational success is getting the right people on the bus. A bus full of excellent people can go anywhere and accomplish anything. That is certainly the key element to creating the best and most efficient teams in our business. In my opinion, talent is more important than experience. When I was first hired into my role at a new property, my boss at the time said to me, "I will not let you fail. Because if you fail, I've failed." That message was very powerful for me and made me realize that indeed I was becoming a part of a team and I was not alone in the process. I try to pass this same message along to each new person I hire.

The gaming and hospitality industry is growing exponentially. Many new properties will be opening in the next few years. Talented people will be an even more vital resource. In order to accommodate the need for people and talent as the company grows, MGM MIRAGE has invested in several different programs to find and develop top talent.

The first program, MAP (Management Associate Program), is open to recent college graduates. It is a six-month immersion program where they learn about each and every department on the property and tackle specific jobs in each department. Upon graduating from MAP, employees are placed in entry-level management positions and continue to learn about various departments and how they interact.

The MGM MIRAGE Hospitality Internship Program is another exciting program where college juniors, during the summer prior to their senior year, are placed with a department that interests them. This paid-internship program provides valuable experience and allows them to discover areas of interest they might ultimately like to pursue for a career.

Internally, the company is also working to promote and engage current line-level employees through a program called REACH. Participants are paired with two mentors: one in their current department, and one in another division. This allows them to get two different perspectives on work and career development. REACH participants work on projects to increase their potential for career development and promotion.

As a manager who oversees a team of people, I know how important it is to constantly work to develop the potential of your employees and create an environment where learning and development can occur. It often has been said that you cannot move on and get promoted until you have developed someone to take your place. So employee development is a never-ending challenge.

Chapter Outline

I n today's fast-paced global economy, the sink-or-swim approach to handling new hires is unacceptable. Turning an outsider into a productive insider requires a welcoming atmosphere and instructive orientation and training. This chapter provides a systematic approach for planning orientation. We will also explore specific recommendations for a smooth and effective employee orientation program. The goal is to allow newly hired employees to move in the right direction rather than floundering in doubt, uncertainty, and unproductive confusion.

We begin with an overview of the value and importance of planning for your new hire's first day, week, and month. You will learn about steps you can take prior to the new employee's arrival and what to include in an orientation plan. In addition, we discuss the importance of clarifying expectations from the beginning. New employee orientations are a lot like first impressions; you rarely get a second chance. Make the effort to plan a great orientation for your new hire, and you will quite likely be rewarded with a valuable team member.

The Value of Planning New Employee Orientation

Planning for a new hire's arrival prior to his/her first day has a positive impact on the entire organization, including your new employee. The new **employee orientation** is an opportunity to introduce and welcome your new hire and begin the transition from new employee to contributing team member. Implementing a formal orientation will help your new employee assimilate more quickly into the organization. See Figure 5.1 for an example of the first page of an employee orientation checklist that reinforces the organization's commitment to welcoming new employees.

Involving your team members will generate excitement within the team and organization as everyone awaits the arrival of the new person. Planning for your new hire's first day, week, and month will be the first step in setting the newcomer up for success. In addition, this type of planning ultimately leads to higher levels of retention, motivation, and job satisfaction.[1]

Involving Current Employees

Orientation planning can be a good experience for your current employees if you include them in the process. Involving your current employees will give them the satisfaction of making a valuable contribution. Ultimately, it can lead to a more comprehensive orientation plan because they may pinpoint details you have overlooked. In addition, by including them now, they will be better prepared for the arrival of the new employee and have some time to reflect on how this change will affect them. Finally, and perhaps most importantly, when new employees arrive and discover how prepared you are for their first day, week, and month, they are more likely to feel welcome and needed.

Involving your current employees will allow them to feel a sense of value and contribution and will ultimately lead to a more comprehensive plan.

The Orientation Period

Orientation does not happen in a day. A person can only absorb a limited amount of information during a hectic first day. This is especially true for a person in a whole new

---

FIGURE 5.1 Sample employee orientation checklist
Source: Carol Broderick, Joanne Fraysse, Glee Tuttle, and Linda Watkins, University of California, San Francisco Human Resources, October 15, 2002, http://tep.ucsf.edu/files/NewEmpCklst.pdf (accessed April 26, 2008). Reprinted by permission.

employee orientation
an opportunity to introduce and welcome your new hire and begin the transition from new employee to contributing team member.

New Employee Checklist

For: _____

Date of Hire: _____

Supervisor/Manager _____

Payroll/Personnel Analyst _____

Welcome! We believe that Orientation is a process, not just an event. Our intent is to have the new employee:

- Feel at ease and welcome.
- Obtain a good grasp of the organization's history, mission and values.
- Understand the functions of different units, divisions and departments.
- Understand what the organization expects in terms of work and behavior.
- Know everything necessary to start performing his/her job.
- Know who and where to go to for help with work matters.
- Know the policies and procedures of the organization and of the new employee's department.
- Feel a part of the organization's family.

This checklist details many of the activities that need to take place in the new employee's first six months with the organization.

Cathy © 1996 Cathy Guisewite. Reprinted with permission of *Universal Press Syndicate*. All rights reserved.

situation. For example, students' heads spin with an overload of stimulation during their first day on campus. Therefore, it is important to prepare a detailed list of items new employees must attend to within their orientation period, covering a week, a month, or more. Plan to cover two or three main points or topics during one session rather than cramming ten or twelve items into a day. By spacing orientation training out over several days, you also provide time for new employees to process the information and ask questions.

Items to Address Ahead of Time

In addition to preparing a detailed orientation training plan, there are two main areas that you need to address prior to the new hire's first day on the job. One is determining any forms, documentation, and other information that can be distributed to the new hire in advance. The other involves focusing on factors within the organization. What resources, equipment, training, computer access, and work space will the new person need? These items can be planned for and in most cases secured and set up prior to the new hire's arrival.

Company Forms and Information

Prior to the new employee's first day on the job, there are many items for a supervisor to consider. Paperwork can often be time consuming and can make for a very unproductive first day. To avoid a dull first day, get it done ahead of time. Have new hires complete necessary paperwork—such as payroll forms, identification card authorizations, and other company specific documents—prior to their first day. In addition, many companies provide new employees with handbooks, training manuals, product brochures, menus, and other relevant information prior to their first day to give them a chance to learn about their new workplace.

Braithwaite Communications, a marketing communications firm located in Philadelphia, goes a step further than the traditional documentation. They give new hires an iPod a couple of weeks prior to their first day. Included on the iPod is information about the company and personal greetings from some of the firm's employees. This prerecorded approach to orientation appears to be a good investment because, in all likelihood, employees will retain the information on their iPods long after their first day. Hugh Braithwaite believes the free iPod delivered in advance leads to new hires arriving with "higher morale and positive energy."[2] This generous method may be too costly for some organizations. Still, the idea of letting new hires know you are looking forward to their arrival is a positive step toward a good first day on the job.

KNOWLEDGE TO ACTION

Choose a company or nonprofit organization with which you are familiar. Then explain which topics should be included on a recording of the organization's new employee orientation audio file that can be downloaded to MP3 players.

Resources and a Pre-arrival Checklist

There are typical resources and items that all employees in an organization need, regardless of their jobs, and there are resource needs that are unique to particular positions. Review each of the areas in this section and add items that are unique to your organization.

> *You may find it helpful to develop a pre-arrival checklist that includes documents, items, and actions that are necessary for each employee.*

You may find it helpful to develop a **pre-arrival checklist** that includes documents, items, and actions needed before the employee begins working. See Figure 5.2 for an example of a pre-arrival checklist.

STANDARD ITEMS FOR ALL NEW EMPLOYEES

Orientation checklists are often broken down into a couple of sections. The first section can be for all employees, regardless of their position, and would include standard information such as (1) offer letter, (2) phone call, (3) forms, (4) benefit packet, (5) companywide announcement, and (6) schedule.[3] Let us take a closer look at these items:

- **Offer letter.** Personally send (or have human resources send) the offer letter immediately following the individual's verbal acceptance.

- **Phone call.** Call your new employees a couple of days prior to their start date to welcome them. Let them know the plan for their orientation, where to report, and at what time. Tell them where they can park and what it might cost. If possible, follow the phone call with an e-mail summarizing the information. If you cannot be available to greet new hires personally, provide them with the name of the person who will be present to meet them at the start of their first day.

- **Forms.** Prepare a set of forms that every new hire must complete. If these are available electronically, consider e-mailing the forms to the new hire in advance.

- **Benefits.** Provide a copy of the benefits packet so new hires can review this information and discuss the options with their families.

- **Companywide announcement.** Send an announcement to everyone in the company (or relevant department or unit) a day or two prior to the new employee's first day. Provide a brief biography of the person, describe the newcomer's job responsibilities, and ask everyone to introduce themselves as they welcome the new person.

pre-arrival checklist
a checklist for new employees that includes documents, items, and actions needed before the employee begins working.

FIGURE 5.2 Sample pre-arrival checklist

Source: Carol Broderick, Joanne Fraysse, Glee Tuttle, and Linda Watkins, University of California, San Francisco Human Resources, October 15, 2002, http://tep.ucsf.edu/files/NewEmpCklst.pdf (accessed April 26, 2008). Reprinted by permission.

- Designates who is responsible for performing the task, the new employee ("EE") or another departmental staff member ("DEPT"). If the Supervisor/Manager will be delegating this task, indicate to whom the task has been delegated.

BEFORE THE NEW EMPLOYEE'S FIRST DAY		Responsibility		
Task	Resources	EE	DEPT	Done
Send offer/welcome letter.	Sample Letter Tip: Include a copy of the job description with the letter.		?	☐
Notify unit personnel/payroll/benefits representative of hire.			?	☐
Prepare new employee packet including: • Agenda for the first week • UCSF Mission and Principles of Community Statements (included in campus new employee orientation) • UCSF Organizational Chart (included in campus new employee orientation) • UCSF Code of Conduct (included in new employee orientation) • Departmental Organizational Chart • Departmental mission, vision, and values • Departmental phone/e-mail directory • Buddy Program Information • Emergency Procedures	http://www.ucsf.edu/about ucsf/history_philosophy/mission.html (UCSF Mission and Principles of Community Statements) http://chancellor.ucsf.edu/orgchart.pdf (UCSF Organizational Chart) http://ucsfhr.ucsf.edu/policies/finalcc.pdf (UCSF Campus Code of Conduct) Buddy Program information		?	☐
Notify departmental information technology (IT) contact of hire, provide list of required software/hardware. Request e-mail setup.			?	☐
Notify departmental telecommunications contact of hire. Request phone hookup and voicemail setup.			?	☐
Prepare employee work area, including: • Ordering any needed desk supplies & furniture • Ordering a nameplate • Assigning Keys and keypad codes			?	☐

Make lunch plans for employee's first day.			?	☐
Identify UCSF employee who will be the new employee's buddy: Give buddy his/her buddy packet.	Buddy Program information		?	☐
Identify employee(s) with similar responsibilities to function as the new employee's coach/mentor for work-related processes & procedures.			?	☐
Add employee to department and/or unit organizational contact and routing lists.			?	☐
Prepare new hire paperwork (payroll & benefits information).	New Hire Paperwork Checklist		?	☐
Prepare parking permit information/paperwork (if applicable).			?	☐
Set up timesheet(s).			?	☐
Install appropriate hardware/software.			?	☐
Establish e-mail.			?	☐
Complete phone and voice mail setup.			?	☐

■ **Master schedule.** Schedule meetings, appointments, and training sessions with other employees ahead of time. Keep a master calendar for new employees so they will know from day one where they need to be on each day.

KNOWLEDGE TO ACTION   Imagine that you have just been hired for your dream job. Write the announcement that your new company should send to all relevant employees announcing that you have been hired.

POSITION-SPECIFIC ITEMS

The second section of the orientation checklist contains position-specific information such as (1) uniforms, (2) identification badges, (3) business cards, (4) work space, (5) telephone, (6) e-mail, and (7) computer and printer. Each of these items is examined in greater detail below:

■ **Uniforms**. If a uniform is required, let the new hire know what options are available and what the cost will be.

■ **Identification badges**. If a photo identification badge is required, let the employee know ahead of time when the photo will be taken. If a photo is not required, consider ordering the name badge in advance so it is available on the employee's first day. Another option is to provide a temporary badge until the employee has completed orientation.

■ **Business cards**. If the person will be working in a position requiring contact with customers, vendors, or business partners, consider ordering business cards ahead of time. This allows the employee to present a professional image to customers and clients and provides a sense of being part of the team.

■ **Work space**. If the position is office-based, determine which office or cubicle the person will occupy. Take the extra time to clean this space (including the insides of drawers and cabinets). Check for necessary office supplies such as desk calendar, pens, pencils, paper clips, tape dispenser, stapler, scissors, and note pad. Also, determine if any furniture needs to be replaced or new furniture added.

■ **Telephone**. If the employee will have a personal telephone and/or a company cell phone, have it set up ahead of time. Determine features the employee will need, such as caller ID, long-distance calling, speaker phone, hands-free headset, call waiting, and voice mail. Provide a copy of the user manual for the telephone and a copy of the company's phone directory. Be sure to add phone usage and etiquette to the training plan.

■ **E-mail**. Have the employee's e-mail account created in advance so that you can immediately begin reinforcing training with appropriate e-mail communication. In addition, this will give the employee access to companywide e-mails from day one. Remember to review company policies and guidelines for appropriate use of company e-mail.

■ **Computer and printer**. Determine if the employee will need a laptop or desktop computer. Identify what printer the person will use, either local or networked. Also decide what software applications and network files the person will need. Coordinate setup and access with the technology person in your company or unit in advance, as it may take a couple of weeks for the proper equipment to be ordered and configured properly. Add the appropriate hardware and software application training to your training plan.

When you are prepared and have everything ready to go, you are demonstrating for your new employees excellent organizational skills and your commitment to setting them up for success.

Each company will have unique additional items for these lists. The point is to carefully anticipate your new employees' needs prior to their arrival. When you are prepared and have everything ready to go, you are demonstrating for your new employees excellent organizational skills and your commitment to setting them up for success.

Fostering Realistic Employee Expectations

An **expectation** is defined as the act of looking forward or anticipating, often with the prospect of a good future or profit. Companies like Ernst & Young develop employee expectations through their realistic job previews.[4] However, not all companies are as successful in this area. As a result, unmet expectations are major source of frustration for new employees.[5] This occurs for two reasons: (1) companies and supervisors do not follow through on commitments and promises and (2) new employees have unrealistic expectations because of faulty assumptions. Both of these situations can be avoided with clear communication and frequent follow-up.

Communication Is Key

To begin with, when you make an offer, take the time to give a realistic job preview, as discussed in Chapter 4. While covering the appealing and exciting aspects of the job, be sure to mention the less desirable aspects such as cleaning, on-call responsibilities, or the need to work weekends.[6] Additionally, outline the orientation plan with a detailed schedule so the new person will know what to expect. Finally, if you make commitments or promises, write them down and prepare a plan for following through. Share this plan with new hires so they know what to expect. For example, you may promise to allow new employees to shadow you for a day. However, they may not know that you usually schedule this after they have completed the first two weeks of orientation. If a week passes without the promised shadowing activity, a new employee may assume that you forgot about the commitment and become disappointed. The key is to communicate frequently and in detail. Do not assume that the other person is thinking what you are thinking; clarify information and expectations verbally and follow-up in writing.[7]

Invite Feedback and Questions

Another major source of anxiety for new employees is surprises.[8] Anxiety can arise because of changes to schedules, shifts in reporting relationships, or simply overhearing a conversation in the lunchroom that reveals new information about the company and/or its culture. Regardless of the source or the nature of the surprise, it can create uncertainty and doubt in the minds of newcomers. It is unrealistic to expect that you can prevent these types of events from taking place. What you *can* do is answer questions and exchange

expectation
looking forward to or anticipating the prospect of something good in the future.

feedback. **Feedback** is an evaluative response about the result of a process or activity. Keep in mind that most new employees will be reluctant to bring situations to your attention, so you will need to be accessible. Oftentimes, it is as simple as asking new employees if they have any questions or feedback or if they have experienced any surprises.

Meet Often

During your new hire's orientation period, schedule frequent meetings just to touch base. The meetings do not need to be lengthy—fifteen to thirty minutes may be sufficient. However, they should be consistent and frequent. If time and scheduling permits, spend the first fifteen minutes of each day or the last fifteen minutes of each day talking with your new person. During your initial meeting, discuss and set SMART goals with your new hire. As you learned in Chapter 3, SMART goals are specific, measurable, achievable, realistic, and time bound. Be sure to explain the purpose for each goal and how it links to the organization's mission and strategic plan. Decide when to meet again and how you will measure achievements using incremental **milestones** involving key events, turning points, and progress during the first thirty, sixty, and ninety days.[9] Use your subsequent meetings to review the progress on the person's goals and to discuss the status of the orientation plan. Make changes if necessary and invite questions. Ask if the newcomer has encountered any surprises and address his/her concerns or requests. In addition, share formal or informal feedback you have received about the person and invite feedback and suggestions in return. New employees bring a fresh perspective, expertise, industry contacts, and new ideas[10]—invite them to share these with you. Finally, this is a good time to provide positive feedback and reassurance to ward off any insecurity.

The Company Orientation Plan

Starting a new job is difficult. New employees have to rapidly learn while meeting new people, exploring the corporate culture, and figuring out where they fit in. Recall what it was like when you were beginning a new job or starting at a new school. Consider breaking information up into small modules of information and follow up each session with an e-mail restating the content. This, in turn, will provide a handy reference document for the new employee to review later. In addition, you can take several steps to make the newcomer's orientation period more enjoyable and less stressful. Preparing a detailed plan for the orientation period is the first step, beginning with planning for the first day. As Heather Herrod stated in the chapter opener, developing your employees to reach their potential is an ongoing process. Getting them off to a good start is just the beginning!

feedback
an evaluative response about the result of a process or activity.

milestones
important events, turning points, and advances in progress.

First Impressions Are Lasting Impressions: The First Day

Most of us have been told since childhood that first impressions are lasting impressions. In other words, you do not get a second chance at a first impression. Keep this in mind as you plan your employee's first day.[11] See Figure 5.3 for an example of a checklist for an employee's first day. (It follows up Figure 5.2.)

FIGURE 5.3 Checklist for new employee's first day

Source: Carol Broderick, Joanne Fraysse, Glee Tuttle, and Linda Watkins, University of California, San Francisco Human Resources, October 15, 2002, http://tep.ucsf.edu/files/ NewEmpCklst.pdf (accessed April 26, 2008). Reprinted by permission.

ON THE NEW EMPLOYEE'S FIRST DAY		Responsibility		
Task	**Resources**	**EE**	**DEPT**	**Done?**
Send welcome e-mail to staff announcing the new employee's arrival, function and location.	Warm welcome ideas: • Welcome signs/banner at desk • Coffee/donuts or bagels staff get together • Flowers		?	☐
Introduce employee to coworkers and buddy; give brief tour of department.			?	☐
Meet with personnel/payroll/benefits representative to complete new hire paperwork and to receive introduction to employee benefits.		?	?	☐
Complete fingerprint process (if applicable).		?	?	☐
Obtain UCSF employee ID.		?	?	☐
Schedule attendance at orientation programs: 1) Campus New Employee Orientation Program 2) Benefits Orientation	Note: Advance sign-up is required for the Campus New Employee Orientation Program.	?	?	☐
Order business cards.		?	?	☐
Introduce employee to work area, including: • Ergonomic Review (Arrange for/make any needed adjustments.) • Use of phones • Departmental purchasing policies • Computer orientation—common programs & useful websites • Review & set up standard meetings.	Ergosmart diskette available from Departmental Benefit Representative or Disability Management Services.	?	?	☐
Orient employee to worksite: • Coffee room • Bathrooms • Photocopy machines • Fax machines • Supplies • Restaurants • Transportation • Break rooms • ATMs • Vending machines • Location of first aid and emergency supplies • Mail services			?	☐

Most people arrive on their first day eager for information and they observe and absorb everything from appearances to schedules. Imagine for a moment that you are the supervisor scheduled to meet with a new employee at 8:30 A.M. on his/her first day. Rather than getting to work a few minutes early to greet the newcomer upon arrival, you show up at 10:30 A.M., two hours late. How do you think your new employee feels? Most likely, the person will feel unimportant—a message you definitely do not want to send, especially on the first day. The goal is to make the new hire's first day *great*. Try using some of the following suggestions, adding your own as appropriate. You want your new person to feel welcome, valued, and special.

GREET NEW EMPLOYEES PERSONALLY AND BE AVAILABLE

If at all possible, be on site and available during the entire day, even if you have your new employee scheduled to meet with other people. If you tell the new hire to arrive at 9:00 A.M., you should plan to arrive at 8:30 A.M. because people are typically early on the first day of a new job. Have everything prepared the day before just in case you have an emergency and you need someone else to cover for you.

FOOD IS ALWAYS GOOD

Plan to bring in a light breakfast for the entire staff and invite everyone to stop by to welcome the new person and enjoy a cup of coffee, pastry, or fruit. In addition, plan to take the new person out to lunch. You may want to invite other people on the team, the new hire's assigned orientation buddy, and/or a member of the executive team, such as the company president or vice president.

COMPANY PRODUCTS

A memorable first day includes giving new employees company information and promotional items in the form of a welcome basket.[12] You can include marketing materials, product samples, logo coffee mugs, tee shirts, or whatever other items your company has on hand.

THE IDEAL DAY

The ideal day begins with a tour of your facility and the new hire's work area. Proceed with introductions to members of the team and other departments. Next, review the orientation plan and answer questions. Give new employees about an hour to get their desks organized, review literature, and reflect before whisking them off for lunch. After lunch, give them an opportunity to spend time with their assigned orientation buddy so they can get exposed to job activities. Be sure to schedule a fifteen- or twenty-minute meeting at the end of the day to get feedback on the first day, answer any questions, and go over plans for the following day.

The Company Orientation

New employees may be exposed to several aspects of their orientation plan within the first day or two, or the plan may be spread out over several weeks. However, some organizations such as the Children's Hospital of Philadelphia require new hires to attend orientation prior to their first day.[13] Figure 5.4 provides an excellent outline of topics to include in your new employee orientation schedule for the first month.

Large companies often schedule a one-day general orientation for all new employees from all departments. These events are typically organized by the human resources department. As a hiring supervisor, your job is to make sure your new employee knows when and where to report. However, if you are with a company that does not have a formal orientation program, then you will need to plan the

FIGURE 5.4 What a new employee can expect within the first month

Source: Carol Broderick, Joanne Fraysse, Glee Tuttle, and Linda Watkins, University of California, San Francisco Human Resources, October 15, 2002, http://tep.ucsf.edu/files/ NewEmpCklst.pdf (accessed April 26, 2008). Reprinted by permission.

WITHIN THE FIRST MONTH		Responsibility		
Task	**Resources**	**EE**	**DEPT**	**Done?**
Review departmental new employee packet, including: • UCSF Mission and Principles of Community Statements (also included in new-employee orientation) • UCSF Code of Conduct (also included in new-employee orientation) • UCSF Organizational Chart (also included in new-employee orientation) • Departmental Organizational Chart/Problem Resolution Channels • Departmental mission, vision, and values and the connection to UCSF's mission and values • Departmental phone/e-mail directory • Buddy Program Information • Emergency Procedures	http://www.ucsf.edu/about_ucsf/history_philosophy/mission.html (UCSF Mission and Principles of Community Statements) http://chancellor.ucsf.edu/orgchart.pdf (UCSF Organizational Chart) http://ucsfhr.ucsf.edu/policies/finalcc.pdf (UCSF Campus Code of Conduct) Buddy Program	?	?	☐
Review departmental policies and procedures re: • Probationary period • Timesheets • Vocation and sick leave accrual and use • Dress Code • Hours of Work • Work Rules • Attendance Policy • Phone etiquette • Personal phone usage policy • Personal computer usage policy • Performance appraisal process • Merit/salary increase timeline		?	?	☐
Introduce employee to job: • Review Job Description. • Discuss supervisor's style and expectations. • Review performance goals and expectations. • Identify the "players" connected to the position: make appointments with "key players." • Identify the "customers" served by this position: define customer service. • Discuss employee safety. • Review standard meetings the employee needs to attend.		?	?	☐
Identify what training and development activities will be needed in the next six months. Sign up for the appropriate classes.	http://ucsfhr.ucsf.edu/training/index.html (Development & Training Website)	?	?	☐
Meet weekly to complete orientation to work-related tasks and to ask/answer questions.		?	?	☐
Set performance expectations and discuss how and when the employee will be evaluated. Provide feedback on a weekly basis.		?	?	☐
Meet with key players.		?	?	☐
Meet Department Head and/or Chair.		?	?	☐

orientation as well as the appropriate job-specific training. This type of all-day orientation can become boring and tiresome if the participants are sitting for hours listening to people lecture.

Consider mixing in some activities such as a walking tour after lunch, a video, or an interactive game. For example, you could set up a quiz just before lunch, ask questions about what new employees learned during the morning sessions, and give prizes to high scorers.[14] This can be a fun way to reinforce what newcomers have learned. Another idea is to incorporate different approaches to learning. Rather than spoon-feeding employees information via a standard PowerPoint® presentation, create a more stimulating learning experience. For example, to learn about the company mission and vision, organize the new hires into teams and send them on a scavenger hunt to find a current employee who knows the company mission. They have to bring that person back to the orientation to recite the mission and vision and give an example of how their work supports the company mission. Of course, this could be disruptive in a tightly scheduled production situation and could easily get out of hand, so use your best judgment and establish boundaries.

The point is to mix up orientation day so the new people are not sitting in the same chair listening to presentations all day. Give them a chance to talk with one another and offer some experiential learning activity if possible.[15]

When feasible, have the company president or CEO provide the opening remarks and company overview. This sends a powerful message to the newcomers and it is great way for the organization's leader to meet the new team members.

Large organizations often go to the expense of having a high-quality "welcome" video from the CEO or founder. For example, The Men's Wearhouse CEO, George Zimmer, delivers a welcome message via video to every new employee using the company's StarCast New Hire Portal. With over 11,000 employees, this type of investment in new employee orientation has contributed to *Fortune* magazine repeatedly including The Men's Wearhouse on its list of "100 Best Companies to Work For."[16]

To prepare for your company orientation, consider providing each new employee with a personal folder. See Figure 5.5 for examples of what to include in this folder. In addition, remember to begin the day by sharing the agenda.

FIGURE 5.5 Checklist for orientation folders

Orientation Folders

Include in the folder:
- An agenda for the day
- Names, titles, and contact information for all of the presenters and other participants
- A copy of the organization's mission and vision statements
- A copy of the organizational chart
- An employee handbook
- Benefit information
- A master calendar including company paid holidays and major events
- Recent press releases
- A copy of the most recent company newsletter
- Handouts from the guest speakers scheduled
- A notepad and pen

The following sections explain what should be included in a general company orientation.

COMPANY BACKGROUND AND OVERVIEW

One of the best ways to kick off an orientation session is to begin by talking about the organization. It gets everyone focused and energized, and it is helpful for employees to know the history of the organization and its mission, vision, and goals.[17] This is also a good opportunity to share the company's customer service philosophy and quality standards. In addition, you want employees to know the organizational structure and the names and faces of the executives. Therefore, it is ideal when a top executive presents this overview session in person or via video.[18]

EMPLOYEE BENEFITS

Employee benefits include non-salary compensation such as health, life, and disability insurance; vacation and personal leave; and employee stock option and retirement plans. Health insurance has become so complex that it is very helpful for new employees to get an explanation of their options along with associated fees. If you have a human resources person or benefits specialist, ask her/him to be present at this session. In addition, ask the human resources or benefits specialist to prepare a document outlining the cost of each benefit to the employee as well as the employer's contribution. Insurance benefits are one of the fastest-growing expenses for companies, and employees tend to recognize and appreciate them more when they know the actual costs associated with each benefit.

Also include a discussion about other benefits available, such as employee discounts, retirement plans, fitness center privileges, child care, and any other benefits your organization makes available.

HOURS OF OPERATION AND IMPORTANT DATES

Provide an overview of the organization's typical business hours. Give new employees a list of the observed holidays as well as any other important dates. For example, many manufacturing sites close for a week between Christmas and New Year to conduct inventory and maintenance. Let employees know if they will be required to take their annual leave during this week. If the company has any mandatory meetings, these should be listed. Also consider dates for corporate events such as major sales or promotions.

INCLEMENT WEATHER

Review the company's inclement weather policy and procedure. If you typically provide updates via television or radio, let new employees know which stations to check. If you follow the protocol of other organizations, let employees know the names and where to go for updated information. For example, a day care center may choose to close if the local school system closes for the day; day care employees should be instructed to check the school system's website or local media outlets for updates on school closing information.

EMERGENCY PREPAREDNESS AND SAFETY

Personal safety for all employees is a common goal for most organizations. In fact, safety training has become mandatory in many organizations. However, every

employee benefits
non-salary compensation such as health, life, and disability insurance; vacation and personal leave; and employee stock options and retirement plans.

company has different risks because various jobs create different levels of exposure. The important point is to review safety protocol with all new employees, including precautionary measures and incident reporting procedures. In addition, you want to review with employees how to handle potential emergencies. These include events such as robbery or fire as well as individual illness or injury.

LEGAL ISSUES

Employers can be held liable for the actions of their employees. Therefore, it is important to let new hires know how the company defines appropriate and acceptable behavior. Items to include in this discussion include policies regarding sexual harassment,[19] computer use, e-mail and phone use, confidentiality of corporate and customer information, intellectual property rights, theft, alcohol and drug use, and other relevant legal topics. In addition, some companies may require employees to sign conflict-of-interest statements.

KNOWLEDGE TO ACTION

Team up with one or two of your classmates. Select a company or nonprofit organization that everyone is familiar with to answer the following.

1. How do you suggest the company notify employees of closings and delays?

   _____

2. What topics should be included in the company's emergency preparedness and safety plan?

   _____

Job-Specific Orientation

Along with the general company overview, there are typically items to review with new hires that are unique to the department and to the position for which the person has been hired. Listed below are common items to include in a job-specific orientation. Because each company, department, and job is different, you will need to add some of your own items to this list.

DEPARTMENT'S MISSION AND GOALS

Review the department's goals and share your plan for achieving these goals.

Each department or division serves a primary purpose within an organization. If the department has a formal mission or statement of purpose, review these items with new hires and let them know how these support the overall mission of the organization. Also, review the department's goals and share your plan for achieving these goals.

JOB FUNCTIONS

In most cases, the new hire had a chance to review the job description during the interview process. However, it is a good idea to provide the person with a copy of the job description during the first week. It is also helpful to take the extra time to go over each item in detail and provide examples of actual tasks associated with job duties listed on the job description.

This supervisor is taking the time to personally introduce her new employees to the rest of the team. What a wonderful way to be welcomed into a new organization!
© Image Source Black/Jupiter Images

INTRODUCTIONS AND TOUR

During the first few weeks, new employees are challenged with learning new skills, procedures, and people. To make this easier, consider preparing two reference documents. You can refer to one of these documents as "Whom do you call?" This reference document should list the names, phone numbers, and e-mails of key members of the organization and team. Include vital contacts in human resources, benefits, payroll, information technology, purchasing, and security, as well as members of the immediate team or department.

The other document can be titled "A day in the life." Ask your current employees to help you prepare a one- or two-page preview of a typical day in your department. This document is a nice way to acquaint newcomers to potential problems and how they are typically handled.

Be sure to introduce new employees to people on the "Whom do you call?" list. Also introduce new employees to their assigned "orientation buddy" and give them time to get acquainted.

POLICIES AND PROCEDURES

New employees may receive a copy of the company's policies and procedures manual during the general orientation. However, it is the supervisor's responsibility to be sure they fully understand the relevant policies and procedures.

If there are additional policies and procedures for your department, take the time to go over them in detail. It is important to review security and safety items on the first day. Clarify for new hires the rules and expectations regarding the use of e-mail, the Internet, their telephone and/or cell phone, company vehicles, purchasing cards, and any other company-supplied resources they may or may not use for personal business. This is also the time to let new hires know the department's expectations for work schedules, overtime, breaks, lunch, requesting vacation and personal days, communicating absence in the event of illness or emergency, and the policy for attendance and punctuality. If you have a dress code, standards for appearance and/or conduct, and rules regarding parking, displaying an employee ID, or other relevant items, communicate these policies as well.

The Orientation Training Plan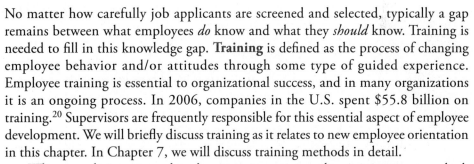

No matter how carefully job applicants are screened and selected, typically a gap remains between what employees *do* know and what they *should* know. Training is needed to fill in this knowledge gap. **Training** is defined as the process of changing employee behavior and/or attitudes through some type of guided experience. Employee training is essential to organizational success, and in many organizations it is an ongoing process. In 2006, companies in the U.S. spent $55.8 billion on training.[20] Supervisors are frequently responsible for this essential aspect of employee development. We will briefly discuss training as it relates to new employee orientation in this chapter. In Chapter 7, we will discuss training methods in detail.

When you design an employee's orientation training plan, it is important to look at it from two perspectives. The first and most obvious is to design a plan that prepares the person to do the job he/she was hired to do. The second and less obvious is from the new employee's perspective. As we discussed in Chapter 4, retention and turnover can be very costly and disruptive to an organization. Two reasons why employees choose to stay are a feeling of attachment to the company and sense of support for the employee.[21] Therefore, one of your goals is to create an orientation training plan that fosters an environment where new employees feel they want to stay and contribute.[22] This begins by understanding what new employees experience.

The New Hire's Perspective

Typically, new hires experience three stages of adjustment when they begin a new job: anticipation, reality, and decision. [23]

ANTICIPATION

It is human nature to formulate expectations and to anticipate certain events, behaviors, and responses for a new job. For a supervisor, the challenge is to understand these expectations and gauge their accuracy. Begin by asking your new hire these basic questions:

- What do you expect? Why?
- What are three things you are most looking forward to in this position?
- What are three things that you are worried about in this job?

training
using guided experiences to change employee behavior/attitudes.

Gathering this information will help you modify your training plan to address any concerns or misinformation the person may have.

REALITY

The next stage of adjustment sets in after a few weeks, when new hires begin to evaluate their experience in earnest. Your goal is for them to feel secure, important, and accepted so they become productive, long-term employees.[24] This is going to require the supervisor to strike a balance by providing just enough support, feedback, and supervision to nurture new employees without "micromanaging." Open and honest two-way communication is one of the keys to striking the right balance. Employees who began their new job with unrealistic expectations may be feeling disappointed or let down. On the other hand, they may have anticipated very little support and no orientation, so their experience may be far better than they had imagined. Regardless of where your employee is on this spectrum, it is important to discuss how she/he is feeling. This will provide you with insight and it will allow you both to define realistic expectations.

DECISION

The final stage is when new hires decide whether or not they like their job. If you are consistently and frequently talking with your new hire and soliciting feedback from existing members of your team, you should be receiving some clues as to how the person is feeling. The newcomer may need more training, more challenging work, or less supervision. Or, the job may simply not be a good fit. The important aspect of this cycle is that supervisors recognize the different phases in the adjustment process and be prepared to adapt or change as necessary.

The Buddy System

The **buddy system** is the process of assigning new hires a mentor to help set them up for success.[25] The buddy should be carefully selected and his/her role should be recognized during his/her end-of-year performance evaluation. One of the primary roles of a buddy is to be shadowed by a new hire. Job shadowing allows new hires to acquire knowledge about their job and company. The ideal buddy has a very positive and enthusiastic attitude, combined with excellent job skills and comprehensive knowledge of the job functions and the organization. Meet with the buddy prior to the new hire's start date to review the orientation training plan and to get the buddy's input and suggestions.

In addition to the job shadowing and formal job knowledge, the buddy also helps the new hire learn the "unwritten rules" about the department and the organization. New employees need to learn both technical skills as well as social information as they begin to adapt to their new environment.[26] Understanding office politics and how to fit in can have a positive impact on the new hire's decision to stay. The buddy is a newcomer's "go to person" when you are not available or when the newcomer feels unsure about asking you certain questions. Another role for the buddy is to help the new person establish a network of relationships with stakeholders, including coworkers, contractors, customers, and vendors. The buddy is usually aware of each

buddy system
the process of assigning new hires a mentor or buddy to help set them up for success.

person's expertise and interests and can encourage knowledge sharing, thus providing an opportunity for bonding and team building. Establishing positive relationships with coworkers typically helps with retention when the new hire feels a stronger sense of connection and commitment to the organization.[27]

The key to setting up a productive buddy system is to establish parameters and formal communication channels. The new hire can ask the buddy anything. But if it relates to policies or job responsibilities, the newcomer must validate the information with the supervisor. In addition, you want to be clear with the buddy about her/his role in helping the new person adapt to a new job, department, and corporate culture. Importantly, it is not the buddy's job to supervise the new person. The buddy is there to serve as a resource and to communicate with you regarding how well the new hire is progressing and advise you if the newcomer needs additional training or coaching.

The key to setting up a productive buddy system is to establish parameters and formal communication channels.

The Training Plan

Every position is different; therefore, every training plan will need to be tailored to some extent. However, there are some common elements to include as you begin to plan for training your new hire. One of the items that is difficult to gauge is how long it will take for new hires to become independent and productive. On average, "it ranges from eight weeks for clerical jobs to twenty weeks for professionals to more than 26 weeks for executives."[28]

First, identify the detailed list of job functions and tasks the person will be asked to perform. You may want to break this down into primary and secondary duties. This approach will allow you to focus initial training on primary duties and then expand the employee's responsibilities and training over time. To prepare the list of functions, reference the employee's job description and invite input from your existing staff. Do not assume that someone with experience in the field does not need training. For example, if you are a supervisor at a restaurant and you hire a new server who has previous experience, you may assume that she needs very little training. However, every restaurant is unique, with different employee expectations. In addition, formal and informal training varies. Therefore, it is important to take the extra time to show your new hire how things are done at your restaurant.

Once you have the detailed list of topics for training, identify who will conduct the initial training and determine how much time it will take. Review the plan with the trainer(s) prior to each training session. Discuss your expectations and clarify how you will determine that the new employee has been successfully trained. You want to emphasize good training techniques and consistency. Be sure to connect each training element to the job function and explain how they support the mission and goals for the department and the organization.

When new hires arrive, meet with them individually first to review the orientation training plan, and then meet with everyone involved in the training to clarify expectations. Let them all know how to communicate with you if they feel they need more or less time for training in a particular area. Also, provide new employees with a master check-off list and explain how you plan to assess their independence in each area. Let them know from the beginning that your approach to training includes the four ingredients of a good training program—goal setting, modeling (or explaining), practice, and feedback—discussed in Chapter 7.

Sales Training

Every employee has some sort of selling to do. How each person influences sales is slightly different. However, all new hires should have some basic company sales training included in their orientation. For example, a person hired to work as a mechanic at a car dealership will have contact with customers. Although this employee's primary job is servicing vehicles, it is helpful for him/her to learn about the newest models. Such information may come in handy if a customer asks the mechanic about a specific feature found only on a new model. It is helpful to teach employees the unique features and benefits of the company's products and services, and how they match up against the competition. In addition, it is essential to train them in excellent customer service from the beginning. Review how customers should be treated, how to handle complaints, how to listen, and how to ask questions.[29]

The Culture

During the recruitment process, most employers try to hire candidates who are well qualified and who will be a good fit. That good fit often centers on the **corporate culture,** the shared values, traditions, customs, philosophy, and policies of a corporation.[30] Orientation is the perfect time to share the company's cultural values, although they need to be consistently reinforced over time.[31] In today's competitive environment, your corporate culture needs three elements to recruit and retain the best and brightest: entrepreneurship, an owner/businessperson mindset, and a cause-driven environment.[32]

Developing an entrepreneurial culture encourages employees to be creative problem solvers whose pervasive attitude is to offer innovative ideas and suggestions rather than complaints.[33] This, combined with the owner/businessperson mindset, leads to informed employees who are more empowered and hold themselves to a higher standard. This approach also gets employees involved and participating in organizational decisions, something many employees indicate that they value and look for at work.[34] The third feature of an effective corporate culture involves creating a cause-driven environment where employees unite to achieve an inspiring, shared, and exceptional vision.[35] By developing a team with a strong sense of purpose, you foster a sense of community that typically leads to an environment where people trust and respect one another—two key components to high-achieving teams. A shared sense of urgency also helps, particularly when project deadlines loom.

Although every organization's culture is different, creating an environment where employees are valued, recognized, and rewarded is essential. Encouraging employees to innovate, take initiative, and unite in achieving excellence will lead to greater job satisfaction, retention, and results.

corporate culture
the shared values, traditions, customs, philosophy, and policies of a corporation.

THEY SAID IT BEST

Your youth is one of the main things you bring to the table. Share your energy and excitement. It will cost you nothing extra to have a passionate personality. Find a way to share your unique perspective with your new colleagues. You understand things about technology and culture that my generation only reads about. Use this to your advantage.

—JIM McCANN, CEO 1-800-Flowers.com

Source: USA Today, May 21, 2007, 7B.

Measuring Progress

During a new hire's orientation period, the supervisor should attempt to provide a nurturing environment. This is accomplished by providing training, resources, and support. It also involves giving the new person enough freedom and independence to grow, develop confidence, and demonstrate competence in her/his new role. One of the challenges the supervisor faces is monitoring progress and performance, but not micromanaging or "checking up" excessively on the person. Developing agreed-upon measures and reporting tools can help minimize the perception of over-supervising.

The 5:15 Report

The **5:15 report** was originally developed as an operations management tool. It is equally effective with orientation updates. The name *5:15* is derived from the idea that it should take fifteen minutes to prepare the report and five minutes to read. The actual content and format will vary depending upon the nature of the job and the type of organization. However, all 5:15 reports should contain certain basic information, including achievements, challenges/barriers, recommended solutions, and plans for the next time period.[36] A 5:15 report for a new employee during the orientation period may include a section on goals, including milestones achieved or other progress indicators. It might also include any scheduling changes and unanticipated training problems. In addition, it should include a brief summary of his/her plans for the next week. The new employee and the supervisor should agree ahead of time about the format, frequency, and general content of the report. Ideally, the new hire submits a 5:15 report to the supervisor at the end of each week.

One of the benefits of using this format is that it puts the new employee in charge of monitoring and reporting his/her progress. The supervisor does not have to ask how the individual is progressing because the information is proactively reported. This leads to a perception that the employee is in control, rather than the supervisor constantly asking questions and over-supervising. It also provides a consistent and structured method for assessing goals, training, and progress.

5:15 report
a reporting tool that allows employees to share significant information with their supervisor in a concise manner.

Goals and Measures

One of the initial steps every supervisor should take with their new employees is to schedule time to establish training goals. This gives the new employee something to strive for, and it provides the supervisor with measurable expectations. As you learned in Chapter 3, goals should conform to the SMART model. It is helpful to prepare training goals with the training plan as a reference. Take each skill, topic, or content area and develop a SMART goal. For example, if you supervise a retail shoe store, SMART goals for your new hire might include the following:

- Within one week, I will demonstrate my ability to accurately measure a customer's shoe size, including length and width, to properly fit them with the correct shoe.
- Within two weeks, I will demonstrate my ability to place new inventory in the stock room according to shoe brand, model, color, and size to provide quick and easy retrieval and re-stocking of shoes.

The new employee's training plan will include time to learn these new skills and to practice them, in order to gain confidence in doing them independently. Part of the plan also includes identifying when and how the newly acquired skills/knowledge will be assessed. You may choose to have another employee validate that the new hire has mastered the skill, or you may ask for a demonstration of the newcomer's ability. In some cases, you can directly observe the end result (e.g., visiting the stock room after the employee has completed her/his inventory to determine if all of the items are properly placed).

There are two aspects to assessing goal achievement. The first and most obvious is evaluating whether or not new hires can demonstrate a new skill or articulate new knowledge. This is fairly objective and fact-based—either they can or they cannot. The second element is less obvious, and far more subjective. How skillfully and professionally did they achieve the goal? Measuring quality can be difficult. For example, if we go back and evaluate the two SMART goals for the shoe clerk, the first is measuring a customer's shoe size. One feature of this goal that is implied, but not stated, is that the measurement is made without hurting or offending the person. A trainee may be able to measure a customer's shoe size, but if this is done while offering negative comments such as, "wow, your feet are really wide for a woman," the business will probably lose a customer. Additional training is in order. With the second goal, involving stocking inventory, the trainee may get the inventory stored, but in a hard-to-find or unsafe manner. The new employee's perception of stacking boxes neatly may be entirely different from yours. Therefore, goals, training, and evaluation need to include qualitative as well as technical measures.

Performance Expectations

performance appraisal
evaluating job performance as a basis for personnel decisions.

Performance appraisals can be effective and satisfying if systematically developed and implementation techniques replace haphazard methods. For our purposes, **performance appraisal** is the process of evaluating individual job performance as a basis for making objective personnel decisions.[37] This definition intentionally excludes occasional coaching, in which a supervisor simply checks an employee's work and gives immediate feedback. Although personal coaching is fundamental to good management and is essential during the orientation period, formally documented appraisals are needed both to ensure that opportunities and rewards are equitably distributed and to avoid prejudicial treatment.[38] Any systematic evaluation process needs to be anchored to the organization's philosophy and approach toward performance appraisals. In addition to reviewing the job description with your new hire, it is important to explain performance expectations. Provide a copy of the appraisal form you will be using to assess job performance along with the key indicators, measures, and criteria.

The Value of Discussing Performance Appraisal Criteria During Orientation

As we have mentioned before, new employees tend to thrive when they clearly understand what is expected of them. They also tend to be more focused and perform at a higher level when they understand how their performance will be assessed. Let them know from the beginning how you plan to measure and/or assess each item on the performance evaluation form. Explain the criteria you have established and what you consider to be key indicators, invite their input to enhance these items, and make them meaningful for the individual.[39] This will reduce the employee's anxiety and the element of surprise that employees often associate with performance evaluations. Performance appraisals are discussed in more detail in Chapter 6.

Formal Performance Appraisals

Most organizations conduct a formal performance appraisal for each employee on an annual basis. However, during the new hire's orientation/probation period, a supervisor may conduct abbreviated performance appraisals after the first three months, six months, and year. These "mini" evaluations should be documented and reviewed with the employee. It is important to discuss with your new employees how and when you plan to formally evaluate their job performance.

Informal Performance Evaluations

Informal performance assessment is part of the supervisor's coaching role and it should occur much more frequently than the formal performance appraisal. New employees especially need frequent coaching and positive and constructive feedback. This ongoing evaluation of performance allows employees to make improvements promptly without floundering until a formal performance appraisal. Providing new hires with consistent, constructive feedback will help them stay on track to become outstanding team members. Remember to let them know from the beginning how and when you plan to assess their progress and performance. Just as they need to know what you expect from them, it is important that they know what to expect from you.

Compensation and Evaluations

compensation
money or other rewards paid to employees for their service to the organization.

Some organizations link **compensation**, including wages, salaries, and other rewards, with performance evaluations. Others keep them separate. Let your new hires know what sort of linkage exists and how their performance evaluation could impact their compensation.

Discussing job functions and performance indicators should be an ongoing process with your new employees. One important step toward setting your new hires up for success is letting them know what is expected of them from the beginning. By reviewing the job description, functions, performance evaluation criteria, indicators, and training plan, you are clarifying expectations. This gives new hires the opportunity to ask questions as they embark on their journey to becoming valuable members of your team.

One important step toward setting your new hires up for success is letting them know what is expected of them from the beginning.

KNOWLEDGE TO ACTION

1. Why do you think it is important to clarify performance expectations during a new employee's orientation?

   _____

2. What unintended or negative consequences do you think are possible if a supervisor fails to let employees know how and when their performance will be evaluated?

   _____

Orientation and Training for the Virtual Employee

In today's global economy, more and more workers are too geographically dispersed for standard orientation and training. But these workers still need the same information as on-site employees, including general business knowledge, department and job-specific information, and a sense of the cultural values of the organization.

The Travel Option

If you have one or two virtual employees, you may choose to pay their travel expenses to bring them to your home office for a compressed orientation. However, if you have several virtual workers and/or they are located in other parts of the world, it may be too costly and unrealistic to pay for travel. In this case, you need to design the virtual orientation and training program.

Content and Format for the Virtual Orientation

The content will be consistent with the orientation plan described in this chapter. But your delivery of this information will change dramatically. Following the model of distance learning in academic environments, create an online community for your virtual employees. Create learning modules for each content area. Each module should include an outline of the learning objectives, relevant documents and reference guides, and videos, which may include product demonstrations or executive presentations.

Virtual office workers need orientation and training, too. New employees who are in a different geographic location need just as much training, if not more, than employees located in the same office as their supervisor. This employee is learning about the company through videos, pod-casts, and other technologies that can effectively and efficiently deliver training and orientation to remote workers.

© Klaus Tiedge/Getty Images/Blend Images

Virtual Training

If new employees are expected to have tangible items in front of them while completing a training module, make sure you send them well in advance. For example, you may be responsible for technical support for a new cell phone device. In order to provide call center support twenty-four hours a day, you have hired workers overseas to answer calls at night. They should have the actual phone device in their hands before they begin the training program. In addition, it is still important to maintain frequent communication with them, to establish a buddy system, and to define goals and measures.

It may be more difficult to assess virtual employees' skills and abilities, so you may need to use alternative tools. One approach is to build an online quiz tool to accompany each learning module. You can set this up so that they cannot advance to the next module until they have successfully passed the quiz for the current module. In addition, you can "test" call them to see how they respond to you or one of your team members. You may also require that they have video capability so they can record themselves demonstrating their skills.

Regardless of whether your new hires report to the home office every day or live on the other side of the world, they should all have an orientation period to help them succeed. Orientation training provides the opportunity to learn about the company and its products, services, and people, along with its corporate culture. This knowledge and experience contribute to a well-prepared employee who can have a positive impact on the organization.

SUMMARY

1. Planning ahead for a new hire's arrival prior to his/her first day is one way to make sure the newcomer feels a sense of welcome, value, and importance—all of which are key ingredients for employee retention. Involving current employees in the planning process leads to more effective training plans while giving staff a chance to make valuable contributions to the team.

It also gives them time to anticipate the arrival of the new employee and to reflect on how this change will affect them.

2. Prior to a new hire's arrival, determine which forms, documentation, and company materials can be distributed in advance. Also determine the equipment, training, computer access, work space, and other resources the

newcomer will need. Order these items and have them set up prior to the new hire's arrival. The universal pre-arrival checklist includes items such as (1) offer letter, (2) welcome phone call, (3) forms, (4) benefits package, (5) announcement, and (6) schedule. The job-specific list may include items such as (1) uniform, (2) identification badge, (3) business cards, (4) work space, (5) telephone, (6) e-mail, and (7) computer equipment.

3. Realistic job expectations that are fulfilled contribute to employee satisfaction and retention. Previewing their job responsibilities in detail and providing an outline of the orientation plan—including a schedule—will help new employees know what to expect. Clarify information and expectations verbally and in writing. In addition, invite questions and feedback to be sure your expectations are aligned with those of your new employees.

4. The orientation plan includes an overview of general company information, such as (1) the history of the company and its mission and vision, strategic plan, and goals, (2) employee benefits, (3) hours of operation, (4) emergency preparedness and safety plans, and (5) legal issues. The job-specific component of orientation includes (1) the department's mission, purpose, and goals, (2) overview of job functions, (3) introduction to team members and other department, (4) facilities tour, and (5) an overview of policies and procedures. People from all areas of the company should be involved in orientation, including executives, the immediate supervisor, and other team members.

5. A good orientation training program includes an introduction to company policies and procedures while also providing training that relates directly to the job functions and tasks the person will be asked to perform. Using the buddy system will help the person acclimate to the corporate culture and integrate into the organization more quickly.

6. Orientation progress should be assessed with the SMART (specific, measurable, achievable, realistic, and time bound) goals. Assessing goal achievement involves evaluating whether or not new hires can demonstrate new skills or articulate their new knowledge combined with measuring the quality of their work. A 5:15 report provides employees with a reporting tool to share significant information with their supervisor in a concise manner. It should contain some basic information, including (1) achievements, (2) challenges/barriers, (3) recommended solutions, and (4) plans for the next reporting time period.

7. A performance appraisal is the process of evaluating individual job performance as a basis for making objective personnel decisions. It is important to include a discussion on this topic during the orientation period so employees know what to expect. This reduces the employee's anxiety and the element of surprise that employees often associate with performance evaluations. New employees thrive, are more focused, and perform at a higher level when they understand how their performance will be assessed. Explain how and when their performance will be measured and what criteria and key indicators will be used to assess their performance.

8. In today's global economy, virtual workers still need orientation and training. If possible, employees can travel to the home office for a condensed orientation. Otherwise, a virtual training plan can be offered using technology and modifying the standard orientation plan. Develop learning modules for virtual training that include (1) reference documents, (2) video demonstrations, (3) assessment tools, and (4) resource materials to provide a sound distance learning environment.

TERMS TO UNDERSTAND

5:15 report, p. 139
buddy system, p. 136
compensation, p. 141
corporate culture, p. 138

employee benefits, p. 132
employee orientation, p. 121
expectation, p. 126
feedback, p. 127

milestones, p. 127
performance appraisal, p. 140
pre-arrival checklist, p. 123
training, p. 135

QUESTIONS FOR REFLECTION

1. What are three things that you would want an employer to do to set you up for success as a new hire?

2. What are three techniques a company supervisor can use to help a new hire feel welcome, valued, and special?

3. Why is it important to clarify expectations with your new hire?

4. How does the employee's performance appraisal fit into the orientation period? Why is this important?

5. If you just started in a new job, what are two methods you can use to keep your new supervisor informed about your progress and orientation?

6. How would you orient and train a new employee who lives in another country with a time zone that is eight hours earlier than yours?

HANDS-ON ACTIVITIES

GENERAL COMPANY ORIENTATION

Choose a company (this can be the company you work for, an organization you are familiar with, or your dream company) and prepare a general orientation plan.

1. Prepare a detailed list of items you will include in the general company orientation. Identify which handouts, reference documents, and other support material will be required to conduct this orientation.

2. Identify who will present each section.

3. Pick one section and develop an interactive session that will achieve the learning objective and at the same time get the employees actively engaged and involved.

JOB-SPECIFIC ORIENTATION

Select a position (this can be your current job, a job you are familiar with, or your dream job) and prepare a job-specific orientation plan.

1. Prepare a detailed list of items you will include in the job-specific orientation. Identify which handouts, reference documents, and other support material will be required to conduct this orientation.

2. Identify who will present each section.

3. Prepare an overview and list of instructions for the new hire's buddy.

4. Pick one of the learning objectives and describe how you will train the person to learn the new behavior/skill.

5. How will you measure their achievement of this learning goal?

Interview an Expert

The purpose of this exercise is to learn from an expert the best practices he/she has developed for new employee orientation and training. Select a person with employee orientation planning and training experience to interview. Your goal is to learn from this person's experience. You may use the questions listed below and/or develop your own. After your interview, prepare a brief summary of the conversation and list their orientation best practices.

Questions

1. What are some things that you do prior to a new employee's first day?

2. Please describe your vision of the perfect first day for a new hire.

3. What are some of the more effective tools and techniques you have used for teaching employees new information about the company and/or their job?

4. How do you assess the quality and effectiveness of your orientation program?

5. Do you use a buddy system? If yes, please describe how the buddy is selected and how these relationships are structured.

6. What do you think are the most important characteristics of an excellent orientation program?

7. Do you have any virtual employees? If yes, how do you structure their orientation?

You may improvise and add or edit questions to fit the situation or the circumstances of your interview. Schedule your interview ahead of time and try to limit it to about 15 minutes. Remember to send a thank-you note to the person you interview.

YOU DECIDE

CASE STUDY 5.1
Orientation Planning

Ken is the supervisor of the Super New Hospital's (SNH) accounting department. He recently hired Maria as a new payroll clerk. She will be starting in two weeks. This is the first time Ken has hired a new employee since joining the SNH last year. His previous employer had a very structured employee orientation program, which he relied on to integrate employees into their new positions and acclimate them to the corporate culture. However, SNH does not have any type of orientation plan. Ken would like to create a comprehensive orientation plan for Maria as he believes that investing time and effort in the beginning leads to long-term employee satisfaction and better job performance.

He has several dilemmas. He is not sure where to start or what to include. He also does not know how to acquire some of the reference materials and resources. In addition, he is still relatively new in his position and he does not want to offend anyone or cause any problems.

Questions

1. If you were Ken, what would you do? Would you choose to develop a comprehensive orientation plan? A general company plan? A job-specific plan? Or no orientation plan at all? Explain your rationale.

2. If you chose to develop a plan, who and what will you include?

3. If you chose not to create an orientation plan, how will you set Maria up for success in her new job?

SUPERVISOR'S TOOLKIT

Select a job/position of your choice, then perform the following tasks.

1. Write a 5:15 report. The report should be no more than two pages long; it should take fifteen minutes to prepare and five minutes to read. A 5:15 report is typically prepared on a weekly basis, particularly during orientation. Depending on the job you choose, the content will be different. However each report should contain the same general information, including achievements, challenges/barriers, recommended solutions, and plans for the next reporting time period.

2. Write two SMART training goals and identify how you will measure a new employee's performance in achieving these goals. What assessment criteria will you use? What role will the employee play in evaluating his/her own performance?

3. Develop a buddy system for employee orientation training for the position you have identified. Write a detailed list of responsibilities for the buddy. Also prepare instructions for the buddy explaining the parameters for the role, including level of authority, decision making, and frequency of communication with you.

CHAPTER **6**

Appraising and Rewarding Performance

Learning Objectives

1. Describe at least five performance appraisal techniques.

2. Explain what makes a performance appraisal legally defensible and discuss the importance of record keeping and confidentiality.

3. Explain how to design a performance appraisal system and explain the value of including employees and customers in the process.

4. Discuss performance measures and assessment criteria.

5. Discuss the "No Surprises" approach to supervision and performance evaluations.

6. Describe various types of employee compensation plans; distinguish extrinsic rewards from intrinsic rewards and list four rules for administering extrinsic rewards effectively.

7. Compare individualized and team rewards and provide examples of each.

Straight Talk from the Field

Bruce Miles is a Warehouse Manager for Costco Wholesale in Overland Park, Kansas.

QUESTION: ***What are your secrets to success in appraising employee performance?***

RESPONSE:

Costco is unique in many ways. It is a multibillion-dollar global retailer with warehouse club operations in eight countries. We are the recognized leader in our field, dedicated to quality in every area of our business and respected for our outstanding business ethics. Despite our large size and explosive international expansion, we continue to provide a family atmosphere in which our employees thrive and succeed. We strive to foster an environment that can be a very good fit for anyone who has a high energy level and a positive attitude. As a manager at Costco, I am charged with managing a fast-paced team environment laced with challenges and opportunities while developing our employees for future growth. In fact, the majority of our management team is promoted from within. Although our business is large, it is relatively simple and can be taught to anyone who has the desire to learn.

One of the challenges for some of our employees is the ability to stay positive—no matter how much is thrown at them at any given time—and the ability to get along with coworkers and management. Good employees make my job very easy! They are the future leaders and they "get it" most of the time and do not need a lot of coaching. It is the employee who has behavior issues that makes my job more difficult. I realize that I do not have the ability to change another individual's behavior, but I do have the ability to influence and encourage him to modify his behavior. This is not always a comfortable experience, but it is essential if I am going to be successful in achieving my goal of developing my employees to reach their potential.

In order to be an effective supervisor or manager, you have to be accurate, timely, honest, and consistent with your communication. There should always be dialogue between you and your employees. If an individual has issues that are affecting her work—she is not getting along with others or not performing satisfactorily—it is important to discuss your concerns with that person immediately. Meet with such employees prior to their performance review. Your

employees deserve the opportunity to improve and it is impossible for them to fix a problem that they are not aware of.

In addition to frequent and timely communication, at Costco we have a formal performance evaluation process that includes a self-evaluation form that employees complete prior to their supervisor's review. The self-evaluation includes an assessment of their strengths, personal leadership and communication skills, initiative, decision making, working with others, development opportunities, results of their annual goals, and new goals for the upcoming year. If the supervisor has given the employee timely feedback and proper coaching, then the individual typically identifies areas for improvement during his self-evaluation. This makes it much easier to address the concern and it is a positive step towards self-improvement. However, if the supervisor has not been consistent throughout the year in addressing concerns in an effective manner, it will be more difficult to present the review and suggest improvements because the employee may not even be aware of his performance issues.

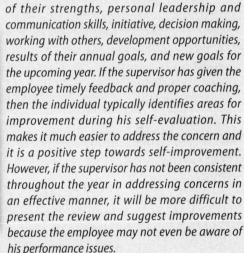

I experienced this situation one time when I had relocated to a different Costco location years ago. Shortly after arriving in my new store, I had to give one of the employees who reported to me her performance review. I had my own observations and suggestions for improvements, but I also solicited feedback from other managers who had worked with this person over the entire year, since it was an annual review. I agreed with the points they brought up, which were consistent with my observations. Our concerns with this employee were all behavior-related, which can often be more difficult to discuss and resolve as employees tend to take this type of assessment very personally. Well, when I delivered the review it generated a lot of emotion from this individual. I worked through the points, being as tactful as possible. I focused on using constructive criticism and suggesting more appropriate behavior. I also provided the employee with specific examples of what I had observed in the

short time I had worked with her. The employee understood the concerns, and I will never forget her response once we were finished with the review: "Thank you for bringing this to my attention. I wish someone would have said something to me sooner, because I would have started working on it a long time ago if I would have only known." It really reinforced in me how important it is to be

timely and consistent with your employees and your peers. You do not have to wait until the annual review to provide feedback.

As a manager who is dedicated to developing people, I believe that effective communication is the key. Employees cannot fix a problem they do not know about. Everyone deserves the opportunity to improve.

Chapter Outline

P erformance appraisals and rewards are discussed together in this chapter because they are inherently linked. Employees' contributions to the organization are typically measured and rewarded during their performance review. When performance appraisal systems are administered properly, they can serve as an effective motivational tool and provide measurable indicators for rewards. However, some rewards are not associated with performance appraisals. For instance, rewards can be tied to special projects or incremental goals. Other rewards are public- and team-oriented, as opposed to performance appraisals that are typically confidential and individual in nature. This chapter focuses on how you can use both of these tools to improve employee performance and goal attainment. It all begins by involving employees from the beginning. This provides them with the opportunity to understand the performance appraisal system, including why and how their performance will be assessed.

Before we get into the main topics of this chapter, it is important to note that feedback and open communication between the supervisor and employees should occur on a frequent and consistent basis. Later in this chapter we will discuss the "No Surprises" approach, which places a great deal of emphasis on frequent two-way communication. According to Dr. John C. Kelly, business

Communication should include spontaneous feedback.

counselor for SCORE (Counselors to America's Small Business)[1], this communication should include spontaneous feedback, weekly one-on-one meetings, monthly companywide meetings to share information, and an annual formal discussion to review goals and action plans.[2] The point is that supervisors do not need to wait until they are giving employees their annual performance appraisal to tell them what they are doing well and where they have room for improvement.

Performance Appraisal

Annual performance appraisals are such a common part of organizational life that they qualify as a ritual. As with many rituals, the participants repeat the historical pattern without really asking the important questions: "Why?" and "Is there a better way?"

Without formal measures, assessment criteria, and goals, it is difficult to recognize and reward good performance.

Unfortunately, when people hear the words "performance appraisal," they often experience negative emotions. In many organizations, the consensus is that supervisors do not like giving them and nobody wants to be on the receiving end. They are perceived as a waste of time and often lead to decreased productivity.[3] However, without formal measures, assessment criteria, and goals, it is difficult to recognize and reward good performance.

Both appraisers and appraisees tend to express general dissatisfaction with performance appraisals. In fact, nearly 75% of the companies responding to a survey expressed major dissatisfaction with their performance appraisal system.[4] This is not surprising, in view of the following observation:

> The annual performance review process, touted by some as the gateway to future prosperity, is, in reality for many companies, nothing more than a fill-in-the-blank, form-completing task that plots an individual's performance against a sanitized list of often generic corporate expectations and required competencies.[5]

Performance appraisals can be effective and satisfying if systematically developed and implemented, replacing haphazard methods. As defined in Chapter 5, a performance appraisal is the process of evaluating individual job performance as a basis for personnel decisions.[6] It is essentially a communication tool, a formal method for exchanging feedback between employees and their supervisors.[7] This definition intentionally excludes coaching, in which a supervisor checks an employee's work and gives immediate praise or instruction. Personal coaching is fundamental to good supervision and is discussed in depth in Chapter 8. This section will focus on formally documented appraisals necessary to ensure that opportunities and rewards are equitably distributed.[8] We will examine two important aspects of performance appraisal: (1) alternative techniques and (2) legal defensibility.

Performance Appraisal Techniques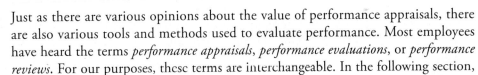

Just as there are various opinions about the value of performance appraisals, there are also various tools and methods used to evaluate performance. Most employees have heard the terms *performance appraisals*, *performance evaluations*, or *performance reviews*. For our purposes, these terms are interchangeable. In the following section,

"This is bad work, Edwards! Bad! Bad! Bad! Bad!"

© The New Yorker Collection, 1995, Mort Gerberg, from cartoonbank.com

we discuss alternative ways of assessing employee performance. Importantly, our focus is on how employees can improve their own job performance.

The list of alternative performance appraisal techniques is long and growing. Appraisal software programs are also proliferating. Unfortunately, many appraisal instruments are simplistic, invalid, and unreliable. If an appraisal is overly simplistic, it will not provide supervisors with a complete assessment of the employee. In general terms, an invalid appraisal instrument does not accurately measure what it is supposed to measure. Unreliable instruments do not measure criteria in a consistent manner. Many other performance appraisal techniques are so complex that they are impractical and burdensome to use. But armed with a working knowledge of the most-popular appraisal techniques, a good supervisor can distinguish the strong from the weak. Once again, the strength of an appraisal technique is gauged by its conformity to the criteria for legal defensibility discussed later. Of course, standard appraisal practices and traditions, such as those in a branch of the military, need to be taken into consideration. For examples of performance appraisal forms, visit the textbook website at www.cengage.com/business/cassidy/.

The following sections discuss some of the appraisal techniques that have been used through the years.

Goal Setting

Within a management-by-objectives (MBO) framework, performance is typically evaluated in terms of formal goals or objectives set at an earlier date. There is room for assessing accomplishment of individual goals as well as overall department and/or organizational goals. When performance goals are being established, it is helpful to include the employee in the process. In addition, by linking the individual's goals to the broader mission and goals of the organization, employees tend to develop a higher level of commitment and a greater sense of purpose and value. Typically, achievement of goals is measured in quantifiable terms. However, you should include a quality component as well. The goal setting technique is a comparatively strong method if desired outcomes are clearly linked to specific behavior. For example, a product design engineer's "output" could be measured in terms of the number of product specifications submitted per month that meet or exceed quality control standards.

Written Essays

With the written essay method, supervisors describe the performance of employees in narrative form, sometimes in response to predetermined questions. Evaluators often criticize this technique for consuming too much time. This method is also limited by the fact that some supervisors have difficulty expressing themselves in writing.

Critical Incidents

Specific instances of inferior and superior performance are documented by the supervisor when they occur. For example, an inferior incident in a restaurant occurs when a customer complains that his chicken is pink and uncooked in the middle. An example of superior performance is when a restaurant critic in the local paper specifically mentions your chef and comments on the exquisite food she enjoyed at your restaurant. Accumulated incidents then provide an objective basis for evaluations at appraisal time. The strength of the critical incidents technique is enhanced when evaluators document specific behavior in specific situations and ignore personality traits.[9]

Graphic Rating Scales

Various behaviors or traits are rated on incremental scales. For example, "Initiative" could be rated on a scale of 1 through 5 (1 = low and 5 = high). This technique is among the weakest when personality traits are being evaluated. However, **behaviorally anchored rating scales (BARS)**, performance rating scales divided into increments of observable and measurable job behavior determined through job analysis, are considered to be one of the strongest performance appraisal techniques. For example, supervisors at credit card issuer Capital One use performance rating scales with behavioral anchors such as: "Do you get things done well through other people?" and "Do you play well as team member?"[10]

Weighted Checklists

behaviorally anchored rating scales (BARS)
performance appraisal scales that are divided into increments of observable, measurable job behavior.

With weighted checklists, evaluators check appropriate adjectives or behavioral descriptions that have predetermined weights. The weights, which gauge the relative importance of the randomly mixed items on the checklist, are usually unknown to the evaluator. Following the evaluation, the weights of the checked items are added or averaged to permit interpersonal comparisons. As with other techniques, the degree of behavioral specificity largely determines the strength of weighted checklists.

Rankings and Comparisons

Coworkers in a subunit are ranked or compared in head-to-head fashion according to specified accomplishments or job behavior. A major shortcoming of this technique is that the absolute distance between evaluated employees is unknown. For example, the employee ranked number one may be five times as effective as number two, who in turn is only slightly more effective than number three. Rankings/comparisons are also criticized for causing resentment among lower-ranked, but adequately performing, coworkers. In 2001, *Fortune* magazine observed:

> In companies across the country, from General Electric to Hewlett-Packard, such grading systems—in which all employees are ranked against one another and grades are distributed along some sort of bell curve—are creating a firestorm of controversy. In the past 15 months, employees have filed class-action suits against Microsoft and Conoco as well as Ford, claiming that the companies discriminate in assigning grades. In each case a different group of disaffected employees is bringing charges: older workers at Ford, blacks and women at Microsoft, U.S. citizens at Conoco.[11]

Ford has since dropped its forced ranking system.[12]

Multirater Appraisal

This is a general label for a diverse array of appraisal techniques involving more than one rater of the evaluated person's performance. The rationale for multirater appraisals is that "two or more heads are less biased than one." One approach that has become popular in recent years is the "360-degree review." In a **360-degree review**, a supervisor is evaluated by his or her boss, peers, and subordinates. The results are typically pooled and are generally presented anonymously.[13] Although 360-degree feedback is best suited for use in management development programs, some companies have turned it into a performance appraisal tool, with mixed results.[14] If 360-degree appraisals are to be successful, they need to be carefully designed and skillfully implemented (for example, see Figure 6.1).

Continuous Improvement Review (CIR)

A unique approach to performance appraisals is the **continuous improvement review (CIR)**, which "focuses the review process on customers, the team and the employee's contribution to system improvements."[15] CIR identifies employees who have helped improve the organization as a whole. Assessment focuses on productivity, quality outcomes, and customer satisfaction.[16]

Making Performance Appraisals Legally Defensible

Lawsuits that challenge the legality of specific performance appraisal systems and the personnel actions that result from them have left scores of human resource

360-degree review
a pooled, anonymous evaluation by one's boss, peers, and subordinates.

continuous improvement review
review process that focuses on customers, the team, and the employee's contribution to system improvements.

FIGURE 6.1 Sample 360° Appraisal Form

Employee: _____   **Date:** _____
Evaluator: _____   **In what capacity do you work with this person?** _____

Management Competency	Referring to ANY of the 11 competencies to the left, list 3 areas of strength and 3 areas for growth. Reference the specific competencies in your response. You may continue on additional blank sheets as necessary.
1. Inclusiveness Promotes cooperation, fairness and equity; shows respect for people and their differences; works to understand perspectives of others; demonstrates empathy; brings out the best in others	*3 areas of strength:*
2. Managing people Coaches, evaluates, develops, inspires people; sets expectations, recognizes achievements, manages conflict, aligns performance goals with university goals, provides feedback, group leadership; delegates	
3. Stewardship and managing resources Demonstrates accountability and sound judgment in managing university resources in open and effective manner; appropriate understanding of confidentiality, university values; adheres to policies, procedures, and safety guidelines	
4. Problem solving Identifies problems, involves others in seeking solutions, conducts appropriate analyses, searches for best solutions; responds quickly to new challenges	
5. Decision making Makes clear, consistent, transparent decisions; acts with integrity in all decision making; distinguishes relevant from irrelevant information and makes timely decisions	
6. Strategic planning and organizing Understands big picture and aligns priorities with broader goals, measures outcomes, uses feedback to redirect as needed, evaluates alternatives, solutions oriented, seeks alternatives and broad input; can see connections within complex issues	*3 areas for growth:*
7. Communication Connects with peers, subordinates and customers, actively listens, clearly and effectively shares information, demonstrates effective oral and written communication skills, negotiates effectively	
8. Quality improvement Strives for efficient, effective, high quality performance in self and the unit; delivers timely and accurate results; resilient when responding to situations that are not going well; takes initiative to make improvements	
9. Leadership Motivates others, accepts responsibility; demonstrates high level of political acumen; develops trust and credibility; expects honest and ethical behavior of self and others	
10. Teamwork Encourages cooperation and collaboration; builds effective teams; works in partnership with others; is flexible	
11. Service focus Values the importance of delivering high quality, innovative service to internal and external clients; understands the needs of the client; customer service focus; shares accountability for results provided	

Supervisors need specific criteria to develop legally defensible performance appraisals.

managers asking themselves, "Will my organization's performance appraisal system stand up in court?" From the standpoint of limiting legal exposure, it is better to ask this question while you are developing a formal appraisal system rather than after it has been implemented. Supervisors need specific criteria to develop legally defensible performance appraisal systems. Fortunately, researchers have discerned some instructive patterns in court decisions.

After studying the verdicts in sixty-six employment discrimination cases in the United States, one pair of researchers found that employers could successfully defend their appraisal systems if they satisfied four criteria:

1. A job analysis was used to develop the performance appraisal system.

2. The appraisal system was behavior-oriented, not trait-oriented.

3. Performance evaluators followed specific written instructions when conducting appraisals

4. Evaluators reviewed the results of the appraisals with the employees being evaluated.[17]

Each of these conditions has a clear legal rationale. Job analysis, which we discussed in Chapter 4 relative to employee selection, anchors the appraisal process to specific job duties, not personalities. Behavior-oriented appraisals properly focus the supervisor's attention on how the individual actually performed his or her job.[18] Performance appraisers who follow specific written instructions are less likely to be plagued by vague performance standards and/or personal bias. Finally, by reviewing employees' performance appraisal results with them personally, supervisors provide the feedback to help them learn and improve. Supervisors who keep in mind these criteria for legal defensibility, as well as the elements of a good appraisal shown in Figure 6.2, are better equipped to develop a sound appraisal system.

FIGURE 6.2 Elements of a good performance appraisal

Elements of a Good Performance Appraisal

Elements to consider include:

1. Goals set by the employee and supervisor during the most recent appraisal.

2. List of specific competencies or skills being measured, with examples of successful behaviors.

3. Ratings scale appropriate to the organization.

4. Space for employee's self-appraisal.

5. Space for supervisor's appraisal.

6. Space for specific comments from the supervisor about the employee's performance.

7. Suggestions for employee development.

8. Goals to meet by the next appraisal date.

Source: Carla Joinson, "Making Sure Employees Measure Up," *HR Magazine* 46 (March 2001): 39. Copyright 2001 by Society for Human Resource Management. Reproduced with the permission of the Society for Human Resource Management, Alexandria, VA in the format Textbook via Copyright Clearance Center.

Record Keeping and Confidentiality

According to the criteria for legally defensible performance appraisals, the evaluator should follow specific written instructions. Specifically, the evaluator needs to document the performance appraisal and any related data such as attendance, productivity, and evidence of superior or inferior work. In addition, individual performance appraisals are a private matter between the supervisor and the employee. **Confidentiality** is essential to maintaining trust between a supervisor and his/her employees. It is important that the actual performance appraisal, related documents, and subsequent conversations remain confidential. Beyond the supervisor and employee, this information should be shared only with a limited number of individuals in the organization, such as human resources specialists, the company attorney, or senior-level management.

KNOWLEDGE TO ACTION

Consider the following scenario:

Mary recently met with her supervisor Nancy for her annual performance appraisal. During the meeting, Mary admitted that she had made a few mistakes because she was rushing too much. She agreed to slow down and check her work more thoroughly in an effort to improve. Mary kept the conversation confidential and did not mention it to anyone. The following week, one of Mary's coworkers said to her, "I hear you agreed to slow down a little so you make fewer mistakes!" Of course, Mary is left to assume that Nancy must have discussed their conversation with others.

1. How do you think Mary feels?

   _____

2. What impact do you think this will have on the relationship between Mary and Nancy?

   _____

3. What do you suggest Nancy do to resolve this situation?

   _____

Making the Appraisal System Relevant

confidentiality
keeping private documents and conversations a secret.

As you just discovered, a variety of techniques can be used to evaluate employee performance. Whether your organization uses a traditional performance appraisal, the CIR model, or a combination of methods, your goal should be to create a tool for improving productivity, quality, and key organizational outcomes. Let us briefly discuss how to make performance appraisals more relevant and acceptable in today's global economy.

Employee Input

As you can see in Figure 6.3, employees' perception of the value, fairness, and timeliness of performance reviews is not very high. One of the ways to counter this trend is to involve your employees in the process of designing the performance appraisal system. This begins by outlining the variables involved in performance appraisals, such as goals, measures, assessment criteria, scoring method, weighting factors (if used), frequency, who conducts the appraisal, an agreed-upon method for modifying variables, and how the appraisal links to rewards and compensation. As you work through the process of defining each of these variables, it is essential that you seek input from your employees. If they help to create the system, they will have a better understanding of how their performance is going to be assessed and they will feel a greater sense of control. In addition, if the process is managed effectively, it can be used as a motivational tool and will no longer perceived as a dreaded, negative experience.

Involve your employees in the process of designing the performance appraisal system.

Customer Input

In addition to employee participation, it is also useful to survey a few of your key customers to determine what they consider to be the most important aspects of their relationship with your department and organization. In this context, the term *customer* refers to both external and internal customers. Incorporating methods to measure how well your employees are doing in the support of the organization's and department's mission, as well as meeting customer expectations, is an important factor in properly aligning performance appraisals with organizational outcomes. Another positive byproduct of this step is that your customers will feel that their opinions are valued and that you care about their satisfaction.

FIGURE 6.3 Employees' perceptions of employee appraisals
Source: Tom Davis and Michael Landa, "Pat or slap? Do appraisals work?" *CMA Management* 73 (March 1999): 24–27.

Employees' Perceptions of Employee Appraisals

Global consulting firm Watson Wyatt Worldwide surveyed 2,004 Canadian workers. The summary of their findings included:

- Fewer than two-thirds of the sampled employees (60%) said that they understand the measures used to evaluate their performance.
- Even fewer sampled employees (57%) thought that their performance was rated fairly.
- Less than half (47%) said that their managers clearly expressed goals and assignments.
- Only about two-fifths of the sample (42%) reported regular, timely performance reviews.
- Even fewer (39%) reported that their performance review was helpful in improving their on-the-job performance and their pay.

Cultural Sensitivity

The U.S. and Canada are individualistic ("me") cultures where people expect to be singled out for evaluation. Such is not the case in collectivist ("we") cultures. Consider, for example, this cautionary tale from global conglomerate ITT:

> Why was turnover so high? That's what ITT China President William E. Taylor wanted to know when he visited the Shanghai sales office three years ago. The local manager had a simple answer for Taylor. . . . If the sales boss gave workers an average "3" on the 1-5 performance scale, they'd stop talking to him and in some cases, quit shortly after. "They're losing face in the organization," the manager lamented. . . .
>
> In southern Europe, the focus on individual performance didn't sit well with the region's more "collective ethos," says James Duncan, director of ITT's talent development. And in Scandinavia, where there's more of "a sense of equality between bosses and workers," says Duncan, some workers asked, "What gives you the right to rate me a 3?"[19]

So what did ITT do? In a radical move, the firm dropped numerical ratings of its employees worldwide. In today's global economy with its global corporations, the old saying "one size shoe doesn't fit everyone" applies more than ever to the area of performance appraisal.

Performance Measures and Assessment Criteria

Designing an effective performance appraisal system takes time and patience. It also requires a willingness to reevaluate the system periodically to determine if the measures, criteria, and methods being used are still effective. Directly related to performance goals are **performance measures**. The development of performance measures involves defining exactly how employees' performance will be evaluated, including progress toward achieving their goals. Regardless of the techniques or methods you choose for performance appraisals, you still need to define how you will measure performance, what criteria will be used, when it will be done, who will be involved in the process, and what method(s) will be employed.

Quality and Quantitative Measures

Methods used to measure performance will vary depending upon the type of industry or organization. Most methods have both **quality measures** and **quantitative measures** (e.g., productivity). For example, suppose you were a supervisor in a book binding factory and you measured performance only in terms of productivity. You rewarded an employee for producing a large number of books in a short period of time. However, when you examined the quality of the end product, you discovered that the employee sacrificed quality for quantity. The books produced had pages stuck together and the edges were uneven, thus setting the stage for customer complaints. So *quality* needs to be measured along with productivity.

Assessment Criteria

As you learned earlier, it is more effective to have **assessment criteria** that are based on standards related to outcomes and behavior, rather than on personal traits

performance measures
measures that determine how an employee's performance will be evaluated.

quality measures
measures of the level of excellence of a product or service.

quantitative measures
quantifiable results, such as productivity.

assessment criteria
the standards used to assess employee performance.

The previous section suggests that supervisors should include a quality component to the performance evaluation to measure both productivity as well as quality.

1. Do you agree or disagree with this recommendation? Explain.

_____

2. What are possible unintended consequences if a supervisor measures only productivity (quantity) without assessing quality?

_____

3. What would happen if the supervisor evaluates only quality without regard for productivity (quantity)?

_____

or characteristics. It is important to have performance evaluation criteria that are consistent with the organization's mission, values, goals, and quality measures. To be effective, the performance appraisal should assess both an individual's performance as well as his or her contributions to team, department, and organizational objectives.

Oftentimes, supervisors fail to discuss assessment criteria with employees. As a result, employees assume that they will be evaluated on the individual tasks they are assigned to complete. Employees are likely to respond with frustration during their evaluation if they do not understand the criteria being used to assess their performance. For example, a hospital nursing assistant thought her performance appraisal would include attendance, arriving on time, being properly dressed, and caring for patients. She had no idea that her performance appraisal would include several of the hospital's key indicators such as employee safety. Furthermore, she did not understand how these items could even be assessed. This is why it is necessary to clearly define performance measures and assessment criteria, and explain them to every employee from the beginning.

Let's use employee safety to illustrate this point in more detail. Many organizations have identified safety as a key performance measure. If an employee follows all of the safety regulations for his organization and he does not have any safety violations or injuries during the year, he earns the top score for that portion of the performance evaluation. Other companies choose to measure both individual and overall organizational performance for safety. Therefore, a portion of the employee's performance appraisal is based on his individual actions, including following the rules and experiencing no injuries. In addition, he is assessed on the overall safety performance for his team and the entire company. Critics would argue that this is unfair and that employees should be evaluated only for their personal safety record. However, proponents of this method believe that when everyone in the organization is focused on overall safety, the outcomes will be even better. There are two primary reasons why this logic works. One reason is that you remove the competitiveness factor. One person is more likely to reach out and help another person learn to adhere to the safety regulations in a more consistent manner. The second reason is that people become more observant and aware of their surroundings. If they notice something that could put a person in harm's way, they are more likely to stop and address it.

To go back to the nursing assistant example for a moment, consider the scenario where a patient walking the halls spilled a cup of water on the floor. If the employee was being measured only on her individual productivity, she may be tempted to call housekeeping and continue on with her patient care. However, if she knew that her assessment criteria included overall safety for all employees, patients, and visitors, she would be much more likely to either stop and clean up the spill or call housekeeping and place a warning for people to avoid the spill.

Scoring Methods

Once employees know what will be assessed, they need to know how it will be measured. Most scoring methods include two components. The first is the weighting of each performance measure and/or assessment. Typically, an organization will put the highest percentage of weight on the elements that are most important for that particular job function. For example, the nursing assistant would probably have the greatest weight or value placed on items related to patient care, with less weight placed on the overall hospital indicators. To be fair, most organizations place the most value on the items the employee has the most control over. Imagine the frustration of being held accountable for things you cannot control!

The second component to scoring is the actual scale used. Frequently, performance evaluations are perceived as subjective and judgmental. It is helpful to define as many objective scoring criteria as possible. Of course, it is almost impossible to avoid some level of subjective assessment. To develop scoring methods, begin by determining the scale you wish to use (see previous section for examples). Regardless of the scale you choose, it is essential that you define each step in your rating system. In addition, determine what, when, and how each item will be assessed. Ideally, employees can conduct their own regular self-assessments to know how they are progressing.

Frequency

Another variable to define is the frequency for measuring each performance indicator. This typically links back to one's performance goals. For example, a salesperson may have a goal to identify ten new prospective clients per week. Clearly, this would be measured weekly. Another goal may be to generate $50,000 in sales revenue per month. Again, it is quite obvious that this would be measured monthly. The individual may also have a goal to learn about new products being offered by the company. The time frame for measuring this is less apparent, as it depends upon how often new products are introduced. For example, this may occur once a year for an automobile dealership. In contrast, a technology firm such as a cell phone manufacturer may introduce new models every month. The frequency of appraisals will depend on the performance measures, goals, and assessment criteria. Although it is important to evaluate performance on a consistent schedule, it is also essential that you strike a balance. You do not want your employees spending more time recording performance than actually doing their jobs.

Who Conducts the Performance Appraisal?

self-evaluation
the process of employees rating their own performance and providing information to their supervisors as part of the performance appraisal process.

Who conducts the performance appraisal depends on the nature of the appraisal system. If a 360-degree evaluation is part of the performance appraisal, then the boss, peers, and subordinates are involved. Other organizations use a combination of **self-evaluation**,

Let employees know at the beginning of the year what to expect.

whereby employees rate their own performance and provide information to their supervisor (for example, see Figure 6.4), along with the supervisor's appraisal. Again, the key is to let employees know right from the start what to expect.

The "No Surprises" Approach to Performance Appraisals and Supervision

Although many of us like surprises in our personal lives involving events such as birthdays or anniversaries, we generally dislike surprises in the workplace. Once again, we are reminded of the importance of the organization's culture and values. By announcing a "No Surprises" philosophy, an organization indicates that open, honest communication in a timely manner is valued and expected. This requires employees to share bad news with their supervisor before it is discovered or brought to their attention by an angry customer. For example, if a hair stylist accidentally drips hair dye on a customer's outfit, it is important to address the mistake when it happens and promptly bring the incident to the supervisor's attention. This provides an opportunity to resolve the situation before the customer leaves the shop. Otherwise, the customer might go home and discover the stain and likely make an "ugly surprise" phone call to the supervisor. Clearly, keeping management informed is one half of the "No Surprises" corporate culture.

The other half of the equation is limiting the surprises that supervisors spring on employees. There will be times when changes occur quickly and employees will be caught off guard. This can lead to negative reactions or resistance. These reactions to surprises and unanticipated events can be avoided by adopting an open, shared communication practice. For example, performance appraisals in most companies are an annual event. They occur on the employee's employment anniversary date or according to a corporate schedule whereby everyone is evaluated at approximately the same time. During the new employee orientation, this information should be shared so employees know when to expect their appraisal. The worst thing you can do to one of your employees is to call him into your office unexpectedly, without fair notice or warning, to conduct his annual performance appraisal.

Employee Compensation and Rewards

All workers, including volunteers who donate their time to worthy causes, expect to be rewarded in some way for their contribution. **Rewards** may be defined broadly as the material and psychological payoffs for performing tasks in the workplace. Supervisors have found that job performance and satisfaction can be improved with properly administered rewards. Rewards today vary greatly in both type and scope, depending on one's employer and geographical location. In fact, a review of comments about the companies named in *Fortune* magazine's annual "100 Best Companies to Work For" list reveals dozens of creative reward programs. For example, OhioHealth, one of the largest healthcare organizations in Ohio, rewards employees for excellence in a wide variety of areas including attendance, customer service, and community service.[20]

rewards
material and psychological payoffs for working.

FIGURE 6.4 Sample Self-Evaluation Form

Name:	Division/Dept:
Job Title:	Evaluation period begin date:
Supervisor:	Evaluation period end date:

Employee signature:		Date:	

☐ Check here if you would like this Worksheet to be included in your Performance Evaluation and your personnel file.

Part I.   Job success factors:
Preparation of the performance evaluation is an interactive process where there is an exchange of information between you and your supervisor. Please provide your supervisor with information related to your performance in any of the job success factors.

Part II.   Goals:
Provide an assessment of your success in reaching the goals set at the beginning of the last evaluation period.

Parts III and IV. Next period's goals and development plan
Describe goals that you would like your supervisor to consider. Include training and other development activities that you believe are relevant to achieving these goals and important to your job performance.

Comments:
List any topics, issues, or problem areas that you wish to discuss with your supervisor during your review.

In this section, we review alternative employee compensation plans, distinguish between extrinsic and intrinsic rewards, and discuss the effective management of extrinsic rewards.

Employee Compensation Plans

Compensation deserves special attention because money is perceived by many as the universal motivator.[21] Moreover, since "labor costs are about two-thirds of total business expenses,"[22] compensation practices need to be effective and efficient. Employee compensation is a complex area fraught with legal and tax implications. Although an exhaustive treatment of employee compensation plans is beyond our present purpose, we can identify major types. Table 6.1 lists and briefly describes ten different pay plans. Two are nonincentive plans, seven qualify as incentive plans, and one plan is in a category of its own. Each type of pay plan has advantages and disadvantages. Therefore, there is no single best plan suitable for all employees. Indeed, two experts at the U.S. Bureau of Labor Statistics say the key words in compensation for the next 25 years will be *flexible and varied*.[23] A diverse workforce will demand an equally diverse array of compensation plans. One such nontraditional plan is a more radical approach that bases employee compensation on market value. In this plan, the company would evaluate what the employee could earn in a similar position with a competitor to decide what the employee is worth.[24]

> *Money is viewed by many as the universal motivator.*

Extrinsic Versus Intrinsic Rewards

There are two different categories of rewards. **Extrinsic rewards** are payoffs granted to the individual by other people. Examples include money, employee benefits, promotions, recognition, status symbols, and praise. The second category is called **intrinsic rewards**, which are self-granted and internally experienced payoffs. Among intrinsic rewards are a sense of accomplishment, self-esteem, and self-actualization.[25] Usually, on-the-job extrinsic and intrinsic rewards are intermingled. For instance, employees often experience a psychological boost when they complete a big project in addition to reaping material benefits.

Improving Performance with Extrinsic Rewards

Extrinsic rewards, if they are to motivate job performance effectively, need to be administered in ways that (1) satisfy active personal needs, (2) foster positive expectations, (3) ensure equitable distribution, and (4) reward results. Let us see how these four criteria can be met relative to the different pay plans in Table 6.1.

extrinsic rewards
payoffs, such as money, that are granted by others.

intrinsic rewards
self-granted and internally experienced payoffs, such as a feeling of accomplishment.

THEY SAID IT BEST

I think a paycheck buys you a baseline level of performance. But one thing that makes a good leader is the ability to offer people intrinsic rewards, the tremendous lift that comes from being aware of one's own talents and wanting to maximize them.

—ABRAHAM ZALEZNIK, Professor Emeritus of Leadership, Harvard Business School

Source: "All in a Day's Work," *Harvard Business Review 79*, special issue, *Breakthrough Leadership* (December 2001): 62.

TABLE 6.1
Guide to Employee Compensation Plans

Pay Plan	Description/Calculation	Main Advantage	Main Disadvantage
Nonincentive			
Hourly wage	Fixed amount per hour worked	Time is easier to measure than performance	Little or no incentive to work harder
Annual salary	Contractual amount per year	Easy to administer	Little or no incentive to work hard
Incentive			
Piece rate	Fixed amount per unit of output	Pay tied directly to personal output	Negative association with sweatshops and rate-cutting abuses
Sales commission	Fixed percentage of sales revenue	Pay tied directly to personal volume of business	Morale problem when sales personnel earn more than other employees, may discourage teamwork
Merit pay	Bonus and/or raise granted for outstanding performance	Gives salaried employees incentive to work harder	Fairness issue raised when tied to subjective appraisals
Profit sharing	Distribution of specified percentage of profits	Individual has a personal stake in firm's profitability	Profits affected by more than just performance (for example, prices and competition)
Gain sharing	Distribution of specified percentage of productivity gains and/or cost savings	Encourages employees to work harder *and* smarter	Calculations can get cumbersome
Pay-for-knowledge	Salary or wage rates tied to degrees earned or skills mastered	Encourages lifelong learning	Tends to inflate training and labor costs
Stock options	Selected employees earn right to acquire firm's stock free or at a discount	Gives individual a personal stake in the firm's financial performance	Can be resented by ineligible personnel; morale tied to stock price; regulators concerned about abuses among top executives
Other			
Cafeteria compensation (flexible benefit plans)	Employee selects personal mix of benefits from an array of options	Tailored benefits package fits individual needs	Can be costly to administer

REWARDS MUST SATISFY INDIVIDUAL NEEDS

Whether it is a pay raise or a pat on the back, a reward has no motivational impact unless it satisfies an active need. Not all people need the same things, and one person may need different things at different times. Money is a powerful motivator for those who seek security through material wealth. But the promise of more money may mean little to a financially secure person who seeks ego gratification from challenging work. As the cost of health care continues to increase, some individuals value paid insurance benefits more than vacation days. In contrast, employees who feel good about their benefits may desire more time off to be with their families. People's needs also vary concerning when and how they want to be paid.

Because cafeteria compensation is rather special and particularly promising, we will examine it more closely. **Cafeteria compensation** (also called *flexible benefits*) is a plan that allows each employee to determine the makeup of his or her benefit package.[26] Because today's nonwage benefits are a significant portion of total compensation, the motivating potential of such a wide range of options can be sizable. It is common to provide employees with an annual statement that outlines the employer's cost for each benefit and the employee's share. Providing employees with the knowledge of how much these items cost the company leads to greater perceived value and appreciation.

Although some organizations have resisted installing cafeteria compensation because of the added administrative expense, the number of programs in effect in the United States has steadily grown. One of the potential reasons for this rise is the positive impact on employee satisfaction.[27] In addition, cafeteria compensation represents a revolutionary step toward fitting rewards to people, rather than offering the same standard plan to everyone regardless of their needs or wants.

EMPLOYEES MUST BELIEVE EFFORT WILL LEAD TO REWARD

According to the expectancy theory, which you will learn more about in subsequent chapters, an employee will not strive for an attractive reward unless it is perceived as being attainable. For example, the promise of an expenses-paid trip to Hawaii for the leading salesperson will prompt additional efforts at sales only among those who believe they have a reasonable chance of winning. Those who believe they have little chance of winning will not be motivated to try any harder than usual. Incentive pay plans, especially merit pay, profit sharing, gain sharing, and stock options, need to be designed and communicated in a way that will foster believable effort–reward linkages.[28] In addition to being attainable, rewards need to be designed to support personal and organizational goals. This includes the use of team rewards, discussed in more detail in the "Team Versus Individualized Rewards" section.

REWARDS MUST BE EQUITABLE

Something is **equitable** if people perceive it to be fair and just. Each of us carries in our head a pair of scales upon which we weigh equity.[29] Figure 6.5 shows one scale for *personal* equity and another for *social* equity. The personal equity scale tests the relationship between effort expended and rewards received. In contrast, the social equity scale compares our own effort–reward ratio with that of someone else in the same situation. We are motivated to seek personal and social equity and to avoid

cafeteria compensation
a plan that allows employees to select their own mix of benefits.

equitable
perceived to be fair.

FIGURE 6.5 Personal and social equity

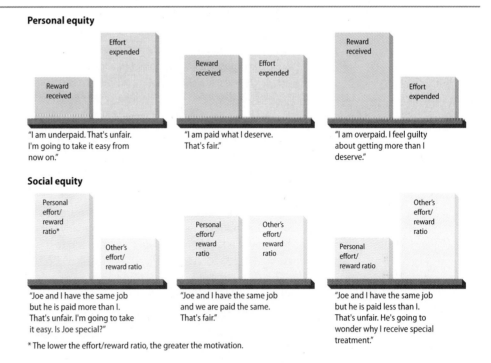

Personal equity

"I am underpaid. That's unfair. I'm going to take it easy from now on."

"I am paid what I deserve. That's fair."

"I am overpaid. I feel guilty about getting more than I deserve."

Social equity

"Joe and I have the same job but he is paid more than I. That's unfair. I'm going to take it easy. Is Joe special?"

"Joe and I have the same job and we are paid the same. That's fair."

"Joe and I have the same job but he is paid less than I. That's unfair. He's going to wonder why I receive special treatment."

* The lower the effort/reward ratio, the greater the motivation.

inequity.[30] Interestingly, research on this topic has demonstrated that inequity is perceived by those who are *overpaid* as well as by those who are underpaid.[31]

Since perceived inequity is associated with feelings of dissatisfaction, anger, and jealousy or guilt, inequitable reward schemes tend to be counterproductive and are ethically questionable. Record-setting executive pay in recent years has been loudly criticized as inequitable, particularly when viewed in combination with pay cuts to lower-level employees and/or pay increases that do not keep pace with the increased cost of living.[32] For example, consider this lopsided situation:

> Biogen Idec Inc. of Cambridge, MA will award 200 top executives nearly 1.2 million shares of stock. The total award is worth about $48 million, or an average of about $241,000 for each of the 200 participants. The restricted-stock plan was disclosed . . . just days after Biogen Idec said it would lay off 650 employees, or about 17 percent of its workforce.[33]

In stark contrast is the CEO of Xilinx, a semiconductor company in San Jose, California, who took a 20% pay cut to help maintain the firm's no-layoff policy during an industry downturn.[34] From a motivational standpoint, which company would you prefer as your employer?

L.M. Baker, Jr., former chairman of Wachovia, the Charlotte, North Carolina–based bank, summed up the motivational importance of reward equity when he said this:

> Most people think motivating people is about pushing others to do what you want them to do, but I've found that the secret to motivating others has really been to adhere to simple values, things like honesty, fairness, and generosity.[35]

Consider the following story from the airline industry, then answer the questions that follow.

Something funny is happening in the aviation industry: Airlines are making money again. But while that's good news for shareholders, it's infuriating pilots and other employees who took pay cuts in the wake of 9/11. Nowhere are pilots as peeved as they are at American, where the airline's 12,000-member Allied Pilots Association has declared war on management.

The pilots' chief complaint: Four years after they voluntarily gave up 23% of their pay along with other concessions to help stave off bankruptcy, top executives of American and parent AMR Corp. have received about a quarter-billion dollars in AMR stock, while employees got only small pay increases. With American poised to have one of its best years ever, its pilots say they just want to make the same as they did in 1992, adjusted for inflation.

1. One of American Airline's executives made this statement about the pilots' complaints: "Our strategic decisions kept the company out of bankruptcy and we deserve to be rewarded for it." How would you respond to this statement?

2. From an employee motivation standpoint, what role does reward equity play in this situation?

Source: Barney Gimbel, "Anger at 30,000 Feet," *Fortune*, December 10, 2007, 32.

LINKING REWARDS TO PERFORMANCE

Ideally, there should be an *if-then* relationship between task performance and extrinsic rewards. Traditional hourly wage and annual salary pay plans are weak in this regard. They do little more than reward the person for showing up at work. Supervisors can strengthen their employees' motivation to work by making sure that those who give a little extra, get a little extra. In addition, piece-rate, sales-commission plans, merit pay, profit sharing, gain sharing, and stock option plans are popular ways of linking pay and performance.[36] The reward should be valued by the employee and in line with the complexity of the project or job.[37]

All incentive pay plans should be carefully conceived because undesirable behavior may inadvertently be encouraged. Consider, for example, what the head of Nucor Corporation, a successful mini-mill steel company, had to say about his firm's bonus system:

> Nucor's bonus system . . . is very tough. If you're late even five minutes, you lose your bonus for the day. If you're late more than 30 minutes, or you're absent because of sickness or anything else, you lose your bonus for the week. Now, we do have what we call four "forgiveness" days during the year when you can be sick or you have to close on a house or your wife is having a baby. But only four. We have a melter, Phil Johnson, down in Darlington, and one of the workers came in one day and said that Phil had been in an automobile accident and was sitting beside his car off of Route 52, holding his head. So the foreman asked, "Why didn't you stop and help him?" and the guy said, "And lose my bonus?"[38]

upervisors need to make sure goals and incentives point people in the right direction.

Like goals, incentive plans may have unintended consequences like this example, where an employee was focused on his bonus and as a result chose not to assist a possibly injured coworker.[39] Consequently, supervisors need to make sure goals and incentives point people in the right direction.

Team-Based Versus Individualized Rewards

The reality is, employees *expect* to receive a pay raise every year. In most instances, a few percentage points cover cost of living increases and a few more percentage points send a message that the employee has done a good job. However, the impact of the annual raise lasts only for the first few paychecks. Thus, the challenge is to keep your employees motivated and reward them during the rest of the year, while at the same time increasing overall performance and results for your entire team.

Team Rewards

When employers choose to reward an entire team for goal attainment and success, they are specifically recognizing the group rather than each individual. The concept of **team rewards**, whereby organizations implement team-based incentive pay as a way of rewarding teamwork and cooperation, has been slow to take hold in the United States. This is primarily for two reasons: (1) it goes against the grain of an individualistic culture and (2) poorly conceived and administered plans have given team-based pay a bad reputation.[40] As a result, there are few examples and limited employee confidence in team-based rewards.

Supervisors can work with their teams to define measurable goals and objectives. These ultimately become the basis for the team's performance measures. Ideally, a team can agree on rewards that are both appropriate and meaningful. This is not always easy because individuals are motivated by different things, thus making agreement about team rewards difficult. This process may require supervisory guidance. In fact, you may choose to prepare a list ahead of time and let each employee vote on his or her top three. As we have mentioned previously, the reward should be in line with the importance and complexity of the objective or project. For example, an accounting firm set a team goal to reduce the number of extensions it had to file on behalf of its income-tax clients by 10%. To achieve this goal, employees were required to place additional follow-up phone calls, take messages, and research client information for one another, and work extra hours prior to the tax filing deadline of April 15. If they met the goal, employees were allowed to choose from a variety of rewards, including:

- an extra paid day off
- a trip to the local amusement park for everyone and their families
- an afternoon for all of the employees to go to a day spa for massages
- a catered luncheon

team rewards
rewards given to a group of employees to recognize team-based goal attainment.

Individualized Rewards ... Beyond the Annual Pay Raise

Unlike team rewards, **individualized rewards** are typically unique and of significant value to the employee. However, like other reward systems, the payoff should be in line with the achievement. You would not want to send an employee on an all-expenses-paid vacation for achieving his first month's sales goal. If he exceeds the sales goal by 20% for the entire year, then you may choose a reward of that magnitude. At the same time, giving him a company coffee mug could be a real letdown. The best approach is to ask your employees what they value the most. Find out what is meaningful to each individual. The reward will vary depending upon the person and the project. See Figure 6.6 for a few examples of rewards that supervisors have used in the workplace.

The key is to discover what is of greatest value to each employee.

As you can see, the possibilities are limited only by management's imagination. Some have no cost associated with them, while others can be costly. The key is to discover what is of greatest value to each employee. Do not assume that what excites you is going to be a great reward for everyone.

How supervisors use rewards also makes a difference. They want employees to know that their exceptional efforts and achievements are being recognized. If supervisors give out too many rewards for minimal effort, they could end up creating an environment of entitlement where employees always expect something extra. Therefore, it is important to be thoughtful and strategic with the distribution of rewards. Sometimes, you may choose to identify the "if-then" relationship ahead of time. For example, *if* the employee is successful in achieving a major training milestone, *then* there is a specific reward. However, it is also very effective to surprise an employee with an unexpected reward if she or he goes above and beyond. These spontaneous types of rewards, if done publicly, can have the added benefit of inspiring other employees.

Whatever you choose to do to recognize and reward your employees, make it meaningful to the individual and appropriate for the achievement.

FIGURE 6.6 Rewarding your employees

Rewarding Your Employees

Examples of rewards you may want to consider offering to employees:

1. RECOGNITION—This item is in all caps to place emphasis on one of the greatest rewards available to supervisors ... and it does not cost a penny. Give credit and recognition OFTEN and in PUBLIC! In addition, ask your boss to send a personal note specifically recognizing the achievement. This lets the employee know that you are giving him credit and it also lets him know that he is valued by upper management.

2. RESPONSIBILITY—Yes, you read that right! Many employees are looking to advance, and an excellent reward is trusting them to take on more visible assignments or greater responsibility. In addition, most employees want work that is challenging and rewarding.

3. FLEXIBILITY—Allow the employee to have an alternative work schedule, taking advantage of flex-time options such as four 10-hour days or letting her telecommute—perhaps working from home one day a week.

4. TRAINING—This may be achieved by offering to pay for a class at a local college, allowing the employee to attend a seminar or conference, or implementing a cross-training situation with another employee.

Other tangible rewards include:

- A gift card to a favorite restaurant or store.
- Paying for a gym membership for a year.
- A technology tool that will improve work efficiency, such as a Blackberry or iPhone.
- An afternoon off to go shopping around the holidays.

individualized rewards
rewards given to individuals to recognize goal attainment unique to the employee.

KNOWLEDGE TO ACTION

Consider the following quotes from a recent article on work/life balance, then answer the questions that follow.

Employees are looking for more than a paycheck in today's competitive work environment.

Striking a balance between work and family life is a top priority, according to a recent survey....

It indicated that more than half of respondents cited flexibility as "very important" to overall job satisfaction.

If you want to keep some of your most valuable players, it may be time to consider instituting family-friendly policies such as flex-time and telecommuting, human-resources experts say.

1. How do you plan to achieve work/life balance in your career?
   _____

2. Which is more important to you, more pay or more leisure time? Explain.
   _____

3. From a supervisor's perspective, what are the pros and cons of flex-time and telecommuting?
   _____

Source: Jamie Herzlich, "Work/Life Balance Tops List," *Arizona Republic*, January 6, 2008, EC1.

This supervisor knows how important it is to recognize his employee's success in front of her peers. This type of public recognition for individual achievement can be a wonderful way to reward the person. It also can serve as a powerful motivator for other team members. Of course, care needs to taken not to embarrass those who are very shy or from cultures where public displays are unwelcome.
© Jon Feingersh/Getty Images/Blend Images

SUMMARY

1. There are a wide variety of performance appraisal methods used to evaluate job performance as a basis for personnel decisions. These methods include (1) goal-setting framework, (2) written essays, (3) critical incidents, (4) graphic rating scales, (5) weighted checklists, (6) rankings and comparisons, (7) multirater appraisals such as the 360-degree review, and (8) continuous improvement review. Many organizations use a combination of these methods as well as computer software to streamline the process.

2. To be legally defensible, performance appraisal systems should satisfy the following criteria: (1) a job analysis was used to develop the performance appraisal system; (2) the appraisal system was behavior-oriented, not trait-oriented; (3) performance evaluators followed specific written instructions when conducting appraisals; and (4) evaluators reviewed the results of the appraisals with the employees being evaluated. Supervisors should document the performance appraisal and any related data such as attendance, productivity, and evidence of superior or inferior work. Individual performance appraisals are a private matter between the supervisor and the employee; therefore, all records and conversations should be kept confidential.

3. Ideally, performance appraisals are a tool to improve productivity, quality, and organizational outcomes. Variables to consider when designing your performance appraisal system include goals, measures, assessment criteria, scoring method, weighting factors for each component, frequency, who conducts the appraisal, an agreed-upon method for modifying variables, and how the appraisal links to rewards and compensation. As you work through the process of defining each of these variables, it is essential that you seek input and feedback from your employees, all levels of management, and your customers.

4. Methods used to measure performance will vary depending upon the type of industry or organization. Most methods have both quality measures (the level of excellence of a product or service) and quantitative measures (the ability to determine an amount such as production). Assessment criteria should be based on outcomes and behavior rather than personal traits or characteristics. Performance evaluation criteria should be consistent with the organization's mission, values, goals, and quality measures.

5. A "No Surprises" philosophy within a company indicates that open, honest communication in a timely manner is valued and expected. One of the worst things you can do to employees is to call them into your office unexpectedly, without notice or warning, to conduct their annual performance appraisal. Instead, let employees know ahead of time when the appraisal will occur. During new-employee orientation, this information should be shared so employees know when to expect their appraisal and what will be evaluated.

6. A diverse workforce will demand an equally diverse array of compensation plans, which may include one or more of the following: (1) hourly wages, (2) contractual salaries, (3) piece rate, (4) sales commission, (5) merit pay, (6) profit sharing, (7) gain sharing, (8) pay-for-knowledge, and (9) stock options. There are two different categories of rewards. Extrinsic rewards are granted by others and include everything from praise to payoffs, such as money. The second category is called intrinsic rewards, which are self-granted and internally experienced payoffs, such as a feeling of accomplishment. If they are to motivate job performance effectively, extrinsic rewards need to be administered in ways that (1) satisfy personal needs, (2) foster positive expectations, (3) ensure equitable distribution, and (4) reward results.

7. Team and individualized rewards should be in line with the importance and complexity of the objective. The possibilities for tangible and intangible rewards for both teams and individuals are endless. Some have no cost associated with them, while others can be quite expensive. The key is to discover what is of greatest value to your employees. Do not assume that what excites you is going to be a great reward for everyone. How you use rewards also makes a difference. While employees should be rewarded for exceptional efforts, too many rewards for minimal effort reduces the value of the recognition. Spontaneous and unexpected rewards, if done publicly, have the added benefit of inspiring other employees.

TERMS TO UNDERSTAND

360-degree review, p. 154
assessment criteria, p. 159
behaviorally anchored rates scales
(BARS), p. 153
cafeteria compensation, p. 166
confidentiality, p. 157

continuous improvement review
(CIR), p. 154
equitable, p. 166
extrinsic rewards, p. 164
individualized rewards, p. 170
intrinsic rewards, p. 164

performance measures, p. 159
quality measures, p. 159
quantitative measures, p. 159
rewards, p. 162
self-evaluation, p. 161
team rewards, p. 169

QUESTIONS FOR REFLECTION

1. Describe a formal method for assessing job performance and explain why this is a necessary part of a supervisor's responsibilities.

2. List four criteria that should be satisfied for your performance appraisal system to be legally defensible.

3. In this chapter, you learned about several performance appraisal methods. Which of these do you think is best? Explain your answer.

4. Many employees and supervisors have a negative perception of performance appraisals. What suggestions do you have for making this important process a positive, motivational experience?

5. Explain the difference between quality measures and quantitative measures. Provide an example of each.

6. Should performance appraisals be linked to compensation? Explain why or why not.

HANDS-ON ACTIVITIES

REWARDS THAT WORK!

Brainstorm with your classmates to develop a list of additional rewards that have not been mentioned already in the chapter.

1. Identify three rewards that are relatively easy for supervisors to distribute and that have little or no financial cost to the organization.

2. Identify three major rewards that supervisors would distribute on a limited basis because they are likely to cost the company in terms of time and/or money.

3. Submit an example of a performance appraisal software application and explain why it would be helpful to a supervisor.

PERFORMANCE APPRAISAL EXAMPLES

Organizations use a wide variety of performance appraisal forms, methods, and software applications. Conduct a brief research project to identify a few that you think are effective.

1. Submit examples of three performance appraisal systems, including associated procedures and forms.

2. Select one of these and explain why you think it is an effective tool.

3. Identify three rewards that supervisors can use to recognize an entire team for its achievement.

Interview an Expert

The purpose of this exercise is to learn from an expert the best practices he/she has developed for appraising and rewarding employees. Identify a supervisor or manager who works for a company that has a formal performance appraisal system in place. Your goal is to learn from this person's experience. You may use the questions listed below and/or develop your own. After your interview, prepare a brief summary of the conversation and list their performance-appraisal and reward-system best practices.

Questions

1. Please describe how you developed your performance appraisal system.
2. What are some examples of assessment criteria that you use?
3. What quantitative performance measures do you use?
4. What quality measures do you use?
5. How are customers involved in the appraisal process?
6. How are employees involved in their performance appraisal?
7. Is compensation linked to performance appraisals? If yes, please explain the connection.
8. What are some of the most effective rewards you have used with individuals? Please explain the situation and how you used it as a motivational tool.
9. What are some of the most effective rewards you have used with teams? Please explain the situation and how you used it as a motivational tool.
10. Do you have any virtual employees? If yes, how do you conduct their performance appraisal?

You may improvise and add or edit questions to fit the situation or the circumstances of your interview. Schedule your interview ahead of time and try to limit it to about 15 minutes. Remember to send a thank-you note to the person you interview.

YOU DECIDE

CASE STUDY 6.1

Evaluating and Rewarding Performance

Margaret is one of the shift supervisors for Clear Lake Boats, Inc. She has been with the company since it started manufacturing boats over ten years ago. Margaret was one of the original designers and also worked on the production line until last year, when she was promoted to supervisor. The company started out small, with only twelve employees and one shift working Monday to Friday from 8:30 A.M. to 5:00 P.M. Clear Lake Boats now has over three hundred employees and runs three shifts a day. Every employee on each shift gets paid the same except for the supervisors, who are paid two dollars more per hour. The night-shift employees get paid a dollar more per hour. There is no performance appraisal system or reward structure in place.

After Margaret was promoted, she asked to take a Principles of Supervision class at the local community college to learn proper supervisory skills and coaching techniques. One of the topics discussed in her class was performance appraisals and reward systems. Although her company has grown quickly and has been very successful, she has noticed a decline in employee morale. Production numbers are also down. Margaret thinks that the lack of a formal performance appraisal system and the standardized pay structure may be part of the problem.

She has been with the company for a long time and she is very fond of the owners, so she does not want to offend them; however, she does want to make a difference and contribute to the company's long-term success.

Questions

1. If you were Margaret, what recommendations would you make to the owners regarding performance appraisals?

2. What recommendations would you make regarding employee compensation?

3. What recommendations would you make regarding recognition and reward systems?

4. What approach would you suggest for implementing your recommendations so that both the employees and the owners support the new performance appraisal system, compensation plan, and reward program?

SUPERVISOR'S TOOLKIT

Select a job/position of your choice to create a performance appraisal system. The system you create should include the following:

1. A procedure document that outlines what will be assessed, what criteria will be used to measure performance (remember quality and quantitative measures), and when and how the evaluation will be conducted.

2. An appraisal form that will be used.

3. The assessment criteria that explain how each measure correlates to level of performance so it is clear how the employee and supervisor will grade or score job performance.

CHAPTER 7

Training: Begin with the End in Mind

Learning Objectives

1. Explain why it is important to initiate a training program.

2. Specify common reasons why companies train.

3. Identify and briefly explain the ingredients of a good training program and the four steps in skill-based and factual training.

4. Describe various training methods.

5. Discuss techniques to reinforce learning.

6. Describe personal variables that impact training.

Straight Talk from the Field

Justin Jones-Fosu is the founder and President/CEO of JS Training Solutions, LLC, in Baltimore, Maryland.

QUESTION . . . *How do you keep a diverse group of individuals engaged and interested in learning during one of your training sessions?*

RESPONSE . . .

There are thousands of training classes occurring around the world every day and a majority of the participants are bored out of their minds. The problem: mundane PowerPoint presentations, monotone presenters, and lecturers who do nothing but . . . well . . . lecture. The participants are sincerely seeking to find knowledge nuggets of gold in a mine of commonplace stuff. This does not have to be the case!

All of my training sessions begin with this question: "Has anyone ever been to a boring presentation?" Immediately, almost all of the hands are raised. People are more than excited to vocalize their experiences with what made past presentations boring, along with what they think could have been improved. I take mental notes of the responses and I vow to the participants that this will not be like the usual training session. What most participants do not realize is that they have already been engaged into a process that continues as long as I or the presenter/facilitator allows it to. This initiates the process of knowledge discovery.

While presenting at a conference of professionals, ages 24 to 58, I generated a dialogue about vision and how it is important for their development, growth, and ultimate life fulfillment. Most of the people were captivated and I thought everything was going well, until I noticed a group of people who were not as interested in the presentation as others. What I had unconsciously done was ignore this uninterested group and focused on the people who were giving me enthusiastic head nods and actively participating. I feared ultimately losing control of the whole group. A quick choice had to be made: (a) continue on with the training and leave the uninterested people behind or (b) make an attempt to inspire and engage this small subgroup and bring them along for the ride. I chose option b.

So I went over to the subgroup and I started a discussion, asking a member of that group questions about her experiences. I included her in an activity, and suddenly everyone in the subgroup was involved. They were asking questions, participating in discussions, and most importantly they were learning! I realized at that moment that in everyday life we make the choice to either tell people what to do, or actively engage them in the discovery process. It is commonly known that people learn from and act more upon things they discover, rather than learning from what they are being told is important.

This simple lesson has led me to search within myself and ask, "Am I this way in real life? Do I give people fish, or do I teach them how to fish? As I lead others, am I just telling them what to do, or am I creating an atmosphere of discovery through involvement, role-plays, and practice?" Effective training for me has been teaching people how to fish, so to speak, and having them demonstrate how they might do it differently.

Consequently, engaging training is not simply a lecture, but an experience of knowledge discovery. Knowledge discovery opens up the portals of people's minds. It allows them to peer into and assess their situations. It aids them in creating solutions and/or learning future action steps—so that they might do things differently, create useful knowledge, and become a better employee and, hopefully, a better person.

I've learned that participants are desperately seeking this unique experience through their different learning styles. Some desire quotes, while others would like to learn through action. Some want to ponder more about their own lives and conduct introspective assessments, while still others want to see the vibrancy of a passionate PowerPoint presentation. I make a valiant effort to give them an experience with a mixture of it all. After all, just like in supervising, you should not treat every person the same, because each person has her or his own process of knowledge discovery. If there is good facilitation and participants truly desire to learn, they can gather their own knowledge nuggets. Those treasures will last longer than a boring lecture!

Chapter Outline

One of the primary roles of a supervisor is to assess employee training needs and make arrangements to meet those needs. Much of this effort focuses on the newly hired. Regardless of how carefully job applicants are screened and selected, typically a gap remains between what employees *actually* know and what they *should* know. Consequently, one of the leading reasons why organizations conduct training is to fill new employees' knowledge gaps. Training methods vary widely, depending upon the circumstances. In this chapter, we will introduce several training techniques. We will also examine the characteristics of a multigenerational workforce, including various learning styles and their impact on corporate training. Keep in mind that supervisors also spend time with their employees informally training, coaching, and mentoring.

It is important to note that in many large organizations, the human resources department typically partners with supervisors to coordinate formal training. However, in smaller organizations, the immediate supervisor has responsibility for assessing training needs, setting training goals, identifying training methods, and conducting the actual training.

The Need for Training

Most organizations offer some form of employee training, either in a formal program or informally on-the-job, or a combination of both. Frequently, companies attempt to balance the needs of the organization with the employee's personal goals. According to a report published by the American Society for Training and Development, supervisors and training professionals should "encourage employees at all levels to take personal ownership of their professional development."[1] Nonetheless, it is a supervisor's responsibility to guide and assist employees in achieving professional development goals.[2]

In 2006, companies spent more than $56 billion on training, according to the *Corporate Learning Factbook*.[3] Huge as this number sounds, it still is not nearly enough. How the money was spent is also a problem. Most of it was spent by big companies training already well-educated managers and professionals.[4]

The Plight of Small to Medium-Sized Enterprises (SMEs)

A significant training shortfall exists for companies with fewer than one hundred employees, frequently classified as small to medium-sized businesses (SMEs). The training picture for SMEs is cloudy due to a lack of data on informal training, as opposed to formal employee training initiatives.[5] The importance of training in SMEs was underscored in a recent research study published in the *Journal of Small Business Management*:

> The perceived importance of training to improvements in productivity, sustained competitive advantage, and ultimately to firm performance has led governments in various countries to invest considerable resources into programs that encourage management and employee training in small to medium-sized enterprises (SMEs).[6]

Most organizations believe that training contributes to increased employee productivity.

It is clear from this report that most organizations believe that training contributes to increased employee productivity and ultimately to their competitive advantage. However, the report goes on to state that although there is perceived importance, there is a lack of commitment or execution:

> Despite the perceived importance of training to improved SME performance, there is a general reluctance among SMEs to provide formal training. Employee training in SMEs is often described as informal, unplanned, reactive, and short-term oriented. Training in SME's is mostly on-the-job with little or no provision for employee development.[7]

Literacy and Basic Skills Training

In addition to the lack of formal training and professional development in SMEs, there is also a significant need for basic skills training in all organizations: large and small, public and private, for profit and nonprofit. This is because we live in a fast-paced, knowledge-driven nation, where our workforce needs to be able to read and assimilate information to continue to meet the demands of employers.[8] The U.S. federal government defines **literacy** as "an individual's ability to read, write, speak the language, compute and solve problems at levels of proficiency necessary to function on the job, in the family of the individual, and in society."[9]

literacy
the ability to read, write, speak the language, and compute/solve problems at a functional level.

Approximately 15% of the adult population living in the United States have no basic literacy skills, and roughly 30% have low basic literacy skills, according to *The National Assessment of Adult Literacy*, a study published by the federal government.[10] As you can see in Figure 7.1, this represents 93 million people—or close to half of

FIGURE 7.1 Percentage of adult literacy in the U.S.

- No basic literacy skills
- Low basic literacy skills
- Good literacy skills

the adult population in America—who lack the literacy skills, including fundamental communication skills, needed to function effectively in the workforce. As a result, many supervisors are faced with the challenge of training employees who have a difficult time reading, writing, and performing basic numerical calculations. It is essential, therefore, that supervisors use a variety of tools in training their employees. For example, employees who cannot read will require more emphasis on demonstrations, verbal explanations, and the use of symbols. Consider the following situation:

> At City Fresh Foods, CEO Glynn Lloyd likes to hire from the neighborhood. And because the 12-year-old food-service company is headquartered in Boston's polyglot [multilingual] Dorchester neighborhood, Lloyd's payroll resembles a mini-United Nations. Some 70 percent of his 65 employees are immigrants, from places like Trinidad, Brazil, Nigeria, the Dominican Republic, and Cape Verde, off the West Coast of Africa. They speak half a dozen languages, not to mention the myriad cultural differences. . . .
>
> The highest hurdle, of course, has been communication. Lloyd tried overcoming it by providing about 40 hours of ESL [English as a second language] classes to his workers so that all 65 of them would use English. But that bar seemed too high, so Lloyd has lowered it. Instead, he requires his employees to learn the more limited language of City Fresh Foods—terms like "delivery ticket," "checkout sheet," and "ice packs."[11]

In addition to offering literacy training programs on-site, companies can turn to educational institutions such as local community colleges. Remedial education and basic skills training for personnel are good for both the employer and the employee.

Begin with the End in Mind: Why Companies Train

Training is the process of teaching employees new skills or knowledge and changing employee behavior and/or attitudes through some type of guided experience. Keep in mind that the object of training is *learning*. Learning requires thoughtful preparation, carefully guided exposure to new ideas or behaviors, and motivational support.[12]

*The object of training is **learning**.*

Although training needs and approaches vary, supervisors can get the most out of their training budgets by following a few guidelines. Before we discuss these guidelines in detail, it is important to understand the common thread that weaves all of these elements together. This is the notion that everything about the training program needs to relate to the desired outcome: *What new knowledge, skill, or behavior is expected as the end result of this learning experience?*

This is like baking a peach pie, with the desired outcome being a delicious pie. Steps to achieve this outcome include selecting ripe peaches, peeling and preparing them properly, making the dough to be used in the crust (including measuring and mixing all the ingredients properly), combining the ingredients in a visually pleasing manner, and then baking for the proper length of time at the correct temperature.

Creating an effective training program requires a similar balance of planning the whole process, mixing the elements correctly, and achieving the desired outcomes. An effective training program includes constant reminders of the desired outcomes. That's why this chapter and section are titled "Begin with the End in Mind."

training
the process of teaching new skills or knowledge and changing behavior/attitudes through guided experience.

Why Companies Train

Shhh! Serious teaching and learning in progress. This supervisor is providing her trainees with a highly effective learning environment that combines personal instruction with hands-on learning and immediate feedback.
© Davis Barber/PhotoEdit

Among the many reasons why companies train employees are everything from legal compliance to customer satisfaction. In addition to new employee training and orientation, companies also rely on training to launch new products or services and introduce new technology. Training is needed for introducing changes to policies and/or procedures, cross-training, and general staff development.

Employee retention is another key reason why organizations train. One of the most effective ways to reduce employee turnover is to allow and, in most cases, pay for employees to attend professional training and development courses. Such training, including leadership/management development programs for supervisors and managers, may be in-house or in other venues.

A common thread in all of this is a desire to help employees develop new skills, improve existing capabilities, or acquire new knowledge—a win-win situation for the individual and the organization. Companies focused on performance management systematically link strategy and organizational goals with individual performance. As a result, these organizations implement training programs as part of their companywide strategy for excellence.

Aetna is a good example:

> In the last several years, Aetna has implemented a corporate-wide business process that integrates corporate goal setting, operational goals, individual performance plans, and learning. This process . . . ties learning programs directly back to these corporate goals through the Performance Management process.[13]

In other words, companies will prepare a training plan that emphasizes learning that, in turn, supports the organization's goals. One of the challenges with this approach is balancing the needs and expectations of the employer with the developmental interests of the employee.[14] Common reasons why companies train employees are described in this section. They include (1) new employee orientation, (2) performance improvement, (3) implementing change, (4) new technology, (5) company/product knowledge, (6) cross-training, (7) legal compliance and discouraging sexual harassment, (8) safety, and (9) general team building.[15]

NEW EMPLOYEE ORIENTATION

As we discussed in Chapter 5, new employee orientation training provides the new hires with the opportunity to learn about their new company and acquire job-specific skills. This is typically a combination of skill development and factual learning. New employee orientations are necessary to get newcomers on a productive track as soon as possible.

PERFORMANCE IMPROVEMENT

Companies such as Trostel Whitewater Molding, based in Whitewater, Wisconsin, are committed to continuous improvement and innovation. They have been recognized for their excellence at work and are repeat winners of the prestigious Wisconsin Forward Award.[16] Trostel's vision includes the following:

> Our growth will be stimulated by quality, productivity, technological and innovative excellence and will provide opportunities and personal development for our employees.[17]

In other words, Trostel's vision includes a commitment to its employees to have access to education and training opportunities for personal development. Organizations such as Trostel that are focused on performance improvement invest in training for their employees' personal development and to improve their skills for better job performance. This type of training is frequently planned as a result of, or as an integral part of, the employee's performance appraisal process. No one is perfect or superhuman; therefore, everyone has room for improvement. This may include learning new techniques and/ or learning how to perform existing tasks more efficiently. In addition, there may be quality reasons for performance improvement training.

For example, an international hotel chain has a large department dedicated to telephone customer service and reservations. After conducting a satisfaction survey, the hotel learned that callers were frequently not satisfied with their reservation experience. One of the issues cited was unmet expectations. Specifically, customers were told that they would receive a confirmation e-mail; in fact, fewer than half of the customers surveyed actually received one. The company did some research and determined that one of the sources of the problem was insufficient training about the reservation system software. The employees were not purposely skipping a task; in fact, they assumed that the e-mails were being sent. Further investigation revealed that employees learned the system informally from other employees, faulty information and all. This example reinforces the need for formal, structured training programs with measurable outcomes.

IMPLEMENTING CHANGE

Organizations also need a companywide training approach when implementing major changes. This approach may be used for big changes such as expansion, downsizing, sale of the company or division, merger, or acquisition. It is also frequently used to educate employees about changes to company policies and procedures. In addition, some organizations use this approach in problem solving and decision making that ultimately leads to change.

We often hear that older employees are less comfortable with change than their younger coworkers. However, a report by the Center for Creative Leadership, a nonprofit, educational institution based in Greensboro, North Carolina, indicates that, "people from all generations are uncomfortable with change."[18] This conclusion reinforces the need for a planned, companywide training strategy for implementing change.

NEW TECHNOLOGY

As a sign of the times, one of the most common reasons for employee training today is to implement new technology. New technologies can range from Web-based software applications for financial managers to digital imaging machines in hospitals. Staying current with hardware and software advances and other new technologies requires an ongoing commitment to training.

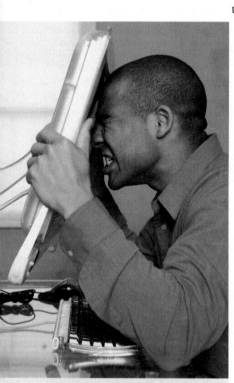

Change is not always easy! Whether the organization is implementing new technology tools or a new product, employees can become frustrated with the learning process. Effective supervisors anticipate and prepare for challenges associated with implementing change. Providing sufficient training and a supportive environment for learning are two keys to success.

© Photodisc/Getty Images

COMPANY/PRODUCT KNOWLEDGE

Successful companies tend to develop new products and/or services and continue to improve their core offerings. Companywide training initiatives that introduce employees to new or improved products and services are foundation stones of success. Such training can cover product use, benefits, profiles of the typical buyer, and how the product will be sold, shipped, and serviced.

CROSS-TRAINING

Many organizations, particularly small to medium-sized businesses, have just one or two individuals who are properly trained to perform certain functions or tasks. Organizations invest in cross-training to provide opportunities for employees to grow and also to avoid workflow interruptions if someone is absent. **Cross-training** is the process of learning a new skill or task that is typically the responsibility of a coworker.

For instance, there is a candy factory specializing in dark chocolate candies embossed with customers' logos. Only one person knows how to create and apply corporate logos to the chocolates. These specialized visual images are prepared with computer technology and printed using an all-natural cocoa butter application. The edible logos are applied when the chocolates are at a precise temperature. Although this company has only twelve employees, and its training budget is very small, it should invest in cross-training. At least one or two additional people need to learn the logo application technique so production does not shut down in the event of illness, vacation, resignation, or retirement. The logo specialist, in turn, should be cross-trained in other relevant skills.

LEGAL COMPLIANCE

Legal compliance is an unglamorous but nonetheless important reason for training. Topics include sexual harassment, security awareness, safe food handling, accounting and tax regulations, confidentiality (company/patient/customer records), hazardous waste handling and disposal, appropriate use of e-mail and other company resources, and more.

SAFETY

Certain industries—including manufacturing, construction, police and fire protection, shipping, oil and natural resources, and health care—have higher-than-average risks of injury and/or illness. Dramatic evidence of hazardous work conditions can be seen by watching the Bering Sea crab fisherman on the Discovery Channel's program, *Deadliest Catch*. Safety-conscious organizations make an effort to keep both employees and customers safe and prevent accidents. An excellent example of this is Port Kembla Steelworks, located outside of Sydney, Australia. The company has achieved remarkable results in employee safety. In fact, Port Kembla received the 2007 Occupational Health and Safety Excellence Award in recognition of its incredible safety record. The company's 6,000 employees and contractors work on average 13 million hours per year. The company was rewarded for the incredible 14.9 million hours worked, without a lost time injury.[19] Port Kembla's safety record is recognized internationally as the best within the steel industry.[20] Remarkable results like Port Kembla's do not happen by chance; they are the result of rigorous safety training.

cross-training
training in a new skill or task that is typically the responsibility of a coworker.

TEAM BUILDING

Finally, team-oriented training can enrich the corporate culture and foster team spirit. Team-building training can focus on teamwork skills as well as achieving key team results. Team building can reinforce camaraderie and relationship building, particularly if everyone in a department or work unit participates in the training together. This is true for both small and large organizations. For example, a relatively small health and wellness center closes its offices twice a year to allow all of the employees to attend professional development sessions together. Learning as a team reinforces a spirit of collaboration. In service organizations, a positive outcome of team building can be higher-quality customer service. Team-building training also helps develop a common vocabulary and awareness of best practices.

KNOWLEDGE TO ACTION   In the previous section, you learned about several reasons why companies choose to train. Pick one of the reasons given and identify three specific examples of training in the workplace that are related to the topic you selected.

Why Employees Learn

Now that we have covered why companies train, we need to turn our attention to learning—the other side of the training equation. It is important to explore the question, "why do employees learn?" The challenge is determining why the training is relevant and meaningful for employees and what will motivate them to learn. As their supervisor, you will need to discover these very personal indicators. You will also need to explain to trainees why the training is important and how their new knowledge and/or skill will benefit both them and the organization. We will explore employee motivation in much more detail in Chapter 8. For this discussion about training, we will focus on two common employee motivators for training: rewards and career goals.

> *The challenge is determining why the training is relevant and meaningful for employees and what will motivate them to learn.*

REWARDS AND BENEFITS

People, like their fingerprints, are unique. Therefore, it is necessary for supervisors to work with each person to identify how the proposed training will benefit him/her *personally*. Employees may ask if they will receive a pay raise or bonus or perhaps better hours or more responsibility. It is important to recognize what each employee values and do your best to link successful completion of the training to a reward or benefit the employee believes is worth the effort. You also want to connect the training opportunity to both the company's mission and objectives and the individual's goals and interests. As you probably know from personal experience, if you are not interested, you are far less likely to learn and achieve at a high level.

CAREER GOALS AND PROFESSIONAL DEVELOPMENT

Does the training directly relate to the individual's personal career path? A "yes," in the perception of the trainee, will spark her interest in the training and pump up her motivation to learn. Part of the supervisor's role is to coach and mentor. Knowledge of your employees' career aspirations and professional development goals is essential. They may not be aware of what opportunities are available to them and how certain training programs may help them advance.[21] This is where your role as coach and advisor may have a significant impact on your employees' commitment to learning new skills and gaining knowledge through training.

KNOWLEDGE TO ACTION

Reflect for a moment on a situation when you wanted to learn a new skill. What inspired or motivated you to want to learn?

_____

How can you use this insight and knowledge to be a more effective supervisor and trainer?

_____

THEY SAID IT BEST

I am always ready to learn, although I do not always like being taught.
—WINSTON CHURCHILL, Former British Prime Minister

Source: "They can learn their own way," *Training & Coaching Today* 68 (May 15, 2007): NA. *InfoTrac OneFile.* Thomson Gale. Anne Arundel Community College. 30 July 2007.

The Ingredients of a Good Training Program

As we learned from Justin Jones-Fosu, in the chapter opener, good trainers get individuals engaged in the learning process to foster *knowledge discovery*. Desired outcomes of the training also need to be specified at the start. In this section, you will be introduced to the basic elements of a good training program. You will also discover some important modifications, depending upon whether the learning objectives involve skills or facts.

Training Principles

Before we get to the nuts and bolts of developing a training program, it is important to briefly discuss a few basic principles about training. Kathleen A. O'Halloran summed it up nicely when she said:

All people are similar, people learn by doing, and learning can be enjoyable.

The truths about people and training include: all people are similar, people learn by doing, and learning can be enjoyable. Nearly all people involved in the training process need to feel acknowledged and need reassurance.[22]

In other words, it is okay to have some fun, while reminding trainees that it is normal to feel uncertain, embarrassed, and even intimidated at the thought of learning a new task or skill. In addition, keep in mind that everyone is unique to a certain extent and they will express their feelings in different ways, or perhaps not at all. But just about everyone seeks feedback. A little reassurance can go a long way in building confidence and reducing stress and anxiety.

It's okay to have some fun! Successful supervisors recognize how important it is to provide their employees with feedback when they do a good job. They also foster a positive environment where individuals enjoy what they do and look forward to learning.
© Huntstock, Inc/Alamy

Guidelines for Training

Along with engaging the employee in the training process and providing reassurance are seven guidelines for developing a training program: (1) maximize the similarity between the training situation and the job situation, (2) provide as much experience as possible in the task being taught, (3) provide a variety of examples when teaching concepts or skills, (4) label or identify the important features of a task, (5) make sure that general principles are understood before expecting knowledge transfer, (6) make sure that the trained behaviors and ideas are rewarded in the job situation, and (7) design the training content so that trainees can see its applicability.[23] Every training program should be designed using these guidelines in order to maximize retention and transfer of learning to the job.

MAKE THE TRAINING SIMILAR TO THE JOB

Maximize the similarity between the training situation and the job situation. "Real world" experience truly is the best teacher. However, depending on budget, time, and task constraints, this may not be feasible. Other variables to consider in determining how to replicate a job situation include the cost of equipment, the level of complexity and technical skill required, and the risk factors involved.

For example, a low-risk, low-cost training experience that realistically replicates a job situation can be found in a retail clothing store. During a slow time in the store, the supervisor can work with the trainee on how to handle common customer interactions. Among them would be how to find the proper size, provide fashion consultation, and handle special requests or complaints. The supervisor may even choose to shadow the employee while he practices with real customers. By being close at hand, the supervisor can quickly answer questions or offer assistance while the trainee gains confidence (and, importantly, not lose a customer in the process).

An example of a higher-cost, more risky situation is teaching someone to safely operate a piece of heavy equipment, such as a hydraulic car lift in an automotive repair center. Life and limb are at risk with such equipment.

A similar training experience with high levels of complexity, risk, and potential cost that most of us can relate to is learning to drive a car. Learning this new skill usually begins by observing someone else driving in a safe manner while complying with traffic laws. The student driver also is likely to have classroom instructions, maybe watch a film, and perhaps take a test drive in a simulator before actually getting behind the wheel of a vehicle. When the new driver practices for the first time, it is usually in a vacant parking lot, not on the freeway during rush hour! With practice, the novice typically develops into a competent, confident driver ready to experience busy roads with traffic signals and parking challenges.

PROVIDE HANDS-ON EXPERIENCE

As the old saying goes, "Practice makes perfect." Provide as much experience as possible with the task being taught. When individuals are learning a new skill, it is essential that they have time to practice—preferably as close to the initial training as possible. In addition, it is helpful to reinforce learning through frequent repetition. To return to our driving example, if the student driver gets to practice her skills in a vacant parking lot for seven days, she will learn more quickly than someone who practices once a week for seven weeks.

When discussing computer training, Leigh Buchanan, editor-at-large of *Inc. Magazine*, made this observation: "If more than a day elapses between the class and heavy-duty application of the new system, our brains are wiped clean."[24] Promptly, frequently, and consistently applying what you are being taught greatly enhances learning.

PROVIDE VARIOUS EXAMPLES

Provide a variety of attention-getting and instructive examples when teaching concepts or skills. Some people learn more effectively by reading, while others need to see or hear something explained if they are to learn. Yet another group of learners needs hands-on experience before they fully understand. Many of us learn through a combination of these styles. So trainees need a variety of examples. In the case of the retail clothing store trainee, the supervisor doing the training could share several customer scenarios to challenge the new employee to learn. For instance, the supervisor might present situations ranging from how to properly measure a customer's shoe size to what to do if someone is shoplifting. Adding real-life stories about previous customer experiences would help to reinforce the message and promote retention.

LABEL OR IDENTIFY IMPORTANT FEATURES

Employees who are trying to absorb new knowledge or learn a new skill may feel overwhelmed. You can reduce their stress and minimize errors by identifying critical steps or important features. Keep instructions as simple as possible, providing direction in a step-by-step fashion. The words and instructions should be concise and the language used should mirror that of the organization, rather than a vendor or topic expert. If the company commonly uses acronyms or jargon to refer to procedures or equipment, then use the same terminology during training and in training documents. The goal is for employees to effectively learn a new skill or procedure, not learn a strange new language.

A checklist is good for developing step-by-step procedure documents. For example, in the driver training situation, you could create a checklist that includes important safety features such as:

- Prior to getting in the car, check to be sure there are no objects such as children's toys or bicycles in the path of the vehicle.
- Make sure there are no children or pets nearby who could accidentally get in the path of the vehicle.
- Before starting the vehicle, make sure the car is in park and the emergency brake is set.

Providing employees with a checklist during training is an excellent way for them to stay focused on the learning objectives and key results. Checklists provide handy reminders of key steps in the process—something that employees can refer back to when they begin to work independently. In addition, checklists can be used by supervisors to make sure that employees are on track. They also eliminate the chance that an important training component is inadvertently left out because the supervisor forgot about it.
© Andersen Ross/Brand X/Corbis

- Check the gas gauge to determine if you have sufficient fuel.
- Verify that you and all passengers have properly fastened seat belts prior to proceeding.

CONFIRM THAT THE BASICS ARE LEARNED

Make sure that general principles are understood before expecting much knowledge transfer. Think back to when you first learned to read—you probably did not instantaneously learn words and sentences. Prior to that stage, you had to learn the basics, beginning with the alphabet. The same concept is true in employee training—you need to provide the basics first. For example, if you are training someone on new point-of-entry software, show him how to enter typical customer orders first. Once he has mastered this basic knowledge, move on to entering special orders. Next, ramp up to making modifications to existing orders. This progressive approach to training allows employees to learn at their own speed and gain confidence as they master each skill level.

KNOWLEDGE TO ACTION   Brainstorm with a few of your classmates to develop a list of methods a supervisor can use to confirm that the employee he/she is training is successfully learning.

USE APPROPRIATE REWARDS

It is vital to make sure that the trained behaviors and ideas are rewarded in the job situation. One of the easiest ways to encourage bad behavior on the job is to reward the wrong thing. USA Waste learned this the hard way when it was fined $65,000 by the Occupational Safety and Health Administration (OSHA) because its safety incentive program caused employees to hide injuries rather than report them. This undesirable outcome was the result of a poorly designed incentive program that rewarded cash based on a variety of measures, including how few safety incidents were reported.[25]

Darrel Storey, safety director at Jordan Contracting in Anaconda, Montana, has suggested that a better method of improving workplace safety is to place major emphasis on employee observation reporting. To encourage this behavior, Storey implemented a safety observation program where employees are rewarded for meeting the established criteria and reporting at least ten safe-working observations per month. As a result, Jordan Contracting has successfully cultivated a corporate culture that embraces safety. The proof? Since the inception of its safety incentive program in 2002, the company has not had an OSHA-recordable employee safety incident. Clearly, focusing on day-to-day employee observations of safe behavior yielded far better results than rewarding the number of reported incidents.

The key learning point here is to properly align rewards with desired outcomes, behaviors, and goals.

SHOW HOW THE CONTENT APPLIES

Design the training content so that the trainees can see its applicability. As we said previously, the learning experience needs to have *meaning* for employees. In addition, the training plan needs to be clearly linked to business goals and objectives.[26] The more employees know about how their training is relevant to business objectives, and how it also benefits them personally, the more quickly they will focus and absorb new knowledge or become proficient at a new skill. To help accelerate learning, it is helpful for employees to know why their training is relevant and how it will be applied in their daily work. Therefore, as the supervisor, you should take a few minutes to explain the value and purpose of the training along with how it is useful to employees in their daily lives.

Skill Development Versus Factual Learning

The ingredients of a good training program vary according to whether skill learning or factual learning is the goal. This section compares these two important goals.

SKILL DEVELOPMENT

Figure 7.2 illustrates the four essential ingredients for skill-based learning: (1) goal setting, (2) modeling, (3) practice, and (4) feedback.[27] We will discuss each of these ingredients in the following paragraphs.

Goal Setting As we have discussed in previous chapters, goal setting establishes a target to aim at. Put another way, it is the desired outcome. For example, imagine that you are training Paula how to research and find articles using the online databases available through the college library. Paula's goal for this activity could be: By next Friday, I will successfully print three articles from online databases, available through the college library, that are current and relevant to my research topic.

Modeling When you are teaching a trainee a new skill, it is important to show the person the proper method to accomplish the task safely and effectively. In other words, you want to demonstrate or model the behavior so it can be learned through observation. Let's continue the previous example where Paula is learning how to find articles online. In this example, as the trainer, you would model for Paula by demonstrating how to search for articles related to specific topics. You would continue by showing her each step in the process as you proceed to finally select and print an article.

Practice The next stage in training is to provide an opportunity for the person to learn by actually performing the new task or skill firsthand. Through this type of practice, the trainee will reveal his/her understanding and competence with the new task. To continue with Paula, after you have demonstrated how to conduct a search, you want

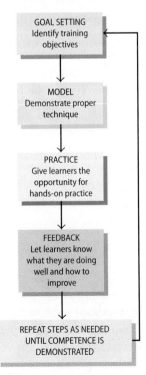

FIGURE 7.2 Four steps for effective skill-based learning

FOUR STEPS FOR
EFFECTIVE SKILL-BASED LEARNING

GOAL SETTING
Identify training objectives

MODEL
Demonstrate proper technique

PRACTICE
Give learners the opportunity for hands-on practice

FEEDBACK
Let learners know what they are doing well and how to improve

REPEAT STEPS AS NEEDED UNTIL COMPETENCE IS DEMONSTRATED

to give her an opportunity to practice what she has just learned from observing you during the modeling stage. By letting Paula sit at the keyboard and make decisions, you are providing her with the necessary hands-on experience to build confidence and independence.

Feedback After learners have had ample opportunity to practice their new skill or task, it is important for the trainer to provide specific, constructive feedback. "You're doing great" sounds nice, but it is not specific enough. Tell learners exactly what they are doing well. For example, if Paula is effectively selecting search words for her online research, then you may want to say, "Good. You have quickly learned how to select search words that lead to relevant articles for your research." In addition, if learners are not demonstrating competence with their new skill, it is essential that the trainer provide specific, corrective feedback to quickly remedy the situation and get them on the right track. Most people are nervous when learning a new skill; therefore, it is important to be sensitive to their feelings. Avoid put-downs like, "No, no, no, you are doing it all wrong!" Instead, start off positively by commenting on what they are doing correctly. Then restate the instructions for properly completing the task by emphasizing the correct method(s). For example, Paula is choosing good search words, but then she is not properly sorting to review the most recent articles first. Point out what she is doing correctly first, then review and model the sorting procedure. After modeling, provide sufficient time for her to practice.

FACTUAL LEARNING

When factual learning is the goal, the same sequence is used, except that in step 2, "meaningful presentation of the materials" is substituted for modeling. Keep in mind that the object of training is learning. Learning requires thoughtful preparation, carefully guided exposure to new ideas or behavior, and motivational support.[28]

KNOWLEDGE TO ACTION As you just learned, practice is one of the key ingredients to learning a new skill. Use this opportunity to practice teaching someone a new skill. Select a task that you can teach to a classmate fairly quickly, such as how to create a playlist on an MP3 player, how to braid hair, how to frost a cake, or how to make a paper airplane.

1. What skill are you teaching?

_____

2. List each step you will take in teaching this skill. Provide specific examples.

_____

Training Methods

Just as there are many reasons to train, there are many methods used to conduct training. In this section, we will discuss a wide array of training methods, including (1) traditional classroom instruction, (2) independent study, (3) face-to-face training,

(4) computer-aided training, (5) simulation techniques (6) on-the-job training, (7) apprenticeships (8) one-to-one training, (9) group training, (10) on-site training, (11) off-site training, (12) outsourcing, and (13) distance learning. Keep in mind that there is no single best method for training. A great deal depends on the knowledge, skill, and experience of the employee along with the focus of the training and the level of urgency. Many organizations, especially large ones, use a combination of methods.

Traditional Classroom Instruction

Traditional instructor-led classroom training remains the most common form of employer-sponsored training reported in the U.S.[29] This format typically is used for topics such as new employee orientation, sexual harassment, safety, product knowledge, technology skills, diversity, and customer service, along with other subjects suitable for groups of employees. Traditional instructor-led training may take place on-site or off-site, and it may be outsourced (each of these is discussed in more detail later).

Independent Study

Independent study, also known as *self-directed learning*, includes the use of books, online reference materials, access to software, and training manuals. One of the biggest benefits is the notion that employees are in control. They can learn when and where they want because these learning tools are typically available 24/7.[30]

Independent study is often used when employees need to acquire a lot of company or industry-specific information and less behavior training is required. For example, this method would probably *not* be an effective method if you need to teach an employee how to operate the new bar code scanner used to check inventory. A good example of when to use independent study is in the financial services industry when an associate has an interest in being promoted to a financial advisor. Providing this employee with instructional manuals and access to relevant computer software, websites, and video clips is an effective way for the person to gain the needed knowledge.[31] In addition, it is a good way to establish that learning is the *employee's* responsibility.

Keep in mind that effective independent study requires the trainee to be focused, highly motivated, and self-disciplined.

Face-to-Face Training

Face-to-face training is usually what comes to mind when people think of instructor-led classroom training. This is probably the most common reference, although informal training typically occurs face-to-face, as does on-the-job training. Face-to-face training may take many forms. It can be one instructor for many students, more than one instructor for one or more students, or it may be one-to-one. Regardless of the ratio, this format features a person (or people) with expertise in the subject being taught. Trainees have the ability to practice the four essential ingredients we described previously by establishing learning goals, modeling (or presenting relevant material), letting learners practice, and providing feedback. Remember what Kathleen O'Halloran said: "People learn by doing." This method frequently provides the opportunity for trainees to learn from their instructor, practice, and get timely feedback in person from their trainer.

Computer-Aided Training

It is important to clarify here that we are referring to computer-*aided* training, not necessarily training about computers. **Computer-aided training** methods include the use of computers, interactive software, video, audio, and Web-based resources to train people in a variety of skills. There are several different computer-aided training models, and new tools are constantly being introduced. See Figure 7.3 for examples of common forms of computer-aided training.

Simulation Techniques

Also known as *virtual reality training*, **simulation techniques** imitate real situations for training. This technique encompasses more than just computer-aided simulation. Of course, computer-aided simulation is frequently used, particularly in high-cost, high-risk training situations such as teaching someone to fly a plane[32] or operate a train. Other simulation techniques are used to help prepare individuals for the real thing. Examples include training fire and rescue personnel how to respond to a fire or accident created in a controlled environment to simulate the actual event.

Practicing new skills in a simulated environment builds confidence without harming people or equipment.

Simulation techniques are also frequently used in the healthcare field to prepare doctors, nurses, and even patients. It may be a medical student learning surgical skills through the use of a computer simulation or a diabetic patient learning how to self-inject medication via a syringe by first practicing on an orange. These simulations teach proper technique without risking harm to the patient.[33] Importantly, practicing new skills in a simulated

---

FIGURE 7.3 Common forms of computer-aided training

Computer-aided Training

1. **Instructor-led in a lab classroom**—uses computers, interactive software, video, audio, and Web-based resources.
2. **Instructor-led distance learning using the Internet**—similar experience to the one provided in a lab classroom, but without face-to-face interaction.
3. **Blended or hybrid learning**—combines face-to-face instruction with online instruction.
4. **Video teleconferencing and videocasting**—frequently used for simultaneous training requiring high-quality visual and audio transmission in a broad geographic area.
5. **Self-directed computer learning**—including Web-based resources, asynchronous video and/or audio files, and interactive software.
6. **Computer simulations**—uses virtual reality to teach computer skills as well as many other skills in a wide variety of industries.
7. **Computer gaming systems**—offers problem-solving-style training with plenty of room for employee interaction, decision making, and rapid feedback (an outstanding tool to keep your millennial generation employees actively engaged and excited to learn).

computer-aided training
training via computers, interactive software, video, audio, and Web-based resources.

simulation techniques
training that imitates real situations.

environment builds trainee confidence without harming people or equipment.

This type of training is frequently combined with other training techniques, such as classroom instruction, before trainees are exposed to an actual simulated training event.

On-the-Job Training

On-the-job training is probably used the most frequently, particularly in small businesses. It typically is the least structured. This method is simply learning a new skill while doing your job. For example, someone working for a paint company is asked to prepare the exterior of a house for a new coat of paint. The trainee is told that the first step is to power wash the house; she is then provided with the necessary equipment and sent off to the home to complete the job. At the job site, the trainee is left to figure out how to properly connect and operate the power washer. In the best-case scenario, someone who knows the equipment accompanies the trainee to the site to provide on-the-job training.

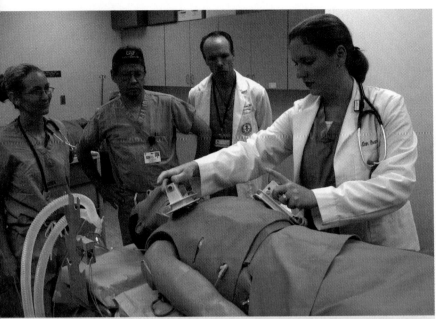

Simulation tools provide trainers with the ability to give students hands-on experience without risking potential harm or injury. In this situation, we see the instructor teaching medical students how to properly use a defibrillator to restart a patient's heart. Can you imagine using this device for the first time, with no training, on a real person? Any volunteers?
© AP Images/Chris O'Meara

On-the-job training can be a cost-effective way to teach employees new skills. However, this method, like all of the others, should follow the four-step process shown in Figure 7.2: (1) goal setting, (2) modeling, (3) practice, and (4) feedback.

Apprenticeship

From a training perspective, the term *apprentice* is most widely recognized among trade and craft unions. An **apprenticeship** is a formal, on-the-job training program that teams an experienced veteran with a person learning the trade. Apprentice programs are common for workers entering trade industries, such as electricians, plumbers, and masons. In many cases, an apprenticeship is required to progress to the next level and ultimately to become licensed in the field.

One-to-One Training

As the name implies, one-to-one training is simply one trainer and one trainee. This may be structured as a formal training program, or it may be part of a mentoring program where the mentor also acts as a trainer.

This ratio of one-to-one is a highly effective method of training because the trainer can focus all of his time and energy on one person. This allows him to quickly assess the trainee's ability and learning style and adjust the training content and delivery accordingly. But one of the disadvantages of one-to-one training is that it can be very expensive, compared to other training methods.

on-the-job training
learning a new skill while doing your job.

apprenticeship
a formal, on-the-job training program that teams an experienced veteran with a person learning the trade.

Group Training

In contrast to one-to-one training, **group training** involves one or more trainers and more than one trainee. Group training can be a cost-effective training method that also provides for a team building experience if desired. Delivery methods for group training include instructor-led (in-person or online), videocasting, or on-the-job. Instruction should be delivered using a combination of methods in an effort to appeal to various learning styles and to keep the group interested. Figure 7.4 provides quick tips for group training.

On-Site Training

On-site training means it is conducted on company property. The trainer may have to travel, but the trainees typically attend sessions at their regular place of work. For organizations with multiple locations, such as a bank with several branches, the training may take place at one location and require some trainees to travel. There are obvious cost advantages to using existing facilities and minimizing travel expenses. The primary downside is the potential for distractions among trainees who are close to their normal work areas. (Of course, with cell phones, text messaging, personal digital assistants, and wireless computers, today's employees can be distracted by their work *anywhere*.)

Off-Site Training

Unlike on-site training, off-site training occurs at a location other than the employee's place of business. This may include training at a vendor's facility, a hotel or conference center, a technical or trade school, or a college or university. The advantage to off-site training is that everyone tends to stay more focused on learning—particularly if they are required to turn off their cell phones, PDAs, etc. The main disadvantage is the cost and inconvenience of travel.

FIGURE 7.4 Tips for leading group training

Tips for Leading Group Training

Plan ahead—know your audience and why they are attending training.

Provide an agenda—use a roadmap in training.

Have clear goals for the training—explain learning objectives.

Take steps to minimize stress and anxiety—don't use tests, if possible.

Use several delivery methods in short, concise segments:

- Written instructions
- Demonstrations
- Video clips
- Computer technology tools where appropriate
- Group discussion
- Real-world examples
- Hands-on activities
- Problem-solving challenges

Provide the opportunity for two-way feedback—adapt delivery as needed.

Remember to have some fun!

group training
training that involves one or more trainers and more than one trainee.

Outsourcing

Companies often have their own professional trainers on staff, or they use their own internal experts to conduct employee training. The benefit to using your own trainers is that they know your company—its procedures, culture, jargon, and methods. Using company employees is typically less expensive than outsourcing. There is one negative: while training, inside experts are not able to carry out their regular duties, which hits productivity.

An alternative method is outsourcing the training to an expert or experts from another company or organization. The advantage to hiring qualified external trainers is that they typically have access to the most current techniques and resources. In addition, a fresh new face is often helpful in getting employees excited to learn. This can also backfire if the employees do not trust the trainer or do not have confidence in their knowledge or ability. Hiring external organizations to conduct training can also be quite expensive. Therefore, the key is to outsource training to companies or educational institutions with a proven track record to get the best results from your investment. Talk to other people in your industry and ask for references prior to signing a contract. Don't forget to identify measurable training outcomes to use in assessing the effectiveness of their training.

Distance Learning

Distance learning was mentioned earlier as part of computer-aided training, because most distance learning today requires some form of technology. In addition to using computers and the Internet (the most common vehicle for distance learning), companies are also training employees with Podcasts via iPods. A more expensive option is televised training using closed-circuit systems, satellite transmissions, or local television carriers, including cable companies. Many of these distance learning opportunities are now being structured in an "on-demand" format.

Companies continue to embrace distance learning because it can efficiently deliver standardized training to many employees nationally or globally. The savings in both travel time and expenses can be considerable.[34] Distance learning provides a flexible format for modifying materials quickly, compared to hard-copy training manuals. It also gives trainees greater control over when and where they learn. This can be very empowering and motivating. Still, some training experts argue that the cost of developing distance learning programs is not any cheaper than traditional methods and does not automatically lead to more effective learning.

 **KNOWLEDGE TO ACTION**   Earlier in the chapter you identified three specific examples of training in the workplace that are related to a particular reason why companies choose to train their employees. Review your three examples of training. Then pick one of the examples you listed and choose two training methods that you think would be most effective for helping employees learn.

distance learning
training delivered via computer technology, the Internet, televisions, satellites, and other media.

Techniques to Reinforce Learning

As you know, people learn by doing and they get better with practice. Therefore, it is essential that time and opportunity for practice are incorporated into every training plan. In addition, it is important that practice and application of new information occur as close to the time of training as possible. As we have learned, most people begin to forget if they do not have a chance to practice what they have just learned.

People learn by doing and they get better with practice.

Trainers can use several strategies to reinforce learning. These include (1) experiential learning activities, (2) various communication tools, and (3) timely feedback.

Experiential Learning Activities

In addition to the simulation methods discussed earlier, other techniques can be used to provide hands-on experience. These **experiential learning** techniques include role playing and scenario-based training.

ROLE PLAYING

Role playing involves interpersonal contact, making it a particularly effective technique for service-oriented organizations. This method involves staging a particular work-related activity and having the trainee play a role for realistic practice. An example would be teaching a nurse how to conduct a preliminary examination of a patient. The nurse would practice an examination on the instructor or another classmate playing the role of a patient. The mock patient could offer more precise and instructive feedback than would a real patient.

SCENARIO-BASED TRAINING

Scenario-based training is similar to role playing. Supervisors can create a realistic situation to supplement training in the classroom or online. For example, schools typically have an emergency response training program, including documented procedures for handling crisis situations. Teachers, administrators, and support staff are usually retrained once a year on these procedures. Next, the students are trained. To make the training realistic, the principal creates different scenarios, generally involving some role playing. In one scenario, a person might play the role of a stranger entering the school grounds and walking the halls. Properly trained students and staff should report the intruder to the office, which, in turn, should announce a secret code to have all teachers lock their classrooms.

Communication Tools

experiential learning
hands-on simulation, role playing, or scenario-based training.

role playing
staging a work-related activity to give the trainee realistic practice.

Training can be reinforced through the use of effective communication tools such as written instructions, photos or visual images, and video instruction.

WRITTEN INSTRUCTIONS

Written instructions provide an overview of how the skill or knowledge supports the overall company mission or objective, along with step-by-step directions. If any references (computer resources, websites, and in-house experts) can be used to answer questions, they should be included at the end of the document.

PHOTOS OR VISUAL IMAGES

Photos or visual images can be incredibly helpful to people who are learning new tasks. Seeing what the end product should look like makes the process far easier to learn and subsequently practice.

VIDEO INSTRUCTION

Video instruction takes visual learning to another level because it involves live action. Imagine the impact on a trainee if you show her a video of her peers performing the task. This technique is used frequently in production and sales and service training.

Timely Feedback

Recall that the fourth step in an effective training plan is feedback. As a trainer, you want to reassure your trainees quickly and reinforce what they are doing correctly, while at the same time preventing them from developing bad habits. This means observing trainees during the learning process, as a basis for providing positive and constructive feedback. Techniques for providing effective feedback are discussed in detail in Chapter 10.

In addition to feedback from the trainer, feedback from other trainees can be quite useful if it occurs in a non-threatening, supportive, and collaborative learning environment. This type of peer review may require the trainer's initial facilitation. However, once people get to know one another and build relationships and trust, they will be more open to sharing and providing constructive feedback.

Self-assessment can be a highly effective feedback tool. This is often accomplished through the use of audio or video recordings. Suppose a salesperson is participating in a role-playing session that is being videotaped. The trainee has the chance to practice in a "high-attention," "low-risk" environment. Like an elite athlete, the trainee can review the tape to critique what was done well and discuss potential improvements. This is far better than the trainer constantly pointing out errors and flaws.

It is essential that employees receive feedback in a timely fashion.

Regardless of the feedback tool(s) you select, it is essential that employees receive feedback in a timely fashion. This will effectively reinforce a positive learning experience and will minimize the opportunities to develop bad habits.

Personal Variables That Impact Learning

You must consider a wide variety of personal and organizational variables when determining how and when to train employees. High on the list are trainees' personal qualities and characteristics, including their learning styles and cultural differences.

Additionally, there many variables to consider when determining which specific training methods and tools to use.

Learning Styles

As you can see in Figure 7.5, there are four major **learning styles** or channels (modalities) for learning: visual, auditory, tactile-kinesthetic, and kinesthetic. As mentioned previously, the best way to learn varies by individual. Most people tend to retain what they have learned if they have hands-on experience during the training period with ample opportunity for practice. In fact, roughly half of all learners are classified as kinesthetic or experiential and close to 40% of learners are visual.[35] However, that does not render the other learning modalities less effective. It is usually beneficial to train employees using a combination of techniques.

FIGURE 7.5 Learning styles

Four Major Channels Of Learning

Visual

Visual learners learn through seeing. With their primary perceptual preference being visual, they can typically recall what they have read or observed. They prefer to look at illustrations or watch others doing something, rather than listening only. They are the learners who usually take and make lists.

They learn best from visual displays, including pictures, charts, graphs, diagrams, overhead transparencies, videos, flip charts, and handouts. In addition, they tend to be more productive when their environments are neat.

Auditory

Auditory learners prefer to listen. They are usually able to memorize what they hear and tend to be very attentive when information is presented in this way. Written information may have little meaning to these learners. They search for meaning and interpretation in lectures or speeches by listening to tone of voice, pitch, speech, and other special signals.

They learn best through presentations, discussions, talking things through, and just listening to what others have to say. These learners need to be told what to do rather than having them read directions.

Tactile-kinesthetic

Tactile-kinesthetic learners need to write things down. They like to incorporate their fine motor skills. These learners like to take notes as they listen and keep their hands busy.

They learn best through a hands-on approach and by actively exploring their environment. They are the learners who appreciate hands-on activities.

Kinesthetic

Kinesthetic learners need to use their bodies in the learning process. They need to do, not just watch or listen, to gain understanding. They are hands-on learners. These learners often enjoy projects, videos, or computer software that allow them to be directly involved in the lesson.

They learn best when they are totally involved. They need to be involved in activities that allow them to move and explore. Acting, drama, the use of manipulatives, playing, designing, and building are excellent examples of kinesthetic learning.

Source: Fitzroy Farquharson and Bernadette Carithers, "Four Major Channels of Learning," 2008 at http://faculty.valencia. cc.fl.us/ffarquharson/learning_styles/ (accessed May 30, 2008). Reprinted by permission of the authors.

learning styles
channels/modalities for learning, including visual, auditory, tactile-kinesthetic, and kinesthetic.

Cultural Differences

The U.S. workforce becomes more diverse everyday. With this diversity comes the recognition that one action or behavior may be appropriate to one person and terribly offensive to another person. Cultural and/or religious differences have a significant impact when planning training programs, particularly role-playing activities and hands-on activities. Ask participants if they are comfortable with the planned activities. Let them know that if they are not comfortable with any aspect of the training program, they may express their concerns to the instructor without fear of embarrassment or humiliation. Any food served during full-day or half-day training sessions raises diversity issues. Be sure to accommodate various dietary needs and restrictions. It is always a good idea to include a vegetarian option.

Generational (Age) Differences

Generational differences in both learning styles and expectations are having major impacts on organizational training and education. One indication of things to come is the use of MP3 players in employee orientation and training programs.

Members of each generation are shaped by the significant events of their time (see Table 7.1). Generations exhibit different personality traits and learning preferences. Keep in mind that these are general characterizations for instructional purposes, not mindless stereotypes. There are always exceptions. Still, supervisors need to be aware of the generational profiles when adapting their training programs and management styles. Chapter 8 explores how these characteristics influence employee motivation. For now, we are going to focus on how to design your training and educational programs to serve the particular needs of each generation.

BABY BOOMERS

Baby boomers seem to have a love/hate relationship with authority. Consequently, they may not respond well to a highly structured training session with an authoritarian leader. A workable alternative is traditional classroom-style learning with plenty of time and opportunity for interaction, including ice-breakers, small group activities, and discussions and debates. Role playing is probably not a good idea.[36] But providing them with plenty of written instructions along with copies of articles from respected authors/publications should work. Remember to begin by outlining the training and explaining the desired outcomes and impact.

GENERATION X

Gen Xers are the independent latchkey kids who are results-oriented and interested in maintaining a healthy work/life balance. It will be important for them to know from the beginning why the training is relevant and how it fits into the big picture. They are self-directed and learn best by doing. You will want to allow time for social interaction and try to foster a fun learning environment. Visual stimulation should be incorporated into your training program to keep Gen Xers engaged and interested.[37]

TABLE 7.1
Generational Differences: Baby Boomers, Generation X, and the Millennials (Generation Y)

	Baby Boomers	Generation X	Millennials
Born between	1946–1964	1965–1980	1981–2000
History and society	• Vietnam • Prosperity • Television • Suburbia • Civil rights • Women's liberation	• Watergate • Latchkey kids • High divorce rate • 1980s Wall Street • MTV • Social Security crisis • Corporate layoffs	• Computers • The Internet • School shootings • Terrorist attacks • Diversity • Extracurricular activities • 1990s economic boom
Individual characteristics	• Willing to go the extra mile • Optimistic • Positive • Love/hate relationship with authority • Idealistic • Want to have it all • Change	• Independent • Results-oriented • Skeptical • Work/life balance • Self-reliant • Pragmatic • Earn my respect	• Idealistic • Confident • Collective • Socially minded and active • Achievement-oriented • Structured • Immediacy
Learning preferences	• Print/paper • Respected sources/journals • Highlighter and note taking • Face time • Learning is passive activity • What are results? • Impact?	• Internet first, books second or third • Seek information: ask questions • Require experts to earn respect • Socialize with peers • Remain self-reliant, self-directed • What is relevance? • Benefits?	• Tune out the uncomfortable or boring • 24/7 multimedia • Seek sound, color, and humor • Learn collaboratively • Seek interactivity • Value integrity • Expect leaders to listen and respect their ideas
Training perspective	Tell me WHAT to do.	Show me HOW to do it.	WHY do I need to learn this?

Note: This table is intended to provide a general overview of generational differences. Each of the topics mentioned is not applicable to everyone within each generational category.

Sources: Linda G. Keidrowski, "Whose Generation Is It, Anyway?" *Small Business Times* (February 2, 2008), http://www.biztimes.com/news/2008/2/8/whose-generation-is-it-anyway (accessed April 12, 2008); Anne Houlihan, "The New Melting Pot: How to Effectively Lead Different Generations in the Workplace," *Supervision* 68 (September 2007): 10–11; Mary E. Brady, "Managing a Multigenerational Workforce," *Women's Digest*, http://www.womensdigest.net (accessed April 12, 2008); Lin Kroeger, "Adult Learning Styles & Motivation: How Might Generation Xers and Millennials Influence Corporate Training?" (Stratford, Ontario: PWD Consulting, Inc., 2007): 1–13; Amy Glass, "Boomers, Gen X, and Millennials: Managing the Generations," (Jenkintown, PA: Brody Communications Ltd., 2006): 1–12; Gerry Davis, "Managing a Multi-Generational Workforce" (Chicago: Heidrick & Struggles): 1–5; and "Managing A Multigenerational Workforce," *The Diversity Manager's Toolkit*, www.diversitytoolkit.com (accessed April 12, 2008).

MILLENNIALS, OR GENERATION Y

This idealistic, achievement-oriented generation has grown up with immediate access to their friends, family, and information thanks to digital information technology. In the age of 24/7 access, they expect rapid response and reliability. Multitasking is part of their natural fabric because they simultaneously talk on their phones, instant message on their computer, and listen to music on their MP3 players.[38] They are part of a complex social network on the Internet. Members of this generation expect to be trained for their jobs, and they expect to get immediate and continual feedback.[39]

It is safe to assume that the most effective training for Millennials will be available in a flexible, accessible fashion where they have room to choose how they will complete the training. Room for group collaboration, with a high degree of interaction, and the use of interactive media delivered in short bursts, will keep their attention far better than long lectures.[40]

Which Method Is Best?

Determining the best training methods for you and your organization is a never-ending challenge. As you have just learned, you need to consider your trainees' learning styles, culture, and generational profile. Supervisors will be challenged to train a diverse group of employees likely to include individuals from each of the generational profiles just described. Therefore, it is essential that you begin any group training with an explanation of your training approach. Mention that you will be using different teaching modalities in an effort to appeal to various learning styles.

In addition, there are several other variables to consider when choosing your training method(s), including:

- The learning objectives for the training
- Type of industry
- Type of training (skill or knowledge)
- The level of risk and complexity
- The cost of training
- The financial impact or potential risk of not training
- The level of readiness of your employees (their interest and desire to learn)
- The knowledge and experience of your employees
- The amount of time available
- The level of urgency in the organization to complete the training
- The availability of necessary resources to conduct training

In summary, there is no one best method for training. In fact, the most effective training typically encompasses the use of several different methods. Remember to link your training to the organization's goals and identify why the learning experience will be of interest and value to your employees. Finally, make the learning experience enjoyable. Have some fun and remember that mistakes are a valuable learning resource. The key is to learn from these mistakes while striving for excellence in your training program, work, and life.

SUMMARY

1. Companies initiate training programs to achieve organizational goals. Of primary importance is the fact that training contributes to employee retention. In addition, training and education promote employee development and literacy, which are good for businesses of all sizes.

2. There are several reasons why companies train employees, including (1) new employee orientation, (2) performance improvement, (3) implementing change, (4) new technology, (5) company/product knowledge, (6) cross-training, (7) legal compliance (8) safety, and (9) general team building. Employees engage in learning activities if they understand the value of the training, how it will benefit them personally, and/or how it well help them advance their careers.

3. Guidelines for developing a training program include (1) maximizing the similarity between the training situation and the job situation, (2) providing as much experience as possible in the task being taught, (3) providing a variety of examples when teaching concepts or skills, (4) labeling or identifying the important features of a task, (5) making sure that general principles are understood before expecting knowledge transfer, (6) making sure that the trained behaviors and ideas are rewarded in the job situation, and (7) designing the training content so that trainees can see its applicability. In addition, training programs should minimize stress and anxiety and provide reassurance to the trainees. Follow these steps for skill-based training: (1) goal setting, (2) modeling, (3) practice, and (4) feedback.

4. There is no one best training method. Formal training methods include (1) traditional classroom instruction, (2) independent study, (3) face-to–face training, (4) computer-aided training, (5) simulation techniques (6) on-the-job training, (7) apprenticeship, (8) one-to-one training, (9) group training, (10) on-site training, (11) off-site training, (12) outsourcing, and (13) distance learning. In most organizations, a combination of several different methods is used.

5. Trainers use several strategies to reinforce learning, including (1) experiential learning activities such as role playing and the use of scenarios; (2) various communication tools such as written instructions, photos, and video; and (3) timely feedback that incorporates self-assessments and video/audio critiques.

6. Selecting training methods involves assessing personal qualities and characteristics of your employees, including their (1) learning styles, (2) cultural backgrounds, and (3) generational profile (Baby Boomer, Generation X, or Millennial). The four major learning styles (channels/modalities) for learning are visual, auditory, tactile-kinesthetic, and kinesthetic. Other variables to consider when choosing your training methods include (1) the learning objectives for the training, (2) type of industry, (3) type of training (skill or knowledge), (4) the level of risk and complexity, (5) the cost of training, (6) the financial impact or potential risk of not training, (7) the level of readiness of your employees, (8) the knowledge and experience of your employees, (9) the amount of time available, (10) the level of urgency in the organization to complete the training, and (11) the availability of necessary resources to conduct training.

TERMS TO UNDERSTAND

apprenticeship, p. 193
computer-aided training, p. 192
cross-training, p. 183
distance learning, p. 195

experiential learning, p. 196
group training, p. 194
learning styles, p. 198
literacy, p. 179

on-the-job training, p. 193
role playing, p. 196
simulation techniques, p. 192
training, p. 180

QUESTIONS FOR REFLECTION

1. Why are companies choosing to initiate training programs? What impact does literacy training have on today's supervisor?

2. What are some of the more common types of training programs?

3. When would simulation training be the best choice for training?

4. List and explain the four essential ingredients for skill-based learning.

5. How does traditional classroom instruction differ from distance learning online? What do these two methods have in common?

6. Explain the difference between on-site and off-site training and describe the pros and cons of each.

HANDS-ON ACTIVITIES

CREATE YOUR OWN TRAINING PROGRAM

Plan for and conduct a training session for your classmates to teach them a new skill. Pick a skill that you are familiar with and feel comfortable teaching others. Examples of topics include how to tie a knot, how to create an origami figure, or how to download a song to your MP3 player. Prepare a training plan that includes the following:

1. An outline of your training plan to share with your professor. Remember the four steps for effective skill-based learning: goal setting, modeling, practice, and feedback. Plan your training to encompass these elements.

2. A training document to hand out to each student to use during the training session and reference later while practicing. This document should provide an explanation of the overall training goal and/or learning objectives (remember to begin with the end in mind). In addition, you should provide simple, step-by-step instructions with illustrations or pictures if appropriate.

3. A list of resources and equipment necessary to conduct the training, along with a plan for how you will make arrangements for each participant to have the necessary tools to effectively learn.

Interview an Expert

The purpose of this exercise is to learn from an expert his/her approach to successful employee training. Identify a supervisor or trainer who works for a company that conducts formal training. If possible, choose someone working in an industry where you have personal interest or are already working. Your goal is to learn from this person's experience, tools, and techniques that have been effective. You may use the questions listed below and/or develop your own. After your interview, prepare a brief summary of the conversation and list the person's strategies, tools, and techniques for effective training.

QUESTIONS

1. How are training needs assessed in your organization?
2. What role does the supervisor play in this process?
3. What are the most common reasons why you conduct training?
4. What are the most common training methods used?
5. What steps do you take in preparing a training plan?
6. What are some of the challenges or obstacles you face in delivering training?
7. How do you overcome these?
8. How do you modify/adapt your training depending on the age of your learners?
9. What do you think are the keys to a successful training experience?

You may improvise and add or edit questions to fit the situation or the circumstances of your interview. Schedule your interview ahead of time and try to limit it to about 15 minutes. Remember to send a thank-you note to the person you interview.

YOU DECIDE

CASE STUDY 7.1

Preparing to Train a Diverse Group of Employees

Anne is the kitchen supervisor at Poppy's Pancake House, which is a popular spot for breakfast and lunch with students in the college town where it is located. Anne is responsible for training and supervising all of the prep cooks, line cooks, and dishwashers. Poppy is opening another restaurant in a county about two hours north. The population in this new location is a mix of young families and baby boomers entering retirement. From a marketing perspective, Poppy thinks the location is ideal. However, Anne is concerned about the prospects for hiring experienced kitchen staff. Most of her current employees are students who she can easily relate to, as she just graduated from the local college's culinary school last year. In fact, many of the cooks working for her were recruited from her culinary classes, so they needed very little training.

Poppy is taking care of the initial recruiting effort for the new location to allow Anne time to stay focused on training one of her current cooks to become the assistant manager and run the kitchen in the original pancake house while she gets the new restaurant up and running. The new restaurant opens next month, and Anne needs to begin training her new staff. Poppy has hired five new employees: Jeanine, a mother of two who can only work from 9:00 A.M. to 11:00 A.M. while her children are in pre-school; Tony, a recent high school graduate who has been working at the diner up the road and plans to attend culinary school next year; Julie, a woman in her fifties who has never worked outside the home before but has many years of experience cooking for her family; Colin, a retired Army mess cook in his forties; and Esther, a woman in her thirties who was previously a sales representative for a large wholesale food distributor and decided she wanted to get back in the kitchen.

Anne must now prepare a training plan to teach her new employees safe food handling and storage; the ingredients and preparation for each of the menu items; and the procedures used to serve the customers food hot and quick.

Questions

1. If Anne came to you and asked for advice about how to prepare her training plan, what guidelines would you tell her to follow in preparing her plan?

2. Anne is uncomfortable training the employees in their thirties, forties, and fifties. What suggestions do you have for her to be prepared to successfully train each of these age groups?

3. One of the specialty items on the menu is the children's happy-face pancake. How would you suggest Anne structure training to teach her new cooks how to prepare this menu item?

SUPERVISOR'S TOOLKIT

One of the ways to increase learning is to decrease the stress and anxiety employees have about training and education and try to make the training enjoyable. Prepare a couple of documents to add to your supervisor's toolkit that outline tips and best practices for aspects of training.

1. Prepare a document that lists various methods a trainer can use to reduce employees' stress and anxiety before and during training.

2. Prepare a document with a list of tips for making your training sessions fun and interactive.

CHAPTER 8

Motivation and Coaching— It's Okay to Have Some Fun!

Learning Objectives

1. Discuss employee motivation and related myths about what motivates employees.

2. Compare different motivation theories and discuss their relevance for supervisors.

3. Describe the components of goal setting.

4. Describe techniques that can be used to support employee motivation.

5. Explain the supervisory role of coaching and the difference between training and coaching, and discuss components involved in developing a productive coaching relationship.

6. Describe strategies for developing peak performers through coaching and delivering effective feedback.

Straight Talk from the Field

Jeanne Crane has more than 30 years of experience coaching and training with expertise in supervision, leadership, and organizational behavior. Crane Coaching and Consulting is located in Canandaigua, New York.

QUESTION: *How do you approach employee coaching?*

RESPONSE:

To be a successful coach, there are two sets of people you need to understand: upper management, including your boss, and your subordinates. It is essential that you know what your manager wants and how he or she wants to receive information from you. You also need to understand your employees—what motivates them, what they are good at, what they need to learn, and how they learn best. Coaching is all about pinpointing a problem, helping the person to recognize the problem, and then working together to overcome the problem.

In my company, we call employees who have room for improvement Smart Martians. This is not because we think supervisors should look at their employees as though they are from another planet, but rather they should realize that their employees simply may be unaware. A technique or desirable behavior may seem obvious and easy to the supervisor. However, the employee may not have experienced it before. Therefore, we begin the coaching process by helping the employee to pinpoint the skill area needing improvement. There are several effective techniques you can use to lead a person to self-discovery. Coaching will be easier and better received if your employees recognize the need for improvement on their own, rather than you telling them what they are doing wrong.

Two of my favorite techniques are the use of video and relevant analogies. Let's explore each of these in more detail. Videotaping can be a fantastic way of helping employees find their blind spots—undesirable behaviors they are not aware of. For example, I was working with the sales manager at a car dealership who was learning how to coach his sales team to achieve better results. We videotaped the salespeople in action in several different situations. After watching the film clips of themselves, the team members were able to quickly identify the mistakes they made in approaching customers and handling certain situations. Thanks to this performance feedback, the sales manager's employees were eager to learn and much more coachable.

Another effective technique is using analogies to help an employee pinpoint a problem. The key to success with this technique is to find something that is relevant to the employee. Ideally, you use an example involving an area where the employee has had success. One employee might identify with a sports analogy, for example, while another would find a parenting situation more meaningful. Of course, this second technique requires you to learn about your employees so you can adapt your style to them.

In situations where I don't know a lot about my audience, I like to use tennis as an example. Even if people don't play tennis, they are usually familiar with the court and the basic rules. Through tennis, employees and supervisors can learn to be proactive and anticipate. Good tennis players don't waste energy running around the court without a plan. Instead, they anticipate where the opponent will hit the ball next and they get into position to be ready. Importantly, they prepare by practicing and conditioning prior to taking the court. These tennis principles can be applied to supervisors in the workplace. Invest time and energy in practice and preparation and you will flourish. Teach your employees how to anticipate and be ready for a variety of situations and problems and they will succeed.

To reinforce the need to understand both your employees and your manager, consider this example from one of my clients. I was hired to help a very talented supervisor in an information technology department. We'll call him Dave. He leads an *innovative, hard-working team of computer programmers. His team leadership style is very personal and informal. However, he reports to an executive who has a formal, crisp, and concise style. Although Dave was doing a good job in his day-to-day work, he was losing credibility with upper management. After spending time on the job site, I discovered that Dave did not understand his manager's expectations and he did not recognize the need to adapt his style to the situation. Through the use of a relevant analogy, Dave was able to recognize his blind spot. This personal exploration provided Dave with the insight he needed to modify his behavior, improve communication, and ultimately rebuild his manager's confidence. Dave was a Smart Martian who simply*

did not have the experience to know he needed to understand his manager's expectations.

The takeaway lesson is to invest time in learning about your employees so you can use relevant analogies and metaphors. Find out what your manager wants and needs from you. Understand your manager's preferences and adapt your style to deliver information in a format she or he is comfortable with. Finally, if possible, use self-discovery tools such as video feedback to help employees pinpoint skill areas that need improvement. Remember, most employees are simply Smart Martians who need your guidance and wisdom to achieve success.

Chapter Outline

One of the primary roles of a supervisor is to ensure that employees perform their jobs in an efficient and effective manner. Employees need to be motivated to achieve their personal goals, team goals, and organizational goals. Another important role of a supervisor is being a coach. In this chapter, we will explore the process of coaching. But first, we need to understand the basics of employee motivation.

There are lots of myths and opinions about the supervisor's role in employee motivation. Fortunately, psychologists and other researchers have been studying work motivation for decades. There is value in learning about a few of these theories to give you a sense of the complex combination of factors that motivate work behavior. This background will help you with the difficult task of figuring out how to motivate and coach your employees.

Employee Motivation: Myths and Motivators

Motivation is typically referred to as an employee's desire or drive to achieve. The question that is frequently debated is, "can supervisors really motivate employees?" Those who believe that supervisors cannot motivate employees will argue that a supervisor's job is to create a working environment where people will motivate themselves. According to this line of thinking, motivation comes only from within. On the opposite side of this debate are those who believe that supervisors can "motivate" employees with appropriate words, actions, and decisions.

Regardless of which position you might take, the fact of the matter is that employee motivation is essential to organizational success. In today's competitive corporate environment, more and more organizations are embracing this reality. For example, American Express, an industry leader and repeat company on *Fortune* magazine's list of the "100 Best Companies to Work For," has a new training program available to its management team: *Leadership: Inspiring Employee Engagement.*[1] Organizations such as American Express recognize that to inspire their employees they must understand what motivates them.

KNOWLEDGE TO ACTION

1. Do you agree or disagree with the statement that supervisors cannot motivate employees, people motivate themselves? Explain.

2. Reflect on a personal experience where someone was supervising your activities or leading a team. This may be at work, in a volunteer capacity, or through extracurricular activities. Did the leader's words, actions, and decisions impact your motivation? Explain.

Myths About Employee Motivation

Despite the importance of this topic, several myths persist—especially among new supervisors. Before looking at what supervisors can do to foster employee motivation, we need to address some common myths (see Table 8.1).

Employee Motivation and Job Performance

Job performance requires both personal motivation and the ability to get the job done.

motivation
an employee's desire or drive to achieve.

Figure 8.1 (on page 211) presents an overview of the model for individual motivation as it relates to job performance. As you can see, job performance requires *both* personal motivation and the ability to get the job done. Occasionally, we will hear supervisors state that an employee failed because he was not motivated, when in fact the person was not sufficiently prepared with proper training and experience to be successful. For example, all the motivation in the world will not enable a computer-illiterate person to sit down and create a spreadsheet using a computer. Ability and skills—acquired through education, training, and/or on-the-job experience—are also necessary.

TABLE 8.1
Clearing Up Common Myths About Employee Motivation

Myth	Reality
Myth #1—"I can motivate people"	Not really—they have to motivate themselves. However, you can set up an environment that fosters self-motivation. The key is knowing how to set up such an environment for your employees.
Myth #2—"Money is a good motivator"	Not really. Certain things like money, a nice office, and job security can help people from becoming *less* motivated, but they usually don't help people to become *more* motivated. However, there are always exceptions; therefore, it is important that you understand the motivations of each of your employees.
Myth #3—"Fear is a good motivator"	Fear is a great motivator—for a very short time. That's why a lot of yelling from the boss won't seem to "light a spark under employees" for an extended period of time.
Myth #4—"I know what motivates me, so I know what motivates my employees"	Not really. Different people are motivated by different things. I may be highly motivated to earn time away from my job to spend more time with my family. You may be motivated much more by recognition of a job well done. People are not motivated by the same things. Again, a key goal is to understand what motivates each of your employees.
Myth #5—"Increased job satisfaction means increased job performance"	Research shows this isn't necessarily true. Increased job satisfaction does not necessarily mean increased job performance. If the goals of the organization are not aligned with the goals of employees, then employees aren't effectively working toward the mission of the organization.
Myth #6—"I can't comprehend employee motivation—it's a science"	Not true. There are some very basic steps you can take that will go a long way toward supporting your employees to motivate themselves toward increased performance in their jobs.

Source: Carter McNamara, *Basics About Employee Motivation (Including Steps You Can Take)*, Copyright 1997–2007, Carter McNamara, MBA, PhD, Authenticity Consulting, LLC. Reprinted with permission.

An individual's motivational factors are (1) needs, (2) satisfaction, (3) expectations, and (4) goals. Supervisors have a direct impact on their employees because these factors are affected by challenging work, rewards, and participation.[2] Individual motivators will vary. Therefore, it is essential that supervisors take the time to understand what motivates each of their employees. This exploration includes examining each of the factors just mentioned. Remember, every individual is unique to some extent. Setting employees up for success should include an assessment of their skills and abilities, as well as an awareness of their motivational factors.

FIGURE 8.1 Individual motivation and job performance

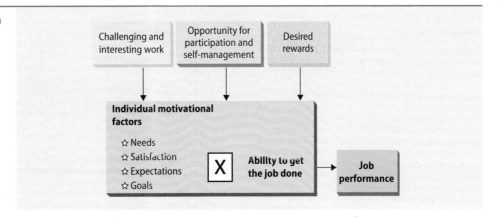

In this chapter, we review five basic theories to provide you with a framework for understanding how people are motivated.

Important Motivation Theories

Among the many different theories of motivation, five have emerged as the most influential over the years: (1) Maslow's hierarchy of needs theory, (2) Herzberg's two-factor theory, (3) job enrichment theory, (4) expectancy theory, and (5) goal-setting theory. Each approaches the motivation process from a different angle, each has supporters and detractors, and each teaches important lessons about motivation at work.

Maslow's Hierarchy of Needs Theory

Psychologist Abraham Maslow proposed that people are motivated by a predictable five-step hierarchy of needs.[3] Maslow's message was simply this: people always have needs, and when one need is relatively fulfilled, others emerge in a predictable sequence to take its place. From bottom to top, **Maslow's hierarchy of needs theory** includes (1) physiological, (2) safety, (3) social, (4) esteem, and (5) self-actualization needs (see Figure 8.2). According to Maslow, most individuals are not consciously aware of these needs, yet we all supposedly proceed up the hierarchy of needs, one level at a time.

PHYSIOLOGICAL NEEDS

At the bottom of the hierarchy are needs based on physical drives such as food, water, and sleep. Fulfillment of these lowest-level needs enables the individual to survive, and nothing else is important when these bodily needs have not been satisfied.

SAFETY NEEDS

After our basic physiological needs have been satisfied, we next become concerned about our safety from the elements, enemies, and other threats. Unemployment assistance is a safety net for those between jobs. Insurance also helps fulfill safety needs.

Maslow's hierarchy of needs theory
a theory of motivation stating that when one need is relatively fulfilled, another emerges in sequence to replace it.

FIGURE 8.2 Maslow's hierarchy of needs theory

Sources: Data for diagram drawn from A. H. Maslow, "A Theory of Human Motivation," *Psychological Review* 50 (July 1943): 370–396.

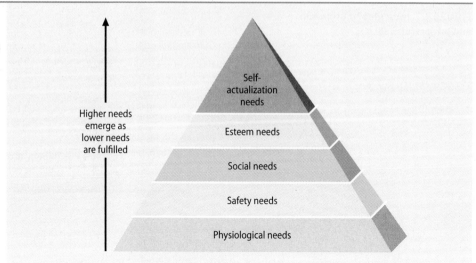

Higher needs emerge as lower needs are fulfilled

Self-actualization needs

Esteem needs

Social needs

Safety needs

Physiological needs

SOCIAL NEEDS

This category is a powerful motivator of human behavior. People typically strive hard to achieve a sense of belonging with others. At this level, people are satisfying their needs for love, affection, and the sense of belonging.

ESTEEM NEEDS

People who are comfortable with themselves and perceive themselves as worthwhile are said to possess high self-esteem.[4] Self-respect is the key to esteem needs. Much of our self-respect, and therefore our esteem, comes from being accepted and respected by others. It is important for those who are expected to help achieve organizational objectives to have their esteem needs relatively well fulfilled. But esteem needs cannot emerge if lower-level needs go unattended.

SELF-ACTUALIZATION NEEDS

At the very top of Maslow's hierarchy is the open-ended category of self-actualization needs. It is open-ended because, as Maslow pointed out, it relates to the need "to become more and more what one is, to become everything that one is capable of becoming."[5] One may satisfy this need by striving to become a better supervisor, plumber, nurse, or musician. According to one writer, the self-actualizing supervisor has the following characteristics:

1. Has warmth, closeness, and sympathy.
2. Recognizes and constructively shares negative information and feelings.
3. Exhibits trust, openness, and candor.
4. Does not achieve goals by power, deception, or manipulation.
5. Does not project his or her own feelings, motivations, or blame onto others.
6. Does not limit horizons; uses and develops his or her body, mind, and senses.
7. Is not rationalistic; can think in unconventional ways.
8. Is not conforming; regulates behavior from within.[6]

A truly self-actualized individual is more of an exception than the rule.

Granted, this is a tall order to fill. It has been pointed out that "a truly self-actualized individual is more of an exception than the rule in the organizational context."[7] Whether competitive organizations need more self-actualized individuals is subject to debate. On the positive side, self-actualized employees might help break down barriers to creativity and steer the organization in a new direction. On the negative side, too many unconventional nonconformists could wreak havoc on a typical administrative organizational structure.

RELEVANCE OF MASLOW'S THEORY FOR SUPERVISORS

Behavioral scientists who have attempted to test Maslow's theory in real life claim that it has some deficiencies.[8] Edward E. Lawler III, director of the University of Southern California's Center for Effective Organizations, made this observation:

> Which higher-order needs come into play after the lower ones are satisfied and in which order they come into play cannot be predicted. If anything, it seems that most people are simultaneously motivated by several of the same-level needs.[9]

Although Maslow's theory has not stood up well under actual testing, it teaches supervisors one important lesson: *unfulfilled* needs, not fulfilled ones, motivate an individual. Effective supervisors understand that each individual is motivated by a unique combination of unfilled needs. Because challenging and worthwhile jobs and meaningful recognition tend to enhance self-esteem, the esteem level probably presents supervisors with the greatest opportunity to motivate better performance.

For a dramatic real-life illustration of Maslow's hierarchy, consider the aftermath of Hurricane Katrina and, in particular, the people who were stranded outside the New Orleans convention center.

> These unfortunate souls were interviewed continuously during their ordeal by the national media and you could watch Maslow's theory in action as the days passed. Their first concern during early interviews was that they had no food or water and only the clothes on their backs.
>
> Once they started receiving food and water, their attention turned to their environment and the fact that it was dangerous. People were being attacked and their few meager possessions stolen.
>
> Authorities rounded up the people causing these problems and safety became less of a concern. Then, the displaced victims of this natural disaster began to focus on where friends, neighbors, and relatives were and whether they were safe.
>
> As information started to filter down to them that the people they were concerned about were accounted for, they finally reached the point where esteem needs were important to them. They had been living for days in filth, without any sanitation facilities or trash removal. Reporters often heard complaints such as: "We're being treated like animals," which spoke directly to the self-esteem issues raised by their situation.
>
> We never saw self-actualization, but the situation did climb Maslow's ladder right up through self-esteem.[10]

Herzberg's Two-Factor Theory

Frederick Herzberg proposed a theory of employee motivation based on satisfaction.[11] His theory implied that a satisfied employee is motivated from within to work harder and that a dissatisfied employee is not self-motivated. Herzberg's research uncovered two classes of factors associated with employee satisfaction and dissatisfaction (see Table 8.2). As a result, his concept has come to be called **Herzberg's two-factor theory.**

DISSATISFIERS AND SATISFIERS

Herzberg compiled his list of dissatisfiers by asking a sample of about 200 accountants and engineers to describe situations in which they felt exceptionally bad about their jobs. An analysis of their responses revealed a consistent pattern. Dissatisfaction tended to be associated with complaints about the context of their jobs. *Job context* refers to factors in the immediate work environment such as company policies, supervision, and working conditions.

Herzberg then drew up his list of satisfiers, factors responsible for self-motivation, by asking the same accountants and engineers to describe situations in which they felt exceptionally good about their jobs. Again, a patterned response emerged. However, this time different factors were described, such as the opportunity to experience achievement, receive recognition, work on an interesting job, take responsibility, and experience advancement and growth. Herzberg observed that these satisfiers centered on the nature of the task itself. Employees appeared to be motivated by *job content*— that is, by what they actually did all day long. Consequently, Herzberg concluded that enriched jobs were the key to self-motivation. The work itself—not pay, supervision, or some other environmental factor—was the key to satisfaction and hence motivation.

IMPLICATIONS OF HERZBERG'S THEORY

By insisting that satisfaction is not the opposite of dissatisfaction, Herzberg encouraged supervisors to think carefully about what actually motivates employees. For example, you may have an employee who is not dissatisfied with her pay or

Herzberg's two-factor theory
the theory that employee motivation involves two factors: sources of satisfaction and dissatisfaction.

TABLE 8.2
Herzberg's Two-Factor Theory of Motivation

Dissatisfiers:	Satisfiers:
Factors mentioned most often by *dissatisfied* employees	Factors mentioned most often by *satisfied* employees
1. Company policy and administration 2. Supervision 3. Relationship with supervisor 4. Work conditions 5. Salary 6. Relationship with peers 7. Personal life 8. Relationship with subordinates 9. Status 10. Security	1. Achievement 2. Recognition 3. Work itself 4. Responsibility 5. Advancement 6. Growth

Source: Adapted and reprinted by permission of the Harvard Business Review. An exhibit from "One More Time: How Do You Motivate Employees?" by Frederick Herzberg (January–February 1968). ©1968 by the Harvard Business School Publishing Corporation; all rights reserved.

working conditions but is not particularly motivated to work hard because the job itself lacks challenge.

Companies such as Barry-Wehmiller, a large packaging and manufacturing company located in St. Louis, Missouri, recognize this. In fact, Barry-Wehmiller's chief executive officer, Bob Chapman, has been characterized as "chief inspiration officer." Chapman views people as central to the success of any organization. He offers this observation:

> My concern is clearly that business—the most powerful engine in our country—has lost its touch with people. At Barry-Wehmiller, we decided instead of looking at sales or size or revenue, we were going to measure success by the way we touch the lives of people.[12]

Chapman has clearly made a commitment to empowering his employees. He has given every supervisor the power to "inspire, motivate, and to send people home each day healthy and fulfilled."[13] To send employees home fulfilled each day and to motivate them requires meaningful, interesting, and challenging work.

Herzberg believed that money is a weak motivational tool because, at best, it can only eliminate dissatisfaction. Eliminating dissatisfaction is not the same as motivating. His theory emphasizes the need for supervisors to evaluate the motivational potential of meaningful work, which paves the way for job enrichment.

Job Enrichment Theory

In general terms, **job enrichment theory** calls for redesigning a job to increase its motivating potential. Two job-design experts have proposed that managers address the question, "How can we achieve a fit between persons and their jobs, which fosters *both* high work production and a high-quality organizational experience for the people who do the work?"[14] Table 8.3 provides a list of five core dimensions of work that lead to job enrichment. Unlike job enlargement, which merely combines equally simple tasks, job enrichment builds more complexity and depth into jobs by introducing planning and decision-making responsibility normally carried out at higher levels. Managing an entire project can be very challenging and motivating. Scott Nichols, a home construction foreman, had this to say about his job:

> I find it very rewarding. Just building something, creating something, and actually seeing your work. . . . You start with a bare, empty lot with grass growing up and then you build a house. A lot of time you'll build a house for a family and you see them move in, that's pretty gratifying. . . . I'm proud of that.[15]

It is important to note that not all employees will respond favorably to enriched jobs. Only those with the necessary knowledge and skills, plus a desire for personal growth, will be motivated by enriched work. Furthermore, in keeping with Herzberg's two-factor theory, dissatisfaction with factors such as pay, physical working conditions, or supervision can neutralize enrichment efforts. Researchers have reported that fear of failure, lack of confidence, and lack of trust in the supervisor's intentions can stand in the way of effective job enrichment. However, job enrichment can and does work when it is carefully thought out, when management is committed to its long-term success, and when employees desire additional challenge.[16]

job enrichment theory
redesigning a job to increase its motivating potential.

TABLE 8.3
Job Enrichment

Core Dimension of Work	Definition
1. Skill variety	The degree to which the job requires different activities in carrying out the work, involving the use of different skills and talents.
2. Task identity	The degree to which the job requires completion of a "whole" piece of work; that is, doing a job from beginning to end with a visible outcome.
3. Task significance	The degree to which the job has a substantial impact on the lives of other people, internal and external to the organization.
4. Autonomy	The degree to which the job provides substantial freedom, independence, and discretion to the individual in scheduling the work and in determining the procedures to be used in completing the job.
5. Job feedback	The degree to which carrying out the work activities required by the job provides the individual with direct and clear information about the effectiveness of his or her performance.

Sources: J. Richard Hackman and Greg R. Oldham, *Work Redesign* (Reading, MA: Addison-Wesley Publishing Company, 1980): 78–80; John W. Medcof, "The Job Characteristics of Computing and Non-Computing Work Activities," *Journal of Occupational and Organizational Psychology* 69 (June 1996): 199–212; Joan R. Rentsch and Robert P. Steel, "Testing the Durability of Job Characteristics As Predictors of Absenteeism over a Six-Year Period," *Personnel Psychology* 51 (Spring 1998): 165–190; "Job Enrichment: Increasing Job Satisfaction," Copyright, Mind Tools Ltd, 1995–2008, Mind Tools website, http://www.mindtools.com/pages/article/newTMM_81.htm (accessed May 7, 2008).

Expectancy Theory

Practical experience shows that people are motivated by many different things. Fortunately, expectancy theory, based largely on Victor H. Vroom's 1964 classic, *Work and Motivation*, effectively deals with the highly personalized rational choices that individuals make when faced with the prospect of having to work to achieve rewards. The term **expectancy** refers to the subjective probability (that is, the belief) that one thing will lead to another. Work-related expectancies, like other expectations, are shaped by ongoing personal experience.

A BASIC EXPECTANCY MODEL

Although Vroom and other expectancy theorists developed their models in somewhat complex mathematical terms, the descriptive model in Figure 8.3 is helpful for basic understanding. In this model, one's motivational strength increases as one's perceived effort-performance and performance-reward probabilities increase. This is not as complicated as it sounds.

The perceived effort-performance probability refers to the expected outcome from a given amount of effort. For example, estimate your motivation to study if you

expectancy
the subjective belief that one thing will lead to another.

FIGURE 8.3 A basic expectancy model

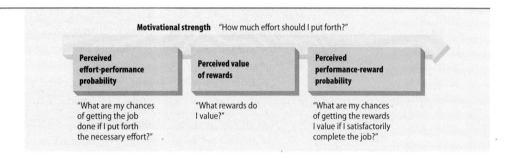

expect to do poorly on a quiz no matter how hard you study. You have a low effort-performance probability in this situation.

The perceived performance-reward probability involves the expected reward from your performance. Using the quiz example, estimate your motivation to study if you know that the quiz will not be graded. This creates a low performance-reward probability.

Now compare that estimate with your motivation to study if you believe you can do well on the quiz with minimal study (high effort-performance probability) and that by doing well on the quiz your course grade will significantly improve (high performance-reward probability). Like students, employees are motivated to expend effort when they believe it will ultimately lead to rewards that they value. This expectancy approach not only appeals strongly to common sense; it also has received encouraging research support.[17]

RELEVANCE OF EXPECTANCY THEORY FOR SUPERVISORS

According to expectancy theory, expectations of relationships between effort and performance, and between performance and reward, determine whether motivation will be high or low. Although these expectancies are in the mind of the employee, they can be influenced by the employee's supervisor, upper management's actions, and organizational experience. Training, combined with challenging but realistic objectives, helps give people the idea that they can get the job done if they put forth the necessary effort. However, perceived effort-performance probabilities are only half the battle. Listening skills enable supervisors to discover each individual's perceived performance-reward probabilities. Employees tend to work harder when they believe they have a *good chance* of getting personally *meaningful rewards*. Both sets of expectations require supervisor attention. Each is a potential barrier to work motivation.

> *Employees tend to work harder when they believe they have a* good *chance* of getting personally *meaningful rewards.*

Goal-Setting Theory

Think of two or three of the most successful people you know personally. Their success may have come via business or professional achievement, politics, athletics, or community service. Chances are, they got where they are today by being goal-oriented. In other words, they committed themselves to (and achieved) progressively more challenging goals in their professional and personal lives.[18] The fact that you are reading this book is a good indicator that you are taking college-level courses to achieve a personal goal—perhaps a degree, certificate, promotion, or other career advancement.

A prime example of a goal-oriented person is Martina Navratilova, the Hall of Fame tennis star and champion of 18 Grand Slam tournaments:

> Now that I am playing doubles, I want to be the best doubles player I can be right now. And that means doing everything I can to get to that point. You set your goals and then break it down and try to figure out how to get there. Then it becomes a palatable, doable daily routine.
>
> You say, "OK, how was my serve?" This is where I can make it better. "How is my level of fitness?" Well, I am in shape, but I could have better endurance. And then you get into the solution. Maybe I need to start running more long distance or I need to practice more of my backhand down the line or I need to think more about strategy.[19]

Biographies and autobiographies of successful people in all walks of life generally attest to the virtues of goal setting. Accordingly, goal setting is acknowledged today as a respected and useful motivation theory.

Within an organizational context, **goal setting** is the process of improving individual or group job performance with formally stated objectives, deadlines, or quality standards.[20] Research also supports this theory, as evidenced by the review and analysis of thirty-five years of research on goal-setting theory by two experts in the field. Edwin A. Locke and Gary P. Latham offered this conclusion:

> In short, goal-setting theory is among the most valid and practical theories of employee motivation in organizational psychology.[21]

A GENERAL GOAL-SETTING MODEL

Thanks to motivation researchers such as Locke, Latham, and others, there is a comprehensive body of knowledge about goal setting.[22] Important lessons from goal-setting theory and research are incorporated in the general model in Figure 8.4. This model shows how properly conceived goals trigger a motivational process that improves performance. In fact, according to Locke and Latham:

FIGURE 8.4 Model of how goals can improve performance

goal setting
the process of improving individual or group job performance with formally stated objectives, deadlines, or quality standards.

With goal-setting theory, specific difficult goals have been shown to increase performance on well over 100 different tasks involving more than 40,000 participants in at least eight countries working in laboratory, simulation, and field settings. The dependent variables have included quantity, quality, time spent, costs, job behavior measures, and more.[23]

PERSONAL OWNERSHIP OF CHALLENGING GOALS

In Chapter 3, we discussed the importance of writing SMART goals and how goal effectiveness is enhanced by *specificity, difficulty*, and *participation*. Measurable and challenging goals encourage an individual or group to stretch while striving to attain progressively more difficult levels of achievement. For instance, parents or employers who are paying a college student's tuition are advised to specify a challenging grade-point goal rather than to simply tell the student, "Just do your best." Otherwise, at the end of the semester when the student ends up with Cs or Ds, he could simply say, "Well, I did my best!" It is important to note that goals need to be difficult enough to be challenging, but not impossible. Impossible goals hamper performance; they can become a convenient excuse for not even trying.[24]

Participating in the goal-setting process gives the individual personal ownership. From the employee's viewpoint, it is "something I helped develop, not just my boss's wild idea."

GOALS AND FEEDBACK

Feedback lets the person or group know if things are on track or if corrective action is required to reach the goal. Feedback on performance operates in concert with well-conceived goals. An otherwise excellent goal-setting program can be compromised by a lack of timely and relevant feedback. Researchers have documented the motivational value of matching *specific goals* with equally *specific feedback*.[25] Sam Walton, the founder of Wal-Mart, was a master of blending goals and feedback. For example, consider this exchange between Sam Walton and an employee during one of his regular store visits.

> A manager rushes up with an associate in tow.
> "Mr. Walton, I want you to meet Renee. She runs one of the top ten pet departments in the country."
> "Well, Renee, bless your heart. What percentage of the store [sales] are you doing?"
> "Last year it was 3.1 percent," Renee says, "but this year I'm trying for 3.3 percent."
> "Well, Renee, that's amazing," says Sam. "You know our average pet department only does about 2.4 percent. Keep up the great work."[26]

HOW DO GOALS ACTUALLY MOTIVATE?

Goal-setting researchers say goals perform a motivational function by doing the four things listed in the center of Figure 8.4. A goal motivates by:

1. Directing one's attention to a specific target.

2. Encouraging one to exert effort toward achieving something specific.

3. Encouraging persistence through a challenging goal that requires sustained or repeated effort.

4. Fostering the creation of action plans and strategies to bridge the gap between the current state and the desired outcome.

PRACTICAL IMPLICATIONS OF GOAL SETTING

The model of performance improvement in Figure 8.4 is generic and has a wide range of applications, from athletics to academics to the workplace. The motivational mechanics of goal setting are the same, regardless of the targeted performance. If you learn to be an effective goal setter in school, that ability will serve you well throughout your life. For a refresher, review the goal-setting techniques discussed in Chapter 3.

Anyone tempted to go through life without goals should remember the smiling Cheshire Cat's good advice to Alice when she asked him to help her find her way through Wonderland:

"Would you tell me, please, which way I ought to walk from here?"
"That depends a good deal on where you want to get to," replied the Cat.
"I don't much care where—" said Alice.
"Then it doesn't matter which way you walk," said the Cat.
"—so long as I get somewhere," Alice added as an explanation.
"Oh, you're sure to do that," said the Cat, "if you only walk long enough."[27]

Motivation in Action: Techniques to Support Employee Motivation

Michelle Peluso, CEO of Travelocity, supports the theory that money is only a short-term motivator. While discussing employee motivation and the need to inspire great customer service, she shared this insight:

People internalize compensation for a few hours or days, but it doesn't fire them up to get out of bed every morning, unless of course it's bonus day. Seriously, you don't get up saying, "I've got great compensation." You go to work because you believe in the people around you, your peers, your colleagues, and when you believe your company does something great for your customers.[28]

How will you get your employees fired up? Start with these five guiding principles from management expert Carter McNamara, co-founder of Authenticity Consulting, based in Minneapolis.

1. Motivating employees starts with motivating yourself
Enthusiasm is contagious. If you're enthusiastic about your job, it's much easier for others to be too.

2. Always work to align goals of the organization with goals of employees
Ensure that employees have input in goal setting and understand how they fit in with organizational goals.

3. Key to supporting the motivation of your employees is understanding what motivates each of them
Each person is motivated by different things. Find out what really motivates each of them by asking them, listening to them, and observing them.

4. Recognize that supporting employee motivation is a process, not a task
If you look at sustaining employee motivation as an ongoing process, then you'll be much more fulfilled and motivated yourself.
5. Use organizational systems (i.e., policies and procedures)
Use reliable and comprehensive systems in the workplace to help motivate employees.[29]

Also consider this quote from Oren Harari, recognized by *The Financial Times* as one of the "Top 40 Business and Management Minds in the World"[30]:

> If as a group [your employees are] not showing initiative, creativity, excitement, and accountability, then all your sticks, carrots, posters, win-one-for-the-Gipper speeches, and little parties with balloons won't make much difference. Instead, . . . examine the actual work environment you've created, and then change it accordingly.[31]

These top six professional motivational categories from the *Journal of Career Planning and Employment* provide additional practical advice:

- Acknowledgment and respect
- Camaraderie and fun
- Compensation
- Flexibility and time off
- Increased responsibility and challenge
- Personal and professional development[32]

KNOWLEDGE TO ACTION

1. Make a list of your own top five motivators.

2. Now, work in groups with your classmates to compare lists. What do you have in common? What is unique? Are there any surprises?

Supervisory Roles: Beginning with Coaching

Creating organizational systems and working with employees to develop goals are just the beginning of the motivational process. To encourage employees to achieve their goals and to become peak performers, supervisors also need to act as coaches, counselors, and disciplinarians. In this section, we will focus on coaching. The roles of counselor and disciplinarian are discussed in Chapter 11.

Helping and Coaching: What's the Difference?

Supervisors who *help* their employees tend to create weak, dependent, and passive people. In contrast, supervisors who *coach* create strong, self-confident, and proactive individuals.[33] This concept reinforces Chinese philosopher Kuan-tzu's famous statement, "If you give a man a fish, he will have a single meal. If you teach him how to fish, he will eat all his life."[34] **Coaching** involves guiding employees when learning a new task, skill, or information and connecting the "How" with the "Why." By explaining the facts or why something is important and necessary, coaches provide the employee with relevant information. This higher level of understanding encourages the individual to perform a particular task a certain way, or to appreciate the value and relevance of achieving a specific goal. Effective coaches have the ability to connect the "How" with the "Why." This suits today's younger employees very nicely.

Cultivating a Productive Coaching Relationship

Just as farmers and gardeners prepare the soil prior to planting, supervisors need to build a relationship of trust prior to coaching. This process does not occur overnight. It is a progressive experience that builds on events, interactions, communication, and decisions over time. Therefore, it is important for supervisors to always be truthful and follow through on commitments. Little reminders of that commitment can help. For example, if you make a commitment to research a question an employee has about tuition reimbursement and get back to her by the end of the week, you may want to begin your conversation or e-mail with, "As promised, here is the information you requested . . . ." This is a subtle reminder to your employee that you "walk the talk." The key is to be *genuine* in looking for opportunities to set your employees up for success. Once employees know you have integrity and can be trusted, they are much more likely to respond in a positive manner to your coaching efforts.

> *The key is to be genuine in looking for opportunities to set your employees up for success.*

Lou Holtz, the Hall of Fame college football coach, has three components to his proven philosophy for success: (1) a winning attitude, (2) a positive self-image, and (3) set a higher standard.[35] Each of these is relevant to cultivating a productive coaching relationship with your employees.

A WINNING ATTITUDE

Henry Ford once said, "If you think you can, you will . . . if you think you can't, you won't."[36] Lou Holtz continues this line of thinking with his emphasis on attitude and his belief that each of us is in control of our attitude and the choices we make. According to Coach Holtz:

> You have the power to think, to love, to create, to imagine, to plan. The greatest power you have is the power to choose. Wherever you are today, you're there because you choose to be there. We also choose the attitudes we have.[37]

> *When people believe in themselves and their ability to attain a goal, they are far more likely to achieve it.*

When people believe in themselves and their ability to attain a goal, they are far more likely to achieve it.[38] One key thing supervisors do when coaching is help people recognize that they have choices and control over their own attitudes and belief system. Whether employees believe they can learn a new task or take on more responsibility depends on their attitude. Coaches can help employees to put these goals in perspective and develop a positive attitude by asking simple questions such as:

coaching
guiding employees when learning a new task, skill, or information and connecting the "How" with the "Why".

- Why is achieving this goal important to you?
- How will your new skill have a positive impact on the organization?
- How will achieving this goal prepare you for career advancement or future opportunities?

A POSITIVE SELF-IMAGE

Another key ingredient for success is a positive self-image. When you feel good about yourself and believe in your abilities, those around you will sense this and generally have a positive perception of you. This may lead to more opportunities or, in a coaching situation, greater success as your positive self-image will have a positive impact on your employees. As the supervisor, your employees will look to you to foster a positive environment. Your attitude and how they perceive you are indeed contagious. So it is important to project a positive self-image. In addition, you need to assure your employees that you have confidence in their ability to get the job done. They may not have a positive self-image yet. But expressing your belief in their potential to learn and achieve can help them move forward in their journey to success.

KNOWLEDGE TO ACTION

You cannot be a parent, a manager, a leader, a teacher, or a coach and be effective if you don't have a good self-image. We're going to make mistakes and oftentimes, we're going to make many—but let's learn and let's benefit from them. Do what's right and avoid what's wrong. It's that simple. Sometimes we blame everybody and everything around us to the point where it gets ridiculous.

Lou Holtz, "Setting A Higher Standard," *Get Motivated Workbook, 25th Anniversary Commemorative Edition* (Tampa, FL: Get Motivated Seminars, Inc., 2006): 22.

1. Do you agree or disagree with Lou Holtz's comments above? Explain.

   _____

2. How do you think supervisors should respond when one of their employees makes a mistake?

   _____

Clearly, one aspect of developing a positive self-image is to learn from your mistakes and move on. You cannot dwell on the past, nor can you allow your employees to focus on their failures. Instead, celebrate success as often as possible. A good exercise to practice personally and to teach your employees is how to end each day on a positive note. Regardless of how bad the day may have been, there is always at least one positive. Sure, there are days when the positives may be a little hard to identify. Nevertheless, at the end of every day, pause for five minutes to reflect on what you did that was good. A few questions to help you (and your employees) get started include:

- What did I do today to help a customer, coworker, family member, or friend?
- What step(s) did I take toward completing a goal?

- What did I learn today? (New knowledge and skills are always worth celebrating.)
- How did the work that I did today contribute to our team's success?
- Why is the work that I am doing important to me, my company, and/or our customers?

PROJECTING A POSITIVE IMAGE

Life leads too many people down a negative path where they dwell on their mistakes and shortcomings. Effective coaches refocus people on solving problems, learning from mistakes, and moving ahead. Good coaching helps employees recognize their contributions and how they are vital to organizational success. Encouraging employees to celebrate incremental achievements can contribute to a better self-image.

Coaches have to lead by example.

Importantly, coaches have to lead by example. If you are sincere in your actions, do the right things for the right reasons, treat people with respect, act with integrity, and work hard, you are likely to get the same in return from your employees. But if you are insincere, rude, and disrespectful, you will be a poor role model for your employees to imitate. The point is, "the people with whom you work reflect your own attitude."[39] You get what you give.

SET A HIGHER STANDARD

Lowering the bar has never brought out the best in people. In fact, research shows that people want to use their talents to make a difference and to create new solutions to existing problems.[40] Creating an environment where employees are accountable for their actions, have a sense of autonomy, and feel challenged, can lead to excellent results. It is essential that you recognize the achievements of your employees. Give them credit for their contributions. There is nothing worse than having a supervisor steal your idea or take credit for your work. Give credit where credit is due.

Most supervisors want to see their employees succeed. As result, it is tempting to lower your standards or to make things easier when an employee is struggling with a new task. Fight this urge and commit to coaching them through the tough times. In addition, keep your own personal standards high. When you tackle a difficult problem or accomplish a challenging goal, your confidence naturally increases and those around you will respect your tenacity.

Although this concept of leading by example and setting high standards may be a bit over-simplified, it is a solid one. Invest in your people and set a good example and you will develop highly effective performers. Of course, this type of development does not happen randomly, just as the farmer's crop does not miraculously grow. Coaching takes time and effort.

We have all heard the phrase, "The grass is greener on the other side of the fence." It is generally not true. Dean Minett, hospitality legend and general manager for Ascott International, has an alternative perspective. He observed that, "The grass is greenest where it is watered. In other words, things grow where effort is made to grow them."[41] This is a good way to think about coaching and helping your people to grow and develop.

Coaching and developing your employees is a lot like watering your lawn. Dean Minett summarized this concept nicely when he said, "The grass is greenest where it is watered. In other words, things grow where effort is made to grow them." Effective supervisors understand this concept as they invest the necessary time and resources to help their employees grow and develop.

© Jupiter Images/Comstock Images/Alamy

Strategies for Developing Peak Performers

Supervisors yelling at their employees when mistakes are made is all too common, but is it effective? The short answer is "no." People generally resent and resist such harsh treatment. Of course, the nature of the situation and the level of urgency may necessitate direct orders and immediate action. Examples include an emergency room crisis or a police officer responding to a robbery. This section focuses on how to effectively coach your employees in ordinary working conditions (not urgent crisis situations).

Creating a Safe Environment

Coaching begins with a conversation. It is essential that your employees know you do not expect perfection. You expect their best effort to meet goals and in return you will give your best. Let them know that you realize everyone is human and capable of making mistakes. The key is what happens when a mistake occurs. It is important that employees feel comfortable bringing mistakes to your attention. Remember the "no surprises" philosophy discussed in Chapter 6? Your opening conversation prior to coaching is a great place to reinforce this concept. Dealing constructively with mistakes needs to be focused on the organization's mission and driven into the organization's culture. For instance, this is how Michael Dell, founder of the computer powerhouse bearing his name, explains his company's secret to steady growth:

> We all make mistakes. It's not as though at any given time, Dell doesn't have some part of the business that's not working for us as it should. But we have a culture of continuous improvement. We train employees to constantly ask themselves: "How do we grow faster? How do we lower our cost structure? How do we improve service for customers?"[42]

What happens the first time an employee brings a mistake to your attention will make or break your coaching relationship. If you react with a tirade about his incompetence, do you think he will come to you the next time something goes wrong? No one likes to be the proverbial messenger with bad news who gets shot.

A better approach is to use errors as "teachable moments." When we take a step back and put most mistakes into perspective, they are not as catastrophic as our first reaction might indicate. Therefore, it is important to quickly put the situation into perspective and reassure your employee that the mistake is not the end of the world. Instead, find a way to help him learn from his mistake so it is not repeated. The employee also needs to understand the consequences of the mistake within the context of the bigger picture.

THEY SAID IT BEST	*You're going to make mistakes in life. It's what you do after the mistake that counts.*
	—BRANDI CHASTAIN, World Cup Soccer Star
	Source: Lorraine A. DarConte, ed., *Lessons for Success* (New York: MJF Books, 2001).

Timing Matters

Supervisors are challenged to balance many roles and manage their time effectively. Some choose to actually schedule time on their calendars for coaching. Oftentimes, this works out fairly well. This helps supervisors to be proactive coaches rather than reactive "fire fighters." This accomplishes two goals: (1) the coaching session is planned and, typically, objectives and strategies are well thought out, and (2) there is usually less emotion involved, a potential barrier to effective learning.

Another approach to coaching, often used in conjunction with the proactive planned approach, is to leverage defining moments, also known as *learning moments* or *teachable moments*. These coaching opportunities are spontaneous, unplanned events that may include one or more of the following characteristics: (1) conflict, (2) resonance, and (3) surprise.

CONFLICT

When people read the word **conflict**, it often brings to mind a battle or similar uncomfortable situation. However, when handled in a respectful manner, conflict can be a very creative, productive experience in the workplace. In addition, conflict can provide excellent coaching opportunities. The conflict may center on many factors in the workplace. It may be a personality conflict among coworkers, or it could be conflicting opinions about how to solve a problem. Regardless of the nature of the conflict, one common characteristic is that there are at least two different sides to a situation. This creates an opportunity for supervisors to demonstrate patience, while encouraging exploration of alternative ideas and opinions.

RESONANCE

Resonance is often referred to as the "aha moment" when "the mental light bulb goes on." These moments are characterized by the employee recognizing new knowledge or realizing something for the first time. For example, an office equipment sales supervisor had been emphasizing for months the importance of everyone reading their e-mails each morning for the company's daily bulletin. One team member continued to check her e-mail randomly, every other day at best. In addition, she usually waited until the end of the week to submit her customer orders. As a result, she missed her chance to earn a fifty dollar bonus on every order placed one day because she failed to read the e-mail announcement and did not submit any orders that day. Her initial response was predictably an emotional mix of anger, disappointment, and frustration. However, after the employee had a chance to reflect, she remarked to her supervisor, "Now I know why you kept telling us to check our e-mails everyday." Such recognition strengthens the trust and respect between supervisor and employee. In addition, it provides the supervisor with valuable coaching opportunities to emphasize other important procedures.

"Aha, I've got it!" One of the most exciting and rewarding times for a supervisor is when an employee experiences that "aha moment." That's when the light bulb flashes and they say, "Oh … now I understand!" or "I have a great idea!".

© John Lund/Getty Images/Photodisc

conflict
a situation in which there are at least two different sides.

resonance
the moment when an employee recognizes new knowledge or realizes something for the first time.

SURPRISE

Surprises in the workplace are usually not received with joy and enthusiasm. In fact, most people respond to surprises like they do to change. The emotional reaction is often reflected in comments such as, "I hate surprises!" or "Why do they always spring things on us at the last minute?" On the positive side, surprises can turn into wonderful coaching moments. When employees are surprised, they will usually react either with a negative response that deflects responsibility or with a positive reaction that recognizes an opportunity to try something new.

For example, imagine that you are the supervisor of a Web page development group at a high-tech firm. You have a client coming into the office tomorrow morning to preview his new company website in a face-to-face meeting. Andy has been the team leader on this project. He is the primary person who has been working with the client and he is scheduled to present the new website. Oh, no, he calls to say his wife is going into labor and he will be absent tomorrow. You surprise Lexie, another member of the Web development team, by asking her to take over as team leader and prepare to meet with the client tomorrow. As a coach, your job is to wait and evaluate where and how Lexie needs you to assist in moving forward. In this case, Lexie is confident with her knowledge about the project, but is very uncomfortable meeting with the client because she has never presented before. One excellent coaching strategy to use in this situation is to provide Lexie with the opportunity to practice her presentation with you in private. This will allow you to give her constructive feedback to help her improve her presentation, build her confidence, and enhance her promotability.

Coaching Through Exploration and Inquiry

Most people do not like to be micromanaged. Good coaches realize this and will structure their interactions with their employees to allow them to figure problems out on their own. This begins by putting situations into proper perspective so the employee understands how the results will impact the organization. Then the supervisor needs to shift from the person doing the talking to coaching through exploration and inquiry. **Inquiry** involves asking questions, listening, and observing behavior. General questions to ask include:

- What do you think?
- How do you feel?
- What are you going to do about that?

Another form of inquiry focuses more narrowly on behavior. The question has four possible endings: start, stop, continue, and change. You may use one or more in preparing your inquiry. Typically, the question begins with a specific reference such as, "As a result of your new knowledge, what will you . . ."

- start?
- stop?
- continue?
- change?

inquiry
asking questions, listening, and observing.

FIGURE 8.5 How messages are communicated

Source: Elizabeth Rapoport, "Learning Curves: Corporate Horse Whisperer," *Delta Sky* (August 2007).

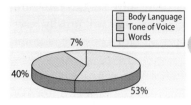

This approach allows your employees to explore the consequences and impact of their knowledge, skills, and actions. Also, the nature of the question leads them to think about their behaviors as a result of the event. One of the outcomes of this process is that employees will connect their learning with *action*, typically a goal for coaching. Remember, you want to help them to understand *why* and *how*.

How You Communicate Matters

Communication is at the heart of coaching. So it is important to understand the three basic components of a message and their impact. As you can see in Figure 8.5, only 7% of your message is based on the words you choose. The rest of your message is communicated through your body language and tone of voice.[43] In Chapter 10, we explore communication in detail. For now, just keep in mind that *what* you say matters, but *how* you say it matters much more.

Coaching in a Virtual Environment

Now that we appreciate the importance of body language and tone of voice, you may be wondering what to do if you rarely, if ever, see your employees. Certainly, coaching becomes more challenging when it is not face-to-face. A slightly different approach is needed in that case. One of the best ways to coach is by asking questions. In our coverage of exploration and inquiry, we described information gathering and behavior-oriented questions. These techniques can be used and actually expanded upon in a virtual coaching role. As previously discussed, you can use general questions to gain a better understanding of what your employee is experiencing and feeling.

General questions in a virtual environment need to be followed by questions that are more specific and in-depth. For example, instead of asking the general question, "What do you think?" you may want to make it more specific. For example: "What do you think about the new online application form we will be using? Do you think the drop-down box with the product codes is adequate?"

The goal is to gain a better sense of how your employees are feeling about their work and what they are thinking. Frequently, employees will initially respond with one- or two-word answers. For example, when asked, "How do you feel about the change?" the first response is often, "I feel fine," when in fact the employee may feel a high level of anxiety, uncertainty, or fear. Continue to ask questions until you get a complete picture of the situation. This information will prepare you to provide focused, productive coaching.

Communicating Effective Feedback

Providing employees with feedback is a major aspect of coaching. Feedback is typically positive, reinforcing good behavior, or it is in the form of constructive criticism, redirecting the employees to correct their errors.

POSITIVE FEEDBACK

Unfortunately, most employees receive inadequate positive feedback. As a coach, it is essential that you let your team members know when they are doing a good job. For **positive feedback** to be effective, your communication should be unique, timely, and specific. Rather than simply telling one of your employees that she is doing a good job, carefully phrase your feedback to be unique and specific to her. Once again, you need to be genuine and credible if you are to be trusted. Consider for a moment this scenario where you are a supervisor in a retail store. A customer is paying for his $32 purchase and hands your employee, Kathleen, $42 by mistake. You observe Kathleen catching the mistake and giving the customer back $10. Shortly after the customer leaves the store, you should let Kathleen know she did a good job with the honest transaction. You may choose to say something like, "Kathleen, thank you for demonstrating our company values of honesty and integrity. Did you see the look on that customer's face when you gave him back the $10? That was great. Keep up the good work!"

Catching people doing something *right* requires coaches and supervisors to take the time to observe. Other techniques for positive feedback include sharing customer comment cards or letters. It is amazing how good people feel when their efforts are noticed and appreciated. It also provides a source of pride and motivation. Although some people may get embarrassed, most people like being praised in front of others.

CONSTRUCTIVE CRITICISM

Coaches are challenged with balancing constructive criticism with positive feedback. When employees are constantly told what they are doing wrong and they never hear what they are doing right, they tend to lose enthusiasm for their work. Therefore, it is important to carefully choose when and how to provide constructive criticism. A general rule-of-thumb is to never criticize an employee in front of other people. This can be very embarrassing and may damage the positive relationship of trust you have worked so hard to establish. Similar to positive feedback, you want **constructive criticism** to focus on the desired behavior rather than the person.

The "Ritz-Carlton Way" is an excellent example. According to Simon Cooper, the president of Ritz-Carlton,

> ...his company strives to engage its staff to increase employee satisfaction and improve customer service. One of the ways they achieve this is through effective coaching. They don't focus on what employees have done wrong but instead seek to help them improve on a given task. Supervisors use staff meetings to publicly praise employees. Criticism is done in private. One supervisor suggested sandwiching constructive criticism among the praise. "You did a great job this week cleaning the coffee pot," he would say, "but you're still struggling here. Let's work together on improving it." By offering the criticism in the middle of praise, he inspires his employees to exceed the expectations of the hotel's guests.[44]

positive feedback
positive communication that is unique, timely, and specific.

constructive criticism
criticism that is specific and focused on the desired behavior.

Keys to Successful Coaching

As you contemplate your role as supervisor and coach, reflect on the ten values of a successful StaffCoach™ (see Figure 8.6).[45] Remember, like any other new skill, learning to become an effective coach will take time and practice. Let your employees

KNOWLEDGE TO ACTION

If you slather it on when just a "nice job" will do, employees and coworkers will doubt your sincerity—or think you're surprised by their competence.

A corollary: **Be specific**. *People respect a boss who knows which tasks are toughest to pull off.*

Pat the right back. *Nothing makes employees more cynical than the boss's public praise of someone whose work on a project was minimal or nonexistent.*

Source: Kerry J. Sulkowicz, "Analyze This," *Business Week*, December 24, 2007, 21.

1. Personally, how important is supervisory feedback to you doing your best on the job?

   _____

2. What experience have you had with positive, inadequate, or inappropriate feedback from your boss? Explain what happened.

   _____

Learning to become an effective coach will take time and practice.

know you are developing your coaching skills and invite their feedback. Let them coach you.

Learning to be a good coach takes time, just as the results of your coaching will take time. Be patient, practice, and celebrate the incremental successes!

KNOWLEDGE TO ACTION

1. Which of the coaching skills, attributes, and values listed in Figure 8.6 have you currently mastered or developed well?

   _____

2. How can you develop more confidence in the other coaching skills, attributes, and values that you did not list previously?

   _____

FIGURE 8.6 The 10 values of a successful StaffCoach

Source: Micki Holliday, *Coaching, Mentoring & Managing* (Franklin Lakes, NJ: Career Press, 2001), 3.

The 10 Values of a Successful StaffCoach™

1. **Clarity**—giving and receiving accurate communication.
2. **Supportiveness**—a commitment to stand with and behind team members.
3. **Confidence building**—personal commitment to build and sustain the self-image of each team member.
4. **Mutuality**—a partnership orientation whereby everyone wins or no one wins.
5. **Perspective**—focus on the entire business enterprise.
6. **Risk**—encouragement of innovation and effort that reduces punishment for mistakes and fosters learning by doing.
7. **Patience**—going beyond the short-term business focus to a view of time and performance that balances long-term gain and business imperatives.
8. **Involvement**—genuine interest in learning about individuals in order to know what incentives, concerns, and actions will inspire them.
9. **Confidentiality**—an ability to protect information of all team interactions and cause a sense of trust and comfort with the individuals.
10. **Respect**—ongoing mutual respect.

SUMMARY

1. Motivation relates to an employee's drive and desire to accomplish a task or goal. Common myths about employee motivation are (1) I can motivate people, (2) Money is a good motivator, (3) Fear is a good motivator, (4) I know what motivates me, so I know what motivates my employees, (5) Increased job satisfaction means increased job performance, and (6) I can't comprehend employee motivation—it's a science. Job performance requires *both* personal motivation and the ability to get the job done.

2. The individual's motivational factors are (1) needs, (2) satisfaction, (3) expectations, and (4) goals. They are affected by challenging work, rewards, and participation. Although there are dozens of different theories of motivation, five have emerged as the most influential: (1) Maslow's needs hierarchy theory, (2) Herzberg's two-factor theory, (3) job enrichment theory, (4) expectancy theory, and (5) goal-setting theory. Job performance requires both personal motivation and the ability to get the job done.

3. Goal setting is acknowledged today as a respected and useful motivation theory. Within an organizational context, goal setting is the process of improving individual or group job performance with formally stated objectives, deadlines, or quality standards. Properly conceived goals trigger a motivational process that improves performance.

4. To support employee motivation, supervisors should attempt to understand and implement the following principles: (1) Motivating employees starts with motivating yourself, (2) Align goals of the organization with goals of employees, (3) Understand what motivates each of your employees, (4) Recognize that supporting employee motivation is a process, not a task, and (5) Support employee motivation by using organizational systems (for example, policies and procedures)—don't just count on good intentions.

5. To help employees achieve their goals, supervisors also act as coaches. The primary difference between training and coaching is that training focuses on "How" while coaching focuses on "Why." Effective coaches have the ability to connect the "How" with the "Why." Supervisors should build a relationship of trust prior to coaching. This is a progressive experience that builds on events, interactions, communication, and decisions over time. Be truthful and follow through on commitments, have a winning attitude and a positive self-image, and set a higher standard for you and your team.

6. Effectively coaching your employees to become peak performers begins by creating a safe environment. Coaches use both a proactive planned approach and a strategy of leveraging defining moments, also known as learning moments or teachable moments. These coaching opportunities are spontaneous, unplanned events that may include one or more of the following characteristics: (1) conflict, (2) resonance, and/or (3) surprise. Successful coaching includes (1) clarity, (2) supportiveness, (3) confidence building, (4) mutuality, (5) perspective, (6) risk, (7) patience, (8) involvement, (9) confidentiality, and (10) respect. In addition, coaches use specific and timely positive feedback and constructive criticism.

TERMS TO UNDERSTAND

coaching, p. 222
conflict, p. 226
constructive criticism, p. 229
expectancy, p. 216
goal setting, p. 218
Herzberg's two-factor theory, p. 214
inquiry, p. 227
job enrichment theory, p. 215
Maslow's hierarchy of needs theory, p. 211
motivation, p. 209
positive feedback, p. 229
resonance, p. 226

QUESTIONS FOR REFLECTION

1. Can supervisors motivate employees? Why or why not?

2. One of the common myths about motivation is that money is always a good motivator—why is this a myth?

3. You learned about several motivation theories in this chapter. Pick one or more that you think are most relevant for supervisors and explain why.

4. List and explain five guiding principles for supporting employee motivation.

5. Explain the difference between training and coaching.

6. Describe what is involved in developing a productive coaching relationship with your employees.

HANDS-ON ACTIVITIES

WHAT VALUES ARE IMPORTANT FOR OVERALL SUCCESS?

List two or three values that you think are essential for overall success in coaching and explain why.

PRACTICING POSITIVE FEEDBACK

For each value you named in the previous activity, answer the following:

1. What does _____ look like, sound like, act like?

2. What happens when _____ occurs?

3. How does that affect our coaching relationship?

4. What doesn't _____ look like, sound like, act like?

5. What happens when _____ does not occur?

6. How does that affect our coaching relationship?

For example, if you named "positive feedback" as an essential value, fill in each blank with "positive feedback" and answer the questions. Now, use your own examples and go through the list of questions.

Interview an Expert

The purpose of this exercise is to learn from an expert his/her approach to employee motivation. Identify a supervisor or manager to interview. If possible, choose someone working in an industry in which you have a personal interest or are already working. Your goal is to learn from this person's experience and discover tools and techniques that have been effective in motivating his/her employees. You may use the questions listed below and/or develop your own. After your interview, prepare a brief summary of the conversation and list their strategies, tools, and techniques for effective employee motivation.

Questions

1. Do you believe supervisors can motivate employees?

2. How do you support employee motivation?

3. What do you think are the most effective motivators?

4. How do you know what motivates your employees?

5. Does an employee's ability have anything to do with job performance, or do you think success is primarily driven by the employee's level of motivation?

6. How do you modify/adapt your approach depending on the age of your employee?

7. What do you think are the keys to successfully motivating employees?

You may improvise and add or edit questions to fit the situation or the circumstances of your interview. Schedule your interview ahead of time and try to limit it to about 15 minutes. Remember to send a thank-you note to the person you interview.

YOU DECIDE

CASE STUDY 8.1
Motivating and Rewarding Your Employees

Susan is the store manager for one of the largest toy stores in the country. Her store is located next to the Galleria Mall in Houston, Texas. As a result, it is difficult to hire good employees because they are competing with other retail stores in the mall. In addition, since Susan has taken over as store manager, several employees have quit. Jack, one of the shift supervisors, believes that employees are leaving because Susan changed the reward structure. The old reward system that was in place allowed employees to choose from one of four incentives if the store achieved its monthly sales goal. The rewards included a paid day off, tuition reimbursement for up to $500 per course, a $200 bonus, or the opportunity to be trained to work in another area of the store.

Susan believes everyone is motivated by money, so she has designed a cash-based incentive program with a complex formula that no one seems to fully understand. It appears that the maximum bonus an associate can earn is $200, although so far no one has achieved this. In addition, the employees have heard through the grapevine that the supervisors are getting paid $300 bonuses and Susan, the store manager, is getting a $500 bonus per month even if the sales goals are not met.

To make matters worse, employees just completed their quarterly inventory and have determined that the volume of theft (or inventory shrinkage) has increased by 12% since last quarter and is up 20% compared with the same time period last year. Jack is concerned that this increased loss of inventory is because employees are stealing from the store as their inventory control measures and surveillance at the door makes it difficult for customers to steal merchandise.

Jack does not want to leave the store, but he is finding it more and more difficult to keep his employees motivated and productive in their jobs.

Questions

1. If you were asked to help Susan learn about employee motivation and job performance, how would you proceed?

2. What would you do if you were in Jack's shoes?

3. Do you think the change in the reward system may be having an impact on employee job performance, retention, and/or loyalty? Explain why or why not.

4. If this were your store, what would you do to support employee motivation?

*S*UPERVISOR'S TOOLKIT

One of the ways to be successful as a coach is to have a positive relationship with your team members. As you develop your supervisory skills, learning how to build long-term relationships of trust with your team members is essential. Prepare a couple of documents to add to your supervisor's toolkit that outline tips and best practices for building relationships with team members and for various aspects of coaching.

1. Identify at least three things you can do to cultivate a positive relationship with your team members.

2. Coaching can be challenging, particularly for new supervisors. Describe at least three strategies you will use to be an effective coach.

CHAPTER 9

Building a Positive, Creative, and Productive Work Environment

Learning Objectives

1. Discuss strategies for developing an organizational "attitude standard."

2. Identify techniques you can use to generate new ideas and encourage creativity.

3. Discuss strategies to cultivate a positive work environment.

4. Explain strategies that can be implemented in the workplace to encourage healthy habits that reduce stress and absenteeism.

5. Describe how conflict and failures can contribute to a positive, creative, and productive work environment.

Straight Talk from the Field

Walter Nelson is Vice President of Architecture and Planning and a Senior Project Manager for A. Epstein and Sons, a large multidiscipline Design/Build firm in Chicago, Illinois.

QUESTION: *How do you generate new ideas, encourage creativity, and support your commitment to the environment?*

RESPONSE:

*A*s Marvin Gaye asked in his 1971 classic, Mercy Mercy Me (The Ecology), "What about this overcrowded land, how much more abuse from man can she stand?" A prophetic question in the 70s and an urgent call for action today. As stewards of spaceship earth, it is incumbent upon all of us to search for ways to reduce our carbon footprint. In response to the increasing scientific evidence of global warming, architects, engineers, and builders across the country are signing on to the 2030 Challenge: to begin designing and constructing buildings that have a zero carbon footprint, so that by the year 2030 all new buildings will be energy neutral. The growing emphasis on sustainable "green design" is a direct outgrowth of this challenge. My firm has made "green design" a priority and has mandated that all of our projects incorporate elements of sustainable design, and that we work with and educate our clients to achieve this end.

This new emphasis on sustainable design has caused me to rethink my project management techniques. There are really three critical issues in this effort: recognizing and embracing the need for sustainable design, partnering with enlightened clients, and developing an integrated sustainable design methodology. Unlike most Architecture/ Engineering firms, we are a fully integrated design firm with all engineering disciplines "in-house," including Architecture, Interior Design, Structural Design, Civil Engineering, Mechanical, Electrical, Plumbing and Fire Protection Engineering, and Construction Management. Having all of these resources in-house allows us to fully integrate the design effort from the onset of the project and provide our client a more effective and coordinated design effort. This is the critical element in successful sustainable design.

The success of projects is also rooted in a design methodology that fosters an exciting work environment, facilitates integrated design, and encourages the free exchange of new ideas. One technique that has been particularly successful for me is to conduct project brainstorming sessions and design workshops where design ideas from team members are thrown out and recorded without editorial comment or evaluation. The compiled list is evaluated against the project scope and project budget at a later time. I have found that amazingly creative and "out of the box" thinking occurs at these sessions.

Successful integrated sustainable design requires ideas, input, and consensus from all of the project stakeholders. I select my in-house project team members based on their depth of experience with similar projects and their ability to think "out of the box." Project teams consist not only of our in-house engineers and architects, but often include specialty consultants and owner's representatives. A project team may consist of 16 or more individuals. The value and importance of each project team member's input is reinforced as an integral part of the success of the project.

I schedule a project kickoff meeting to discuss the design parameters, the project schedule, and scope of work. The project team members are encouraged to reach a consensus on milestone dates and project deliverables, which form the foundation of our project plan. Our project plan becomes our tool for evaluating conformance to project goals.

I use weekly team design meetings to facilitate coordination between disciplines and to provide a forum to discuss design ideas and project issues. Each discipline presents its design concepts for review and discussion with the project team, and team members are encouraged to give input on the design and to discuss the pros and cons of the design solution. Weekly project meetings are critical in facilitating interdisciplinary project coordination and also help to reinforce project momentum.

We also schedule regular client workshops to present and discuss updated designs and budgets. Our client is encouraged

235

to interact with the project team members to discuss and give input on design concepts. Our primary goal is to keep the level of enthusiasm up and our client engaged and informed.

As architects, we strongly believe in saving our planet one building at a time and partnering with educated and enlightened clients, creative technical people, and supportive municipalities and governmental agencies. Signing on to the 2030 Challenge is the first step. Deciding to pursue thoughtful sustainable design is the next step. Developing a methodology for integrated sustainable design and achieving measurable success is our goal. I am currently working with an in-house sustainable design committee that has been tasked to review the ways that projects are managed and to come up with tangible action items to implement in a comprehensive integrated sustainable design strategy. It is truly an exciting endeavor.

Chapter Outline

Organizations use various approaches to foster a positive work environment to encourage learning and experimentation. Walter Nelson and his colleagues at A. Epstein and Sons are energized by the need to creatively help save the planet—a mind-boggling challenge. In this chapter, we will explore ways supervisors can energize employees. In addition, we will discuss elements of an attitude standard that can be used in any organization. Supervisors who recognize the value of positive work attitudes develop standards and measures to reward those attitudes and behaviors. Another vital step toward a productive work environment involves creativity. Almost all supervisory problems require a healthy measure of creativity as supervisors mentally take a situation apart, rearrange the pieces in new configurations, and look beyond normal frameworks for solutions. This process is like turning the kaleidoscope of one's mind.

Developing an Organizational Attitude Standard

Supervisors (and customers) frequently comment on their employees' **attitude**, their viewpoint, perspective, feelings, and disposition (good or bad). Yet attitude is too often ignored during performance evaluations. One way to encourage good behavior and a positive work attitude is to develop an "attitude standard" for your organization, and then assess and hold employees accountable for their attitudes.[1]

Employees' attitudes largely determine their behavior and productivity at work. Both good and bad attitudes are contagious. So it is important to foster a positive environment and quickly address any demonstration of a negative attitude.

Good or bad, attitudes can be contagious.

A good work attitude is essentially a free asset with a positive impact on the organization's bottom line. Conversely, a bad attitude is an expense and has negative impacts.[2] An **attitude standard** is a set of expected employee behaviors for fostering a positive, friendly, creative, and professional corporate culture where employees are pleasant to everyone, including customers, vendors, and each other.

William Cottringer, Ph.D., business consultant, sport psychologist, college professor, and author, has identified six personal characteristics that should be included in an organization's attitude standard: (1) friendliness, (2) positivism, (3) teamwork, (4) enthusiasm, (5) responsibility, and (6) professionalism.[3]

Friendliness

Friendliness is exhibited with a simple smile, an act of kindness, good-natured humor, and social pleasantries. Its opposite is found in the employee who frowns, seems to always be angry or defensive, blames others, spreads malicious gossip, and/or is overly serious. Linda Kaplan Thaler and Robin Koval, authors of the book *The Power of Nice: How to Conquer the Business World with Kindness*, recommend that people, "exercise their '*nice*' muscles every day for a week, by doing five nice things that yield no personal gain."[4]

Positivism

Positivism is demonstrated by employees with a "can do" attitude who get things accomplished. This sharply contrasts with the negative employee who exhibits cynicism and pessimism, which can drain the creative energy out of any team.

Teamwork

Teamwork occurs when employees leverage individual strengths and talents and embrace individual differences to work together to achieve organizational goals. Teamwork requires people to get along and to share the credit instead of individuals doing things their own way and taking full credit. Productive teams ultimately achieve much better long-term results than individuals working independently, especially in today's high-tech global economy.

---

attitude
a person's viewpoint, perspective, feelings, and disposition.

attitude standard
a set of expected employee behaviors for fostering a positive, friendly, creative, and professional corporate culture.

friendliness
trait exhibited with a simple smile, an act of kindness, good-natured humor, or social pleasantries.

positivism
a "can do" attitude that leads to getting things accomplished.

teamwork
employees leveraging individual strengths and talents and tolerating individual differences to work together to achieve organizational goals.

A positive attitude and a sincere smile on your face make hard work more enjoyable. They also lead to better results and more productive teamwork. Exercise your "nice" muscles and practice your "can do" attitude. It is amazing how a simple smile will lighten the weight on your shoulders. Try it today!
© Somos/Veer/Getty Images

Enthusiasm

Enthusiasm is exhibited when employees enjoy their work, do not complain or talk negatively, are self-motivated and eager to learn, and see problems as challenges and opportunities rather than obstacles. It also is very contagious. Norman Vincent Peale summed this concept up nicely by saying, "There is a real magic in enthusiasm. It spells the difference between mediocrity and accomplishment."[5]

Responsibility

Employees with a sense of responsibility are committed and hold themselves accountable for their actions. **Responsibility** is exhibited when employees follow up on their commitments, do what they say they are going to do, have a sense of urgency, and go above and beyond what is expected of them.

Professionalism

Professionalism refers to high standards of performance and quality along with integrity and pride in the work. Employees with professionalism communicate openly and honestly, and they respect themselves and other people. They are persistent in achieving the established goals without compromising quality or integrity.[6] Like a great painter or sculptor, they take pride in their craft.

Igniting the Creative Spark

enthusiasm
employees enjoy their work, do not complain or talk negatively, are self-motivated and eager to learn, and see problems as challenges and opportunities rather than obstacles.

responsibility
employees follow up on commitments by doing what they say they are going to do, having a sense of urgency, going above and beyond what is expected, and holding themselves accountable.

professionalism
high standards of performance and quality along with integrity and pride in the work.

creativity
the ability to generate new ideas to support the organization's mission and goals.

As Walter Nelson indicated in the chapter opener, one of the characteristics he looks for when selecting team members is their ability to "think outside the box." When we hear the word *creativity,* we often reflect on this phrase. What does this really mean? In most organizations, out-of-the-box thinking is another way to say they are looking for new ideas. **Creativity** is the ability to generate new ideas to support the organization's mission and goals. This may be a new product or service, or it may be a better way to accomplish a task. According to a management consultant who specializes in creativity:

> Creativity is a function of knowledge, imagination, and evaluation. The greater our knowledge, the more ideas, patterns, or combinations we can achieve. But, merely having knowledge does not guarantee the formation of new patterns; the bits and pieces must be shaken up and interrelated in new ways. Then, the embryonic ideas must be evaluated and developed into usable ideas.[7]

Creativity is often subtle and may not be readily apparent to the untrained eye. But the combination and extension of seemingly insignificant day-to-day breakthroughs can lead to significant organizational progress.

Identifying general types of creativity is easier than explaining the mental process. One pioneering writer on the subject isolated three overlapping domains of creativity:

1. If you were asked to create an attitude standard for your workplace, team, or group, what elements would you include?

    _____

2. Pick one of the items listed above and explain how you would measure or assess your employees to determine if they are meeting the standard.

    _____

art, discovery, and humor.[8] These have been called the "ah!" reaction, the "aha!" reaction, and the "ha-ha!" reaction, respectively.[9]

The discovery ("aha!") variation is most relevant to management. Entirely new products and businesses can spring from creative imagination and innovation. For example, consider the evolution of MP3 players. These devices are not just the product of technological advances; it took imagination to conceive the idea of connecting a compact portable music player to a computer with Internet access to purchase music online. This revolutionary development is an example of creativity that changed the entire music industry.[10]

Workplace Creativity: Myth and Modern Reality

Recent research has shattered a long-standing myth about creative employees. According to the myth, creative people are eccentric nonconformists. But Alan Robinson's field research paints a very different picture. He concluded that "only three out of six hundred" innovators they studied were actually nonconformists. "The rest were more like your average corporate Joe, much more 'plodding and cautious' than most managers would expect."[11] Thus, creative self-expression through unconventional dress and strange behavior does not necessarily translate into creative work and marketable products.

Today's supervisors are challenged to create an organizational culture and climate capable of bringing to the surface the often hidden creative talents of *every* employee. In the Internet age, where intellectual capital is the number-one resource, the emphasis is on having fun in high-energy work environments. For example, Theresa Garza, a vice president and general manager at computer-maker Dell, seeks to generate enthusiasm and encourage employees to invest their creative energy into their work. Garza recently observed, "It's people who have momentum, who are working hard, and who are excited to be here."[12]

Learning to Be More Creative

Some people naturally seem to be more creative than others. But that does not mean that those who feel the need cannot develop their creative capacity. It does seem clear that creative ability can be learned, in the sense that our creative energy can be released from the bonds of convention, lack of self-confidence, and narrow thinking. We all have the potential to be more creative.

Creative ability can be learned.

The best place to begin is by trying consciously to overcome what creativity specialist Roger von Oech calls *mental locks*. The following mental locks are attitudes that get us through our daily activities, but tend to stifle our creativity:

1. *Looking for the "right" answer.* Depending on one's perspective, a given problem may have several right answers.

2. *Always trying to be logical.* Logic does not always prevail, given human emotions and organizational inconsistencies, ambiguity, and contradictions.

3. *Strictly following the rules.* If things are to be improved, arbitrary limits on thinking and behavior need to be questioned.

4. *Insisting on being practical.* Impractical answers to "what-if" questions can become the stepping-stones to creative insights.

5. *Avoiding ambiguity.* Creativity can be stunted by too much objectivity and specificity.

6. *Fearing and avoiding failure.* Fear of failure can paralyze us into not acting on our good ideas. This is unfortunate because we learn many valuable and lasting lessons from our mistakes.[13]

7. *Forgetting how to play.* The playful experimentation of childhood too often disappears by adulthood.

8. *Becoming too specialized.* Cross-fertilization of specialized areas helps to define problems and generate solutions.

9. *Not wanting to look foolish.* Humor can release tensions and unlock creative energies. Seemingly foolish questions can enhance understanding.

10. *Saying, "I'm not creative."* By nurturing small and apparently insignificant ideas, we can convince ourselves that we are indeed creative.[14]

KNOWLEDGE TO ACTION

1. Do you agree or disagree with the statement, "Creativity can be learned"? Explain.

2. Describe a situation when you felt like you were experiencing a mental lock or you were having a difficult time generating ideas. What steps did you take (or should you have taken) to get beyond the lock?

If you and your employees can conquer these mental locks, then you will be ready to implement creativity tools in the workplace. However, the concept of thinking outside the box requires employees to take a step back and look at the big picture first by answering the question: what are the mission and goals? Then, let the fun begin! By looking at the organization, its customers, challenges, or day-to-day tasks with a different perspective, employees can come up with all kinds of new ideas. Some of these ideas may grow, while others may be considered too outrageous or unrealistic (at least for now). So how do you get your creative juices flowing and inspire your employees to think outside the box? Consider using the techniques discussed in the following sections.

Create a New Perspective

One of the most effective ways to get out of a rut and ignite your creative spark is to change your perspective. Creating a **new perspective** involves using a different approach to identify, analyze, and correlate data in an effort to generate fresh ideas. This may be accomplished in a variety of ways, including rearranging furniture, taking a different route to work, or visiting another area or country. Some are simple and can be accomplished in a matter of minutes at no cost, whereas others such as foreign travel may be expensive and require more planning. Changing scenery is also great for brainstorming sessions with your employees. Consider meeting off-site at a local park or restaurant to help spark new ideas. A few specific suggestions for changing perspective are discussed next.

CHANGE YOUR PATTERNS

Most of us develop habits and patterns over time that become routine. A change in routine forces us to alter our perspective. This may lead us to discover something new and exciting, or it may require us to adapt to a challenging situation (new traffic patterns, for example). Creativity expert and author Michael Michalko suggests that you make a list of habits and over a period of time (a week, a month, etc.) consciously try to change your routine.

- Take a different route to work or to your college class.
- Change your sleeping hours.
- Listen to a different radio station each day.
- Read a different newspaper.
- Make new friends.
- Try different recipes or restaurants.
- Change your reading habits. If you normally read nonfiction, read fiction. If you normally read *Fast Company*, try reading *Sports Illustrated*, *Pink Magazine*, or *Black Enterprise*.
- Change your break habits. If you usually drink coffee, drink juice.
- Take a bath instead of a shower.
- Watch a different television news broadcaster.[15]

REARRANGE YOUR SPACE

Whether at home or work, rearranging the furniture will force you to view the world from a different angle. This may be just enough to see an obvious idea that you have been overlooking for weeks or months. In addition, people will react to the change in your space with questions and comments, which may lead to an unanticipated but fruitful brainstorm. If you don't have the option of rearranging the furniture, try working in another room or, weather permitting, take your pen and paper or wireless laptop outside. A change in scenery will bring a fresh perspective that can lead to very productive idea generation.[16]

TRAVEL

Traveling to another country, state, or city can lead to many mind-altering experiences. Learning about other cultures, including their food and rituals, can cultivate a host

new perspective
a different approach used to identify, analyze, and correlate data in an effort to generate fresh ideas.

of fresh ideas. However, you do not have to travel far to gain a new perspective. If you are home or at work and you need a source for fresh ideas, try visiting places you normally don't visit, such as a:

- Museum
- Toy store
- Shopping mall
- Park or botanical garden
- Retirement community
- Recreation facility
- Bowling alley
- Library
- Book store
- Flea market
- Craft show
- Trade show (home/garden, recreational vehicle, sports memorabilia, etc.)[17]

Consider the story of candy maker George Smith:

George Smith made candy on a stick in the early 1900s. Competition was fierce. He tried hard to find a new marketing twist to differentiate his stick candy from others. One day, he decided to take a break and went to the race track. One of the finest racehorses of the day was racing, and he bet a substantial amount of money on it. The horse won. The name of the horse was Lolly Pop. Smith named his stick candy "lollipops" and made candy history.[18]

> *Experience places and people that are not part of your day-to-day life to spark fresh ideas.*

The point is to experience places and people that are not part of your day-to-day life to spark fresh ideas and give you a new perspective. This requires an open mind and the willingness to view random objects to see how they might connect. Approaching creativity in this fashion will take time, practice, patience, curiosity, and the desire to have a little fun while looking at life through a different set of lenses.

Brainstorm

Brainstorming occurs when many people generate and share ideas in a nonjudgmental setting. This technique can be particularly effective when working with teams; however, individual brainstorming can also be a productive source of creativity and innovation. Here are some brainstorming methods to consider.

SET A DAILY QUOTA FOR IDEAS

Identify a challenge or opportunity you are working on and set a quota for yourself, a minimum number of ideas you must generate each day that are related to your challenge. Frequently, people pile new ideas onto previous ones in building-block fashion. Of course, there is no rule that says you must stop generating ideas once you've reached your daily quota. But it is not fair to bank the extras for tomorrow. The rationale behind quotas is that the more ideas you generate, the more likely you

brainstorming
having many people generate and share ideas in a nonjudgmental setting to solve problems.

are to identify the best idea for the situation. Inventor Thomas Edison used a quota system to help him identify new ideas, which resulted in 1,093 patents.[19]

INVOLVE NEW PEOPLE

If your brainstorming sessions are getting stale and you keep getting the same results, try including new people. If you have student interns working in your organization, invite them to participate.[20] They may be just what the group needs to come up with a new idea or solution. If you are in another city or town, eat at a local restaurant and strike up a conversation with residents from the area to learn more about cultural interests, industry, and education in the region.

KEEP AN IDEA LOG

Maintain an idea log or journal where you record details about your ideas. You may find it helpful to divide your journal into work-related categories and personal ideas. Your idea log/journal entries may include one or more of the following:

- A description of the idea
- Diagrams or illustrations
- Where you were when you came up with the idea
- The day, date, and time
- Whom you were with or talking to
- How this idea connects with a problem or opportunity

Brainstorming in nature. What on Earth could they be talking about—perhaps renewable energy sources, or maybe a green marketing campaign? The point is to give your brainstorming sessions fresh energy with a change of scenery. You don't necessarily have to head for the mountains; simply conduct your brainstorming sessions in fresh new locations. Getting close to the customer, for instance, can inspire great new ideas. Where do your best ideas pop up?
© moodboard RF/photolibrary

- Questions you will need to think about and answer
- Any other relevant information about your idea[21]

Use your idea log or journal to capture your initial thoughts. In addition, revisit your previous entries to add to your original idea. Reading your entries at a different time and/or in a different place will typically lead to more specific thoughts, questions, and revelations.

ASK A LOT OF QUESTIONS

Curiosity can lead to many ideas. That's how children learn—by asking questions about *everything*! Asking a variety of people about their thoughts and opinions—including strangers, friends, customers, and coworkers—can trigger undreamed-of ideas. Reflecting on why a service is delivered in a certain way or how a product works is just the beginning. Put yourself in an open and creative frame of mind with the thought, "I wonder . . . ," and then fill in the blank.

For example, "I wonder how we can bring in more customers between 9:00 A.M. and 11:00 A.M.," or "I wonder where I can advertise to recruit experienced staff to work from 1:00 P.M. to 9:00 P.M. on weekends." You are sure to think of some new ideas by asking various individuals these types of questions.

KNOWLEDGE TO ACTION

Brainstorm with your classmates. Figure 9.1 offers tips for brainstorming; consider reviewing this with your group prior to getting started with the questions below.

1. Use the preceding "I wonder. . . .?" questions as a model to follow when brainstorming with your classmates to generate a list of two or three leading, open-ended questions you can use to help generate ideas.

   _____

2. Who might you ask these questions if you were attempting to generate ideas for recruiting new employees for your organization?

   _____

FIGURE 9.1 Tips for brainstorming
Source: Robert Sutton, "Eight Tips for Better Brainstorming" *BusinessWeek*, July 28, 2006, http://www.businessweek.com/innovate/content/jul2006/id20060726_517774.htm (accessed March 16, 2008). Reprinted by permission of the author.

Tips for Brainstorming

During your brainstorming sessions for school and work, consider following these guidelines.

1. Use brainstorming to combine and extend ideas, not just to harvest ideas.

Andrew Hargadon's *How Breakthroughs Happen* shows that creativity occurs when people find ways to build on existing ideas. The power of group brainstorming comes from creating a safe place where people with different ideas can share, blend, and extend their diverse knowledge. If your goal is to just "collect the creative ideas that are out there," group brainstorms are a waste of time. A Web-based system for collecting ideas or an old-fashioned employee suggestion box is good enough.

2. Don't bother if people live in fear.

As Sigmund Freud observed, groups bring out the best and the worst in people. If people believe they will be teased, paid less, demoted, fired, or otherwise humiliated, group brainstorming is a bad idea. If your company fires 10% of its employees every year, for instance, people might be too afraid of saying something "dumb" to brainstorm effectively. It is better to have them just work alone.

3. Do individual brainstorming before and after group sessions.

Alex Osborn's 1950s classic *Applied Imagination*, which popularized brainstorming, gave advice that is still sound:

Creativity comes from a blend of individual and collective "ideation." Skilled organizers tell participants what the topic will be before a brainstorm. I once went to a session on how to give an "itch-less haircut," and, at the suggestion of the organizer, took a preliminary trip to a salon where I asked the stylist for a cut as "itch-free as possible" to jumpstart my thinking. At the brainstorm, I reported how tightly the stylist wrapped the cape around my neck and how she put talcum powder all over me—effective, if uncomfortable and messy measures.

4. Brainstorming sessions are worthless unless they are woven with other work practices.

Brainstorming is just one of many practices that make a company creative, and it is of little value if it's not combined with other practices—such as observing users, talking to experts, or building prototype products or experiences—that provide an outlet for the ideas generated. Some of the worst "creative" companies are great at coming up with new ideas, but never actually get around to implementing them.

5. Brainstorming requires skill and experience both to do and, especially, to facilitate.

In all of the places where brainstorming has been used effectively—Hewlett-Packard, SAP's Design Services Team, the Hasso Plattner Institute of Design at Stanford (or "The d.school"), the Institute for the Future, Frog Design, and IDEO—brainstorming is treated as a skill that takes months or years to master. Facilitating a session is a skill that takes even longer to develop. If you hold brainstorms every now and then, and they are led by people without skill and experience, don't be surprised if participants "sit there looking embarrassed, like we're all new to a nudist colony," as one manager told *The Wall Street Journal*. That is how humans act when they do something new and have poor teachers.

6. A good brainstorming session is competitive—in the right way.

In the best brainstorms, people feel pressure to show off what they know and how skilled they are at building on others' ideas. But people are also competitive in a paradoxical way. They "compete" to get everyone else to contribute, to make everyone feel like part of the group, and to treat everyone as collaborators toward a common goal. The worst thing a manager can do is set up the session as an "I win, you lose" game, in which ideas are explicitly rated, ranked, and rewarded.

7. Use brainstorming sessions for more than just generating good ideas.

Brainstorms aren't just a place to generate good ideas. At IDEO, these gatherings support the company's culture and work practices in a host of other ways. Project teams use brainstorms to get inputs from people with diverse skills throughout the company. In the process, a lot of other good things happen. Knowledge is spread about new industries and technologies, newcomers and veterans learn—or are reminded—about who knows what, and jumping into a brainstorm for an hour or so to think about someone else's problem provides a welcome respite from each designer's own projects. The explicit goal of a group brainstorm is to generate ideas. But the other benefits of routinely gathering rotating groups of people from around a company to talk about new and old ideas might ultimately be more important for supporting creative work.

8. Follow the rules, or don't call it a brainstorm.

This is true even if you only hold occasional brainstorms and even if your work doesn't require constant creativity. The worst "brainstorms" happen when the term is used loosely, and the rules aren't followed—or known—at all. Perhaps the biggest mistake that leaders make is failing to keep their mouths shut.

The rules vary from place to place. But Alex Osborn's original four still work: (1) Don't allow criticism; (2) Encourage wild ideas; (3) Go for quantity; (4) Combine and/or improve on others' ideas—along with a couple from IDEO; (5) One conversation at a time; and (6) Stay focused on the topic.

Suspend Judgment

In the daily rush of events, most CEOs, managers, and supervisors become good at assessing a situation and arriving at a conclusion rather quickly. True creativity and innovation require you to suspend judgment and to put the rapid assessment and decisive instincts on hold temporarily.[22] Paul Budnitz, is President of Kidrobot (www .kidrobot.com). According to the company's website: "Kidrobot is the planet Earth's premier creator & retailer of limited edition toys, clothing, mini-figures, artwork & books." For Budnitz, to **suspend judgment** is the practice of separating the idea-generation process from the evaluation of those ideas. Budnitz shared his perspective on the subject:

> You can't say, that's a bad idea or that's a stupid idea. That just shuts you down creatively. We were creating our spring clothing line over the past couple of weeks, and I designed [or co-designed] about 85 percent of it. I made tons of designs for hoodies: the good, the bad, the horrible, the incredibly stupid. We had 200 to 250 designs, just for hoodies.[23]

Roger Martin, Dean of the Rotman School of Management at the University of Toronto, suggests that you "ban the term 'prove it' from your business vocabulary. Anything that is truly innovative can't be proven in the early stages."[24] In other words, give new ideas a chance to develop and grow.

Sleep on It!

You have likely heard the old saying, "**Sleep on it.**" It means walking away from a challenging problem, taking a nap or getting a good night's rest, and coming back to the issue refreshed. Interestingly, some companies are refining this concept.

WHAT THE RESEARCH SAYS

Researchers report that close to 40% of workers studied experienced fatigue during a two-week period, and 66% of these workers indicated that their fatigue contributed to health-related lost productive time. According to this report, "Workers with fatigue cost employers $136.4 billion annually in health-related lost productive time, an excess of $101.0 billion compared with workers without fatigue."[25] In addition, according to a study conducted by NASA, a worker's productivity can increase by up to 34% after taking a short nap.[26] Beyond the positive impact on productivity, researchers have also concluded that napping improves memory and creative thinking while decreasing stress and heart disease. Clearly, this research evidence is causing managers to reconsider the impact of fatigue on their bottom line.

STRUCTURING NAPTIME—OR AT LEAST A LUNCH BREAK

Although the research shows that your brain needs a break, many workers choose to work through lunch rather than stay late. However, skipping lunch can have a negative impact on productivity (plus possibly violate labor laws for nonexempt employees). According to Phyllis Korkki, "What your brain really needs in the middle of the day is a nap."[27] Yes, you read that right, a *nap*. In fact, organizations are increasingly receptive to the idea of allowing their employees to sleep on the job! Well-known

suspend judgment
the practice of separating the idea-generation process from the evaluation of those ideas.

sleep on it
taking a break from a challenging problem for a nap or a good night's rest and facing the issue refreshed.

companies—including Nike, Procter & Gamble, and Pizza Hut—have discovered that employee "nap breaks" have increased performance and productivity.[28]

Children in preschool typically take a break during the middle of the day for naptime. Unfortunately, most corporations cannot afford the luxury of having their entire workforce climb into their sleeping bags on the job for forty-five minutes with the lights off. So, how do those progressive companies like Procter & Gamble do it? One method gaining traction is the Sleep Pod, manufactured by MetroNaps, where employees enjoy twenty minutes of shut-eye.[29] Other less elaborate means include "crashing" on a yoga mat with your head on a comfy pillow hidden under your desk. People have also been known to bring in fleece blankets and soothing music to make their naptime more comfortable.

Regardless of the method, supervisors need to develop a written policy for "Nap Breaks" to be sure naptime is not abused or misused and that the results are productive. Although the research shows that most people are more alert, energetic, and productive after a twenty-minute nap, not everyone experiences positive results. Therefore, it may be best to conduct a pilot test to gauge how you and your employees will react and to assess the overall impact on the bottom line.

The Experiential Approach

In the **experiential approach**, employees figuratively walk in the customers' shoes and experience first-hand what the customers are going through. The innovative firm, IDEO, considered "one of the planet's most influential design firms,"[30] focuses on a

Nap time! Researchers tell us that 20 minutes of shut-eye can reinvigorate employees and increase personal productivity. Whether using sophisticated Sleep Pods or simple yoga mats for this progressive employee benefit, supervisors need to establish policies and procedures for making nap breaks part of a productive day. Cookies and milk, anyone?
© Ausloeser/photolibrary

experiential approach
walking in your customers' shoes and experiencing firsthand what your customers are going through.

human-centered process to look for opportunities to design new products or improve products and/or business processes. Rather than sitting in an office brainstorming about different ideas, IDEO employees with educational backgrounds in everything from sociology and psychology to anthropology go into the field to experience first-hand what consumers are going through.[31] This provides much greater insight than a survey or focus group ever could. IDEO is credited with creating the first computer mouse for Apple Computer and the first laptop for Grid Systems. The company also works in low-tech areas such as toothpaste tube design and patient-admitting procedures for hospital emergency rooms.[32] IDEO has an approach that CEO Tim Brown refers to as **Design Thinking**, which involves experiencing the world first-hand in an effort to generate new ideas.

Design Thinking has three main components: (1) empathy, (2) prototyping, and (3) storytelling.[33]

1. **Empathy** involves experiencing the world firsthand. The goal is to go out into the field to see personally what consumers are experiencing. Truly understanding how customers interact with your product or service requires more than just asking them what features they like or dislike. To illustrate this point, consider the following IDEO project:

   Specialized Bicycle Components, a California bike accessory company, came to IDEO looking for new approaches to the common water bottle. So the company sent a team of researchers into the foothills above Stanford University in Palo Alto to watch bikers using their water bottles in action. The observers quickly came to two conclusions: First, reattaching a water bottle to a bike is a tricky move when you're also trying to keep your eyes on the road ahead. The IDEO solution was a water bottle with a tapered bottom and a rubber friction ring to make it easier to grip. Second, bikers used a two-step process with the water bottle: pull the nozzle out with their teeth and squeeze the bottle. So, using the human tricuspid heart valve and a bit of inspirational biomimicry, the IDEO team designed a simple self-sealing valve that opens only when squeezed.[34]

2. Rapidly **prototyping** an idea and exposing it to users is the second aspect of design thinking. The key is to create a prototype quickly and inexpensively.[35] It does not have to be fancy or elaborate; the goal is to allow users to see, touch, and otherwise experience the new idea.

3. **Storytelling** is the third step in design thinking. This stage helps people to understand and connect with new ideas.[36] The story can be told through the use of film or in person with both designers and users included. To successfully share a new idea, consider two significant points identified by researchers at Stanford and UCLA:
   - The more passionate the person is who is presenting the idea, the more successful the pitch.
   - Involving the decision maker in the creative process provides the opportunity for the boss to think she/he came up with the idea, which usually leads to the boss approving the idea.[37]

In addition to these suggestions, it is always helpful to explain how the new idea will benefit the company and the boss. You want to be sure they understand how the

Design Thinking
experiencing the world firsthand to generate new ideas.

empathy
experiencing and understanding the world firsthand.

prototyping
making a model of something to test an idea.

storytelling
helping people understand and connect with new ideas.

implementation of your idea will make them look good. Finally, acknowledge that your idea remains unproven, but remind decision makers of previous success stories to give them the reassurance they need to take a chance and move forward with your idea.[38]

Fostering a Positive Work Environment

One of the challenges supervisors face is balancing serious, focused work effort with time for fun and creative activities. In fact, many wonder if there is time for anything but dedicated effort to get the day-to-day tasks completed. However, scientific data suggest that workers are more likely to achieve organizational goals, with less turnover and absenteeism, in a **positive work environment** where they are happy. This, in turn, contributes to increased productivity. The key is happy employees who are peak performers and work well with team members to achieve organizational goals. Ideally, employee satisfaction leads to less turnover and absenteeism. Consistent attendance by high-achieving workers will also contribute to an increase in productivity.[39]

Supervisors can do a whole host of things to increase employee satisfaction and performance. In this section, we will discuss seven strategies organizations use: (1) be good corporate citizens; (2) create a signature experience; (3) develop fair and equitable personnel policies and procedures; (4) create an environment that celebrates achievement; (5) allow employees to have a voice; (6) make learning, creativity, and innovation part of your corporate culture; and (7) make employee and customer satisfaction a way of life. Keep in mind that these may not all be feasible or appropriate for your work environment. Use what you can, get creative, and come up with a few of your own ideas—perhaps through a brainstorming session with your team!

Be Good Corporate Citizens

There is a correlation between employee satisfaction and their perception of the company's social responsibility.

When Sirota Survey Intelligence recently polled 1.6 million workers, 71% of the respondents believed their organization is socially responsible and they view their senior managers as having high integrity. Researchers concluded that there is a correlation between employee satisfaction and their perception of the company's social responsibility.[40] Let us explore some low-cost ways you can help your company demonstrate good corporate citizenship and foster a positive work environment for your team.

GET GREEN!

Many organizations start with a basic recycling program on site and then graduate to other environmentally friendly initiatives such as roof gardens, car pooling and public transportation programs, telecommuting options, and more. The Chesapeake Bay Foundation (CBF) is dedicated to improving the health of the Chesapeake Bay. Therefore, it is not surprising that the foundation cultivates an environmentally friendly corporate culture.

Employees working at the CBF headquarters in Annapolis, Maryland, take great pride in their work and their workspace. Their building has been recognized

positive work environment where happy employees achieve organizational goals with less turnover and absenteeism, thus contributing to increased productivity.

as the greenest building in the world. It includes recycled materials and renewable wood such as bamboo flooring. In addition, the building designers made a conscious effort to create a warm environment that connected employees with the natural elements they are committed to protecting. This is achieved through features such as open workspaces with plenty of exposure to windows, allowing employees to soak up incredible views of the beach and bay. While looking at nature's bounty is a wonderful benefit, CBF takes it a step further by encouraging employees to walk the wooded grounds and kayak in the bay. Locker-room facilities are available for those employees who wish to commute to work by bike or choose to take advantage of outdoor activities. They also have an on-site lunch program that reduces vehicle use, and they provide access to hybrid-powered vehicles for employee use.[41]

Clearly, CBF demonstrates a commitment to the environment and to creating a warm and inspiring workspace. Although your company headquarters may not sit on the shores of the Chesapeake Bay, you can still use some of CBF's ideas such as providing on-site lunches to reduce travel. This program not only benefits the environment, it also provides the opportunity for employees to socialize and strengthen relationships.

KNOWLEDGE TO ACTION

An early leader in sustainability efforts, DuPont was able to reduce its greenhouse emissions by 72% from 2000 to 2004. That proved good for the environment and good for DuPont. "We avoided costs of over $3 billion by holding our energy use 6% below 1990 levels, while production increased," says Chad Holliday, DuPont's chairman and chief executive officer.

Source: Alan Cohen, "Sustaining the Future," Special advertising section, *Fortune*, December 10, 2007, S4.

1. "The green business movement is just a passing fad not to be taken seriously." How would you respond to this opinion?

   _____

2. What environmentally friendly practices do you engage in regularly in your own life?

   _____

VOLUNTEER

Most organizations encourage employees to be active in their communities. It could be mentoring a young student or helping your local Habitat for Humanity chapter to build a home. When these efforts are recognized, it reinforces the value to the community and instills a sense of pride in the employee(s) involved. Volunteer activities also can be a great team-building opportunity for your employees. For example, employees at a technology firm decided to forgo the annual holiday party and gift exchange. Instead, they volunteered their time and money to improve the conditions at one of the local YWCA's safe houses for victims of domestic violence. The employees donated money to buy needed supplies and furnishings. They gave the interior a fresh coat of paint and completely rebuilt the children's playroom in the house.

Nonprofit organizations serving communities around the world need this type of volunteer effort. It is a wonderful way to make a difference and also to create a sense of pride and camaraderie for your employees. You may have the resources to allow your employees to volunteer during their typical work day, or you may need to ask that they volunteer their own time. Either way, it is important to recognize their efforts and celebrate their contributions. Consider adding community service to your performance appraisal form.

Create a Signature Experience

As discussed in Chapter 4, recruitment and retention can be challenging for supervisors. Retention often involves letting employees know that they are valued members of the team. In addition, it is important that employees' values, dreams, and goals do not conflict with the organization's mission, vision, and values. One of the ways you can reinforce your company's story and emotionally connect with your employees is to create a signature experience.[42] Such an event differentiates the company, reflects its values, and represents the culture of the organization.[43]

For the eleventh consecutive year, Austin, Texas-based Whole Foods Market has appeared on *Fortune's* list of the "100 Best Companies to Work For." One of the reasons may be the company's signature experiences, beginning with team-based hiring. Whole Foods' website explains this process as follows:

> Team member participation in group interviews is one way we put our culture of empowerment into action. The team interview process is an effective way to make hiring decisions because the diversity of participants brings all of the different aspects of the

Volunteers worked together in 2008 to construct playground equipment for the new Denby Park in Norfolk, Virginia. The volunteers, from several local car dealerships, the Chrysler Foundation, and the City of Norfolk, teamed up with KaBoom, a national organization dedicated to putting a playground within walking distance of every child in America. Let's hear it for "people power!"
© AP Images/Gary C. Knapp

roles and responsibilities of the position to the table. In addition, the process educates both the interviewers and the candidates by giving insight into all the expectations and challenges of the job.

The process of selecting a new Whole Foods Market team member doesn't end with the hiring process! During your orientation period (typically 30–90 days) you will attend orientation and training classes, and you and your team leader will discuss your progress.

If your team leader then recommends that you be considered for team membership, your fellow team members will vote on whether to add you to their team. The team vote process empowers team members to share in the building of a quality team and strengthens communication. The criteria used to vote a new member onto a team are positive job performance, adherence to policies and procedures, excellent customer service skills, and teamwork.[44]

Develop Fair and Equitable Personnel Policies and Procedures

Human resources professionals, managers, and supervisors will tell you that employee pay and performance appraisals are confidential. However, the reality is that employees will gossip. Therefore, it is essential to have well-documented personnel policies and procedures. These policies and procedures should also be fair and equitable for all employee categories. This includes a policy that ties employees' salaries, bonuses, and promotions to performance. These items should also be consistent with the contribution the employee makes to the organization.[45] This requires policies and procedures that recognize and reward employees for exceptional performance, while not penalizing those who are good—but not great—workers. Employees' *perceptions* about personnel policies are important. Therefore, it is worth the extra time to meet with employees to explain policies and procedures, invite their input and suggestions, and answer their questions.

Create an Environment That Celebrates Achievement

Another way to foster a positive work environment is to celebrate success. You do not have to wait for the organization or your team to achieve a major milestone. It is great for team morale to celebrate the completion of an incremental goal, no matter how small. In addition, it is a nice boost to employees' self-esteem and confidence when they are recognized for their contributions and/or for reaching personal goals. Celebrations should be in line with the accomplishment. For example, if you are the sales supervisor for a car dealership, a handwritten note to an employee after she sells her first car and an announcement at the next staff meeting is appropriate. In comparison, if the team has a record month, then a more substantial celebration is in order, such as hosting a catered lunch. How you choose to celebrate will depend on you and your employees. What is meaningful and valued as a reward for one person may mean a lot less to another. It is important to learn what motivates each individual employee as you plan to celebrate and reward performance.

To foster a positive work environment, celebrate success.

Allow Employees to Have a Voice

Listen to your employees. They are the front line of your organization and they typically have the most contact with your customers. As a result, they understand better than most what your customers like and dislike. In addition, they have great insight into what is efficient and effective about organizational policies and procedures. Yet, supervisors often feel they need to have all the answers and do not invite their subordinates to share their ideas. By listening to your employees, you will ultimately end up with better ideas that will be implemented with greater success because your employees were part of the process. In addition, your employees will be happier because they will feel like they are contributing and making a difference. This increases their sense of worth to the organization and is a source of pride and self-confidence. You want your employees to know that you value and respect their opinions.

You may not agree with all of your employees' ideas and opinions. However, it is still important to let them share what they are thinking. Even if you disagree, you are giving them the chance to be heard and they are giving you the chance to explain your decisions in an effort to get their buy-in. Being open, honest, and up-front with employees will earn their respect. Inviting their input and giving them credit where credit is due will demonstrate your *respect* for them.

THEY SAID IT BEST	*Listening and responding to suggestions from employees and customers was the key to winning.*
	—SHELLY REESE, *USA TODAY,* referring to Baldridge Award Winner, Wainwright Industries
	Source: "Listening Quotes," HighGain website http://www.highgain.com/html/listening_quotes_1.html (accessed June 20, 2008).

Creativity and Learning Should Be Part of the Culture

Work specialization usually leads to efficiency and quality, but it can also turn talented employees into bored, unengaged workers. Allowing them to learn new skills or gain new knowledge can keep them interested and challenged. Encouraging creativity and innovation is another way to keep employees interested. In addition, fostering an environment where employees feel safe trying new things will lead to discovery, innovation, and failures—because not every new idea actually works. Allowing people to learn from their mistakes in an effort to generate new ideas is a common characteristic of successful and creative organizations. Of course, in the long run, these strategies will also contribute to a more productive workforce, which strengthens the organization.

Jeneanne Rae of Peer Insight, an innovation-focused consulting firm in Alexandria, Virginia, summed these concepts up nicely when she said, "Company leaders have to be the ones pushing for innovation by accepting failure and promoting learning through experimentation."[46] Supervisors can help by reinforcing this corporate culture of creativity.

KNOWLEDGE TO ACTION

1. What do you think are the benefits to an organization that permits mistakes?

   _____

2. What do you think are the drawbacks or potential risks to the organization that permits mistakes?

   _____

Employee and Customer Satisfaction: A Way of Life

Some companies may focus on customer satisfaction, while others choose to focus on their employees' satisfaction. Making both of these a part of the organization's culture will increase the odds that you have a positive working environment.

Organizations that focus on employee satisfaction share the philosophy that a happy workforce will take good care of the customer. In comparison, companies focusing on customer satisfaction believe that, if their employees are doing a good job, then their customers will be happy. Both of these approaches are valid and have worked for very successful companies. Still, when you combine them, it creates a powerful force that ultimately can lead to both loyal customers and loyal employees.

Infusing the spirit of customer satisfaction can contribute to employee satisfaction, particularly if the team's goals and reward system include a performance indicator that measures customer satisfaction. In addition, fostering an environment where employees know that they too are valued and their satisfaction is also important will usually create an environment where they exceed expectations and reach their potential. Whole Foods Market co-president and chief operating officer Walter Robb emphasized this point with this observation: "One of our core values at Whole Foods Market is Team Member happiness and excellence, and we believe our innovative and egalitarian work environment is a major factor in our success as a company." A. C. Gallo, Whole Foods' co-president and chief operating officer, emphasized this point when he added: "From opening up our benefits package to a company-wide vote and encouraging experimentation with new products and innovative ideas to achieve our mission, our Team Members have a voice to participate in shaping the direction of the company and their future."[47]

Although Whole Foods Market provides an excellent example of the ideal customer/employee experience, it is also worth noting that you may not be able to satisfy every employee or customer. The key is to be realistic while seeking to understand and fulfill employee and customer expectations.

Healthy Habits Reduce Stress and Absenteeism

Employee retention and productivity are essential for organizations to achieve their goals and objectives. Of course, this requires that employees are actually working. Turnover and absenteeism are two factors that can have a serious negative impact on the efficiency and effectiveness of a team.

We live in a fast-paced society that embraces technological advances and other changes at a rapid rate. In many ways, this is a good thing. But this pace can also lead to difficulty balancing work and family. In fact, a report published by the U.S. Department of Labor indicated that the number of hours parents spent with their children declined by 22 hours per week or 14% over a ten-year period (the study looked at data from 1989 to 1999).[48] Consistent with these findings are results from a 2007 survey conducted by CareerBuilder.com indicating that 25% of working mothers are not satisfied with their work-life balance.[49]

It seems fairly obvious that encouraging on-the-job safety along with healthy habits—including plenty of rest, maintaining a good diet, exercising, and balancing work and family—will reduce stress and minimize absenteeism. What many forget to factor in is employee safety outside of work. According to Elizabeth Wilson of the National Safety Council, off-the-job injuries cost employers more than work-related injuries. She also noted that there is a noticeable increase in the number of injuries at the beginning of summer.[50] As a result, some companies are including safety tips along with health and wellness programs to reduce absenteeism due to injuries sustained outside of work.

Stress is another hidden cost to employers. According to a survey conducted by the American Management Association, 81% of employees indicate that at least once a week they suffer from stress. The estimated cost in the form of absenteeism, reduced productivity, turnover, medical expense, and other consequences adds up to approximately $300 billion annually in the U.S.[51]

In this section, we will discuss a few of the many programs organizations are putting in place to encourage healthy habits and reduce stress. Of course, companies implement these initiatives because they care about their employees. As a win-win situation, these programs also improve performance, productivity, recruitment, and retention.

Health and Wellness *Can* Begin at Work!

There is a growing trend among employers to support and promote healthy lifestyles and wellness.

Many supervisors probably view health and wellness as a personal issue that is best addressed at home. However, according to Archelle Georgiou, M.D., of United Health Group, "there is a growing trend among employers to support and promote healthy lifestyles and wellness for employees and their families."[52] These efforts include a wide range of initiatives, such as:

- On-site fitness centers
- Healthier food choices in the cafeteria
- Group exercise classes before work, at lunch, and after work
- Personal coaching to help employees to quit smoking or lose weight

As a supervisor, your role is to support your employees in achieving their goals. In addition, you can organize some fun group activities. For example, consider getting members of your team together for a thirty-minute "walk and talk" during lunch. If you and the members of your team work at computers all day, organize a group stretch break a few times a day to get everyone out of their chairs to loosen up the joints and to give their hands and wrists a break. Another quick and easy way to get your blood flowing is to take the stairs instead of riding the elevator. One supervisor purchased pedometers and created a competition within her team with a prize going to the person who walked the most steps over a thirty-day period. Each

Kirstie Foster, a corporate public relations manager for General Mills, runs on a treadmill in the company's fitness center at company headquarters in Golden Valley, Minnesota. General Mills is on *Working Mother* magazine's annual list of the 100 best companies for working mothers.
© AP Images/Ann Heisenfelt

month, they had a contest with an award for the winner. Get creative, involve your employees, and have some fun! As exercise experts remind us, "move it or lose it."

Time Management

One of the pressing challenges most workers face today is managing their time. There are two factors contributing to this phenomenon: (1) the desire to balance work and home/family and (2) the desire for exceptional results.[53] The first factor involves a feeling of guilt if they miss an important event in their child's life, such as a soccer game, school play, or field trip. Guilt can increase a person's overall stress level. Both of these factors also contribute to some of the behaviors discussed previously, such as skipping lunch. Rather than taking a few minutes out of each day to plan, set and evaluate goals, and prioritize, many people just jump right into their day

Time management involves understanding what needs to get done and having a plan to get everything accomplished within the time allotted. Good time management requires people to be honest with themselves in identifying their "time wasters" and minimizing these interruptions. Keys to effective time management include:

- Establishing SMART goals with clearly defined tasks, timelines, and due dates.

- Scheduling time for daily planning. This includes planning for all aspects of your life, including work-related as well as personal goals and activities.

- Prioritizing your "to do" list. Each day brings new challenges, which often include a change in plans. It is important to take a moment to revisit your original plan and re-prioritize the list.

- Focus your investment of time on the important, essential tasks and activities.

- Eliminate or minimize the time wasters. These may include interruptions, inefficient operational procedures, and/or responding to e-mail every minute of every day (consider scheduling blocks of time during the day to review e-mail rather than reacting to each new e-mail when it arrives[54]). The same goes for checking cell phone, voice mail, and text messages.

- Get organized! By organizing your office, your files (both online and hard copies), your schedule, your activities, and your home life, you will become more efficient and feel more in control.

KNOWLEDGE TO ACTION

1. Describe a period in your life when you felt like you were in complete control of your time. You had sufficient time for work, school, family, recreation, and your other interests. What were the keys to your success in managing your time?

_____

2. What steps can you take today to improve your time management?

_____

time management
the process of identifying what needs to get done and having a plan to get everything accomplished within the time allotted.

If you never seem to have enough time, keep a time journal for a week. Record what you do throughout the day. The simple act of recording your daily activities will raise your awareness about how you are spending your time. This insight will help you regain control of your time and will help you refocus on your priorities and goals. Consider using the template provided in Figure 9.2. Make an effort to record at least four entries

FIGURE 9.2 Time journal template

Name: _____

Date: _____

Priorities/Goals: _____

Time	Description of activity	Minutes	Comments
7:00 a.m.			
8:00			
9:00			
10:00			
11:00			
12:00 noon			
1:00 p.m.			
2:00			
3:00			
4:00			
5:00			
6:00			

Activity Summary and Analysis

Activity	Total Time in Minutes/Day	Comments

per hour, including everything from time spent on the phone, e-mailing, socializing, talking with customers, fixing a piece of equipment, replenishing stock, and responding to interruptions. At the end of the day, add up the number of minutes spent on similar activities and analyze the information. Try to identify areas where you can gain back time by reducing interruptions and/or increasing efficiency.[55]

Use Technology Wisely

The latest technology hyped in the media often leads people to purchase and implement gadgets without considering the trade-offs. One of the goals in reducing stress is to use technology to support operational efficiency, but not to let it consume or control you. For example, consider the common wireless devices that serve as a cell phone, media player, and computer. These devices allow users to text message, phone, and exchange e-mail from just about anywhere. High-performing employees often feel that they cannot turn off these devices because they may miss an important e-mail message. (Ask a BlackBerry user if he could live without it for a week.) However, what this creates is a 24/7 employee who is always on the job. As you learned earlier in this chapter, the brain needs a break—and so do your employees. Create policies and procedures that encourage people to turn off their work-related technology unless they are working or are scheduled to be on-call or available for a special project.

In addition, evaluate the information technology tools available today in an effort to identify solutions that may make your job and/or life easier or more efficient. Prior to implementing any new technology, consider the positive impacts it will have and balance them against any negatives.

Balance Work with Family/Home

It can be difficult to balance the demands of work with your obligations at home. However, with a little planning it can be done. As a supervisor, encourage your employees to find this balance. Corporations are helping employees strike a balance through several work-based initiatives, including:

Balancing family and work is a major challenge for today's employees and supervisors as advances in information technology have made connecting with the workplace easier. Successful supervisors work with employees to clarify expectations and develop policies to maximize employee productivity and minimize disruption to employees' personal lives. Frequently, employees request the option to telecommute and accept responsibility for remaining productive while working from home. "Mmmm, dinner smells good!"

© Plattform/Getty Images/Johner Images Royalty-Free

- Nontraditional schedules, such as four 10-hour days.
- Flexible scheduling where work day start and end times can vary.
- Job sharing.
- Telecommuting.
- On-site child care services.
- Errand and dry-cleaning pick-up and delivery services.[56]

The goal is to be sure that the work gets done, while also providing employees with flexibility to manage their lives. In many cases, it does not matter where or what time of day the work gets done, as long as it is high-quality and on time. For example, consider this situation at Best Buy:

> Jason Dehne's brother called him one day in March and asked if he might like to have lunch and then visit the annual auto show in downtown Minneapolis. Without even checking his schedule, Dehne—a human resource manager of retirement and wealth strategies at Best Buy—agreed to the plan. The brothers spent a blissful Tuesday afternoon walking through showrooms full of the latest vehicles.
>
> The story might not seem unusual if it were not for the fact that Dehne did not need to inform his boss of his whereabouts—he knew his boss could not care less. Nor did he feel guilty about it, since his job allows him to work wherever and whenever he wants as long as he completes projects on a timely basis.

Dehne participates in the consumer electronics retailer's novel Results-Only Work Environment (ROWE) program, which allows almost all of its 4,000 corporate employees to have the same freedom.[57]

Laugh a Little!

Laughter and stress reduction go hand in hand. Have you ever seen a person cracking up with laughter and exhibiting signs of stress at the same time? Probably not. Part of the reason for this is because it is difficult to take ourselves too seriously while we are laughing.

Lighten up! Laughter is indeed often the best medicine. Relieve stress, unite a group, and increase creativity by infusing a little humor in the workplace. Think of humor as seasoning on food—you want to enhance the taste without killing the flavor.
© PhotoAlto/Alamy

One of the sources of stress is being overly sensitive to criticism or failure. Everyone makes mistakes. The key is to learn from your mistakes and, when appropriate, lighten up a little and laugh at yourself. If you have ever heard a child fall into a belly rumble laugh, you know it is truly contagious. No matter how frustrated or unhappy you are, laughter is a great way to release some negative energy and stress.

In addition, it can help you make better decisions. For instance, ask someone to tell you a good joke the next time you have a big decision to make. Cornell University psychology professor Alice M. Isen believes that positive affect, or being in a good mood, helps you make better decisions and solve problems more creatively.[58] This does not imply that work is all fun and games or a big joke. Racism and sexual harassment, for example, often wear a mask of humor but are no laughing matter. However, Dr. Isen's claim suggests that lightening up the mood a little, taking yourself a little less seriously, and letting the laughter loose can improve performance and reduce stress.

How Conflict and Failure Can Be Good at Work

Conflict and failure are two terms that immediately generate negative thoughts. In the case of "conflict," you can readily picture coworkers arguing about an issue. "Failure" might bring about an image of an employee hanging his head in shame while his supervisor yells at him. Although these scenarios may play out in some organizations, successful supervisors realize that they can use conflict and failure in a positive fashion to improve performance outcomes.

How Can Conflict Be Good?

Many supervisors wrongly assume that employees who do not voice their disapproval or negative opinion are in agreement and supportive. However, what they may be experiencing is a lack of employee interest.[59] This type of apathy can lead to a decline in performance and productivity. Researchers suggest that a lack of conflicting opinions over issues is likely to lead to poor decision making. This sounds rather ominous. However, you can create positive conflict that can lead to much better solutions and decisions.

The key to managing *constructive* conflict is to foster an environment of trust and mutual respect. The individuals involved should know one another and respect one another's skills, knowledge, and expertise. Every person's opinions should be heard and respected. Everyone must also be prepared to speak the truth and hear the truth. This open and honest approach requires people to emotionally detach themselves from their ideas. An alternative opinion or criticism should not be taken personally. From the other side, it is important to criticize the idea or action, not the person or personality. The overriding goal as a supervisor is to facilitate a dialogue where people contribute conflicting ideas in the spirit of excellence, where everyone is striving for the best possible solution, product, or service. Starting the conversation with a clarification of the common goal, along with a review of ground rules for sharing one's thoughts and listening to other people's ideas, is essential. In addition, if a decision is to be made, outline how you will proceed through the information-sharing process to ultimately make the final decision.

Feeding Off of Failures

Sir James Dyson, inventor of the best-selling vacuum cleaner in America, said:

> I made 5,127 prototypes of my vacuum before I got it right. There were 5,126 failures. But I learned from each one. That's how I came up with the solution. So I don't mind failure . . . .
>
> You should admire the person who perseveres and slogs through and gets there in the end.[60]

Rather than focusing all of your energy on the negative aspects of failure, pause for a moment and look at failure as fuel for the future. Creativity and innovation are about discovery, and not all new discoveries work out. However, we can learn a lot from this exploratory journey if we open our minds to the possibilities and find what is good in an otherwise bad situation.

To turn failure into fuel for the future, supervisors need to create a safe environment where employees feel comfortable experimenting. Additionally, you need to try to foster a culture of learning where your employees thrive on new knowledge, experiences, and discovery. You may need to develop some guidelines and parameters for your team. For example, it is probably not a good idea to set a new employee free on a project using $10,000 worth of resources to explore possibilities. Therefore, you should outline the process along with expectations. Providing your employees with clear, achievable goals along with the freedom to chart their own course as they embark on their challenge are ingredients for success.

Turn failure into fuel for the future.

Part of the process of learning from failures is to effectively debrief and/or analyze a project. The key is to understand through failure that you can discover opportunities for improvement. However, in some cases the source of failure may be a situation that is beyond control or repair, in which case you may choose to shut down that idea. This information should be shared with coworkers so others do not waste their time and resources. In addition, it is important to move forward with the new knowledge learned from the experience as future initiatives are launched.

One of the keys to turning failure into fuel is fostering an environment where experimentation and discovery are part of the organization's culture.

SUMMARY

1. One way to encourage good behavior and a positive work attitude is to develop an attitude standard for your organization and then assess and hold employees accountable for their attitudes. Employee's attitudes largely determine their behavior and productivity at work, and they are often contagious. Six personal characteristics that should be included in an organization's attitude standard are (1) friendliness, (2) positivism, (3) teamwork, (4) enthusiasm, (5) responsibility, and (6) professionalism.

2. Creativity and idea generation requires employees to take a step back and look at the big picture first by answering the question: what are the mission and goals? Then, by looking at the organization, its customers, challenges, or day-to-day tasks with a different perspective, employees can come up with all kinds of new ideas. A few techniques to get you started include: (1) create a new perspective by changing patterns, habits, and routines, rearranging your space, and traveling; (2) brainstorming by involving new people, establishing idea quotas, keeping an idea log, and asking a lot of questions; (3) suspend judgment by separating idea generation from the evaluation of those ideas; (4) sleep on it by taking a break or even a nap; and (5) use the experiential design thinking approach to experience the world firsthand and walk in your customers' shoes.

3. Cultivating a positive work environment is a challenge as supervisors attempt to balance serious, focused work effort with time for fun, creative activities. The rewards are happy employees who are peak performers contributing to the achievement of organizational goals with less turnover and absenteeism. Seven strategies organizations have used to increase employee satisfaction and performance include: (1) being good corporate citizens; (2) creating a signature experience; (3) developing fair and equitable personnel policies and procedures; (4) creating an environment that celebrates success; (5) allowing employees to have a voice; (6) making learning, creativity, and innovation part of your corporate culture; and (7) making employee and customer satisfaction a way of life.

4. Healthy habits can reduce stress and absenteeism at work. Most supervisors encourage on-the-job safety; however, they forget about off-the-job injury prevention programs. Many organizations are implementing health and wellness programs at work to encourage exercise and nutrition. Other topics to consider include time management, technology use, flexible scheduling and other work/life balance initiatives, and incorporating a little laughter into your work environment because these programs typically improve employee performance, productivity, recruitment, and retention.

5. Successful supervisors realize that they can use conflict and failure in a positive fashion to improve performance outcomes. The key to managing constructive conflict is to foster an environment of trust and mutual respect. This open, honest approach requires people to emotionally detach themselves from their ideas. The goal is to facilitate a dialogue where people contribute conflicting ideas in the spirit of excellence, where everyone is striving for the best possible solution, product, or service. Creativity and innovation are about discovery, and not all new discoveries work out. However, we can learn a lot from this exploratory journey if we open our minds to the possibilities and find what is good in an otherwise bad situation. One of the keys to turning failure into fuel is fostering an environment where experimentation and discovery are part of the organization's culture and where employees feel safe trying new things. In addition, you need to try to foster a culture of learning where your employees thrive on new knowledge, experiences, and discovery.

TERMS TO UNDERSTAND

attitude, p. 237
attitude standard, p. 237
brainstorming, p. 242
creativity, p. 238
design thinking, p. 248
empathy, p. 248
enthusiasm, p. 238

experiential approach, p. 247
friendliness, p. 237
new perspective, p. 241
positive work environment, p. 249
positivism, p. 237
professionalism, p. 238
prototyping, p. 248

responsibility, p. 238
sleep on it, p. 246
storytelling, p. 248
suspend judgment, p. 246
teamwork, p. 237
time management, p. 256

QUESTIONS FOR REFLECTION

1. Why is an attitude standard an important tool for supervisors to use and include in employee performance appraisals?

2. Can supervisors teach employees to be creative? Why or why not?

3. The research indicates that one way to foster a positive work environment is to be good corporate citizens. Do you agree or disagree? Why?

4. Identify five ways that you can gain a new and different perspective by changing your patterns.

5. Explain what is meant by the term *work/life balance*. What does it mean to *you*?

6. What responsibility do you think companies and supervisors have to help their employees achieve work/life balance?

HANDS-ON ACTIVITIES

INSPIRING PERSONAL CREATIVITY

1. Identify a problem, challenge, or a potential new opportunity. Create an idea log related to this project. Include in your idea log:
   a. A brief description of the idea.
   b. The date and time.
   c. The location where you came up with the idea.
   d. The person(s) you were with or talking to (if anyone) when you generated the idea.
   e. Any other relevant information that may be useful in evaluating the idea later.

2. Change your perspective.
   a. Pick five ways to alter your routines and/or habits for a week.
   b. Document prior to making the changes things you anticipate will be different and how that will impact you.
   c. Proceed with your changes and document your experience, how you felt, and the overall impact.
   d. As a supervisor, how do you think the concept of changing perspective may be useful in the workplace?

CORPORATE CITIZENSHIP—GOING GREEN

Select a company or nonprofit organization with which you are familiar. Then answer the following questions. Be sure to explain your answers and provide examples.

1. Create a list of the organization's environmentally friendly policies, practices, and procedures. Answer the following questions for each item on the list.
   a. Are there any extra financial costs to the organization to implement the policy, practice, or procedure?

b. Are there any cost savings or other financial benefits?

c. Are there any hidden or intangible costs (such as extra time or effort)?

d. Are there any hidden or intangible benefits for implementing these environmentally friendly initiatives?

2. Create a list of policies, practices, and/or procedures you believe the organization should implement to become more environmentally friendly.

3. As a supervisor, how do you think going green and being a good corporate citizen impact employees?

Interview an Expert

The purpose of this exercise is to learn from an expert the approach used to cultivate a positive work environment. Identify a supervisor or human resources manager to interview. If possible, choose someone working in an industry in which you have a personal interest or are already working. Your goal is to learn from this person's experience and discover tools and techniques that have been effective in fostering an environment where employees are happy, turnover is low, and productivity/ goal achievement is high. You may use the questions listed below and/or develop your own. After your interview, prepare a brief summary of the conversation and list the strategies, tools, and techniques the person uses to create a positive work environment.

QUESTIONS

1. Do you believe employee satisfaction and happiness have an impact on retention?

2. What relationship (if any) does employee satisfaction and happiness have on performance and productivity?

3. When you think of the ideal positive work environment, what comes to mind?

4. What are some strategies and techniques that you and/or your organization use to foster a positive work environment?

5. How do you get employees involved with these initiatives?

6. What are the biggest challenges in balancing a serious, focused work environment with time for learning, creativity, and fun?

7. What do you think are the keys to creating a culture where employee and customer satisfaction are a way of life?

You may improvise and add or edit questions to fit the situation or the circumstances of your interview. Schedule your interview ahead of time and try to limit it to about 15 minutes. Remember to send a thank-you note to the person you interview.

YOU DECIDE

CASE STUDY 9.1
Idea Generation

Matt is a supervisor for a regional economic development agency. There are three main aspects to his job: (1) attract businesses that are currently located in other states to move to the area, (2) retain and help existing employers in the area, and (3) support aspiring entrepreneurs who want to start new businesses. Matt's performance has always been measured based on the number of jobs and total revenue generated by the region's companies. Therefore, he typically spends most of his time trying to attract large businesses from other areas to move into his region. This strategy has worked for him in the past because large companies are more likely to have more jobs and higher revenue, which reflect nicely in his performance measures.

Recently, Gretchen was hired as the new Regional Director, and she has added another performance measure for Matt: total number of new businesses started in the region. Matt has never spent much time focusing on helping start-up companies. However, two of his employees, Kelly and Beth, previously worked for small-business development councils in other cities. In addition, Matt's new boss, Gretchen, has prior experience working with entrepreneurs. Matt's first task is to prepare a list of possible outreach activities and education programs the agency can offer to help aspiring entrepreneurs successfully launch their business start-ups.

Questions

1. How would you suggest Matt get started in generating ideas for possible outreach activities?

2. What are a few specific techniques Matt can use by himself to spark creative ideas?

3. What are a few specific techniques he can use to involve Kelly, Beth, and perhaps Gretchen?

4. How would you suggest he generate ideas for potential education topics that can help aspiring entrepreneurs?

5. How might the experiential design thinking approach be useful?

*S*UPERVISOR'S TOOLKIT

Fostering a positive work environment and encouraging creativity involves promoting a healthy, productive work environment that embraces good conflict. As you develop your supervisory skills, you will learn how to inspire creativity, reduce stress, and improve team performance. Prepare a few documents to add to your supervisor's toolkit that outline tips and best practices for promoting health and wellness, reducing stress and achieving work/life balance, and encouraging positive conflict.

1. Most supervisors would like to reduce their employees' stress and absenteeism; one way to accomplish this is by improving employees' health and safety. Identify at least three ways to promote health and wellness at work.

2. Another factor that contributes to employee stress is balancing work with family/home. What are examples of corporate initiatives that you would consider in an effort to help employees strike a balance?

3. Many supervisors want to avoid conflict at all cost. However, conflict can be a sign of a very positive, productive team. How can you encourage constructive conflict in the workplace?

CHAPTER 10

Communication: Around the World in 60 Seconds

Learning Objectives

1. Analyze cultural differences and the impact on supervisory communication.

2. Explain the communication process and discuss how variables such as global cultural diversity and media richness impact communication.

3. List traits of effective communicators and discuss the power of affirmations and visualization.

4. Explain techniques for effective listening, including overcoming barriers to communication.

5. Compare proactive and reactive language.

6. Discuss the importance of modifying the message and delivery to suit the audience.

Straight Talk from the Field

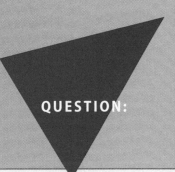

Sandie Anderson is the Communications Manager for Comcast's Bay Shore Group. Comcast's headquarters are located in Philadelphia, Pennsylvania.

QUESTION: *What is your approach to communicating with a diverse workforce and how do you adapt your message for your audience?*

RESPONSE:

*A*s the country's largest provider of cable services—and one of the world's leading communications companies—Comcast now connects more than 21 million people nationwide. We have more than 90,000 employees who want to work alongside the best of the best, people who believe that different perspectives and backgrounds, as well as innovation and growth opportunity, should be all in a day's work.

As the communications manager for the Bay Shore Group, I am responsible for communicating with close to 900 of these employees serving customers in Delaware and Maryland. We consider our workforce to be incredibly diverse for a variety of reasons, most importantly because of each person's unique perspective and job responsibilities. In our region, we have business operations people such as accountants, programmers, and warehouse personnel. We also have an administrative group that is responsible for human resources management, government relations, and community affairs. However, our largest group of employees, approximately 85%, work on the front lines as account executives handling customer phone calls and as technicians working in the field. One of my challenges is to ensure that all of these employees receive important company information, consistently and without interrupting the customer experience.

My Approach

As an industry leader in communication technology, Comcast uses video, Web links, and other forms of technology to communicate with employees and customers. However, technology is not an effective medium for communicating with the majority of our employees because most of these people are working out in the field, not sitting in front of a computer all day. Therefore, I have found personal communication to be the most effective way to communicate with our workforce. We empower managers and front-line supervisors to deliver information to their teams and to provide two-way communication between the staff and upper management. Supervisors also conduct one-on-one connection meetings with each of their employees. During these meetings, they encourage individuals to share their ideas, comments, and suggestions for improvement. Supervisors use these meetings to discuss each person's career path. In addition, they take time to share information about the company, their division, and their team.

Adapting the Message

My job is to work with the managers and supervisors to develop a consistent message that is also relevant for their particular areas. One message for the entire company does not work. Instead, I design three or four versions of the same basic message. Each version is adapted for the intended recipients. The message must be relevant to the workforce. I take time to identify how the information will impact them personally. It is essential that I prepare a message that highlights how the new information will make their jobs easier, will benefit their customers, or will provide opportunities for growth.

The Delivery

In addition, all key messaging points are designed to be clear, concise, and direct. One of my goals is to "remove the noise" from the message and simply focus on the key points. In a perfect world, all of our supervisors and managers would deliver the message consistently. However, people have unique perspectives and filter the information based on their role and expertise. As a result, I spend time with our leaders providing coaching and feedback in an effort to ensure all corporate communication is consistent, clear, concise, direct, and appropriate for the intended audience.

267

Employee Feedback

Another method we use to communicate with our employees is through large group meetings held twice a year. Prior to each of these meetings we ask people, "What's on your mind?" We invite employees to submit questions, comments, and suggestions in advance. This provides us with the opportunity to address the topics that are of interest to the workforce. It also gives us the chance to dispel rumors and keep everyone informed and up-to-date on our new products and services.

To learn more about what employees are thinking, the company sends out an annual electronic survey with approximately twenty categories. Effective communication is one of the categories the company evaluates. This is another way that we gather information to determine what is working and what needs improvement. We strive to encourage effective two-way communication throughout the organization. However, everything we do is within the context of customer service. I will never compromise our customer's experience just to make my job of communicating with the workforce a little easier.

As a leader in the communications industry, Comcast recognizes the value of technology in enabling fast, convenient, cost-effective communication. However, I have found that there are times when personal communication is the most effective method for me to ensure that a clear, concise, and direct message is communicated to our diverse workforce in the field.

Chapter Outline

Virtually every supervisory function involves some form of communication. Planning, recruiting, and training all require a lot of communicating, as do scheduling, coaching, delegating, decision making, and problem solving. Organizational cultures would not exist without communication. Studies have shown that both organizational and individual performance improve when supervisory communication is effective.[1] Given today's team-oriented organizations, where work needs to be accomplished with and through other people, over whom a supervisor all too often has no direct authority, communication skills are more important than

Virtually every supervisory function involves some form of communication.

ever. In fact, a recent survey of 133 executives revealed that communication is the most desired skill for managers and supervisors.[2]

Thanks to technology, we can communicate quickly and inexpensively. But the ensuing torrent of messages has proved to be a mixed blessing for supervisors and their employees. Complaints of information overload are common today. As marketing executive Hilary Billings has observed:

> There's a growing realization that we're all becoming victims of the technological devices that were supposed to make our lives simpler. The proliferation of laptops, PDAs, and pagers means that we're working harder and harder to keep up with our own inventions. The price of being available 24-7 is the loss of time for reflection, creative thinking, and connections with our loved ones—the things that are really important for our emotional and spiritual lives.[3]

Advances in technology, along with increased workforce diversity, create more opportunities for cross-cultural communication. This process is sometimes complex and, if handled improperly, can lead to misunderstandings and conflict.

As you can see, effective communication involves many variables. This chapter will provide you with a comprehensive explanation of the communication process. You will learn valuable strategies and techniques to successfully communicate with your employees, managers, coworkers, and customers around the world.

Culture Matters When Communicating in Today's Global Economy

Management scholar Keith Davis defined **communication** as "the transfer of information and understanding from one person to another person."[4] Communication is inherently a social process. Whether one communicates face-to-face with a single person or with a group of people via the Internet, it is a social activity involving two or more people. Cultural diversity plays a huge role in this complex process. So we need to discuss the role of culture before learning more about the communication process.

The Cultural Imperative

In this section, we define the term *culture*, identify basic cultural dimensions, and explore important cross-cultural differences. **Culture** is a population's taken-for-granted assumptions, values, beliefs, and symbols that foster patterned behavior about how a given collection of people should think, act, and feel as they go about their daily affairs.[5] A central aspect of this definition is the notion of *taken-for-granted-assumptions*. These are aspects of our daily lives and our culture that become second nature. Most people have these so deeply ingrained in their subconscious mind that they are unaware of their assumptions. This applies to people from different cultures around the globe.[6] Keep in mind that although our cultural assumptions are common knowledge to those in our own society, they may be entirely different elsewhere. Therefore, it is essential to recognize and value differences as you build relationships with employees and business partners from other cultures.

communication
the transfer of information and understanding from one person to another person.

culture
a population's taken-for-granted assumptions, values, beliefs, and symbols that foster patterned behavior.

In earlier chapters, we called corporate culture *social glue* that binds members of the organization together. Similarly, but at a broader level, societal culture acts as a social glue made up of norms, values, attitudes, role expectations, taboos, symbols, heroes, beliefs, morals, customs, and rituals. Cultural lessons are imparted from birth to death via role models, formal education, religious teachings, and peer pressure. Cultural roots run deep and have profound impacts on behavior. They are not readily altered. Therefore, it is important to be mindful of organizational values *and* respect cultural differences. Maxine Fechter, a human resources consultant with New York–based People Equities, explains the emphasis on tolerance at the multinational company:

> Honesty, integrity, and individual respect were cornerstones wherever we did business, and applied to both our employees and our customers. At the same time, we respected the cultural mores of each individual country, and so how these values were communicated or behaviors practiced were society specific.[7]

Nine Dimensions of Culture from the GLOBE Project

The GLOBE (Global Leadership and Organizational Behavior Effectiveness) project was conceived by Robert J. House, a University of Pennsylvania researcher. It is a massive ongoing effort in which researchers assess organizations in their own cultures and languages with standardized instruments to collect data from around the world, building a comprehensive model. The network encompasses more than 150 researchers in 62 countries. If things go as planned, the database will provide important information about the similarities and differences across the world's cultures.[8] More importantly, it promises to provide guidelines for international managers. Thanks to the first two phases of the GLOBE project, we have a research-based list of key cultural dimensions (see Table 10.1).

Other Sources of Cultural Diversity That Impact Communication

There are no right or wrong elements of cultural diversity, only cross-cultural differences.

There are no right or wrong elements of cultural diversity, only cross-cultural differences. The goal is for supervisors to understand these differences and how they impact communication and relationship building.

INDIVIDUALISM VERSUS COLLECTIVISM

This distinction between "me" and "we" cultures deserves closer attention because it encompasses two of the nine GLOBE cultural dimensions in Table 10.1. People in **individualistic cultures** focus primarily on individual rights, roles, and achievements.[9] The United States and Canada are highly individualistic cultures. Meanwhile, people in **collectivist cultures**—such as Egypt, Mexico, India, and Japan—rank duty and loyalty to family, friends, organization, and country above self-interests. Group goals and shared achievements are paramount to collectivists: personal goals and desires are suppressed. Importantly, individualism and collectivism are extreme ends of a continuum, along which people and cultures are variously distributed and mixed. For example, in the United States, one can find pockets of collectivism among Native Americans and recent immigrants from Latin America and Asia. This helps explain why a top-notch engineer

individualistic cultures cultures that emphasize individual rights, roles, and achievements.

collectivist cultures cultures that emphasize duty and loyalty to collective goals and achievements.

TABLE 10.1
Nine Cultural Dimensions from the GLOBE Project

Dimension	Description	Countries scoring highest	Countries scoring lowest
Power distance	Should leaders have high or low power over others?	Morocco, Argentina, Thailand	Denmark, Netherlands, South Africa (black sample)
Uncertainty avoidance	How much should social norms and rules be used to reduce future uncertainties?	Switzerland, Sweden, Germany (former West)	Russia, Hungary, Bolivia
Institutional collectivism	To what extent should society and institutions reward loyalty?	Sweden, South Korea, Japan	Greece, Hungary, Germany (former East)
In-group collectivism	To what extent does the individual value loyalty to his/her family or organization?	Iran, India, Morocco	Denmark, Sweden, New Zealand
Assertiveness	How aggressive and confrontational should one be with others?	Germany (former East), Austria, Greece	Sweden, New Zealand, Switzerland
Gender equality	How equal are men and women?	Hungary, Poland, Slovenia	South Korea, Egypt, Morocco
Future orientation	How much should one work and save for the future, rather than just live for the present?	Singapore, Switzerland, Netherlands	Russia, Argentina, Poland
Performance orientation	How much should people be rewarded for excellence and improvement?	Singapore, Hong Kong, New Zealand	Russia, Argentina, Greece
Humane orientation	How much should people be encouraged to be generous, kind, and fair to others?	Philippines, Ireland, Malaysia	Germany (former West), Spain, France

Source: Adapted from discussions in Robert J. House, Paul J Hanges, Mansour Javidan, Peter W. Dorfman, and Vipin Gupta, eds. *Culture, Leadership, and Organizations: The GLOBE Study of 62 Societies* (Thousand Oaks, CA: Sage, 2004).

 **KNOWLEDGE TO ACTION**

Imagine that your organization just hired a new supervisor who is in the process of moving to the United States from Morocco. He speaks fluent English, but he has never lived or worked in America. He will be supervising five women and three men. Brainstorm with your classmates about the following:

1. Are there any cultural dimensions listed in Table 10.1 that could potentially be a source of misunderstanding due to cultural differences? Explain.

2. Based on Table 10.1 and the information above, make a list of topics you think should be included as part of the new supervisor's cultural training.

Today's organizations recognize the value of a diverse workforce. Through diversification of employee backgrounds and knowledge, companies can enjoy a competitive advantage. Supervisors working for these organizations embrace cross-cultural differences. Their challenge is to understand individual differences and to help their employees appreciate those differences. This knowledge-building process will foster stronger relationships and more effective communication among team members.

© Andersen Ross/Barnd X Pictures/Jupiter Images

born in China might be reluctant to attend an American-style recognition dinner where individual award recipients are asked to stand up for a round of applause.

TIME

Time has been referred to as a silent language of culture.[10] Specifically, **monochronic time** refers to perceiving time as a unidimensional straight line divided into standard units such as seconds, minutes, hours, and days. In monochronic cultures, including North America and northern Europe, everyone is assumed to be on the same clock and time is treated as money. The general rule is to use time efficiently, be on time, and above all, do not waste time. In contrast, **polychronic time** involves the perception that time is flexible, elastic, and multidimensional.[11] Latin American, Mediterranean, and Arab cultures are polychronic. Supervisors in polychronic cultures such as rural Mexico see no problem with loosely scheduled, overlapping office visits. For example, a monochronic American arriving 10 minutes early for an appointment with a regional Mexican official could resent having to wait another 15 minutes. The American perceives the Mexican official as slow and insensitive. The Mexican official believes the American is self-centered and impatient.[12] Different perceptions of time are responsible for this collision of cultures.

monochronic time
the perception that time is a line divided into standard units.

polychronic time
the perception that time is flexible, elastic, and multidimensional.

KNOWLEDGE TO ACTION

Misunderstandings because of time and individual perceptions of time have long been a source of conflict. What steps can a supervisor take to avoid potential misunderstandings related to time for the following situations?

1. Every employee is required to complete the safety training course by the end of the year. The course is available online in three separate modules and there is a test at the end. The supervisor will be on vacation from December 21 to January 3, so he wants everyone to complete the training before he leaves. He has people on his team from various parts of the world, including South America, the Mediterranean, Mexico, and the United States. How should he communicate with his team to be sure everyone understands the deadline?

_____

2. Leslie is ordering a replacement part for a unique and very expensive piece of equipment that is used to cut metals for custom work her company performs. They need the part by next Tuesday and it is being sent from Latin America, which means it probably needs to be shipped today or tomorrow at the latest. The e-mail confirmation she receives indicates that it will be sent "right away." How should Leslie respond to this e-mail to be sure the part reaches her company on time?

_____

INTERPERSONAL SPACE

People in a number of cultures, including Arab and Asian cultures, prefer to stand close when conversing. An interpersonal distance of only six inches is very disturbing to a northern European or an American, accustomed to conversing at arm's length. Cross-cultural gatherings in the Middle East often involve an awkward dance as Arab hosts strive to get closer while their American and northern European guests back away to maintain what they consider to be a proper distance.

LANGUAGE

Foreign language skills are the gateway to true cross-cultural understanding. Translations are not an accurate substitute for conversational ability in the local language.[13] In addition, there often is not time for computer software translations or the availability of a human translator. As the immigrant population continues to grow in the U.S., a supervisor likely will have at least one employee who comes from a country where English is not the primary language.

RELIGION

Awareness of a business colleague's religious traditions is essential for building a lasting relationship. Those traditions may dictate dietary restrictions, religious holidays, and worship schedules, which are important to the devout and represent cultural minefields for the uninformed. For instance, in some countries such as Israel, "Burger King restaurants—unlike McDonald's—do not offer cheeseburgers in order to conform to Jewish dietary laws forbidding mixing milk products and meat."[14] From a scheduling perspective, particularly if you are conducting business with employees located in different countries, it is helpful to know

Religious traditions may dictate dietary restrictions, religious holidays, and worship schedules.

their scheduling traditions. For example, the official day of rest in Iran is Thursday; in Kuwait and Pakistan it is Friday.[15] In Israel, the official day off is Saturday.

Components of the Communication Process

The communication process is a chain made up of identifiable links (see Figure 10.1). Links in this process include sender, encoding, medium, decoding, receiver, and feedback.[16] The essential purpose of this process is to send an idea from one person to another in a way that will be understood by the receiver. Like any other chain, the communication chain is only as strong as its weakest link.[17]

Encoding

The act of thinking takes place within the privacy of your brain and is greatly affected by how you perceive your environment. However, when you want to pass along a thought to someone else, an entirely different process begins. This second process, communication, requires that you, the sender, package the idea for understandable transmission. Encoding occurs at this point. The purpose of **encoding** is to translate internal thought patterns into a language or code that the intended receiver of the message should be able to understand.

Supervisors usually rely on words, gestures, or other symbols for encoding. Their choice of symbols depends on several factors, one of which is the nature of the message itself. Is it technical or nontechnical, emotional or factual? Perhaps it could be expressed better with colorful Microsoft PowerPoint slides rather than words, as in the case of a budget report. To express skepticism, merely a shrug of the shoulders may be enough. More fundamentally, will the encoding help get the attention of busy and distracted people?[18]

As you learned in the previous section, cultural diversity necessitates careful message encoding. In the global marketplace, where language barriers may hamper communication, e-mail and software translation programs can make the encoding process a bit easier. However, it is still important to take the time to research the recipient's culture in an effort to effectively encode your message. As this recent

FIGURE 10.1 The basic communication process

encoding
translating internal thought patterns into a language or code that the intended receiver of the message will understand.

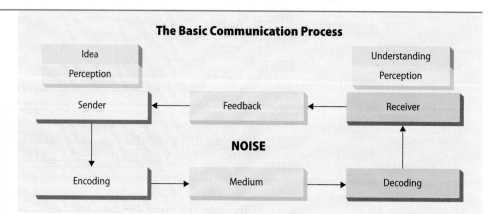

example illustrates, there really is no fully adequate substitute for firsthand knowledge of the local culture and language:

> The seasoned banker from Rhode Island and the junior banker from Brazil seemed to be worlds apart on the surface. But when Merrill Lynch managing director Kerry Cannella and young associate Selma Bueno joined forces on their first deal, they made a potent cross-cultural duo.
>
> Merrill Lynch was representing Brazilian investors selling their stake in a multibillion-dollar Latin American company to potential U.S. investors. The deal was moving slowly, with both sides cautious.
>
> Then Cannella and Bueno stepped up the pace. They jetted between New York and Brazil many times. Bueno analyzed financial papers in Portuguese. She put together an offering document for investors. She picked classy hotels and restaurants, translated during negotiations, and made both sides feel more at ease with each other.
>
> With the help of Bueno's business and social skills, the bankers finally closed the deal—in the hundreds of millions of dollars—to everyone's satisfaction.[19]

Selecting a Communication Medium

Supervisors can choose among a number of transmission media or forms of communication. A **communication medium** is the form of transmission. Today's communication media include face-to-face conversations, telephone calls, e-mails, instant messaging (IM), memos, letters, computer reports, network file sharing, photographs, bulletin boards, blogs, meetings, organizational publications, and others. Communicating with those outside the organization opens up further possibilities, such as news releases, press conferences, and advertising on television and radio or in magazines, in newspapers, and on the Internet.

CROSS-CULTURAL SENSITIVITY

As with encoding, the importance of selecting an appropriate medium is magnified in both internal and external cross-cultural dealings.[20] Remember that cultural traditions can have a significant impact on employee communication patterns and their behavior. In addition, sensitivity to cross-cultural differences is imperative for people who do business in other countries. Indeed, cross-cultural sensitivity is vital to each of us on a daily basis because we live in a world where 3 out of every 100 people (more than 174 million) live outside the country of their birth.[21]

A CONTINGENCY APPROACH

A contingency model for media selection was proposed by Robert Lengel and Richard Daft.[22] It pivots on the concept of media richness. **Media richness** is the capacity of a given medium to convey information and promote learning. Media vary in richness from high (or rich) to low (or lean). Face-to-face conversation is a rich medium because it:

1. Simultaneously provides *multiple information cues*, such as message content, tone of voice, facial expressions, and body language.
2. Facilitates immediate *feedback*.
3. Is *personal* in focus. A personal phone call is a relatively rich medium, while a voice-mail message is not as rich.

communication medium
the form of transmission used such as telephone calls, e-mails, or instant messaging.

media richness
the capacity of a given medium to convey information and promote learning.

In contrast, posted bulletins and general computer reports are lean media–that is, they convey limited information and foster limited learning. Lean media–such as general e-mails–provide a single cue, do not facilitate immediate face-to-face feedback, and are impersonal.

A supervisor's challenge is to match media richness with the situation. Choosing the best method to communicate is based on several variables. Included among them are the level of urgency and complexity of the information, the sensitivity of the content, and the nature of the sender's relationship with the recipients. Nonroutine problems or highly sensitive topics are best handled with rich media such as face-to-face, telephone, or video interactions. Lean media are appropriate for routine communication

Examples of mismatched media include reading an entire company report to employees during a staff meeting (*data glut* and a waste of precious time) or announcing a layoff through an impersonal e-mail (*data starvation* and emotionally insensitive). The latter situation would have a major impact on job performance for both the employees whose jobs are being eliminated and those who will remain employed. Consider this recent example from RadioShack Corp. Management chose to notify 400 employees via e-mail that the company was eliminating their jobs. Another retailer decided to fire an employee via text message.[23] Can you imagine being on the receiving end of these poor media-selection decisions?

Test your ability to match the message with the most appropriate transmission media in the following Knowledge to Action exercise.

KNOWLEDGE TO ACTION

Complete the following by matching the message with the communication transmission media you think is most appropriate for the type of message being sent.

Type of Message	Choose the Best Match	Transmission Media
1. Performance counseling and/or appraisal.		a. E-mail
2. Plans to lay off 50 employees by the end of the year.		b. Face-to-face, one-on-one in person
3. Last-minute change in plans, the meeting will start at 3:00, not 1:00 as originally scheduled.		c. Face-to-face, group meeting in person
4. Announcing plans for the company's annual holiday party.		d. Company website posting
5. Promotional notice advertising new product.		e. Phone call

See end of chapter for correct answers.

Decoding

Even the most expertly fashioned message will not accomplish its purpose unless it is understood. After physically receiving the message, receivers begin **decoding** it or translating the packaged message into a format they can comprehend. If the message has been properly encoded, decoding will take place rather routinely. However, perfect encoding and decoding are nearly impossible to achieve in our world of many languages, cultures, jargon, and slang. American sports jargon is particularly troublesome in cross-cultural business dealings. Take baseball jargon, for instance:

> Executives from Qingdao to São Paulo must know what it means to "make a pitch," and if they don't know what it takes to develop a "home-run" product, they had better know how to "manufacture runs" by "choking up" and "playing small ball in the late innings."
>
> Huh? Business is so rife with the jargon that it makes foreigners wonder what Americans are smoking when they throw around baseball in a business context, like "throwing smoke." "Around the horn" has nothing to do with shipping. "Pickles" don't come from a Vlasic jar. "Chin music" doesn't come from an iPod, and "ringing someone up" has nothing to do with an iPhone.[24]
>
> (Note: A baseball-loving classmate can translate this jargon, if needed.)

Also, the receiver's willingness to receive the message is essential for successful decoding. If the receiver knows the language and terminology used in the message, she is more likely to decode it correctly. It also helps if the receiver understands the sender's purpose, the background of the situation, and other variables such as level of urgency. Effective listening is also critical to the success of decoding. Listening skills are discussed in detail later in this chapter.

Feedback

Verbal or nonverbal feedback from the receiver to the sender is required to complete the communication process. Without feedback, senders have no way of knowing whether their ideas have been accurately understood. Knowing whether others understand us affects both the form and content of our follow-up communication. Employees consistently underscore the importance of receiving timely and personal feedback from management. Therefore, it is essential that supervisors provide specific feedback to employees through coaching and timely communication to reinforce positive employee behavior and to curtail any undesirable behavior.

Noise

decoding
translate the packaged message into a format that the receiver can comprehend.

noise
any interference with the normal flow of understanding from one person to another.

Noise is not an integral part of the communication process; however, it may influence the process at any or all points. As the term is used here, **noise** is any interference with the normal flow of understanding from one person to another. This is a very broad definition. A few examples of noise include (1) garbled technical transmission, (2) negative attitudes, (3) a speech impairment, (4) misperceptions, (5) illegible print or pictures, (6) telephone static, (7) partial loss of hearing, (8) poor eyesight, and (9) lies.[25] A person's level of understanding tends to diminish as the volume of noise increases. In general, the effectiveness of organizational communication can be improved in two ways:

■ Steps can be taken to make verbal and written messages more understandable. For example, you can review your message with one of your employees or have someone else proofread a written message to be certain your intended message is clearly understood.

■ At the same time, noise can be minimized by foreseeing and neutralizing or accommodating potential sources of interference.

KNOWLEDGE TO ACTION

1. Select one of the examples of noise that may interfere with the sending and receiving of a message. Identify two things you can do to eliminate this noise or make accommodations to reduce the interference it may cause.

2. Imagine that one of your sources of noise is frequent interruptions. What are two steps you can take to reduce this source of noise?

Communication Strategies

Companies spend a lot of time and energy on planning new products, information technology decisions, financial decisions, and marketing strategies. They spend much less, if any, time preparing organizational communication strategies. Hence, organizational communication tends to be haphazard and often ineffective. As an individual supervisor, you may not be able to change the entire communication culture of your organization. However, you can be key to implementing a more systematic approach.[26] This section introduces five basic communication strategies, with an eye toward improving the overall quality of organizational communication.

A Communication Continuum with Five Strategies

A team of authors led by communication expert Phillip G. Clampitt created the communication strategy continuum shown in Figure 10.2.

Communication effectiveness is the vertical dimension of the model and ranges from low to high. A message that is communicated via any of the media discussed earlier is effective if the sender's intended meaning is conveyed fully and accurately to the receiver. The horizontal dimension of Clampitt's model is the amount of information transmitted, ranging from great to little. Plotted on the resulting grid are five common communication strategies. Let us examine each one more closely.

■ *Spray & Pray.* This is the organizational equivalent of a large lecture section in which passive receivers are showered with information in the hope that some of it will stick. Supervisors employing the Spray & Pray strategy assume "more is better." Unfortunately, as employees who are swamped every day by corporate

FIGURE 10.2 Clampitt's communication strategy continuum

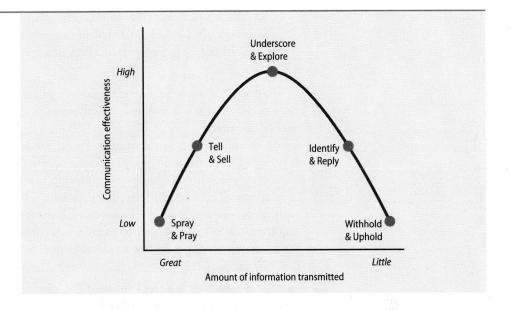

e-mail directives and announcements will attest, more is *not* necessarily better. This strategy suffers from being one-way, impersonal, and unhelpful because it leaves receivers to sort out what is actually important or relevant.

- *Tell & Sell*. This strategy involves communicating a more restricted set of messages and taking time to explain their importance and relevance. Top executives often rely on Tell & Sell when introducing new strategies, merger plans, and reorganizations. A potentially fatal flaw arises when more time is spent polishing the presentation than assessing the receivers' actual needs.

- *Underscore & Explore*. With this give-and-take strategy, key information and issues closely tied to the organization's success are communicated. Priorities are included and justifications are offered. Unlike the first two strategies, this one is two-way. Receivers are treated as active rather than passive participants in the process. Feedback is generated by "allowing employees the creative freedom to explore the implications of those ideas in a disciplined way."[27] Listening, resolving misunderstandings, building consensus and commitment, and addressing actual or potential obstacles are fundamental to success in the Underscore & Explore strategy.

- *Identify & Reply*. This is a reactive and sometimes defensive strategy. Employee concerns about prior communications are the central focus here. Employees are not only viewed as active participants, they essentially drive the process because they are assumed to know the key issues. According to Clampitt and his colleagues, "Employees set the agenda, while executives respond to rumors, innuendoes, and leaks."[28] Those using the Identify & Reply strategy need to be good listeners.

- *Withhold & Uphold*. With this communication strategy, you tell people what you think they need to know only when you believe they need to know it. Secrecy and control are paramount. Because information is viewed as power, it is rationed and restricted. In this command-and-control management style, those in charge uphold their view of things when challenged or questioned. The Withhold & Uphold communication strategy virtually guarantees rumors and resentment.

In organizational life, one can find hybrid combinations of these five strategies. But usually there is a dominant underlying strategy. That particular strategy may or may not be effective.

Both ends of the continuum in Figure 10.2 are problematic. At the Spray & Pray end of the continuum, employees are overloaded with too much information. In contrast, at the Withhold & Uphold end, employees are left out of the communication loop all together. The challenge for supervisors is to strike the right balance. This requires you to focus on the core issues and determine what information is most important for your employees to receive.[29] Accordingly, supervisors should adhere to the following set of guidelines when selecting a communication strategy appropriate to the situation:

- Avoid Spray & Pray and Withhold & Uphold.
- Use Tell & Sell and Identify & Reply sparingly.
- Use Underscore & Explore as much as possible.

Merging Communication Strategies and Media Richness

Present and future supervisors who effectively blend media richness and communication strategies are on the path toward improved organizational communication. The trick is to select the richest medium possible (given resource constraints) when employing the Tell & Sell, Identify & Reply, and Underscore & Explore strategies.[30]

"Step One: Climb the ladder. Step Two: Guess what you're expected to do. Step Three: You're wrong."

© Ted Goff

Traits of Effective Communicators

When you think about people you consider to be effective communicators, some specific traits probably come to mind. Of course, these are not the same for everyone, but there are some notable characteristics instructive for all supervisors. Let's start with first impressions. Contrary to popular belief, they do matter and, as the saying goes, *you don't get a second chance at a first impression.* Therefore, consider a few keys to creating a good first impression. Most of these factors have more to do with nonverbal communication than with what you actually say. For example, making (nonglaring) eye contact with a person sends a message that you are sincere and honest. Smiling while reaching out to shake a person's hand shows a human touch that helps to create a genuine connection.[31]

Making (nonglaring) eye contact with someone sends a message that you are sincere and honest.

THEY SAID IT BEST

Use the Platinum Rule;
"Treat others the way they want to be treated."
This ensures that your customer will be treated in a way that meets his or her needs.
—LAURIE BROWN, International Trainer and Consultant

Source: Laurie Brown, "When Good Customer Service Rules Go Bad," *Supervision* 68 (September 2007): 9.

Staying Focused and Achieving Results

Laurie Brown's Platinum Rule takes the famous Golden Rule an additional step. Although Brown's emphasis is on customer service, the Platinum Rule also applies to how you treat your employees and managers. Keep the Platinum Rule in mind as you consider the ten tips in Figure 10.3 for staying focused and working toward your potential.[32]

The Power of Visualization and Affirmations

You probably have heard athletes describe how they pictured themselves achieving success in their sport. It could have been an ice skater landing the perfect jump or a golfer making a putt. This technique can also make a big difference in the business world.[33] **Visualization** is creating a picture in your mind of the desired outcome. In other words, it is "like running a movie through your mind for which you are the actor and director."[34] Think of visualization as mental rehearsal for real-life events.

Visualization is a powerful communication tool for supervisors because it enhances the ability to communicate effectively. The key is to visualize every aspect of the scenario or goal, including your facial expression, tone of voice, body language, and appropriate feedback from your audience. You can use this technique to prepare for a big presentation, for a customer interaction, or a coaching session with one of your employees. Visualizing the exchange will allow you to sharpen your focus, relieve stress, and gain confidence.

visualization
creating a picture in your mind of the desired outcome.

FIGURE 10.3 Quick tips for staying focused and achieving results

Source: Adapted from Frank Savarese, CPA, CFP, "It's All About Leadership, Managing Human Capital," *Business Owners Guide to Financial Management*, 10. Savarese is the Managing Partner at Weyrich, Cronin & Sorra, Chartered ~ Certified Public Accountants & Financial Consultants, www.wcscpa.com, (accessed July 13, 2008)

Ten Tips for Staying Focused and Achieving Results

1. **Treat others with respect.** It is better to err on the side of being too formal than risk being too informal, particularly with employees, coworkers, customers, vendors, and management.

2. **Keep promises and commitments.** As a supervisor, it is essential that your employees trust you and think you are reliable. One of the best ways to reinforce this is to do what you say you are going to do. In addition, it is far better to deliver a day early than a day late. Make every effort to never miss a due date.

3. **Be accountable for decisions.** It is often easier to shift responsibility to someone else, particularly if the decision is not popular or the desired results are not achieved. Set the example and hold yourself accountable.

4. **Report information honestly.** Attempting to skip over details that reflect poorly on you or your team will ultimately catch up with you. It is far better to be direct and honest.

5. **Admit mistakes.** Supervisors may feel like they need to do everything right; however, the reality is that we are all human. If you make a mistake, own up to it, learn from it, and do what it takes to correct the situation.

6. **Maintain a safe and healthy workplace.** It is important to foster an environment where people feel safe and where malicious gossip is unacceptable. The grapevine can be positive; however, unfortunately it is often very destructive. It is a supervisor's job to keep this informal communication in check.

7. **Stand up for strongly held beliefs and principles.** Another very difficult task for supervisors is to disagree with management or employees. However, if you remain focused on the mission of the organization and remain true to your values and the company's values, it will pay off in the long run.

8. **Treat customers and employees with dignity at all times.** There are times when employees may show up late or do everything wrong. You may want to just scream at them for behaving badly; however, it is essential that you never lose your temper and always treat everyone with dignity.

9. **Recognize and appreciate everyone at all levels.** When people get promoted through the ranks and take on more responsibility, they may fall into a negative pattern of behavior where they treat people at other levels in the organization differently. Be aware of the potential for this to happen and aim to recognize each person for her/his unique abilities and contributions.

10. **Be humble.** As you achieve success, you are quite likely to feel good about your accomplishments. Occasionally, you may even receive special recognition for your achievements. Don't let it go to your head. Give credit where credit is due and share the stage with your team whenever possible. Rather than saying, "I did this," say, "We did this" when appropriate, or specifically name and acknowledge individuals for their contribution.

Visualizing is seeing things happen before they actually happen. When you visualize, you form vivid pictures in your conscious mind. Those pictures of your goals or objectives are kept alive until they sink into your subconscious mind. When they reach the subconscious mind, untapped energies are released to help visualized pictures become reality.[35]

Of course, just like accomplished athletes who diligently practice their sport, supervisors will need to practice using this technique. Start with a few relatively simple scenarios to get comfortable with the process and then graduate to more complex or difficult situations.

Positive affirmation statements, used in conjunction with visualization, can lead to great results. An **affirmation statement** is the process of putting positive thoughts, beliefs, goals, and/or desires into words to increase the likelihood of success. In the

affirmation statement
the process of putting positive thoughts, beliefs, goals, and/or desires into words to increase the likelihood of success.

FIGURE 10.4 The S.O.F.T.E.N. technique

Source: Marjorie Brody, "Learn to Listen: Closing the Mouth and Opening the Ears Facilitates Effective Communication," *Incentive* 178 (May 2004): 57–59.

S.O.F.T.E.N. Technique

Smile—Facial expressions can be the difference between inviting and discouraging communication.

Open posture—Body language can make or break a dialogue. Don't cross your arms.

Forward lean—This body position indicates interest and invites communication.

Tone—The sound of your voice speaks volumes. Show enthusiasm with pitch and inflection.

Eye communication—Making eye contact shows you are paying attention.

Nod—Demonstrating agreement or understanding provides feedback that you are listening.

next section, we will discuss the importance of listening to your employees. If one of your goals is to value your employees' ideas, an example of an affirmation statement to support this goal might be: *"I will listen to my employees' suggestions with genuine interest and enthusiasm."*

Now, combine this affirmation statement with a visual image. Can you see yourself smiling, making eye contact, nodding, and providing positive feedback to encourage your employees to share their ideas? This may seem far-fetched and hard to imagine right now, but give it a try. With practice, you are very likely to enjoy positive results. In addition, try using the S.O.F.T.E.N. technique described in Figure 10.4.

Communicating for Success

Larry King, host of the long-running show *Larry King Live*, has conducted over 40,000 interviews during his broadcasting career spanning more than fifty years.[36] He has been called the "master interviewer."[37] Here is what King says about his success:

> To be a good speaker, you must be a good listener. This is more than just a matter of showing interest. Careful listening makes you better able to respond when it's your turn. Good follow-up questions are a mark of a good conversationalist.
>
> Don't ask "yes or no" questions. Ask "what-if" questions, especially those that require a moral or philosophical response. And ask "why?" It's the greatest question ever asked and will keep a conversation lively and interesting.[38]

Of course, King was referring to his career in broadcasting and the need to generate interesting dialogue as a television talk show host. However, his comments are relevant for supervisors as well. Extract his key points:

- Listen carefully.
- Ask good follow-up questions.
- Don't ask "yes" or "no" questions.
- Ask "what-if" questions.
- Ask "why?"

If you follow these recommendations, you will gain a better understanding of your customers and employees. Additionally, you will reinforce your commitment to developing and sustaining mutually beneficial relationships that embrace open and honest communication. Consider this story of a hair salon owner who failed to listen to her two employees' suggestions. The hair stylists made repeated attempts to help increase business. Unfortunately, the owner consistently failed to listen, which ultimately led her employees to quit in frustration. The two hair stylists went on to start their own thriving business where they encourage employees to make suggestions. The skills they demonstrated were their ability to listen, to relate to their employees, and to "imagine what you would want for yourself if you were in their shoes."[39]

It does not matter whether you own the business or supervise the evening shift at a huge company, the point is to listen to your employees, invite their suggestions, and leverage their creativity to help your company prosper.

The Art of Listening

Almost all training in oral communication in high school, college, and management development programs is focused on effective speaking. But what about listening, the other half of the communication equation? Listening is the forgotten component in communication skills training. This is unfortunate, since the most glowing oration is a waste of time if it is not heard. Listening takes place at two steps in the verbal communication process. First, the receiver must listen in order to decode and understand the original message. Then the sender becomes a listener when attempting to decode and understand subsequent feedback. Identical listening skills come into play at both ends.

We can hear and process information more quickly than we can talk. According to researchers, our average rate of speaking is about 125 words per minute, whereas we are able to listen to about 400 to 600 words per minute.[40] Thus, listeners have up to 79% slack time during which they can daydream or alternatively analyze information and plan a response. Effective listeners know how to put that slack time to good use. However, unlike math or science, there is no exact formula for listening. Most people are not born great listeners, so it takes practice and a commitment to improve.

Before discussing techniques for effective listening, let's review some common barriers to listening.

Barriers to Effective Listening

High on the list is misunderstanding the intended message. Often, this is attributed to cultural differences and language barriers.[41] However, there are several other factors involved for both the sender and the receiver of the message that center on feelings, attitudes, assumptions, beliefs, and values.[42]

A few common variables that contribute to communication break-downs include:
- Your relationship to the other person (colleague, supervisor, employee, friend or enemy).
- The response or information you want to hear or expect.
- What you assume the other person already knows or believes.
- How high your need is for the other person's approval or respect.
- How knowledgeable or credible you assume the other person is.[43]

As much as 93% of communication is conveyed through nonverbal signals.

In addition, research shows that 93% of communication is conveyed through nonverbal signals (tone of voice, facial expression, and body language).[44]

Nonverbal signals to be aware of that may have the unintended consequence of shutting down communication include:

- Lack of eye contact.
- Fidgeting.
- Crossed arms.
- Interrupting.
- Checking your PDA or cell phone.
- Looking around the office or flipping through papers.[45]

Techniques for Effective Listening

Keeping these common barriers to effective listening in mind, let us take a look at how to improve your listening skills. You will need to practice, set the example, and take the time to teach your employees. By teaching others, you will reinforce your own understanding, and your employees will appreciate your effort to learn more about their thoughts and ideas.

By teaching others, you will reinforce your own understanding.

First, and perhaps most important, begin with an open mind. Erase any preconceived thoughts or expectations and allow yourself to focus on the person speaking and the message he is trying to convey. Set the tone from the beginning by letting the person know what he can expect from you as the listener. As Larry King said, ask good open-ended questions beginning with words like "what if" or "why?" rather than "yes or no" questions. Then follow up with relevant, insightful questions to demonstrate that you have been paying attention and understand the topic being discussed. Tolerate silence. Listeners who rush to fill momentary silence cease being listeners.

Practice self-awareness. It is important that you know your biases and attempt to correct for them. Try to avoid premature judgments about what is being said, and avoid being defensive. Indra Nooyi, Pepsico's CEO who was born in India, suggests that you listen with "positive intent." Her approach is to say, "Wait a minute. Let me really get behind what they are saying to understand whether they're reacting because they're hurt, upset, confused, or they don't understand what it is I've asked them to do."[46] Clearly, this approach will reduce misunderstandings.

Good listening also requires you to "read between the lines." This will help you decipher what the speaker is saying, not through words, but rather, through nonverbal communication. If there appear to be inconsistencies between the content of the message and nonverbal cues, it is probably worth following your hunch and asking a few more questions. For example, an employee might tell you that she is excited to cross-train and learn someone else's job, yet she looks down at the floor while

They say a picture can tell a thousand words. What is the body language saying in this office photo? Who is being aggressive? Who is being defensive? Who is nervous or afraid? Body language is a major part of communication. Supervisors need to know how to read body language and adjust their communication style accordingly. If the finger pointer in this scene is the supervisor, a less confrontational private meeting would seem to be in order.

© ColorBlind Images/Corbis

FIGURE 10.5 Quick tips for improving your listening skills

Source: Adapted from Marjorie Brody, "Learn to Listen: Closing the Mouth and Opening the Ears Facilitates Effective Communication," *Incentive* 178 (May 2004): 57–59.

Tips for Improving Your Listening Skills

Eliminate distractions
- Stay away from the phone.
- Turn off your cell phone and/or PDA.
- Establish a method to let people know you are in a meeting and are not to be interrupted.

Clean up the clutter
- Remove any unrelated documents or paperwork from the meeting area.

Take notes
- Write down keys words or ideas.
- Note questions for later (to avoid interrupting).
- Let the person(s) know you will be taking notes.

Paraphrase the speaker
- Provide verbal verification such as, "Your idea to publish a company newsletter, to be sent once a month by e-mail, is excellent." This technique will help you to stay alert and it will let the speaker know you are paying attention. In addition, this type of validation can help avoid misunderstandings.

Assume an uncomfortable position
- Sit on the edge of your chair, be poised for action—in other words, don't sit back and recline in a comfortable chair where you can become too passive.

W.I.I.F.M.: Ask yourself, "What's in it for me?"
- Listen as if you are required to report the information back to others.
- Take mental notes.

telling you this. You may want to explore this disconnect because her body language is not consistent with her words.

In addition, practice the tips in Figure 10.5 provided by Marjorie Brody, author, speaker, consultant, and coach to Fortune 1,000 executives.

Proactive Language Versus Reactive Language

In Chapter 9, you learned about fostering a creative and positive working environment. Effective communication is central to achieving a high-performance workplace. One of the keys is to shift your perspective from being reactive to proactive. This requires using proactive language rather than reactive language.

Reactive Language

Reactive language tends to be negative, with an undertone of failure and a sense of defeat from the start. It is often characterized by a feeling of hopelessness, as if one has no control. In fact, you may not control the entire situation, but you do control your choices in preparing for and ultimately responding. Stephen Covey captured this concept with these observations:

> The language of reactive people absolves them of responsibility.
>
> A serious problem with reactive language is it becomes a self-fulfilling prophecy. People become reinforced in the paradigm that they are determined, and they produce evidence to support the belief. They feel increasingly victimized and out of control, not in charge of their life or their destiny. They blame outside forces—other people, circumstances, even the stars—for their own situation.[47]

How do you know if you or one of your employees has fallen into a reactive mode? Look for common reactive and self-defeating language statements such as:

- There's nothing I can do.
- That's just the way I am.
- He makes me so mad.
- They won't allow that.
- I have to do that.
- I can't.
- I must.
- If only.[48]

Proactive Language

The ideal scenario is for a supervisor to have a positive, proactive attitude that is shared by their employees. This goes back to the "can do" attitude discussed in the last chapter. Rather than focusing on what they cannot control, proactive people tend to focus on what they can control or at least influence. They accept responsibility for the situation and are determined to take action to move forward in resolving a problem or overcoming an obstacle.

Examples of proactive language include:

- Let's look at our alternatives.
- I can choose a different approach.
- I control my own feelings.
- I can create an effective presentation.
- I will choose an appropriate response.
- I can make a difference here.
- I choose.
- I prefer.
- I will.[49]

These statements clearly illustrate a sense of *personal* control. Proactive individuals illustrate through their action and their language that they have choices and alternatives.

KNOWLEDGE TO ACTION

Consider the following scenarios and replace the reactive language with a more proactive response.

1. Mari is a supervisor at the local pet store. She does not have to work every day, but she is ultimately responsible for staffing. She is scheduled to have Saturday off to attend a football game with friends. Around 9:00 A.M., one of her employees calls her at home to say he is sick and he is not going to be able to go to work. She calls her friend to say, "I have to go into work today, so I can't attend the football game." What do you think would be a more proactive response to this situation?

_____

2. Kane is the supervisor at an electronic game store. A customer walks into the store and asks to pick up her game console that she ordered last week. Kane informs the customer that it has not arrived yet. The customer expresses her dissatisfaction, to which Kane responds, "There is nothing I can do." What do you think would be a more proactive response to this situation?

_____

If you have a tendency to be reactive, try replacing a reactive phrase with a proactive one. With time and practice, your world can change significantly.

Adapting the Message to the Audience

Many factors influence communication styles and determine whether or not a communication experience is effective. These variables include age, gender, education level, ethnic background, geographic location, and where we were raised and educated. It can be difficult to take all of these variables into consideration when communicating with someone. But the more aware of and responsive to these factors you are, the more likely you are to be clearly understood.

Cultural Differences

As mentioned throughout this chapter, culture and language *do* matter in today's global economy. For a person born and raised in the United States (a monochronic culture), the phrase, "Right away," will carry different meaning than for someone born and raised in a polychronic culture. This subtle yet important difference can lead to misunderstanding and negative consequences. So rather than asking the person to place a follow-up call to a customer *right away* (which, culturally, could mean anything from this very minute to by the end of the week), it is better to be specific. A clearer message would ask the employee to place a follow-up phone call to the customer by the close of business at *5:00 P.M. today*. This leaves no room for cross-cultural misinterpretation.

Vocabulary and Effective Writing

Another common error supervisors make is using sophisticated language employees do not understand. It is essential to assess the education level and reading comprehension skills of your employees. The vocabulary you use when speaking or writing needs to be easily understood by all employees, regardless of their language skills and education. Anything you put in writing should be clear. Good writing is part of the encoding step in the basic communication process. If it is done skillfully, potentially troublesome barriers can be surmounted. The publication editor for heavy-equipment manufacturer Caterpillar offers four helpful reminders:

1. *Keep words simple.* Simplifying the words you use will help reduce your thoughts to essentials; keep your readers from being "turned off" by the complexity of your letter, memo, e-mail, or report; and make it more understandable.

2. *Don't sacrifice communication to rules of composition.* Most of us who were sensitized to the rules of grammar and composition in school never quite recovered from the process. As proof, we keep trying to make our writing conform to rigid rules and customs without regard to style or the ultimate purpose of the communication.

3. *Write concisely.* This means expressing your thoughts, opinions, and ideas in the fewest number of words consistent with composition and smoothness. But don't confuse conciseness with mere brevity; you may write briefly without being clear or complete.

4. *Be specific.* Vagueness is one of the most serious flaws in written communication because it destroys accuracy and clarity, leaving the reader to wonder about your meaning or intent.[50]

Age Matters

Researchers have spent countless hours analyzing and characterizing the Baby Boomers, Generation X, and Generation Y. What they have learned is that there are some differences, but not everyone fits the stereotypes. So what is a supervisor to do? Start by asking each employee for input and suggestions on the most effective way to communicate with him/her. Ask specific questions about things like feedback and praise. For example, does the person prefer to receive praise in public or in private, and how often?

Research indicates that Baby Boomers need less praise because they perceive their paycheck to be a reward. Meanwhile, younger employees who grew up in a world of constant praise from their parents and teachers have come to expect the same treatment at work.[51]

Recognizing and Valuing Individuality

The key to adapting your message to your employees is to appreciate that each employee is unique to a certain extent. Regardless of their age, ethnic background, or education level, they will have individualized styles and preferences. Take the time to learn about each individual employee and you will become a much more effective communicator.

Communicating with Groups

The challenge of adapting your message to meet the needs of a group grows along with the size and diversity of that group. A good rule-of-thumb is to err on the side of basics and simplicity. Define terms or other complex concepts even if you are confident many of the people know what you are talking about. It is essential to establish a baseline of knowledge. Choose simple words presented in a concise manner. Try to limit your message to one or two main points. With more than three main points, you risk losing people's attention. If possible, solicit feedback to be sure everyone understands before moving to the next topic. Slow down and repeat difficult ideas if nonverbal feedback indicates confusion.

A good rule-of-thumb is to err on the side of basics and simplicity.

Effective communication is an ongoing challenge requiring supervisors to make a commitment to continuous learning and practice. There will always be a need to verify that the sender and receivers have "connected." Choosing the best transmission channel, combined with appropriate language, will increase the probability of successful communication. Are we clear?

SUMMARY

1. Cultural differences have an impact on communication, so supervisors need to be aware of nine cultural dimensions, including perceptions of power, collectivism, gender, assertiveness, people, and the future. They also need to be sensitive to differences in language, religion, interpersonal space, and perceptions of time.

2. The communication process involves the transfer of information and understanding from one person to another via a chain of links, including (1) sender, (2) encoding, (3) medium, (4) decoding, (5) receiver, and (6) feedback. Cross-cultural differences that impact communication include (1) perception of time, (2) interpersonal space, (3) language skills, (4) religion, and (5) cultural traditions and values. Communication media along with rich and lean media also have an impact. A supervisor's challenge is to match media richness with the situation by choosing the best method to communicate based on several variables, including (1) the level of urgency and complexity of the information, (2) the sensitivity of the content, and (3) their relationship with the recipient(s). Of the five communication strategies discussed, Spray & Pray and Withhold & Uphold should be avoided, Tell & Sell and Identify & Reply should be used sparingly, and Underscore & Explore should be used as much as possible.

3. Effective communicators share many common traits. They tend to (1) treat others with respect, (2) keep promises and commitments, (3) be accountable for decisions, (4) report information honestly, (5) admit mistakes, (6) maintain a safe and healthy workplace, (7) stand up for strongly held beliefs and principles, (8) treat customers and employees with dignity at all times, (9) recognize and appreciate everyone at all levels, and (10) be humble. In addition, they frequently use visualization techniques and affirmation statements to achieve results. They are also good listeners who don't ask "yes or no" questions; instead, they ask open-ended questions, such as "what if?" or "why?" They also ask good follow-up questions.

4. Effective listening begins with an open mind when listeners erase any preconceived thoughts or expectations and allow themselves to focus on the person speaking and the message the speaker is trying to convey. Good listeners also tolerate silence, try to avoid premature judgments, and "read between the lines" to decipher what the speaker is "saying" through nonverbal communication. Tips for improving listening skills include (1) eliminate distractions, (2) clean up the clutter, (3) take notes, (4) paraphrase the speaker, (5) assume an uncomfortable position, (6) listen with intent, and (7) use the S.O.F.T.E.N. technique.

5. Reactive language tends to be negative with an undertone of failure and a sense of defeat before you even get started. Proactive people tend to focus on what they can control. Through their action, their language, and their choices, they also accept responsibility. Examples of proactive statements include (1) Let's look at our alternatives, (2) I can choose a different approach, (3) I control my own feelings, (4) I can create an effective presentation, (5) I will choose an appropriate response, (6) I choose, (7) I prefer, and (8) I will.

6. Another important aspect of effective communication is adapting the message to the audience. The ideal situation provides ample opportunity for the speaker to learn about the audience, whether it is one person or a diverse group. Variables to consider that have an impact on how the message is prepared and delivered include (1) age, (2) gender, (3) education level, (4) ethnic background, (5) geographic location, and (5) where they were raised and educated.

TERMS TO UNDERSTAND

affirmation statements, p. 282
collectivist cultures, p. 270
communication, p. 269
communication medium, p. 275
culture, p. 269

decoding, p. 277
encoding, p. 274
individualistic cultures, p. 270
media richness, p. 275
monochronic time, p. 272

noise, p. 277
polychronic time, p. 272
visualization, p. 281

QUESTIONS FOR REFLECTION

1. How does the global economy and workforce diversity impact communication on the job?

2. Explain the communication process and identify each of the major links in this chain.

3. List five barriers to effective listening and identify a strategy to overcome each.

4. Explain what nonverbal signals are and describe how they may affect communication between supervisors and their employees.

5. Do you think affirmations and visualization techniques contribute to a person achieving his/her goals and/or desired outcome? Why or why not?

6. Explain how proactive language can be used to improve the relationship between supervisors and employees.

ANSWERS TO KNOWLEDGE TO ACTION EXERCISE (PAGE 276)

Type of Message	Choose the Best Match	Transmission Media
1. Performance counseling and/or appraisal.	b	a. E-mail
2. Plans to lay off 50 employees by the end of the year.	c	b. Face-to-face, one-on-one in person
3. Last-minute change in plans: the meeting will start at 3:00, not 1:00 as originally scheduled.	e	c. Face-to-face, group meeting in person
4. Announcing plans for the company's annual holiday party.	a	d. Company website posting
5. Promotional notice advertising new product.	d	e. Phone call

HANDS-ON ACTIVITIES

MEDIA RICHNESS

1. Explain the concept of media richness.
2. List four or five specific transmission media.
   a. For each method, provide an example from your personal experience. Describe the nature of the message content.
   b. Describe how the message was conveyed and analyze whether or not you think the appropriate method was selected for the situation. If the method was appropriate, explain why. If the method was not appropriate, what would have been a better medium for the situation?

AFFIRMATIONS AND VISUALIZATION

1. Describe a goal you would like to achieve.
2. Write an affirmation for this goal.
3. Now visualize the achievement of this goal. Describe this visual image in detail. Approach this as though you are describing a scene from a movie. Include details such as where you are physically, who is with you, what are the expressions on each person's face, how are you feeling, etc.
4. Use magazine clippings, illustrations, photography, and your own sketches to illustrate this scene on a piece of paper.

CASE STUDY 10.1

Recognizing and Overcoming Communication Barriers

Cari Lyn has worked for Springbreak Scooters for three years. She started out on the manufacturing floor while taking college courses at the local university. She graduated last May with a bachelor's degree in business management. When she shared this information with her coworkers and boss, no one seemed to notice or care. She was planning to start looking for another job when she received a notice that Brad, one of the supervisors, was leaving and the company was accepting applications for the position.

Although she had no formal supervisory experience, she decided to apply. Cari Lyn believed that her experience as a team leader for her section provided her with hands-on experience leading people and accomplishing goals. In addition, she was familiar with the team, which included a balanced mixed of age, gender, and ethnic diversity. Their education levels varied as well: three had associates degrees, one had a bachelor's degree, and the rest had a high school diploma or equivalent.

During the interview process, Rich (the day-shift floor manager) and Daphne (the plant manager) asked fairly typical questions. Then they surprised Cari Lyn by sharing that productivity on first shift had been declining over the last year, primarily because the previous supervisor's communication style was defensive. He would frequently say, "There's nothing I can do to increase productivity."

Daphne also shared that she had met with Brad's team after he left to get a better understanding of their concerns. There were a couple of common complaints. Everyone agreed that Brad, who had a Ph.D. in engineering, would always use technical terms when it was not necessary and seemed to talk down to people. He never listened to them and would always blame everyone else for his mistakes. Daphne concluded the interview by requesting that Cari Lyn prepare a communication strategy report that included a list of potential barriers to communication as well as Cari Lyn's suggestions for improving communication and her overall strategy for effectively communicating with this team to ultimately improve productivity.

Questions

1. How would you suggest Cari Lyn begin?

2. What are a few specific communication barriers that Daphne mentioned when referring to the previous supervisor?

3. How should Cari Lyn avoid these barriers?

4. What other suggestions do you think Cari Lyn should make for improving communication?

5. What should her strategy be for communicating effectively with her new team?

SUPERVISOR'S TOOLKIT

Most people would agree that there is always room for improvement with our communication skills. Supervisors are not only striving to improve their personal communication skills but are also teaching their employees these same skills. Prepare a couple of documents to add to your supervisor's toolkit that outline tips and best practices for effective communication related to the following situations.

1. If you are coaching an employee who consistently demonstrates negative communication and uses reactive language, identify three communication techniques you can teach him to help shift his communication style to be more effective and at the same time help shift his attitude to be more positive and proactive.

2. In this chapter you learned about noise. List three or four common sources of noise in the workplace and identify strategies to reduce and/or eliminate them. How can you teach your employees to follow your lead in reducing noise?

FILM STUDY

Choose a movie you have never seen before from the list provided by your professor.

1. Prior to watching the movie, write down information about your expectations, why you chose the film, how you expect to feel after watching the movie, what you anticipate happening during the movie, what you hope doesn't happen, and any other thoughts you have.

2. After watching the film, write down your reactions and analysis. What surprised you, how did you feel, how do these compare with your original expectations?

3. How did communication, personal biases, and expectations play a role in the film?

4. How can you apply what you have learned through this experience to your workplace and supervisory role?

5. How do variables such as expectations and biases impact our communication, actions, and decisions?

6. What can you do to improve your communication skills and reduce the effects of these variables?

CHAPTER 11

Behavior in the Workplace: The Bad and the Ugly

Learning Objectives

1. Identify strategies to help an underachieving employee improve performance.

2. Explain the concept of progressive discipline.

3. Discuss how a supervisor should approach terminating an employee.

4. Identify common sources of negative conflict at work and describe how to manage these situations.

5. Discuss how to handle difficult situations with your employee.

David Buck is president of Castle Security Group, a private investigative agency serving the business community throughout Maryland.

QUESTION:

What can supervisors proactively do to protect their business from losses caused by their own employees?

RESPONSE:

*A*s you may know, the majority of a company's losses are typically from employee theft. In many cases, organizations have inefficient systems in place to manage and minimize risk, or even worse, they do not follow their own potentially effective systems.

The old saying "An ounce of prevention is worth a pound of cure" is especially fitting when supervisors are dealing with the consequences of their employees' bad behavior. Let me tell you a story to help you understand how easily supervisors can be fooled into believing they have great employees who would never lie or steal.

An owner of a distribution business called our private investigative agency when he discovered a sizable loss after noticing several months of declining profits. After some initial review of the company's sales figures, everything began to point to one of his best salespeople. Let's call her Susan. Susan was well liked and trusted by her customers, as well as by her coworkers. She was professional in her interactions and the way she dressed. She was good at turning in her reports and keeping everyone "in the loop." She was also a thief. Upon further investigation, a clever deception was revealed. Susan had gone to some of her customers who paid cash and told them that the company was implementing a new computer system that still had a few glitches. Susan told her customers that they might see some errors on their monthly statements showing a higher balance owed than was correct, but that they shouldn't worry because she was "on top of it."

She went to her credit manager and told her that she was working with these same customers who were experiencing some tight times. But she said their business was sound and, if the credit manager would extend their credit, Susan would make sure they paid their bills. She then went to her sales manager and told

him that she was working through some credit issues with her customers and that she had already met with the credit manager. She assured her sales manager that she would be able to increase sales with these customers in the future.

See where this is going? $80,000 later, our client calls us because profits are dropping steadily.

After our client confronted Susan regarding this situation, she disappeared. A week later, we located her and led the police to the bar where we found her. They escorted her out in handcuffs. Our client never recovered his money from Susan, but because the company prosecuted her, it was able to make a claim against its insurance policy.

What can you learn from my client's experience?

1. **Inspect what you expect.** Have a system of checks and balances in place to evaluate and manage your processes. We all get busy and want to trust our employees to follow through and do what we want them to. The vast majority of them do. But if you have built a system that is overly dependent on any given employee instead of the process itself, you are creating an opportunity for the dishonest employee.

2. **"Trust, but verify."** I borrowed this phrase from President Ronald Reagan, who understood that ultimately the boss is accountable. This is true for every organization. It applies to both your business processes and your employees.

3. **Hire smart.** In addition to interviews and references, consider taking the extra steps to access information about the candidate, such as criminal records, background checks, credit checks, and drug testing. Keep in mind that the prospective employee will need to consent to most

of these pre-employment measures. However, access to criminal records and sexual offender databases involve public records and do not require consent. At a minimum, do criminal background checks on all employees. Once again, "An ounce of prevention is worth a pound of cure."

Consider the distribution company in my story about Susan. As we later discovered, if the company had conducted a simple background check on Susan before she was hired, it

would have found that she already had a criminal conviction on her record for theft from a former employer. The comparatively small cost of a background check could have saved the owner $80,000 and a lot of wasted time and energy. Would my client still have hired her? Maybe, maybe not. But if he had hired her with this knowledge, I bet he would have watched the numbers more closely.

Chapter Outline

The terms *discipline, conflict, poor performance*, and *termination* tend to be associated with powerful negative emotions. Most supervisors do not enjoy handling difficult situations and will often avoid addressing them. But most problems do not just go away. In this chapter, you will learn how to work with underachieving employees in an effort to help them reach their potential. We will also discuss specific remedial techniques such as progressive discipline and action plans. Unfortunately, there are times when these strategies are not effective and the best decision is to terminate an employee.

Prior to taking any major personnel action, you should consult with your manager and/or human resources department. It is wise to seek their guidance in resolving difficult employee situations. If you are unsure, request input from an attorney, preferably one with expertise in personnel law. If your company employs union members, familiarize yourself with the specific terms of the labor contract.

Getting Underachievers on Track

> *The first step in addressing poor performance is to openly and honestly assess the situation with the person.*

Most supervisors have great expectations when they hire new employees. During the interview process, the person has done or said something to stand out from the other applicants. This may involve his knowledge, experience, communication skills, or a combination of these variables. A disappointing day in the life of a supervisor is when she realizes that a new hire is not living up to her expectations. The employee is underachieving and his performance is not meeting expectations. In all fairness, the first step in addressing poor performance is to openly and honestly assess the situation with the individual. This process involves discussing the following topics with the employee: (1) expectations, (2) performance measures, (3) resources, (4) training, (5) obstacles, and (6) action plan.

Expectations

As you learned in Chapter 5, one of the keys to setting employees up for success is clarifying expectations. When you feel an employee is not reaching her potential, take the time to discuss and clarify expectations with her. Rather than merely restating your expectations, a good approach is to ask your employee an open-ended question such as, "please describe for me what you think are your primary job responsibilities and what you think is expected of you."[1] This provides valuable insight into what the employee thinks and gets her involved in the conversation.

If their response to this question is accurate and you both agree on the expectations, then you are ready to move on to a discussion about performance measures. If your expectations are different from those the employee just described, then you need to review the employee's job description with her and reiterate your expectations. It is also helpful to provide the employee with this information in writing so it can be referenced later.

Performance Measures

subjective performance measures
measures based on personal feelings and opinions.

objective performance measures
measures based on quantifiable data.

Subjective performance measures are based on personal feelings and opinions. For example, you may feel an employee is not working hard enough. If this is an opinion that is based on your intuition, observation, and feelings, it is a subjective method of assessing productivity. A more effective method of assessing employee performance is through the use of objective measures. This is because **objective performance measures** are based on quantifiable data. In order to assess employee productivity, you will need to identify measurable outcomes. This will vary by job and industry. Manufacturing provides a good example. Employee performance can be measured objectively by counting the number of items produced during a shift. To ensure that quality is not sacrificed for quantity, the performance measure should apply only to the number of items that pass final inspection.

Regardless of the industry, the performance measures should be standardized, data driven, and objective.[2] It is essential that employees understand how their performance will be measured. Again, ask an open-ended question such as, "How and when can your performance be measured?" If the employee knows the performance measures, attention turns to whether or not the individual has the proper resources and training to be successful.

KNOWLEDGE TO ACTION

One of the ways that supervisors set their employees up for success is by avoiding the use of subjective measures, clarifying expectations, and establishing mutually agreed-upon performance measures that are objective.

1. Provide two examples of subjective performance measures.

_____

2. Now replace these with two examples of objective performance measures (remember that these should be quantifiable).

_____

Resources

Busy supervisors often *assume* that their employees have the necessary resources to be successful. **Resources** are the items employees need to get their jobs done successfully, such as access to information, people, and technology. The truth is that employees, particularly new workers, are often uncomfortable asking for additional resources. Cost can be a big issue. For example, a salesperson might request a new laptop to complete customer transactions in the field. Employees also may be reluctant to ask for access to necessary information or people with particular expertise. By analyzing whether or not your employees have the resources they need, you may discover opportunities to improve organizational efficiency by streamlining processes or implementing more advanced technology tools. A simple question to ask to assess this situation is, "Do you have what you need to do your job?"[3] Also recognize that employees may have the resources, but lack adequate training.

Training

New hires and recently promoted employees face the same challenge of mastering a new job. You may believe you provided adequate training, yet they still are not accomplishing the work to your satisfaction. In most situations, you should give the employee the benefit of the doubt and develop a retraining plan.[4] This plan should be anchored to specific milestones, with dates and an outline of how training success will be determined. If you conducted the employee's initial training, you may want to partner with another supervisor for the retraining or bring in a senior employee to mentor the new person through the learning process.

If the first training program was not effective, simply repeating the same routine could be a waste of everyone's time. This presents a good opportunity to evaluate and improve your training processes. In addition, you may want to consider supplementing traditional training by using the coaching techniques described in Chapter 8. It is

resources
the items employees need to get their jobs done successfully.

A river guide would never dream of taking rafters into white water without lifejackets and paddles, right? Employees are just like these rafters—they depend on their supervisor to set them up for success. Supervisors need to assess what's ahead and provide the necessary equipment, training, and resources for their teams to achieve success efficiently and safely.
© Stockbyte/Getty Images

important to find out how the employee feels about his skills. Simply ask, "Have you been adequately trained?"[5]

Obstacles

Your employee may experience **obstacles** or challenges that hinder his/her ability to accomplish the job. The best way to learn about this is to ask. Consider an open-ended question such as, "Is something happening that is interfering with your ability to achieve your goals?"[6] It is important for employees to feel safe and comfortable giving you honest feedback, because *you* may be the source of the problem.[7] Care also needs to be taken when receiving feedback about another employee, because your response can reinforce employee behavior (good or bad).

> *It is important for employees to feel safe and comfortable giving you honest feedback.*

For example, consider the scenario where Marti is the supervisor of a billing office for a medical practice. Dustin and Trish are responsible for processing all of the insurance claims. They have recently fallen behind schedule and are unlikely to achieve their monthly goals. When Marti questioned each of her employees in private to learn more about the delays, she received specific feedback from both. Trish reminded Marti that the computers had been down for three days last week for repairs. Meanwhile, Dustin reported that Trish had been showing up late every day, implying that the delay in the schedule was her fault. If Marti responds to Dustin's

obstacles
challenges that hinder an employee's ability to accomplish the job.

feedback with a judgmental remark such as, "That is unacceptable; we'll bring that to end right now!" She runs the risk of alienating Trish and sending a message to Dustin that he can place blame on others. A better response from Marti is, "Dustin, thank you for bringing this to my attention. We'll meet as a team this afternoon to create a plan for getting back on schedule. In the interim, I'll talk with Trish to find out if there is something going on in her personal life that is contributing to her tardiness. Do you know if she is working through lunch or staying late to make up her time?" This sends a message to Dustin that his feedback is valued, but there is more information to be gathered and it becomes a private matter between the supervisor and the other employee.

Marti should follow up with a private conversation with Trish, and she should meet with Dustin and Trish together to discuss strategies to get back on schedule. In addition, during the next department meeting she should remind employees that any schedule changes should be approved by her in advance.

THEY SAID IT BEST	*Retain absolute faith that you can and will prevail in the end, regardless of the difficulties, AND at the same time confront the most brutal facts about your current reality, whatever they might be.*
	—JIM COLLINS
	Source: Jim Collins, *Good to Great* (New York: HarperCollins, 2001), 88.

Action Plan

The final step in getting your poor performer to meet your expectations is to prepare an action plan. List individual steps, including a detailed description of what is to be done, who is responsible, the measure or indicator (in other words, how you will know it is complete), and a due date. The action plan is the employee's road map to success, with checkpoints along the way.

For example, in the case of Marti working with Trish and Dustin to get back on the schedule, the action plan should include a specific "to do" list, including the number of claims to be submitted, who is responsible, and a due date. See Table 11.1 for a sample action plan for Trish and Dustin.

Supervisors need to review action plans regularly with the employee(s) involved to make sure they are reaching key milestones. As you prepare the action plan, it is important to discuss contingency plans outlining alternatives in case things get off track. For example, with Marti's situation, she will need a handy back-up plan if the computers go down again. Perhaps Trish and Dustin could use the computers in another department. More importantly, employees should know the consequences

TABLE 11.1
Sample Action Plan

Task Description	Measure	Person Responsible	Due Date	Notes
Submit at least 95% of bills for services between February 1 and February 15 to Medicare.	Total number of Medicare patient visits during this time period.	Trish	Feb. 22	Strive for 100%! It is understood that there are usually a few accounts where authorization or doctor's orders are pending.
Submit at least 95% of bills for services between February 1 and February 15 to all other insurance carriers, excluding Medicare claims.	Total number of non-Medicare patient visits during this time period.	Dustin	Feb. 22	Strive for 100%! It is understood that there are usually a few accounts where authorization or doctor's orders are pending.

if they fail to implement the plan and improve their performance, particularly in situations where they are not getting the job done. One of the consequences of failing to improve performance may be immediate termination. A more likely scenario is to begin progressive discipline.

Progressive Discipline

After working hard with an employee to help him get on track, you may feel a sense of despair and a desire to fire him when he remains stalled. Both in fairness to the team and as a legal matter, it is important to follow a predetermined process. If you are unsure, ask your manager or a human resources representative for a copy of the employee manual and/or policy regarding employee discipline. Remember to document everything in the employee's personnel folder, regardless of the situation. A minor infraction may be resolved and never reoccur, or it could be the beginning of a downward spiral in performance. Noting each incident will allow you to evaluate the employee's performance over time in an objective and comprehensive fashion.

Many companies use progressive discipline, also referred to as *corrective discipline*. Because there are too many possible scenarios to cover here, Figures 11.1 and 11.2 provide examples of minor and major infractions.

We outline a framework for progressive discipline in this section. These are general guidelines, because each situation you will encounter is unique and warrants careful examination of the facts. **Progressive discipline** is typically a four-stage process: (1) counseling, (2) written warning, (3) suspension, and (4) termination.[8] It is not uncommon for an employee to be the subject of multiple written warnings and suspensions for various infractions.

progressive discipline
a four-stage process of disciplinary action beginning with a verbal warning, then a written warning, suspension, and finally termination.

Counseling

Violations of company policies or procedures are generally considered minor infractions. Step one is to teach the employee the proper method, appropriate rules to

FIGURE 11.1 Examples of minor infractions

Source: Adapted from University of North Texas Policy Manual, Section: Performance Counseling and Discipline, last updated 06/04, http://www.unt.edu/policy/UNT_Policy/volume1/1_7_1.html (accessed May 11, 2008).

Examples of Minor Infractions

This list is not exhaustive.

1. Unexplained, inexcusable, or unauthorized absence or tardiness.
2. Failure to notify supervisor as soon as possible on first day of absence.
3. Failure to observe assigned work schedules (starting time, quitting time, rest and lunch periods).
4. Soliciting or collecting contributions for any purpose on company premises without management permission.
5. Selling or offering for sale, on company premises, any article or service without management permission. Employees may not use company time or equipment to profit from or promote a personal business.
6. Unsatisfactory work performance.
7. Loafing or other abuse of time during assigned working hours.
8. Interfering with any employee's work performance or duties by talking or other distractions.
9. Leaving regularly assigned work location without notifying immediate supervisor.
10. Minor violations of safety rules.
11. Discourteous treatment of the public or of other employees.
12. Engaging in excessive visiting, personal conversations, or use of the telephone for personal business.
13. Accepting any gifts or favors that influence or tend to influence the performance of duties or the granting of service or favors to other company personnel, applicants, clients, or other persons.
14. Failure to follow any reasonable instructions issued by supervisor related to performing job tasks and/or other duties.
15. Using personal, political, or religious beliefs to harass or intimidate others on company premises.

KNOWLEDGE TO ACTION

Brainstorm with your classmates to identify additional items that can be added to the lists of infractions in Figures 11.1 and 11.2.

1. Identify at least five additional infractions to add to the minor infractions list.

_____

2. Identify at least five additional infractions to add to the major infractions list.

_____

counseling

sharing the supervisor's expectations for correct behavior and explaining the consequences of failing to improve.

follow, and/or techniques to use. Following the first infraction, you have the opportunity to coach the employee through counseling. **Counseling** involves sharing your expectations for correct behavior and informing the employee about the consequences for not improving. A major challenge for supervisors during the counseling stage is balancing the warning with encouragement. The goal is for the employee to know what is wrong and be inspired to improve. This conversation should be conducted in private, never in front of other employees or customers. However, you might choose to have your supervisor or a human resources person

FIGURE 11.2 Examples of major infractions

Source: Adapted from University of North Texas Policy Manual, Section: Performance Counseling and Discipline, last updated 06/04, http://www.unt.edu/policy/UNT_Policy/volume1/1_7_1.html (accessed May 11, 2008).

Examples of Major Infractions

These typically result in suspension or termination. This list is not exhaustive.

1. Any act that might endanger the safety or lives of others.
2. Refusal or failure to perform a major assignment, task, or function in an effective and efficient manner.
3. Willful, deliberate, or repeated violation of company safety rules.
4. Falsifying any company records.
5. Punching the time card for another employee or allowing yours to be punched by another employee.
6. Deliberately or negligently abusing, destroying, damaging, or defacing company property, tools, or equipment.
7. Gambling on company premises.
8. Fighting on company premises (any employee directly involved).
9. Bringing and/or consuming liquor, marijuana, narcotics, or any illegal substances on company premises; or reporting for duty under the influence of liquor, marijuana, or narcotics.
10. Carrying firearms or other dangerous weapons on company premises.
11. Disclosure of confidential information to unauthorized persons.
12. Dishonest or unethical actions, theft, misappropriation or unauthorized use of company funds or property, or failure to report knowledge thereof. (Knowledge is witnessing the dishonest or unethical act or receiving direct information regarding the act.)
13. Failure to abide by company and/or departmental policies and rules.
14. Insubordination or willful disobedience.
15. Flagrant or repeated minor rule violations.

present to witness the conversation and potentially facilitate the dialogue. See Figure 11.3 for a handy employee counseling checklist.

Written Warning

If an employee fails to correct the situation within the agreed-upon time, the next step is to provide her with a written warning. The content is similar to what we discussed for the counseling stage, with everything documented in writing. Then go over the content of the written warning in detail during a private meeting with the individual. In addition, if you have not already done so, this is the time to develop an action plan. Written warnings typically include:

- A summary of the situation, including the dates and nature of past discussions related to the issue.
- Specific expectations, including measures and timelines.
- Consequences if expectations are not met.
- A signature line for the employee to acknowledge receipt and understanding of the written warning. One copy should be filed in the employee's personnel folder, and another copy should be given to the employee.[9]

FIGURE 11.3 Employee counseling checklist

Source: Adapted from Indiana University Human Resources Services, Progressive Discipline Training, Indiana University website, last updated July 26, 2002, http://www.indiana.edu/~uhrs/training/ca/progressive.html (accessed March 21, 2008).

Employee Counseling Checklist

Counseling, also referred to as a *verbal warning,* is the first step in the progressive discipline process. Explain this to the employee and let him/her know the situation is serious but you believe it can be corrected.

Document the counseling session. Although the warning itself is not being delivered in a written format, the circumstances leading up to the counseling, as well as the fact that the verbal warning took place, should be noted in the employee's personnel file.

Clarify expectations. Review the company policies and procedures including performance standards. After reviewing these documents and reiterating your expectations, request that the employee explain in detail his/her understanding, including modifications in behavior, decisions, and actions to improve performance and correct the situation. In addition, consider working with the employee to prepare an action plan.

Listen. Give the employee a chance to share his/her perspective. Make it clear that you do not care to hear excuses but you are willing to listen in an effort to understand. You may discover a situation where the employee acted in the best interest of the company and the situation warrants a policy change rather than discipline.

Establish a timeline. Work with the employee to determine how quickly you expect the changes or corrections to be implemented. In some cases, it may be immediate; in others, the employee may need a week or two.

Explain the consequences. Let the employee know the potential positive consequences if improvement occurs, such as more hours on the schedule or increased opportunities for more responsibility. In addition, share with the employee the potential negative consequences if the situation is not corrected. Maintaining a friendly manner while conveying a serious verbal warning can be difficult. Consider reviewing your planned conversation with your manager or a human resources professional prior to meeting with the employee.

Suspension

Depending upon the circumstances and company policy, organizations may suspend an employee with or without pay. Employee suspensions are used in two ways. One is the third step in progressive discipline. In this case, the employee is suspended for a short period of time if performance fails to improve after the written warning. The purpose of a suspension is to give employees time to reflect on their actions with the expectation that performance will improve when they return to work. This is similar to detention or suspension for school children.

> *The purpose of a suspension is to give employees time to reflect on their actions with the expectation that performance will improve.*

A *major* infraction is the second reason for a suspension (refer back to Figure 11.2 for examples). With serious situations, suspensions allow time for a complete investigation rather than immediate termination. For example, if a supervisor discovers that an employee is stealing, but needs to fully investigate the circumstances before firing the employee, the supervisor may choose to suspend the person. This is a more cautious approach that provides the employer with time to gather facts prior to making a final decision.[10]

Day of Decision Making

Instead of suspending employees, which can be a negative experience, some companies are using the Day of Decision Making approach. In this situation, companies give the employee a paid day off to reflect on his actions and what he wants to do. Does the employee want to stay and work hard, or is the position too demanding? When the employee returns to work the next day, he meets with his supervisor to discuss his decision. If the employee chooses to leave, he walks out immediately. If the employee chooses to stay, the supervisor and employee write an action plan together.[11]

Termination

Termination is the final step when other remedial attempts have failed. Of course, there are certain circumstances that warrant immediate dismissal. Terminating an employee encompasses many variables. It is important to be sure the situation is handled properly to minimize the risk of a lawsuit and to reduce the negative impact on coworkers. Because this is such an important and complex area, the next section deals with properly handling employee terminations.

Terminating an Employee

Termination means firing an employee. It occurs immediately. What are a few reasons you think a supervisor would be justified in firing an employee immediately without progressive discipline? Common answers to this question include lying; stealing; failure to report for work; arriving for work intoxicated; using illegal drugs or drinking alcohol on the job; flagrant misuse of company resources; sexual misconduct with another employee, customer, or vendor; and sleeping while at work. The list goes on.

Policies, Procedures, and the Law

Before making any decisions or taking action, it is essential that you familiarize yourself with company policies and procedures along with federal, state, and local personnel laws. If you are a business owner or you aspire to own a business in the future, be sure to have personnel-related policies documented. In addition, if you have employees who are union members, you also need to comply with the terms and conditions of their employment under the union contract.

Surveys indicate that 78% of small business owners have kept an employee too long.

Firing an employee is difficult for most supervisors and business owners. According to a survey conducted in 2007, 61% of small business owners indicated that it was tough to fire someone and 78% revealed that they had kept an employee too long. Retaining a poor performer can negatively impact both coworkers and the organization. In Chapter 13, we cover legal issues in more detail. For this discussion, it is important to know that most states recognize the principle of employment at will. **Employment at will** means an employer can terminate an employee at any time without explanation or cause.[12] However, termination of an employee must not be based on discrimination or revenge.

termination
firing an employee.

employment at will
an employer can terminate an employee at any time without explanation or cause.

Classifications protected from discrimination include:

- Race
- Religion
- Sex (gender)
- Pregnancy
- Sexual orientation
- Age (unless there is a legal maximum age, such as for airline pilots)
- Physical or mental disability[13]
- National origin[14]

Moreover, you cannot terminate an employee for refusing to follow orders that will break the law or for **whistle blowing**, reporting corporate fraud, or other illegal and unethical behavior. It is also illegal to fire a person for filing a worker's compensation claim if he or she has been injured on the job.[15]

Tips for Terminating Employees

A few ways to reduce the likelihood of an unlawful discharge lawsuit and make the process a little less stressful include: (1) offer a warning, (2) script it out, (3) get to the point, (4) focus on the future, (5) stay in control, and (6) follow the Golden Rule.[16]

- **Offer a warning.** As we mentioned in the progressive discipline section, let the employee know what she needs to do and the timeframe to implement the changes necessary. Clarifying expectations reduces the opportunity for excuses and eliminates the "I didn't know" defense. This step forces supervisors to take a moment to reflect and will eliminate a snap decision in the heat of the moment that may be regretted later. A good rule of thumb is: "Do not fire an employee in anger."[17]

- **Script it out.** Once you have made the decision to fire the employee, consult with human resources and/or your manager to prepare for the termination meeting. Confidentially communicate with your technology person to make arrangements to have the employee's computer access disabled during the meeting. Depending on the circumstances, you may want to make sure that security is available in case the meeting does not go well.

- **Get to the point.** Keep the meeting short. You have made your decision, so there should be no negotiations. Maintain a professional, respectful demeanor. The person will be leaving without a job; she does not need to be humiliated. Jonathan Segal, a partner with the law firm WolfBlock, recommends this empathetic yet direct phrase, "I'm sorry we find ourselves in this position."[18]

- **Focus on the future.** You have made it clear that there will be no negotiations and your decision is final. Therefore, you should redirect the conversation to what remains to be discussed. The employee may request a letter of recommendation or for you to be a reference. Follow your company's policies and be honest with the employee about how her request will be handled.

whistle blowing
an employee's reporting of corporate fraud or other illegal and unethical behavior.

In addition, make arrangements for the employee to return any company-owned property such as keys, cell phones, uniforms, laptops, or documentation.

- **Stay in control.** Although employee terminations should never come as a surprise, most employees still appear shocked at the news. This may lead to an unexpected emotional reaction. It is a good idea to have a box of tissues handy. It is also advisable to have another supervisor or manager in the room, who can serve as a witness and, if necessary, assist in handling the situation or calling security if the employee becomes hostile. The old saying, "Prepare for the worst and hope for the best," definitely applies here.

- **Follow the Golden Rule.** Try to imagine what it would be like to be in the employee's situation. Although there is no room for negotiation, there is still room to help the person maintain dignity and self-esteem.[19]

There are various theories about the best time to schedule a termination meeting. It is usually less disruptive to the rest of the team if you schedule it at the end of the day.[20] There are some who think Friday afternoon is best, while others say Monday morning is most appropriate.[21] From a supervisor's perspective, it is usually best to schedule the meeting as soon as possible once the termination decision is made.

Provide a termination letter during the meeting. In most cases, it is best to limit the letter to the terms of the dismissal such as final pay, how unpaid leave will be handled, and whether or not the employee can expect to receive a COBRA letter with information regarding continuation of medical insurance. A limited number of states require an employer to disclose specific reasons for the termination.[22]

It's Not Over Yet

After you conclude the termination meeting with an employee, it is important to remain with him while he packs up his personal belongings. Be prepared for this and have a few boxes available. Once the employee has packed up and said his good-byes, escort him to the parking lot. It is common for security personnel to handle this transition phase.

Immediately following the employee's departure, meet with your staff briefly to announce the decision. Answer general questions in an effort to assure the remaining good performers that they are not next. But avoid disclosing any details about the terminated employee's situation.[23]

Negative Conflict

Negative, dysfunctional, or destructive conflict can be a drain on productivity and may ultimately lead to a decline in employee morale and increased turnover. Therefore, it is essential that supervisors recognize the sources of negative conflict and address them quickly so they do not become part of the organization's culture.

Negative conflict can be a drain on productivity.

Common sources of negative conflict are: (1) poor communication, (2) competition, (3) personality differences, (4) diverse opinions, and (5) inequity, either perceived or real.

Poor Communication

Poor communication is probably the number one source of conflict in the workplace. This includes situations when there is little or no communication because supervisors, employees, and their coworkers fail to effectively exchange information. As you learned in the last chapter, effective communication involves listening, encoding your messages so that they are easily understood, and using media appropriate to the situation.

SHARING INFORMATION

Workplace communication frequently breaks down because people fail to share information. This may occur for a variety of reasons. A few are inadvertent, such as when an employee or supervisor does not realize their knowledge is valuable to others. They also may not take the time to communicate what they assume everyone already knows. You need to encourage employees to share more frequently and to verify that everyone has the information they need. Let them know that it is better to communicate a little too much than not enough.

In other situations, people may choose not to share their knowledge because they believe it gives them power or prestige. In this unfortunate situation, you may need to do a lot of coaching to break the negative cycle. It can be difficult to convince employees that they actually become more powerful by sharing their knowledge and expertise. If you discover that your employees continue to withhold information, you will need to quickly take action to correct this behavior before it impacts your team and the organization.

ASSUMPTIONS

When an employee begins a sentence with the words, "I assumed…," it usually flags a communication breakdown. Assuming your employees understand a new sales policy or that they are communicating effectively with customers is risky. It takes only a few extra minutes to give your assumptions a "reality check" to prevent costly miscommunication.

KNOWLEDGE TO ACTION

People in the workplace frequently make assumptions. The good news is that many times their assumptions are correct. The bad news is that employees also wrongly assume, which can produce negative consequences for the organization.

1. Have you ever wrongly assumed something or been on the opposite side of a situation where someone assumed you knew and you did not? How did you handle it?

   _____

2. As a supervisor, what steps can you take to avoid or correct false assumptions among your employees?

   _____

TRUST BUT VALIDATE

The grapevine and other informal sources of information can also lead to misunderstandings and costly errors. A common explanation for a bad job or poor decision is that "someone" gave the erring employee incorrect information. For example, a new employee scheduled a doctor's appointment for her son during work hours. She asked one of her coworkers if she should request vacation time or record her absence as sick leave hours on her time sheet. The coworker said she didn't know, but if she was in the same situation, she would use her sick leave. The employee recorded her absence as sick leave in violation of company policy and was reprimanded. As computer specialists like to say, "garbage in, garbage out."

This scenario was easily preventable by following a simple rule: **trust but validate**. Rather than assuming that the information is correct, confirm the facts with an appropriate source. When in doubt, check with your immediate manager or supervisor. In the preceding example, the employee should have checked with the supervisor or human resources professional. If the topic or issue is significant, it is a good idea to get your validation in writing via an e-mail or a copy of the relevant policy or procedure. Supervisors need to teach their employees the "trust but validate" method. Let them know that decisions based on misinformation that they failed to validate are unacceptable. Strive for a "no excuses" environment where your employees are accountable for obtaining and distributing accurate information.

LISTENING

We thoroughly discussed listening skills in the last chapter because ineffective listening leads to frequent miscommunication. When people fail to listen, they often make poor decisions based on inaccurate information. It is essential that supervisors and their employees practice good listening skills to foster a healthy exchange of information. Review the specific techniques in Chapter 10 with your employees to improve their listening skills.

Competition

A close-knit team that helps beat competing companies is a dream come true for management. Unfortunately, many organizations have created an environment where employees compete destructively against one another. This may be for limited resources or for rewards, promotion, or recognition.

COMPETING FOR RESOURCES

Although they are a fact of life for supervisors, limited resources breed competition. Managers and supervisors often end up competing for budget allocations for items such as new equipment, additional positions, or funds for employee training. It can be a challenge for supervisors to balance the needs of the company with the needs of employees.

To manage this type of competition, it is important for all employees to have a clear line of sight to the organization's mission and goals. Accordingly, they need to know the strategic priorities and how their jobs and budget requests support the

trust but validate
confirming facts with an appropriate source rather than assuming information you have received from a coworker or third party is correct.

This telephone tussle gives the phrase "please hold" a whole new meaning! When employees compete or, in this case, fight over resources in the workplace, productivity, attitudes, and employee satisfaction quickly go down the drain. Supervisors are challenged to distribute resources fairly to avoid this sort of conflict.

© Holger Winkler/zefa/Corbis

achievement of the organization's goals. Supervisors need to communicate openly throughout the process. For example, if you have to deny an employee's request to attend a training class, it is helpful to explain how expenditures are prioritized and how they fit into the company's overall planning.

FOSTERING COMPETITION

A measure of internal competition can be healthy. Fair and balanced competition can be a source of motivation, productivity, and teamwork. For example, a company may create a quarterly sales competition with a nice reward for the top salesperson. A supervisor also may choose to create team competitions with incentives to encourage teamwork, camaraderie, and increased productivity. This may include a bonus for everyone on a call-center team when it beats all the other teams on a monthly performance indicator. By rewarding the entire team, individuals may be more inclined to help one another during peak hours rather than focusing on their own individual goal and reward.

When the structure or terms of the competition are unfairly weighted to benefit one person or group, then the competition becomes a source of conflict. In addition, if employees perceive any favoritism or bias towards one individual, the culture can quickly sour.

Therefore, it is essential that supervisors structure competitions in a fair and impartial fashion. Consider involving employees in the initial creation. If they help develop the criteria, rules, and rewards, they are far more likely to be enthusiastic about the competition.

RECOGNITION AND PROMOTION

Competition for coveted promotions is common. Because supervisors are limited in the number of promotions they can award, they need to find other ways to recognize and reward employees. One the best ways to build good behavior is through positive reinforcement. A low-cost method many supervisors use to acknowledge excellent performance is verbal and written praise. Verbal recognition may occur in a private conversation or during a staff meeting. When this method is used in public, perhaps at a meeting or in front of other employees, it can motivate others to achieve the same level of excellence as the person being praised. However, this method can backfire quickly if the person receiving the recognition does not deserve it. If you choose this method of public recognition, be sure to use it often and spread the praise around to your entire team. Otherwise, employees may become jealous and compete for your attention. You should also check the facts to be sure you are giving credit to the appropriate person(s).

Another common occurrence in the workplace is employee advancement. Promoting from within can be a good move because you are familiar with the employee, his work ethic, and capabilities. Because he is familiar with the organization, his training will proceed more quickly than if you hire from the outside. The downside to this approach is the internal competition that can occur between employees. You may experience a situation where two or more employees apply for the same position. But you can choose only one. Quite naturally, the individuals who are not selected will be disappointed and potentially harbor feelings of resentment and anger. It is essential that supervisors explain the mechanics of the entire process, to foster the perception of fairness and even-handedness. The supervisor should meet privately with each person who applied to inform them of the decision and to reinforce the importance of their contributions to the overall of success of the organization. It is also important to congratulate the person selected in a public forum, such as a staff meeting or official e-mail announcement.

Personality Differences

You likely have been in a situation where two people simply did not like each other; perhaps in a class, on a team, or at work. It is often hard to say precisely why they did not like each other. Usually, it centers on subtle personality differences. One person may be very gregarious and loud, while the other person is reserved and quiet. If these two people fail to understand and appreciate each other's strengths and contributions to the team, then they could hamper the team's success.

There are lots of tools and techniques for analyzing personality types. However, you do not need to spend a lot of money bringing in consultants to tell you how diverse your employees are. The simple fact is that everyone is unique and each person has his/her own style with perceived strengths and limitations. The key is to make an effort to understand all of your employees and leverage their unique strengths to benefit the team. By setting the example that you value the unique qualities and characteristics of your people, you will send a message to your employees that you embrace their diverse personalities. The disastrous flip side to this is when supervisors want everyone to be a mirror image of themselves. This inevitably leads to conflict, resentment, and a lack of productivity.

Everyone is unique and each person has his/her own style with perceived strengths and limitations.

Diverse Opinions

Diverse opinions and values can lead to conflict. Your employees' opinions and values have probably been influenced by a variety of factors, including their upbringing, education, and work experience. Your challenge is to make it safe for people to voice their opinions in a respectful manner. That paves the way for positive conflict and dialogue rather than negative conflict, angry put-downs, and hostile debates.

It is important to establish a framework for sharing opinions. Begin by focusing the conversation on achieving a goal or solving a problem. Make it clear that each person's opinion matters and there are no dumb ideas. Explore opposing viewpoints. Make an attempt to understand each perspective and how the person arrived at their conclusion. As the supervisor, it is your job to quickly cut off any personal attacks or demeaning comments directed at an individual. Racist and sexist comments are definitely out of bounds. Your words and actions set the tone, so be clear that you want to hear from everyone and that disagreement is okay as long as individuals can articulate why they support a different position.

Good companies have become great companies by welcoming diverse opinions and respectful disagreements. A prime example is Grand Circle Corporation, a Boston-based international travel company:

> In addition to arranging "life changing" trips to exotic locales for Americans age 50 and older, Grand Circle employees are expected to practice "open and courageous communication" in their dealings with each other and with management.
>
> Grand Circle defines "open and courageous communication" as being willing to ask tough questions, give constructive feedback to others and accept such feedback without defensiveness. . . .
>
> Marielle Arguello, a worldwide training manager at Grand Circle, admits the environment is not for everyone. "It's uncomfortable to be open and courageous," she says. In addition to giving and receiving feedback, "you can't just complain. You are expected to make recommendations for solutions" to the problems you identify.
>
> Further, at monthly corporate meetings, Grand Circle employees are expected to bring up "non-discussables" (described by CEO Alan Lewis as "things you don't want to hear") and get answers to their questions from the executive team.
>
> Nothing is off limits.[24]

Inequity

Whenever an employee believes that she is being treated unfairly, her performance will probably decline and you are quite likely to observe negative behavior in the workplace. Unfortunately, it does not matter whether the employee is right or not. You may be treating everyone exactly the same; however, the fact that the employee *perceives* unequal treatment makes it a problem to address quickly. Feelings and perceptions of **inequity** can come from a variety of sources, including the topics we just discussed: promotion, competition, and diverse opinions.

Failure to deal with perceived inequity can generate internal conflict for the employee and possibly corrode teamwork. You may believe that you do not have to defend yourself or your decisions to your employees. However, to build a positive and productive team, it is helpful to take the time to explain your decision-making process.

For example, if you decide to let only one of your employees telecommute by working from home two days a week, explain your rationale to everyone. Without disclosing private information, let your team know that this employee made the request based on personal circumstances. Explain that you have agreed to implement the telecommuting arrangement on a trial basis and you may consider extending the opportunity to others in the future. Reinforce that one of the major factors you considered when agreeing to this schedule is the person's long history as an outstanding performer. Point out to everyone that the job can be performed on the individual's own home computer at no additional costs. In addition, his work product is easy to quantify and the quality can also be objectively measured. Finally, agree on a format for effective communication during this transition. Answer questions as openly and honestly as possible, but do not turn the conversation into a debate. Your goal is to help employees to understand how or why a decision is made and not to defend the actual decision.

inequity
when employees believe they are being treated unfairly.

Dealing with Difficult Situations

Difficult situations at work include everything from harassment to employee theft. Supervisors need to be able to read the warning signs and respond appropriately. There are far too many trouble spots to cover in detail here. For a foundation of understanding, this section is broken down into seven major categories: (1) workplace violence, (2) personal hygiene and body art, (3) behavior/attitude, (4) theft, (5) substance abuse, (6) verbal abuse, and (7) harassment.

Violence in the Workplace

Hopefully, you will never be faced with violence in the workplace. Yet it does all too often occur. In fact, according to the U.S. Department of Labor, violent acts are among the top three causes of workplace fatalities.[25] How can you reduce the risk of employee conflict escalating to violent behavior? First, learn to recognize warning signs and threats.

THREATS

Threats are usually made verbally or through gestures, actions, or a combination.[26] There are three categories of threats: (1) direct, (2) conditional, and (3) veiled.[27]

1. **Direct**. Easiest to identify as they create a sense of immediate danger; however, they do not always lead to violence. For example, "I'm going to kill you."

2. **Conditional**. Fairly clear and present an imminent danger; they usually link the threat to a change or consequence. For example, "If you don't stop giving me warnings, I'm going to get even."

3. **Veiled**. Imply violence rather than explicitly state the threat; they may create a threatening situation in which a subject feels intimidated. For example, "I know where you live."[28]

TAKING ACTION

Since it is difficult to know whether or not an employee is simply venting, it is best to take any threat seriously and immediately report it to your manager and security or the police. Do not confront the individual in the heat of the moment. This could make the situation worse. Instead, meet with your manager and/or authorities to determine the appropriate course of action. Your goal is to maintain a safe and productive work environment for everyone, while remaining fair and objective as you examine the facts surrounding the perceived threat.

Take any threat seriously.

ASSESSING EMPLOYEE BEHAVIOR: THE VIOLENCE CONTINUUM

Most supervisors want a safe work environment for their employees. Unfortunately, there are situations where individuals demonstrate aggressive or violent behavior. A goal for supervisors is to identify employee behavior that may lead to more aggressive and/or violent actions. By recognizing these symptomatic acts early, supervisors can be proactive and address the situation before it escalates.

TABLE 11.2
The HARM Model

The HARM Model HARM Term	The Violence Continuum Examples
Harassment	Irritating, inappropriate conduct, such as slamming doors or telling lies about a coworker.
Aggression	Hostile behavior, such as slamming a door in someone's face.
Rage	Inappropriate physical and visible behavior, such as pushing someone or leaving a "hate" note.
Mayhem	Physical violence or destruction of property.

Source: Frank E. Rudewicz, "The Road to Rage: Workplace Violence Grows Out Of Escalating Patterns of Aggressive Behavior That Managers Must Be Trained to Recognize and Stop," *Security Management* 48 (February 2004): 40–47.

Frank E. Rudewicz, senior managing director and counsel at Decision Strategies in Hartford, Connecticut, provides a concise list of guidelines for assessing behavior. He refers to this as the HARM model: (1) harassment, (2) aggression, (3) rage, and (4) mayhem.[29] See Table 11.2 for an overview of this framework.

Ideally, coworkers will intervene at the harassment stage to prevent more aggressive behavior and/or workplace violence.

OTHER POTENTIAL WARNING SIGNS

Analyzing employee behavior is a significant challenge for supervisors. Most supervisors face fairly routine employee issues, such as attendance problems, mood swings, and poor overall performance. The cause of each of these could be something as simple as a minor illness or something more serious that could lead to violence.[30] Regardless of the reason, each of these issues warrants action by the supervisor. Let's use attendance as an example.

If an employee is arriving late for work or missing work on a consistent basis, it usually is a symptom of a broader problem. The reason for the change in attendance may be a work-related issue. For example, the employee might have problems with a harassing coworker (a factor in the HARM model). On the other hand, the reason for missing work or arriving late could be a family-related issue; perhaps child-care arrangements have changed. Changes in attendance can also be a sign of medical problems or substance abuse.

Whenever an employee demonstrates changes in behavior, such as mood swings, attendance problems, or a decline in performance, it is important to recognize that these may be either a key warning sign or simply a temporary situation that can be quickly and easily resolved. Later in this chapter, we will discuss how to handle these situations.

Personal Hygiene and Body Art

Personal hygiene is one of those areas that most supervisors avoid discussing with employees unless there is a complaint by a customer or other employees. You can

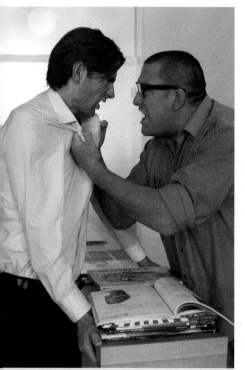

Make no mistake, this is criminal assault and battery! Get help immediately, call security or the police to get assistance in breaking up this dangerous situation. Prompt disciplinary action should follow. Regardless of the reason for the argument, there is no place for violence in the workplace. This is a zero-tolerance issue.

© Christoph Wilhelm/Getty Images/Digital Vision

save an employee from continued embarrassment by talking with the individual in private. Talking with an employee about personal cleanliness, including appearance and body odor, can be very awkward. This is particularly true in cross-cultural situations. If handled improperly, the person can be deeply offended and emotionally defensive. Therefore, it is important to approach the conversation in a sensitive manner. Remember the Golden Rule and try to imagine how you would feel if you were in the employee's place. It is very helpful to have the support of a written policy regarding general appearance and cleanliness, as well as stated limitations on facial hair, piercings, tattoos, and use of colognes. In fact, an estimated 22% of Americans have tattoos.[31]

> Daria Juran, office manager for Express Personnel staffing agency in Phoenix, said her company directly addresses body art. "We absolutely never ignore tattoos or piercings," she says.
>
> "Typically, people aren't resistant to hearing they need to cover up a tattoo, or to remove piercing jewelry," she said. "But it does limit job opportunities."[32]

KNOWLEDGE TO ACTION

Personal hygiene problems in the workplace is an area where many supervisors will choose to avoid the conversation because it is awkward and/or embarrassing. Consider the scenarios below and describe how you would handle the situation. Remember the Golden Rule and keep in mind that different cultures have different perspectives and traditions that may be contributing factors.

1. Body Odor. If you have an employee who has body odor or is using heavy perfume and/or cologne that is offensive to coworkers and customers, what would you do?

   _____

2. Appearance. If you work in a setting where personal appearance is important and there is a dress code because employees frequently interact with customers—such as a real estate office, retail store, or restaurant—and your employee's clothes are wrinkled or inappropriate, what would you do?

   _____

Bad Attitudes

Inevitably, some employees will display a bad attitude. They can be rude to customers or coworkers and insubordinate to their supervisors. The good news is that supervisors do not have to accept this behavior. It is helpful to create an "attitude standard" (refer back to our discussion in Chapter 9). An attitude standard establishes a baseline of expectations for employee conduct. In the absence of a documented attitude standard, you can still describe to all of your employees the characteristics of a positive attitude. If an employee consistently demonstrates a bad attitude, it is futile to sit back and hope it goes away. As difficult as it may be, you need to address the situation before the individual's negativity contaminates the entire workplace. Remember, attitudes are contagious—both good and bad.

Initiate this change by meeting privately with the employee to explain that you have concerns about his negative behavior and attitude. Clarify your expectations and provide examples of how he can demonstrate a positive attitude. Share a few examples of when he displayed a bad attitude and the negative impacts this behavior had on coworkers and productivity. Although the employee's bad attitude may be obvious to everyone else, individuals who are confronted with the information are generally surprised. They often are completely unaware of how they are perceived by others. In these cases, put your coaching hat on and work with your employee to improve. Agree on an action plan for a better attitude. A good idea is to include a gesture or code word you can use to signal the employee when he begins to display a negative demeanor. This secret code will help avoid embarrassment in front of others while nipping the problem in the bud. The action plan should also include time lines for incremental improvement along with consequences if the negative behavior does not change. Consequences may include reassignment of duties or disciplinary action.

Theft

Most supervisors and small business owners trust their employees and perceive a low risk of theft or other fraudulent behavior. If they are experiencing a loss of inventory, managers tend to believe it is a result of thieves from outside the company. But, in many cases, the culprit is an employee. In fact, small companies (100 or fewer employees) are more likely to have employees stealing from them than their larger counterparts.[33] According to a report published by the Association of Certified Fraud Examiners, the median loss due to employee theft for small businesses in 2006 was $190,000.[34] The unfortunate reality is that employees sometimes steal. They will take cash, inventory, and even checks. Supervisors are the first line of defense in reducing opportunities for fraud, deception, and theft.

> *The unfortunate reality is that employees sometimes steal.*

Here are a few steps you can take that will be cost-effective for the company: (1) create checks and balances, (2) use the element of surprise, (3) turn on the controls, (4) when theft does happen, take action and maintain trust, (5) hire smarter,[35] (6) take proactive measures, and (7) get help from your employees.

CREATE CHECKS AND BALANCES

Design your work systems to create a separation of duties. For example, in a retail environment, the person handling receipt of cash, checks, and credit card payments should not be the same person who reconciles the register and ultimately does the bank deposits. In addition, separate responsibilities for different aspects of the reporting process. Develop a routine to reconcile all of the variables, including comparing cash deposits with daily sales reports.[36]

Compare sales volumes for the same day and time of the week when different people are working the register. For example, compare total sales for every Thursday from 3:00 P.M. to 10:00 P.M. over a three- to six-month period of time. You will also need to track who is working the register for each time slot. This is a fairly easy spreadsheet to create, and it can quickly raise a red flag. It was through this method that the owners of a boutique shoe store figured out who was stealing from them. It took further investigation to prove the employee theft, but this quick analysis pointed them in the right direction.[37]

Are your employees stealing from you? Successful supervisors create checks and balances to reduce the opportunity for employee theft. In addition, proper hiring and training can help minimize illegal behavior. Rewarding team members for reporting their co-workers is another effective way to catch a thief.
© Denkou Images/Alamy

USE THE ELEMENT OF SURPRISE

People who resort to theft are often desperate and clever. They will learn your systems and find ways to beat the system. Therefore, you need to catch them off-guard. In the retail environment, you may decide to stop in just before closing to close out the register. In other instances, changing purchasing limits or doing random checks can identify a white-collar criminal within.

Consider, for example, a regional bank with approximately two hundred employees that decided to hand-deliver every employee's paycheck. This happened somewhat by accident as the bank had just switched over to a new payroll-processing company, and the format for the checks and direct deposit notices had changed. Bank officials wanted the transition to go smoothly for the employees, so they decided to visit each branch office to answer any questions or concerns. At the last minute, they chose to actually deliver the employees' paychecks at the same time. This last-minute decision caught the human resources director off-guard and ultimately led to her demise.

What bank officials learned when they hand-delivered the checks is that the human resources director had created an employee record and generated paychecks for a relative who never worked at the bank. When there was one paycheck left over and no department or branch linked to the account, officials knew something was wrong. It took a few days of research before the human resources director finally confessed. The bank had been paying this nonemployee for over a year before the fraud was discovered.[38]

TURN ON THE CONTROLS

Computer applications are becoming more sophisticated and offer more security features. Unfortunately, some organizations either are not aware of how to use these tools or they choose to disable them. Security features can help prevent theft when used properly. For example, consider the restaurant that learned this lesson the hard way when an employee modified entries in the point-of-service (POS) system and stole cash from the register. This company now uses the software system's security features to prevent theft by limiting employee access only to authorized modules.[39]

WHEN THEFT DOES HAPPEN, TAKE ACTION AND MAINTAIN TRUST

As expected, each of the employees in the previous examples lost their job and was prosecuted. In one case, in addition to paying financial penalties, the thief went to jail.[40] By taking action, you are sending a message to your employees, prospective employees, and customers that there are serious consequences for stealing.

This brings us to the issue of *trust*. Most employees want to be trusted by their supervisor and indeed are trustworthy. But blind trust without proper controls is foolhardy. Michael Powell learned this lesson the hard way in the chain of bookstores he founded when an employee's used-book purchasing scheme cost him $60,000. According to Powell:

> The incident was a watershed for me and my staff dispelling any naïveté we may have had about crime. We realized that not only can theft happen; it will happen. At the same time, dealing with the matter forced us to revisit our basic values and managerial

philosophies. We believe that the modern demands of business call for empowered and fully flexible staff, and we know that such a staff will often have to handle valuable commodities and money. We also believe that most people are not going to abuse our trust if they are put in a position with a reasonable amount of review and responsibility.[41]

HIRE SMARTER

As emphasized in Chapter 4, hiring the right people can have a positive impact on employee retention and organizational performance. You can reduce the odds of hiring employees who end up stealing from your business by taking the time to check their references and conducting comprehensive background checks.[42]

PROACTIVE MEASURES TO REDUCE THEFT

Consider taking proactive measures to reduce the temptation for employees to steal. Many restaurants and hotels provide employees with meal allowances. Other retailers offer significant discounts or bonuses to employees. Your policies and procedures need to clearly state what employees can and cannot have for free and what the consequences are for stealing. If your employees are serving customers who are friends and family, remind them that giving away a cup of coffee or a scoop of ice cream is stealing. Imagine if every employee consumed or gave away ten dollars worth of merchandise or services every day. The impact on the bottom lines of our nation's small businesses would be staggering.

TO CATCH A THIEF—GET HELP FROM YOUR EMPLOYEES

Your employees are often the first to know if someone is stealing merchandise or putting cash in their pockets. Make it easy for employees to report this theft without concern for retaliation. Whenever possible, try to keep their identity confidential so the thief never knows who reported them. Create incentives, either individual or team rewards, if goals for reducing theft are reached. For example, some companies will provide an end-of-year bonus for all employees if the goal for inventory shrinkage (theft) is achieved. The bonus amount is often based on the amount of money the company has saved due to better inventory control. The point is to work with your team to change the culture from one of distrust and a sense of entitlement to steal to one of pride and satisfaction in achieving organization goals.

Substance Abuse—Drugs in the Workplace

Employees who are using illegal drugs have an incredibly negative impact on organizations. Attendance problems, accidents, and diminished productivity and quality are just a few of the issues supervisors experience as a result of employees on drugs. You may be thinking, "No problem, I won't supervise anyone who uses drugs." However, the odds that you will either supervise or work side-by-side with a substance abuser are greater than you think. An estimated 75% of illegal-drug users are employed. Worse yet, one out of every five workers between the ages of eighteen and twenty-five uses drugs at the worksite (see Figure 11.4).[43] Methamphetamine (meth) appears to be the drug of choice.[44]

FIGURE 11.4 Substance abuse among workers aged 18 to 25
Source: T. L. Stanley, "Workplace drug testing and the growing problem of Methamphetamines," *Supervision* 68 (August 2007): 3–6

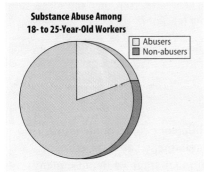

Substance Abuse Among 18- to 25-Year-Old Workers
☐ Abusers
■ Non-abusers

Although supervisors are not expected to be experts in the signs and symptoms of substance abuse, some helpful warning signs are listed in Figure 11.5. Consider implementing a comprehensive program to promote a drug-free workplace that includes (1) an assessment of the problem, (2) policy development, (3) employee education, (4) supervisor training, (5) employee assistance programs, and (6) drug testing.[45]

Verbal Abuse

It is hard to find a supervisor who doesn't have a "war story" about dealing with **verbal abuse.** Such abuse may be from a manager, customer, or employee. These experiences usually involve a person launching into a verbal assault that might include personal insults, threats, and inappropriate language. These emotional outbursts are usually accompanied by yelling and nonverbal displays such as slamming doors or throwing things.

What can you do if you are the recipient of an emotional explosion leading to verbal abuse? Begin by remaining calm and in control. If you feel threatened in any way, calmly step back and call security immediately. Avoid any sudden movements that could be misinterpreted as hostile or threatening. Let the person vent, as long as it is safe and he is not damaging equipment or endangering people. When the person begins to calm down, acknowledge his feelings with a statement such as, "Obviously, you're upset; this is a tough problem."[46]

Your goal is to diffuse the anger and determine the source of the problem in an effort to bring long-term resolution to the situation. It is often helpful to request permission prior to gathering information and asking questions. This approach shifts the nature of the conversation from a threatening inquisition to a scenario where the person who is upset feels in control. Continue the conversation until the person reveals the source of the emotional reaction. The person may not fully realize what triggered the tantrum. The debriefing process may take time. If you feel threatened or uncomfortable, request assistance from your manager or a human resources associate.[47]

FIGURE 11.5 Ten warning signs of employee meth use in the workplace
Source: T. L. Stanley, "Workplace drug testing and the growing problem of Methamphetamines," *Supervision* 68 (August 2007): 3–6.

Ten Warning Signs of Employee Meth Use in the Workplace

1. Extreme talkativeness
2. Declining productivity
3. Extreme and rapid weight loss
4. High energy levels or restlessness
5. Deterioration in personal appearance
6. Damaged working relationships with peers
7. Stealing money or pilfering from company
8. Temper outbursts and unusual mood changes
9. Sudden increase in absenteeism and tardiness
10. Combative and unreasonable attitude toward supervisors

verbal abuse
a verbal assault including personal insults, threats, and inappropriate language.

KNOWLEDGE TO ACTION

How aware are you of signs of verbal abuse?

1. List four or five characteristics of verbal abuse.

_____

2. Reflect on a situation when you witnessed these actions (if not in person, then consider a scene from a movie). How did you feel and what was your reaction?

_____

Harassment

The term *harassment* conjures up different images for different people. Some immediately think of sexual harassment. Others think of harassment based on ethnicity, age, or lifestyle. We discuss harassment in more detail in Chapter 13 because many harassment cases have significant legal implications. Sadly, in some areas such as racial-harassment lawsuits, complaints are increasing.[48]

If an employee is suspected of harassment, your role as supervisor is not to analyze or interpret her behavior by trying to be a therapist. Instead, you should gather facts and observe the employee's actions. Importantly, focus on her performance and the job. For example, rather than spending a lot of time and energy analyzing the reasons for a harassment claim, discuss specific performance issues such as her uncooperative behaviour. Be careful not to attack the individual's personality. Remind her of the overall goals for the organization and how vital her role is in achieving those goals. Explain to her the importance of teamwork and cooperation.

Your plan for correcting the problem should emphasize the desired behavior. Rather than saying, "Don't be a troublemaker," describe the preferred outcome, "Be a good team player."

You cannot control other people's behavior or emotions the way you can control your own actions, emotions, and decisions.

Remember, you cannot control other people's behavior or emotions. But you can control your own actions, emotions, and decisions. Remain calm, be aware of the entire situation, and focus on the facts when dealing with challenging and difficult situations. Visualize the outcome you desire and then work with your team to achieve it.

SUMMARY

1. The first step to helping an underachieving employee reach his/her potential and address poor performance is to openly and honestly assess the situation with the person. Begin this improvement process by reviewing the following topics with the employee: (1) clarify expectations, (2) define performance measures, (3) identify necessary resources, (4) determine if the employee has had adequate training, (5) identify obstacles, and (6) prepare an action plan.

2. Progressive discipline typically has four stages: (1) counseling, (2) written warning, (3) suspension, and (4) termination. One of the challenges during the counseling stage is for supervisors to balance the warning aspects with encouragement so the employee continues to feel confident and capable while also clearly understanding that the problematic actions are not acceptable. If an employee fails to correct the situation, the next step is a

written warning; this may be the time to develop an action plan. Lack of improvement after the written warning leads to suspension. After other attempts to work with the employee to improve performance have failed, the final step is termination.

3. Most states recognize employment at will, which allows an employer to terminate an employee at any time without explanation or cause. However, you may not terminate an employee based on discrimination or revenge. A few ways to reduce the likelihood of a lawsuit and make the process of terminating someone less painful include (1) offer a warning, (2) script it out, (3) get to the point, (4) focus on the future, (5) stay in control, and (6) follow the Golden Rule.

4. Negative conflict can be a drain on productivity and may ultimately lead to a decline in employee morale and increased turnover. Common sources of negative conflict include (1) poor communication, (2) competition, (3) personality differences, (4) diverse opinions, and (5) inequity, either perceived or real. To avoid these situations, encourage better communication through information sharing, clarifying assumptions, and effective listening. In addition, foster positive competition while reducing battles for limited resources. Create an environment where diverse opinions and personality differences are embraced and a spirit of equality, integrity, and fairness permeate the organization.

5. Difficult situations at work include everything from harassment to employee theft. As a supervisor, it is important to see the warning signs and to know how to handle the situation. Seven common categories include (1) workplace violence, (2) hygiene factors, (3) behavior/attitude, (4) theft, (5) substance abuse, (6) verbal abuse and (7) harassment. Each of these areas is unique, with different warning signs and recommended approaches. Focus on performance and be careful not to make personal attacks. Corrective action should focus on the desired behavior.

TERMS TO UNDERSTAND

counseling, p. 302
employment at will, p. 305
inequity, p. 312
objective performance measures, p. 297

obstacles, p. 299
progressive discipline, p. 301
resources, p. 298
subjective performance measures, p. 297

termination, p. 305
trust but validate, p. 309
verbal abuse, p. 319
whistle blowing, p. 306

QUESTIONS FOR REFLECTION

1. Explain the difference between subjective and objective performance measures. Which of these is more effective for supervisors to use with their employees? Why?

2. What is an action plan? When would you consider using one?

3. Describe your understanding of employment at will.

4. List and explain why it is important for supervisors to be aware of eight protected classifications commonly identified in discussions about workplace discrimination.

5. Explain whistle blowing. Do you think employers should be permitted to fire a person for blowing the whistle? Why or why not?

HANDS-ON ACTIVITIES

PROGRESSIVE DISCIPLINE

1. Explain the concept of progressive discipline.

2. List the four steps typically involved in progressive discipline.
   a. Explain each step in detail.
   b. Select an example from your personal experience or from a situation you have read about where an employee was disciplined.
   c. Describe how the situation was handled and analyze whether or not you think the appropriate steps were selected for the situation.
   d. If yes, explain why. If no, what would have been a more appropriate way to approach the situation?

THEFT IN THE WORKPLACE

Unfortunately, employee theft is a difficult situation that many supervisors have to deal with and work to prevent.

1. What size business is most likely to experience employee theft? Explain why.

2. Select a business that you are familiar with. Provide a brief description of the business including the number of employees, its primary line of business, and a description of how the business sells to its customers.
   a. What are three steps the business can take to reduce theft?
   b. Explain in detail how you would implement each of these steps.

Interview an Expert

The purpose of this exercise is to learn from an expert his/her approach to handling difficult situations in the workplace, including discipline, termination, theft, and other common challenges. Identify a supervisor, manager, or human resources professional to interview. If possible choose someone working in an industry where you have a personal interest or are currently employed. Your goal is to learn from this person's experience and discover tools and techniques that have been effective in dealing with difficult circumstances. You may use the questions listed below and/or develop your own. After your interview, prepare a brief summary of the conversation and list their strategies, tools, and techniques for handling difficult situations in the workplace.

Questions

1. Describe a situation where you had to discipline an employee.

2. How did you approach the employee?

3. What disciplinary steps did you take?

4. Has an employee ever stolen from your company? If so, how did you discover the theft and how did you handle the situation?

5. What systems do you have in place to reduce the likelihood of employee theft?

6. Have you experienced verbal abuse or harassment at work? Please describe the scenario and discuss how you handled it.

7. What are the biggest challenges in helping a poor performer improve?

8. You may improvise and add or edit questions to fit the situation or the circumstances of your interview. You may also request copies of relevant policies, procedures, and forms. Schedule your interview ahead of time and try to limit it to about 15 minutes. Remember to send a thank-you note to the person you interview.

YOU DECIDE

CASE STUDY 11.1
Making Difficult Decisions at Work

Lorena has been a police officer with the Pleasanton Police force for eleven years. Until last year, she was primarily assigned to foot patrol in the downtown business and shopping district. Merchants and other locals knew her by name and commented on her firm yet fair approach to maintaining a safe place for people to work, live, and shop. The safety rating in her jurisdiction was always rated as excellent, with fewer than ten violent crimes per year and fewer than five robberies per year.

Last year, one of the patrol officers retired and the sergeant asked Lorena to change assignments from foot patrol downtown in the commercial district to car patrol in one of the outlying neighborhoods. Lorena was ready for a change, so she agreed. She even offered to walk the downtown patrol with her replacement to introduce him to local merchants. Derek, a relatively new member of the police force, was selected to take over the downtown foot patrol. Lorena spent a half day with him showing him around the commercial district.

At first, everything seemed to be going along fine. Lorena was enjoying her new assignment, and Derek reported to her that criminal activity in the commercial district was down. However, after six months the sergeant called Lorena into his office to discuss a confidential matter. He noticed in his quarterly report that violent crimes and robberies were on the rise in the downtown area. He expressed concern and asked Lorena for her opinion. She offered to go chat with some of the downtown merchants to see if they had any observations or information to share. What she learned was shocking. The merchants told her that Derek was involved with an illegal gambling operation. Instead of patrolling the streets, he was focusing his time on collecting gambling debts.

Questions

1. If you were Lorena, would you report Derek? Why or why not?

2. If you were Derek's supervisor, how would you handle this situation once you found out about the illegal gambling operation?

SUPERVISOR'S TOOLKIT

Verbal abuse is one of the more common concerns in the workplace. The scenarios vary widely from a customer yelling at an employee to an irate manager screaming at a subordinate. Supervisors are frequently caught in the middle of unwelcome verbal exchanges. Prepare a couple of documents to add to your supervisor's toolkit that outline tips and best practices for effectively recognizing verbal abuse and for managing the situation.

1. List four or five characteristics of verbal abuse.

2. If someone is being verbally abusive, what actions should you take?

3. What type of demeanor should you exhibit?

4. What type of language should you use?

5. What should be the focus of your message and comments to the abusive person?

6. How can you help your employees to become more aware of their actions to avoid being perceived as verbally abusive?

7. What can you do to help your employees be prepared to handle a situation if someone is verbally abusive to them?

CHAPTER 12

Staffing: Planning, Scheduling, and Outsourcing

Learning Objectives

1. Identify tools and techniques for estimating staffing needs.

2. Discuss strategies for scheduling employees.

3. Compare alternative scheduling options.

4. Discuss strategies for implementing alternative schedules.

5. Explain the concept of contingency planning and discuss the value of cross-training.

6. Explain outsourcing, off-shoring, and globalization.

7. Discuss the unique challenges associated with staffing foreign positions and list strategies for setting expatriates up for success.

Straight Talk from the Field

Maury Chaput is co-owner of the Canine Fitness Center located in Crownsville, Maryland. The center offers swimming, fun, and fitness for dogs through a wide variety of services.

QUESTION: *How do you staff your business to ensure customer satisfaction while keeping your operating costs under control?*

RESPONSE:

In virtually any business, staffing is an integral part to its success. Typically, a client's first point of contact is with a staff member. The staff member represents the owners of the business and should embody the purpose and goals that inspired the owners to open the business. Supervisors must work with their employees to be sure they understand the organization's vision and goals, as well as their personal role in helping the company achieve success.

Our business, the Canine Fitness Center, opened in November 2002. It consists of three family owners and seven part-time employees. When choosing a staff member, we look for a person who values our clients' experience (both canine and human) at the center. Our first employees—who are still with us—are two of our enthusiastic dog-lover friends. From the beginning, they understood the customer service side as well as the pool and building maintenance side of our business.

As time passed, we have added several part-time employees. Most were customers prior to applying for employment, and they love what we do. Several are dog-loving early retirees from professional positions. The staff members develop bonds with the dogs and their owners. They enjoy playing fetch with a Labrador Retriever; they cherish the satisfaction of seeing an arthritic German Shepherd regain mobility.

At the center, we have unique staffing challenges. Our high-demand appointment times are weekday mornings and evenings and all day Saturday. Mid-afternoons during the week are less busy. However, customers frequently call at the last minute to schedule a swim for their dog. We do our best to accommodate these requests. Of course, we prefer that the client schedule in advance, but we realize that some of our customers simply cannot plan ahead.

When it comes to staffing, flexibility is the key to success for both the employee and the employer. We generate work schedules two weeks ahead, but frequently call upon the staff to come in earlier or stay later to meet our clients' unpredictable schedules. We are also mindful of our staff's needs and strive to be flexible with their schedules as well. This joint effort between us and our staff has allowed us to retain dedicated employees who represent our business well. Another important ingredient to our success in balancing our needs with our employees' preferences is frequent, open communication. We make a concerted effort to anticipate demand and plan accordingly. In return, we ask that our employees schedule personal appointments that do not conflict with their work schedules.

The center's operating costs are very high. Staffing with part-time employees allows us to keep our prices at a reasonable level. If we hired full-time employees and paid benefits, our prices might be out of reach for many people.

We also reward our employees in other small ways. For example, employees can bring their dogs to swim at no charge once a week. They also receive a 25% discount in our gift shop. The Saturday staff is provided with coffee, donuts, and lunch.

We value our staff and strive to treat them as we ourselves would want to be treated. We listen to their comments and suggestions. Our business is a joint effort between owners and staff. We achieve success by working together to make each appointment at the Canine Fitness Center a special time for all of our clients (both animal and human).

Chapter Outline

S**taffing** encompasses everything from hiring to recognizing and developing individual talent to meet organizational needs. Staffing has long been an integral part of the supervisory role. Like other supervisory activities, such as planning and organizing, the staffing function has grown throughout the years. Early definitions of staffing focused narrowly on hiring people for vacant positions. Today, the traditional staffing function involves the acquisition, retention, and development of people.[1] It also involves balancing individual strengths and personal interests with the overall needs of the organization. This underscores the point that people are valuable resources who require careful nurturing along with training and coaching.

Moreover, global opportunities and competitive pressures have made the skillful supervision of human resources more important than ever.[2] The purpose of this chapter is to help you understand and apply concepts that will help you make effective staffing and scheduling decisions.

> *Global opportunities and competitive pressures have made the skillful supervision of human resources more important than ever.*

Estimating and Planning for Staffing Needs

staffing
hiring employees and recognizing and developing individual talent to meet organizational needs.

Staffing requires supervisors to analyze the day-to-day needs of the organization and anticipate business fluctuations that may impact scheduling. This can be a difficult and complex process in many industries. There are some important variables we need to consider before looking at specific tools for forecasting and estimating staffing needs.

Staffing and Scheduling Variables

Important variables to consider when estimating your staffing and scheduling needs are (1) seasonal impact, (2) market fluctuations, (3) environmental factors, and (4) availability of labor.

SEASONAL IMPACT

Mention seasonal impact and most people think of the end-of-the-year shopping rush that retail stores experience. Of course, this significantly impacts retailers' staffing programs. There are seasonal fluctuations in other sectors of the economy as well. For instance, the health care industry must deal with flu season each year. Increased demand for flu vaccinations and more visits to medical facilities for treatment necessitate seasonal staffing adjustments to meet the demand.

KNOWLEDGE TO ACTION

Brainstorm with your classmates to identify seasonal variables.

1. Select a local organization or business that everyone in your group is familiar with.

   _____

2. What are two seasonal variables that can impact the staffing for this business?

   _____

MARKET FLUCTUATIONS

What is happening in the marketplace? This includes your local geographic area as well as the general economy. Assume there is a recession looming and economists are predicting a decline in consumer spending. This could mean lower demand for your product or service, which will have an impact on operations and staffing needs. For example, if you are responsible for scheduling massages, facials, and other services at a day spa, economic forecasts may help you determine the number of staff you need to meet projected lower demand.

Other market fluctuations may be the result of a popular or trendy item on the market. For example, if your store sells the leading computer game console, accessories, and games, then you should anticipate higher demand and adjust your staffing plans accordingly.

ENVIRONMENTAL FACTORS

It is important for supervisors to remain abreast of environmental factors that may impact their business.

Local weather can wreak havoc on an outdoor wedding. Wedding planners have highly flexible staffing needs. Supervisors in other weather-impacted industries pay attention to broad geographic areas. For example, during hurricane season, building-material, tree-service, and electrical-utility companies closely monitor weather patterns to respond quickly to sudden demand.

Aside from the weather, environmental factors may include major events involving local sports teams, agricultural harvests, or schools. For example,

Troy Lee of Reynoldsburg, Ohio, shouts out an Ohio State University football cheer at The Buckeye Hall of Fame Cafe in Columbus, Ohio. Bar managers called in extra servers, checked their DirecTV connections, and stocked up on buffalo wings and beer for the first OSU football game of the season as fans without access to the new Big Ten Network were expected to crowd into restaurants and bars to cheer on their favorite team.
© AP Images/Jay LaPrete, File

every restaurant and hotel in the Columbus, Ohio, area is aware of the Ohio State University Buckeye's football schedule. They know that their businesses will be incredibly busy during home-game weekends, and they staff accordingly. Other local businesses, such as a furniture store, may be negatively impacted by the throng of sports fans. Staying connected and becoming aware of current events can play a major role in effectively planning for staffing needs.

AVAILABILITY OF LABOR

When you need more staff, it is essential to have previously evaluated the local labor market. This will greatly facilitate forecasting. This evaluation includes both the demand for labor as well as the labor supply. Local unemployment figures are an indicator of local labor supply. As Figure 12.1 shows, if unemployment is declining, there will be fewer job seekers. On the other hand, when unemployment goes up, more people will be looking for work.

Another method you can use to assess supply and demand for labor is to review the local Help Wanted ads in newspapers and online for positions similar to those you need to fill. After analyzing the advertisements for a few weeks, you will begin to see trends. If you see the same company advertising for the exact same job for several weeks in a row, a natural conclusion is that this company is having a difficult time finding a qualified candidate for that position. Another way to assess supply and demand for labor is to contact local colleges and universities. Talk with their

FIGURE 12.1 Correlation between unemployment and labor supply

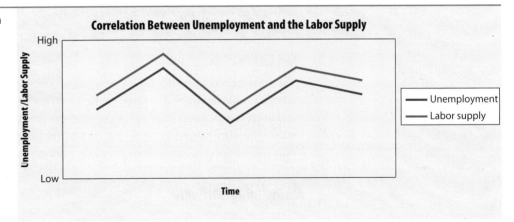

job placement specialists to get their sense of the situation. If there are a lot of job openings and a limited number of qualified candidates, you may have difficulty filling your positions.

KNOWLEDGE TO ACTION

Use your current job or the position you would like to have to answer the following:

1. What are two ways that you can determine the demand for employees to work in this position in your geographic area?

2. How can you assess the available supply of qualified workers for this position?

Estimating and Forecasting

There is no exact science to estimating and forecasting staffing requirements. However, there are a few tools you can use to improve the accuracy of your estimates. In short, learn from history and incorporate current information. A combination of these two sources of information can help you prepare a plan for staffing that yields positive results.

HISTORICAL DATA

One of the most effective methods for forecasting demand and estimating staffing needs is to evaluate historical records. Look at your **historical data,** such as sales or office visits along with staffing figures from prior years. It is instructive to break this down into blocks of time throughout the day, for various days of the week, or for seasonal slack or busy periods. For example, if you are a supervisor in a retail store and you are forecasting for the day after Thanksgiving, evaluate your past sales figures in one-hour increments. Review the number of employees who worked and think about customer satisfaction levels in past periods. Were the lines at the cash register too long? Were associates available to answer questions and provide adequate

historical data
figures from prior years, such as sales and employee staffing.

assistance? Incorporate your past experience with numerical data to create an initial estimate of staffing needs.

NEW INFORMATION

The next step is to factor in any new information that is available. This information relates to the variables discussed earlier: market fluctuations, environmental factors, and your own sources. For example, perhaps this year the company is doing a major marketing campaign featuring big discounts for purchases made before 10:00 A.M. This information is essential to properly forecast staffing needs.

Scheduling Software

As with many complex tasks, computer technology can make your job easier. In small organizations, a supervisor may simply use a spreadsheet to prepare schedules and track hours. This approach may take a few extra minutes to complete, but in the long run, it could end up saving the company money by avoiding overtime.

Larger organizations must use specialized, complex computer applications to successfully schedule human resources properly. Consider the highly regulated airline industry. Pilot scheduling would be difficult, if not impossible, without the use of computer software to track flying hours and configure the sophisticated travel logistics inherent in the industry.

Keep in mind that computer software, while helpful, also has limitations. For example, many systems are designed to coordinate routine schedules, but are not equipped to handle extenuating circumstances or unique requests. Therefore, supervisors cannot relinquish 100% of the scheduling responsibility to a computer. Definitely take advantage of information technology to increase your efficiency and effectiveness. But remember that you are ultimately responsible for the end result—a schedule that optimizes resources, achieves organizational goals, and does not erode morale.

> *Computer software can be helpful, but it also has limitations.*

Employee Scheduling

Balancing the needs of the organization with the personal preferences of each employee is a tough challenge for supervisors. In service businesses where customers can show up without appointments, such as a nail salon or auto repair shop, it can be difficult to gauge demand. This directly impacts a supervisor's ability to determine the proper number of employees to schedule. If too many people are scheduled, the company loses money. For example, consider a hair salon or barber shop. If a supervisor schedules too many hair stylists for a shift, there will be times when employees are sitting around with nothing to do.

Conversely, understaffing can lead to frustrated customers, increased stress among staff members, and lost revenue. The goal for every supervisor is to achieve the right balance with the correct level of employees scheduled. Ultimately, you want to have the proper number of people with the necessary skills to meet the needs of

Barber David Phan waits for customers at Michael's Barbershop in Wahiawa, Hawaii. Despite military haircuts costing only $6.25, the nine chairs at the shop were empty. Business got bad when 10,000 soldiers of the 25th Infantry Division from nearby Schofield Barracks were deployed to Iraq and Afghanistan. Wahiawa businesses, most of which are mom-and-pop shops, have suffered.
© AP Images/Ronen Zilberman

the organization and its customers. Visit the textbook website at www.cengage.com/business/cassidy for examples of various schedules.

We will begin this section by examining how to determine staffing priorities and scheduling strategies from the company's perspective.

Staffing Priorities and Scheduling Strategies

Staffing needs and priorities will vary by industry and company size. The following information can be used as general guidelines as you develop an approach to scheduling that is appropriate for your organization. In the end, every company wants to achieve organizational goals and deliver excellent customer service. As discussed in Chapter 7, properly trained employees are one of the keys to success. Another important factor is to be sure there are the proper numbers of employees working to meet the level of demand. This is true whether you are working in retail, hospitality, manufacturing, emergency services, or health care. Guessing the correct number can be very difficult. Fortunately, there are some helpful techniques for estimating and forecasting that you can use to anticipate staffing requirements. We will discuss them later in the chapter.

Be sure there are the proper numbers of employees working to meet the level of demand.

There are additional important variables to consider when supervisors are preparing their staffing plans. These include (1) expertise, (2) experience, (3) level of trust, (4) reliability, (5) availability of resources, (6) limitations, and (7) extenuating circumstances.[3]

EXPERTISE

Evaluating the requirements for specially trained personnel involves comprehensive knowledge about the products and/or services being offered. Supervisors also need to have a thorough understanding of each employee's abilities, including their experience, training, licenses, certifications, language skills, and any other indicators of expertise in a particular area.

Additionally, you need to be aware of customer expectations. Are there certain areas where customers expect employees to provide assistance or service? What unique skills are necessary? For example, consider an auto repair shop that offers everything from routine services such as oil changes and tire rotations to complex engine repairs. If a customer has a hybrid-powered vehicle, she may need to schedule an appointment far in advance due to a limited number of mechanics who have been trained to work on these unique vehicles.

Preparing a workload schedule is similar to doing a puzzle. All the pieces need to fit together. With scheduling, employees must be available to serve the full range of customer needs. This will create more balance and ultimately serve the organization and its customers more effectively.

EXPERIENCE

In addition to level of expertise, it is important to consider each person's length and depth of experience, both inside and outside the organization. One good strategy is to achieve a mix of experience on teams and shifts, with at least one experienced person in each group to assist less-experienced coworkers. Although they all may be well-qualified, familiarity with the organization's policies and procedures can be critical to successfully handling a difficult situation.

For example, imagine that you are the nursing supervisor on the pediatric floor at a hospital. You have several nurses who have been working with you for more than ten years, and you have three nurses with less than six months at the hospital. All of the nurses have expertise in pediatric nursing because they have completed specialty training and received additional certifications in this area. However, the three new nurses have far less experience in your hospital. Your goal is to avoid scheduling the three newcomers together. A better approach is to have each one working on a shift with the more experienced nurses.

LEVEL OF TRUST

Supervisors commonly rely on their instincts to determine whom they can trust, especially with newer employees. Trust is a fragile thing that takes time to develop (and an instant to destroy). Your trust in various employees is an important consideration in scheduling. For instance, whom do you trust to handle things properly when you're not around? As a supervisor, it is difficult to control what happens in your absence. So you want to establish a high level of trust in all of your employees. One of the best ways to begin to build this trust is to progressively give team members more responsibility. It is essential that you believe in your employees and their ability to get the work done in your absence.

Important byproducts of building trust in your workplace are *teamwork* and *cohesiveness*. Take this heart-warming situation in Wilmington, Delaware, for example:

> Wendi Pedicone, who works in internal communications, was diagnosed with breast cancer about two years ago. The mother of four credits her employer with leading to the diagnosis: The cancer was detected after her company, AstraZeneca, reminded her to schedule an annual on-site mammography and exam.
>
> "I attribute my being alive to AstraZeneca," she says. She had chemotherapy, radiation, and surgery.
>
> Pedicone says she was able to transition in and out of work by communicating clearly with team members and clients, sending bi weekly updates about treatments to coworkers, and leaning on colleagues for practical assistance such as meals for her family.
>
> Coworkers pitched in, she says, by delivering meals to her home for months.[4]

Work scheduling is much easier when a climate of trust prevails.

RELIABILITY

Similar to trust, you learn about an employee's reliability over time. If you have concerns about a person's ability to arrive on time for work, do not schedule this employee to work during critical times such as store openings. As we discussed in the last chapter, it is important to address the unacceptable behavior immediately and begin the progressive discipline process if necessary. Your stars can become frustrated very quickly if they are repeatedly scheduled to work with an unreliable problem employee.

AVAILABILITY OF RESOURCES

Do schedules need to be adjusted because of limited access to equipment? Typical situations include manufacturing, health care, banking, and telemarketing. As we mentioned earlier, from an organizational perspective, you want to efficiently use all available resources to meet customer demand. Consider the hair salon once again. It would not be cost-effective to simply schedule a hair stylist to cover every station every hour the shop is open. But attempting to schedule additional staff during peak hours could also create problems if there are not enough stations available.

Another workable strategy, particularly in service businesses, is to schedule according to employees' specialized skills. For example, during busy times at the hair salon, the supervisor may schedule a person to focus on shampooing customers' hair, while having other employees focus on cutting and styling hair. This optimizes specialized expertise.

LIMITATIONS

Scheduling also requires supervisors to be aware of various limitations governed by local, state, or federal laws, company policies, and/or union contracts. (Legal issues are discussed in more detail in Chapter 13.)

Overtime and other wage-related topics are common areas for concern and warrant careful evaluation during the scheduling process. If you frequently have some employees working overtime and getting paid time and a half while other employees are working only twenty or thirty hours per week, you need to evaluate your scheduling methods. It may be that the person working overtime has unique skills that are required to meet customer needs. If this is the case, it could pay to cross-train another employee in these areas or hire an additional person.

Paying people overtime can be used as an occasional incentive to fill scheduling gaps or cover for someone at the last minute. When it becomes part of routine scheduling, it can prove too costly. From a personnel perspective, overtime for extended periods of time can lead to employee burnout, a decline in productivity, and high turnover.

Limitations dictated by external sources can impact scheduling. For example, the U.S. Federal Aviation Administration determines the number of hours pilots may fly and the minimum number of crew members that are required based on the number of passengers. The trucking business, emergency services, and other industries where safety is a major concern, have predetermined rules for employee scheduling.

In addition, there may be requirements for licensing or certification to work in specific areas or to operate certain pieces of equipment. Specific laws govern the hiring of workers under the age of eighteen. (These are reviewed in detail in the next chapter.) It is essential that supervisors are aware of these limitations when preparing the schedule. If you are in the hospitality industry, there are mandates about who can serve alcohol, thus limiting who can work in specific roles.

Ultimately, supervisors must learn about their industry, understand labor laws, and be familiar with company policies and procedures regarding overtime, holiday pay, age requirements, and other limitations that may impact scheduling.

EXTENUATING CIRCUMSTANCES

Another common challenge facing supervisors is adapting the schedule to accommodate **extenuating circumstances**. These special situations often involve injury or temporary physical limitations such as pregnancy. How a supervisor adapts the schedule will vary by industry and job requirements. Similar to limitations, there may be legal issues and/or company policies and procedures that need to be referenced prior to accommodating an employee's request due to extenuating circumstances.

Take, for example, a fire fighter with a broken ankle in a cast—she obviously cannot respond to an emergency call. However, she may be able to take on other duties such as answering calls or preparing computer reports. If this same situation involved an office worker, such as an accountant who was unable to drive, the supervisor may choose an alternative scheduling arrangement such as telecommuting.

Regardless of the situation, extenuating circumstances should be evaluated on a case-by-case basis. They need to be reviewed with your manager or human resources professional prior to scheduling to be sure your plan is legally compliant and in accordance with company policies.

extenuating circumstances
special situations that impact scheduling, such as an injury, or temporary physical limitations, such as pregnancy.

Employee Preferences for Scheduling

Most employees are more than happy to tell their supervisor when they want to work. The challenge for supervisors is to create a system where everyone can express their preferences with the understanding that they will be given fair consideration during the scheduling process. It is important for supervisors to help their people appreciate the complex nature of staffing and to realize that their requests may not always be granted.

RECEIVING AND PRIORITIZING REQUESTS

To avoid any perceptions of favoritism or inequity, create a procedure that includes an employee request form for work schedules. Let your employees know when you typically prepare the schedule and give them due dates for requests. In addition, create a method for prioritizing your employees' scheduling requests. They should understand that the needs of the company come first. Your next priority level may be based on their level of seniority or on the order in which the requests were submitted. Involving employees in the creation of the prioritization system is a good idea. This will give them an opportunity to contribute and will reduce their skepticism and/or criticism of the process.

Create a method for prioritizing your employees' scheduling requests.

VACATIONS AND HOLIDAYS

Requests for vacations and holidays pose unique challenges that may require a separate system, particularly in industries that operate twenty-four hours a day, seven days a week, such as hospitals and emergency services.

Begin by asking for volunteers to sign up for holiday coverage. People may observe different religious holidays or they may have plans to celebrate with family at another time. You may want to provide an incentive for working during the major holidays that most people request to take off. Perhaps you pay double time or offer an extra personal day that can be used in the future.

After exhausting the volunteer sign-up, you will probably have to proceed with assigning staff to work on holidays. Keep schedules from year to year to be fair in the long-term rotation. Prepare these schedules well in advance to allow employees time to plan and potentially negotiate trades with coworkers.

Determine how decisions will be made and communicate this in advance. Identify when vacation requests are due to you and let employees know when you will notify them if they have been approved or not. People may need to make advance travel arrangements and reservations. Do your best to respond to requests as quickly as possible. In many organizations, all of the vacation scheduling is completed a year in advance. This allows time for employees to make firm plans. Regardless of the system you choose, it is essential that you explain the process to employees and let them know how requests are being evaluated and ultimately approved. Once again, transparency, participation, and fair treatment breed trust.

PROCEDURE FOR CHANGES

Consider requiring any scheduling changes to be pre-approved by you.

Inevitably, there will be requests for changes to the schedule. You will need to develop a procedure for handling these requests and making modifications to the schedule. At a minimum, you should consider requiring any scheduling changes to be pre-approved by you.

Alternative Scheduling Options

There are many scheduling alternatives being used by businesses, government agencies, and nonprofit organizations. Common **alternative schedule options** are (1) flexible schedule, (2) job sharing, and (3) telecommuting. We take a closer look at each in this section. But first, there are important factors to consider prior to implementing an alternative schedule (see Figure 12.2).

Flexible Schedule

According to a national poll of executives, a flexible schedule was identified as the benefit employees valued the most (see Figure 12.3 for the survey results).[5] Based on these results, it is easy to understand why companies are either offering or considering this option.

The definition of flexible schedules varies widely from one organization to the next. Listed below are a few examples of how flexible schedules have been implemented in the workplace.

- **Modifying the start and finish time to the work day.** For example, at one company everyone normally works from 8:30 A.M. to 5:00 P.M. One employee asked to start work at 7:00 A.M. so he could leave by 3:30 P.M. to pick his children up from school.

  A more flexible interpretation of this practice allows employees to decide from day to day when they want to arrive for work and when they want to leave. This option is readily abused and should be limited to trusted and highly motivated professionals whose job outcomes are easily measured.

- **Modifying the number of hours worked per day.** For example, rather than working eight hours per day, five days per week, an employee works a compressed work week—ten hours a day, four days per week.

FIGURE 12.2 Questions to consider prior to implementing an alternative scheduling option

Source: "Be Willing to Bend: Execs Say Flexible Schedules Most-Valued Staff Benefit," *Westchester County Business Journal*, August 9, 2004, 4.

alternative schedule options flexible schedule, job sharing, and telecommuting.

Questions to Consider Prior to Implementing an Alternative Scheduling Option

1. How will it affect customer service?
Staggering work hours might allow you to accommodate employee schedules while being more available to customers. However, if your business has certain peak periods, you may want all personnel available during those times.

2. How strong is the employee work ethic?
Flexible schedules work best for self-motivated professionals, particularly if they'll be doing their jobs when no one else is around.

3. How dependent on teamwork is the organization?
If impromptu meetings are where the best ideas are born, you'll want to ensure significant overlap in employee schedules.

FIGURE 12.3 Most-valued employee benefits

Source: "Be Willing to Bend; Execs Say Flexible Schedules Most-Valuded Staff Benenfit," *Westchester County Business Journal,* August 9, 2004, 4.

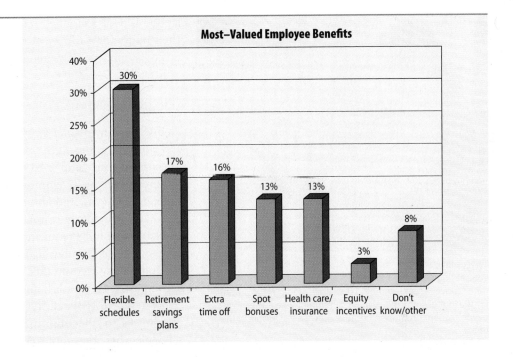

Most–Valued Employee Benefits

- **Modifying the days of the week.** For example, rather than working the typical Monday through Friday, a person may work five different days, including one or both weekend days. This could be five consecutive days, or a mix.

Job Sharing

As the title suggests, job sharing is when two people share the responsibilities of one job. This situation requires both individuals to be knowledgeable and highly effective in their jobs. In addition, outstanding communication among the two people and their supervisor is essential. Frequently, job sharing schedules will be structured so that one person works Monday, Tuesday, and Wednesday and the other person works Wednesday, Thursday, and Friday. The overlap on Wednesday allows for information sharing and updates. Sharon Cercone and Linda Gladziszewski, working mothers who share a human resources job at PNC Financial Group in Pittsburgh, follow that scheduling routine except that they alternate Wednesdays.

> They talk or exchange messages several times a day, and more often on Wednesdays. They check in at night. They keep project notes and a phone log, and even describe the body language of those with whom they meet. "We overcompensate so people understand that we don't let anything fall through the cracks," says Sharon. "We make references to our notes when talking to others." The back-and-forth can add up to three hours to their weekends, but, says Linda, "We know the arrangement could end at any time, so whatever we can do, we do." They even schedule face time; collcagues tease them about planning lunches weeks ahead.[6]

New employees are not good candidates for job sharing because it requires experience, job knowledge, and trust. This scheduling alternative has proven to be

Telecommuters enjoy many benefits, including reduced commuting time and expenses. However, one of the downsides for employees set on climbing the career ladder is the potential for the "out of sight, out of mind syndrome," where they may be overlooked for promotion because they are less visible in the office.

© Directphoto.org/Alamy

a good way of retaining excellent workers who want to reduce their hours for a variety of reasons, such as attending college, raising a family, or care giving.

Telecommuting

As discussed in Chapter 4, when an employee works from home and connects to the office via information technology, it is called **telecommuting**. Similar to job sharing, this scheduling option requires trustworthy employees who have demonstrated their skills, motivation, and ability to produce quality results. This alternative obviously is not appropriate for retail, hospitality, or health care jobs requiring face-to-face customer or patient service. But telecommuting is an excellent option for computer programmers, accountants, and other professionals who can accomplish their jobs at home.

There are still relatively few organizations that allow employees to telecommute full-time. Most offer a hybrid schedule where the employee comes into the office three or four days a week and telecommutes a day or two a week. Employees set on climbing the career ladder generally prefer the visibility of physically being in the office and having face-to-face interaction with the boss. One of the concerns for telecommuters is being overlooked for promotion, as they fall victim to the "out of sight, out of mind syndrome."[7]

As fuel costs rise and overall operating costs for commercial space increase, we may see more companies encouraging telecommuting to reduce their expenses and improve their employees' quality of life.

Implementing Alternative Schedules

If you decide to implement one or more of these options, be sure to refer back to the scheduling variables discussed earlier. Pay particular attention to company policies, procedures, legal issues, and/or regulatory compliance areas.

There are three essential elements to your implementation plan: (1) communication, (2) a pilot program, and (3) outcome measures.

Communication

Once you and your employee(s) have agreed on an alternative schedule, it should be clearly documented. Part of this document will be a communication plan, including a description of how and when they will report to you. It should specify how coworkers will be updated and list relevant contact information.

telecommuting
working from home via information technology.

It is important to coordinate the alternative scheduling arrangement with other employees. Coworkers do not need to know the personal circumstances that led to approval of the request for an alternative schedule. But they *do* need to know that a structured alternative scheduling plan is in place. If you fail to communicate this effectively, the rest of your team may assume incorrectly that the employee is showing up late, leaving early, or not available. If you choose to share this information in a meeting, consider following it up with a brief e-mail or memo. Anticipate other employees making "me too" requests, and decide in advance how you will handle these inquiries.

Pilot Program

Even the best of plans do not always turn out as expected. Sometimes, the unexpected is a pleasant surprise and the situation turns out better than anticipated. However, there can be undesirable consequences as well that may require modifications or termination of the alternative schedule. Therefore, it is best to begin any new alternative schedule with a **pilot program** for a designated period of time to evaluate actual practice. This allows everyone involved to try it and make any necessary modifications before implementing it on a longer-term basis.

Pilot projects typically last three to six months. During this period of time, communication should occur frequently. In addition to the regular business-related information exchanges, the supervisor and employee should schedule weekly discussions to critique the new scheduling arrangement. Coworkers and other people who are directly affected by the change need to be consulted. Incorporate the feedback to improve the situation if necessary.

It is important to agree ahead of time on the measures and indicators that will be used to evaluate the pilot. In addition, determine when and how you will make a decision to allow the scheduling arrangement to continue or be terminated.

Outcome Measures

How will the employee's performance be measured when he/she is working an alternative schedule? Identifying pre- and post-pilot measures is helpful in assessing the impact (positive or negative) of the scheduling change.

Clearly defined expectations and measurable outcomes are essential elements of alternative scheduling.

pilot program
a designated trial period to evaluate a project prior to full implementation.

Job sharing may require the measurement of cohesive teamwork, in addition to accountability for individual results. In the case of telecommuting, quantifiable outcomes need to be measured (e.g., clients contacted, units sold, etc.). This benefits both the employee and the supervisor and helps counter any misperception that the person is "getting nothing done" while working at home. As with all job performance, clearly defined expectations and measurable outcomes are essential elements of productive alternative scheduling.

KNOWLEDGE TO ACTION

1. Which alternative work scheduling option is most appealing to you? Why?

2. What steps would you take to ensure that you meet your work goals and that your manager knows you are achieving your goals successfully?

Contingency Planning and Cross-Training

Contingency planning focuses on preparing for the unexpected. The unexpected can be anything from employee illness to unanticipated growth. Although the circumstances may vary, the problem is the same—you have a scheduling gap to fill. How you anticipate and respond to these scenarios will differ. A good way to begin this process is to ask "what-if" questions as they relate to scheduling. For example:

- What if my only skilled welder gets hurt?
- What if my third-shift supervisor goes into labor early?
- What if my only bilingual employee does not show up?

Asking questions such as these amount to "looking for trouble." Answering them will help you be prepared for whatever happens on the scheduling front.

Planning for Employee Absences

Every supervisor will eventually receive that dreaded call when an employee phones to say he will not be coming to work. (All too often, it happens during busy periods, when you can least afford a disruption.) Their reason may be illness or injury, a sick child, or a flooded basement. Of course, what matters at this point is how prepared you are to adapt the schedule to accommodate the gap created by this person's absence.

Preparing a scheduling contingency plan allows you to respond quickly to the situation. For example, consider a commercial airline's contingency planning for pilots. Imagine if a pilot called in sick and there was no contingency plan for a quick replacement. A cancelled flight would mean lost revenue and unhappy customers. However, having a reserve pilot on stand-by, as a result of contingency planning, could keep operations running smoothly despite the surprise staffing disruption. Many hospitals and emergency medical technician teams have similar contingency plans.

Cross-Training

In many cases, the supervisor is the backup for an absent employee. But this is not always feasible for extremely busy supervisors. Cross-training is a good solution for the occasional absence due to illness, injury, or whatever. **Cross-training** involves teaching another employee the skills and knowledge necessary to cover for a coworker. Although cross-training requires an additional commitment of time and resources, it can be an excellent complement to contingency planning. Constant cross-training is key to Best Buy's "customer centricity" strategy that prepares its retail salespeople to assess and meet the needs of a steadily more diverse customer base:

> Best Buy is encouraging its outlets to go off script. . . . When multiplied by Best Buy's more than 900 stores, the retailer believes such bottom-up insights could have an outsize impact on sales growth. In a sense, the national chain is trying to go hyper-local, asking on-the-ground employees to spot fresh customer groups—North Carolina retiree clubs, newly returned soldiers in Georgia—that would otherwise pass far below the radar at Best Buy's headquarters in Minneapolis.[8]

contingency planning
planning that focuses on preparing for the unexpected.

cross-training
teaching another employee the skills and knowledge necessary to cover for a coworker.

This empowerment, along with cross-training, makes Best Buy's sales staff flexible, versatile, and interchangeable. Consequently, a surprise absence is not a big problem.

Unanticipated Growth

Too much business is a good thing, right? Not when unanticipated growth leaves supervisors with a staffing shortage. Paying employees overtime may help temporarily, but it is not an effective long-term solution. The use of contingent workers or temporaries may be the best solution if there is not enough time to hire full-timers.[9] This approach also is useful during seasonal peaks in business, such as the holidays in retail and early spring for tax accounting firms.

Contingency planning is like insurance—hopefully, you will never need it, but if you do, you will be glad you have it. Just ask the famous Aflac duck!

Outsourcing, Globalization, and Off-shoring

A more controversial approach to staffing is outsourcing (including off-shoring). Potential benefits include cost savings, increased productivity, and creating a global around-the-clock operation.[10] Along with the benefits come new challenges for supervisors. Quality, communication, and privacy issues head the list.[11]

Outsourcing

According to a federal report, **outsourcing** occurs when organizations shift work previously performed by company employees to an outside entity. Business functions such as payroll processing, bookkeeping, technology services, human resources management, and marketing and public relations are just a few of the many areas presently being outsourced. In some instances, companies may outsource certain business functions to their competitors. For example, Yahoo is outsourcing some of its Web search advertising sales to Google.[12] This trend is not limited to private industry. Federal, state, and local governments also are contracting out certain aspects of their agency functions to outside vendors.

Globalization

Figuratively speaking, the globe is shrinking in almost every conceivable way. **Globalization** involves networks of finance, transportation, and communication that tie the people of the world together as never before. Companies have to become global players just to survive, let alone prosper. Although we typically read about computer companies and manufacturing, few industries remain unaffected by this global phenomenon. Hospitality and food services have experienced incredible opportunities for growth. Consider one of the most well-known fast-food companies as an example. McDonald's "is the leading global foodservice retailer with more than 30,000 local restaurants serving nearly 52 million people in more than 100 countries each day," according to its website.[13]

outsourcing
shifting work to outside entities.

globalization
networks of finance, transportation, and communication that closely link the people of the world together.

Thanks to modern telecommunication and information technology, the dream of working from the beach is now a reality. "Let's see—wireless laptop computer, iPod, hammock, bathing suit, sunscreen—okay, I'm all ready for work." How ready are you to be a productive member of today's globalized mobile workforce?

© John Lund/Paula Zacharias/Getty Images/Blend Images

Thanks to modern information technology, entrepreneurial ventures can be global players from the very start. A prime example is Vast.com, based in San Francisco:

> Vast launched a year ago in its present form and now employs 25 people who work across five time zones, four nations, and two continents—all of which makes it a particularly striking example of a growing breed of startup that can best be described as a micro-multinational. According to the United Nations, in 1990 there were about 30,000 multinational companies. Today there are more than 60,000, and while the number of multinational companies continues to grow, their average size is falling. As micro-multinationals proliferate, they're creating an entirely new form of corporate organization—one with powerful advantages for startups and entrepreneurs.[14]

The dream of working from the beach has finally arrived! In fact, Ivko Maksimovic, Vast.com's Serbian chief technology officer, lives in the Dominican Republic because he enjoys reporting in wirelessly from the Caribbean island's unspoiled white sandy beaches.

On the dark side, some worry about giant global corporations eclipsing the economic and political power of individual nations and their citizens. This may be a valid concern if you analyze multinational companies such as ExxonMobil Corporation, whose total revenue was $372.8 billion in 2007.[15] This extraordinary figure exceeds the gross national product of many countries around the world.

Off-Shoring

One aspect of globalization is the controversial practice of off-shoring. "**Off-shoring** refers to the shifting abroad of business activities or processes. Off-shoring can be a subset of outsourcing, if the new supplier of the outsourced activity is located in a foreign country."[16]

Despite a flood of attention in recent years, this practice has been going on for decades. Hundreds of thousands of jobs in textile, steel, and consumer electronics industries are long gone from the United States, and call center jobs are going fast. Thanks to the broadband Internet, skilled jobs in areas such as computer hardware and software engineering, architecture, tax return preparation, and medical diagnosis are being off-shored to well-educated workers in India, China, the Philippines, and Russia. For example, consider Acxiom Corporation of Little Rock, Arkansas:

> The data mining company showed a PowerPoint presentation to potential buyers earlier this year that projected savings of almost $25 million in the next fiscal year from "offshoring" jobs. And if 100% of the cost initiatives are realized, the annual after-tax savings will be $58.8 million in fiscal year 2011—a hefty boost to the bottom line for a company that had a net income of $70.7 million in its last fiscal year.[17]

off-shoring
outsourcing business activities or processes to foreign countries.

Forrester Research projects that 3.4 million U.S. services jobs will move offshore by 2015.[18]

IMPACT ON *YOUR* FUTURE

The fact that American companies may choose to off-shore is not all bad news for U.S. workers. It does not necessarily equate to lost jobs in the U.S.[19] In fact, Stan Lepeak of the Meta Group makes this observation:

> In the bigger picture, one job gain in India does not relate to one job in the United States. . . . The United States might employ fewer programmers here, but it will employ more managers and a variety of new roles will be created to manage these new relationships.[20]

A good education and marketable skills are excellent insurance against being victimized by off-shoring.

So there will be opportunities in the U.S. for higher-paying supervisory and managerial positions. Although this topic remains front-page news and has found its way into political debates, keep in mind that you are in control of your own personal career and how this trend ultimately affects you. The key point here is that a good education and marketable skills are the best insurance against having your job off-shored to a foreign country.

IMPACT ON LESS-DEVELOPED COUNTRIES

Increased off-shoring has had an impact on global labor supply and demand. The consequences for the foreign operations are predictable—labor costs are rising, recruitment is more competitive, and retention is more difficult.

> In India, a popular location for offshored technology jobs, labor costs are increasing at a rate of about 30% a year . . . and the turnover rate there is also around 30% annually.[21]

Also, as currency exchange rates fluctuate, labor-cost advantages for foreign operators will come and go.

Supervisory Implications

Think you will never experience an outsourcing or off-shoring situation first-hand? Outsourcing and off-shoring will remain stark realities for the foreseeable future.

Learn about communication protocols, culture, and customs in the country where your off-shoring activities are taking place.

Regardless of whether the work is contracted out to a company down the road or halfway around the world, supervisors will need to skillfully coordinate their efforts with outsiders. This effort will require excellent communication along with well-defined quality control measures and clear expectations. Coordinating work efforts with contractors located in other parts of the world will require you to learn about communication protocols, culture, and customs in the countries where your off-shoring activities are taking place.

Staffing Foreign Positions

In our global economy, a successful foreign experience is becoming a required stepping-stone to top management.[22] This may vary from a two- or three-week visit overseas several times a year to an assignment that lasts several years. In addition to private industry, many government agencies and contractors require foreign assignments for career advancement and/or higher pay. Unfortunately, Americans reportedly have a higher-than-average failure rate. Failure in this context means foreign-posted employees perform so poorly that they are sent home early or they voluntarily go home early. Estimates vary widely, from a modest 3.2% failure to an alarming 25%.[23] Whatever the failure rate, *any* turnover among employees on foreign assignments is expensive, considering that it costs an average of $1 million to $2 million to send someone on a three- to four-year foreign assignment.[24] Employers should protect this investment by doing a better job of preparing employees for foreign assignments. Toward that end, let us examine what can be done to improve the odds of success.

The Expatriate Experience

Although historically a term for banishment or exile from one's native country, **expatriate** today refers to a person who lives and works in a foreign country. Living outside the comfort zone of one's native culture and surroundings can be immensely challenging–even overwhelming.[25] Expatriates typically experience some degree of **culture shock**, defined as feelings of anxiety, self-doubt, and isolation brought about by a mismatch between one's cultural expectations and reality. Psychologist Elisabeth Marx discovered that most employees experience some form of culture shock during the first seven weeks in their new surroundings.[26] Those who view culture shock as a natural part of living and working in a foreign country are better equipped to deal with it.

In addition, experience has shown that, upon the expatriate's arrival at the foreign assignment, family sponsors or assigned mentors can effectively reduce culture shock.[27] Sponsors and mentors ease the expatriate and his/her family through the first six months by answering basic but important questions and by serving as cultural translators.

Another significant challenge for expatriates is separation from family members. Workers assigned overseas often leave their families, spouses, or partners behind. This can increase stress, particularly when children are involved. The employee frequently feels guilty about leaving the other parent burdened with all of the responsibility for managing the house and caring for the children. This is one of the more common reasons cited by employees who request an early return from their foreign assignment.

THEY SAID IT BEST

I've always thought of travel as a university without walls.
—ANITA RODDICK, Founder of the Body Shop
Source: As quoted in Saren Starbridge, "Anita Roddick: Fair Trade," *Living Planet* 3 (Spring 2001): 92.

expatriate
a person who lives and works in a foreign country.

culture shock
feelings of anxiety, self-doubt, and isolation brought about by a mismatch between one's cultural expectations and reality.

Cross-Cultural Training

As we discussed in Chapter 10, *culture* is the unique system of values, beliefs, and symbols that fosters patterned behavior in a given population. It is difficult to distinguish the individual from his or her cultural context. Consequently, people tend to be very protective of their cultural identity. Careless defiance of cultural norms

TABLE 12.1
Five Basic Cross-cultural Training Techniques

Technique	Explanation
Documentary programs	Trainees read about a foreign country's history, culture, institutions, geography, and economics. Frequently, video presentations, Internet searches, and tutorials are also used.
Culture assimilator	Cultural familiarity is achieved through exposure to a series of simulated intercultural incidents or typical problem situations. This technique has been used to quickly train those who are given short notice of a foreign assignment.
Language instruction	Conversational language skills are taught through a variety of methods. Months, sometimes years, of study are required to master difficult languages. A 2006 survey of 431 human resources specialists provided this window on the future: *. . . knowledge of foreign languages, cultures and global markets will become increasingly important for graduates entering the U.S. workforce. When asked to project the changing importance of several knowledge and skill needs over the next five years, 63% of the survey respondents cited foreign languages as increasing in importance more than any other basic knowledge area or skill.* At the present time, nearly 81% of Americans speak only English.
Sensitivity training	Experiential exercises teach awareness of the impact of one's actions on others.
Field experience	Extensive firsthand exposure to ethnic subcultures in one's own country or visits to foreign countries to heighten awareness.

Sources: List adapted from "Diverse Landscape of the Newest Americans," *USA Today*, December 4, 2006, 8A; Roslie L. Tung, "Selection and Training of Personnel for Overseas Assignments," *Columbia Journal of World Business* 16 (Spring 1981): 68-78; Lyn Glanz, Roger Williams, and Ludwig Hoeksema, "Sensemaking in Expatriation—A Theoretical Basis," *Thunderbird International Business Review* 43 (January–February 2001): 101–119; and "Cross-cultural Training Helps Offshore Issues," *USA Today*, October 5, 2006, 1B.

or traditions by outsiders can result in personal insult and put important business dealings at risk. Fortunately, cultural sensitivity can be learned through cross-cultural training.

Cross-cultural training is defined as any form of guided experience aimed at helping people live and work comfortably in another culture. Five basic cross-cultural training techniques, ranked in order of increasing complexity and cost, are (1) documentary programs, (2) culture assimilator, (3) language instruction, (4) sensitivity training, and (5) field experience (see Table 12.1 for details).

cross-cultural training
any guided experience aimed at helping people live and work comfortably in another culture.

KNOWLEDGE TO
ACTION

Brainstorm with your classmates. Choose a foreign country where something other than English is the primary language to use as a basis for this discussion. You do not need to have in-depth knowledge of the country.

1. If you were asked to work in this country for a period of six months to one year, what would you do to prepare in advance?

2. If you were asked to host an employee from this country at your business located in the United States, what steps would you take in preparing cross-cultural training to help the person acclimate to your culture and customs?

FIGURE 12.4 Cultural adjustment checklist

Cultural Adjustment Checklist

- Are you continuing to make progress in the local language (if applicable)? Can you communicate with local people in everyday situations?
- Are you starting to be able to read the cultural signals of the local people that differ from yours and to understand what they mean in context?
- When you are with local people, are you learning to adapt your behavior to their cultural expectations?
- Do you have more positive than negative feelings about the local people and culture?
- Do you get regular exercise, and have you found other ways to reduce the stress of living overseas?
- Does your home feel like a comfortable oasis amidst the foreign environment?
- Do you maintain regular contact with people back home?
- Do you have a network of people you can turn to in an emergency or if you need support in other ways?
- Have you made friends outside the narrow circle of colleagues from your home country?
- Do you regularly get out and do things in your free time rather than isolating yourself at home?
- Do you feel that you know your way around and can find what you need?
- Do you feel as if you have a reason to get up in the morning? Is your work (whether paid or unpaid) meaningful and satisfying?
- Have you found enjoyable things to do in your free time, especially activities that were not possible back home?
- Do you view your overseas assignment as an opportunity for personal growth, rather than an unpleasant duty?

Source: Excerpt from Melissa Brayer Hess and Patricia Linderman, *The Expert Expatriate: Your Guide to Successful Relocation Abroad* (Boston, MA: Intercultural Press, 2007): 195. Reprinted by permission.

Regardless of your company's resources, the key is to have a systematic approach to cross-cultural training. The cultural adjustment checklist in Figure 12.4 can be shared with employees headed on foreign assignments. It is also useful for many major lifestyle dislocations, such as adjusting to a new college, city, or organization.

SUMMARY

1. Estimating and staffing can be a difficult and complex process in many industries. A supervisor's goal is to anticipate business fluctuations that may impact scheduling. Variables to consider include (1) seasonal impact, (2) market fluctuations, (3) environmental factors, and (4) availability of labor. Evaluating historical data and incorporating new information will improve the accuracy of forecasting. Computer software applications are another tool available to supervisors to assist in estimating, forecasting, and scheduling.

2. A common scheduling goal for supervisors is to balance the needs of the organization with the personal preferences of each employee while ensuring the proper numbers of people with the necessary skills are scheduled. Variables to consider when supervisors are preparing their staffing plans include (1) expertise, (2) experience, (3) level of trust, (4) reliability, (5) availability of resources, (6) limitations, and (7) extenuating circumstances. To avoid any perceptions of favoritism or inequity, create a scheduling system with a format and procedure for all of your employees to submit their scheduling requests. Requests for vacations and holidays pose unique challenges that may require a separate system. Any scheduling changes should be pre-approved by the supervisor.

3. There are many scheduling alternatives in use by small, medium, and large organizations, including government agencies and private firms. A few common options are (1) flexible schedule, (2) job sharing, and (3) telecommuting.

4. Three essential elements to implementing an alternative schedule are (1) communication, (2) pilot programs, and (3) outcome measures.

5. Contingency planning focuses on preparing for the unexpected. The unexpected can be anything from employee illness to unanticipated growth. Begin this process by asking "what-if" questions related to scheduling. Cross-training is a potential solution for the occasional absence due to illness or injury. Unanticipated growth may require more sophisticated planning, including the use of contingent workers or temporary employees. Cross-training involves teaching another employee the skills and knowledge necessary to cover for a coworker.

6. For both private firms and the federal government, outsourcing shifts or redistributes jobs among employers, but does not necessarily reduce the number of jobs in the United States. Off-shoring can be a subset of outsourcing, if the new supplier of the outsourced activity is located in a foreign country. Globalization involves networks of finance, transportation, and communication that have tied the people of the world together as never before. Potential benefits of outsourcing and off-shoring include cost savings, increased productivity, and expanding business operations to function twenty-four hours a day, seven days a week. However, along with these potential benefits, there are new challenges for supervisors, including quality control, communication, and privacy issues.

7. Staffing foreign assignments can be difficult for Americans, who have a higher-than-average failure rate when posted overseas. One of the reported reasons for this failure is the inability to overcome culture shock. Employers can take several steps to help set their expatriate employees up for success in their new host nation. Assigning a family sponsor or mentor has helped expatriates adapt more quickly to their new surroundings. In addition, cross-cultural training—defined as any guided experience aimed at helping people live and work comfortably in another culture—has proven to be very helpful. Five basic cross-cultural training techniques, ranked in order of increasing complexity and cost, are (1) documentary programs, (2) culture assimilator, (3) language instruction, (4) sensitivity training, and (5) field experience.

TERMS TO UNDERSTAND

alternative schedule options, p. 336
contingency planning, p. 340
cross-cultural training, p. 345
cross-training, p. 340
culture shock, p. 344

expatriate, p. 344
extenuating circumstances, p. 334
globalization, p. 341
historical data, p. 329
off-shoring, p. 342

outsourcing, p. 341
pilot program, p. 339
staffing, p. 326
telecommuting, p. 338

QUESTIONS FOR REFLECTION

1. When preparing a schedule, do you think it is more important to accommodate individual employee preferences or prioritize the organization's needs? Explain your answer.

2. What are examples of limitations/restrictions a supervisor should consider when preparing a schedule?

3. If an employee wants to negotiate a change in schedule with a coworker, should the supervisor be involved? Explain.

4. Compare and contrast outsourcing with off-shoring. What do they have in common and what is different?

5. How is globalization impacting supervisors today?

6. Explain what an expatriate is and describe three things you can do to help one of your employees succeed if she/he is assigned to work in another country.

HANDS-ON ACTIVITIES

ALTERNATIVE WORK SCHEDULES

1. List three different types of alternative schedule options.

2. For each option, describe a job that you think would be appropriate for this arrangement.

3. Identify three steps a supervisor should take when implementing an alternative schedule for the first time.

4. Describe how the supervisor will evaluate the performance in each of the alternative scheduling options.

ESTIMATING AND FORECASTING

Select a business, nonprofit organization, or government agency that you are familiar with. Imagine that you have been hired to assist this organization in estimating its staffing needs for next year.

1. List the variables that you will evaluate in preparing your forecast.

2. Explain how this information will be used and why it is relevant.

3. List other tools you would recommend using to estimate and prepare the schedule.

PREPARING FOR AN ASSIGNMENT OVERSEAS

Imagine that you work for a company that has offices around the world.

1. Select a country that you would be interested in transferring to with your employer. You will be assigned to work at this location for one year.

2. Research to identify at least ten things you did not previously know about this country.

3. What are three things that will be difficult for you to adjust to?

4. How can you prepare for this assignment to reduce the culture shock?

Interview an Expert

*T*he purpose of this exercise is to learn from an expert his/her approach to handling staffing situations and preparing contingency plans. Identify a supervisor or manager to interview who is responsible for preparing staffing schedules. If possible, choose someone working in an industry where you have a personal interest or are currently employed. Your goal is to learn from this person's experience and discover tools and techniques that have been effective in scheduling employees. You may use the questions listed below and/or develop your own. Keep in mind that some of these questions may not be applicable for certain industries. After your interview, prepare a brief summary of the conversation and list their strategies, tools, and techniques for staffing and contingency planning.

You may want to consider interviewing two people. Interview one person from a work environment where staffing is required during multiple shifts, such as a hospital that needs coverage 24 hours a day, 7 days a week or perhaps a manufacturing environment that runs two or three shifts per day. In contrast, the other person you interview could be from an office environment, such as an insurance company, accounting firm, or technology business, where staffing needs will be slightly different.

Questions

1. What are the biggest staffing challenges for you?

2. Describe your scheduling system.

3. How do you balance organizational needs with employee preferences?

4. Do you have any formal contingency plans?
   a. If yes, please describe.
   b. If no, how do you handle unanticipated situations, such as a key person calling in sick?

5. How do you prioritize and ultimately approve requests for personal leave?

6. Do you have a different system for scheduling vacations and holidays?

7. Do you offer any alternative scheduling options such as flex-time, job sharing, or telecommuting?
   a. If yes, please describe.
   b. If no, have you tried this in the past?

8. Would you mind sharing your worst scheduling experience and describe how you handled the situation?

9. What do you think are the most important variables to consider when preparing a staffing schedule?

You may also want to ask the person if he/she will share copies of company policies and procedures related to the topics discussed. Try to limit your interview to about 15 minutes. As always, remember to follow-up with a written thank-you note to the person you interviewed.

YOU DECIDE

CASE STUDY 12.1
Preparing a Staff Schedule

Jacoby is the supervisor at Health and Wellness Children's Hospital. Although he has worked at the hospital for many years, this is his first year as the supervisor on the pediatric intensive care unit (PICU). The schedule was completed by the previous supervisor up through June 30. It is now March, and employees are beginning to submit requests to take time off later in the summer; one employee is already requesting the week prior to Thanksgiving. Jacoby is new to scheduling and he did not receive any training or orientation from the previous person. The PICU staffing ratio is one nurse for every two patients; the average patient census is twelve, although the unit has capacity for sixteen. The PICU is open 24 hours a day, 365 days a year.

Questions

1. How would you suggest Jacoby begin this process?
2. What variables should he consider?
3. How should he respond to the requests he is receiving from employees for vacation leave?
4. How should he plan for holiday coverage?
5. Should he prepare any contingency plans?
   a. If yes, how would you recommend he proceed?
   b. If no, why not?

SUPERVISOR'S TOOLKIT

Prepare a manual of policies and procedures related to topics covered in this chapter. Use the list of topics below to get started and add your own ideas that are relevant and appropriate for the type of work that interests you. If you currently work, begin by gathering samples from your employer. Many companies also post this information on the Internet; therefore, an online search is likely to yield good results. You may also include policies and procedures you learned about in the Interview an Expert exercise.

Topics
1. Scheduling
   a. Vacations
   b. Holidays
   c. Overtime
2. Contingency plans
3. Job sharing
4. Telecommuting
5. Flexible schedules
6. Outsourcing

CHAPTER 13

Legal and Ethical Challenges for Today's Supervisors

Learning Objectives

1. List and explain employment and labor laws that should be familiar to all supervisors.

2. List and explain anti-discrimination laws and describe how these impact supervisors today.

3. Differentiate between ethics and the law.

4. Identify and describe four general ethical principles and discuss strategies to encourage ethical behavior in the workplace.

5. Identify five categories of unethical behavior and explain how people rationalize unethical conduct.

6. Discuss the everyday guidelines for ethical behavior.

Straight Talk from the Field

Jan Donald is the media specialist for Franklin High School in Portland, Oregon.

QUESTION: *What steps do you take to ensure your employees are honest and ethical?*

RESPONSE:

*E*very school year I have the opportunity to supervise student workers who serve as library aides. The students' first exposure to my expectations occurs when they read the student handbook (where students go to choose their classes). I include a very brief job description that describes some of the tasks they will be doing as library aides. However, I don't spell out the details for the position until I meet with them. This allows me to explain the job responsibilities to them in person. During this initial orientation, I can share examples and review additional details if necessary. I also ask for their input and questions, which reveals their level of understanding.

There can be a lot of schedule changes in the first week or two of school, so I begin my formal training after students have settled into their routines. Training is mostly hands-on while I am showing them where things are located, but it is also casual enough to get a feel for their interest in the work I need them to do. This also provides me with time to learn more about each of the library aides, to assign them small tasks, and to begin to build a trusting relationship. As you probably know, it takes time to build trust. I see this initial training period as the beginning of this process. I also use this time to reinforce my expectations and values.

I believe that ethical dilemmas occur when values are in conflict. Therefore, I make it a point to be sure that each library aide understands his or her roles and responsibilities. These include handling money and accessing confidential student and faculty information. During their orientation period, I talk with them about discretion, confidentiality, and trust. If they clearly understand the importance of these, they are more likely to behave appropriately, honestly, and ethically while working for me in the library. Unfortunately, there have been times when a library aide has not successfully met my expectations. If an aide proves to be untrustworthy, I ask that student to leave at the semester break.

As part of the new employee training, I tell the library aides what my expectations are. They include:

- to be courteous when helping adults and their peers
- to protect the library user's right to privacy
- to handle money responsibly and to accurately count/report
- to go on deliveries to the correct location without detours and to return promptly
- to maintain confidentiality when delivering tests or statements to a teacher's mailbox

Of course, I cannot constantly observe their behavior. One of the methods I use to assess a library aide's work ethic and performance is to ask teachers and/or counselors for their feedback. Although this process is relatively informal, it provides input from my colleagues, which helps me to determine how well a library aide is performing her or his duties. It is through my own experience and observations, combined with input from others, that I begin to build greater trust and confidence in my library aides. I communicate this to my employees by complimenting them when they have done a good job. If they make a mistake, we talk about how to fix the error and what to do if a similar situation arises in the future.

Another approach I use to help motivate my employees and encourage ethical behavior is to remind them that their work effort in the library is preparation for future employment—whether or not they choose to work in a library—as many of the job skills they are learning are valuable in any position. I offer to write a letter of recommendation and be a referral for them if they do a good job. This is another good reason students would want to be trustworthy, even as an aide. I have done this for many students, and I feel proud that I have given them the opportunity to gain valuable work skills.

In summary, you can never be 100% certain that you have hired honest and ethical workers. My approach in supervising library aides is to clarify my expectations and take time to work with each person individually to reinforce our team values and to build a relationship of trust, which is the foundation for developing honest and ethical employees.

351

Chapter Outline

Highly effective supervisors realize that successful businesses are built with honest and ethical employees. As the first and vital link in the chain of command, the supervisor is often responsible for creating a culture where people treat one another with respect as they strive for excellence. In addition to making sure employment and labor laws are followed, the supervisor must encourage positive behavior and ethical actions. This chapter will provide you with an overview of legal and ethical topics that you are likely to be exposed to at some point during your career. Use this as an opportunity to imagine how you would react if you observe or experience harassment, discrimination, or unethical conduct. Moreover, think of strategies you can use now and in the future to foster a positive and supportive work environment where people are treated fairly.

Employment and Labor Laws

Supervisors need to be familiar with many employment-related laws. The following is not intended to be a comprehensive discussion of these laws, but rather an introduction to key employment and labor laws that are relevant for today's supervisors. This section provides a brief overview of employment and labor laws related to the following: (1) the Occupational Safety and Health Act, (2) fair wages, (3) hiring young workers, (4) new employees, (5) sexual harassment, and (6) intellectual property.

Occupational Safety and Health Act

Occupational Safety and Health Act (OSH Act)
a federal law that assures safe and healthy working conditions.

The **Occupational Safety and Health Act (OSH Act)**, originally passed in 1970 and amended in 2004, is often referred to as OSHA or the OSH Act. The primary purpose of the OSH Act is to assure safe, healthy conditions in the workplace.

The goal of the OSH Act is to reduce employees' work-related injuries and illness.

Congress passed this law for a variety of reasons. Of primary importance to supervisors is the goal to reduce work-related deaths, injuries, and illness. The Act's Section 5, titled *Duties*, requires employers to provide a working environment that is safe and free from recognized hazards that could lead to serious physical harm or death.[1]

Importantly, the OSH Act holds that occupational safety is the responsibility of both the employer and employee. Occupational hazards, threats, and employee exposure vary by industry. The potential risk of injury or illness for a construction worker is far higher than for someone working in a dentist's office. As a result, there are OSH Act guidelines for specific industries, including construction and health care.

Occupational hazards, threats, and exposure include a wide variety of items found in the workplace. For example, a potential occupational hazard is a piece of heavy equipment such as a crane. OSH Act's purpose is to minimize risk by encouraging employers to implement policies and procedures for using all equipment in a safe manner. The goal is to ensure that the operator, as well as people and structures in close proximity, are not at risk. A recent example of threat prevention occurred at the U.S. Postal Service. After discovering that criminals were using the mail to deliver harmful chemicals to human targets, the Postal Service, along with companies handling large volumes of mail, implemented special precautions to keep its workers safe. Employee exposure to toxins is a concern in many industries. High on the list is the health care field. Those working in diagnostic imaging, for instance, may be exposed to unsafe levels of radiation if proper radiology procedures are not strictly followed.

The laws and regulations included in the OSH Act are far reaching, complex, and a challenge to understand and obey. Consequently, the U.S. government created a dedicated agency that is part of the U.S. Department of Labor. The Occupational Safety and Health Administration (OSHA) offers assistance and enforces the OSH Act. In addition, unique programs and resources are available for small businesses to learn about employer responsibilities under this law. Visit the OSHA website at www.osha.gov for comprehensive information about these programs and more, including copies of documents and posters in Spanish and a complete copy of the OSH Act.[2]

Figure 13.1 lists examples of employee rights under the OSH Act. Examples of employer obligations are shown in Figure 13.2, and the most common OSH Act violations are listed in Figure 13.3.

FIGURE 13.1 Employee rights under OSHA
Source: "OSHA and Workplace Safety," Copyright © 2008 FindLaw, http://smallbusiness.findlaw.com/employment-employer/employment-employer-safety/employment-employer-safety-osha-overview.html (accessed May 12, 2008). Reprinted by permission of FindLaw, a Thomson Reuters Business.

Examples of Employee Rights under OSHA

- Review copies of appropriate standards, rules, regulations, and requirements.
- Have access to relevant employee exposure and medical records.
- Request an OSHA inspection.
- Have their name withheld from their employer, if they file a written complaint.
- Not be subject to discriminatory or retaliatory action as a result of their complaint.

FIGURE 13.2 Employer obligations under OSHA

Source: "OSHA and Workplace Safety," Copyright © 2008 FindLaw, http://smallbusiness.findlaw.com/employment-employer/employment-employer-safety/employment-employer-safety-osha-overview.html (accessed May 12, 2008).

Examples of Employer Obligations under OSHA

- Provide work and workplace conditions free from recognized hazards.
- Inform employees of OSHA safety and health standards that apply to their workplace.
- Display in a prominent place the official OSHA poster describing rights and responsibilities under the OSH Act.
- Establish a written, comprehensive hazard communication program that includes provisions for such things as container labeling, material safety data sheets, and an employee training program.
- Inform employees of the existence, location, and availability of their medical and exposure records.

FIGURE 13.3 The ten most common OSHA violations

Source: Scott Clark, "The 10 Most Common OSHA Violations," *Arizona Business Gazette,* July 18, 2002, 4–6.

The Ten Most Common OSHA Violations

1. No written hazard communication program.
2. No information or training on hazardous chemicals.
3. Unprotected electrical conductors entering boxes, cabinets, or fittings.
4. Missing electrical covers and canopies.
5. Tongue guards either missing or not adjusted on abrasive wheel grinders.
6. Hard hats not worn on construction sites.
7. Lack of protection against falls.
8. Lack of portable fire extinguishers.
9. Using unsafe electrical cords.
10. Failure to maintain an OSHA Form 300 Log (work-related injuries and illnesses). Generally, businesses with 11 or more employees in specific industries—including agriculture, construction, manufacturing, transportation, communications, public utilities, wholesale trade, health services, and most retail stores—are required to maintain these logs.

KNOWLEDGE TO ACTION

1. Pick one of the ten most common OSHA violations presented in Figure 13.3 that you think could potentially happen where you volunteer, work, or hope to work someday.

2. What two recommendations would you make to this employer to prevent the OSHA violations you cited in question 1 from happening?

Fair Wages

Fair Labor Standards Act (FLSA)

a federal law that establishes minimum wage, overtime pay, record keeping, and child labor standards.

Another federal law that directly impacts supervisors is the **Fair Labor Standards Act (FLSA)**. In addition to governing child labor standards and record keeping, FLSA establishes the minimum wage for covered nonexempt workers. We will discuss each of these areas in more detail.

These English and Spanish versions of the official OSHA poster describe rights and responsibilities under the Occupational Safety and Health Act. Employers are required to prominently display these posters in the workplace.

© www.osha.gov   © www.osha.gov

MINIMUM WAGE

Many states have their own minimum wage standards that are sometimes higher than the national minimum wage.

The federal government determines the national minimum wage standards. On May 25, 2007, President George W. Bush signed a federal spending bill that increased the minimum wage on a phased-in scale. The first change went into effect on July 24, 2007, increasing the minimum wage to $5.85. See Table 13.1 for the phased-in national minimum wage standards. It is important to note that many states have their own minimum wage standards that are higher than the national minimum wage standards.[3]

Employers who are subject to the FLSA's minimum wage standards are required to post the FLSA's minimum wage poster in a conspicuous place on the work site.

OVERTIME PAY

FLSA also requires employers to pay overtime to eligible nonexempt employees. Recall from our discussion in Chapter 1 that nonexempt employees, according to U.S. labor law, are nonmanagerial employees who are typically paid on an hourly basis. (For more information and examples, visit the U.S. Department of Labor's website at www.dol.gov/elaws/esa/flsa.)

The latest version of this minimum wage poster is available for download free of charge in English, Spanish, or Chinese on the U.S. Department of Labor, Employment Standards Administration, Wage and Hours Division's website at http://www.dol.gov/esa/whd/regs/compliance/posters/minwagep.pdf

© www.wagehour.dol.gov

EMPLOYEE RIGHTS
UNDER THE FAIR LABOR STANDARDS ACT
THE UNITED STATES DEPARTMENT OF LABOR WAGE AND HOUR DIVISION

FEDERAL MINIMUM WAGE

$5.85 PER HOUR   **$6.55** PER HOUR   **$7.25** PER HOUR

BEGINNING JULY 24, 2007   BEGINNING JULY 24, 2008   BEGINNING JULY 24, 2009

OVERTIME PAY At least 1½ times your regular rate of pay for all hours worked over 40 in a workweek.

YOUTH EMPLOYMENT An employee must be at least **16** years old to work in most non-farm jobs and at least **18** to work in non-farm jobs declared hazardous by the Secretary of Labor.

Youths **14** and **15** years old may work outside school hours in various non-manufacturing, non-mining, non-hazardous jobs under the following conditions:

No more than
- **3** hours on a school day or **18** hours in a school week;
- **8** hours on a non-school day or **40** hours in a non-school week.

Also, work may not begin before **7 a.m.** or after **7 p.m.**, except from June 1 through Labor Day, when evening hours are extended to **9 p.m.** Different rules apply in agricultural employment. For more information, visit the YouthRules! Web site at **www.youthrules.dol.gov**.

TIP CREDIT Employers of "tipped employees" must pay a cash wage of at least $2.13 per hour if they claim a tip credit against their minimum wage obligation. If an employee's tips combined with the employer's cash wage of at least $2.13 per hour do not equal the minimum hourly wage, the employer must make up the difference. Certain other conditions must also be met.

ENFORCEMENT The Department of Labor may recover back wages either administratively or through court action, for the employees that have been underpaid in violation of the law. Violations may result in civil or criminal action.

Civil money penalties of up to $11,000 per violation may be assessed against employers who violate the youth employment provisions of the law and up to $1,100 per violation against employers who willfully or repeatedly violate the minimum wage or overtime pay provisions. This law prohibits discriminating against or discharging workers who file a complaint or participate in any proceedings under the Act.

ADDITIONAL INFORMATION
- Certain occupations and establishments are exempt from the minimum wage and/or overtime pay provisions.
- Special provisions apply to workers in American Samoa and the Commonwealth of the Northern Mariana Islands.
- Some state laws provide greater employee protections; employers must comply with both.
- The law requires employers to display this poster where employees can readily see it.
- Employees under 20 years of age may be paid $4.25 per hour during their first 90 consecutive calendar days of employment with an employer.
- Certain full-time students, student learners, apprentices, and workers with disabilities may be paid less than the minimum wage under special certificates issued by the Department of Labor.

For additional information:
1-866-4-USWAGE WHD
(1-866-487-9243)   TTY: 1-877-889-5627   U.S. Wage and Hour Division
WWW.WAGEHOUR.DOL.GOV

U.S. Department of Labor | Employment Standards Administration | Wage and Hour Division

WHD Publication 1088 (Revised June 2007)

The **overtime pay** rate is at least one and one-half times an employee's regular hourly rate. Employees are entitled to overtime pay if they work more than forty hours in a work week. Similar to the minimum wage, some states have additional rules related to overtime pay.[4] See Figure 13.4 for an illustration of how overtime is calculated.

EQUAL PAY ACT

Employee compensation is also subject to the **Equal Pay Act (EPA)** of 1963, a law requiring employers to pay male and female employees equal pay for comparable work. The few exceptions are noted later in this section.

HIRING YOUNG WORKERS

Like wage laws, child labor laws vary by industry and state. Therefore, it is important to research the local laws in your area that are relevant for your business. Regardless of the local laws, all employers are required to maintain records for employees under the age of 19. These records should include employees' birth dates, daily and weekly work hours (including the actual start times), and job descriptions or occupations.[5] A good source document is the U.S. Department of Labor's website *Youth Rules!* The site has special sections for teens, parents, educators, and employers (http://www.youthrules.dol.gov).

The FLSA also includes basic provisions for **child labor standards** that limit the type of work and the hours employees can work based on their age. These include restrictions for youth under age 16 regarding the hours they can work and the type of work they can perform. The provisions also include 17 occupations that are considered too hazardous for any worker under the age of 18. In addition, the FLSA includes specific child labor laws for agricultural businesses, including waivers for workers as young as 10 years old.

overtime pay
the rate paid to employees who exceed forty hours in a workweek; it is at least one and one-half times an employee' regular hourly rate.

Equal Pay Act (EPA)
a federal law that requires employers to pay male and female employees equal pay for comparable work.

child labor standards
limits on the type of work and the hours employees can work based on their age.

TABLE 13.1
National Minimum Wage Standards for Covered Nonexempt Workers

Minimum Pay Rate Per Hour	Effective Date
$6.55 per hour	July 24, 2008
$7.25 per hour	July 24, 2009

Source: "Compliance Assistance: Fair Labor Standards Act," U.S. Department of Labor, Employment Standards Administration, Wage and Hours Division website http://www.dol.gov/esa/whd/flsa/index.htm (viewed May 12, 2008).

FIGURE 13.4 Calculating overtime pay

Calculating Overtime Pay

Employee's Hourly Pay Rate: **$8.00**
Number of Hours Worked This Week: **50**

Regular hours	40 × $8.00	$240.00
Overtime (1.5 × regular pay of 8 = 12)	10 × $12.00	$120.00
Total pay for this week:		$360.00

For most organizations, the list in Figure 13.5 will be relevant. This list provides a sampling of a few of the rules and regulations included in the FLSA to raise your awareness about child labor laws. If you are considering hiring employees under the age of 20, you are strongly encouraged to visit the U.S. Department of Labor's website (http://www.dol.gov) to learn more about specific laws that are applicable to your occupation/industry and state.

EXCEPTIONS TO FLSA STANDARDS

There are certain industries and job classifications that are exempt from the minimum wage and/or overtime pay requirements. For example, salespeople might be paid on

FIGURE 13.5 Basic provisions and requirements of FLSA related to child labor

Source: Adapted from "Youth in the Workplace," U.S. Department of Labor, Office of Compliance Assistance website, http://www.dol.gov/compliance/audience/youth.htm (accessed May 12, 2008).

Basic Provisions/Requirements of FLSA Related to Child Labor

Sixteen is the minimum age for most non-farm work.

Youths age 14 and 15 may work outside of school hours in certain occupations under certain conditions.

Youths of any age may deliver newspapers; perform in radio, television, movies or theatrical productions; work for their parents in solely owned non-farm businesses (except in mining, manufacturing, or in any other occupation declared hazardous); or gather evergreens and make evergreen wreaths.

Permissible jobs and hours of work, by age, in non-farm work are as follows:

- Age 18 or older are not subject to restrictions on jobs or hours.

- Age 16 and 17 may perform any job not declared hazardous, and are not subject to restrictions on hours.

- Age 14 and 15 may work outside school hours in various non-manufacturing, non-mining, non-hazardous jobs under the following conditions:

  - No more than 3 hours on a school day, 18 hours in a school week

  - No more than 8 hours on a non-school day, or 40 hours in a non-school week

  - They may not begin work before 7:00 A.M. or work after 7:00 P.M., except from June 1 through Labor Day, when evening hours are extended until 9:00 P.M.

  - Those enrolled in an approved Work Experience and Career Exploration Program (WECEP) may work up to 23 hours in school weeks and 3 hours on school days (including during school hours.)

Certain industries and job classifications are exempt from the minimum wage and/or overtime pay requirements.

a commission basis, and taxi drivers or truckers might be paid based on the number and length of trips. A special minimum wage standard applies to employees who receive tips. If an employee typically receives more than $30 per month in income from tips, then the employer must pay at least $2.13 per hour in direct wages. In addition, employers must be sure that their employees are earning the hourly minimum wage. Therefore, they are obligated to make up the difference if an employee's income from tips combined with their income from direct wages does not equal the minimum hourly wage.[6]

Exceptions to the equal pay act include:

1. **A seniority system**. For example, two cashiers at a grocery store work the same schedule—same shift and the same days of the week. However, the more senior cashier has been employed at the store for five years, so she earns $7.75 an hour. Her coworker, who has worked at the store for only two years, earns $6.50, based on the seniority system.

2. **Merit system**. Pay raises in a merit system are linked to each individual employee's performance. The better results an employee gets, the more that worker earns. Therefore, you may have two employees who were hired at the same time performing essentially the same work, but one earns more per hour because of superior results.

3. **Earnings based on quantity/quality of production**. For example, a real estate agent may be paid a commission based on an agreed-upon percentage of the sale price of the home he is selling, rather than being paid by the hour.

4. **Differential based on any factor other than gender**. For example, a moving company pays its employees a weekend differential. Therefore, all employees who work on Saturday and Sunday earn fifty cents more per hour, regardless of their gender.[7]

WHAT FLSA DOES *NOT* INCLUDE

We have focused primarily on what is included in the FLSA. However, a variety of employment practices are not included in this law. For example, the FLSA does not require:

- Vacation, holiday, severance, or sick pay
- Meal or rest periods, holidays off, or vacations
- Premium pay for weekend or holiday work
- Pay raises or fringe benefits
- A discharge notice, reason for discharge, or immediate payment of final wages to terminated employees.[8]

COMPLYING WITH FLSA

The FLSA and Equal Pay Act rules can be complex and the penalties significant, with first-time violators potentially fined up to $10,000 and second-time offenders facing potential prison time. Therefore, it is very important to understand the laws and regulations that are relevant to your specific business and the various job

First-time violators of FLSA and the EPA can potentially be fined up to $10,000; second-time offenders face potential prison time.

classifications. Visit the U.S. Department of Labor's Employment Standards Administration Wage and Hours Division at http://www.dol.gov/esa for detailed information. In addition, you may want to print the *Handy Reference Guide to the Fair Labor Standards Act* at http://www.dol.gov/esa/regs/compliance/whd/hrg.htm.

New Employees

When hiring new employees, most supervisors usually think about orientation, training, and scheduling. However, there are some important legal matters to attend to right away. Employers have documentation and reporting responsibilities. Employee orientations and employee manuals must include references to essential policies and procedures, particularly those involving the legal issues mentioned in this chapter.

EMPLOYER REPORTING REQUIREMENTS

The U.S. Department of Health and Human Services Administration for Children and Family requires employers to file a **new hire report**. According to federal law, employers must file six data elements on all new employees within 20 days of their start date (electronic filing has slightly different submission rules). See Table 13.2 for a detailed description of the information required nationally. The federal government uses this information to cross-reference various state and national databases to locate parents who have not paid child support.[9]

TABLE 13.2
New Hire Report

New Hire Report Data Element	Definition
Employer Name	Name associated with the Federal Employer Identification Number (FEIN)
Employer Address	Address associated with the FEIN entity that employs the individual
Federal Employer Identification Number (FEIN)	Nine-digit number assigned to the employer by the Internal Revenue Service
Employee Name	Full name associated with that employee's Social Security number
Employee Address	Current residential address of the new employee
Employee SSN	Nine-digit Social Security number assigned to the employee by the U.S. Social Security Administration

Source: "New Hire Reporting," The U.S. Department of Health and Human Services Administration for Children and Family website, http://www.acf.hhs.gov/programs/cse/newhire/employer/private/newhire.htm (accessed May 12, 2008).

new hire report
a report required by federal law to assist in enforcing child support obligations.

Many states have additional reporting requirements as well. To look up specific requirements for your state, visit the State New Hire Reporting website at http://www.acf.hhs.gov/programs/cse/newhire/employer/contacts/nh_matrix.htm.

DOCUMENTATION REQUIREMENTS

Every employer, regardless of number of employees or geographic locations, must comply with federal income tax withholding and employee eligibility verification. Listed below are the forms that each new employee should complete:

- Form W-4: Federal Income Tax Withholding

  Form W-4 must be completed by the employee on or before his/her first day of work. The employer is obligated to submit the form to the IRS and to process the employee's payroll following the withholding instructions indicated on this form.

- Form I-9: Employment Eligibility Verification Form.

Federal law requires employers to verify an employee's eligibility to work in the United States. Within three days of hire, employers must complete an I-9 form and, by examining acceptable forms of documentation supplied by the employee, confirm the employee's citizenship or eligibility to work in the United States. Employers can only request documentation specified on the I-9 form. Employers who ask for other types of documentation not listed on the I-9 form may be subject to discrimination lawsuits.

Employers do not file the I-9 with the federal government. Rather, an employer is required to keep an I-9 form on file for three years after the date of hire or one year after the date the employee's employment is terminated, whichever is later. The U.S. Immigration and Customs Enforcement (ICE) agency conducts routine workplace audits to ensure that employers are properly completing and retaining I-9 forms, and that employee information on I-9 forms matches government records.[10]

Organizations failing to comply with these requirements are subject to sanctions, including financial penalties/fines.

Sexual Harassment

A great deal of misunderstanding surrounds the topic of sexual harassment because of vague definitions and inconsistent court findings. Nonetheless, it remains a serious problem in the workplace. According to data published by the U.S. Equal Employment Opportunity Commission (EEOC), there were 12,510 charges of sexual harassment filed in 2007, up from 12,025 in 2006. Of these, 16% were filed by males. As you can see in Figure 13.6, the percentage of claims filed by men increased by 5% over the ten-year period. Still, the majority of claims are filed by women.[11]

The term **sexual harassment** refers to unwanted sexual advances or references that create an offensive, hostile, or intimidating work environment. Sexual harassment has both behavioral and legal dimensions. Important among these are the following:

- Although typically it is female employees who are victims of sexual harassment, the victim and the harasser may be a woman or a man and the victim does not have to be of the opposite gender. Both women and men (in the United States) are protected under Title VII of the Civil Rights Act of 1964 (plus various amendments to the Act).

sexual harassment
unwanted sexual advances or references that create a hostile work environment.

FIGURE 13.6 Sexual harassment claims by gender

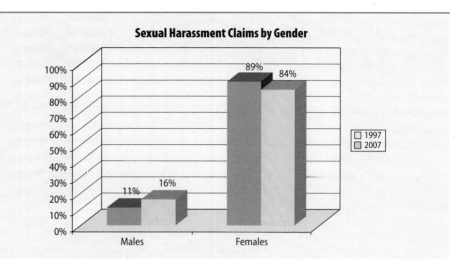

- The harasser's conduct must be unwelcome.

- Sexual harassment includes, but is not limited to, unwanted physical contact. Gestures, displays, joking, and language also may create a sexually offensive or intimidating work environment. This is often referred to as *hostile working conditions.*

- It is the supervisor's job to be aware of and correct cases of sexual harassment. *Ignorance of such activity is not a valid legal defense.*

- The EEOC encourages employers to take a proactive approach, including sexual harassment training that reinforces the company's position that sexual harassment will not be tolerated.[12]

Regardless of whether the alleged harasser is a high-profile professional sports coach or a chef at the local diner, if an employee feels he/she is being harassed, he/she should take action. Begin by letting the harasser know that the behavior is unwelcome and request that the behavior stop immediately.[13] Surprisingly, many harassers fail to recognize that their conduct is offensive; simply letting them know may be enough to put an end to the unwelcome behavior. If this approach is not successful, the employee should report the incident to his/her supervisor and/or human resources office and file a formal complaint. Having witnesses can greatly strengthen a claim of sexual harassment.

Intellectual Property

When you or one of your employees is creating new products that may be classified as **intellectual property** (IP), it is important to clarify who has rights to the IP. But, first let's take a look at what is included in the discussion of intellectual property. Essentially, original items that people create using their imagination and brain power may be considered IP. Examples include:

intellectual property
original or unique items that people create using their imagination and brain power.

- Literary works, such as poems, novels, and lyrics to a song.

- Inventions of any kind, such as a new skateboard or hair dryer.

Consider the following scenario when answering the questions below.
One of your coworkers forwards a joke to you via e-mail. Although it is intended to be funny, the punch line of the joke is sexually explicit. You notice that several of your coworkers (male and female) are included in the e-mail distribution.

1. Imagine for a moment that your first reaction to the e-mail is laughter...you find it harmless and funny. What, if any, would be your response?

2. Now, imagine for a moment that you find the joke personally offensive or you think some of your coworkers may find it offensive. Does this change your response? Explain.

- Works of art, such as a sculpture or painting.
- Symbols and images, such as a team or corporate logo like the Nike swoosh.
- Designs used in commerce, such as original architectural drawings for a new office building.[14]

Among the various types of IP, supervisors need to be aware of these two categories. The industrial property category of IP focuses primarily on patents and trademarks for inventions. A broader category of IP falls under copyright protection for literary works such as books, plays, music, art, and architectural design.[15] How the work is protected from other people using the IP without permission or authorization of the original creator varies.

When there are multiple elements involved, copyright may extend to several parties. Take a song, for example. If David Grohl is working independently (that is, he is not employed by a company) and he writes a song, he can copyright the music and lyrics so that no one can perform or record his song without his permission. In addition, Grohl may demand royalty payments from the musician(s) making the request. If his band, the Foo Fighters, records the song, then everyone participating in the recording can copyright that performance of the song. In addition, if the song is performed live in concert by either the same band members or by touring members, they can copyright the performance, which will prevent the showing of the performance without their authorization.

So who owns that patent or copyright: the employee or the employer? According to intellectual property attorney David Radack, the company automatically owns the rights to any work created by its employee during company time using company resources. Let's use the David Grohl example again. But this time, imagine that he is an employee working for a marketing agency and his job is to write songs for the company to use as promotional pieces

Examples of intellectual property include screenplays, songs, original art, and corporate logos such as the world-famous Google logo pictured here.
© AP Images/Paul Sakuma, file

The company automatically owns the rights to any work created by its employee during company time using company resources.

for their clients. In this case, the company retains ownership of the copyright to these songs, unless a legal agreement has been signed with different arrangements.

The rules and the courts' interpretation of IP rights change when the company pays an independent contractor rather than an employee. If you are working in an industry where this topic is relevant, learn the specific laws and court rulings relative to your type of IP. Additionally, it is a good idea to clearly document intellectual property policies and procedures and have employees sign IP agreements clarifying ownership prior to beginning any work.[16]

Preventing Job Discrimination

Unlawful discrimination is a continuing problem in the workplace. Just look at the front page of a newspaper or check a credible online news source and you are likely to read about a lawsuit or judgment against an employer because of employment discrimination. According to Gilbert Casellas, former chairman of the U.S. Equal Employment Opportunity Commission (EEOC), racial discrimination remains the number one reason for complaints, which has been the case for decades.[17] Meanwhile, other groups of employees with legal protection continue to complain and, in many cases, file suit against employers for discriminatory practices. Discrimination complaints by pregnant women, for instance, rose 14% between 2006 and 2007.[18] Hundreds of cases have either gone to court or ended in out-of-court settlements that involved significant financial compensation.

Federal Anti-Discrimination Laws

Several federal laws are in place to prevent employment discrimination based on a variety of personal attributes and characteristics. The EEOC is responsible for enforcing many of these laws, including:

- **Title VII of the Civil Rights Act of 1964 (Title VII)** prohibits employment discrimination based on race, color, religion, sex, or national origin. This protection later was extended to Vietnam War-era veterans.
- **The Equal Pay Act of 1963 (EPA)** prohibits gender-based wage discrimination for those working in the same establishment under similar working conditions.
- **The Age Discrimination in Employment Act of 1967 (ADEA)** prohibits employment discrimination against persons 40 years of age or older.
- **Title I and Title V of the Americans with Disabilities Act of 1990 (ADA)** prohibit discrimination against qualified individuals with (mental and physical) disabilities. This applies to employers with 15 or more employees.[19]
- **The Family Medical Leave Act of 1993 (FMLA)** requires covered employers to grant eligible employees up to 12 weeks of unpaid leave. According to the U.S. Department of Labor:

Title VII of the Civil Rights Act of 1964 (Title VII)
a federal law prohibiting employment discrimination based on race, color, religion, sex, or national origin.

Age Discrimination in Employment Act of 1967 (ADEA)
a federal law prohibiting employment discrimination against persons 40 years of age or older.

Title I and Title V of the Americans with Disabilities Act of 1990 (ADA)
federal laws prohibiting discrimination against qualified individuals with disabilities.

Family Medical Leave Act of 1993 (FMLA)
a federal law requiring covered employers to grant eligible employees up to 12 weeks of unpaid leave.

Covered employers must grant an eligible employee up to a total of 12 work weeks of unpaid leave during any 12-month period for one or more of the following reasons:

- for the birth and care of the newborn child of the employee;
- for placement with the employee of a son or daughter for adoption or foster care;
- to care for an immediate family member (spouse, child, or parent) with a serious health condition; or
- to take medical leave when the employee is unable to work because of a serious health condition.[20]

It is important to familiarize yourself with relevant local and state laws. Several jurisdictions have expanded the laws mentioned above to prohibit discrimination and harassment based on sexual orientation, status as a parent, marital status, and political affiliation.[21]

The Supervisor's Role in Preventing Discrimination

Supervisors are often the first line of defense in preventing workplace discrimination, beginning with the recruitment and hiring process and continuing throughout an employee's tenure. See Figure 13.7 for the EEOC's list of discriminatory practices prohibited and illegal under Title VII, the ADA, and the ADEA.

Steps a Supervisor Can Take

Make sure your job applications and your interview questions are not discriminatory.

Supervisors cannot control the actions of every person in the organization. But they certainly can take steps to encourage appropriate behavior and reduce employment discrimination practices. The hiring process is one area where employers are frequently exposed to potential discriminatory conduct. This often occurs, not out of malicious intent, but rather because of a lack of

FIGURE 13.7 Discriminatory practices prohibited by law
Source: "Federal Laws Prohibiting Job Discrimination Questions and Answers," The U.S. Equal Employment Opportunity Commission (EEOC) website, www.eeoc.gov/facts/qanda.html (accessed May 12, 2008).

Discriminatory Practices Prohibited by Law

It is illegal to discriminate in any aspect of employment, including:

- Hiring and firing
- Compensation, assignment, or classification of employees
- Transfer, promotion, layoff, or recall
- Job advertisements
- Recruitment
- Testing
- Use of company facilities
- Training and apprenticeship programs
- Fringe benefits
- Pay, retirement plans, and disability leave
- Other terms and conditions of employment

education and training. Part of a supervisor's role is to recruit and screen new employees. Make sure your job applications and your interview questions are not discriminatory, and communicate the importance of this to everyone involved in the interview process. Here are some valuable tips for staying out of trouble during the hiring process:

1. Interview questions and the application form should be focused on job-related skills and work experience.

2. In your advertisements and on your application forms, include a non-discrimination policy statement.

3. Treat each candidate the same. During interviews, ask the same questions and be consistent with your demeanor and nonverbal behavior.

4. Topics to avoid include:

   - Age (this includes indirect lines of questioning that may reveal age, such as, "What year did you graduate from high school?")
   - Marital status
   - Parenting status
   - National origin
   - Religion
   - Affiliations such as political party or organizations
   - Military service (for example, you may not ask the nature of a person's discharge)
   - Arrest record (arrests often do not lead to convictions)
   - Medical history or anything disability-related
   - Race (particularly with online applications and phone interviews where you may never see the person visually—you may not ask for a photo or personal description)[22]

Ethics and the Law Are Not Necessarily the Same Thing

Too many people believe that if something is legal then it must be ethical. For example, consider the story of Javier, the supervisor of a car dealership's maintenance department. Pat, his transmission specialist, is taking three months of unpaid leave (which he is entitled to under FMLA) to have knee replacement surgery. Javier calls Carrie, the supervisor at another dealership, for a referral to a local transmission company he can outsource to while Pat is out on leave. Carrie recommends Master Transmission Specialists. What Carrie fails to reveal is that she and her husband own Master Transmission Specialists. Carrie's referral to her own company is not illegal. However, her failure to disclose her ownership is unethical because she will personally gain from this referral. This is a case of "conflict of interest."

During decision making, evaluate both legal and ethical ramifications.

Ethics is the study of moral obligation involving the distinction between right and wrong.[23] Laws, on the other hand, are typically written or modified and approved by elected government officials. These laws can have unintended consequences. In addition, there are situations where individuals and/or companies

ethics
the study of moral obligation involving the distinction between right and wrong.

are complying with the law but society believes they are acting unethically. As a result, you may encounter situations where ethics and the law are inconsistent. For example, food manufacturers are now required to follow strict rules about what words they can place on packaging because of widespread accusations of misleading advertising and false claims. The government responded by enacting legislation to discourage manufacturers from using misleading tactics. The key learning point here is to consider both legal and ethical ramifications when making decisions.[24]

General Ethical Principles

Your ethical beliefs have been shaped by many factors, including family and friends, the media, culture, schooling, religious instruction, and general life experiences.[25] We use ethical principles both consciously and unconsciously when we deal with ethical dilemmas.[26] Consider the importance of these general ethical principles when facing day-to-day ethical dilemmas.

Never take any action that is not:

- balanced—consider your self-interests with your organization's interests.
- open, honest, and truthful and that you would not be proud to see reported widely in national newspapers and on television.
- kind and that does not build a sense of community, a sense of all of us working together for a commonly accepted goal.
- in compliance with the law, for the law represents the minimal moral standards of our society.[27]

The best way to test your ethical standards and principles is to consider a *specific* ethical question and see which of these principles is most likely to guide your *behavior*. Sometimes, especially in complex situations, a combination of principles will be applicable. See the "You Decide" scenarios at the end of the chapter to practice your ethical reasoning.

KNOWLEDGE TO ACTION

1. Which of the preceding general ethical principles appeals most to you in terms of serving as a guide for making important decisions? Why?

   _____

2. As a supervisor, how can you help your employees to adopt one or more of these principles?

   _____

Encouraging Ethical Conduct

Simply telling managers, supervisors, subordinates, and other employees to be good will not work. Both research evidence and practical experience tell us that words must be supported by action. Four specific ways to encourage ethical conduct within the organization are (1) ethics training, (2) ethical advocates, (3) ethics codes, and

(4) whistle blowing. Each can make an important contribution to an integrated ethics program.

ETHICS TRAINING

According to a survey of 1,001 employees in the United States, only 28% had received any ethics training during the prior year.[28] Clearly, there is an opportunity to improve in this area. Critics of ethics training argue that these education programs are a waste of time because ethical lessons are easily shoved aside in the heat of competition.[29] Ethics training is often halfhearted and intended only as window dressing. When the company culture ignores, promotes, or even rewards improper conduct, no amount of employee training will prevent unethical behavior and ultimately the company's demise.[30] Therefore, it is essential that the guidelines listed below are followed to create a corporate culture that supports the ethics training effort and fosters an ethical organization. Carefully designed and administered, ethics training programs can make a positive contribution. Key features of effective ethics training include:

- Top-management support
- Open discussion of realistic ethics cases or scenarios
- A clear focus on ethical issues specific to the organization
- Integration of ethics themes into all training
- A mechanism for anonymously reporting ethical violations (e.g., an ethics hotline)
- An organizational climate that rewards ethical conduct.[31]

ETHICAL ADVOCATES

An **ethical advocate** is a business ethics specialist who sits as a full-fledged member of the board of directors and acts as the board's social conscience.[32] In some organizations, the job title for this position is the Chief Ethics Officer and/or the Compliance Officer.[33] This person may be asked to sit in on decision deliberations of top management. The idea is to assign someone the specific role of critical questioner to avoid unquestioning conformity. The ethical advocate's role is to test management's thinking about ethical implications during the decision-making process.

CODES OF ETHICS

An organizational **code of ethics** is a published statement of moral expectations for employee conduct and behavior. Some codes specify penalties for offenders. Recent experience has shown ethics training and codes of ethics to be a step in the right direction, but not a cure-all.[34] To encourage ethical conduct, formal codes of ethics for an organization's employees must satisfy two requirements:

1. They should refer to specific practices such as kickbacks, payoffs, receiving gifts, falsifying records, and making misleading product claims. For example, the 2007 recipient of the American Business Ethics Award, Freescale Semiconductor's 12-page Code of Business Conduct and Ethics, includes this statement: "Deliberately

ethical advocate
an ethics specialist who plays a role in top-management decision making.

code of ethics
a published statement of moral expectations for employee conduct and behavior.

misleading messages, omissions of important facts or false claims about our competitors' offerings are never acceptable. We only obtain business legally and ethically. Bribes or kickbacks are not acceptable."[35] General statements about good business practice or professional conduct are ineffective—they do not provide specific guidance and they offer too many tempting loopholes. In comparison, Freescale's code is comprehensive, with specific guidelines for employees, board members, and business partners.

2. An organizational code should be firmly supported by top management and equitably enforced through the reward-and-punishment system. Selective or uneven enforcement is the quickest way to diminish the effectiveness of an ethics code. The effective development of ethics codes and monitoring compliance are more important than ever in today's complex global economy. See Figure 13.8 for a checklist you can use in developing and implementing a code of ethics in your organization.

WHISTLE BLOWING

Detailed ethics codes help supervisors deal swiftly and effectively with employee misconduct. But what should supervisors do when their manager or an entire organization is engaged in misconduct? Yielding to the realities of organizational politics, many supervisors simply turn their backs or claim they were "just following orders." Some supervisors may attempt to work within the system for positive change.[36] Still others will take the boldest step of all, whistle blowing.

FIGURE 13.8 Code of ethics checklist

Source: Checklist adapted from "Code of Ethics," *Charter Management Institute: Checklists: Human Resources, Training and Development* (June 2006); and Adam Santavicca, "Ethics Anyone? Establish a Code of Ethics to Help You and Your Employees Make Great, Fair Judgment Calls," *Smart Business Matters* 2 (Fall 2006): 2.

Code of Ethics Checklist

- Secure the commitment of top management.
- Gain agreement on the primary purpose of the code. Is the code mainly for the benefit of employees, shareholders, or even customers?
- Define statements of values.
- Consider what specific issues need to be covered for your organization.
- Prepare a draft code including:
  - An introduction
  - The organization's mission, objectives, and values
  - Guidance for all stakeholder groups: employees, shareholders, customers, suppliers, and the community
  - Expectations about acceptable behavior
  - Operating principles, with realistic examples
  - A formal mechanism for resolving employee questions.
- Circulate the draft.
- Ensure that the code is clear and understandable.
- Devise an implementation strategy.
- Circulate the final code.
- Establish a procedure for complaints, concerns, and questions.
- Establish a mechanism to review the code.

Recall from Chapter 11 that *whistle blowing* occurs when an employee reports corporate fraud or other behavior that is illegal, immoral, or both. A whistle blower reports perceived unethical practices to outsiders such as the news media, government agencies, or public-interest groups. *Time* magazine named three ordinary women, now famous because of their ethical actions and courage, as their Persons of the Year. These whistle blowers are Sherron Watkins, who foresaw Enron's financial collapse; Cynthia Cooper, who exposed WorldCom's fraudulent accounting practices; and Coleen Rowley, an FBI agent who went public with allegations of a mishandled terrorist lead.[37]

Not surprisingly, whistle blowing is a highly controversial topic among supervisors and managers, many of whom believe it erodes their authority and decision-making prerogatives. Because loyalty to the organization is still a cherished value in some quarters, whistle blowing is criticized as the epitome of disloyalty. Consumer advocate Ralph Nader disagrees: "The willingness and ability of insiders to blow the whistle is the last line of defense ordinary citizens have against the denial of their rights and the destruction of their interests by secretive and powerful institutions."[38] Still, critics worry that whistle blowers may be motivated by revenge.

Whistle blowing generally means putting one's job and/or career on the line, even though many states and the federal government have passed whistle blower protection acts, such as the Sarbanes-Oxley Act.[39] The challenge for today's management is to create an organizational climate in which the need to blow the whistle is reduced. In the final analysis, it is the behavior of individuals that makes an organization ethical or unethical. Organizational forces can help bring about the best in people by clearly identifying and rewarding ethical conduct.

THEY
SAID IT
BEST

Our lives begin to end the day we become silent about things that matter.

—DR. MARTIN LUTHER KING JR.

Source: Richard Lacayo and Amanda Ripley, "Persons of the Year," *Time*, December 22, 2002, http://www.time.com/time/magazine/article/0,9171,401944,00.html (accessed March 7, 2007).

Ethical Behavior Is Up to You

According to a National Business Ethics Survey, "fifty-two percent of employees witnessed at least one example of misconduct within a year." In addition, only "fifty-eight percent of employees surveyed believed their organization had a strong ethical culture, and an astounding forty-two percent believed their organization's ethical culture to be weak."[40] It is evident that supervisors are challenged with raising awareness about unethical actions and fostering a more ethical work environment. This section cites examples of unethical acts and offers guidelines for ethical behavior in the workplace.

Unethical Behavior and Actions

Regardless of a person's religious beliefs, political affiliation, social customs, or legal thinking, certain actions and behaviors are always considered to be unethical in the United States (and in most developed countries around the world). These include:

- *Sexism*—Treating people unequally (and harmfully) by virtue of their gender.
- *Racism*—Treating people unequally (and harmfully) by virtue of their race or ethnicity.
- *Fraud*—Intentional deception that causes someone to give up property or some right.
- *Deceit*—Representing something as true which one knows to be false in order to gain a selfish end harmful to another.
- *Intimidation*—Forcing a person to act against his/her interest or deter from acting in his/her interest by threats or violence.[41]

Rationalizing Unethical Behavior

People are faced with lots of difficult decisions and potentially unethical situations in their personal lives and on the job. In many cases, they will make an unethical decision based on what they believe to be a perfectly logical rationalization. See Figure 13.9 for twelve of the most common rationalizations that can result in unethical decision making.

"Honesty is the best policy, Fernbaugh, but it's not company policy."

© The New Yorker Collection, 1995, Leo Cullum, from cartoonbank.com

FIGURE 13.9 Twelve rationalizations that can result in unethical decision making

Source: Adapted from "Obstacles to Ethical Decision Making: Rationalizations," The Josephson Institute of Ethics, http://josephsoninstitute.org (accessed March 24, 2008).

Rationalizations That Can Result in Unethical Decision Making

1. **If *It's Necessary, It's Ethical***—*Often leads to ends-justify-the-means reasoning.*
2. **The False Necessity Trap**
3. **If It's Legal and Permissible, It's Proper**
4. **It's Just Part of the Job**
5. **It's All for a Good Cause**—*Loosens interpretations of deception, concealment, conflicts of interest, favoritism, and violations of established rules and procedures.*
6. **I Was Just Doing It for You**—*Pits the values of honesty and respect against the value of caring.*
7. **I'm Just Fighting Fire with Fire**
8. **It Doesn't Hurt Anyone**
9. **Everyone's Doing It**
10. **It's OK If I Don't Gain Personally**
11. **I've Got It Coming**—*People who feel they are overworked or underpaid rationalize that they deserve minor "perks," such as favors, discounts, or gifts, and that it is acceptable to abuse sick time, insurance claims, and overtime.*
12. **I Can Still Be Objective**

KNOWLEDGE TO ACTION

Brainstorm with your classmates.

1. Pick one of the rationalizations listed in Figure 13.9. Provide an example of a scenario where an employee may be tempted to use this rationalization.

2. As a supervisor, what steps can you take to prevent an employee from justifying unethical behavior through one of these rationalizations?

A Call to Action

The persistence of unethical behavior in the workplace underscores the importance of the following call to action. It comes from Thomas R. Horton, former president and chief executive officer of the American Management Association.

> In my view, this tide can be turned only by deliberate and conscious actions of management at all levels. Each manager needs to understand his or her own personal code of ethics: what is fair; what is right; what is wrong? Where is the ethical line that I draw, the line beyond which I shall not go? And where is the line beyond which I shall not allow my organization to go?[42]

Each of us can begin the process of improving business ethics by looking in a mirror and leading by example.

Horton's call to action is *personal*. His words suggest that each of us can begin the process of improving business ethics by looking in a mirror and leading by example (see Figure 13.10).[43]

FIGURE 13.10 Ethical guidelines to live by

Source: Adapted from Robert Moment, "Business Ethics," *Veterinary Economics* 46 (November 2005): 24; and Dr. Bruce Weinstein, "Five Easy Principles?" *Business Week*, January 10, 2007, http://www.businessweek.com/print/careers/content/jan2007/ca20070111_219724.htm (accessed March 7, 2007).

Ethical Guidelines to Live by Every Day

1. Be trustworthy—make sure your employees, clients, coworkers, friends, and family can count on you to be honest.
2. Meet your obligations and keep your promises—honor your commitments.
3. Do no harm—this includes other people, your company, other organizations, the environment, and your community at large.
4. Keep an open mind—remember that minds are like parachutes, they only function when open. Ask for input, suggestions, and feedback.
5. Be respectful—always treat others with respect and courtesy regardless of positions, titles, age, or gender.
6. Make things better—contribute in a positive way at work and in your community.
7. Be fair and compassionate.

SUMMARY

1. The employment-related laws that supervisors need to be familiar with include the following: (1) the Occupational Safety and Health Act (OSH Act) promotes safe and healthy working conditions; (2) the Fair Labor Standards Act (FLSA) and the Equal Pay Act (EPA) promote fair wages and equal pay; (3) the FLSA also establishes child labor standards for hiring young workers; (4) the Family Medical Leave Act of 1993 (FMLA) provides the opportunity for unpaid medical leave; (5) Title VII of the Civil Rights Act of 1964 prohibits sexual harassment; and (6) intellectual property (IP) laws determine whether or not an employee has any rights to inventions, literary and artistic works, and symbols, names, images, and designs they have created. Additionally, hiring a new employee triggers several events an employer must follow to remain compliant with the law, including preparation of a new-hire report and completion of immigration and tax-related forms.

2. Several federal laws are in place to prevent employment discrimination based on a variety of personal attributes and characteristics. The U.S. Equal Employment Opportunity Commission (EEOC) is responsible for enforcing many of these laws, including (1) Title VII of the Civil Rights Act of 1964 (Title VII), which prohibits employment discrimination based on race, color, religion, sex, or national origin; (2) EPA, which prohibits sex-based wage discrimination between men and women in

the same establishment who are performing under similar working conditions; (3) the Age Discrimination in Employment Act (ADEA), which prohibits employment discrimination against persons 40 years of age or older; and (4) Title I and Title V of the Americans with Disabilities Act (ADA), which prohibit discrimination against qualified individuals with disabilities.

3. Ethics and the law are *not* the same. You may be in a situation where a person's actions or behavior is legal but would be considered by most to be unethical. On the other hand, there are also circumstances where people have encountered an ethical decision that does not conform to current laws. The point is to approach decision making by evaluating *both* the legal *and* the ethical ramifications.

4. We use ethical principles both consciously and unconsciously when we deal with ethical dilemmas. Ethical principles include (1) balancing self-interests with the organization's interests, (2) being truthful, (3) being kind and building a sense of community, and (4) complying with the law.

5. Regardless of a person's religious beliefs, political affiliation, social customs, or legal thinking, certain actions and behaviors are always considered to be unethical in developed countries, including (1) sexism, (2) racism, (3) fraud, (4) deceit, and (5) intimidation. People commonly rationalize unethical behavior by saying it is

necessary, legal, just part of the job, for a good cause, unselfish, fighting fire with fire, a common practice, or an entitlement.

6. Seven everyday guidelines for ethical behavior are (1) be trustworthy, (2) keep your promises, (3) do no harm, (4) keep an open mind, (5) be respectful, (6) make things better, and (7) be fair and compassionate.

TERMS TO UNDERSTAND

Age Discrimination in Employment Act of 1967 (ADEA), p. 363
child labor standards, p. 356
code of ethics, p. 367
Equal Pay Act (EPA), p. 356
ethical advocate, p. 367
ethics, p. 365

Fair Labor Standards Act (FLSA), p. 354
Family Medical Leave Act of 1993 (FMLA), p. 363
intellectual property, p. 361
new hire report, p. 359
Occupational Safety and Health Act (OSH Act), p. 352

overtime pay, p. 356
sexual harassment, p. 360
Title I and Title V of the Americans with Disabilities Act of 1990 (ADA), p. 363
Title VII of the Civil Rights Act of 1964 (Title VII), p. 363

QUESTIONS FOR REFLECTION

1. What laws are in place to provide fair and equitable wages?

2. If a person's actions are legal, are they ethical? Explain why or why not.

3. What three legal obligations does an employer have when hiring a new employee?

4. If an employee of a company is required to invent new products as part of her job that she is paid for,

does she automatically own the intellectual property rights to these items? Explain why or why not.

5. What are the potential risks to an employee if he chooses to "blow the whistle"? What protections does the employee have?

6. What are seven ethical guidelines to live by?

HANDS-ON ACTIVITIES

DISCRIMINATION CASES

Research workplace discrimination to identify three different cases that have gone to court or been settled between an employee and her/his employer. Identify cases based on various types of discrimination, such as gender, race, and age. In addition, try to include examples from different industries, such as financial services, hospitality, manufacturing, health care, and retail.

1. What was the legal reasoning behind each of the complaints?

2. What was the final outcome for each of the cases?

3. What can you do to prevent similar situations from happening with one of your employees?

INTERVIEW QUESTIONS THAT AVOID ILLEGAL DISCRIMINATION

Briefly describe a job that interests you. Imagine for a moment that you are the supervisor hiring for this position.

1. Make a list of five interview questions that would be legal and acceptable to ask a candidate who has applied for this position.

2. Make a list of five interview questions that would *not* be legal or acceptable.

Interview an Expert

*F*or this chapter's interview assignment, try to identify a person who has expertise in one of the areas we have discussed. For example, perhaps you or a family member knows an OSHA employee—interviewing this person about an actual case will provide firsthand knowledge about the complaint and resolution process. You can also try to interview an attorney with expertise in personnel and/or employment law. Another possibility is the ethics officer for a local business. If you do not have access to any of these types of workers, consider interviewing a human resources person or a manager who has many years of experience. Choose questions from the following list that are relevant and, of course, add your own:

Questions

1. How do you promote a safe and healthy workplace?
2. Has anyone at your organization ever been injured or become ill as result of working conditions?
   a. If yes, what were the circumstances?
   b. What was done after the incident to prevent a reoccurrence?

3. Have you or someone you know ever had an employee, coworker, or boss do something illegal and/or unethical?
   a. If yes, please describe the situation.
   b. What was your reaction? How did the person involved react when the illegal action was brought to light?
4. Have you or someone you know ever been the victim of discrimination or harassment?
   a. If yes, what were the circumstances?
   b. What did you (or the person involved) do?
   c. Would you do anything different if a similar situation arose?
5. What do you think companies should do to eliminate discriminatory employment practices?

You may also want to ask the person to provide copies of company policies, procedures, and documents related to the topics discussed in this chapter, including the company code of ethics (if applicable). As always, remember to follow up with a written thank-you note to the person you interviewed.

CASE STUDY 13.1
Ethical Decision Making

For each of these ethical scenarios, explain how you would handle the situation and specify which ethical principles apply.

1. You receive too much change from the cashier in a restaurant.
2. You witness a friend at work stealing merchandise.
3. You overhear a supervisor from another department making sexual advances toward one of his employees.

4. Your job requires you to choose the company to supply your business with office supplies. You are given a $200 gift card to the local mall from one of the office supply company's salespeople in hopes that you will decide to purchase from her company.
5. You are traveling on business with another coworker, who tells you how to cheat on your expense report to get reimbursed for money you did not spend.

SUPERVISOR'S TOOLKIT

For this project, select a company you are familiar with or an industry you are interested in. One of the goals for supervisors is to encourage employees to abide by the law and to make ethical decisions. To assist you in conducting an ethics training session with your employees, it will be helpful to provide them with a few reference documents. Prepare the following documents to use during your ethics training session:

1. Guidelines for ethical decision making. This document should include a brief explanation of each guideline/principle, along with an example that is relevant for your workplace.

2. A code of ethics. This document should be introduced to employees as a draft or working document where their feedback and suggestions for adding, deleting, or modifying are encouraged. Your code of ethics should include:

   a. An introduction.
   b. The organization's mission, objectives, and values.
   c. Guidance for all stakeholder groups: employees, shareholders, customers, suppliers, and the community.
   d. Expectations about acceptable behavior.
   e. Operating principles, with realistic examples.
   f. A formal mechanism for resolving employee questions.

CHAPTER 14

Harnessing the Power of Information Technology and the Internet

Learning Objectives

1. Discuss technology tools and information systems.

2. Describe potential risks associated with information systems and list steps a supervisor can take to protect employee and customer data.

3. Describe technology's impact on productivity.

4. Discuss computer monitoring and surveillance programs organizations are using to track employees.

5. Discuss common Internet resources, the impact they have on individuals and companies, and steps to get started using them.

6. Identify strategies to leverage technology, information systems, and the Internet for positive results.

Straight Talk from the Field

Lisé Johnson is an Executive Vice President at Xplana, an education technology company based in Boston, Massachusetts.

QUESTION: *What role does information technology play in the management and operation of your company?*

RESPONSE:

*X*plana Learning is a development and services company known for its innovative thinking and technology. That reputation, however, underlies our greatest challenge—keeping our staff at the forefront of thinking and technologies in our markets.

Our company focuses on the broad education market and we have a stated strategy of working across as many channels as possible within that market. Whereas most of our competitors specialize in a particular product area or market segment, we have developed a full suite of learning products and services that include learning platforms, e-books, learning simulations, podcasts, and editorial services. These solutions span multiple markets—traditional K-20 learning, career education, and corporate training.

At Xplana, the emphasis on diversity not only applies to what we do, but to who is doing it—we have an extremely diverse group of employees from numerous cultures and with various backgrounds and skill sets from around the world. This diversity means that everyone in our company—from sales and marketing to development and production—needs to remain at the leading edge of multiple market, technology, and cultural trends. Our management team expects every employee to have an awareness of what the future may hold and how that potential future affects our work and that of our clients.

We realize that our employees have strong formal educations in their various areas of expertise, and we know that they can remain current in those areas through formal training courses and attending conferences. What is more difficult, however, is making sure that our production staff is aware of trends in social networking and how that might affect their work around e-books or professional development courses. In other words, it is relatively easy to keep programmers up to speed on the latest nuances of Java or Flash development. It is far more difficult to help them

stay abreast of the "softer" knowledge that is also important to our success.

At Xplana, our expectations around this familiarity with softer knowledge dictates that our management team place a high value on "informal learning"—the unstructured and user-determined acquisition of knowledge—and instill this goal within each and every employee. We understand the need to expose our employees to a variety of information sources and experiences, to let them choose topics they are interested in, and to allow them different avenues for exploring that information.

Of course, as an agile technology company, we find that the best way to foster informal learning at our company is through . . . technology! We design our efforts around the different online production and communication tools our employees are already using in their work each day.

Here are the basic technologies we use to drive our informal learning efforts:

- Company websites—Part of our informal learning strategy includes an emphasis on our own products and the technologies they utilize. We use our public company website and our internal Web intranet to facilitate awareness and communication around those products.

- Blogs—We produce a daily blog posting called "Bits and Pieces" that lists news articles and blog postings for the day that are related to what we believe are important trends. We group these by category so that our employees can select the resources that interest them.

- Wikis—We create Wiki discussions on important products that allow our developer, designer, and production staffs to collaborate on new ideas and innovations. In this way, we foster dialogue that combines our core work and forward-thinking trends.

- *Instant Messaging (IM)—We encourage our teams to engage in ongoing, immediate discussions at the idea level via our internal chat client, Jabber. Our managers are charged with using this technique to prevent our people from becoming so engrossed in their work that they lose sight of the big picture.*
- *E-mail—We "blast" hot ideas to our staff regularly via e-mail. We target specific groups within the company with these and try to touch all of our different interest groups each week.*

The key to our informal learning program is that it is driven by our executive management team and is coordinated carefully to drive our company vision internally. Naturally, we augment

our virtual program with face-to-face informal sessions as well. We hold regular brainstorming sessions and encourage open conversation in our common lunch area. We also maintain an open-office layout that fosters impromptu discussions and planning.

Success with an informal learning strategy like ours is dependent on planning. We have learned over the years that it's not enough to put bright people in an open space and to give them fun projects. Even with that kind of a setup, a loss of energy can occur and workers can become less collaborative and open to new ideas over time. In order to maintain a freshness and eagerness for new ideas, Xplana carefully crafts its vision and structures purposeful informal learning around that vision.

Chapter Outline

*T*echnology is a term that ignites passionate debate in many circles these days. Some blame technology for environmental destruction and cultural fragmentation. Others view technology as the key to economic and social progress. It is likely that each view contains important messages.

Technological advances facilitated the evolution of society into the industrial age and later into the information age. This has created a much higher level of dependence on computer technology and information systems in a wide variety of industries including construction, health care, and education.[1] One of the major challenges for supervisors is to leverage computer technology, information systems, and the Internet to improve overall performance in a cost-effective manner.

In this chapter, we will introduce a variety of information technology tools that supervisors commonly use. We also will discuss strategies for taking full advantage of these tools. In addition, you will learn about a few downsides to technology, potential risks, and how to protect employee and customer data.

Technology and Information Systems at Work

As a competitive necessity today, most managers use some form of computer information technology to operate their businesses. In the hospitality industry, everything from reservation systems to menu planning is done by computer. In the retail sector, purchasing, inventory management, sales, and accounting are all dependent on computers. In health care, doctors, nurses, and other service providers are using computers to assist in diagnosing and tracking patient illnesses as well as billing insurance companies and patients. The point is that information technology systems have become the backbone for organizations around the world. This section provides an overview of various types of information technology being used today. It is not intended to be a comprehensive discussion about computers, nor is it a complete list of information technology tools available or on the horizon.

Technology in General

For our purposes, **technology** is defined as all the tools and ideas available for extending the natural physical and mental reach of humankind. A central theme in technology is the practical application of new ideas. For supervisors, these new ideas can frequently lead to increased productivity and quality improvement. However, they also present challenges from both a human resources management perspective as well as with operational logistics.

Technology tools in the workplace include a wide variety of applications such as electronics, robots, imaging, and communication. These tools are designed to make humans more efficient and effective. Additionally, they often are developed to promote employee safety. Take, for example, the security screening job at airports. Without technology tools such as metal detectors and imaging devices, screeners would have to complete the same tasks manually. It would take them much longer to go through each passenger's belongings by hand while risking exposure to hazardous items such as sharp objects or dangerous chemicals. Technology tools, in this case, also create a less intrusive experience for the traveler (e.g., a quick walk through a body scanner versus an embarrassing strip search). This is just one everyday example of how technology tools can be used to increase productivity.

technology
all the tools and ideas available for extending the natural physical and mental reach of humankind.

computer information systems
the combination of data input, processing, and output.

Computer Information Systems

Information technology tools have become indispensable in today's workplace. **Computer information systems** automate data input, processing, and output for end users inside and outside the organization. For supervisors with jobs that rely on computerized information systems, it is essential to be familiar with the functioning and control of those systems.

Jamile, for example, is the auto claims department supervisor for a major insurance company. Her firm's computer applications are designed specifically for auto insurance companies. Jamile leads a team of ten data entry clerks. Their job is to type in information related to the claim. This is the *input* step and the data elements include the name, address, phone number, and policy number of the insured and the responsible party (if different). Other key input data include the year, make, and model of the vehicle; the date of the accident; the cost for repairs; and the status (either total loss or pending repair). The next step is for the computer to verify the eligibility of the insured and to compute the amount to be paid for the claim. This is the automated *processing* function. Based on certain variables such as age of the car and type of policy, the software application will determine how much should be paid. It will then reduce the amount by the deductible to arrive at a final payment. (In pre-computer days, this stage was tediously and slowly done by hand.) The resulting information is transferred automatically and electronically to the accounts payable department to issue a check—this is the *output* function.

If a data entry clerk makes a keystroke mistake or if the wrong table is used to calculate the loss, the erroneous final amount calculated can be costly. (Computer specialists refer to this as "garbage in–garbage out.") Therefore, Jamile needs to verify the accuracy of input data. This may simply involve visually scanning a report listing every claim, including the age of the vehicle, the type of loss, and the policy category. If the dollar amount exceeds a certain range, it could be flagged for review. Alternatively, Jamile could do a random quality check to compare the data entry worksheets with the computer report to verify that the information was entered properly. A third way to check the accuracy of input data would be to review the formulas in the tables once a month or quarterly.

> *Regardless of the industry, it is important to validate that your computer input, processing, and output components are working properly.*

Regardless of the industry, it is important to validate that your computer input, processing, and output components are working properly. Plan for periodic reviews because computer software updates or hardware changes can adversely impact the integrity of your information system.

KNOWLEDGE TO
ACTION

1. How can computer information systems be used by supervisors to increase efficiency and effectiveness?

   _____

2. What are the potential risks to the organization by introducing these?

   _____

Protecting Information Systems

computer crime
using computer technology to steal or cause harm to another person or company.

According to an FBI survey, computer abuses such as computer viruses, data corruption, and lost revenue led to $1.6 trillion in damages.[2] As we discussed in the Chapter 13, not everyone is honest or ethical. **Computer crime** occurs when a person uses computer technology to steal or cause harm to another person or company.

Most computer security breaches are not random or external attacks, but rather the acts of current or former employees

This threat places added responsibility on supervisors and their employees to protect their organization's information systems and data from theft or other attacks. It is also important to recognize that most computer security breaches are *not* random or external attacks, but rather the acts of current or former employees. In fact, according to a recent survey, 33% of information security breaches are by employees and another 28% are the result of business partners.[3]

Not all of these attacks are malicious or even on purpose. Some occur because of employee errors or lack of training. A survey by the Computing Technology Industry Association found that human error was the cause of information security breaches nearly 60% of the time. These errors can be as simple as an employee unknowingly infecting the company's network with a virus by connecting his infected laptop or downloading an unfiltered e-mail attachment.[4]

Potential Risks

Computers and information systems are exposed to potential theft or damage in a wide variety of ways. We examine the most common sources of security breakdowns in this section. Meanwhile, people engaged in computer crime continue to come up with new and innovative ways to gain access to information systems. Therefore, it is essential to be aware and keep your security systems current.

COMPUTER VIRUS

A **computer virus** is a malicious software parasite that can damage applications, erase data and files, or shut down entire systems. This is probably one of the oldest and most well-known ways to violate computer systems. Although most people are aware of viruses, and most companies have installed virus protection software, users routinely put their computers and their employer's computer information systems at risk. When a computer virus invades an organization, it can lead to anything from irritating distractions to more severe problems such as crashing the entire system or providing access to criminals.

INTERNAL THEFT OF DATA

In retail settings, one of the greatest threats to profitability is employee theft of inventory. In knowledge-based organizations, **employee data theft** is a major concern. Employee data theft can occur when employees use computers to steal confidential data. Employees steal data to sell it or use it for their own gain with a future employer. This is not unique to large corporations or government agencies. While considering the following two examples, imagine how this could occur in your organization and what you could do to avoid it.

computer virus
a malicious software parasite that can damage programs, erase data and files, or shut down entire systems.

employee data theft
the act of employees stealing confidential data.

- The first case involves two competing Dodge car dealerships. Three ex-employees are accused of returning to their former dealership to break in to the computer database and steal customer lists in an effort to benefit their new employer. At risk is a settlement ranging from $853,000 to $2.6 million. As of 2008, this case is pending a decision by the New Jersey Supreme Court.[5]

"Remember all that top secret data you were storing on our web page?"

© Ted Goff

■ The second case involves a database administrator working for a firm that provides check authorization services to financial institutions and merchants. He pleaded guilty to stealing approximately 8.5 million customer records and then selling them for $580,000. He will incur financial penalties and jail time for his crime.[6]

EXTERNAL HACKING

External hacking occurs when the computer criminal gains access to an organization's system from the outside, either by finding an entry point or stealing an employee's log-in information. One of the more widely publicized cases occurred at TJX Company. The owner of TJ Maxx, Marshalls, HomeGoods, AJ Wright, Winners, and HomeSense stores lost at least 45 million customer records, including their credit card information. External hackers had access to the company's computer databases for more than 18 months. Estimates for a financial settlement range from $40 million to $150 million, plus the potential loss of loyal customers.[7]

COMPUTER HARDWARE THEFT

In some cases, valuable information ends up in the wrong hands because computer hardware is lost or stolen. Consider, for example, the case of a U.S. Department of Veterans Affairs employee whose company laptop and external hard drive was stolen from his home. The computer equipment held the "unencrypted names, social security numbers and birth dates for about 26.5 million veterans."[8]

external hacking
computer criminal gains access from outside the organization to steal confidential data or cause harm.

How to Reduce the Risk

Unless you are a computer professional or supervisor in information technology, you may feel a little overwhelmed at this point. What can you possibly do to prevent computer security breaches? In fact, there are several steps you can take to minimize the risk of an accidental or malicious attack.

POLICIES AND PROCEDURES

Follow the policies and procedures developed by your organization to reduce the risk of being a victim of a computer attack.

The first and most obvious step is to follow your organization's policies and procedures to reduce the risk of being a victim of a computer attack. These will frequently include restrictions on access to data, requirements for training, and guidelines for logging onto the network. If your company does not have any formal policies or procedures related to computer information systems, consider working with your technology employees to develop these important guidelines.

PASSWORDS AND VERIFICATION

Here are a few basic rules about passwords:

1. Do not write them down!
2. Do not share them with anyone.
3. Use different passwords for your home accounts and your work accounts.
4. Change your passwords frequently.
5. Use a variety of letters, numbers, and symbols in your password.
6. Never use recognizable names or dates, such as your children's names, birthdates, anniversary dates, etc.

Additionally, some organizations use a second mode of verification such as a key card.[9] If you have one of these devices, do not lend it to anyone or leave it unsecured.

Corporate computers are only as secure as employees habitually keep them. When employees post log-in names and passwords on their monitors, the perception of a secure computer network ends up being nothing more than a false illusion in the executive suite.
© Turbo/zefa/Corbis

encryption
the process of converting data from plain text to a cipher text, a difficult-to-interpret format.

LOG OUT

Require all employees to log out when they get up from their computer, even if it is only for five minutes. You may want to ask if your computer technology staff can automatically log an employee off of the system if his/her computer has been idle for a specified period of time, such as fifteen or twenty minutes.

PROTECTING DATA—ENCRYPTION

Encryption is the process of converting data from plain text to a cipher text, a difficult-to-interpret format using complex computer algorithms. Through these reversible encryption algorithms and encryption keys, companies protect the integrity, authenticity, and privacy of their systems. Organizations should consider encrypting all confidential data, including customer records, employee information, and competitive data. This is particularly important for information being sent as an e-mail attachment or data stored on a laptop, handheld computer, or other portable device.[10] Also, if your software has the capability to password protect individual files, take advantage of that feature to add another layer of protection.

ACCESS CONTROL

As mentioned earlier, most security breaches are committed by employees or former employees. Therefore, it is important to limit access to information. Work with your information systems staff to restrict employee access to certain data or portions of key databases. For example, all supervisors may need access to the timesheet portion of the payroll system; however, supervisors do not need to view their employees' social security numbers or other confidential data. In addition, create a computer system security log listing all employees and their data access limitations. If you have a situation where an employee has become disgruntled or her performance is declining, you may want to limit her access to intellectual property or confidential information such as customer lists or product information.[11]

E-MAIL, WEBSITES, AND OTHER PLACES WHERE VIRUSES HIDE

Do not open any e-mail from an unknown sender unless it is a requirement of your job. Keep your virus scanning software current and actively running. Be cautious when providing any privileged information on the Internet. By simply answering a survey or signing up for a free offer, you may be exposing the organization's entire system to a potential attack.

TRAINING, TRAINING, TRAINING

The cost of security breaches can be extraordinary. It may be challenging to find time to provide employees with computer security training; however, the risk of not properly training them is far worse.

This is where it is good to heed the old saying, "An ounce of prevention is worth a pound of cure!" As we learned earlier, the cost of security breaches can be extraordinary. It may be challenging to find time to provide busy employees with computer security training. But the risk of not properly training them could become a much bigger headache. Every organization will have unique aspects to its training program depending on the information systems, data elements, and mobility of the workers. See Figure 14.1 for topics to include in your computer security training.

Update your policies, procedures, and guidelines at least once a year. It is important to conduct refresher training as well, since people have a tendency to get busy and may forget about the necessary steps to maintain a secure computing environment.

FIGURE 14.1 Computer security training

Source: Adapted from Dan Kaplan, "Back to School: As Data Becomes More Prevalent, Enterprises Must Provide Employee Security Awareness Training Courses," *SC Magazine* (June 2006): 38–42; and Kevin McKeough, "Inside, and Outside, Jobs; Looking to Protect Your Business? Better Search for Leaks on Both Sides," *Crain's Chicago Business* 30 (February 26, 2007): 18.

Computer Security Training

- Review company policies and procedures.
- Explain why information and data security is important to the organization.
- Discuss the secure nature of the information and data.
- List potential consequences to the company and to each individual if there is a breach.
- Review of guidelines:
  - Passwords
  - Logging out
  - Encryption

The Computer's Impact on Productivity and Supervision

One of the great debates going on in cubicles across America is over personal computer use at work and the overall impact technology has on productivity. According to Salary.com's 2007 Wasting Time Survey, "the average employee spends 1.7 hours of a typical 8.5-hour workday on activities unrelated to the job. Almost 35% of respondents said they spend time on the Internet for personal reasons. . . ."[12] Many argue that this has a negative impact on productivity and profitability. In contrast, proponents for permitting employees to use their computers for personal use view this activity as a break rather than a waste of time. They further argue that allowing employees time to take care of personal business on the Internet may actually save time and improve productivity. Author David H. Freedman offered the following enlightened perspective:

> *"The average employee spends 1.7 hours of a typical 8.5-hour workday on activities unrelated to the job."*

> If you have a significant percentage of employees who are genuinely shirking their responsibilities via constant, mindless Web surfing, you really should consider the possibility that open Web access isn't even close to being your biggest problem. As HR expert Robert Cenek puts it: "Folks ought to be working hard because they're attracted to the work they're doing." And management's key job is make sure employees are motivated in this way.[13]

Complicating this debate is the observation that employees in the Internet age are spending far more personal time on work-related activities than in the past. In fact, a study conducted by the University of Maryland's Smith School of Business and Rockbridge Associates, a Virginia-based market research firm, revealed that "employees spend an average of 3.7 hours per week on the Web for personal activities at work and 5.9 hours a week online at home doing work-related tasks."[14]

So what is the impact of computer information technology on productivity? Technology advocates argue that computer tools have increased productivity, while critics say the opposite. Of course, the results and opinions vary by industry. Let's examine both sides of this important debate.

Information Technology's Positive Impact on Productivity

Information technology has helped a wide variety of industries achieve greater productivity and a higher level of accuracy. Consider, for example, the Pirelli Tire Company, where integration software made it possible to connect over 100 different software programs together. The positive outcomes: a reduction in inventory expenses and improved customer service because inventory and order systems are now linked to 2,000 tire dealers.[15]

From economists to futurists, a common theme is that technology has had a positive impact on productivity. Futurists Marvin J. Cetron and Owen Davies have made these observations about technology, the future, and productivity:

> Computers are fast becoming part of our environment, rather than just tools we use for specific tasks. With wireless modems, portable computers give us access to networked data wherever we go.

Robots are taking over more and more jobs that are routine, remote, or risky.

By 2010, artificial intelligence, data mining, and virtual reality will help most companies and government agencies assimilate data and solve problems beyond the range of today's computers.

New technologies should continue to improve the efficiency of many industries, helping to keep costs under control.[16]

Brookings Institute economists Jack E. Triplett and Barry P. Bosworth identify information technology as contributing to productivity growth in the huge service sector. This includes major industries such as finance, telecommunications, and transportation, thanks to greater speed, portability, and declining costs.[17]

THEY

SAID IT

BEST

The first rule of any technology used in a business is that automation applied to an efficient operation will magnify the efficiency. The second is that automation applied to an inefficient operation will magnify the inefficiency.

—BILL GATES, Co-founder, Microsoft Corp.

Source: www.billgatesmicrosoft.com (December 30, 2007).

Information Technology's Negative Impact on Productivity

The cost of workplace distractions is estimated to be around $650 billion a year![18] Consider for a moment the experience of a former marketing manager at Wellfleet Communications (now Bay Networks), who discovered one of his employees spending half his day surfing the Web, paying bills, and disturbing other employees. No surprise, the employee was terminated.[19] With stories like this, it is easy to understand why critics argue that modern computer information systems, along with access to the Internet, have overloaded employees while offering too many distractions from work.

The list of complaints include:

- *E-mail*—The volume, the amount that is unwanted, the risk of viruses, expectation for a rapid response, potential misunderstandings, and impersonal nature of the messages put this one at the top of the list.[20]

- *Constant connection*—With the availability of wireless access and advances in portable technology devices such as iPhones and BlackBerries, many employees feel they can never get away from the office. These "electronic leashes" can negatively impact productivity, as well as increase stress levels and erode job satisfaction.[21]

- *Information quality*—The Internet instantly puts a world of information at our fingertips. This is both good and bad. The downside is that we must filter through massive volumes of information that is often inaccurate and outdated to find anything useful.[22]

- *Rapid obsolescence and the learning curve*—New technology often creates improvements and opportunities, but at a price (not just the dollar amount paid for the hardware and software). Most new technology takes time to implement and learn. The more complex the application, the more likely the company is to pay for training. Less sophisticated applications still take time to learn how to use effectively. The big question is: will each new wave of information technology be worth the time and energy required to learn and implement?

KNOWLEDGE TO ACTION

1. What can you do to minimize the negative impact e-mail has on your personal productivity and the productivity of others?

2. Brainstorm with your classmates—what do you think will be the next revolutionary technology to impact personal productivity in the workplace?

Monitoring Employees

In addition to concerns about information technology's impact on productivity, there has been a lively debate over how far to go in monitoring employees' activities. Opponents view computer surveillance as an invasion of privacy, corporate spying, and a possible violation of civil liberties.[23]

Employer Surveillance Practices

Ninety-two percent of all U.S. employees have been electronically monitored by their bosses.

It may surprise you to know that 92% of all U.S. employees have been electronically monitored by their bosses, according to a recent study.[24] For a closer look, consider the results of a survey conducted by the American Management Association and the ePolicy Institute (See Figure 14.2):

- 76% of the companies monitor and review website connections.
- 55% store and review employee e-mail.
- 51% use video surveillance.
- 36% monitor keystrokes and time spent on the computer.[25]

Companies are also using global positioning system (GPS) technology to track workers' movements and the amount of time spent on breaks.[26] For example, U.S. Foodservice is using GPS-enabled Nextel phones to monitor employee timesheets, jobs, and locations. This technology is also being used by government agencies such as the Massachusetts State Highway Department, which issued GPS phones to over 2,000 snow plow contractors to monitor their travels.[27]

FIGURE 14.2 Employees under surveillance

Source: "Tips on Keeping Workplace Surveillance from Going Too Far," *HR Focus* 83 (January 2006): 10.

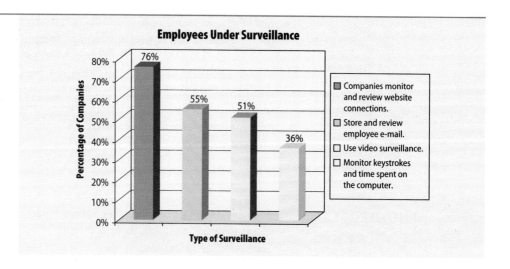

Consequences

As employee monitoring and surveillance have increased over the years, so too have the consequences for offenders. For example:

- A large national bank fired two employees for forwarding a picture of a well-known female politician's head superimposed on a bare-breasted woman's body.

- A major chemical company fired 24 employees for sending e-mails with sexual or threatening content.

- A regional health system organization in Illinois fired 6 employees, including a vice president, for Internet and e-mail abuse.[28]

Finding a Balance

Most employees resist or resent monitoring because the practices are not fully disclosed or explained. If your company has a monitoring program in place, consider following these steps to improve acceptance:

- Tell employees what surveillance equipment and monitoring is in place.

- Reassure employees that no video recordings will be conducted in private areas, such as bathrooms and locker rooms.

- Post notices where video surveillance is in place.

- Explain why and how surveillance and monitoring technologies are being used (emphasize employee safety and theft reduction).

- Make available and discuss related policies and procedures.[29]

A WABC-TV news truck leaves the company building on West 67th St. in New York City. News trucks at the station were equipped with global positioning systems, raising concerns among the station's union workers about privacy issues. It's a growing workplace controversy as companies steadily embrace the GPS technology already in use to track everything from wayward teens to sex offenders.

© AP Images/Adam Rountree

KNOWLEDGE TO
ACTION

eTelemetry, which provides tech departments with network monitoring services, came out with a new version of hardware that some might consider creepy. It gives managers desktop access to details about the online activities of the people they supervise—data previously reserved for IT.

The hardware lets managers set up e-mails to alert them when a worker has been surfing excessively, view which sites employees have visited that day, and compare individuals' bandwidth use.

Source: Jena McGregor, "A Way to Tell If They're Slaving Away or Surfing," *Business Week*, January 14, 2008, 56.

1. Do you think this an infringement of employee privacy rights? Explain.
   _____

2. In your view, what are the general boundaries for a fair and reasonable company Internet use policy?
   _____

The Impact of the Internet

The Internet has revolutionized how we work, learn, socialize, shop, and more.

There is no question that the Internet has revolutionized how we work, learn, socialize, shop, and live. Blogs, social networking websites such as MySpace and Facebook, and video sharing sites such as YouTube have changed how individuals communicate and use computers for business and pleasure. The impact on corporate America continues to expand as these types of websites gain popularity and acceptance. Internet resources are directly affecting supervisors in the areas of communication, recruitment, research, sales, and customer service.

Internet Resources

The rapid growth in tools available to anyone with access to the Internet is amazing. Users can find information on just about any topic imaginable. People can communicate with customers across the world or friends across the street in real time—the possibilities seem endless. The benefits of these advances are extraordinary for business people, students, activists, politicians, law enforcement, and the average citizen. Of course, there are also potential negative consequences if the users are careless or fall victim to a malicious computer attack. In this section, we highlight four of the more common Internet resources affecting organizations and supervisors today: (1) blogs, (2) social networking, (3) video sharing, and (4) reference sites.

BLOGS

The term **blog** is short for *Web log*. A blog is essentially an electronic diary made available via the Internet. Many blogs are organized around a particular topic, and they may have multiple authors.[30] As Lisé Johnson described in the chapter opener, her company Xplana posts a daily blog called "Bits and Pieces" to communicate important trends and information to employees.

blog
an online diary, used to share business knowledge, personal information, and more.

More than 175,000 new blogs are created every day where people share independent thoughts and ideas.[31] Corporations such as Xplana are using this medium to reduce e-mail and post information in a private, members-only blog to be shared and discussed with coworkers. In addition, public blogs are going beyond personal interests and hobbies. From a business perspective, this open forum for communication can be a marketing bonanza or an absolute nightmare.[32] Here are two examples from opposite ends of the spectrum to illustrate this point.

The first story is about a new product, the Voltaic Backpack, increasing sales as a result of the buzz created on various blogs.

> Entrepreneur Shayne McQuade received an early sample of his company's solar-powered backpack, which can charge the wearer's cell phone and other gadgets. He asked a friend—who runs a blog with a niche audience called Treehugger—to blog about it. The mention on Treehugger didn't by itself produce a huge word-of-mouth epidemic. But another blogger higher up the blogging ecosystem picked up the story from Treehugger and blogged about the backpack on his Cool Hunting blog, which was then read by Gizmodo, one of the most popular blogs on the Internet for cool stuff and gadgets. Once the backpack was featured on Gizmodo, the orders poured in![33]

The second story demonstrates how blogs can bring negative and unwanted attention to a company and ultimately impact business decisions.

> Take the recent case of Greenpeace vs. Gorton's. The activist group in March flamed the seafood merchant on its website, claiming that Gorton's was linked to whale hunting in the Antarctic; the parent company of Gorton's owns about a third of the company that owns the Japanese whaling fleet that hunts in Antarctica. The word quickly spread through the blogosphere. Greenpeace included anti-Gorton's banners and HTML coding that bloggers could put on their own blogs to help raise awareness of the situation.
>
> A month later, Greenpeace reported on its site that Gorton's parent company, Nissui, said it would sell its share of the whaling fleet. A note on the Greenpeace site read, "As our web wizard Adele put it, 'We moused them into submission.'"[34]

Blogs can be very powerful and can have a significant impact on a business's success, decision making, and marketing strategy.

As you can see from these contrasting cases, blogs can be very powerful and can have a significant impact on a business's success, decision making, and marketing strategy. In addition, prospective employees conducting online research are quite likely to be influenced by blogs written about a company, its products, its customer service, and how it treats its employees.

SOCIAL NETWORK SITES (SNS)

social network sites
websites used by members to create personal profiles, post messages, manage address books, and share photos and videos.

Social network sites (SNS) support a wide variety of interests, people, and cultures. Some sites are public and center around hobbies, sports, and common interests such as environmentalism, religion, or politics. Other sites are private and access is limited to members of a particular community of interest. SNS typically provide the opportunity for members to create personal profiles, post messages, manage address books, share photos and videos, and more.[35] The top-ranked social networking sites include MySpace, Multiplay, Bebo, Vox, Facebook, and Facebox. In addition to these traditional SNS, there are thousands of sites dedicated to special interests, such as Flixter for movie buffs, Dogster for dog lovers, and Librarything for the avid reader.[36]

Although SNS originally were formed for personal and social reasons, business-oriented networking sites such as Doostang, Linkedin, and Xing have emerged to appeal to professionals between the ages of 25 and 65. MySpace and Facebook changed their business models to also welcome business users.[37] If you are responsible for recruiting, consider joining a virtual job fair hosted by local chambers of commerce and other trade associations.[38]

Companies such as Dow Chemical are installing official social networking sites for their alumni, retirees, and employees to improve communication and relationships.[39] Nonprofit organizations also are taking advantage of this technology to attract new donors and volunteers. They are using their social networks to share information about the charity and its operations, while fostering a sense of community among existing supporters.[40]

In addition to the official sites, many unofficial SNS are dedicated to a particular product or company, such as Starbucks, Gap, and American Eagle Outfitters.[41] According to Forrester Research analyst Peter Kim,

> The posts on blogs and social networking sites are beginning to really influence customer decisions, and that will have a ripple effect on consumer purchases. Bloggers and social networks keep ideas in the public mindset; think about the influence that can have over brands.[42]

This is not news to product managers like Jana Eggers, general manager for Intuit Quickbase, who finds this new technology to be an excellent source of customer feedback. While comparing this to traditional focus groups, Eggers said, "You're getting people who are more passionate about the product rather than people who are willing to get paid to give their opinion."[43]

These virtual communities of strangers, friends, coworkers, consumers, and enthusiasts are changing the nature of interpersonal relationships. Although the initial applications in the business community were primarily focused on product marketing and promotion, organizations are also beginning to use SNS sites for team collaboration, recruitment, and retention efforts.

This is the area where supervisors can probably have the greatest impact. Imagine creating a site for your team where people can keep one another updated about work-related projects, schedules, and customer information. This alone would improve employee performance. Now, add to this the social aspects of SNS—people who know one another on a more personal level tend to build stronger relationships and subsequently work together more effectively. If your work team's site lets employees post personal information such as birthdays, photos of their families and/or pets, favorite restaurants or recipes, or movie and video game reviews, they are more likely to bond. What worries management is the potential for employees to waste a significant amount of work time on these sites. Therefore, it is important to establish ground rules and boundaries as part of your implementation plan.

VIDEO SITES

Top video sharing sites include YouTube, MySpaceVideo, Gotuit, Meta Café, Motionbox, Revver, vSocial, iFilm, and Eyespot.[44] The entertainment industry is leveraging technology to provide on-demand video, music, and audio. In turn, companies are making instructional videos available online, including product demonstrations and corporate training material.[45]

IBM CEO Sam Palmisano took this concept one step further when he conducted a virtual meeting using a Second Life meeting space. He spoke with 7,000 employees from Beijing, China. Palmisano presented himself via an avatar (an online representation of an individual) when he spoke to the group and then responded to questions from employees who were also participating in the meeting using their own avatars.[46] Although this approach may seem a bit too high-tech for some, it was a great way for the technology company leader to grab the attention of his employees and meet "face-to-face" in virtual reality. Julie Fason Holder, corporate vice president for marketing and sales, human resources, and public affairs at Dow Chemical, anticipates using these information technology tools in ways no one has imagined yet. In discussing this topic, she said, "I'm sure we're at the beginning."[47]

KNOWLEDGE TO ACTION

1. How can you use blogging, social networking, and/or video sharing to be a more effective supervisor?

_____

2. What are some of the drawbacks to using these tools in the workplace?

_____

REFERENCE SITES

One of the common misconceptions about **reference sites** on the Internet is that the information they provide is accurate. These sites include online dictionaries,

Rosie Goergen, left, Mark Hilburn, center, and Kara Garman spend time in their communications class navigating through a virtual world in "Second Life" at the University of Nebraska at Omaha. "Second Life" is an online virtual world with more than 12 million residents, created by San Francisco–based Linden Lab. Companies such as IBM are experimenting with this technology to communicate with their employees and customers.
© AP Images/Dave Weaver

reference sites
websites providing information on a variety of topics.

encyclopedias, and sources for research data. It is essential for users to identify primary sources whenever possible and to consult multiple reliable sources to verify the accuracy of posted information. In addition, check the date the information was prepared and posted. Internet authors will frequently post information and never update or remove outdated material. Particularly when researching current events and science and technology, it is important to identify updated sources of information for your research. Figure 14.3 lists the top online encyclopedias.

The availability of reference tools such as dictionaries and encyclopedias online has both positive and negative aspects. The great thing about these accessible tools is that they are updated and maintained in real time, so in theory they should be current and relevant. In comparison to their hard-copy printed counterparts, this is a significant improvement. Still, the downside is that many online reference sites have too few qualified people to edit and/or validate information posted, thus inaccurate or misleading postings occur.[48]

Online research allows students, businesspeople, and anyone searching for information the freedom and flexibility to conduct their research when and where they choose. Of course, as with any online activity, users should proceed with caution. Some websites may ask for personal information prior to permitting the user access to content. Before providing any information, verify the credentials and validity of the website. Importantly, never give personal information such as your address or phone number unless it is a secure site that you are familiar with (e.g., a professional organization with a password-protected, members-only site). Most people providing Internet content likely are credible, honest, ethical individuals. Unfortunately, there are those with criminal or malicious intent. A good motto to live by on the Internet is "Trust but Verify!"

A good motto to live by on the Internet is "Trust but Verify!"

FIGURE 14.3 Top online encyclopedias

Source: LibrarySpot.com, a free virtual library resource center for educators and students, librarians and their patrons, families, businesses, and just about anyone exploring the Web for valuable research information. Published by StartSpot Mediaworks, Inc. in the Northwestern University/Evanston Research Park in Evanston, Ill., located on the web at http://www.libraryspot.com/features/encyclopedia.htm (accessed May 12, 2008).

Top Online Encyclopedias*

- Britannica (http://www.britannica.com)
  Britannica.com includes a portion of the content from the print edition. You can also simultaneously search for reviews of the 125,000 hand-picked reference sites, related books, and current articles from magazines.

- Encarta (http://encarta.msn.com)
  This free encyclopedia from Microsoft contains 17,000 articles and more than 2,200 photos, illustrations, maps, charts, and tables. You can also access the World Atlas and the World English Dictionary, a "talking dictionary" replete with audio files.

- Encyclopedia (http://www.encyclopedia.com)
  This site offers more than 50,000 articles from *The Concise Columbia Electronic Encyclopedia* (Third Edition). Encyclopedia.com offers 170,000 links, including cross-referenced articles and other sites. You can also access articles and images from the Electric Library for a fee.

- Wikipedia (http://en.wikipedia.org/wiki/Main_Page)
  Anyone across the globe can add content to this free reference website. With an infinite number of contributors, Wikipedia remains very much up-to-date. Articles are created or updated within minutes or hours of an event.

*Authors' note: The Internet is a dynamic medium that is changing every day. The websites and URLs referenced in this book were accurate at the time of publication and are subject to change.

Tips for Getting Started

After reading this section, you may be thinking it is time for your company to catch the wave. Before getting started, however, first determine why a social network or blog is a good move for your business and specify the primary purpose for this initiative. Consider asking the following questions:

1. Do you want to improve or build better customer relationships?
2. Do you want to increase your knowledge management capabilities?
3. Do you want to facilitate sales or recruitment?
4. Do you want to increase your personal and corporate visibility to gain more brand awareness or business opportunities?
5. Do you want to build a community in which ideas and information can be exchanged and discussed?
6. Do you want to hold one-on-ones or engage in multiple conversations at the same time?
7. Do you want to use certain tools or applications?
8. How will you get customers, partners, colleagues, employees, and prospective employees and customers to interact with your site?
9. How will you integrate with other social networks?
10. How will you monitor and censure content/conversations and what the legal implications and user guidelines are?[49]

Once you have answered these questions, start small. Like any other new technology project, it is best to conduct a pilot test first. Assess the results, make appropriate modifications, and then proceed with a full implementation. For example, you may want to begin with a small team of people to test the concept of a companywide blog. Below are a few suggestions for launching your blogging initiative:

1. Create a "safe haven" for employees to experiment with blogging. Set up a private blog on your intranet or start a blog that's password-protected.
2. Select a permanent home for your blog—the Web address you choose should be one that you will be happy with for years to come and is not linked to a service provider.
3. Identify a scalable, flexible, and user-friendly blog platform such as WordPress, Drupal, or Movable Type.
4. Decide on a posting schedule. Try to post at least three times a week.
5. Build relationships with respected bloggers. Post on their blogs and consider attending blogger conferences like BlogOn and Blog Business Summit.[50]

Validity and Reliability

Ongoing concerns with all of these Internet resources are the validity and reliability of the information. Many blogs and websites are uncensored, meaning that people are free to post their own personal thoughts, opinions, ideas, images, and more. This, of course, promotes engaging dialogue and supports democratic ideals. However, it also creates an environment where misinformation can be posted and quickly spread. Misinformation on the Internet is difficult to contain. Other concerns about the ease of access to information on the Internet are the potential for copyright violations and the unauthorized reproduction of content and/or images.

Leveraging Information Technology for Positive Results

Employees and supervisors from a variety of industries can identify technology tools that have improved their performance and/or productivity. In this section, we have selected a few examples that are relevant for supervisors to illustrate how information technology tools can have a positive impact on your organization.

Performance Evaluation Software

As mentioned in Chapter 6, a key supervisory role is conducting employee performance evaluations. Although your assessment of employee performance will involve personal observation, customer feedback, and other measures, computer software can make this process much more efficient and consistent. Several evaluation applications are available to small, medium, and large organizations. They are designed to help supervisors complete the evaluation process in a timely and consistent manner. In addition, the automated features provide reminders and reporting functionality to make trend analysis and workforce assessment easy enough to do on a weekly or monthly basis, rather than just once a year. Not only does this make evaluations easier for supervisors, but employees also seem to prefer this automated approach.[51]

Intranets

Similar to the well-known Internet, companies and government agencies are using intranets to communicate with their employees. Although an **intranet** is based on the same technology as the Internet, the big difference is that access is limited to a specific group such as a company's employees. These websites are being used to post policy and procedure manuals, conduct online training, and allow access to human resources applications such as internal job postings and personnel management tools. What makes this so appealing to employees is that, in most cases, they can access their company's intranet from anywhere (and any time) they have Internet access. This is particularly helpful when employees want to review items such as benefits or insurance information.[52]

Telecommuting

intranet
based on the same technology as the Internet, with access limited to a specific group.

As we discussed in Chapter 4, offering the option to work from home provides employees with flexibility and typically leads to greater job satisfaction. In addition, "78% of global executives believe telecommuters are as productive as or more

1. What are a few examples of ways you can use your company intranet to communicate more effectively with your employees?

_____

2. How else can you use the Internet, a company intranet, or blogs to have a positive impact on team building?

_____

productive than employees who work in the office."[53] Wireless technology, Voice-over Internet Protocol (VoIP), webcams, video phones, and online collaboration tools have made this option more realistic and cost-effective for a growing number of companies and their employees.[54]

Deciding to Implement Information Technology

All the technology tools discussed in this chapter provide options and benefits for both the employer and the employee. The key to evaluating these for potential implementation is to assess the potential return on investment to determine if it is worth the time, energy, and expense to implement and train employees.

As you have learned in this chapter, technology can have a positive impact on quality, performance, and productivity. But it also can lead to distractions and negative impacts. Your role as supervisor is to determine what is best for you, your team, and your organization. It is your job to help foster a "safe computing" environment.

SUMMARY

1. Technology tools in the workplace are designed to promote safety and to help employees to be more efficient and effective. Examples include applications such as electronics, robots, imaging, and communication. Computer information systems use computer technology for data input, processing, and the output or production of useful information.

2. Protecting information systems should be a priority. Potential threats include (1) computer viruses, (2) internal theft of data, (3) external hacking, and (4) theft of computer hardware. To reduce the risk, organizations should develop (1) policies for information systems security, (2) password

and authentication guidelines, (3) login and logout procedures, (4) encryption standards, (5) access control, (6) Internet and e-mail regulations, and (7) an ongoing training program.

3. Technology has changed the way people work, communicate, entertain, and socialize. Advocates argue that technology has had a positive impact on productivity, while opponents believe that the volume of e-mail and information available on the Internet combined with constant connectivity provide more distractions.

4. Companies are monitoring employee computer use, including website connections, e-mail, keystrokes

and time spent on the computer. In addition, many organizations also have video surveillance in place. The key is to implement company security initiatives with employee support and buy-in.

5. The rapid growth in Internet tools allows users to find information on just about any topic imaginable. The benefits of these advances are extraordinary for business people, students, and the average citizen. Of course, there are also potential negative consequences if the users are careless or fall victim to a malicious computer attack. Internet resources that are affecting business people

today include (1) blogs, (2) social network sites, (3) video sharing, and (4) reference sites.

6. Examples of computer technology tools that supervisors can use to positively impact their organization include (1) performance evaluation software to complete the evaluation process in a timely and consistent manner; (2) telecommuting options that provide employees with the flexibility to work from home; and (3) a company or department intranet to post policy and procedure manuals, conduct online training, and communicate with employees.

TERMS TO UNDERSTAND

blog, p. 389
computer crime, p. 380
computer information systems,
　p. 379

computer virus, p. 381
employee data theft, p. 381
encryption, p. 383
external hacking, p. 382

intranet, p. 395
reference sites, p. 392
social network sites, p. 390
technology, p. 379

QUESTIONS FOR REFLECTION

1. What are the primary reasons for implementing technology tools in the workplace?

2. Why should supervisors be concerned about computer hackers?

3. Identify three forms of employee monitoring being used today and discuss the pros and cons of each.

4. How have computers had a positive impact on productivity?

5. What are three complaints users have about information technology that have a negative impact on productivity?

6. What is an intranet and how can it be used to improve organizational efficiency and effectiveness?

HANDS-ON ACTIVITIES

INTERNET RESEARCH

The Internet has changed how people work, learn, and communicate. In this chapter, we discussed various resources, including blogs, social networking sites, video sharing, and reference sites.

1. Visit one of the reference sites listed in this chapter and research a topic of interest to you that is related to supervision and business.

2. Write down the topic you selected and report on your findings. Include in your report a

discussion about the specific content, such as definitions, examples, comparisons to similar topics, identification of reference sources, and anything else you observed during this experience.

3. Considering that this is only one source and it may have been posted without editorial review or verification, how can you validate the accuracy of the information?

BLOGGING

Blogging is a way for people to share their opinions and knowledge about a topic on the Internet.

1. Identify a business blog and look for a thread related to supervision, leadership, motivation, productivity, technology, or another topic discussed in this class.

If you have never visited a blog before, try starting with one of the following blogs:

- http://www.businessweek.com/the_thread/ blogspotting/
- http://www.gizmodo.com
- http://www.lifehack.org

2. Discuss the content of the original posting as well as the additional comments posted.

3. How can a blog be beneficial or detrimental to a company?

Interview an Expert

Choose between five and ten friends, family, coworkers, and/ or strangers to interview about information technology resources impacting supervisors and businesspeople today. You may use the questions below and/or add your own. Prepare a brief summary of your findings and what you learned from the people you interviewed.

Questions

1. What information technology tool is most useful to you at work? Please explain why.

2. What computer technology tool is the biggest distraction and/or has a negative impact on your productivity? Explain your answer.

3. Do you know if your boss monitors your computer activity or uses video surveillance? How do you feel about this?

4. Do you have a profile or page posted on a social networking site? If yes, how often do you visit this site and what are your primary activities?

5. Have you ever read and/or posted to a blog? If yes, how many times? What was your reason for blogging?

6. What are your favorite Internet reference sites? Why?

7. What do you think are the biggest technology threats?

8. How do you protect yourself and your computer from a malicious attack?

9. How can the Internet be used to help employers be more efficient and/or effective in achieving their goals?

YOU DECIDE

CASE STUDY 14.1
Responsible Blogging and Social Networking for Work

Mimi is the supervisor for a local electronics store that also sells and installs home theaters. The store has a loyal following and an excellent reputation. The business recently expanded, which required the hiring of three new people. Eldrick, one of the new employees, has outstanding skills and expertise with all of the products the store sells. He is also a regular Internet user, blogger, and social networker. He is very enthusiastic about his new job. In fact, he placed a lengthy posting on his MySpace page describing the store, his coworkers, and a few of the customers. He did not use anyone's name, but he used enough details that people familiar with the store knew whom he was talking about. One of his comments described his boss as "really nice and pretty hot." Mimi learned about the posting from a customer.

Questions

1. If you were Mimi, how would you handle this situation?

2. How can Mimi leverage Eldrick's interest in Internet resources to benefit the store?

3. What are the potential consequences if Mimi ignores this situation?

SUPERVISOR'S TOOLKIT

One of the responsibilities supervisors have is to foster a safe computing environment. Company computers and the data stored on these systems are vulnerable to attacks from current and former employees as well as external hackers. Prepare a few documents related to safe computing that you can add to your supervisor's toolkit.

1. Develop a list of information systems security policies and procedures that you think every office should have.

3. What guidelines should be followed in creating passwords?

3. What are three steps you can take to protect your computers from a malicious attack by an external hacker?

CHAPTER 15

It's All About People and Self-Awareness

Learning Objectives

1. Define self-awareness and discuss the importance of knowing one's strengths and limitations.

2. Discuss the value of self-awareness in communicating at work, identifying the need for change, and achieving peak performance.

3. Describe self-assessment tools you can use to discover your learning style, assess your communication skills, and identify what motivates you.

4. Compare tangible skills to soft skills, and identify tools you can use to learn about you and your employees' interests, talents, knowledge, and skills.

5. Analyze assessment results to become a more effective supervisor and identify strategies for using information about your employees to set them up for success.

Straight Talk From the Field

Michael Mallette is now retired after a career that spanned 40 years. During his 18 years at Motorola, Mike held a diverse array of managerial and executive positions in personnel, sales, and marketing.

QUESTION: *From your career-long perspective, what can you tell us about the importance of supervisors and managers knowing their own strengths and limitations?*

RESPONSE:

At one point in my career at Motorola, I was the firm's sales director in Japan. One question that seemingly always arose when being given any performance review was, "What do you want to be when you grow up?" I was always comfortable with saying "I have no idea! All I can hope for is to be given a meaningful and challenging job, have the opportunity to make a positive contribution, and be fairly rewarded for it."

Following two years as a drafted Military Policeman in the U.S. Army, I accepted a position as the Customer Service Manager for an engineering company that manufactured aircraft evacuation slides and U.S. Coast Guard–approved rescue equipment. After a year in that position, I was asked to assume the job of Production Control Manager, where I was responsible for scheduling all of the plant's manufacturing. From there I moved on to sales. After five years, I had an "epiphany" that resulted in my returning to graduate school to get a masters degree in psychology and then a teaching certificate that resulted in me teaching high school English for five years.

Then came another epiphany! Early one morning, I was correcting some papers in the faculty office and came to the conclusion that I could very well be reviewing ". . . these very same papers forty years from now!" So, later that day, I called a good friend of mine who was an executive at Motorola. I asked him if he knew of anyone in the employment office who might grant me a courtesy interview so that I could determine if there were opportunities at Motorola for which I might qualify. He agreed to meet and told me to bring a résumé. I will always be grateful to him for taking it and calling a contact he had in Recruiting and Staffing and arranging my first interview with a gentleman named Don Schepp. This fortunate circumstance resulted in my first position at Motorola.

Don Schepp and I shared an immediate affinity for each other. Don had been a recruiter for Motorola for many years. He later told me that he had agreed to interview me only as a favor to my friend; he had no positions for which he was actively recruiting. In the course of our conversation, we determined that, based on my experience, there were many potential areas for which I might qualify. All of a sudden, Don said, "What would you think about doing what I do?" I was so naïve that I immediately thought to myself, "Can this really be a full-time job?" But I was smart enough to skip that question and simply responded, "That sounds exciting. What can you tell me about it?"

Don said he was about to get a new boss, a former peer who had just been promoted from his previous position as Manager of College Recruiting. The new boss would be looking to hire a replacement for his previous position: "Would that hold any appeal for me?" I immediately said, "Yes!"

Well, about eight weeks later, after many, many interviews and my constant follow-up as to the status of the position, I was offered the job and immediately accepted it.

My initial interviewer, Don Schepp, and I became very close friends, now working as peers on the same staff. As I did throughout my career, I used to get to work around 5:30 in the morning, well before most other employees. This made the 2–3 hours before the start of the actual work day my most productive. Don used to arrive early as well, usually about 7:00 A.M. He would wander over to my office and we would have coffee and talk. I respected Don and considered him to be absolutely one of the finest human beings I've ever met. But Don had one character flaw that I always found amusing: Don always saw the glass as being significantly less than "half-full." His first reaction to any idea was always negative. "That was tried

401

before—it failed." "That would never work." "Ha! You'll never be able to 'sell' that."

One morning Don arrived at my door, leaned his head around the corner, and said with a big grin "You son of a gun!"

I kind of flinched and asked, "What did I do?" He came in, sat down, and started talking. "I was driving in this morning and was thinking of all the changes that have occurred around here since you came—and all of them have been successful. I got to thinking . . . with every one of these ideas, I told you they would never work. Then I realized, you've been pumping me for information every morning! I believe I've been pretty important in all of this."

I looked at this wonderful man and said "Don, I can't begin to tell you how important!! You've been invaluable. When you were telling me all the things we couldn't do, you were actually telling me about all the things we could do! You provided the solutions by telling me where all the 'land mines' were, the history of any previous attempts, and where all of the pitfalls were. I would never have been able to do all this without you and I will always be grateful." We just sat there in silence, smiling at each other, both content with our relationship.

The lessons I learned from this experience remained with me for the rest of my career.

NAÏVETÉ is never a weakness, but a major strength. What is required is but a modicum of intelligence and a creative mind. Bolster that with the ability to work with others so as to capitalize on and learn from their knowledge and experience. To gain the support of your associates, you must be willing to admit your own lack of knowledge and experience. This will require a certain measure of self-confidence and humility. But if you are comfortable with this, you then can provide a vision of where you wish to go and garner their support in the achievement of significant goals.

True DIVERSITY goes far beyond race or gender. It is the ability to capture all the strengths of our fellow employees, by valuing their opinions, capitalizing on their intelligence and experience, and focusing their strengths and supporting them on achieving the "vision" you've provided.

Chapter Outline

There are a wide variety of self-assessment and professionally administered tools available today that evaluate everything from learning styles to communication skills. Although these tools can be helpful to supervisors when hiring, coaching, and training employees, they need to be used with caution, because no tool is a perfectly valid and reliable predictor of actual job performance.

One of the keys to personal improvement and professional growth is an accurate assessment of our own strengths and limitations. The assessment tools we discuss in this chapter will help you improve the accuracy of your personal evaluation and improve your self-awareness. In addition, you can use many of these tools with your employees to help them achieve their goals and improve performance.

In this chapter, we discuss the value of self-awareness and introduce a few assessment tools you can use in the workplace. We will also suggest ways to incorporate knowledge gained from these evaluations to become a more effective supervisor.

Self-Awareness

Self-awareness has been identified as an essential skill for succeeding as a supervisor and organizational leader in the twenty-first century.[1] Before we embark on a discussion about the value of self-awareness, let's take a moment to examine this encompassing term. NHS Institute for Innovation and Improvement defines **self-awareness** as "knowing your own strengths and limitations and understanding your own emotions and the impact of your behavior on others in diverse situations."[2] What this definition emphasizes is that individuals are capable of understanding their personal strengths and limitations and how they affect others.

THEY SAID IT BEST

Self-awareness enables us to stand apart and examine even the way we "see" ourselves—our self-paradigm, the most fundamental paradigm of effectiveness. It affects not only our attitudes and behaviors, but also how we see other people.
—STEPHEN R. COVEY

Source: Stephen R. Covey, *The 7 Habits of Highly Effective People* (New York: Free Press, 2004), 66–67.

Positive Psychology

A key aspect of the ongoing self-assessment process is identifying your personal strengths. In fact, many researchers and psychologists believe that the best way to improve performance is to focus on your strengths, potential, and capabilities.[3] Psychologist Tom Muha observes that when people focus on their positive attributes, personal change and improvement begin to take place. He emphasizes that if people focus on creating positive interactions, they will naturally reduce the number of negative thoughts and interactions they experience. In fact, according to Muha, "People who surpass the 5:1 threshold of positive to negative interactions have the highest levels of success and satisfaction."[4] In other words, if you strive for at least five positive interactions or experiences for every one negative interaction, you will significantly increase your

When people focus on their positive attributes, personal change and improvement begin to take place.

self-awareness
knowing your own strengths and limitations, and your impact on others.

chances for a successful and satisfying life. These interactions can be with other people or with activities (e.g., when working independently on a project). This is why it is so important to focus on setting your employees up for success. The more positive interactions they have with both their coworkers and their work, the more likely they are to achieve their goals.[5]

Strength Assessment

In essence, Muha is suggesting that supervisors and employees can achieve better results and be happier workers by focusing on their individual strengths and the positive characteristics of their team members. Rather than generating negative energy by pointing out people's flaws and errors, supervisors need to generate positive, productive energy by leveraging people's strengths.

Many people have a difficult time initially identifying their strengths. Confusion often arises because individuals are not sure what is meant by the term *strength*. In this chapter, we refer to *strengths* as any personal attributes that help a person achieve success. Examples of personal strengths include general abilities such as being a good listener, problem solver, or creative thinker. They also include personality characteristics such as being patient, energetic, and enthusiastic. Additionally, strengths may involve specific skills such as computer programming, welding, or cutting hair. The point is to identify the things you do well along with your personal attributes that contribute to your overall ability to achieve your goals. The other reason why people have a difficult time identifying their strengths is because they are reluctant to appear boastful. However, it is important to recognize your positive characteristics because they are the foundation for your success. This level of self-awareness will allow you to make career and personal decisions that leverage your strengths and minimize the impact of any limitations.

KNOWLEDGE TO ACTION

1. Make a list of three of your strengths and/or positive attributes.
    _____

2. Select one of your strengths and make a list of reasons why this is of value to your current employer or will be of value to a future employer.
    _____

Now, think about how your strengths are useful and beneficial to you at work. To illustrate this point, imagine that you are a supervisor in a college advising department. You have identified *good listener* as one of your strengths. Reflect for a moment on how being a good listener is valuable at work. Listed below are a few possible statements. Consider adding your own ideas for why it would be valuable to have a supervisor in the advising department who is a good listener.

■ I am able to serve our students better because I take the time to listen and really learn what their needs are before making any recommendations.

■ I also think it helps me as a supervisor as I am able to learn more about my employees, their ideas, and their interests. This actually allows our entire team to be more successful.

Limitations Can Lead to Opportunity

Many of us can prepare a list of personal limitations or weaknesses rather quickly. As mentioned above, identifying our strengths is more difficult. This difference traces at least partly to a cultural emphasis on achievement and high standards. We have a tendency to be harder on ourselves when analyzing our own performance. As with strengths, it is important to identify and confront our limitations. Many weaknesses can be overcome through education and training. For example, a person may identify her lack of experience and confidence with public speaking as a limitation, particularly if she plans on a career involving presentations. However, individuals can take a limitation like this and ultimately turn it into a strength by learning and practicing. There are some weaknesses and/or limitations that are more difficult to turn into a strength. These often involve emotional triggers. For instance, a supervisor acknowledged that one of his limitations was low tolerance for dishonest people. He had one employee who would make mistakes and then fabricate excuses and blame other employees for the errors. The supervisor was aware of his impatience and recognized that an employee lying to him triggered an angry emotional response that he needed to control.

Emotional Triggers

Self-aware individuals know which situations, actions, and outcomes trigger positive or negative emotions.

Self-aware individuals know which situations, actions, and outcomes trigger either positive or negative feelings and emotions. As the previous example illustrated, the supervisor was aware of the fact that lying triggered his angry emotional reaction. The key to managing emotional triggers is recognizing how we handle the reaction and understanding the impact this reaction has on the people around us. Impacts on others can range from creating fear to building confidence.

Self-aware people take the time to evaluate themselves and their life experiences. They also reflect on various situations and how they react to them. This includes examining their decisions, choice of words and actions, along with their feelings and emotions.[6] This is not a one-time event. Instead, it is a lifelong journey to remain self-aware as part of a personal commitment to continuous improvement.

As a supervisor, you need to be aware of your own strengths as well as the skills and attributes of your employees. We will look at self-assessment tools in more detail.

KNOWLEDGE TO ACTION

1. Make a list of three of your personal limitations.

   _____

2. How can you turn these weaknesses into strengths?

   _____

Getting Started with Self-Assessment

No assessment tool is 100% accurate.

Assessment tools, whether they are self-administered or handled by an expert in the field, need to be viewed as just one step in the journey to becoming more self-aware. No assessment tool, even a professionally administered one, is 100% accurate. Many survey-style tools rely on subjective questions and answers that change depending on the person's mood or status at work. Supervisors and managers may incorrectly use assessment tools on their own to make personnel decisions. But, when used properly, evaluation tools can provide an excellent baseline for discussion and improving overall self-awareness. In fact, the results of personal assessments are just the start.

The ideal scenario for completing the self-assessment process involves:

- Completing the assessment
- Evaluating the results
- Reflecting on your personal goals
- Reflecting on organizational goals
- Meeting with your supervisor
- Preparing an action plan—this should incorporate feedback and insight from assessments to leverage your strengths and identify steps to improve areas you deem appropriate for personal improvement
- Discussing plans with your supervisor for follow-up and receiving ongoing feedback

Supervisors need to follow this process with each of their employees. It is essential that everyone understand that the assessment tools will not be used in a negative manner. The reason for participating is to identify strengths and styles, and to look for opportunities to benefit both the individual and the organization. Companies frequently have their employees do assessments in groups and teams. Emily Dancyger King, director of executive training at banking giant Citigroup, observed, "It's a very powerful lever for change, for them to become a high-performing group, if they understand what each other's styles are and how they interact."[7]

It is essential that everyone understand that the assessment tools will not be used in a negative manner.

The Value of Self-Awareness

Self-aware supervisors, managers, and organizational leaders ultimately achieve better results with a happier workforce. As a bonus, they enjoy greater personal satisfaction. They also are better prepared to respond to challenges, solve problems, and handle adversity.[8] Self-aware supervisors and employees are of great value to the organization. Three major benefits of self-awareness are (1) improved communication, (2) positive change, and (3) peak performance.

Increasing Self-Awareness Through Good Communication

Supervisor who are in touch with their own strengths and emotions are better equipped to communicate with employees, peers, managers, and customers. They

Successful supervisors and their employees recognize the value of self-awareness. When team members assess their skills and abilities, they are better prepared to take advantage of their strengths and contribute to the team's success. Shortcomings become one's learning agenda. In addition, groups comprised of self-aware individuals are typically more effective in achieving their goals in an enjoyable environment where everyone shares in the positive results.

© Radius Images/Jupiter Images

also are in a much better position to help develop their people. A significant portion of a supervisor's success in achieving organizational goals is tied to individual and team performance. Therefore, it is essential for all members of high-performing teams to be engaged, self-aware, and mindful of one another's strengths and limitations. By communicating openly and honestly about team members' skills and abilities, people are more likely to help one another accomplish a task or goal. If someone (including the supervisor) makes a mistake in this sort of positive climate, people are more likely to work together to solve the problem rather than wasting time placing blame. As we said earlier, increasing the positive experiences that arise from a focus on strengths will achieve better results than generating negative energy.

Recognizing Triggers Can Lead to Positive Change

Another benefit to being self-aware as a supervisor is that it improves your ability to understand your emotional triggers. Recognizing behavior or actions that make you angry is an essential first step in developing a balanced approach to supervision. Once you know your triggers, you can anticipate your reaction and proactively turn a negative experience into a more positive, effective event. For example, suppose you have an employee who never turns in his end-of-month reports on time. Your routine response to his lateness is to yell at him or send him a flaming e-mail. As you practice your self-awareness skills, however, you realize your emotional response to the employee's failure to meet the reporting deadline is a combination of anger and frustration. In fact, you may even take it personally, as a clear sign of disrespect. The employee now expects you to yell at him. So your angry outbursts do not get the desired result. As a self-aware supervisor, you have the opportunity to take your broader knowledge and use it for positive change. We will discuss specific strategies for implementing positive change through self-awareness later in this chapter.

Peak Performance

peak performance
when individuals are at their best, working at their highest level to achieve their goals.

When you have achieved the level of **peak performance**, you are working at your best. You are focused, efficient, and achieving your goals. You are "in the zone," so to speak. Do you know how to get to that level? Do you even know when you are at your best? Many do not, but it is important for people to recognize when they are most productive and when it may be time to take a break and get refreshed. Self-aware individuals know their peak performance times, their ideal work setting, and what reenergizes them.[9] The goal is to personally recognize and benefit from this information.

As a supervisor, it is important that you solicit this information from your employees. This will help you set them up for success by scheduling them to work during their peak times or switching them to activities that increase their energy levels and creativity. For example, some of your classmates and coworkers may be "morning people." Others are more productive at night. If possible, try to schedule your most difficult or challenging tasks during your peak times. Each individual's life has a natural rhythm—so work with it, not against it.

KNOWLEDGE TO ACTION

1. At what time of day are you most productive and creative? Explain why.

   _____

2. What changes can you make in managing your academic, work, and social life to take advantage of your peak times and ideal work locations?

   _____

Personal Discovery

As mentioned earlier, the use of self-assessment tools is not an exact science. The results are primarily based on diverse responses to subjective questions. However, these tools certainly can provide insight into personal patterns, preferences, and perceptions. Successful individuals recognize the value of lifelong learning. As you strive for continuous improvement throughout your career, knowing your learning style(s) will help you achieve your goals in a more effective and efficient manner. In this section, we introduce three different tools for personal discovery: (1) your learning style, (2) your communication skills, and (3) what motivates you. In addition, we will provide an overview of several widely used assessment tools available today that are typically administered by specially trained and/or certified individuals.

Learning Styles

Recall from Chapter 7 our discussion about learning styles (also referred to as *channels* or *modalities*). In this section, we explore three frequently assessed styles: visual, auditory, and kinesthetic. We will explain these styles in more detail and provide suggestions for how to use this information to improve your learning. But first take a few moments to complete the *VAK (visual-auditory-kinesthetic) learning style indicators self-test* in Table 15.1 to discover your learning style(s).

VISUAL

Visual learners can typically recall what they see, read, or observe and they prefer to look at pictures or watch others demonstrating a skill, rather than simply being told how to do something. Therefore, lectures, podcasts, and audio instruction are probably not going to be as helpful. Learning through demonstrations, photos, diagrams, film, and handouts is more effective for the visual learner.

TABLE 15.1
Learning Styles Survey

This VAK learning style indicators assessment can be used as a questionnaire or 'test' to assess your own preferred learning style or styles, or the VAK learning styles of your people. Score each statement and then add the totals for each column to indicate learning style dominance and mix. Your learning style is also a reflection of the type of person you are—how you perceive things and the way that you relate to the world. This questionnaire helps you to improve your understanding of yourself and your strengths. **There are no right or wrong answers**. Simply select one response for each item and total the three columns. The column with the highest total is your preferred learning style.

VAK learning style indicators		Visual	Auditory	Kinesthetic
1	When seeking travel directions I...	look at a map	ask for spoken directions	follow my nose or maybe use a compass
2	When cooking a new dish I...	follow a recipe	call a friend for explanation	follow my instinct, tasting as I cook
3	I tend to say...	"show me"	"tell me"	"let me try"
4	When shopping generally I tend to...	look and decide	discuss with shop staff	try on, handle, or test
5	Learning a new skill I...	watch what the teacher is doing	talk through with the teacher exactly what I am supposed to do	like to give it a try and work it out as I go along by doing it
6	Choosing from a restaurant menu I...	imagine what the food will look like	talk through the options in my head	imagine what the food will taste like
7	When concentrating I...	focus on the words or pictures in front of me	discuss the problem and possible solutions in my head	move around a lot, fiddle with pens and pencils, and touch unrelated things
8	I remember things best by...	writing notes or keeping printed details	saying them aloud or repeating words and key points in my head	doing and practicing the activity, or imagining it being done
9	When explaining something to someone, I tend to...	show them what I mean	explain to them in different ways until they understand	encourage them to try and talk them through the idea as they try
10	My main interests are...	photography or watching films or people-watching	listening to music or listening to the radio or talking to friends	physical/sports activities, fine wines, fine foods, or dancing
11	Most of my free time is spent...	watching television	talking to friends	doing physical activity or making things
12	I find it easiest to remember...	faces	names	things I have done
	Totals	**Visual**	**Auditory**	**Kinesthetic/physical**

Adapted from ©VAK learning styles self-test: Victoria Chislett MSc and Alan Chapman 2005. Not to be sold or published. Sole risk with user. This learning styles self-assessment tool is a rough guide to individual learning styles only—it is not a scientifically validated instrument. With thanks also to Anita Mountain and Chris Davidson for their advice in creating this tool.

Source: © V. Chislett MSc & A. Chapman, 2005. From http://www.businessballs.com/vaklearningstylestest.htm. More details and tests at www.businessballs.com.

To improve retention, visual learners typically diagram concepts, color-code groups of material, and use symbols or pictures to link information to images. If they are taking a test, they will often recall the information by first remembering the image or picture and then the associated information.[10] Most people are visual learners, and everyone tends to learn more when both visual and auditory methods are combined.[11]

AUDITORY

Auditory learners are verbal learners. They are far more likely to retain information that they have heard. Subtle differences in speech patterns such as speed, volume, and tone or point of emphasis contribute to their understanding of the message. Material presented in writing is less useful. However, they can benefit from writing down or outlining what they have heard. In addition, learning in teams or groups where concepts are discussed is effective in reinforcing concepts. In contrast to visual learners, who prefer to be shown what to do, verbal learners would rather be told how to do something.[12] Podcasts, phone conversations, and audio recordings are effective tools for auditory learners.

KINESTHETIC

Kinesthetic learners are considered to be experiential, hands-on people. Rather than listening, reading, or observing, they learn by doing. Kinesthetic learners thrive in lab-type settings, simulators, and role playing. Every opportunity they have to personally engage in an activity helps them to learn and retain new information.[13] Not surprisingly, kinesthetic learners may have a difficult time sitting still for long periods of time. For example, a three-hour lecture would be very tedious for them. On the other hand, spending three hours working with a group on a challenging real-life project would be much more productive and enjoyable.

THE IMPORTANCE OF LEARNING STYLES

So why is it important to understand your personal learning style(s)? By understanding how you learn best, you can take advantage of your strengths and compensate for your limitations. This applies to both school and on-the-job activities.

For example, students who consider themselves visual learners, because they learn best from reading and viewing pictures and images, can enhance their learning by using handouts, diagrams, and images in their textbook for review. Similarly, visual learners at work are likely to learn their job more quickly if they refer to training

KNOWLEDGE TO
ACTION

1. How do you learn best? Which of the learning modalities appeals to you the most?

_____

2. With this knowledge, what modifications can you make in your reading, note taking, classroom participation, and studying to be a more effective and efficient student?

_____

manuals with diagrams and photos or by watching a video demonstrating how to operate a piece of equipment.

Communication Skills

As you know, effective communication skills are vital to supervisory success. Most people are good at a certain aspect of communication. For example, some people are excellent presenters, while others are good listeners. A fortunate few are masters of all forms of communication. To see where you stand, complete the self-test in Table 15.2 to assess your communication skills.

TABLE 15.2
Communication Assessment

Are You a Good Communicator?

The following test, devised by Theo Theobald and Cary Cooper, authors of *Shut Up and Listen: The Truth About How to Communicate at Work,* will help you to discover how good your communication skills are. You can then look at the diagnostic solutions to improve your performance. Choose option a, b, or c from each question and then check your score.

1. When other people are talking to you, do you tend to:
   a. devote your entire attention to them?
   b. listen to them, but your mind wanders from time to time?
   c. rarely listen, with your mind wandering a lot?

2. When presenting a case, do you tend to:
   a. ensure that the people listening are given ample opportunity to intervene?
   b. sometimes allow people to intervene when you notice they want to?
   c. like to finish before taking any questions or clarifications?

3. In trying to convince people to do something, do you tend to:
   a. present only rational arguments?
   b. present rational arguments but use some emotional messages?
   c. appeal to them on an emotional level?

4. Before communicating an important message to people at work, do you tend to:
   a. plan thoroughly what you will say?
   b. think through what you are going to say but not plan it precisely?
   c. do little planning, go with the flow, and communicate in the here-and-now?

5. If somebody had not performed well on a job and you were the boss, would you:
   a. be fairly assertive and direct about his or her performance?
   b. try to communicate the problem calmly but also with some assertiveness?
   c. try to support the person and let him or her know what was done wrong?

6. If you had to fire some people at work, would you:
   a. let the personnel officer do it?
   b. leave most of the responsibility with personnel but offer the opportunity for discussion with yourself?
   c. see each of them face to face?

7. When you arrive at work, do you tend to:
   a. plan all your communications by listing the meetings, e-mails, and calls you need to make?
   b. respond to what comes in throughout the day?
   c. do some planning but build in a contingency for unexpected incoming tasks?

8. Do you view text messaging as:
   a. a way of keeping in touch with friends to make social arrangements?
   b. the primary method of keeping colleagues updated?
   c. a way of alerting workmates to important news?

(continues)

9. Do you think the use of good spelling and grammar is:
   a. a must in communication?
   b. an outdated concept because communication is now less formal?
   c. nice, but not essential?

10. In vital decision-making meetings, do you tend to:
    a. talk more than you listen?
    b. listen more than you talk?
    c. do both in equal measure?

SCORING

	Answer Option = Value		
Question	a	b	c
1	3	2	1
2	2	3	1
3	1	3	2
4	3	2	1
5	2	3	1
6	1	2	3
7	2	1	3
8	2	1	3
9	3	1	2
10	1	3	2

What your score indicates:

21–30

You are already a good communicator—thoughtful, passionate, and prepared to listen. You take time to consider how the other party is feeling and are committed to improving your communication continually, both in its style and in your command of new technologies.

11–20

You have a good instinct for communication, which will serve you well in most business situations. Most of the time, you have planned fairly well but take time to think about what you are portraying to others. You are assertive in your actions. Occasionally you may feel you have not presented your best side, or may have failed to justify your arguments because you have not had sufficient time to think them through.

1–10

Although you understand the basics of communication, you need to take some time to fine-tune your style. You feel that there are too many occasions when other people don't seem to understand your point, or take up a contrary stance for no good reason. You may often get bogged down with information overload and need to find ways of filtering incoming messages to free up more time. It might be that you are not making the best use of the available technology and could do with brushing up on tools and techniques.

Source: "Are you a good communicator? Public appointments," Sunday Times (London, England) (April 18, 2004): 13.

How can you apply these results in the workplace? If you scored high (between 21 and 30), take advantage of your outstanding communication skills and let people know about your skills. Let your manager know that effective communication is one of your strengths and discuss how your talents may benefit the organization. Consider volunteering for activities that require good communication skills. If you scored lower on the scale, you really have two options: (1) passively accept this information and move on or (2) actively identify opportunities to learn, practice, and ultimately improve your communication skills. This second option will require further investigation to determine where to focus your energy. Perhaps you are an excellent listener, but you are not as effective explaining your ideas.

If you are a supervisor, it can be instructive to ask your employees to complete the survey in Table 15.2 to gain a better understanding of their communication skills. This will facilitate placing them in work situations best suited to their skills. In addition, you can use this knowledge to fine-tune your employees' personal development plans.

KNOWLEDGE TO ACTION

1. Reflect on your communication survey results to determine where your limitations are.

2. Brainstorm with your classmates to identify learning experiences and other opportunities to improve in these areas.

What Motivates You?

Understanding what motivates your employees is essential for effective supervision.

As you learned in Chapter 8, understanding what motivates you is one of the keys to achieving your goals. Accordingly, understanding what motivates your employees is essential for effective supervision. Use the exercise, Work Values Quiz, in Table 15.3 to assess what kind of work and work conditions you like. The Work Values Quiz can also help you determine your work motivations, your preferred work setting, how you like to interact with others, and your work style.

You may complete this quiz without using the scoring system. This does not diminish its value, as this is an excellent tool for increasing your self-awareness and expressing your individuality. Review your responses and evaluate your current situation. Are your academic, work, and social decisions consistent with your motivators? In other words, if your answer to "I'm motivated by work that allows me to help other people, either individually or in small groups" was "Important," are you currently working in an area that provides this opportunity? If not, what changes do you need to make?

Keep this tool handy and reassess at least once a year. As we get older, our interests and motivators will frequently change as our priorities change and we gain on-the-job and life experience. Moreover, this is an excellent tool to use with your employees to discover more about what their interests and what motivates each of them. You may want to incorporate this self-assessment tool into your annual review, goal setting, and personal-development meetings with your people. If you would like to complete this survey online and have the scoring results, go to Canada's Job Training Website at https://www.jobsetc.ca/toolbox/quizzes/values_quiz.do?lang=e.

Professional Assessment Tools

HR-Guide.com lists over thirty personality tests and more than one hundred skill-specific aptitude tests used to evaluate everything from accounting knowledge to singing skills

TABLE 15.3
Work Values Quiz

Your values are important clues to what kind of work and work conditions you would like. The Work Values Quiz can help you determine your work motivations, your preferred work setting, how you like to interact with others, and your work style.

Contains 33 questions. Approximate completion time: 10 minutes

My Work Motivations	Important	Somewhat Important	Not Important
The idea of making money motivates me a great deal.	☐	☐	☐
I'm motivated by work that allows me to help other people, either individually or in small groups.	☐	☐	☐
I'm not interested in managing other people. I'm motivated by work that allows me to manage just myself.	☐	☐	☐
Money is not as important to me as a personal sense of satisfaction.	☐	☐	☐
I want work that absorbs me, even if it takes up my leisure time.	☐	☐	☐
I'm motivated by work that will improve the world.	☐	☐	☐
It's important to me to get public recognition for the work that I do.	☐	☐	☐
I'm motivated by work that will lead to a management position.	☐	☐	☐
I want work that leaves me leisure time for my family and friends.	☐	☐	☐

My Preferred Work Setting	Important	Somewhat Important	Not Important
I would like to travel and experience different cultures and places.	☐	☐	☐
I want a calm, peaceful work setting.	☐	☐	☐
I would like to work outside all or some of the time.	☐	☐	☐
I like work that is physically challenging.	☐	☐	☐
I prefer indoor work.	☐	☐	☐
I want work that challenges my intellectual capacities.	☐	☐	☐
I want work that doesn't involve travel.	☐	☐	☐
I enjoy a workplace with lots of fast-paced activity.	☐	☐	☐

How I Like to Interact with Others	Important	Somewhat Important	Not Important
I like to work independently with little or no supervision.	☐	☐	☐
I like work that lets me persuade or negotiate with others.	☐	☐	☐
I like to compete and put my skills and abilities against others.	☐	☐	☐
I would like to work with the public.	☐	☐	☐
I want work where I set and meet my own personal goals.	☐	☐	☐
I want work where I get to interact with a team of other people.	☐	☐	☐
I prefer to work away from the public.	☐	☐	☐
I want work where I can influence the attitudes or opinions of others.	☐	☐	☐

My Work Style	Important	Somewhat Important	Not Important
I like work where I can solve problems and decide how things should be done.	☐	☐	☐
I enjoy work that has fixed hours and a set schedule.	☐	☐	☐
I want work with responsibilities that change frequently.	☐	☐	☐
I want work that lets me use my creativity to think up new ways to do things.	☐	☐	☐
I want the freedom to work to my own schedule.	☐	☐	☐
I enjoy work that requires attention to detail and accuracy.	☐	☐	☐
I prefer a work situation where my responsibilities are the same every day.	☐	☐	☐
I want a work situation that's exciting and high-pressured.	☐	☐	☐

Source: Service Canada, Canada's Job and Training Website, http://www.jobsetc.ca/toolbox/quizzes/values_quiz.do?lang=e. Reproduced with the permission of the Minister of Public Works and Government Services, 2008.

(*American Idol*, anyone?). There are also tests that assess physical abilities, intelligence, memory, and other cognitive skills.[14] You may have heard of a few of the more common tests, such as the Myers-Briggs Type Indicator, the Tracom Social Style Model, the Predictive Index, and the Watson-Glaser Critical Thinking Appraisal.[15] In fact, your college or university may offer students the opportunity to take one or more of these tests and receive free consultation. Check with your advising and counseling office to learn about available services.

From a professional standpoint, you or your company may be considering using one of these tools now or in the future. Prior to selecting one or more of the tests, take the time to identify your goals and objectives for the project. This will help you narrow down which of the tests may be appropriate for your initiative. It is also helpful to get references from similar organizations and discuss how they used the assessment results for positive change.

Skills Inventory Tools

This looks stressful, doesn't it? Although assessment tests and pre-employment exams can be excellent tools for supervisors to learn more about the individuals they are evaluating, they can be stressful to the test taker. Make an effort to reduce anxiety and let the person know how the test results will be incorporated into the evaluation process.
© Bill Aron/PhotoEdit

Along with the self-assessment tools just examined, there are a variety of ways to identify your skills, talents, and strengths. These tools also can be used to learn more about your employees. Ask them to complete their own skills inventory and use the results to prepare plans for staffing, training, professional development, and future opportunities. Below is a brief overview of two useful personal inventory tools.[16] For each of the areas presented below, make a list of your skills and then self-evaluate your level of ability or mastery for each.

Skills Inventory Part 1 – Tangible (Hands-On) Skills

Tangible skills are readily observed and evaluated physical capabilities. Examples of tangible trade skills include welding, cooking, carpentry, driving, equipment operation and/or maintenance, and product assembly. Tangible office skills include typing, software programming, and creating spreadsheets. The list of tangible skills is potentially very long. Take a moment to write down all of your tangible skills, even if they appear to have no direct relationship with your career aspirations. You may discover someday that these skills are transferable to another job or industry.

Table 15.4 provides an example of a tangible skills inventory form to be used for your own self-assessment and/or employee assessments. You can use this to determine roles and responsibilities and to discuss training opportunities.

tangible skills
readily observed physical capabilities such as welding, cooking, carpentry, driving, and equipment operation.

soft skills
intangible skills such as communicating, leading, managing conflict, creativity, critical thinking, and problem solving.

Skills Inventory Part 2 – Intangible (Soft) Skills

Soft skills are arguably as important as tangible skills. **Soft skills** are wide ranging and include just about everything not considered a tangible skill. Examples of intangible skills are communicating, leading, managing conflict, creativity, critical thinking, problem solving, and financial management. Let's take a closer look at essential intangible skills for supervisors.

TABLE 15.4
Tangible Skills Inventory

In addition to listing skills, include in the Notes column additional information such as professional certifications or courses you have completed. In the Level of Mastery column, rate yourself on a scale of 1 to 3.

1 = beginner, entry-level, still need assistance with certain tasks
2 = intermediate, comfortable completing most tasks independently
3 = advanced, complete tasks independently, comfortable training others

Skill	Notes	Level of Mastery (1–3)
Forklift driver	Certified 12/01/08	2

COMMUNICATION SKILLS

As you know from completing your communication assessment, this area is of critical importance to supervisors. **Communication skills** encompass the ability to exchange information by speaking, listening, reading, and writing. Among the many examples are public speaking and making presentations, writing reports, reading, listening, receiving feedback, and articulating a thought or vision. Ideally, you want to prepare a list of your skills that demonstrates your ability to communicate effectively by exchanging information with employees, managers, and customers.

PROBLEM SOLVING

Supervisors are frequently challenged to solve problems on the job. It may be a customer complaint, an issue with a supplier, or a personnel problem. Soft skills generally associated with **problem solving** include assessing situations, gathering facts, investigating, validating information, identifying potential solutions, evaluating and weighing options, and making decisions.

INTERPERSONAL SKILLS

As we have noted throughout this book, supervision is all about accomplishing organizational goals through cooperative effort. Successful supervisors have excellent interpersonal skills. High on the list of essential interpersonal skills are interviewing, training/teaching, demonstrating trust, maintaining a positive and encouraging demeanor, being understanding yet firm, being compassionate, and resolving conflicts.

Use Table 15.5 to prepare your soft skills inventory. This tool is slightly different than the tangible skills inventory because it provides the opportunity to assess consistency and effectiveness. As with the tangible skills inventory, the soft skills

communication skills
the ability to exchange information by speaking, listening, reading, and writing.

problem solving
assessing a situation, identifying potential solutions, and ultimately making a decision.

TABLE 15.5
Soft Skills Inventory

List each of your soft skills. You may want to group related items together. For example, you may want to list all of your communication skills together. In the Notes column, you can include additional information such as specific examples of events or situations when you have demonstrated this skill; you can also identify courses or other learning opportunities that helped you develop these skills.

In the Consistency column, rate yourself on a scale of 1 to 3:
1 = sometimes
2 = most of the time
3 = always

In the Level of Effectiveness column, rate yourself on a scale of 1 to 3:
1 = occasionally achieve desired outcome
2 = usually achieve desired outcome
3 = always achieve desired outcome

Not all of the assessment categories may be relevant for every skill you identify. In addition, you may choose to add additional columns to track progress, list goals, or identify action items.

Skill	Notes	Consistency	Level of Effectiveness
Public speaking	Completed Dale Carnegie Workshop—08/21/09 (need more practice)	2	2

inventory is an excellent tool for supervisors to use with their employees to gain a better understanding of perceived soft skills.

The reflective exercises in this chapter will give you a better idea of where you excel and where you need a plan for learning new skills or improving in key areas. Remember to be realistic—embrace your talents and be honest about your limitations and developmental needs. Let us conclude by reviewing strategies for leveraging strengths in the workplace.

Be realistic and embrace your talents.

KNOWLEDGE TO ACTION

1. What are two of your most valuable tangible skills that are beneficial in your current job or are relevant in the career you plan to pursue? Explain why.

   _____

2. What are two of your most valuable soft (intangible) skills that are beneficial in your current job or are relevant in the career you plan to pursue? Explain why.

   _____

Leveraging Strengths in the Workplace

Learning about yourself and your employees is really just the beginning of a long journey of growth and development. What matters most is what you do with this information. There are a variety of ways to leverage the knowledge gained through personal and employee assessments. In this section, we start with an individual focus and self-reflection on skills and talents. Attention then turns to an example of how to implement change. We wrap up with how to help your employees use their self-awareness in a positive way.

You Have Become More Self-Aware—Now What?

After completing some self-assessments, taking the time to reflect, and perhaps incorporating feedback from a performance evaluation, most supervisors will have become more self-aware. The obvious question is, "Now what?" Our answer is twofold.

USE YOUR BEST SKILLS AND TALENTS

Find opportunities to put your skills and talents to use in an effort to help the organization.

First you want to put yourself in a position to fully exploit your talent. For example, if you have determined that you are a highly effective presenter, talk with your manager about getting opportunities to speak in front of groups. You may want to suggest ideas for presenting to customers, community members, higher-level management, or other employee groups. The point is to find opportunities to use your skills and talents to help the organization.

I'll help! These are magic words to any supervisor. Effective teams benefit from individuals volunteering to share their time, knowledge, and talents. "Find a need and fill it" are good words to live by, both on and off the job.
© Cultura/Alamy

ADDRESS YOUR LIMITATIONS

There is an old saying, "You can't be all things to all people." In other words, it is unrealistic to expect to be good at everything. During the assessment process, most people will identify a few limitations. Individuals in supervisory roles can choose to ignore their limitations, or they can be proactive by either improving themselves or hiring people who can do what they can't.[17]

- **Improve**—If you believe improving yourself is essential to your future success, then you need a personal growth and development plan.

- **Hire**—Surround yourself with people who have different talents, strengths, interests, and passions. Forming a diverse team with complementary skills is an important first step toward individual and organizational success.

Implementing Positive Change Through Self-Awareness

Let's return to our earlier example of the employee who turns in his end-of-month reports late. As a result of reflection and self-assessment, the supervisor realizes that this behavior triggers an angry, emotional response. Shifting this negative situation into a positive and productive experience will require a conscious effort to change. Here are some specific recommendations:

- Schedule a time to meet with the employee rather than yelling at him the first chance you get. This will minimize your emotional reaction and get the employee's attention (because something is different this time). You are not yelling at him as he walks down the hallway. Instead, you are inviting him to meet with you to discuss his strengths and your concerns. Ask him to come with a list of his strengths, positive attributes, and areas where he thinks he can improve. You've got him thinking.

- During your meeting, focus primarily on the person's strengths and contributions to the organization, rather than simply berating him for turning paperwork in late.

- Ask your employee how you can leverage his strengths to help the team or department become more efficient and effective.

- Of course, take some time to explore the pattern of lateness. You may be surprised to discover that the employee is fully aware of his chronic lateness. Perhaps he is just struggling with time management and planning because the reports are due on the last day of the month and his team typically has an increased workload during that week. You may never know unless you ask. Once you have a better understanding of the reason for the behavior, you can assess the situation with an eye toward problem solving. Evaluate the following:

  - Is it essential that the employee turn in the report on the last day of each month?

  - If the schedule cannot be changed, how can you help the employee turn in the reports on time? Perhaps you could team him up with another employee who is an exceptional planner and time manager?

■ The circumstances will be unique for each scenario. The key is to begin with a better understanding of your reaction to the situation, followed by a conscious effort to focus on the employee's strengths and how they contribute to overall success. By opening this positive and constructive dialogue, you are far more likely to arrive at a mutually beneficial solution. At the same time, you are also building a long-term relationship of trust with your employee.

Setting Your Employees Up for Success

As Michael Mallette said in the chapter opener, "true diversity goes far beyond race or gender. It is the ability to capture all the strengths of our fellow employees, by valuing their opinions, capitalizing on their intelligence and experience, and focusing their strengths and supporting them on achieving the 'vision' you've provided." This involves understanding their skills, talents, motivators, and interests. There are two primary areas where supervisors typically use this information to set their employees up for success: (1) job assignments and (2) professional-development planning.

JOB ASSIGNMENTS

One strategy for leveraging assessment results is to use this information when making job assignments. Complete an inventory of all of the tasks and responsibilities within your area. Include in this document a list of the skills necessary to be effective in completing these assignments. Next, list all employees and their skills, including levels of mastery. Assessment-driven job assignments are just plain good management.

PROFESSIONAL-DEVELOPMENT PLANNING

Another good use for personal assessment data is in identifying opportunities for growth and improvement. Imagine for a moment that you are the supervisor at a local insurance agency. One of your file clerks has a desire to become an insurance agent. However, during the assessment process she scored low in verbal communication, one of the essential skills for selling insurance. Rather than telling the employee she does not have the skills to be an agent, encourage her professional development. You can use the assessment information to discuss an action plan for the employee to improve her communication skills. Your organization may offer training programs, or you can suggest she attend courses or workshops. Once she has made the effort to learn about effective communication, provide her with the opportunity to practice her newly learned skills. Also consider mentoring her or teaming her up with one of your most talented agents who is an outstanding communicator.

Invest the time to learn about your employees' goals, skills, talents, and strengths.

As a supervisor, you have a unique opportunity to help other people achieve their own personal goals while also contributing to the overall success of the organization. Invest the time to learn about your employees' goals, skills, talents, and strengths. You will be better prepared to *set them up for success* while helping your team increase its efficiency and effectiveness.

SUMMARY

1. One of the essential skills for succeeding as an organizational leader and supervisor in the twenty-first century is self-awareness. Self-awareness is defined as knowing your strengths and limitations and understanding your emotions and the impact of your behavior on others in diverse situations. Self-aware individuals know what situations, actions, and outcomes trigger positive and negative emotions. Assessment tools provide useful information that can be used to leverage strengths and identify steps to improve areas where there are limitations. No assessment tool is 100% accurate. Therefore, it is essential that everyone understand that the assessment tools will not be used in a negative manner.

2. When supervisors and their employees are self-aware, there is value added to the organization. The benefits of self-awareness include (1) improved communication, (2) positive change, and (3) peak performance. Self-aware supervisors, managers, and organizational leaders ultimately achieve better results with a happier workforce, and they experience a higher level of personal satisfaction. Additionally, they are better prepared to respond to challenges, solve problems, and handle adversity.

3. Self-assessment tools can provide insight into personal patterns, preferences, and perceptions. As you strive for continuous improvement throughout your career, consider retaking the personal-discovery surveys in this chapter, including: *VAK Learning Style Indicators Self-Test, Are You a Good Communicator?*, and the Work Values Quiz. In addition, you may have the opportunity to take one of the commercially available assessment tools, such as the Myers-Briggs Type Indicator, the Tracom Social Style Model, the Predictive Index, or the Watson-Glaser Critical Thinking Appraisal.

4. Tangible skills can be observed and include skills such as welding, cooking, carpentry, driving, equipment operation, typing, software programming, and creating spreadsheets. Soft or intangible skills are quite broad and include just about everything that is not considered a tangible skill, such as communication skills, leadership, creativity, critical thinking, and problem solving. Skills inventory lists are used to identify various skills and to assess consistency, effectiveness, and level of mastery.

5. Learning about yourself and your employees is really just the beginning. What matters most is what you do with this information. There are a variety of strategies and options to leverage the knowledge gained through personal and employee assessments. Find opportunities to put your skills and talents to use, address limitations with proactive steps to improve or hire someone with the skills and talents you lack, and implement positive change. In addition, use assessment results to set employees up for success. This involves understanding their skills, talents, motivators, and interests. There are two primary areas where supervisors typically use this information: (1) job assignments and (2) professional-development planning.

TERMS TO UNDERSTAND

communication skills, p. 417
peak performance, p. 407

problem solving skills, p. 417
self-awareness, p. 403

soft skills (intangible skills), p. 416
tangible skills, p. 416

QUESTIONS FOR REFLECTION

1. Why is it beneficial for all employees to increase their self-awareness?
2. How can self-assessment tools be used by supervisors to set their employees up for success?
3. What steps can you take as a supervisor to use self-assessment tools to become more effective in your job?

4. What are some of the limitations of self-assessment tools?
5. How might you use the Work Values Quiz in a supervisory role?

HANDS-ON ACTIVITIES

STRENGTH ASSESSMENT

Review your list of strengths, tangible, and intangible skills that you started earlier in this chapter.

1. Add additional items to each of these lists.
2. Now add to these lists specific examples of how each of your positive attributes (strengths and skills) will benefit you in the future as a supervisor in the workplace.

SELF-ASSESSMENTS ONLINE

Visit one or more of the following websites to complete the free online assessment. Answer the questions below. (With permission from your instructor, you may identify another free or fee-based online survey tool to complete.)

Career Assessment
• The Princeton Review Career Quiz
  http://www.princetonreview.com/cte/quiz/

Learning Styles
• North Carolina State University, Index of Learning Styles Questionnaire
  http://www.engr.ncsu.edu/learningstyles/ilsweb.html

Personality Type
• Keirsey Temperament Sorter
  http://www.keirsey.com/

Motivation and Emotion
• Riso-Hudson Enneagram Type Indicator (RHETI) sample test
  http://www.9types.com/rheti/homepage.actual.html

After completing one of these assessments, answer the following questions:

1. What results are consistent with your self-perception and expectations?
2. Are there any surprises? Anything you were not aware of or did not expect?
3. How can you use the results of the survey and your increased self-awareness as a student to improve performance and/or to plan your career?

Interview an Expert

Ask five people who represent a diverse group (different ages, genders, ethnic backgrounds, etc.) to complete the Work Values Quiz that you completed earlier in the chapter.

Questions

1. After receiving everyone's results, prepare a brief report identifying what they have in common and what is different.

2. Were you surprised by any of the responses? Why or why not?

3. How is this information useful and relevant to supervisors?

YOU DECIDE

CASE STUDY 15.1
Employee Assessment

Frances was recently hired by a small local restaurant. The restaurant owners recruited Frances from another company because of her successful experience with expansion and opening new locations. One of her first objectives is to learn as much as possible about her current employees. She wants to quickly select a few top performers to be part of a team dedicated to opening new stores. Frances needs people who are not only technically good at their jobs—whether it is cooking, serving, or bartending—she also needs people who have excellent communication skills and are good problem solvers. In addition, she needs to prepare a training plan for her team members; therefore, she needs to have an idea of how they learn best.

Frances is trying to decide the most efficient method for learning about the current employees to decide who

she wants to recruit for her team. One approach she is considering is to shadow each person for a day. Another idea she has is to use one or more assessment tools. However, she has never used an assessment tool, so she is not sure what to use and how to get started.

Questions

1. How do you think Frances should proceed?

2. What are the benefits of shadowing a person?

3. What are the downsides to observing someone all day?

4. What assessment tool(s) would you recommend? Explain why and how she should use the results.

SUPERVISOR'S TOOLKIT

In this chapter, you have discovered a few tools for learning about yourself and your employees. Working in teams, prepare a list of resources available to supervisors and managers that may be helpful in increasing their own personal self-awareness as well as that of their employees. You may use the Internet or personal interviews with supervisors, friends, and family to discover what tools individuals and companies are using in this area. Your goal is to gain an understanding of tools and techniques available in an effort to develop your own strategy for encouraging self-awareness.

References

CHAPTER 1

1. This material is from the 'Lectric Law Library website at http://www.lectlaw.com (accessed April 13, 2008).
2. Tim Barnett, "Management Functions," in *Encyclopedia of Management*, 5th edn., ed. Marilyn M. Helms (Detroit: Gale, 2006): 493–495. *Gale Virtual Reference Library*. Gale. Anne Arundel Community College, Arnold, MD, http://go.galegroup.com.ezproxy.aacc.edu/ps/start.do?p=GVRL&u=aacc_ref (accessed February 2, 2008). Also see Henri Fayol, *General and Industrial Administration* (London: Isaac Pitman & Sons, Ltd., 1949).
3. Jenny Mero, "The Human Game Boy," *Fortune*, March 19, 2007: 50.
4. Paul Cherry, "Jump-Start Your Staff's Zest to Do Their Best," *Supervisor*, December 2007: 12–13; and "Boss 2.0, Redefining Role of Supervisors in Today's Work Environment," *The Baltimore Sun* December 3, 2006: H1.
5. Jeremy B. Dann, "How to Find a Hit as Big as Starbucks," *Business 2.0*, May 2004: 66.
6. Doris Christopher, *The Pampered Chef* (New York: Doubleday, 2005): 3.
7. As quoted in Anne Fisher, "Putting Your Mouth Where the Money Is," *Fortune*, September 3, 2001: 238.
8. Daniel Goleman, *Emotional Intelligence* (New York: Bantam Books, 1995); Michaela Davies, Lazar Stankov, and Richard D. Roberts, "Emotional Intelligence: In Search of an Elusive Construct," *Academy of Management Review*, 24 (April 1999): 325–345.
9. Daniel Goleman, *Emotional Intelligence* (New York: Bantam Books, 1995); Davies, Stankov, and D. Roberts, "Emotional Intelligence: In Search of an Elusive Construct."
10. Michelle Neely Martinez, "The Smarts That Count," *HR Magazine* 42 (November 1997): 72.
11. "The Numbers, It Takes 25 Minutes to Regain Your Focus After an Office Interruption," *Spirit* 16 (January 2007): 66.
12. Barbara Hagenbaugh, "More Employers Recruit the Military Work Ethic," *USA Today*, February 16, 2007: B1. For related reading, see Mark Henricks, "Joining the Ranks, Returning Veterans Are Proving to Be Powerful New Hires," *Small Business Success [America's Small Business Resource]* 21 (Fall 2006): 14.
13. BNET Business Directory, "Business Definitions for: Globalization," Copyright © 2008 CNET Networks, Inc., http://dictionary.bnet.com/definition/Globalization.html (accessed June 7, 2008).
14. "Off-Shoring: An Elusive Phenomenon," *A Report by a Panel of the National Academy of Public Administration for the U.S. Congress and the Bureau of Economic Analysis* (Washington, DC, January 2006): 8–10; also see "Off-Shoring: New Challenges and Opportunities in an Expanding Global Economy," *A Report by a Panel of the National Academy of Public Administration for the U.S. Congress and the Bureau of Economic Analysis* (Washington, DC, July 2007): 1–24.
15. Ibid.
16. Doug Brown and Scott Wilson, "Outsourcing Survival Tips," *American School Board Journal*, October 2007: 37–38; Chris Wood, "The Outsourcing Option: More Attractive Than Ever," *The Public Manager: The New Bureaucrat* 28 (Spring 1999): 43–46; and "Service Offshoring and Productivity: Evidence from the United States," *Research-Technology Management* 49 (Nov-Dec 2006): 65.
17. Brian Hook, "Time to Focus on Core Functions OUTSOURCING/OFFSHORING: Brian R Hook Finds the Cheapest Option Might Not Always Be the Best Solution. (FT REPORT—DIGITAL BUSINESS)." *The Financial Times*, March 14, 2007: 3. *Academic OneFile*. Gale. Anne Arundel Community College, Arnold, MD, http://find.galegroup.com.ezproxy.aacc.edu/itx/start.do?prodId=AONE (accessed February 2, 2008); Nikki Swartz, "Offshoring Privacy: When Companies Offshore Business Processes, They Are Putting Consumers' Most Sensitive Personal Information at Risk—and There's Little Consumers Can Do About It." *Information Management Journal* 38 (Sept-Oct 2004): 24–27; and Skip Corsini, "Outsourcing," *Journal of Property Management* 66 (May 2001): 66.
18. Art Bauer, "Point and Click Technology and the Power of the Desktop: Changing and Improving the Way Today's Managers Manage," *Supervision* 59 (Sept 1998): 16–17.
19. Jean Consilvio, "Balancing Act: Achieving Harmony in Work and Personal Time Isn't a Feat That IT Workers Can Accomplish Alone. These Best Places Make It a Team Effort of Managers and Staff," *Computerworld*, June 9, 2003: 34.
20. Gerry Johnsen, "Contact Center Virtualization: Requirements for Effective Team Supervision and Quality Management," *Customer Interaction Solutions* 25 (August 2006): 48–52. Also see Anita Dennis, "A Firm Without Walls: What Happens When

Practitioners Decide the Rents are Cheaper in Cyberspace?" *Journal of Accountancy* 180 (December 1995): 63–64.

21. Michael Schrage, "Big Brother Evolves: Monitoring Your Salespeople's Performance with Technology Can Be a Means to Success," *Sales & Marketing Management* 156 (June 2004): 23.

22. Kristina Dell and Lisa Takeuchi Cullen, "Snooping Bosses," *Time*, Sept 11, 2006: 62.

23. B. J. Hodge, William P. Anthony, and Lawrence M. Gales, *Organizational Theory: A Strategic Approach*, 5th ed. (Upper Saddle River, NJ: Prentice-Hall, 1996): 10.

24. Adapted from Edgar H. Schein, *Organizational Psychology*, 3rd ed. (Englewood Cliffs, NJ: Prentice-Hall, 1980): 12–15.

25. David Stires, "A Darker View of Starbucks," *Fortune*, November 13, 2006: 197.

26. Adam Smith, *The Wealth of Nations* (New York: Modern Library, 1937): 7.

27. For example, see Jay R. Galbraith and Edward F. Lawler III, "Effective Organizations: Using the New Logic of Organizing," in *Organizing for the Future: The New Logic for Managing Complex Organizations*, eds. Jay R. Galbraith, Edward E. Lawler III, and Associates (San Francisco: Jossey-Bass, 1993): 293–294. Related research is reported in Kees van den Bos, Henk A. M. Wilke, and E. Allan Lind, "When Do We Need Procedural Fairness? The Role of Trust in Authority," *Journal of Personality and Social Psychology* 75 (December 1998): 1449–1458.

28. Elliot Jaques, "In Praise of Hierarchy," *Harvard Business Review* 68 (January-February 1990): 127.

29. Marc Cecere, "Drawing the Lines," *Harvard Business Review* 79 (November 2001): 24.

30. Doris Christopher, *The Pampered Chef* (New York: Doubleday, 2005): 2.

31. Ibid., 3.

CHAPTER 2

1. Inspired by the definition in Andrew J. DuBrin, *Leadership: Research Findings, Practice and Skills*, 2nd ed. (Boston: Houghton Mifflin, 1998), 2. Also see Francis J. Yammarino, Fred Dansereau, and Christina J. Kennedy, "A Multiple-Level Multidimensional Approach to Leadership: Viewing Leadership Through an Elephant's Eye," *Organizational Dynamics* 29 (Winter 2001): 149–163.

2. Linda Baker, "I'm Bad! I'm Slick!" *Fast Company* 125 (May 2008): 104.

3. Council for Excellence in Management Leadership, Inspired Leadership Research Project (Research conducted by the Chartered Management Institute), *Inspired Leadership: Insights into people who Inspire exceptional performance* (United Kingdom: DTI, UK Government, 2006): 5.

4. We are grateful for the content suggestion from David L. Batts, Ed.D., Assistant Professor, East Carolina University, Greenville, NC.

5. The risks of shifting styles are discussed in Thomas L. Brown, "Managerial Waffling: In Politics-or in Business-Waffling Suggests Bad Leadership," *Industry Week*, January 18, 1993, 34; and Oren Harari, "Leadership vs. Autocracy: They Just Don't Get It!" *Management Review* 85 (August 1996): 42–45.

6. Dexter Roberts, "China Goes Shopping," *Business Week*, December 20, 2004: 34.

7. Bill Repp, "Leadership Flexibility Gets Results," *The Capital*, August 28, 2007: B4–B5.

8. Irgens, O. M. "Situational Leadership: A Modification of Hersey and Blanchard's Model." *Leadership & Organization Development Journal* 16 (Feb 1995): 36(4). *Academic OneFile*. Gale. Anne Arundel Community College, Arnold, MD, http://find.galegroup.com.ezproxy.aacc.edu/itx/start.do?prodId=AONE (accessed February 3, 2008); and Bill Repp, "Leadership Flexibility Gets Results," *The Capital, August* 28, 2007: B4–B5.

9. Kenneth H. Blanchard and Paul Hersey, "Great Ideas Revisited," *Training & Development* 50 (January 1996): 42(6). *Academic OneFile*. Gale. Anne Arundel Community College, Arnold, MD, http://find.galegroup.com.ezproxy.aacc.edu/itx/start.do?prodId=AONE (accessed February 3, 2008).

10. Ibid.

11. Charles W. Blackwell and Jane Whitney Gibson, "A Conversation with Leadership Guru, Paul Hersey," *Journal of Leadership Studies* 5 (Spring 1998): 143. *Academic OneFile*. Gale. Anne Arundel Community College, Arnold MD http://find.galegroup.com.ezproxy.aacc.edu/itx/start.do?prodId=AONE (accessed February 3, 2008); Kenneth H. Blanchard and Paul Hersey, "Great Ideas Revisited," *Training & Development* 50 (January 1996): 42(6). *Academic OneFile*. Gale. Anne Arundel Community College, Arnold, MD, http://find.galegroup.com.ezproxy.aacc.edu/itx/start.do?prodId=AONE (accessed February 3, 2008); and O. M. Irgens, "Situational Leadership: A Modification of Hersey and Blanchard's Model," *Leadership & Organization Development Journal* 16 (February 1995): 36(4). *Academic OneFile*. Gale. Anne Arundel Community College, Arnold, MD, http://find.galegroup.com.ezproxy.aacc.edu/itx/start.do?prodId=AONE (accessed February 3, 2008).

12. Fred E. Fiedler, "Job Engineering for Effective Leadership: A New Approach," *Management Review* 66 (September 1977): 29.

13. For an excellent comprehensive validation study, see Michael J. Strube and Joseph E. Garcia, "A Meta-Analytic Investigation of Fiedler's Contingency Model of Leadership Effectiveness," *Psychology Bulletin* 90 (September 1981): 307–321.

14. Fred. E. Fiedler and Martin M. Chemers, *Leadership and Effective Management* (Glenview, IL: Scott, Foresman, 1974): 91.

15. Robert J. House and Terence R. Mitchell, "Path-Goal Theory of Leadership," *Journal of Contemporary Business* 3 (Autumn 1974): 85. An updated path-goal model is presented in Robert J. House, "A Path-Goal Theory of Leadership: Lessons, Legacy, and a Reformulated Theory," *Leadership Quarterly* (Autumn 1996): 323–352.

16. Jan P. Muczyk and Bernard C. Reimann, "The Case for Directive Leadership," *Academy of Management Executive* 1 (November 1987): 301–311.

17. Adapted from House and Mitchell, "Path-Goal Theory of Leadership," 83.

18. For path-goal research, see Abduhl-Rahim A. Al-Gattan, "Test of the Path-Goal Theory of Leadership in the Multinational Domain," *Group & Organizational Studies* 10 (December 1985): 429–445; Robert T. Keller, "A Test of the Path-Goal Theory of Leadership with Need for Clarity As a Moderator in Research and Development Organizations," *Journal of Applied Psychology* 74 (April 1989): 208–212; John E. Mathieu, "A Test of Subordinates' Achievement and Affiliation Needs As Moderators of Leader Path-Goal Relationships," *Basic and Applied Social Psychology* 11 (June 1990): 179–189; and Retha A. Price, "An Investigation of Path-Goal Leadership Theory in Marketing Channels," *Journal of Retailing* 67 (Fall 1991): 339–361.

19. Leonard D. Schaeffer, "The Leadership Journey," *Harvard Business Review* 80 (October 2002): 42–43.

20. Bruce J. Avolio and Surinder S. Kahai, "Adding the 'E' to E-Leadership: How It May Impact Your Leadership," *Organizational Dynamics* 31 (2003): 325–338.

21. Larry Spears, "Reflections on Robert K. Greenleaf and Servant-Leadership," *Leadership & Organizational Development Journal* 17 (December 1996): 33.

22. For more on servant leadership philosophy, see Robert K. Greenleaf, *Servant Leadership: A Journey into the Nature of Legitimate Power and Greatness* (New York: Paulist Press, 1977); and Walter Kiechel III, "The Leader As Servant," *Fortune*, (May 4, 1992): 121–122.

23. "The Servant Leader" by Chris Lee. Reprinted with permission from the June 1993 issue of *Training* magazine. *Training* magazine article used with permission of Nielsen Business Media, Inc.

24. David Leon Moore, "Wooden's Wizardry Wears Well," *USA Today*, March 29, 1995: 1C-2C. Also see "The Wizard Turns 90," *USA Today*, October 11, 2000, 10C; Jerry Useem, "A Manager for All Seasons," *Fortune*, April 30, 2001, 66–72; and Chuck Salter, "Attention, Class!!!" Fast *Company* 53 (December 2001): 114–126.

25. Larry Spears, "Reflections on Robert K. Greenleaf and Servant-Leadership," *Leadership & Organizational Development Journal* 17 (December 1996): 33–36.

26. Ibid.

27. Leader to Leader Institute, "Leadership Breakthroughs from West Point," a Special Supplement to *Leader to Leader* (San Francisco: Leader to Leader Institute and Wiley Subscription Services, Inc., A Wiley Company, Jossey-Bass, 2005): 89.

28. For an excellent elaboration of this definition, see David Horton Smith, "A Parsimonious Definition of 'Group': Toward Conceptual Clarity and Scientific Utility," *Sociological Inquiry* 37 (Spring 1967): 141–167. The importance of social skills in today's diverse workplace is discussed in Robert A. Baron and Gideon D. Markman, "Beyond Social Capital: How Social Skills Can Enhance Entrepreneurs' Success," *Academy of Management Executive* 14 (February 2000): 106–116.

29. Linda N. Jewell and H. Joseph Reitz, *Group Effectiveness in Organizations* (Glenville, IL: Scott, Foresman and Company, 1981): 20; Jean Lipman-Blumen and Harold J. Leavitt, "Hot Groups 'with Attitude': A New Organizational State of Mind," *Organizational Dynamics* 27 (Spring 1999): 63–73; and Lynn R. Offermann and Rebecca K. Spiros, "The Science and Practice of Team Development: Improving the Link," *Academy of Management Journal* 44 (April 2001): 376–392.

30. The following discussion of the six stages of group development is adapted from Linda N. Jewell and H. Joseph Reitz, *Group Effectiveness in Organizations* (Glenview, IL: Scott, Foresman and Company, 1981): 15–20. Also see Artemis Chang, Prashant Bordia, and Julie Duck, "Punctuated Equilibrium and Linear Progression: Toward a New Understanding of Group Development," *Academy of Management Journal* 46 (February 2003): 106–117.

31. Ed Gash, "More Training Than Camp," *Training* 43 (December 2006): 7; and Gary A. Ballinger and F. David Schoorman, "Individual Reactions to Leadership Succession in Workgroups," *Academy of Management Review* 32 (January 2007): 118–136.

32. Spencer E. Ante, "The New Blue," *BusinessWeek*, March 17, 2003: 81–82.

33. Jerry Useem, "What's That Spell? Teamwork!," *Fortune*, June 12, 2006: 65–66; Timothy S. Kieslling, Louis D. Marino, and R. Glenn Richey, "Global Marketing Teams: A Strategic Option for Multinationals," *Organizational Dynamics* 35 (2006): 237–250; Jeanne Brett, Kristin Behfar, and Mary C. Kern, "Managing Multicultural Teams," *Harvard Business Review* 84 (November 2006): 83–91; Paul Falcone, "Inheriting a New Team," *HR Magazine* 51 (December 2006): 95–98; and Boris Groysberg and Robin Abrahams, "Lift Outs: How to Acquire a High-Functioning Team," *Harvard Business Review* 84 (December 2006): 133–140.

34. Robert T. Teller, "Cross-Functional Project Groups in Research and New Product Development: Diversity, Communications, Job Stress, and Outcomes," *Academy of Management Journal* 44 (June 2001): 547–555; and Kay Lovelace, Debra L. Shapiro, and Laurie R. Weingart, "Maximizing Cross-Functional New Product Teams' Innovativeness and Constraint Adherence: A Conflict Communications Perspective," *Academy Management Journal* 44 (August 2001): 779–793.

35. Dori Jones Yang, "Grace Robertson: Piloting a Superfast Rollout at Boeing," *BusinessWeek*, August 30, 1993: 77.

36. Three kinds of trust are discussed in Douglas A. Houston, "Trust in the Networked Economy: Doing Business on Web Time," *Business Horizons* 44 (March–April 2001): 38–44.

37. Stephanie Armour, "Employees' New Motto: Trust No One," *USA Today*, February 5, 2002: 2B; Del Jones, "Do You Trust Your CEO?" *USA Today*, February 12, 2003: 7B; Eric Krell, "Do They Trust You?" HR Magazine 51 (June 2006): 58–65; and Margery Weinstein, "Trust Us—Really," *Training* 43 (November 2006): 14.

38. Deborah L. Duarte and Nancy Tennant Snyder, *Mastering Virtual Teams: Strategies, Tools, and Techniques That Succeed*, 3rd ed. (San Francisco: Jossey-Bass, 2006).

39. Michelle Conlin, "The Easiest Commute of All," *Business Week*, December 12, 2005: 78–80; and Jennifer Taylor Arnold, "Making the Leap," *HR Magazine* 51 (May 2006): 80–86.

40. Kim Kiser, "Working on World Time," *Training* 36 (March 1999): 28–34.

41. The information contained in the following section is based on discussions in Jack Gordon, "Do Your Virtual Teams Deliver Only Virtual Performance?" *Training* 42 (June 2005): 20–26; Deborah L. Duarte and Nancy Tennant Snyder, *Mastering Virtual Teams: Strategies, Tools, and Techniques That Succee*d, 3rd ed. (San Francisco: Jossey-Bass, 2006); and Arvind Malhotra, Ann Majchrzak, and Benson Rosen, "Leading Virtual Teams," *Academy of Management Perspectives* 21 (February 2007): 60–70.

42. Steve Bates, "Unique Strategies Urged to Keep 'Emerging Leaders,'" *HR Magazine* 47 (September 2002): 14; and Carol Hymowitz, "The Confident Boss Doesn't Micromanage or Delegate Too Much," *Wall Street Journal*, March 11, 2003: B1.

43. As quoted in Laurel Shaper Walters, "A Leader Redefines Management," *Christian Science* Monitor, September 22, 1992: 14. For Frances Hesselbein's ideas about leadership, see Roundtable Discussion, "All in a Day's Work," *Harvard Business Review* 79 (Special issue: *Breakthrough Leadership*, December 2001): 54–66.

44. Janice Mack Talcott and Kate B. Peterson, "You Can't Do It All! (Empowering Jewelry Store Employees)," *Jewelers Circular Keystone* 169 (April 1998): 180(4).

45. Tom Davis and Michael J. Landa, "Developing Trust," *CMA Management* 73 (October 1999): 48(4).

46. Martin Tillman, "Help! My Team Won't Accept Empowerment!" *Defense AT & L* 33 (May-June 2004): 32(4).

47. Larry Bossidy, "The Job No CEO Should Delegate," Harvard Business Review 79 (March 2001): 46–49; and Sharon Gazda, "The Art of Delegating: Effective Delegation Enhances Employee Moral, Manager Productivity and Organizational Success," *HR Magazine* 47 (January 2002): 75–78.

48. Sharon Gazda, "The Art of Delegating: Effective Delegation Enhances Employee Moral, Manager Productivity and Organizational Success," *HR Magazine* 47 (January 2002): 75–78.

49. "How Conservatism Wins in the Hottest Market," *Business Week*, January 17, 1977: 43.

50. The delegation styles of selected U.S. presidents are examined in Edward J. Mayo and Lance P. Jarvis, "Delegation 101: Lessons from the White House," *Business Horizons* 31 (September-October 1988): 2–12.

51. Alex Taylor, III, "Iacocca's Time of Trouble," *Fortune*, March 14, 1988: 79, 81.

52. Adapted from William H. Newman, "Overcoming Obstacles to Effective Delegation," *Management Review* 45 (January 1956): 36–41; and from Eugene Raudsepp, "Why Supervisors Don't Delegate," *Supervision* 41 (May 1979): 12–15. Also see Gary Yukl and Ping Ping Fu, "Determinants of Delegation and Consultation by Managers," *Journal of Organizational Behavior* 20 (March 1999): 219–232.

53. Practical tips on delegation can be found in Douglas Anderson, "Supervisors and the Hesitate to Delegate Syndrome," *Supervision* 53 (November 1992): 9–11; and Michael C. Dennis, "Only Superman Didn't Delegate," *Business Credit* 95 (February 1993): 41.

54. For more on initiative, see Michael Frese, Wolfgang Kring, Andrea Soose, and Jeanette Zempel, "Personal Initiative at Work:

Differences Between East and West Germany," *Academy of Management Journal* 39 (February 1996): 37–63; and Alan L. Frohman, "Igniting Organizational Change from Below: The Power of Personal Initiative," *Organizational Dynamics* 25 (Winter 1997): 39–53.

55. Peter F. Drucker, *Managing the Non-Profit Organization* (New York: HarperCollins, 1990), 117; and Jim Holt, "Management Master," *Management Review* 88 (November 1999): 15.

CHAPTER 3

1. John Evan Frook, "E-Champs: Bluedot Chief Guides Firm's Metamorphosis" *B to B*, June 11, 2001: 11.

2. Scott Adams, "Dilbert's Management Handbook," *Fortune*, May 13, 1996: 104.

3. Based on R. Duane Ireland and Michael A. Hitt, "Mission Statements: Importance, Challenge, and Recommendations for Development," *Business Horizons* 35 (May-June 1992): 34–42. Also see Barbara Bartkus, Myron Glassman, and R. Bruce McAfee, "Mission Statements: Are They Smoke and Mirrors?" *Business Horizons* 43 (November-December 2000): 23–28.

4. As quoted in Jon Talton, "What in Blazes Has the Chief Done? Create a Model for Managers," *Arizona Republic*, January 27, 2002: D1.

5. See Thomas W. Porter and Stephen C. Harper, "Tactical Implementation: The Devil is in the Details," *Business Horizons* 46 (January-February 2003): 53–60.

6. Susan M. Heathfield, "Strategic Planning Pitfalls—to Avoid," *About: Human Resources*, http://humanresources.about.com/od/leadership/qt/strgc_plan_13.htm (accessed February 17, 2008).

7. "How to Implement Strategic Planning: Vision Statement, Mission Statement, Values," *About: Human Resources*, http://humanresources.about.com/od/strategicplanning1/a/implement_plan.htm (accessed February 17, 2008).

8. Ibid, P. 434, 6.

9. Ken Blanchard, "Building High Performing Teams®, Strengthening Virtual Teams Overview," The Ken Blanchard Companies, www.kenblanchard.com, http://www.kenblanchard.com/img/pub/pdf_virtualteams_overview.pdf (accessed February 17, 2008).

10. Linda Nacif, "The Secret to Setting & Achieving Your Goals," *Supervision* 68 (August 2007): 18–20; Guy Kawasaki, "The Art of Execution," *Entrepreneur*, September 2007: 26; Amy Jones, "Get Ready, Get Set, Go!" *Get Motivated Workbook* (Get Motivated Seminars, 2006): 46–47; Bryan S. Schaffer, "The Nature of Goal Congruence in Organizations," *Supervision* 68 (August 2007): 13–17; and Cynthia Kersey, "Become Unstoppable," *Success From Home* 3 (April 2007): 50–53.

11. As quoted in Charles Fishman, "Fred Smith," *Fast Company*, 48 (June 2001): 66.

12. See "Planning and Goal Setting for Small Business," *Management and Planning Series* MP-6, (Washington, DC: U.S. Small Business Administration): 3–4.

13. Anthony P. Raia, *Managing by Objectives* (Glenview, IL: Scott, Foresman, 1974): 24.

14. Susanne Beier, "Setting Goals," imdiversity website, http://www.imdiversity.com/Villages/Woman/careers_workplace_employment/

beier_set_career_goals.asp (accessed February 17, 2008); and Charles W. Prather, "The Dumb Thing About SMART Goals," *Research Technology Management* 48 (September-October 2005): 14–15.

15. Charles W. Prather, "The Dumb Thing About SMART Goals."

16. Amy Jones, "Get Ready, Get Set, Go!" *Get Motivated Workbook* (Get Motivated Seminars, 2006): 46–47.

17. For example, see Donna J. Abernathy, "A Get-Real Guide to Time Management," *Training and Development* 53 (June 1999): 22–26; and Martin Delahoussaye, "Houston, Problem Solved," *Training* 39 (June 2002): 24.

18. George Matyjewicz, "The A-B-C Priority System for Time Management," *Etailers Digest* (September 24, 2002), http://www.etailersdigest.com/resources/Specials/time_management.htm (accessed February 17, 2008); also see Alan Lakein, *How to Get Control of Your Time and Your Life* (New York: P.H. Wyden, 1973).

19. Richard Koch, *The 80/20 Principle: The Secret of Achieving More with Less* (New York: Currency Doubleday, 1998): 4.

20. See Barbara Moses, "The Busyness Trap," *Training* 35 (November 1998): 38–42; and Stephen Bertman, "Hyper Culture," *The Futurist* 32 (December 1998): 18–23.

21. Rich Karlgaard, "Peter Drucker on Leadership," *Forbes*, November 19, 2004, http://www.forbes.com/2004/11/19/cz_rk_1119drucker_print.html (accessed June 8, 2008).

22. Marion E. Haynes, *Project Management —From Idea to Implementation* (Menlo Park, CA: Crisp Publications, Inc., 1989): 41–42.

23. Tom Peters, "What Gets Measured Gets Done," Tom Peters Company, originally posted April 28, 1986, http://www.tompeters.com/col_entries.php?note=005143&year=1986 (accessed February 17, 2008).

CHAPTER 4

1. Spherion® press release, "Workers on the Move: Nearly One-Quarter in the U.S. Voluntarily Changed Jobs Last Year, According to Latest Spherion Survey," Spherion website, http://www.spherion.com/press/releases/2007/snapshot-voluntary-job-change.jsp (accessed April 26, 2008).

2. Kay Gilley, "Agency Culture and Supervisor Key to Tackling High Turnover," *Policy & Practice* 64 (September 2006): 25.

3. John Dooney, "SHRM® Human Capital Measure of the Month: New Hire Quality," MITTONMedia website, www.mittonmedia.com (accessed April 13, 2008); and Erika Welz Prafder, "Hiring Your First Employee," *Entrepreneur* magazine website, http://www.entrepreneur.com/humanresources/hiring/article83774.html (accessed April 26, 2008).

4. Steve Hillmer, Barbara Hillmer, and Gale Roberts, "The Real Cost of Turnover: Lessons from a Call Center," *Human Resources Planning* 27 (September 2004): 34–42; and Terry Taylor, "The True Cost of Turnover and How to Prevent It," *Journal of Property Management* 58 (November-December 1993): 20–23.

5. Anat Rafaeli, "Pre-Employment Screening and Applicants' Attitudes Toward and Employment Opportunity," *The Journal of Social Psychology* 139 (December 1999): 700. Also see Jonathan A. Segal, "Urine or You're Out," *HR Magazine* 39 (December 1994): 30–37. For more on psychologically based pre-employment tests, see

6. Scott L. Martin and Loren P. Lehnen, "Select the Right Employees Through Testing," *Personnel Journal* 71 (June 1992): 46–48.

6. Steve Hillmer, Barbara Hillmer, and Gale Roberts, "The Real Cost of Turnover: Lessons from a Call Center," *Human Resources Planning* 27 (September 2004): 34–42. Also see Terry Taylor, "The True Cost of Turnover and How to Prevent It," *Journal of Property Management* 58 (November-December 1993): 20–23.

7. Spherion® press release, "Spherion Survey Shows Dip in Overall Worker Confidence for Sixth Consecutive Month; Workers Still Feel Secure in Current Jobs," Spherion website http://www.spherion.com/pressroom/index.php?s=43&item=529 (accessed April 26, 2008).

8. Spherion® press release, "Workers on the Move: Nearly One-Quarter in the U.S. Voluntarily Changed Jobs Last Year, According to Latest Spherion Survey," Spherion website, http://www.spherion.com/press/releases/2007/snapshot-voluntary-job-change.jsp (accessed April 26, 2008). Also see "Why Workers Change Jobs," *USA Today*, March 8, 2007: B1.

9. Bob Levoy, "Payroll Cuts Pose Problems. You're Looking for Improved Profitability but Could End Up with High Turnover and Service Breakdowns," *Veterinary Economics* 47 (January 2006): 16.

10. Rieva Lesonsky, "Hire Away: Tips for Hiring Your First Employee," *Small Business Success* 20 (Spring 2006) (Small Business Administration, Washington, DC): 62.

11. Wendell Williams, "How to Leave the Interviewing Stone Age: Three Criteria to Use in Making Interviews More Predictive of Performance," *Electronic Recruiting Exchange* (July 18, 2006): 1–2.

12. Rieva Lesonsky, "Hire Away: Tips for Hiring Your First Employee," *Small Business Success* 20 (Spring 2006) (Small Business Administration, Washington, DC): 62; and John C. Kelly, "What Will He or She Do on a Daily Basis?" *Chamber News* 9 (February 2007): 5.

13. Ibid.

14. John C. Kelly, "What Will He or She Do on a Daily Basis?" *Chamber News* 9 (February 2007): 5.

15. Jim Hopkins, "7 Steps to Better Hiring," *USA Today*, June 21, 2006: 2B; and Donald D. DeCamp, "Are You Hiring the Right People?" *Management Review* 81 (May 1992): 44–48.

16. Ibid, P. 435, 14.

17. Hopkins, "7 Steps to Better Hiring;" and Patricia G. Roth and Philip L. Roth, "Reduce Turnover with Realistic Job Previews," *The CPA Journal* 65 (September 1995): 68–70.

18. The U.S. Equal Employment Opportunity Commission (EEOC) website, www.eeoc.gov/policy/laws.html (accessed April 26, 2008).

19. The U.S. Equal Employment Opportunity Commission (EEOC), "Federal Laws Prohibiting Job Discrimination Questions and Answers," EEOC website, www.eeoc.gov/facts/qanda.html (accessed April 26, 2008).

20. "$40 Million Paid to Class Members in December 2005 in Abercrombie & Fitch Discrimination Lawsuit Settlement," *AFjustice.com*, a newsletter from the national law firm of Lieff Cabraser Heimann & Bernstein, LLP, copyright © 2007 Lieff

Cabraser Heimann & Bernstein, LLP, http://www.afjustice.com, (accessed April 26, 2008).

21. See "Study Suggests Bias Against 'Black' Names on Resumes," *HR Magazine* 48 (February 2003): 29; and Jared M. Mellot, "The Diversity Rationale for Affirmative Action in Employment after Grutter: The Case for Containment," *William and Mary Law Review* 48 (December 2006): 1091–1259.

22. Howard Fineman and Tamara Lipper, "Spinning Race," *Newsweek*, January 27, 2003: 26–29; and Roger O. Crockett, "Memo to the Supreme Court: 'Diversity is Good Business,'" *Business Week*, January 27, 2003: 96.

23. R. Roosevelt Thomas, Jr., "From Affirmative Action to Affirming Diversity," *Harvard Business Review* 68 (March-April 1990): 114. For an interview with R. Roosevelt Thomas, see Ellen Neuborne, "Diversity Challenges Many Companies," *USA Today*, November 18, 1996: 10B. Also see William Atkinson, "Bringing Diversity to White Men," *HR Magazine* 46 (September 2001): 76–83.

24. Lin Grensing-Pophal, "A Balancing Act on Diversity Audits," *HR Magazine* 46 (November 2001): 87–95; Jennifer Merritt, "Wanted: A Campus That Looks Like America," *Business Week*, March 22, 2002: 56–59; and Keith A. Caver and Ancella B. Livers, "Dear White Boss," *Harvard Business Review* 80 (November 2002): 76–81.

25. "Jobcenter Plus Says Diversity is Now a Business 'Imperative,'" *Financial Adviser*, February 14, 2008; Chuck Salter, "Diversity Without the Excuses," *Fast Company* 62 (September 2002): 44. Also see Jeremy Kahn, "Diversity Trumps the Downturn," *Fortune*, July 9, 2001: 114–116; and Orlando C. Richard, "Racial Diversity, Business Strategy, and Firm Performance: A Resource-Based View," *Academy of Management Journal* 43 (April 2000): 164–177.

26. As quoted in Chuck Salter, "Diversity Without the Excuses," *Fast Company* 62 (September 2002): 44. Also see Jeremy Kahn, "Diversity Trumps the Downturn," *Fortune*, July 9, 2001: 114–116; and Orlando C. Richard, "Racial Diversity, Business Strategy, and Firm Performance: A Resource-Based View," *Academy of Management Journal* 43 (April 2000): 164–177.

27. Joel Schettler, "Equal Access to All," *Training* 39 (January 2002): 44.

28. U.S. Department of Labor, Bureau of Labor Statistics, "Unemployment Data 1988–2008," Bureau of Labor Statistics website, http://www.bls.gov/webapps/legacy/cpsatab7.htm (accessed June 14, 2008); and Stephen Barr, "A Troublesome Decline in Disability Hiring," *The Washington Post*, January 17, 2008: D4.

29. For an inspiring case study of a blind sports reporter, see Robert Davis, "Friends 'Know of Nothing He Can't Do,'" *USA Today*, October 25, 1999: 10A. Also see Sandra Block, "Deaf Investors Make Themselves Heard," *USA Today*, December 6, 2003: 3B.

30. For more, see Michael T. Zugelder and Paul J. Champagne, "Responding to the Supreme Court: Employment Practices and the ADA," *Business Horizons* 46 (January-February 2003): 30–36; and U.S. Department of Justice, Civil Rights Division,

Disability Rights Section, "A Guide to Disability Rights Laws," http://www.usdoj.gov/crt/ada/cguide.htm#anchor62335 (accessed April 26, 2008).

31. The U.S. Equal Employment Opportunity Commission, "Job Applicants and the Americans with Disabilities Act," EEOC website, http://www.eeoc.gov/facts/jobapplicant.html (accessed April 26, 2008).

32. As quoted in "Quality Workers," *The Baltimore Sun Careerbuilder Section*, July 29, 2007: H1.

33. J. J. Ramberg, "Doing Good: Cause and Effect," *Entrepreneur*, February 2008: 23.

34. The U.S. Equal Employment Opportunity Commission, "Job Applicants and the Americans with Disabilities Act," EEOC website, http://www.eeoc.gov/facts/jobapplicant.html (accessed April 26, 2008).

35. Ibid.

36. John Williams, "Enabling Technologies," *Business Week*, March 20, 2000: 68,70; Otis Port, "Artificial Eyes, Turbine Hearts," *Business Week*, March 20, 2000: 72–73; and Sacha Cohen, "High-Tech Tools Lower Barriers for Disabled," *HR Magazine* 47 (October 2002): 60–65.

37. Michael P. Cronin, "This Is a Test," *Inc. Magazine*, August 1993: 64–68; Stephanie Armour, "Test? Forget the Test—You're Hired," *USA Today*, August 8, 2000: 1B; Matt Murray, "More Help, More Security, Less Testing," *Wall Street Journal Sunday*, May 27, 2001: D7; and Dave Patel, "Testing, Testing, Testing." *HR Magazine* 30 (February 2002): 112.

38. Scott B. Parry, "How to Validate an Assessment Tool," *Training* 30 (April 1993): 37–42.

39. Deniz S. Ones, Chockalingam Viswesvaran, and Frank L. Schmidt, "Comprehensive Meta-Analysis of Integrity Test Validities: Findings and Implications for Personnel Selection and Theories of Job Performance," *Journal of Applied Psychology* 78 (August 1993): 679–703; Kevin R. Murphy, "Why Pre-Employement Alcohol Testing is Such a Bad Idea," *Business Horizons* 38 (September-October 1995): 69–74; Jenny C McCune, "Testing, Testing 1-2-3," *Management Review* 85 (January 1996): 50–52; Deniz S. Ones and Chockalingam Viswesvaran, "Gender, Age, and Race Differences on Overt Integrity Tests: Results Across Four Large-Scale Job Applicant Data Sets," *Journal of Applied Psychology* 83 (February 1998): 35–42; and Stephanie Clifford, "The New Science of Hiring" *Inc. Magazine*, August 2006: 90–98.

40. U.S. Department of Labor, Employment Standards Administration, Wage and Hours Division, http://www.dol.gov/esa/whd/flsa/index.htm, (accessed April 26, 2008).

41. "Hiring Young Workers," NOLO website, http://www.nolo.com/article.cfm/ObjectID/04B502E2-8B27-4AD4-B937A344BC7D23F9/ (accessed April 26, 2008).

42. See Jim Collins, *Good to Great: Why Some Companies Make the Leap and Others Don't* (New York: Harper Business, 2001); and Jim Collins, "Good to Great," *Fast Company* 51 (October 2001): 90–104.

43. Based on "What Are CEOs Thinking?" *USA Today*, May 3, 2001, 1B. Also see Alison Stein Wellner, "Employers Join Forces to

Recruit," *HR Magazine* 46 (January 2001): 86–96; Peter Cappelli, "Making the Most of On-Line Recruiting," *Harvard Business Review* 79 (March 2001): 139–146; Jeffrey Pfeffer, "Fighting the War for Talent is Hazardous to Your Organization's Health," *Organizational Dynamics* 29 (Spring 2001): 248–259; and Jim Meade, "Recruiting Software Can Streamline Hiring Process," *HR Magazine* 46 (September 2001): 139–140.

44. As quoted in Ruth E. Thaler-Carter, "Diversify Your Recruitment Advertising," *HR Magazine* 46 (June 2001): 95.

45. "How Workers Found Their Latest Jobs," *USA Today*, February 3, 2003: 1B. Also see "Job Hunting the Old-Fashioned Way," *Business Week*, February 17, 2003: 10.

46. Ryan McCarthy, "'Help Wanted' Meets 'Buy It Now': Why More Companies are Integrating Marketing and Recruiting," *Inc. Magazine*, November 2007: 51–52; and Stephanie Armour, "This is Job Recruiting?" *USA Today*, March 26, 2007: 1–2.

47. Rieva Lesonsky, "Hire Away: Tips for Hiring Your First Employee." *Small Business Success* 20 (Spring 2006) (Small Business Administration, Washington, DC): 62; and Ryan McCarthy's "'Help Wanted' Meets 'Buy It Now': Why More Companies are Integrating Marketing and Recruiting," *Inc. Magazine*, November 2007: 51–52.

48. David H. Freedman, "The Monster Dilemma: Posting Jobs on the Web is Easy. It's Sifting Through Hundreds of Resumes That's a Pain," *Inc. Magazine*, May 2007: 77–78.

49. Steve Hamm, "Children of the Web," *Business Week*, July 2, 2007: 58.

50. Erin White, "Theory & Practice: Employers are Putting New Face on Web Recruiting," *Wall Street Journal*, January 8, 2007: B3.

51. Jim Hopkins, "Job Seekers Show Rather Than Tell: Websites Showcase Video Resumes." *USA Today*, April 25, 2007: 3B; and "Screen Saver: CareerBuilder.com Launches Free Video Resume Service," *The Baltimore Sun Careerbuilder Section*, July 29, 2007: H1.

52. Jena McGregor, "Beware of That Video Resume," *Business Week*, June 11, 2007: 12.

53. Stephanie Armour, "This Is Job Recruiting?" *USA Today*, March 26, 2007: 1–2.

54. Mark Henricks, "Where to Find That Perfect New Employee? Ask the Ones You Already Have," *Entrepreneur*, May 2007: 89–90.

55. Ibid.

56. Stephanie Armour, "This Is Job Recruiting?" *USA Today*, March 26, 2007: 1–2.

57. "Companies Roll Out the Welcome Mat for Moms Returning to Work," *The Capital*, August 19, 2007: B2.

58. Fred Vogelstein, "Google @ $165: Are These Guys for Real?" *Fortune,* December 13, 2004: 106, 108.

59. Timothy S. Bland and Sue S. Stalcup, "Build a Legal Employment Application," *HR Magazine* 44 (March 1999): 129–133.

60. Jim Hopkins, "Small Businesses Take Steps to Protect Themselves," *USA Today*, November 14, 2001: 6B. Also see Mary Beth Marklein, "Is There Any Truth to Today's Resumes?" *USA Today*, February 4, 2003: 1D–2D; and "The List: Resumegate," *Business Week*, February 10, 2003: 10.

61. Mathew L. MacKelly, "Employer Liability for Employer References," *Wisconsin Lawyer* 81 (April 2008), http://www.wisbar.org/AM/Template.cfm?Section=Home&CONTENTID=71179&TEMPLATE=/CM/ContentDisplay.cfm (accessed April 26, 2008); and Nicole Chiappini and Jane H. Graham, "New Law Protects Employers from Liability for Giving Good Faith Job References," *Employment Law Notes: Sebris Busto James* (May 2005), http://www.sebrisbusto.com/publications/getEmploymentLawNotes.asp?employmentlawnote_id=0505 (accessed April 26, 2008).

62. Stephanie Clifford, "The New Science of Hiring" *Inc. Magazine* 28, August 2006: 90–98.

63. Ibid.

64. Laura Egodigwe, "Finding the Right Fit: Firms using complex tools to hire workers," *Black Enterprise*, September 21, 2006, http://www.blackenterprise.com/cms/exclusivesopen.aspx/id/1894&p=1 (accessed June 15, 2008).

65. Nanea Kalani, "Don't Lower Hiring Standards in Tight Job Market" *Pacific Business News*, February 2, 2007, http://pacific.bizjournals.com/pacific/stories/2007/02/05/focus2.html?jst=pn_pn_lk (accessed June 15, 2008).

66. Dr. John C. Kelly, "Interviewing Job Candidates," *The Capital,* February 3, 2008: B3.

67. Nick Stafieri, "Interviewing Techniques: Looking for That Perfect Employee," *SuperVision* 68 (May 2007): 3–5.

68. Ibid.

69. Carole J. Bolster, "Take This Job and Love It," *Healthcare Financial Management* (January 2007): 56–60.

70. Kirstin Dorsch, "Video Hiring Tools Puts Interviews Online," *Jacksonville Business Journal*, January 19, 2007, http://jacksonville.bizjournals.com/jacksonville/stories/2007/01/22/story5.html?page=2 (accessed June 15, 2008).

71. Spherion® press release, "Workers on the Move: Nearly One-Quarter in the U.S. Voluntarily Changed Jobs Last Year, According to Latest Spherion Survey," Spherion website, http://www.spherion.com/press/releases/2007/snapshot-voluntary-job-change.jsp (accessed April 26, 2008).

72. Sheri Qualters, "Telecommuters Are Reaching Out to Sue Their Employers," *The National Law Journal*, December 15, 2006, http://www.law.com/jsp/article.jsp?id=1166090716179 (accessed June 15, 2008).

73. Sharon Baltes, "Teleworking Continues to Grow, but Some Employers Still Leery," *Business Record—Des Moines*, November 22, 2004: 1–4; Paula B. Thomas and R. Earle Thomas, "Nontraditional Scheduling: A Vehicle for Attracting and Retaining 'The Brightest and the Best,'" *The CPA Journal* 59 (November 1989): 74–79; and Sandra A. Sullivan, "Flexibility as a Management Tool," *Employment Relations Today* 21 (Winter 1994): 393–406.

74. Amy Saltzman, "One Job, Two Contented Workers," *U.S. News & World Report*, November 14, 1988: 74–76; and Paula B. Thomas and R. Earle Thomas, "Nontraditional Scheduling: A Vehicle for Attracting and Retaining 'The Brightest and the Best,'" *The CPA Journal* 59 (November 1989): 74–79.

75. Sandra A. Sullivan, "Flexibility as a Management Tool." *Employment Relations Today* 21 (Winter 1994): 393–406.

CHAPTER 5

1. "Orientation and Training of New Employees," *About: Human Resources* http://humanresources.about.com/od/orientation/Orientation_and_Training_of_New_Employees.htm (accessed April 26, 2008).
2. Mark Henricks, "You Know the Drill...or Do You? The Latest Training Tools Might Surprise You," *Entrepreneur*, April 2007: 24.
3. Cheri A. Young and Craig C. Lundberg, "Creating a Good First Day on the Job: Allying Newcomers' Anxiety with Positive Messages," *Cornell Hotel & Restaurant Administration Quarterly* 37 (December 1996): 26–34.
4. Dr. John Sullivan, "Best Practices in Recruiting: 2008 ERE Award Winners," ERE Media website, http://www.ere.net/articles/db/1B20B5A0D31949F2AF734CEDCA0A3F16.asp (accessed May 3, 2008).
5. Cheri A. Young and Craig C. Lundberg, "Creating a Good First Day on the Job: Allying Newcomers' Anxiety with Positive Messages," *Cornell Hotel & Restaurant Administration Quarterly* 37 (December 1996): 26–34.
6. Patricia G. Roth and Philip L. Roth, "Reduce Turnover with Realistic Job Previews," *The CPA Journal* 65 (September 1995): 68–70.
7. Lynne M. Connelly, "Welcoming New Employees," *Journal of Nursing Scholarship* 37 (Summer 2005): 163–165.
8. Cheri A. Young and Craig C. Lundberg, "Creating a Good First Day on the Job: Allying Newcomers' Anxiety with Positive Messages," *Cornell Hotel & Restaurant Administration Quarterly* 37 (December 1996): 26–34.
9. Chris Penttila, "Hire Away, How to Bring New Hands on Deck—and Keep Them There," *Entrepreneur*, June 2007: 20.
10. Keith Rollag, Salvatore Parise, and Rob Cross, "Getting New Hires Up to Speed Quickly: The Key to Making New Employees Productive Quickly, Known as "Rapid On-boarding," Is to Help Immediately Build an Informational Network With Co-workers," *MIT Sloan Management Review* 46 (Winter 2005): 35–42.
11. John F. McGillicuddy, "Making a Good First Impression," *Public Management* 81 (January 1999): 15–19.
12. "Hire the BEST!" *Get Motivated Workbook* (2007): 67.
13. The Children's Hospital of Philadelphia, The Joseph Stokes Research Institute http://stokes.chop.edu/careers/before_work/ (accessed May 3, 2008).
14. John F. McGillicuddy, "Making a Good First Impression," *Public Management* 81 (January 1999): 15–19.
15. Mary Alice Ragsdale and John Mueller, "Plan, Do, Study, Act Model to Improve an Orientation Program," *Journal of Nursing Care Quality* 20 (July-September 2005): 268–273.
16. "100 Best Companies to Work For 2007," *Fortune* http://money.cnn.com/magazines/fortune/bestcompanies/2007/snapshots/90.html (accessed May 3, 2008); David Dreeszen, "Men's Wearhouse Arrives in Sioux City," *Sioux City Journal*, November 3, 2007 http://www.siouxcityjournal.com/articles/2007/11/03/news/top/054e3fbbf80ed74b86257387007e9f8d.prt (accessed May 3, 2008); and StarCast Solutions http://www.starcast.net/solutions/newhire.html (accessed May 3, 2008).

17. Marilyn Moats Kennedy, "Is Your Orientation Program and Adhesive or a Solvent?" *Physician Executive* 27 (January 2001): 64–67.
18. Pamela F. Weber, "Getting a Grip on Employee Growth," *Training & Development* 53 (May 1999): 87–93.
19. Brigid Maynahan, "Creating Harassment-Free Work Zones," *Training and Development* 47(May 1993): 67–70.
20. Data from Margery Weinstein, "Learning Dollars," *Training* 44 (April 2007): 6.
21. James Kochanski and Gerald Ledford, ""How to Keep Me"—Retaining Technical Professionals," *Research-Technology Management* 44 (May 2001): 31.
22. Zandy B. Leibowitz, Nancy K. Schlossberg, and Jane E. Shore, "Stopping the Revolving Door (Orientation Programs for Reducing Turnover of New Employees)," *Training & Development* 45 (February 1991): 43–51.
23. Gene Powell, "Hoard Your Gold: Cultivate a Workplace That Attracts and Sustains the Best and the Brightest—an Asset No Company Can Afford to Lose," *Journal of Property Management* 69 (May-June 2004): 46–49.
24. Gene Powell, "Hoard Your Gold: Cultivate a Workplace That Attracts and Sustains the Best and the Brightest—an Asset No Company Can Afford to Lose," *Journal of Property Management* 69 (May-June 2004): 46–49.
25. Marilyn Moats Kennedy, "Is Your Orientation Program and Adhesive or a Solvent?" *Physician Executive* 27 (January 2001): 64–67 and "Hire the BEST!" *Get Motivated Workbook* (2007): 67.
26. Zandy B. Leibowitz, Nancy K. Schlossberg, and Jane E. Shore, "Stopping the Revolving Door (Orientation Programs for Reducing Turnover of New Employees)," *Training & Development* 45 (February 1991): 43–51.
27. Keith Rollag, Salvatore Parise, and Rob Cross, "Getting New Hires Up to Speed Quickly: The Key to Making New Employees Productive Quickly, Known as "Rapid On-Boarding," Is to Help Immediately Build an Informational Network with Co-workers," *MIT Sloan Management Review* 46 (Winter 2005): 35–42.
28. These numbers are for external hires. Internal transfers get up to speed about twice as fast. See R. Williams, "Mellon Learning Curve Research Study" (New York: Mellon Corp., 2003); and Keith Rollag, Salvatore Parise, and Rob Cross, "Getting New Hires Up to Speed Quickly: The Key to Making New Employees Productive Quickly, Known as "Rapid On-Boarding," Is to Help Immediately Build an Informational Network with Co-workers," *MIT Sloan Management Review* 46 (Winter 2005): 35–42.
29. Gwen Moran, "Be the Brand," *Entrepreneur*, February 2007: 77. See also Rieva Lesonsky, "Now Presenting 10 Steps to Making a Successful Sales Presentation," *Small Business Success* 20 (Spring 2006): 64 and Kim T. Gordon, "Warm Up to Cold Calls," *Small Business Success* 20 (Spring 2006): 68.
30. *Webster's New Millennium*™ *Dictionary of English, Preview Edition* (v 0.9.7) Copyright © 2003–2007 Lexico Publishing Group, LLC.
31. Pamela F. Weber, "Getting a Grip on Employee Growth," *Training & Development* 53 (May 1999): 87–93.

32. Donald D. DeCamp, "Are You Hiring the Right People?" *Management Review* 81 (May 1992): 44–48 and Oren Harari, "Attracting the Best Minds," *Management Review* 87 (April 1998): 23–27.

33. Oren Harari, "Attracting the Best Minds," *Management Review* 87 (April 1998): 23–27.

34. Pamela F. Weber, "Getting a Grip on Employee Growth," *Training & Development* 53 (May 1999): 87–93.

35. Oren Harari, "Attracting the Best Minds," *Management Review* 87 (April 1998): 23–27.

36. The 5:15 report was originally developed and used as a management tool at Johns Hopkins Home Care Group in Baltimore, MD.

37. Karen McKirchy, *Powerful Performance Appraisals: How to Set Expectations and Work Together to Improve Performance* (Franklin Lakes, NJ: Career Press, 1998) and Carla Joinson, "Making Sure Employees Measure Up," *HR Magazine* 46 (March 2001): 36–41.

38. William S. Swan and Philip Margulies, *How to Do a Superior Performance Appraisal* (New York: Wiley, 1991).

39. Sharon Mattingly, "Getting Your Talent in Shape," *Personnel Today,* October 17, 2006, http://www.humanresourcesmagazine.com.au/articles/40/0C045F40.asp?Type=60&Category=919 (accessed June 15, 2008).

CHAPTER 6

1. SCORE webpage, http://www.score.org (accessed April 28, 2008).

2. John C. Kelly, "Be a Manager and Leader, Not a Scorekeeper," *Chamber News* 9 (May 2, 2007): 5.

3. Mary K. Pratt, "No More Job Reviews: Subtle Changes in Focus Can Transform the Dreaded Performance Review into an Opportunity to Build Better IT Employees, Teams, and Organizations," *Computerworld*, April 2, 2007: 29; Tom Davis and Michael Landa, "Pat or Slap? Do Appraisals Work?" *CMA Management* 73 (March 1999): 24–27; W. Timothy Weaver, "Linking Performance Reviews to Productivity and Quality," *HRMagazine* 41 (November 1996): 93–99; and John C. Kelly, "Be a Manager and Leader, Not a Scorekeeper," *Chamber News* 9 (May 2, 2007): 5.

4. David Stamps, "Performance Appraisals: Out of Sync and As Unpopular as Ever," *Training* 32 (August 1995): 16. Also see Lori Ashcraft and William A. Anthony, "Turn Evaluations into Mentoring Sessions: Performance Evaluations Don't Have to Be Dreadful," *Behavioral Healthcare* 274 (April 2007): 8–10; and Tom Coens and Mary Jenkins, *Abolishing Performance Appraisals: Why They Backfire and What to Do Instead* (San Francisco: Berrett-Koehler, 2000).

5. Tammy Galvin, "The Weakest Link," *Training* 38 (December 2001): 8. Also see Lin Grensing-Pophal, "Motivate Managers to Review Performance," *HR Magazine* 46 (March 2001): 44–48.

6. Lori Ashcraft and William A. Anthony, "Turn Evaluations into Mentoring Sessions: Performance Evaluations Don't Have to Be Dreadful," *Behavioral Healthcare* 27 (April 2007): 8–10; Karen McKirchy, *Powerful Performance Appraisals: How to Set Expectations and Work Together to Improve Performance* (Franklin Lakes,

NJ: Career Press, 1998); and Carla Joinson, "Making Sure Employees Measure Up," *HR Magazine* 46 (March 2001): 36–41.

7. John C. Kelly, "Be a Manager and Leader, Not a Scorekeeper," *Chamber News* 9 (May 2, 2007): 5; and Ashcraft and Anthony, "Turn Evaluations into Mentoring Sessions: Performance Evaluations Don't Have to Be Dreadful."

8. For EEOC guidelines during performance appraisal, see William S. Swan and Philip Margulies, *How to Do a Superior Performance Appraisal* (New York: Wiley, 1991); also see Equal Employment Opportunity Commission, "The U.S. Equal Employment Opportunity Commission, Meeting of May 16, 2007—on Employment Testing and Screening: Statement of Lawrence Ashe, Rafuse & Hill, LLP," EEOC website http://www.eeoc.gov/abouteeoc/meetings/5-16-07/ashe.html (accessed April 28, 2008).

9. For related research, see Todd J. Maurer, Jerry K. Palmer, and Donna K. Ashe, "Diaries, Checklists, Evaluations, and Contrast Effects in Measurement of Behavior," *Journal of Applied Psychology* 78 (April 1993): 226–231.

10. Alan M. Webber, "How Business Is a Lot Like Life," *Fast Company* 45 (April 2001): 135.

11. Mathew Boyle, "Performance Reviews: Perilous Curves Ahead," *Fortune,* May 28, 2001: 187. Also see Del Jones, "More Firms Cut Workers Ranked at Bottom to Make Way for Talent," *USA Today,* May 30, 2001: 1B-2B; and Jim Goodnight, "Make Your Employees Love to Work for You," *Business 2.0* 3 (January 2003): 97.

12. David Kiley and Del Jones, "Ford Alters Workers Evaluation Process," *USA Today*, July 11, 2001: 1B; and Earle Eldridge, "Ford Settles 2 Lawsuits by White Male Workers," *USA Today*, December 19, 2001: 3B.

13. Jai Ghorpade, "Managing Five Paradoxes of 360-Degree Feedback," *Academy of Management Executive* 14 (February 2000): 140–150; Angelo S. DeNisi and Avraham N. Kluger, "Feedback Effectiveness: Can 360-Degree Appraisals Be Improved?" *Academy of Management Executive* 14 (February 2000): 129–139; John Day, "Simple, Strong Team Ratings," *HR Magazine* 45 (September 2000): 159–161; and Suzanne G. Scott and Walter O. Einstein, "Strategic Performance Appraisal in Team-Based Organizations: One Size Does Not Fit All," *Academy of Management Executive* 15 (May 2001): 107–116.

14. See Frank Shipper, Richard C. Hoffman, and Denise M. Rotondo, "Does the 360 Feedback Process Create Actionable Knowledge Equally Across Cultures?" *Academy of Management Learning and Education* 6 (March 2007): 33–50; and the second Q&A in Jack Welch and Suzy Welch, "The Importance of Being There," *Business Week*, April 16, 2007: 92.

15. W. Timothy Weaver, "Linking Performance Reviews to Productivity and Quality," *HR Magazine* 41 (November 1996): 93–99.

16. Ibid.

17. Adapted from Hubert S. Field and William H. Holley, "The Relationship of Performance Appraisal System Characteristics to Verdicts in Selected Employment Discrimination Cases," *Academy of Management Journal* 25 (June 1982): 392–406. A more recent analysis of 51 cases that derived similar criteria can be

found in Gerald V. Barrett and Mary C. Kernan, "Performance Appraisal and Terminations: A Review of Court Decisions Since *Brito v. Zia* with Implications for Personnel Practices," *Personnel Psychology* 40 (Autumn 1987): 489–503.

18. For more, see Ashcraft and Anthony, "Turn Evaluations into Mentoring Sessions: Performance Evaluations Don't Have to Be Dreadful." Dick Grote, "Painless Performance Appraisals Focus on Results, Behaviors," *HR Magazine* 43 (October 1998): 52–58; and Peter Gwynne, "How Consistent Are Performance Review Criteria?" *MIT Sloan Management Review* 43 (Summer 2002): 15.

19. Excerpted from Jena McGregor, "Case Study: To Adapt, ITT Let's Go of Unpopular Ratings," *Business Week*, January 28, 2008: 46.

20. Robert Levering and Milton Moskowitz, "100 Best Companies to Work For: The Rankings," *Fortune*, February 4, 2008: 77.

21. Eric Garner, "Motivate Your Team to Top Performance," MarketingSource website, http://www.marketingsource.com/articles/view/3207 (accessed April 28, 2008); and Pamela Kruger, "Money—Is That What You Want?" *Fast Company* 24 (May 1999): 48–50.

22. James C. Cooper and Kathleen Madigan, "The Second Half Should Be Healthier," *Business Week*, August 13, 2001: 26.

23. Craig Miller, "The Advantages of Online Recognition," *HR Magazine* 47 (October 2002): 86–92; and Michelle Conlin, "The End of One Size Fits All?" *Business Week*, December 16, 2002: 90–92.

24. John C. Kelly, "Be a Manager and Leader, Not a Scorekeeper." *Chamber News* 9 (May 2, 2007): 5.

25. Paul Falcone, "Motivating Staff Without Money," *HR Magazine* 47 (August 2002): 105–108; and Paul Falcone, "Doing More with Less," *HR Magazine* 48 (February 2003): 101–103.

26. Bill Leanorad, "Perks Give Way to Life-Cycle Benefits Plans," *HR Magazine* 40 (March 1995): 45–48; and Robert Kuttner, "Pensions: How Much Risk Should Workers Have to Bear?" *Business Week*, April 16, 2001: 23.

27. Jason Kolysher and Christopher Westcott, "Emerging Benefits Focus on Flexibility," *Canadian HR Reporter* 20 (December 17, 2007): 20, 27; "Cafeteria Plan Statistics for Companies with More Than 100 Employees," FEBCO website, http://febco.com/articles/cafeteria_statistics.html (accessed April 28, 2008); Alison E. Barber, Randall B. Dunham, and Roger A. Formisano, "The Impact of Flexible Benefits on Employee Satisfaction: A Field Study," *Personnel Psychology* 45 (Spring 1992): 55–75.

28. David Fiedler, "Should You Adjust Your Sales Compensation?" *HR Magazine* 47 (February 2002): 79–82.

29. For more, see David A. Bowen, Stephen W. Gilliland, and Robert Folger, "HRM and Service Fairness: How Being Fair with Employees Spills Over to Customers," *Organizational Dynamics* 27 (Winter 1999): 7–23; and Matt Bloom, "The Performance Effects of Pay Dispersion on Individuals and Organizations," *Academy of Management Journal* 42 (February 1999): 25–40.

30. A good overview of equity theory can be found in Robert P. Vecchio, "Models of Psychological Inequity," *Organizational Behavior and Human Performance* 34 (October 1984): 266–282.

31. J. Stacy Adams and Patricia R. Jacobsen, "Effects of Wage Inequities on Work Quality," *Journal of Abnormal and Social Psychology* 69 (1964): 19–25; and Jerald Greenberg and Suzyn Ornstein, "High Status Job Title As Compensation for Underpayment: A Test of Equity Theory," *Journal of Applied Psychology* 68 (May 1983): 285–297. For more on this topic see, Sarah Brown and John G. Sessions, "Some evidence on the relationship between performance-related pay and the shape of the experience-earnings profile," *Southern Economic Journal* 72 (January 2006): 660– 677.

32. For example, see Jerry Useem, "Have They No Shame?" *Fortune*, April 28, 2003: 56–64.

33. "Biogen Details Executive Stock Awards in Wake of Layoff Plans." *Boston Globe*, September 17, 2005, General OneFile. Gale. Anne Arundel Community College (accessed March 9, 2008).

34. Based on Robert Levering and Milton Moskowitz, "100 Best Companies to Work For," *Fortune*, January 2003: 43.

35. As quoted in "Moving Mountains," *Harvard Business Review* 81, special issue: *Motivating People* (January 2003): 43.

36. Marc Knez and Duncan Simester, "Making Across-the-Board Incentives Work," *Harvard Business Review* 80 (February 2002): 16–17: and Steve Bates, "Now the Downside of Pay for Performance," *HR Magazine* 47 (March 2002): 10.

37. Ed Lisoski, "If You Can't Measure It You Can't Manage It," *Supervision*, 59 (June 1998): 8–11.

38. George Gendron, "Steel Man: Ken Iverson," *Inc. Magazine*, April 1986: 47–48.

39. Stephen Rubenfeld and Jannifer David, "Multiple Employee Incentive Plans: Too Much of a Good Thing?" *Compensation & Benefits Review* 38 (2006): 35–40; Alfie Kohn, "Why Incentive Plans Cannot Work," *Harvard Business Review* 71 (September-October 1993): 54–63. Also see Peter Nulty, "Incentive Pay Can Be Crippling," *Fortune*, November 13, 1995: 23; Robert Eisenberger and Judy Cameron, "Detrimental Effects of Reward," *American Psychologist* 51 (November 1996): 1153–1166; Alfie Kohn, "Challenging Behaviorist Dogma: Myths About Money and Motivation," *Compensation & Benefits Review* 30 (March-April 1998): 27, 33–37; and Del Jones, "CEO Pay Takes Another Hit," *USA Today*, March 10, 2003: 5B.

40. Eric Garner, "Motivate Your Team to Top Performance," MarketingSource website, http://www.marketingsource.com/articles/view/3207 (accessed April 28, 2008); Peter V. LeBlanc and Paul W. Mulvey, "How American Workers See the Rewards of Work," *Compensation & Benefits Review* 30 (January-February 1998): 24–28; and Louisa Wah, "Rewarding Efficient Teamwork," *Management Review* 88 (February 1999): 7.

CHAPTER 7

1. "Guidelines for Coaching and Mentoring," *Training & Development* 51 (August 1997): 23.

2. Dr. Gary Bradt, "Don't Manage Time, Invest It in People," *Supervision* 68 (August 2007): 8–9.

3. Joseph Kornik, "A Numbers Game," *Training* 43 (December 2006): 4; and Margery Weinstein, "Learning Dollars," *Training* 44 (April 2007): 6.

4. Joseph Kornik, "A Numbers Game," *Training* 43 (December 2006): 4.

5. Bernice Kotey and Cathleen Folker, "Employee Training in Smes: Effect of Size and Firm Type—Family and Nonfamily," *Journal of Small Business Management* 45 (April 2007): 214–238.

6. Ibid.

7. Ibid.

8. "President Urged to Add Literacy to Competitiveness Plan," *Report on Literacy Programs* 18 (February 9, 2006): 21; and Robert Wedgeworth, "America's Welfare Depends on Improved Literacy Rates (Letter to the Editor)," *Chronicle of Philanthropy*, 18 (July 20, 2006).

9. Nicole Lewis, "Building a Nation of Readers," *Chronicle of Philanthropy*, 18.13 (April 20, 2006): NA. *Academic OneFile*. Gale. Anne Arundel Community College. 28 Oct. 2008.

10. Robert Wedgeworth, "America's Welfare Depends on Improved Literacy Rates," *Chronicle of Philanthropy*, 18.19 (July 20, 2006): NA. *Academic OneFile*. Gale. Anne Arundel Community College. 28 Oct. 2008; and Nicole Lewis, "Building a Nation of Readers," *Chronicle of Philanthropy*, 18.13 (April 20, 2006): NA. *Academic OneFile*. Gale. Anne Arundel Community College. 28 Oct. 2008.

11. Excerpted from Joshua Hyatt, "Found in Translation: How to Make the Multicultural Work Force Work," *Inc. Magazine*, October 2006: 41–42.

12. Liz Simpson, "Great Expectations," *Training* 39 (February 2002): 40–44; Steve Thomas, "ROK Science," *Training* 38 (December 2001): 72; Evaluating Training Programs Is Covered in "Why Training Doesn't Work," *Training* 35 (February 1998): 24; Donna J. Abernathy, "Thinking Outside the Evaluation Box," *Training & Development* 53 (February 1999): 19–23; and Dean R. Spitzer, "Embracing Evaluation," *Training* 36 (June 1999): 42–47.

13. Joseph Bersin, "The Convergence of Learning and Performance Management: Has Talent Management Arrived?" *Bersin & Associates Industry Report* V2.0 (October 2006): 13, and Chris Howard, "Performance-Driven Training: Enterprise Performance Management at Aetna," Bersin & Associates (December 2004), www.elearningresearch.com.

14. Rana Sinha, "Whose Needs Matter More: Learner or Employer?" *Training* (April 19, 2007).

15. Tammy Galvin, "2001 Industry Report," *Training* 38 (October 2001): 54.

16. The Wisconsin Forward Award, http://www.forwardaward.org/winners.html (accessed May 4, 2008); and the Trostel Company, http://www.trostel.com (accessed May 4, 2008).

17. Trostel Vision Statement, http://www.trostel.com/about/about_items.html#mission (accessed May 4, 2008).

18. "General Truths," *Training* 44 (June 2007).

19. "Community Safety and Environment Report 2007," BlueScope Steel, http://csereport2007.bluescopesteel.com/health_safety/award_winning_performance.html#cs6 (accessed May 4, 2008).

20. Ibid.

21. "Guidelines for Coaching and Mentoring," *Training & Development* 51 (August 1997): 23.

22. Kathleen A. O'Halloran, "Three Simple Principals," *Training & Development Journal* 44 (October 1990): 15–18.

23. Kenneth N. Wexley and Gary P. Latham, *Developing and Training Human Resources in Organizations* (Glenview, IL: Scott, Foresman, 1981): 75–77.

24. Leigh Buchanan, "Train in Vain," *Inc. Magazine*, April 2007: 144.

25. Bill Sims, Jr., "Is Your Incentive Program a Ticking Time Bomb?" *Reward and Recognize Now*, http://www.rewardandrecognizenow.com/articles/taxmag.htm (accessed May 4, 2008).

26. Carroll Lachnit, "Training Reinvented: At Rockwell Collins, a Three-Year Learning Program Overhaul Cut Costs by Nearly 40 percent Annually, and Delivered More Training to More Employees. Here's How It Was Done," *Workforce* 81 (October 2002): 114–127.

27. Wexley and Latham, *Developing and Training Human Resources in Organizations*. Also see Diana Hird, "What Makes a Training Program Good?" *Training* 37 (June 2000): 48–52; and Natalie Shope Griffin, "Personalize Your Management Development," *Harvard Business Review* 81 (March 2003): 113–119.

28. Evaluating training programs is covered in, "Why Training Doesn't Work," *Training* 35 (February 1998): 24; Donna J. Abernathy, "Thinking Outside the Evaluation Box," *Training & Development* 53 (February 1999): 19–23; Dean R. Spitzer, "Embracing Evaluation," *Training* 36 (June 1999): 42–47; Steve Thomas, "ROK Science," *Training* 38 (December 2001): 72; and Liz Simpson, "Great Expectations," *Training* 39 (February 2002): 40–44.

29. Holly Dolezalek, "2005 Industry Report: Training Magazine's Exclusive Analysis of Employer-Sponsored Training in the U.S." *Training* 42 (December 2005): 14–24; and Tammy Galvin, "2001 Industry Report," *Training* 38 (October 2001): 54.

30. "They Can Learn Their Own Way," *Training & Coaching Today* 68 (May 15, 2007).

31. John Unkles, "What's New in Corporate Education? E-learning Is Now the Front-runner in Corporate Education. But Does This Signal the End of Face-to-Face Training?" *Journal of Banking and Financial Services* 117 (October-November 2003): 2–4.

32. James Careless, "Low-cost Options," *Rotor & Wing* Nov. 1, 2005, http://www.aviationtoday.com/rw/training/simulators/1829.html (accessed October 28, 2008).

33. Jason Park, Helen MacRae, Laura J. Musselman, Peter Rossos, Stanley J. Hamstra, Stephen Wolman, and Richard K. Reznick, "Randomized Controlled Trial of Virtual Reality Simulator Training: Transfer to Live Patients," *American Journal of Surgery* 194 (August 2007): 205–212; and R. L. Kneebone, D. Nestel, C. Vincent, and A. Darzi, "Complexity, Risk and Simulation in Learning Procedural Skills," *Medical Education* 41 (August 2007): 808–815.

34. Ibid, P. 441, 31.

35. "Learning Styles," The University of Illinois Extension, http://www.urbanext.uiuc.edu/succeed/04-learningstyles.html (accessed May 4, 2008).

36. "General Learning Styles," UWExtension, University of Wisconsin, January 2006, excerpts from: Julie Coates, "Generational Learning Styles," LERN Books (October 31, 2006).

37. Ibid.

38. Diana Oblinger, "Boomers, Gen-Xers & Millennials: Understanding the New Students," *Educause* (July/August 2003): 37–47.

39. Linda G. Keidrowski, "Whose Generation Is It, Anyway?" *Small Business Times*, February 2, 2008, http://www.biztimes.com/news/2008/2/8/whose-generation-is-it-anyway (accessed May 4, 2008); Marianne Bhonslay, "Working Knowledge: As Gen Y enters the Labor Market, Retailers Seek New Training and Motivation Methods," *Sporting Goods Business* 40 (June 2007): 8–10; Julius Steiner, "Six Steps to Guaranteeing Generation Y Productivity," *Supervision* 68 (July 2007): 6–7.

40. Steiner, "Six Steps to Guaranteeing Generation Y Productivity;" and "General Learning Styles," UWExtension, University of Wisconsin, January 2006, excerpts from: Julie Coates, "Generational Learning Styles" LERN Books (October 31, 2006).

CHAPTER 8

1. "100 Best Companies to Work For 2008," *Fortune,* http://money.cnn.com/magazines/fortune/bestcompanies/2008/snapshots/62.html (accessed May 10, 2008); and Carmine Gallo, "Your New Title: Chief Inspiration Officer," *BusinessWeek*, January 4, 2008, http://www.businessweek.com/print/smallbiz/content/jan2008/sb2008014_303969.htm (accessed May 10, 2008).

2. Gardiner Morse, "Why We Misread Motives," *Harvard Business Review* 81 (January 2003): 18; Robert N. Llewellyn, "The Four Career Concepts," *HR Magazine* 47 (September 2002): 121–126; and Thad Green, "Three Steps to Motivating Employees," *HR Magazine* 45 (November 2000): 155–158.

3. A. H. Maslow, "A Theory of Human Motivation," *Psychological Review* 50 (July 1943): 370–396; Ron Zemke, "Maslow for a New Millennium," *Training* 35 (December 1998): 54–58; and Robin Marantz Henig, "Basic Needs Met? Next Comes Happiness," *USA Today*, January 2, 2001: 11A.

4. Gene Koretz, "The Vital Role of Self-Esteem," *BusinessWeek*, February 2, 1998: 26; Donald G. Gardner and Jon L. Pierce, "Self-Esteem and Self-Efficacy Within the Organizational Context: An Empirical Investigation," *Group & Organizational Management* 23 (March 1998): 48–70; and Perry Pascarella, "It All Begins with Self-Esteem," *Management Review* 88 (February 1999): 60–61.

5. Maslow, "A Theory of Human Motivation," 382.

6. George W. Cherry, "The Serendipity of the Fully Functioning Manager," *Sloan Management Review* 17 (Spring 1976): 73.

7. Vance F. Mitchell and Pravin Moudgill, "Measurement of Maslow's Need Hierarchy," *Organizational Behavior and Human Performance* 16 (August 1976): 348. Self-actualizing executives are profiled in Keith H. Hammonds, "The Mission," *Business Week*, March 22, 1999: 97–107; and Micheline Maynard, "Lutz Gets a Charge Out of New Career," *USA Today*, June 1, 1999: 12B.

8. Ellen L. Betz, "Two Tests of Maslow's Theory of Need Fulfillment," *Journal of Vocational Behavior* 24 (April 1984): 204–220.

9. Edward E. Lawler, *Motivation in Work Organizations* (Monterey, CA: Brooks/Cole, 1973): 34.

10. Professor Charles Wyckoft, Riverside Community College, California. Reprinted with permission.

11. Frederick Herzberg, Bernard Mausner, and Barbara Bloch Snyderman, *The Motivation to Work*, 2nd ed. (New York: Wiley, 1959).

12. As quoted in Carmine Gallo's, "Your New Title: Chief Inspiration Officer," *BusinessWeek*, January 4, 2008, http://www.businessweek.com/print/smallbiz/content/jan2008/sb2008014_303969.htm (accessed May 10, 2008).

13. Carmine Gallo's, "Your New Title: Chief Inspiration Officer," *BusinessWeek*, January 4, 2008, http://www.businessweek.com/print/smallbiz/content/jan2008/sb2008014_303969.htm (accessed May 10, 2008).

14. J. Richard Hackman and Greg R. Oldham, *Work Redesign* (Reading, MA: Addison-Wiley, 1980): 20. Also see Roger E. Herman and Joyce L. Gioia, "Making Work Meaningful: Secrets of the Future-Focused Corporation," *The Futurist* 32 (December 1998): 24–38; and Donna Fenn, "Redesign Work," *Inc. Magazine*, June 1999: 74–84.

15. As quoted in John Bowe, Marisa Bowe and Sabin Streeter, eds., *Gig: Americans Talk About Their Jobs at the Turn of the Millennium* (New York: Crown Publishers, 2000): 30.

16. Deborah J. Dwyer and Marilyn L. Fox, "The Moderating Role of Hostility in the Relationship Between Enriched Jobs and Health," *Academy of Management Journal* 43 (December 2000): 1086–1096; and Amy Wrzesniewski and Jane E Dutton, "Crafting a Job: Revisioning Employees as Active Crafters of Their Work," *Academy of Management Review* 26 (April 2001): 179–201.

17. Peter W. Hom, "Expectancy Prediction of Reenlistment in the National Guard," *Journal of Vocational Behavior* 16 (April 1980): 235–248; John P. Wanous, Thomas L. Keon, and Janina C. Latack, "Expectancy Theory and Occupational/Organizational Choices: A Review and Test," *Organizational Behavior and Human Performance* 32 (August 1983): 66–86; Alan W. Stacy, Keith F. Widaman, and G. Alan Marlatt, "Expectancy Models of Alcohol Use," *Journal of Personality and Social Psychology* 58 (May 1990): 918–928; and Anne S. Tsui, Susan J. Ashford, Lynda St. Clair, and Katherine R. Xin, "Dealing with Discrepant Expectations: Response Strategies and Managerial Effectiveness," *Academy of Management Journal* 38 (December 1995): 1515–1543.

18. Bill Leonard, "College Students Confident They Will Reach Career Goals Quickly," *HR Magazine* 46 (April 2001): 27.

19. As quoted in "Leadership for the 21st Century: Lessons We Have Learned," *Newsweek*, September 25, 2006: 75.

20. Jim Collins, "Turning Goals into Results: The Power of Catalytic Mechanisms," *Harvard Business Review* 77 (July-August 1999): 71–82.

21. Edwin A. Locke and Gary P. Latham, "Building a Practically Useful Theory of Goal Setting and Task Motivation: A 35 Year Odyssey," *American Psychologist* 57 (September 2002): 705–717.

22. Ibid.

23. Ibid.

24. "Stretch goals" are discussed in Shawn Tully, "Why Go for Stretch Targets," *Fortune*, November 14, 1994: 145–158; Strat Sherman, "Stretch Goals: The Dark Side of Asking for

Miracles," *Fortune*, November 13, 1995: 231–232; Gary Bielous, "Stretch Targets: The Art of Asking for Miracles," *Supervision* 57 (October 1996): 16–19; and Kenneth R. Thompson, Wayne A. Hochwarter, and Nicholas J. Mathys, "Stretch Targets: What Makes Them Effective?" *Academy of Management Executive* 11 (August 1997): 48–60.

25. Christopher Earley, Gregory B. Northcraft, Cynthia Lee, and Terri R. Lituchy, "Impact of Process and Outcomes Feedback on The Relation of Goal Setting to Task Performance," *Academy of Management Journal* 33 (March 1990): 87–105.

26. John Huey, "America's Most Successful Merchant," *Fortune*, September 23, 1991: 50.

27. Lewis Carroll, *Alice's Adventures in Wonderland* (Philadelphia: The John C. Winston Company, 1923): 57.

28. As quoted by Carmine Gallo, "Bringing Passion to Starbucks, Travelocity," *BusinessWeek*, January 9, 2008, http://www.businessweek.com/print/smallbiz/content/jan2008/sb2008019_492857.htm (accessed May 10, 2008).

29. Carter McNamara, *Basics About Employee Motivation (Including Steps You can Take)*, Copyright 1997–2007, Carter McNamara, MBA, PhD, Authenticity Consulting, LLC; for more on professional motivation see Jennifer Wilson, "Motivate Your Team: A Simple Question Can Solve the Mystery," *Accounting Today* 20 (September 4, 2006): 22; Oren Harari, "Stop Trying to Motivate Your employees—Part I," *How I See It*, On-Line Articles (November 21, 2000); and Oren Harari, "Stop Trying to Motivate Your Employees—Part II," *How I See It*, On-Line Articles (November 28, 2000).

30. Gary LaBranche, "What Matters," *This Week at Association Forum*, April 23, 2005: http://www.associationforum.org/thisWeekDetail.asp?objectID=4819 (accessed October 28, 2008).

31. Harari, "Stop Trying to Motivate Your Employees—Part I."

32. Wilson, "Motivate Your Team: A Simple Question Can Solve the Mystery."

33. Special thanks to Professor Charles Wyckoft at Riverside Community College, California, for suggesting this perspective.

34. S. Sadi Seferoglu, "Quotes, Proverbs, and Pearls of Wisdom from [the] Internet," http://www.columbia.edu/~sss31/rainbow/quotes.html (accessed May 10, 2008).

35. Lou Holtz, "Setting a Higher Standard," *Get Motivated Workbook* (2006): 22.

36. Joan Marie Whelan, "Create the Change You Want to Become," *Holistic Junction On-Line* (August 13, 2007, Copyright Whelan).

37. Ibid, P. 443, 35.

38. Ibid, P. 443, 36.

39. "17 Inspirational Quotes on People Skills," The Positivity Blog, http://www.positivityblog.com/index.php/2007/04/10/17-inspirational-quotes-on-people-skills/ (accessed May 10, 2008); and Dean Minett, "A Little Water Goes a Long Way," *Hospitality* (January 1, 2007): 22.

40. "USA Today Snapshots®," *USA Today*, February 6, 2007: B1 (source: Ace Hardware survey of 1059 adults 18 and older conducted by Impulse Research.)

41. Minett, "A Little Water Goes a Long Way."

42. As quoted in Thomas A. Stewart and Louise O'Brien, "Execution Without Excuses," *Harvard Business Review* 83 (March 2005): 106.

43. Elizabeth Rapoport, "The Corporate Horse Whisperer," *The Crossings* Feb. 2008: http://www.thecrossingsaustin.com/features/feb08/corporate_horse_whisperer.php (accessed October 28, 2008).

44. Carmine Gallo, "Employee Motivation the Ritz-Carlton Way," *BusinessWeek*, February 29, 2008, http://www.businessweek.com/print/smallbiz/content/feb2008/sb20080229_347490.htm (accessed May 10, 2008).

45. Micki Holliday, *Coaching, Mentoring & Managing* (Franklin Lakes, NJ: Career Press, 2001): 3.

CHAPTER 9

1. William Cottringer, "The Right Work Attitude," *Supervision* 64 (May 2003): 6–8.

2. Ibid.

3. Ibid.

4. Daniel Gross, "Nice Work: In the Corporate Culture, A Little Kindness Won't Hurt You," *US Airways Magazine*, February 2007: 51–53.

5. Jon Reinfurt, "Back Page: Selling for Success," *Small Business Success* (2006): 72.

6. Ibid, P. 443, 3.

7. Sidney J. Parnes, "Learning Creative Behavior," *The Futurist* 18 (August 1984): 30–31; Liz Simpson, "Fostering Creativity," *Training* 38 (December 2001): 54–57; and Polly LaBarre, "Weird Ideas That Work," *Fast Company*, 54 (January 2002): 68–73.

8. Arthur Koestler, *The Act of Creation* (London: Hutchinson, 1969): 27.

9. James L. Adams, *Conceptual Blockbusting* (San Francisco: Freeman, 1974): 35; Dean Foust, "Getting to 'Aha!' *BusinessWeek*, September 4, 2006, 100; and Siri Schubert, "A Duffer's Dream," *Business 2.0* 7 (November 2006): 56.

10. Geoffrey Colvin, "The Imagination Economy," *Fortune*, July 10, 2006: 53.

11. Minda Zetlin, "Nurturing Nonconformists," *Management Review* 88 (October 1999): 30; Diane L. Coutu, "Genius at Work," *Harvard Business Review* 79 (October 2001): 63–68; Ryan Mathews and Watts Wacker, "Deviants, Inc.," *Fast Company*, no. 56 (March 2002): 70–80; and Robin Hanson, "The Myth of Creativity," *BusinessWeek*, July 3, 2006: 134.

12. John Byrne, "The Search for the Young and Gifted," *BusinessWeek*, October 4, 1999: 108. Also see Thomas H. Davenport, Laurence Prusak, and H. James Wilson, "Who's Bringing You Hot Ideas, and How Are You Responding?" *Harvard Business Review* 81 (February 2003): 58–64.

13. Ian Wylie, "Failure is Glorious," *Fast Company*, no. 51 (October 2001): 35–38; and Jena McGregor, "How Failure Breeds Success," *BusinessWeek*, July 10, 2006: 42–52.

14. List adapted from Roger von Oech, *A Whack on the Side of the Head* (New York: Warner Books, 1983). Reprinted with permission.

15. Adapted from Michael Michalko, *Thinkertoys*, 2nd ed, (Berkeley, CA: Ten Speed Press, 2006): 15.

16. "Stepping Outside of the Box to Achieve Extraordinary Results," *Get Motivated Workbook* (2006): 57.

17. Michalko, *Thinkertoys,* 2nd ed, 18; and "Stepping Outside of the Box to Achieve Extraordinary Results," *Get Motivated Workbook* (2006): 57.

18. Michalko, *Thinkertoys,* 2nd ed, 18.

19. Ibid., 12.

20. Karen E. Spaeder, "Creative Sparks: Interns Can Do More Than Stuff Envelopes. The Key to Releasing Their Potential is Recognizing Them as an Important Part of Your Team," *Entrepreneur* (April 2007), http://www.entrepreneur.com/magazine/entrepreneur/2007/april/175806.html (accessed July 13, 2008).

21. Michalko, *Thinkertoys,* 2nd ed, 20.

22. Alison Stein Wellner, "Creative Control, Even Bosses Need Time to Dream," *Inc. Magazine,* July 2007: 40–42.

23. As quoted by Stein Wellner, "Creative Control, Even Bosses Need Time to Dream."

24. Diane Brady, "Ideas that Bloom," *BusinessWeek SmallBiz* (Spring 2006): 47–53.

25. Judith A. Ricci, Elsbeth Chee, Amy Lorandeau, and Jan Berger, "Fatigue in the U.S. Workforce: Prevalence and Implications for Lost Productive Work Time," *Journal of Occupational & Environmental Medicine* 49 (January 2007): 1–10; and Teresa M. McAleavy, "Asleep on the Job," *The Sunday Capital,* May 20, 2007: E3.

26. Teresa M. McAleavy, "Asleep on the Job," *The Sunday Capital,* May 20, 2007: E3.

27. "Lunch is for Sissies," *The Week* 7 (September 7, 2007): 39; Phyllis Korkki, "CAREER COUCH; That Yawn After Lunch Is Perfectly Normal" *New York Times,* August 19, 2007, http://www.nytimes.com/2007/08/19/business/yourmoney/19career.html?n=Top/News/Business/Small%20Business/Human%20Resources&_r=1&oref=slogin&pagewanted=print (accessed July 13, 2008).

28. McAleavy, "Asleep on the Job."

29. Ibid.

30. James M Pethokoukis, "The Deans of Design: From the computer mouse the newest Swiffer, IDEO is the firm behind the scenes," *U.S. News & World Report,* October 2, 2006: 65–68.

31. Ibid.

32. Ibid.

33. Diego Rodgriguez and Ryan Jacoby, "Embracing Risk to Learn, Grow and Innovate," *Rotman Magazine* (Spring 2007): 54–58.

34. Ibid, P. 444, 30.

35. Ibid, P. 444, 30.

36. Ibid, P. 444, 30.

37. Excerpts from James M Pethokoukis, "The Deans of Design: From the Computer Mouse the Newest Swiffer, IDEO is the Firm Behind the Scenes," *U.S. News & World Report,* October 2, 2006: 65–68, copyright 2006 U.S. News & World Report, L.P. Reprinted with permission; and Trevor Thieme, "The Bright Stuff," *Best Life Magazine* (March 21, 2007), http://www.bestlifeonline.com/cms/publish/best-success/The_Bright_Stuff.shtml (accessed July 13, 2008).

38. Trevor Thieme, "The Bright Stuff," *Best Life Magazine* (March 21, 2007), http://www.bestlifeonline.com/cms/publish/best-success/The_Bright_Stuff.shtml (accessed July 13, 2008).

39. Tom Muha, "Happy Workers Good for Business," *The Sunday Capital,* May 20, 2007: F1, F4.

40. "Career Digest: Help Yourself," *The Baltimore Sun,* September 16, 2007: H1.

41. Chesapeake Bay Foundation website, http://www.cbf.org/site/PageServer?pagename=about_sub_careers_why (accessed March 17, 2008).

42. Tamara J. Erickson and Lynda Gratton, "What it Means to Work Here," *Harvard Business Review* 85 (March 2007): 104–112.

43. Ibid.; and Whole Foods Market website, press release, January 23, 2008, http://media.wholefoodsmarket.com/pr/wf/national/pr_01-23-08.aspx (accessed May 4, 2008).

44. Whole Foods Market website, press release, January 23, 2008, http://media.wholefoodsmarket.com/pr/wf/national/pr_01-23-08.aspx (accessed May 4, 2008). Courtesy of Whole Food Market.

45. T. L. Stanley, "Generate a Positive Corporate Culture," *Supervision* 68 (September 2007): 5–7.

46. Diane Brady, "Ideas That Bloom," *BusinessWeek SmallBiz* (Spring 2006): 47–53.

47. Whole Foods Market website, press release, January 9, 2006, http://media.wholefoodsmarket.com/pr/wf/national/pr_01-09-06.aspx (accessed May 4, 2008).

48. Hillary Chura, "Balancing Act: Forward-Thinking Firms Are Making It Easier to Juggle Work and Family Successfully," *Business Work & Family* (March 2006): 108–111.

49. Marcia A Reed-Woodard, "The Balancing Act: How Busy Executives Make Their Lives Work," *Black Enterprise* (February 2007), http://www.allbusiness.com/specialty-businesses/minority-owned-businesses/3949457-1.html (accessed July 13, 2008).

50. Jacqueline Lynn, "Play It Safe," *Entrepreneur,* June 2007: 56.

51. Chris Penttila, "Funny Business," *Small Business Success* 21 (Fall 2006): 41–46.

52. Jorge Cruise, "The Boss Wants You to Stay Healthy," *USA Weekend,* February 23–25, 2007: 4.

53. Joe Robinson, "On the Hot Seat: Fighting "Obsessive-Compulsive Productivity," *Fast Company* (March 2007): 54.

54. Marcia A Reed-Woodard, "The Balancing Act: How Busy Executives Make Their Lives Work," *Black Enterprise* (February 2007), http://www.allbusiness.com/specialty-businesses/minority-owned-businesses/3949457-1.html (accessed July 13, 2008).

55. Steve Pavlina, "Triple Your Personal Productivity," Copyright © 2008 by Pavlina LLC, http://www.stevepavlina.com/articles/triple-your-personal-productivity.htm (accessed March 17, 2008); and Stephen R. Covey, *The 7 Habits of Highly Effective People* (New York: Free Press, 2004): 149–167.

56. Hillary Chura, "Balancing Act: Forward-Thinking Firms Are Making It Easier to Juggle Work and Family Successfully," *Business Work & Family* (March 2006): 108–111; Marcia A Reed-Woodard, "The Balancing Act: How Busy Executives Make Their Lives Work," *Black Enterprise* (February 2007) http://www.allbusiness.com/specialty-businesses/minority-owned-businesses/3949457-1.html (accessed July 13, 2008); and Mark Henricks, "Young at Heart," *Entrepreneur,* March 2007: 30.

57. Excerpted from Frank Jossi, "Clocking Out," *HR Magazine* 52 (June 2007): 46–50.

58. Janet Paskin, "Happily Ever After," *Money*, June 2006: 28.

59. Richard F. Bowman, Jr., "Temptation #4: Harmony Versus Productive Conflict," *The Educational Forum* (Spring 2001), http://findarticles.com/p/articles/mi_qa4013/is_200104/ai_n8951515?tag=artBody;col1 (accessed July 13, 2008).

60. As quoted in Chuck Salter, "Failure Doesn't Suck," *Fast Company*, no. 115 (May 2007): 44.

CHAPTER 10

1. Ale Smiths, Ad Th. H. Pruyn, and Cees B. M. van Riel, "The Impact of Employee Communication and Perceived External Prestige on Organizational Identification," *Academy of Management Journal* 49 (October 2001): 1051–1062; and Lisa Burrell, "The CEO Who Couldn't Keep His Foot Out of His Mouth," *Harvard Business Review* 84 (December 2006): 35–46.

2. "Wanted: Management Skills, "*Training* 41 (November 2004): 19.

3. "Hilary Billings," *Fast Company*, no. 66 (January 2003): 104; James Surowiecki, "Too Much Information," *Fast Company*, 65 (December 2002): 41–42.

4. Keith Davis, *Human Behavior at Work: Organizational Behavior*, 6th ed. (New York: McGraw-Hill, 1981): 399.

5. Nancy J. Adler, *International Dimensions of Organizational Behavior*, (Mason, Ohio: South-Western, 2002): 16–34.

6. As quoted in "How Cultures Collide," *Psychology Today*, July 1976: 69.

7. Karen E. Klein, "Ensuring Harmony Amidst Diversity," *BusinessWeek*, March 8, 2001, http://www.businessweek.com/smallbiz/content/mar2001/sb2001038_686.htm?chan=search (accessed May 10, 2008).

8. Robert House, Mansour Javidan, Paul Hanges, and Peter Dorfman, "Understanding Cultures and Implicit Leadership Theories Across the Globe: An Introduction to Project GLOBE," *Journal of World Business* 37 (Spring 2002): 3–10; Felix C. Brodbeck, Michael Frese, and Mansour Javidan, "Leadership Made in Germany: Low on Compassion, High on Performance," *Academy of Management Executive* 16 (February 2002): 16–29; Jeffery C. Kennedy, "Leadership in Malaysia: Traditional Values, International Outlook," *Academy of Management Executive* 16 (August 2002): 15–26; Robert J. House, Paul J. Hanges, Mansour Javidan, Peter W. Dorfman, and Vipin Gupta, eds., *Culture Leadership, and Organizations: The GLOBE Study of 62 Societies* (Thousand Oaks, CA: Sage, 2004); and Mansour Javidan and Jandani Lynton, "The Changing Face of the Chinese Executive," *Harvard Business Review* 83 (December 2005): 28, 30. Also see George B. Graen, "In the Eye of the Beholder: Cross-Cultural Lessons in Leadership from Project GLOBE: A Response Viewed from the Third Culture Bonding (TCB) Model of Cross-Cultural Leadership," *Academy of Management Perspectives* 20 (November 2006): 95–101; and Robert J. House, Mansour Javidan, Peter W. Dorfman, and Mary Sully de Luque, "A Failure of Scholarship: Response to George Graen's Critique of GLOBE," *Academy of Management Perspective* 20 (November 2006): 102–114.

9. John Schaubroeck and Simon S. K. Lam, "How Similarity to Peers and Supervisors Influences Organizational Advancement in Different Cultures," *Academy of Management Journal* 45 (December 2002): 1120–1136.

10. Allen C. Bluedorn, Carol Felker Kaufman, and Paul M. Lane, "How Many Things Do You Like to Do at Once? An Introduction to Monochronic and Polychronic Time," *Academy of Management Executive* 6 (November 1992): 17–26; and Allen C. Bluedorn and Rhetta L Standifer, "Time and the Temporal Imagination," *Academy of Management Learning and Education* 5 (June 2006): 196–206.

11. Alison Overholt, "The Art of Multitasking," *Fast Company*, 63 (October 2002): 118–125.

12. Gregory K. Stephens and Charles R. Greer, "Doing Business in Mexico: Understanding Cultural Differences," *Organizational Dynamics* 24 (Summer 1995): 39–55; Mike Johnson, "Untapped Latin America," *Management Review* 85 (July 1996): 31–34; and Yongsun Paik and J. H. Derick Sohn, "Confucius in Mexico: Korean MNCs and the Maquiladoras." *Business Horizons* 41 (November-December 1998): 25–33; Laura Petrecca, "Stores, Banks Go Speedy to Win Harried Customers," *USA Today*, December 1, 2006: 1B.

13. Karl Albrecht, "Lost in the Translation," *Training* 33 (June 1996): 66–70; Daniel Pianko, "Smooth Translations," *Management Review* 85 (July 1996): 20; and Rebecca Ganzel, "Universal Translator? Not Quite," *Training* 36 (April 1999): 22, 24.

14. "Burger Boost," *USA Today*, October 11, 1995, 1B; and Michael Arndt, "A Misguided Beef with McDonald's," *Business Week*, May 21, 2001: 14.

15. Based on Figure 2 in Gary Bonvillian and William A. Nowlin, "Cultural Awareness: An Essential Element of Doing Business Abroad," *Business Horizons* 37 (November-December 1994): 44–50.

16. Phillip G. Clampitt, *Communicating for Managerial Effectiveness* (Newbury Park, CA: Sage, 1991): 1–24.

17. Harriet Rubin, "The Power of Words," *Fast Company*, 21 (January 1999): 142–151.

18. Thomas H. Davenport and John C. Beck, *The Attention Economy: Understanding the New Currency of Business* (Boston: Harvard Business School Press, 2001).

19. Edward Iwata, "Companies Find Gold Inside Melting Pot," *USA Today*, July 9, 2007: 1B–2B.

20. Nandani Lynton and Kirsten Hogh Thogrersen, "How China Transforms an Executive's Mind," *Organizational Dynamics* 35 (2006): 170–181; Diane Coutu, "Leveraging the Psychology of the Salesperson: A Conversation with Psychologist and Anthropologist G. Clotaire Rapaille," *Harvard Business Review* 84 (July-August 2006): 42–47; Paula Lehman, "The Evolution of a Diplomat," *BusinessWeek*, September 18, 2006: 74; and Keith Naughton, "The Great Wal-Mart of China," *Newsweek*, October 30, 2006: 50–52.

21. Stacy Lawrence, "Greetings from Planet Vagabond," *Business 2.0* 4 (February 2003): 32.

22. Robert H. Lengel and Richard L. Daft, "The Selection of Communication Media As an Executive Skill," *Academy of Management*

Executive 2 (August 1988): 225–232; John R. Carlson and Robert W. Zmud, "Channel Expansion Theory and the Experiential Nature of Media Richness Perceptions," *Academy of Management Journal* 42 (April 1999): 153–170.

23. Erin Binney, "Is E-mail the New Pink Slip?" *HR Magazine* 51 (November 2006): 32; Adam Lashinsky, "Lights! Camera! Cue the CEO!" *Fortune*, August 21, 2006: 27; Linda Dulye, "Get Out of Your Office," *HR Magazine* 51 (July 2006): 99–101; Kerry J. Sulkowicz, "The Corporate Shrink," *Fast Company*, no. 108 (September 2006): 103; and Kerry Hannon, "Winning Coach Shares Winning Advice for Success," *USA Today*, October 16, 2006: 7B.

24. Del Jones, "Do Foreign Executives Balk at Sports Jargon?" *USA Today*, March 30, 2007, 1B. Also see Stanley Bing, "Corporate Jargon," *Fortune*, March 19, 2007: 44.

25. Bella M. DePaulo, Deborah A. Kashy, Susan E. Kirkendol, Melissa M. Wyer, and Jennifer A. Epstein, "Lying in Everyday Life," *Journal of Personality and Social Psychology* 70 (May 1996): 979–995; and Bella M. DePaulo and Deborah A. Kashy, "Who Lies?" *Journal of Personality and Social Psychology* 70 (May 1996): 1037–1051.

26. John Hamm, "Five Messages Leaders Must Manage," *Harvard Business Review* 84 (May 2006): 114–123; David Robinson, "Public Relations Comes of Age," *Business Horizons* 49 (May-June 2006): 247–256; and Paul A. Argenti and Thea S. Haley, "Get Your Act Together," *Harvard Business Review* 84 (October 2006): 26.

27. Phillip G. Clampitt, Robert J. DeKoch, and Thomas Cashman, "A Strategy for Communicating About Uncertainty," *Academy of Management Executive* 14 (November 2000): 48.

28. Ibid.

29. Ibid.

30. Patricia Digh, "One Style Doesn't Fit All," *HR Magazine* 47 (November 2002): 79–83.

31. Jonathan Benz, "How to Establish Instant Rapport," *Get Motivated Workbook* (2006): 48.

32. Frank Savarese, "It's All About Leadership," *Business Owners Guide to Financial Management*, 10.

33. Michael Kemp, "Visualization Works in Reaching Business Goals," *American Salesman* 45 5 (May 2000): 18.

34. Michael Anthony Holliday, "'Friends, Romans, Countrymen. . . .' In the First of a Series of Articles on Advanced Communication, Michael Anthony Holliday Turns the Spotlight on Presentation Skills," *Training Journal* (Sept. 2007): 33–37.

35. Carl May as quoted in Victor M. Parachin's, "Seven Secrets for Self-Motivation," *Supervision* 60 (January 1999): 3–6.

36. CNN website, http://www.cnn.com/CNN/Programs/larry.king.live/ (accessed March 17, 2008); and Larry King, "Communicating for Success," *Get Motivated Workbook* (2006): 12–13.

37. CNN website, http://www.cnn.com/CNN/anchors_reporters/king.larry.html (accessed March 17, 2008).

38. Larry King, "Communicating for Success," *Get Motivated Workbook* (2006): 12–13.

39. Gladys Edmunds, "Keeping Workers Involved Means Listening to Them," *USA Today*, October 17, 2007: 4B.

40. Data from Cynthia Hamilton and Brian H. Kleiner, "Steps to Better Listening," *Personnel Journal* 66 (February 1987): 20–21. Also see Madelyn Burley-Allen, "Listen Up," *HR Magazine* 46 (November 2001): 115–120.

41. Rebecca Wasieleski, "Communicating with Cross-Cultural Crews," *Concrete Contractor* 7 (April 2007): 56.

42. Paula Butterfield, "What a Listener Hears Isn't Necessarily What Was Said," *Business First-Columbus*, December 15, 2000: A26.

43. Ibid.

44. Elizabeth Rapoport, "The Corporate Horse Whisperer," *The Crossings* Feb. 2008: http://www.thecrossingsaustin.com/features/feb08/corporate_horse_whisperer.php (accessed October 28, 2008).

45. Adapted from Howard Feiertag's "Avoiding Communication Barriers Leads to Successful Sales," *Hotel & Motel Management* 218 (April 21, 2003): 16.

46. "The Best Advice I Ever Got," *Fortune*, May 12, 2008, 74.

47. Stephen Covey, *Seven Habits of Highly Effective People* (New York: Free Press, 2004): 79.

48. Ibid.

49. Ibid.

50. Based on Robert F. DeGise, "Writing: Don't Let the Mechanics Obscure the Message," *Supervisory Management* 21 (April 1976): 26–28. Also see Kenneth W. Davis, "What Writing Training Can—and Can't—Do," *Training* 32 (August 1995): 60–63; David A. Bates, "When Good Writing Goes Bad," *Internal Auditor* 53 (February 1996): 36–38; and Jeffrey Marshall, "How to Write a Perfectly Good Memo," *Harvard Management Communication Letter* 2 (July 1999): 4–6.

51. "The Last Word, A New 'Greatest' Generation," *The Week*, May 11, 2007: 44–45.

CHAPTER 11

1. Jennifer Gill, "How to Help an Underachiever," *Inc. Magazine*, March 2007: 44.

2. T. L. Stanley, "Poor Performance & Due Process (Ways to Deal with Poorly Performing Employees)," *Supervision* 68 (January 2007): 8–12.

3. Ibid, P. 446, 1.

4. T. L. Stanley, "Poor Performance & Due Process (Ways to Deal with Poorly Performing Employees)," *Supervision* 68 (January 2007): 8–12; and Jennifer Gill, "How to Help an Underachiever," *Inc. Magazine*, March 2007: 44.

5. Gill, "How to Help an Underachiever."

6. Ibid.

7. Ibid.

8. Stephanie Davis, "Avoid Being 'The Terminator': Before You Say 'Hasta la Vista,' Use Progressive Discipline to Coach, Counsel Employees," *Ophthalmology Times* 32 (October 1, 2007): 86(2); Indiana University Human Resources Services, Progressive Discipline Training, Indiana University website, last updated July 26, 2002, http://www.indiana.edu/~uhrs/training/ca/progressive.html (accessed March 21, 2008); and Brent T. Johnson, "Implementing Progressive Discipline Policies to Minimize Liability and Improve Employee Performance," Fairfield and Woods, P.C.,

Fairfield and Woods website, http://www.fwlaw.com/progressive
.html (accessed March 21, 2008).

9. Ibid.

10. Ibid.

11. Special thanks to Professor Elaine Madden from Anne Arundel Community College in Arnold, Maryland for suggesting this topic for inclusion.

12. "Ask Inc., Firing" *Inc. Magazine*, November 2007, 69; Chauncey M. DePree Jr. and Rebecca K. Jude, "Ten Practical Suggestions for Terminating an Employee," *The CPA Journal* 77 (August 2007): 62–63; and Kerry M. Richard, "Pruning Poor Performers," *Veterinary Economics* 47 (January 2006): 30.

13. DePree and Jude, "Ten Practical Suggestions for Terminating an Employee." Also see Kerry M. Richard, "Pruning Poor Performers," *Veterinary Economics* 47 (January 2006): 30.

14. Richard, "Pruning Poor Performers;" Davis, "Avoid Being 'The Terminator': Before You Say 'Hasta la Vista,' Use Progressive Discipline to Coach, Counsel Employees;" and Brent T. Johnson, "Implementing Progressive Discipline Policies to Minimize Liability and Improve Employee Performance," Fairfield and Woods, P.C., Fairfield and Woods website, http://www.fwlaw.com/progressive.html (accessed March 21, 2008).

15. Ibid.

16. Chris Penttila, "Buh-Bye, Say Hello to a Better Way of Firing Problem Employees," *Entrepreneur*, September 2007: 28; DePree and Jude, "Ten Practical Suggestions or Terminating nd Employee;" Richard, "Pruning Poor Performers:" Davis, "Avoid Being 'The Terminator': Before You Say 'Hasta la Vista,' Use Progressive Discipline to Coach, Counsel Employees;" and Johnson, "Implementing Progressive Discipline Policies to Minimize Liability and Improve Employee Performance."

17. DePree and Jude, "Ten Practical Suggestions for Terminating and Employee."

18. Penttila, "Buh-Bye, Say Hello to a Better Way of Firing Problem Employees."

19. Ibid.

20. Kerry M. Richard, "Pruning Poor Performers."

21. Chris Penttila, "Buh-Bye, Say Hello to a Better Way of Firing Problem Employees," *Entrepreneur*, September 2007: 28.

22. Richard, "Pruning Poor Performers."

23. Ibid, P. 447, 20.

24. Ann Pomeroy, "Great Communicators, Great Communication," *HR Magazine* 51 (July 2006): 44.

25. Frank E. Rudewicz, "The Road to Rage: Workplace Violence Grows Out of Escalating Patterns of Aggressive Behavior That Managers Must Be Trained to Recognize and Stop," *Security Management* 48 (February 2004): 40–47.

26. Ibid.

27. Ibid.

28. Ibid.

29. Ibid.

30. Ibid.

31. Data from Michelle Archer, "Tome Tracks Our Trends, from Tattoos to Snipers," *USA Today*, September 10, 2007: 9B.

32. As quoted in Patricia Bathurst, "Workplace Policies on Body Art Differ," *Arizona Republic*, October 22, 2006: EC1.

33. C. J. Prince, "To Catch a Thief," *Entrepreneur*, September 2007: 60–62.

34. Ibid.

35. Ibid.

36. Ibid.

37. Personal interview with store manager in Rockville, MD.

38. Personal interview with the bank president in Frederick, MD.

39. Ibid, P. 447, 33.

40. Ibid,

41. Michael Powell, "Betrayal," *Inc. Magazine*, April 1996: 24.

42. Ibid, P. 447, 33.

43. Karen Elliott and Kyna Shelley, "Impact of Employee Assistance Programs on Substance Abusers and Workplace Safety, "*Journal of Employment Counseling* 42 (September 2005): 125–133; and T. L. Stanley, "Workplace Drug Testing and the Growing Problem of Methamphetamines," *Supervision* 68 (August 2007): 3–6.

44. Stanley, "Workplace Drug Testing and the Growing Problem of Methamphetamines."

45. "Addressing Drug and Alcohol Problems at Work: ACTU Policy Provides a Fair and Consultative Approach to Addressing Drug and Alcohol Problems in the Workplace," *The Lamp* 64 (April 2007): 31; and Stanley, "Workplace Drug Testing and the Growing Problem of Methamphetamines."

46. Bill Repp, "Help in Handling a Hothead," *AnneArundelBusinessBreak.com, Capital-Gazette Newspapers* (December 2006): 12.

47. Ibid.

48. Stephanie Armour, "Racial Harassment Lawsuits at Work Go Up," *USA Today*, Friday, October 26, 2007: B1.

CHAPTER 12

1. Gary Kaufman, "How to Fix HR," *Harvard Business Review* 84 (September 2006): 30; Stephen Covey, "Redefining HR's Role for Success," *Training* 43 (October 2006): 56; James C. Wimbush, "Spotlight on Human Resources Management," *Business Horizons* 49 (November-December 2006): 433–436; and Robert J. Grossman, "Measuring the Value of HR," *HR Magazine* 51 (December 2006): 44–49.

2. Robert J. Grossman, "HR's Rising Star in India," *HR Magazine* 51 (September 2006): 46–52.

3. Jenny Whittard and John Burgess, "Working-Time Flexibility and Full-Time Work in a Retail Banking Organization," *Labour & Industry* 17 (April 2007): 119–142; Gary Linden, "All Onboard for Scheduling: Ohio Hospital Rolls Out Scheduling/Staffing Solution for Its Entire Organization, Saving Time and Money," *Health Management Technology* 27 (February 2006): 32–34; Anura deSilva, Kathleen Smith and Sonali Jayawardena, "Demand a Staff Scheduling System That Is Easy to Use, Empowers Your Staff, and Slashes Budgets!" *CARING Newsletter* 10 (Winter 2005): 6–12; and Vinh Quan, "Retail Labor Scheduling: Store Managers Face a Classic O.R. Problem: Ensuring Optimal Staffing to Accommodate Anticipated Sales Volumes and Customer Traffic, While

Meeting a Laundry List of Constraints and Without Blowing the Budget," *OR/MS Today* 31 (December 2004): 32–36.

4. Stephanie Armour, "Cancer Patients Keep On Working," *USA Today*, November 20, 2006: 4B.

5. "Be Willing to Bend: Execs Say Flexible Schedules Most-Valued Staff Benefit," *Westchester County Business Journal*, August 9, 2004: 4.

6. Susan Berfield, "Two for the Cubicle," *BusinessWeek*, July 24, 2006: 90.

7. Special thanks to Professor Elaine Madden at Anne Arundel Community College in Arnold, Maryland, for suggesting the inclusion of this topic.

8. Jena McGregor, "At Best Buy, Marketing Goes Micro," *Business-Week*, May 26, 2008: 52.

9. Fay Hansen, "A Permanent Strategy for Temporary Hires: Part 1 Of 2; As Contingent Workers Become an Essential Part of the Total Workforce, More Companies Are Adopting an Integrated Supply Chain Approach That Cuts Costs and Boosts Flexibility," *Workforce Management* 86 (February 26, 2007): 25; and Gillian Flynn, "Contingent Staffing Requires Serious Strategy," *Personnel Journal* 74 (April 1995): 50–56.

10. Chris Wood, "The Outsourcing Option: More Attractive Than Ever." *The Public Manager: The New Bureaucrat* 28 (Spring 1999): 43–46; "Service Offshoring and Productivity: Evidence from the United States," *Research-Technology Management* 49 (November-December 2006): 65.

11. Nikki Swartz, "Offshoring Privacy: When Companies Offshore Business Processes, They Are Putting Consumers' Most Sensitive Personal Information at Risk—and There's Little Consumers Can Do About It." *Information Management Journal* 38 (September-October 2004): 24–27; and Skip Corsini, "Outsourcing," *Journal of Property Management* 66 (May 2001): 66.

12. "Google CEO Says, 'Nice to Be Working with Yahoo'" Reuters, April 17, 2008, http://www.reuters.com/articlePrint?articleId=U SN1620362320080417 (accessed May 11, 2008).

13. Quoted from McDonald's website, "About McDonalds," http://www.mcdonalds.com/corp/about.html (accessed March 22, 2008).

14. Michael V. Copeland, "The Mighty Micro-Multinational," *Business 2.0* 7 (July 2006): 107–108.

15. Data from "500 Largest U.S. Companies," *Fortune*, May 5, 2008: F1.

16. "Off-Shoring: An Elusive Phenomenon," A Report by a Panel of the National Academy of Public Administration for the U.S. Congress and the Bureau of Economic Analysis (January 2006, Washington, DC): 8–10.

17. Mark Friedman, "Acxiom plans offshoring jobs to save money," *Arkansas Business*, August 27, 2007: 1–4.

18. Business Editors/High Tech Writers, "Forrester Finds Near-Term Growth of Offshore Outsourcing Accelerating; Latest Research Indicates a 40 percent Increase in Jobs Moving Offshore in the Next 18 Months," *Business Wire* (May 17, 2004), http://findarticles.com/p/articles/mi_m0EIN/is_2004_May_17/ai_n6029354/print (accessed May 11, 2008).

19. Diane E. Lewis, "20% Annual Rise in Offshoring Seen; Desire by Firms to Cut Costs Cited," *Boston Globe*, October 13, 2004, http://www.boston.com/business/technology/articles/2004/10/13/20_annual_rise_in_offshoring_seen/ (accessed July 13, 2008).

20. As quoted in ibid.

21. Mark Friedman, "Acxiom Plans Offshoring Jobs to Save Money," *Arkansas Business*, August 27, 2007: 1–4.

22. Dean Foust, "Queen of Pop," *BusinessWeek*, August 7, 2006: 44–51.

23. Data from J. Stewart Black and Hal B. Gregersen: "The Right Way to Manage Expats," *Harvard Business Review* 77 (March-April 1999): 52–63; and Gary S. Insch and John D. Daniels, "Causes and Consequences of Declining Early Departures from Foreign Assignments," *Business Horizons* 45 (November-December 2002): 39–48.

24. Data from Robert O'Connor, "Plug the Expat Knowledge Drain," *HR Magazine* 47 (October 2002): 101–107; and Carla Joinson, "No Returns," *HR Magazine* 47 (November 2002): 70–77.

25. Susan Ladik, "Working Together," *HR Magazine* 50 (June 2005): 86–91; G.Pascal Zachary, "As Easy as ABC? Not Exactly," *Business 2.0* 6 (August 2005): 66; Sidra Durst, "Risky Business," *Business 2.0* 7 (August 2006): 114–115; and Barney Gimbel, "A Master Traveler Tells All," *Fortune*, October 16, 2006: 218, 220.

26. Elisabeth Marx, *Breaking Through Culture Shock: What You Need to Succeed In International Business* (London: Nicholas Brealey Publishing, 2001): 7.

27. See Barbara A. Anderson, "Expatriate Management: An Australian Tri-Sector Comparative Study," *Thunderbird International Business Review* 43 (January-February 2001): 33–51; and Eric Krell, "Budding Relationships," *HR Magazine* 50 (June 2005): 114–118.

CHAPTER 13

1. Public Law 91-596, 84 STAT.1590, 91st Congress, S.2193, December 29, 1970, as amended through January 1, 2004, known as the Occupational Safety and Health Act of 1970, from the U.S. Department of Labor Occupational Safety and Health Administration's website, http://www.osha.gov/pls/oshaweb/owadisp.show_document?p_table=OSHACT&p_id=2743.

2. "OSHA Releases New Workplace Poster: Notice of Employee Rights is Required," *Industrial Engineer* 39 (April 2007): 14.

3. "Compliance Assistance: Fair Labor Standards Act," U.S. Department of Labor, Employment Standards Administration, Wage and Hours Division website, http://www.dol.gov/esa/whd/flsa/index.htm (accessed May 12, 2008).

4. Ibid.

5. "Youth in the Workplace," U.S. Department of Labor, Office of Compliance Assistance website, http://www.dol.gov/compliance/audience/youth.htm (accessed May 12, 2008).

6. *Handy Reference Guide to the Fair Labor Standards Act*, U.S. Department of Labor, Employment Standards Administration Wage and Hour Division (revised July 2007): 4.

7. "The Equal Pay Act of 1963," The U.S. Equal Employment Opportunity Commission's website, http://eeoc.gov/policy/epa .html (accessed May 12, 2008).

8. *Handy Reference Guide to the Fair Labor Standards Act*, U.S. Department of Labor, Employment Standards Administration Wage and Hour Division (revised July 2007): 2.

9. "New Hire Reporting," The U.S. Department of Health and Human Services Administration for Children and Family website, http://www.acf.hhs.gov/programs/cse/newhire/employer/ private/newhire.htm (accessed May 12, 2008).

10. "Ten Steps to Hiring Your First Employee," The U.S. Small Business Administration website, http://www.business.gov/topic/ human_resources/first_employee.html (accessed May 12, 2008); and "New Hire Setup," Intuit Payroll website, http://payroll .intuit.com/payroll_resources/new_hires/index.jhtml?view= forms_and_records (accessed May 12, 2008).

11. "Sexual Harassment Charges EEOC & FEPAs Combined: FY 1997–FY 2007," EEOC website, http://www.eeoc.gov/stats/ harass.html (accessed May 12, 2008).

12. Jathan W. Janove, "Sexual Harassment and the Three Big Surprises," *HR Magazine* 46 (November 2001): 123–130; Margaret M. Clark, "Failure to Cure Harassment Can Be 'Continuing Violation,'" *HR Magazine* 48 (February 2003): 106; and "Sexual Harassment," The U.S. Equal Opportunity Commission website, http://www.eeoc.gov/types/sexual_ harassment.html, last updated May 17, 2007 (accessed May 12, 2008).

13. Sam Smith, "Can't Lay All Knicks' Woes on Thomas," *Chicago Tribune*, December 14, 2007, www.chicagotribune.com/sports/ chi-smith-onnba14dec14,1,5237174.column (accessed May 12, 2008); and Jathan W. Janove, "Sexual Harassment and the Three Big Surprises," *HR Magazine* 46 (November 2001): 123–130.

14. List of examples adapted from, "What is Intellectual Property?" The World Intellectual Property Organization (WIPO) website, http://www.wipo.int/about-ip/en/ (accessed May 12, 2008).

15. Ibid.

16. David V. Radack, "Intellectual Property: Yours or Your Employer's?" *The American Management Association* (November 1997) and the Gale Group (2004); also see "The Intellectual Property Handbook: Policy, Law, and Use," The World Intellectual Property Organization (WIPO) website, http://www.wipo.int/about-ip/en/iprm/index.html (accessed May 12, 2008).

17. Hildy Medina, "The Final Say," *Hispanic Business* (October 2007): 92; also see Stephanie Armour, "Racial Harassment Lawsuits at Work Go Up," *USA Today*, October 26, 2007: B1.

18. Data from Jill Hamburg Coplan, "What to Expect When You're Expecting," *Business Week*, May 26, 2008: 17.

19. The U.S. Equal Employment Opportunity Commission (EEOC) website, www.eeoc.gov/policy/laws.html (accessed May 12, 2008).

20. "Compliance Assistance: Family Medical Leave Act," The U.S. Department of Labor website, http://www.dol.gov/esa/whd/ fmla/ (accessed May 12, 2008).

21. "Federal Laws Prohibiting Job Discrimination Questions and Answers," The U.S. Equal Employment Opportunity Commission (EEOC) website, www.eeoc.gov/facts/qanda.html (accessed May 12, 2008).

22. John H. Dise, Jr., "Avoiding Liability in Employee Selection: Risk of Discrimination Lawsuits," *School and College* 33 (June 1994): 32–33; Laura M. Litvan, "Thorny Issues in Hiring," *Nation's Business*, April 1996: 34–35; Denise Dubie, "Asking the Right Questions; How to Guide an Interview to Get the Information You Need Without Touching on Illegal Topics," *Network World*, November 8, 1999: 54; John Durso, "Interviewing Techniques Must Be Proper," *McKnight's Long-Term Care News* 23 (September 13, 2002): 39; John Durso, "Legal Issues; Don't Ask These Things when Hiring," *McKnight's Long-Term Care News* 23 (October 4, 2002): 14; and George D. Fagan, "Workplace Discrimination: Be Crystal Clear on Anti-discrimination Policies and Procedures So That Managers and Employees Know Exactly Where You—and They—Stand," *Pool & Spa News* 43 (September 3, 2004): 34.

23. Rushworth M. Kidder, "Tough Choices: Why It's Getting Harder to Be Ethical," *The Futurist,* September-October 1995: 29–32.

24. Linda Elder and Richard Paul, *The Miniature Guide to Understanding the Foundations of Ethical Reasoning, Based on Critical Thinking Concepts & Principles,* 3rd ed. (Dillon Beach, CA: Foundation for Critical Thinking, 2005): 11.

25. Marc Gunther, "God & Business," *Fortune*, July 9, 2001, 58–80; and Gary R. Weaver and Bradley R. Agle, "Religiosity and Ethical Behavior in Organizations: A Symbolic Interactionist Perspective," *Academy of Management Review* 27 (January 2002): 77–97.

26. Edward Soule, "Managerial Moral Strategies—In Search of a Few Good Principles," *Academy of Management Review* 27 (January 2002): 114–124.

27. Excerpted from LaRue Tone Hosmer, *Moral Leadership in Business* (Burr Ridge, IL: Richard D. Irwin Publishers, 1995): 39–41.

28. Data from "Ethics Training a Low Priority," *USA Today*, January 29, 2004: 1B.

29. Tom Vanden Brook, "Troops Will Get 'Values' Training," *USA Today*, June 2, 2006: 1A; Greg Farrell, "Bad Harvard Grads are Poster Boys for Ethics Classes," *USA Today*, September 28, 2006: 4B; and the series of articles about ethics education in the September 2006 issue of *Academy of Management Learning and Education.*

30. D. Christopher Kayes, David Stirling, and Tjai M. Nielsen, "Building Organizational Integrity," *Business Horizons* 50 (January-February 2007): 65.

31. Based on Brad Lee Thompson, "Ethics Training Enters the Real World," *Training* 27 (October 1990): 82–94. Also see Greg Farrell and Jayne O'Donnell, "Ethics Training as Taught By Ex-Cons: Crime Doesn't Pay," *USA Today*, November 16, 2005: 1B-2B; and Margery Weinstein, "Survey Says, "Ethics Training Works," *Training* 42 (November 2005): 15.

32. Alynda Wheat, "Keeping an Eye on Corporate America," *Fortune*, November 25, 2002: 44, 46; and Gary R. Weaver, Linda Klebe Trevino, and Bradley Agle, "'Somebody I Look Up

To': Ethical Role Models in Organizations," *Organizational Dynamics* 34 (2005): 313–330.

33. Hannah Clark, "Chief Ethics Officers: Who Needs Them?" *Forbes*, October 23, 2006, http://www.forbes.com/2006/20/23/leadership-ethics-hp-lead-govern-cx_hc_1023ethics (accessed March 8, 2007).

34. Mark Henricks, "Ensuring an Ethical Business," *Entrepreneur Magazine*, December 2006; also see Bruce Horovitz, "Scandals Grow out of CEO's Warped Mind-Set," *USA Today*, October 11, 2002: 1B-2B.

35. "Freescale Receives 2007 American Business Ethics Award," *Business Wire*, September 27, 2007; and Freescale Semiconductor's website: www.freescale.com, December 10, 2007 (link to the Code of Business Conduct and Ethics can be found at http://media.corporate-ir.net/media_files/irol/17/175261/cgov/fsl_code_english052006.pdf , last updated May 2006).

36. Richard P. Nielsen, "Changing Unethical Organizational Behavior," *Academy of Management Executive* 3 (May 1989): 123–130; For information about related cases see, "Wendy Zellner, "A Hero—and a Smoking-Gun Letter," *Business Week*, January 28, 2002: 34–35; Greg Farrell and Jayne O'Donnell, "Watkins Testifies Skilling, Fastow Duped Lay, Board," *USA Today*, February 15, 2002: 1B-2B; and Angus Loten, "CEOs in Slammer," *FastCompany* (December 2006).

37. Richard Lacayo and Amanda Ripley, "Persons of the Year," *Time*, December 22, 2002; Jodie Morse and Amanda Bower, "The Party Crasher," *Time*, January 6, 2003: 52–56; Amanda Ripley and Maggie Sieger, "The Special Agent," *Time*, January 6, 2003: 34–40; and Maria Bartiromo, "The Ones Who Got Away," *Business Week*, June 12, 2006: 98.

38. Ralph Nader, "An Anatomy of Whistle Blowing," in *Whistle Blowing*, ed. Ralph Nader, Peter Petkas, and Kate Blackwell (New York: Bantam, 1972): 7.

39. Valerie Watnick, "Whistleblower Protections Under the Sarbanes-Oxley Act: A Primer and Critique," *Fordham Journal of Corporate & Financial Law* 12 (June 2007): 831–279. The federal Whistleblowers Protection Act of 1989 is discussed in David Israel and Anita Lechner, "Protection for Whistleblowers" *Personnel Administrator* 34 (July 1989): 106. Also see Richard Lacayo and Amanda Ripley, "Persons of the Year," *Time*, December 22, 2002; Neil Weinberg, "The Dark Side of Whistleblowing," *Forbes*, March 14, 2005: 90–98; and Catherine Rampell, "Whistle-Blowers Tell of Cost of Conscience," *USA Today*, November 24, 2006: 13A.

40. As quoted by Adam Santavicca, "Ethics and Company Culture," *Smart Business Matters* 2 (Fall 2006): 2.

41. Linda Elder and Richard Paul, *The Miniature Guide to Understanding the Foundations of Ethical Reasoning, Based on Critical Thinking Concepts & Principles,* 3rd edn., 12.

42. Thomas R. Horton, "The Ethics Crisis Continues: What to Do?" *Management Review* 75 (November 1986): 3. Derek Bok, former president of Harvard University, calls for greater civic mindedness in "A Great Need of the 90's" *Christian Science Monitor*, May 22, 1992: 18.

43. See Kerry Hannon, "How to Build in Values in Building a Business," *USA Today*, July 31, 2006: 6B; Catherine M. Dalton, "When Organizational Values Are Mere Rhetoric," *Business Horizons* 49 (September-October 2006): 345–348; and Alan Wolfe, "Bringing Religion Into Your Company Can Be a Test of Faith—but Not in the Way You Might Expect," *Inc. Magazine*, December 2006: 63–64.

CHAPTER 14

1. Natasa Suman and Mirko Psunder, "Mobile Computing Changing the Traditional Ways of Organizing the Construction Company," *American Journal of Applied Sciences* 5 (January 2008): 42–28; "Futurist: I.T. Key to Productivity," *Health Data Management* 15 (December 2007): 16; V. Klyuev, T. Tsuchimoto and G. P. Nikishkov, "Using a Web-Based System to Support Teaching Processes," *International Journal of Information and Communication Technology Education* 4 (January-March 2008): 72–86; and Stuart Maguire and Udechukwu Ojiako, "Interventions for Information Systems Introduction in the NHS," *Health Informatics Journal* 13 (December 2007): 283–303.

2. Curtis E. Dalton, "Preventing Corporate Network Abuse Gets Personal—Network Access Abuse and Proprietary Corporate Data Theft Are a Recipe for Disaster," *Network Magazine*, February 1, 2001: 56.

3. Kevin McKeough, "Inside, and Outside, Jobs; Looking to Protect Your Business? Better Search for Leaks on Both Sides," *Crain's Chicago Business* 30 (February 26, 2007): 18; also see Kazuhiko Adachi, "Special Supplement: Fight Fraud—the Enemy Within—Companies That Focus on External Criminals Attempting to Steal Their Intellectual Property Assets are Looking in the Wrong Direction. More Often, the Culprits are Inside the Firewall," *The Banker* (December 1, 2006).

4. McKeough, "Inside, and Outside, Jobs; Looking to Protect Your Business? Better Search for Leaks on Both Sides."

5. Michael Booth, "Court Mulls Company's Liability for Employees' Data Theft from Rival," *New Jersey Law Journal*, February 1, 2007, NA.

6. Jaikumar Vijayan, "DBA Admits to Theft of 8.5M Records," *Computerworld*, December 3, 2007: 8.

7. "US: Widespread Acceptance for TJX Computer Breach Deal," *just-style.com* (December 19, 2007); and Jaikumar Vijayan, " TJX Says Breach Costs May Exceed $150 Million: Analysts Content Latest Estimate by Retailer is Woefully Low," *Computerworld*, August 20, 2007: 20.

8. Brian Krebs, "OMB Sets Guidelines for Federal Employee Laptop Security," *Washingtonpost.com* (June 27, 2006); and "This Message Will Self-Destruct," *Risk Management* 53 (August 2006): 6.

9. Krebs, "OMB Sets Guidelines for Federal Employee Laptop Security."

10. Amanda C. Kooser, "Safety First, Keep Your Customer and Employee Data on Lockdown," *Entrepreneur*, June 2007: 32; Bill Roberts, "Risky Business: Protect Employee Data from Security Risks Posed by the Use of Laptops and Mobile Devices,"

HR Magazine 51 (October 2006): 68–74; and Krebs, "OMB Sets Guidelines for Federal Employee Laptop Security."

11. "Expert Tips That Can Help You to Protect Employee Data," *Payroll Manager's Report* 06-06 (June 2006): 1–6; and "Safeguarding Personal Information Calls for a More Comprehensive Approach by Financial Services Institutions," *PR Newswire* (August 8, 2007): NA; and Kazuhiko Adachi, "Special Supplement: Fight Fraud—the Enemy Within—Companies That Focus on External Criminals Attempting to Steal Their Intellectual Property Assets are Looking in the Wrong Direction. More Often, the Culprits are Inside the Firewall," *The Banker* (December 1, 2006).

12. K. C. Jones, "Hardly Working? Survey Exposes the Mind of a Time Waster; The Average Employee Spends 1.7 Hours on Unrelated Work Activities, but Taking a Break Can Help People Recharge Their Batteries to Make it Through the Day," *InformationWeek*, July 25, 2007, http://www.informationweek.com/shared/printableArticle.jhtml?articleID=201201060 (accessed July 14, 2008); Joseph Carroll, "U.S. Workers Say They Waste About an Hour at Work Each Day; Say Their Co-workers Are Unproductive About an Hour and a Half Daily," *Gallup Poll News Service* (September 6, 2007) http://www.gallup.com/poll/28618/US-Workers-Say-They-Waste-About-Hour-Work-Each-Day.aspx (accessed July 14, 2008).

13. David H. Freedman, "Worried That Employees Are Wasting Time on the Web? Here's Why You Shouldn't Crack Down," *Inc. Magazine*, August 2006: 77–78.

14. Ibid.

15. Steve Hamm, Andrew Park, Roger Crockett, and Spencer Ante, "The Tech Challenge," *BusinessWeek,* August 27, 2001, http://www.businessweek.com/magazine/content/01_35/b3746662.htm?chan=search (accessed May 12, 2008).

16. Marvin J. Cetron and Owen Davies, *53 Trends Now Shaping the Future* (Bethesda, MD: The World Future Society, 2005): 18; and "Futurist: I.T. Key to Productivity," *Health Data Management* 15 (December 2007): 16.

17. Hal R. Varian, "Information Technology May Have Been What Cured Low Service-Sector Productivity," *The New York Times*, February 12, 2004: C2.

18. Emily Keller, "Why You Can't Get Any Work Done," *BusinessWeek*, July 19, 2007, http://www.businessweek.com/careers/content/jul2007/ca20070719_880333.htm?chan=search (accessed May 12, 2008).

19. Ibid.

20. John Soat, "E-mail: A Plague of Biblical Proportions," *Informationweek*, February 19, 2007: 18; Edward C. Baig, "What Gets Technology Users Really Peeved?" *USA Today*, April 5, 2007: 3B; Chris Penttila, "Time Out: Never Enough Time? Practice These Simple Time Management Techniques, and Get Your Life Back in Control," *Entrepreneur*, April 2007: 71–73; and Adam Santavicca, "E-mail: Time Saver or Time Waster?" *Smart Business Matters* (Summer 2007): 4.

21. Leigh Buchanan with Kim Kleeman, "I'm Trying to Create a Mental Air Bag Between Me and the Craziness of the Day," *Inc. Magazine*, October 2007: 111–114; Katie Arcieri, "In the Technology Age, Getting Away Can Be Tough," *The Capital*, June 21, 2007, A6; and Lisa Singhania, "Out of the Office but Can't Get Away," *Anne Arundel Business Break* (June 2006): 1, 13.

22. Donna Ferrara, "Technology Productivity and Other Lies," *Risk Management* 48 (July 2001): 37.

23. Illana Ozernoy, "Are You Under Surveillance?" *BestLife*, February 23, 2007, http://www.bestlifeonline.com/cms/publish/finance/Are_You_Under_Surveillance.shtml (accessed July 14, 2008); and "Learning to live with Big Brother; Civil Liberties: Surveillance and Privacy," *The Economist*, September 29, 2007: 63.

24. As quoted by Illana Ozernoy, "Are You Under Surveillance?" *BestLife*, February 23, 2007, http://www.bestlifeonline.com/cms/publish/finance/Are_You_Under_Surveillance.shtml, (accessed July 14, 2008).

25. "Tips on Keeping Workplace Surveillance from Going Too Far," *HR Focus* 83 (January 2006): 10.

26. "Under Close Supervision," *Risk Management* 54 (February 2007): 8.

27. Ben Charmy, "Big Boss Is Watching," *CNET News.com*, September 24, 2004, http://www.news.com/2102-1036_3-5379953.html (accessed May 12, 2008).

28. Ozernoy, "Are You Under Surveillance?"

29. "Tips on Keeping Workplace Surveillance from Going Too Far," *HR Focus* 83 (January 2006): 10.

30. Stephen Spencer, "Blogging for Dollars," *Multichannel Merchant* 6 (June 1, 2005), http://multichannelmerchant.com/mag/blogging_dollars/index.html (accessed July 14, 2008); also see David Greenfield, "Straight from the Source," *Control Engineering* 52 (July 2006): 2.

31. Technorati website, http://technorati.com/about, December 28, 2007 (accessed May 12, 2008).

32. Natasha Spring and William Briggs, "The Impact of Blogging: Real or Imagined? Microsoft Blogging Guru Robert Scoble Talks About What the Technology Means for Companies and How They Can Use Blogs to Their Advantage," *Communication World* 23 (May-June 2006): 28–33; and "Online Publishing—Blogging: Two-Way Conversation," *New Media Age* (October 5, 2006): 25.

33. Spencer, "Blogging for Dollars."

34. Tim Parry, "Defending Yourself Against the Blogs," *Multichannel Merchant* 23 (May 1, 2006), http://multichannelmerchant.com/webchannel/defending_yourself_blogs_05012006/index.html (accessed July 14, 2008).

35. Danah M. Boyd and Nicole B. Ellison, "Social Network Sites: Definition, History, and Scholarship," *Journal of Computer-Mediated Communication*, 13 (2007): article 11; Ed Frauenheim, "Social Revolution: A Wired Workforce Community: Part 1 of 2; Social Networking Technology Is Colliding with the Workplace—whether Employers Like It or Not," *Workforce Management* 86 (October 22, 2007): 1; and "News Analysis: Social Interpretation," *New Media Age* (August 3, 2006): 10.

36. "Social Networking Awards—The Top Social Networks of 2006," *Mashable Social Networking News*, December 24, 2006, http://mashable.com/?p=1536 (accessed December 28, 2007).

37. Aili McConnon, "Social Networking is Graduating—and Hitting the Job Market; How Do the Online Rolodexes Stack Up?" *Business Week*, September 10, 2007, 4; and Ed Frauenheim, "Social Revolution: A Wired Workforce Community: Part 1 of 2; Social Networking Technology Is Colliding with the Workplace—Whether Employers Like It or Not," *Workforce Management* 86 (October 22, 2007): 1.

38. "Recruiting 2.0," *Entrepreneur*, November 2007: 100.

39. Ed Frauenheim, "Social Revolution: A Wired Workforce Community: Part 1 of 2; Social Networking Technology Is Colliding with the Workplace—Whether Employers Like It or Not," *Workforce Management* 86 (October 22, 2007): 1.

40. Anne W. Howard, "Nonprofit Groups Can Take Advantage of Technology," *Chronicle of Philanthropy* 20 (December 13, 2007), http://philanthropy.com/premium/articles/v20/i05/05004102.htm (accessed July 14, 2008).

41. Ed Frauenheim, "Social Revolution: A Wired Workforce Community: Part 1 of 2; Social Networking Technology Is Colliding with the Workplace—Whether Employers Like It or Not," *Workforce Management* 86 (October 22, 2007): 1.

42. As quoted in Laurie Sullivan, "Businesses Tap into Social Networks, Blogs, Video Sharing: Their Interest Is Driven in Part by the Impact That Blogs and Social Networking Sites Are Having on Consumer Decisions and Purchases," *Information Week*, May 30, 2006, http://www.informationweek.com/news/management/showArticle.jhtml?articleID=188700313 (accessed July 14, 2008).

43. Ibid.

44. "Social Networking Awards—The Top Social Networks of 2006," *Mashable Social Networking News*, December 24, 2006, http://mashable.com/?p=1536 (accessed December 28, 2007).

45. Laurie Sullivan, "Businesses Tap into Social Networks, Blogs, Video Sharing: Their Interest Is Driven in Part by the Impact That Blogs and Social Networking Sites Are Having on Consumer Decisions and Purchases," *Information Week*, May 30, 2006, http://www.informationweek.com/news/management/showArticle.jhtml?articleID=188700313 (accessed July 14, 2008); Johna Till Johnson, "Social Networks and the Wisdom of Crowds," *Network World*, October 25, 2007, 15; and Ed Frauenheim, "Social Revolution: A Wired Workforce Community: Part 1 of 2; Social Networking Technology Is Colliding with the Workplace—Whether Employers Like It or Not," *Workforce Management* 86 (Oct 22, 2007): 1.

46. "Face Time?" *Entrepreneur*, June 2007: 86.

47. Frauenheim, "Social Revolution: A Wired Workforce Community: Part 1 of 2; Social Networking Technology Is Colliding with the Workplace—Whether Employers Like It or Not."

48. Johna Till Johnson, "Social Networks and the Wisdom of Crowds," *Network World*, October 25, 2007: 15.

49. Adapted from "Mobile Social Networking: 8 strategies for B-to-B Marketers," *MarketingSherpa.com,* How To #HOW580: December 19, 2007, http://www.marketingsherpa.com/article.php?ident=30270 (accessed December 28, 2007).

50. Adapted from Tim Parry, "Defending Yourself Against the Blogs," *Multichannel Merchant* 23 (May 1, 2006), http://multichannelmerchant.com/webchannel/defending_yourself_blogs_05012006/index.html (accessed July 14, 2008).

51. Mark Henricks, "Rave Reviews: Automation Can Earn You Two Thumbs Up at Employee Evaluation Time," *Entrepreneur*, September 2007: 91–92.

52. "Postal Service Hi-Tech Human Resources Transformation a Success," *US Newswire*, December 18, 2007): NA.

53. "Global Village" *Entrepreneur*, April 2007: 87.

54. Barbara Seale, "Transform Your Life Through Technology," *Success From Home* 3 (April 2007): 14–17; Taylor Mallory, "Virtual Margaret: Companies Go High-Tech So Employees Can Be Virtually Anywhere—Virtually," *Pink Magazine* (August/September 2007): 40–41; and "Meet in the Middle," *Entrepreneur*, November 2007: 56.

CHAPTER 15

1. Carol Tice, "Building the 21st Century Leader," *Entrepreneur*, February 2007: 64–69.

2. NHS Institute for Innovation and Improvement, The Leadership Qualities Framework, http://www.leadershipdevelopment.nhs.uk/framework/personalqualities (accessed March 27, 2008).

3. Tom Muha, "Steps to Keeping Talented Workers," *The Capital*, November 4, 2007: F1-2; Bill Repp, "Use failure as a tool to future success," *The Capital*, October 23, 2007: B4; Tom Muha, "Playing to your strengths," *The Capital*, March 11, 2007: F1, F4; and Carol Tice, "Building the 21st Century Leader," *Entrepreneur*, February 2007: 64–69.

4. Muha, "Playing to your strengths."

5. Ibid.

6. Tice, "Building the 21st Century Leader." NHS Institute for Innovation and Improvement, The Leadership Qualities Framework, http://www.leadershipdevelopment.nhs.uk/framework/personalqualities (accessed March 27, 2008); and "Are You Self-Aware on Workplace Diversity? Take the Mirror Test," *The Virginian Pilot*, November 20, 2005: D2.

7. As quoted in Kelley Holland's, "What a Test Can Say About Your Style," *The New York Times*, August 26, 2007: BU15.

8. Glenn E. Mangurian, "Realizing What You're Made Of," *Harvard Business Review* 85 (March 2007): 125–130; Romanus Wolter, "Did I Do That?" *Entrepreneur*, November 2007: 144–145; and J. R. and Arnold Waddell, "Are Your Employees Afraid of You?" *Supervision* 68 (September 2007): 20–22.

9. Chris Penttila, "Bring on the Night," *Entrepreneur,* April 2007, 32.

10. Richard M. Felder and Barbara A. Soloman, "Learning Styles and Strategies," http://www.ncsu.edu/felder-public/ILSdir/styles.htm (accessed March 27, 2008); and Fitzroy Farquharson and Bernadette Carithers, "Four Major Channels Of Learning," http://faculty.valencia.cc.fl.us/ffarquharson/learning_styles/ (accessed March 27, 2008).

11. Richard M. Felder and Barbara A. Soloman, "Learning Styles and Strategies," http://www.ncsu.edu/felder-public/ILSdir/styles.htm (accessed March 27, 2008).

12. Fitzroy Farquharson and Bernadette Carithers, "Four Major Channels of Learning," http://faculty.valencia.cc.fl.us/ffarquharson/

learning_styles/ (accessed March 27, 2008); and Felder and Soloman, "Learning Styles and Strategies."

13. Liz Bogod, "Learning Styles Explained," http://www.ldpride.net/learningstyles (accessed March 27, 2008); and Fitzroy Farquharson and Bernadette Carithers, "Four Major Channels of Learning."

14. HR-Guide.Com, http://www.hr-guide.com/selection.htm (accessed March 27, 2008).

15. Adrian Furnham, Georgia Dissou, Peter Sloan, and Tomas Chamorro-Premuzic, "Personality and Intelligence in Business People: A Study of Two Personality and Two Intelligence Measures," *Journal of Business and Psychology* 22 (September 2007): 99–110; "Personality Test Reduces Turnover and Saves Hospital Dollars," *Healthcare Financial Management* 60 (July 2006): 24; and Kelley Holland, "What a Test Can Say About Your Style," *The New York Times*, August 26, 2007: BU15.

16. The personal inventory tools in this section are adapted from a variety of skills inventory and employee survey tools from the following sources: "Job Skills Checklist," The Writing Lab & *The Owl* at Purdue University, Copyright 1995–2008, http://owl.english.purdue.edu/owl/resource/626/01 (accessed March 27, 2008); "Worksheet #5—Skills Inventory Worksheet," *Job Search Manual*, SunRaye Enterprises, Copyright 1997–2006, http://www.sunraye.com/job_net (accessed March 27, 2008); "1.5 Identify Your Skills," *Looking for a Job*, The Government of Canada Document No. Y-331-03-04E, http://www.youth.gc.ca/publications/pubstext/looking_e.pdf (accessed March 27, 2008); and Laurie Bassi and Daniel McMurrer, "Maximizing Your Return on People," *Harvard Business Review* 85 (March 2007): 115–123.

17. Tice, "Building the 21st Century Leader."

Glossary

achievement-oriented leadership style a leadership style in which managers set challenging goals, emphasize excellence, and seek continuous improvement

affirmation statement the process of putting positive thoughts, beliefs, goals, and/or desires into words to increase the likelihood of success

affirmative action program (AAP) a program for actively seeking, employing, and developing the talents of groups traditionally discriminated against in employment

Age Discrimination in Employment Act of 1967 (ADEA) a federal law prohibiting employment discrimination against persons 40 years of age or older

alternative schedule options flexible schedule, job sharing, and telecommuting

Americans with Disabilities Act of 1990 (ADA) a federal law prohibiting employers from discriminating against qualified applicants or employees with disabilities

apprenticeship a formal, on-the-job training program that teams an experienced veteran with a person learning the trade

assessment criteria the standards used to assess employee performance

attitude a person's viewpoint, perspective, feelings, and disposition

attitude standard a set of expected employee behaviors for fostering a positive, friendly, creative, and professional corporate culture

authoritarian leader one who retains all authority and responsibility, assigning people to clearly defined tasks; there is primarily a downward flow of communication

behavioral leadership styles patterns of leadership behavior

behaviorally anchored rating scales (BARS) performance appraisal scales that are divided into increments of observable, measurable job behavior

Blanchard and Hersey's situational leadership model a leadership model based on four different leadership styles or characteristics: directing, coaching, supporting, and delegating

blog an online diary, used to share business knowledge, personal information, and more

brainstorming having many people generate and share ideas in a nonjudgmental setting to solve problems

buddy system the process of assigning new hires a mentor or buddy to help set them up for success

cafeteria compensation a plan that allows employees to select their own mix of benefits

chain of command the order of authority that defines who reports to whom

child labor standards limits on the type of work and the hours employees can work based on their age

coach a person who guides employees with instruction, feedback, and encouragement

coaching guiding employees when learning a new task, skill, or information and connecting the "How" with the "Why"

code of ethics a published statement of moral expectations for employee conduct and behavior

collectivist cultures cultures that emphasize duty and loyalty to collective goals and achievements

common goal something of mutual interest that members of an organization strive for

communication the transfer of information and understanding from one person to another person

communication medium the form of transmission used such as telephone calls, e-mails, or instant messaging

communication skills the ability to exchange information by speaking, listening, reading, and writing

compensation money or other rewards paid to employees for their service to the organization

computer-aided training training via computers, interactive software, video, audio, and Web-based resources

computer crime using computer technology to steal or cause harm to another person or company

computer information systems the combination of data input, processing, and output

computer virus a malicious software parasite that can damage programs, erase data and files, or shut down entire systems

confidentiality keeping private documents and conversations a secret

conflict a situation in which there are at least two different sides

constructive criticism criticism that is specific and focused on the desired behavior

contingency plan a back-up plan prepared for a defined scenario or set of circumstances

contingency planning planning that focuses on preparing for the unexpected

continuous improvement review (CIR) review process that focuses on customers, the team, and the employee's contribution to system improvements

controller a person who measures quality and performance

coordination of effort the process of two or more people coordinating mental or physical efforts to accomplish a task

core abilities a list of technical and behavioral skills and personal attributes required for a job

corporate culture the shared values, traditions, customs, philosophy, and policies of a corporation

counseling sharing the supervisor's expectations for correct behavior and explaining the consequences of failing to improve

creativity the ability to generate new ideas to support the organization's mission and goals

cross-cultural training any guided experience aimed at helping people live and work comfortably in another culture

cross-functional team a task group staffed with a mix of specialists who are focused on a common objective

cross-training training in a new skill or task that is typically the responsibility of a coworker

culture a population's taken-for-granted assumptions, values, beliefs, and symbols, which foster patterned behavior

culture shock feelings of anxiety, self-doubt, and isolation brought about by a mismatch between one's cultural expectations and reality

decoding translating the packaged message into a format that the receiver can comprehend

delegation the process of sharing authority and responsibility with someone else

democratic leader one who delegates authority while retaining ultimate responsibility, arranging to have work divided and assigned on the basis of participatory decision making; active two-way communication is common

Design Thinking experiencing the world firsthand to generate new ideas

directive leadership style a leadership style in which managers tell people what is expected of them and provide specific guidance, schedules, rules, regulations, and standards

distance learning training delivered via computer technology, the Internet, televisions, satellites, and other media

diversity a wide range of individual characteristics

division of labor the process of dividing tasks into specialized jobs

80/20 principle the concept that a minority of causes, inputs, or efforts tends to produce a majority of results, outputs, or rewards

emotional intelligence noncognitive skills, capabilities, and competencies that influence a person's ability to cope with environmental demands and pressures

empathy involves experiencing the world firsthand to see personally what consumers are experiencing to gain an understanding of how they interact with your product or service

employee benefits nonsalary compensation such as health, life, and disability insurance; vacation and personal leave; and employee stock options and retirement plans

employee data theft the act of employees stealing confidential data

employee orientation an opportunity to introduce and welcome your new hire and begin the transition from new employee to contributing team member

employee turnover employees leaving a company either because they are asked to or they choose to leave voluntarily

employment at will an employer can terminate an employee at any time without explanation or cause

employment selection test any procedure used in the employment decision process

empowerment making employees full partners in the decision-making process and giving them the necessary tools and rewards

encoding translating internal thought patterns into a language or code that the intended receiver of the message will understand

encryption the process of converting data from plain text to a cipher text; a difficult-to-interpret format

enthusiasm employees enjoy their work, do not complain or talk negatively, are self-motivated and eager to learn, and see problems as challenges and opportunities rather than obstacles

entrepreneurial venture a new or emerging start-up business

Equal Employment Opportunity (EEO) laws federal laws prohibiting employment discrimination based on personal characteristics

Equal Pay Act (EPA) a federal law that requires employers to pay male and female employees equal pay for comparable work

equitable perceived to be fair

ethical advocate an ethics specialist who plays a role in top-management decision making

ethics the study of moral obligation involving the distinction between right and wrong

expatriate a person who lives and works in a foreign country

expectancy the subjective probability that one thing will lead to another

expectation looking forward to or anticipating the prospect of something good in the future

experiential approach walking in your customers' shoes and experiencing firsthand what your customers are going through

experiential learning hands-on simulation, role playing, or scenario-based training

extenuating circumstances special situations that impact scheduling, such as an injury or temporary physical limitations such as pregnancy

external hacking computer criminal gains access from outside the organization to steal confidential data or cause harm

extrinsic rewards payoffs, such as money, that are granted by others

Fair Labor Standards Act (FLSA) a federal law that establishes minimum wage, overtime pay, record keeping, and child labor standards

Family Medical Leave Act (FMLA) a federal law requiring covered employers to grant eligible employees up to 12 weeks of unpaid leave

feedback an evaluative response about the result of a process or activity

Fiedler's contingency theory a leadership model based on the notion that a leader's performance depends on the likelihood that the leader can successfully accomplish the job and the leader's basic objective

5:15 report a reporting tool that allows employees to share significant information with their supervisor in a concise manner

flex-time when an employer permits an employee to work a modified schedule

formal group a collection of people created to do something productive

friendliness exhibited with a simple smile, an act of kindness, good-natured humor, or social pleasantries

globalization networks of finance, transportation, and communication that closely link the people of the world together

goal a commitment to achieve a measurable result within a specified period

goal setting the process of improving individual or group job performance with formally stated objectives, deadlines, or quality standards

group two or more people who share a common identity and purpose

group training training that involves one or more trainers and more than one trainee

Herzberg's two-factor theory the theory that employee motivation involves two factors: satisfaction and dissatisfaction

hierarchy of authority the formal organizational structure that defines positions of authority and decision making

historical data figures from prior years, such as sales and employee staffing

horizontal specialization various divisions of labor across an organization

individualistic cultures cultures that emphasize individual rights, roles, and achievements

individualized rewards rewards given to individuals to recognize goal attainment unique to the employee

inequity when employees believe they are being treated unfairly

inquiry asking questions, listening, and observing

intangible costs expenses that are not easily defined or measured

intellectual property original or unique items that people create using their imagination and brain power

intermediate planning determining subunits' contributions using allocated resources

interviewing assessing job candidates by asking questions about their work experience and potential

intranet based on the same technology as the Internet, with access limited to a specific group

intrinsic rewards self-granted and internally experienced payoffs, such as a feeling of accomplishment

jargon informal terminology unique to a business or industry, often not understood by new employees, customers, and people outside the organization

job analysis identifying task and skill requirements for specific jobs by studying superior performers

job description a document that outlines expectations and skill requirements for a specific job

job enrichment theory redesigning a job to increase its motivating potential

job sharing a situation in which one job gets done by two people

laissez-faire leader one who grants responsibility and authority to a group of individuals, who are told to work problems out themselves; communication is primarily horizontal among peers

leader one who sets the tone for the organization, creates the vision, and inspires others to achieve

leadership the process of inspiring, influencing, directing, and guiding others to participate in a common effort

learning styles channels/modalities for learning, including visual, auditory, tactile-kinesthetic, and kinesthetic

literacy the ability to read, write, speak the language, and compute/solve problems at a functional level

management the process of working with and through others to achieve organizational objectives in a changing environment

managerial functions general administrative duties that need to be carried out in virtually all productive organizations

Maslow's hierarchy of needs theory a theory of motivation stating that when one need is relatively fulfilled, another emerges in sequence to replace it

media richness the capacity of a given medium to convey information and promote learning

milestones important events, turning points, and advances in progress

mission statement defines the primary purpose of an organization, generates a positive image, and provides a focal point for planning

monochronic time the perception that time is a line divided into standard units

motivation an employee's desire or drive to achieve

motivator a person who inspires people to perform at their best and achieve a common goal

new-hire report a report required by federal law to assist in enforcing child support obligations

new perspective a different approach used to identify, analyze, and correlate data in an effort to generate fresh ideas

noise any interference with the normal flow of understanding from one person to another

nonverbal communication facial expressions, posture, eye contact, and other body language

objective performance measures measures based on quantifiable data

obstacles challenges that hinder an employee's ability to accomplish the job

Occupational Safety and Health Act (OSH Act) a federal law that assures safe and healthy working conditions

off-shoring outsourcing business activities or processes to foreign countries

on-the-job training learning a new skill while doing your job

operational planning determining how to accomplish specific tasks with available resources

organization a group of people combining efforts for a common purpose

organizational chart a visual display of an organization's official positions and formal lines of authority

outsourcing when a company or government agency contracts with an unrelated firm to complete work that was previously done internally

overtime pay the rate paid to employees who exceed forty hours in a workweek; it is at least one and one-half times an employee's regular hourly rate

participative leadership style a leadership style in which managers consult with employees to seek their suggestions and then seriously consider those suggestions when making decisions

path-goal theory a leadership model that suggests that leaders motivate their followers by providing clear goals and meaningful incentives for reaching them

peak performance when individuals are at their best, working at their highest level to achieve their goals

performance appraisal evaluating job performance as a basis for personnel decisions

performance measures measures that determine how an employee's performance will be evaluated

pilot program a designated trial period to evaluate a project prior to full implementation

plan an objective plus an action statement

planner a person who evaluates goals, objectives, and future needs to prepare plans that provide the necessary resources and action items to achieve success

polychronic time the perception that time is flexible, elastic, and multidimensional

positive feedback positive communication that is unique, timely, and specific

positive work environment where happy employees achieve organizational goals with less turnover and absenteeism, thus contributing to increased productivity

positivism a "can-do" attitude that leads to getting things accomplished

pre-arrival checklist a checklist for new employees that includes documents, items, and actions needed before the employee begins working

prioritizing ranking goals, objectives, or activities in order of importance

problem solving assessing a situation, identifying potential solutions, and ultimately making a decision

professionalism high standards of performance and quality along with integrity and pride in the work

progressive discipline a four-stage process of disciplinary action beginning with a verbal warning, then a written warning, suspension, and finally termination

prototyping allows users to see, touch, and otherwise experience the new idea

quality measures measures of the level of excellence of a product or service

quantitative measures measures of the ability to determine an amount, such as productivity

reasonable accommodations accommodations for employees with disabilities that do not create "undue hardship" for employers

recruiter one who assists in identifying potential job candidates, screening applications, interviewing, and hiring new employees

recruitment efforts by a company to find and hire qualified workers

reference sites websites providing information on a variety of topics

resonance the moment when an employee recognizes new knowledge or realizes something for the first time

resources the items employees need to get their jobs done successfully

responsibility employees follow up on commitments by doing what they say they are going to do, having a sense of urgency, going above and beyond what is expected, and holding themselves accountable

retention efforts by a company to keep employees; the opposite of employee turnover

rewards material and psychological payoffs for working

role playing staging a work-related activity to give the trainee realistic practice

scheduler a person who prepares the schedule to ensure that proper staffing and resources are available to meet customer needs

self-awareness knowing your own strengths and limitations

self-evaluation the process of employees rating their own performance and providing information to their supervisors as part of the performance appraisal process

servant leader an ethical person who puts others—not herself or himself—in the foreground

simulation techniques training that imitates real situations

situational leadership the concept that successful leadership occurs when the leader's style matches the situation

sleep on it taking a break from a challenging problem for a nap or a good night's rest and facing the issue refreshed

social network sites websites used by members to create personal profiles, post messages, manage address books, and share photos and videos

soft skills intangible skills such as communicating, leading, managing conflict, creativity, critical thinking, and problem solving

staffing hiring employees and recognizing and developing individual talent to meet organizational needs

storytelling told through the use of film or in person with both designers and users included to help people understand and connect with new ideas

strategic planning determining how to pursue long-term goals with available resources

subjective performance measures measures based on personal feelings and opinions

supervisor an individual who typically has the authority to hire, direct, promote, discharge, assign, reward, or discipline other employees

supportive leadership style a leadership style in which managers treat employees as equals in a friendly manner while striving to improve their well-being

suspending judgment the practice of separating the idea-generation process from the evaluation of those ideas

synergy the idea that the whole is greater than the sum of its parts

tangible costs expenses that are easily defined and measurable

tangible skills readily observed physical capabilities such as welding, cooking, carpentry, driving, and equipment operation

team rewards rewards given to a group of employees to recognize team-based goal attainment

teamwork employees leveraging individual strengths and talents and tolerating individual differences to work together to achieve organizational goals

technology all the tools and ideas available for extending the natural physical and mental reach of humankind

telecommuting connecting to one's office via computer technology while working at home

termination firing an employee

360-degree review a pooled, anonymous evaluation by one's boss, peers, and subordinates

time management the process of identifying what needs to get done and having a plan to get everything accomplished within the time allotted

trainer a person who teaches employees and coworkers new information and skills

training the process of teaching new skills or knowledge and changing behavior/attitudes through guided experience

trust a belief in the integrity, character, or ability of others

trust but validate confirming facts with an appropriate source rather than assuming information you have received from a coworker or third party is correct

verbal abuse a verbal assault including personal insults, threats, and inappropriate language

vertical hierarchy another term for "chain of command"

virtual team a physically dispersed task group that interacts primarily by electronic means

visualization creating a picture in your mind of the desired outcome

whistle blowing an employee's reporting of corporate fraud or other illegal and unethical behavior

Index